Abraham Lincoln's log cabin

Built by Abraham Lincoln and his father in 1831, in Coles County, Illinois

ALSO BY SIDNEY BLUMENTHAL

The Strange Death of Republican America

How Bush Rules

The Clinton Wars

This Town (play)

Pledging Allegiance: The Last Campaign of the Cold War

The Reagan Legacy (Editor with Thomas Byrne Edsall)

Our Long National Daydream: A Pageant of the Reagan Years

The Rise of the Counter-Establishment:
From Conservative Ideology to Political Power

The Permanent Campaign

The first photograph of Abraham Lincoln, 1846 or 1847.

A SELF-MADE MAN

The
Political Life
of
Abraham Lincoln,
1809–1849

SIDNEY BLUMENTHAL

Simon & Schuster

New York   London   Toronto   Sydney   New Delhi

Simon & Schuster
1230 Avenue of the Americas
New York, NY 10020

First Simon & Schuster hardcover edition May 2016

SIMON & SCHUSTER and colophon are
registered trademarks of Simon & Schuster, Inc.

For information about special discounts for bulk purchases,
please contact Simon & Schuster Special Sales at
1-866-506-1949 or business@simonandschuster.com.

The Simon & Schuster Speakers Bureau can bring authors to your live event. For more information or to book an event contact the Simon & Schuster Speakers Bureau at 1-866-248-3049 or visit our website at www.simonspeakers.com.

Interior design by Joy O'Meara

Manufactured in the United States of America

10 9 8 7 6 5 4 3 2

Library of Congress Cataloging-in-Publication Data

Names: Blumenthal, Sidney, 1948–
Title: A self-made man : the political life of Abraham Lincoln, 1809–1849 /
    Sidney Blumenthal.
Description: First Simon & Schuster hardcover edition. | New York : Simon &
    Schuster, 2016. | Includes bibliographical references and index.
Subjects: LCSH: Lincoln, Abraham, 1809–1865—Political career before 1861. |
    Lincoln, Abraham, 1809–1865—Political and social views. | Lincoln,
    Abraham, 1809–1865—Childhood and youth. | Lincoln, Abraham, 1809–
    1865—Marriage. | Politicians—Illinois—Biography. | Lawyers—Illinois—
    Springfield—Biography. | Illinois—Politics and government—To 1865. |
    United States—Politics and government—1815–1861. | Presidents—United
    States—Biography. | BISAC: BIOGRAPHY & AUTOBIOGRAPHY /
    Presidents & Heads of State. | HISTORY / United States / Civil War Period
    (1850–1877). | BIOGRAPHY & AUTOBIOGRAPHY / Historical.
Classification: LCC E457.35 .B55 2016 | DDC 973.7092—dc23 LC record
available at http://lccn.loc.gov/2015027339

ISBN 978-1-4767-7725-2
ISBN 978-1-4767-7727-6 (ebook)

For Claire Stone Blumenthal Miller

"All that I am or ever hope to be, I owe to my angel mother."
Abraham Lincoln

CONTENTS

TIMELINE OF MAJOR EVENTS

February 12, 1809:   Birth of Abraham Lincoln

December 1811:   The Lincoln family moves from Kentucky to Indiana

October 5, 1818:   Death of Lincoln's mother, Nancy Hanks Lincoln

December 2, 1819:   Marriage of Thomas Lincoln, Lincoln's father, to Sarah Bush Johnston

August 5, 1822:   Edward Coles elected governor of Illinois, goes on to defeat efforts to legalize slavery in the state

January 20, 1828:   Sarah Lincoln Grigsby, Lincoln's sister, dies in childbirth

December 1828:   Lincoln, on a flatboat trip down the Mississippi River, arrives in New Orleans where he is angered by the sights of slavery

March 1830:   The Lincoln family moves to Illinois

July 1831:   Lincoln settles in New Salem as a clerk in Denton Offutt's store

April 1832:   Lincoln enlists to fight in the Black Hawk War

August 6, 1832:   Lincoln loses his first election for the state legislature

December 10, 1832:   President Andrew Jackson issues his Proclamation Against Nullification

April 1833:   The Berry & Lincoln general store fails, leaving Lincoln in debt

August 4, 1834:   Lincoln is elected to the state legislature

August 25, 1835:   Lincoln's fiancée, Ann Rutledge, dies

January 20, 1836:   Lincoln proposes a bill in the Illinois legislature for emancipation in the District of Columbia

May 25, 1836:   John Quincy Adams launches the fight against the Gag Rule

September 9, 1836:   Lincoln receives his license to practice law

November 1836:   Stephen A. Douglas elected to the state legislature

March 4, 1837:   Martin Van Buren inaugurated as president

April 15, 1837:   Lincoln moves to Springfield, becomes the law partner of John Todd Stuart

November 7, 1837:   Elijah Lovejoy murdered

January 27, 1838:   Lincoln delivers his Lyceum address denouncing Lovejoy's killing

November 7, 1838:   William H. Seward elected governor of New York

April 4, 1841:   President William Henry Harrison dies; John Tyler becomes president

September 22, 1842:   Lincoln's duel with James Shields aborted

November 4, 1842:   Lincoln marries Mary Todd

August 1, 1843:   Robert Todd Lincoln born

August 7, 1843:   Illinois Supreme Court justice Stephen A. Douglas elected to the U.S. House of Representatives

June 27, 1844:   Mormon Prophet Joseph Smith murdered ending the Illinois Mormon War

November 5, 1844:   James K. Polk defeats Henry Clay for president

December 1844:   Lincoln sets up his own law office with William H. Herndon as partner

March 10, 1846:   Edward Baker Lincoln born

May 13, 1846:   Mexican War declared

August 3, 1846:   Lincoln elected to the U.S. House of Representatives

December 13, 1846:   Stephen A. Douglas elected to the U.S. Senate

January 22, 1847:   Lincoln delivers floor speech after introducing his "Spot Resolution" demanding to know exactly where the Mexican War began

April 15, 1848:   Seventy-seven slaves in Washington attempt to escape on a boat called the *Pearl*

September 22, 1848:   Lincoln campaigns for the Whig Party and Zachary Taylor in Boston with William H. Seward

December 1848:   Lincoln authors a bill for emancipation in the District of Columbia that fails to win support and he does not introduce

February 22, 1849:   Salmon P. Chase elected to the U.S. Senate

March 31, 1849:   Lincoln leaves Washington after failing to secure a patronage position, returns to Springfield and will not come back to the capital until twelve years later as president-elect

February 1, 1850:   Edward Baker Lincoln dies

CAST OF MAJOR CHARACTERS

FAMILY

Thomas Lincoln, Father

Nancy Hanks Lincoln, Mother

Sarah Lincoln, Sister

Sarah Bush Johnston Lincoln, Stepmother

Mary Todd, Wife

Ninian W. Edwards, Brother-in-law, son of the first governor of Illinois

Elizabeth Todd Edwards, Sister-in-law

Robert Smith Todd, Mary Todd's father

ILLINOIS

Jack Armstrong, Clary's Grove Boys leader

Edward D. Baker, Illinois legislator, congressman

Justin Butterfield, Chicago lawyer, Whig politician

John Calhoun, Lincoln's supervisor as surveyor, Democratic politician

Peter Cartwright, Preacher and Democratic politician, Lincoln's congressional opponent

Edward Coles, Thomas Jefferson's protégé, James Madison's private secretary, governor of Illinois

David Davis, Illinois legislator, judge, Whig Party stalwart

Stephen A. Douglas, Illinois legislator, judge, congressman, senator

Thomas Ford, Governor of Illinois during the Mormon War

Simeon Francis, Editor, *Sangamo Journal*

Mentor Graham, New Salem schoolteacher

John J. Hardin, Illinois legislator, congressman, Mary Todd's cousin

Dr. Anson Henry, Whig partisan, Lincoln's doctor

William H. Herndon, Lincoln's law partner

Usher F. Linder, Illinois legislator, attorney general, lawyer

Stephen Trigg Logan, Lincoln's second law partner

Denton Offutt, Lincoln's first employer, store owner, and horse whisperer

James Shields, Illinois legislator, U.S. senator, Douglas's ally

Joseph Smith, Mormon Prophet

Joshua Speed, Lincoln's Springfield roommate

John Todd Stuart, Lincoln's early political mentor in the legislature and first law partner

NATIONAL POLITICS

Thomas Hart Benton, Senator from Missouri

Francis Preston Blair, Editor, *Washington Globe*, Democratic political adviser

John C. Calhoun, Congressman, secretary of war, vice president, secretary of state, senator from South Carolina

Henry C. Carey, Pennsylvania businessman, political economist

Henry Clay, Speaker of the House, secretary of state, senator from Kentucky

Jefferson Davis, Senator from Mississippi

Horace Greeley, Editor, *New York Tribune*

Henry J. Raymond, Editor, *New York Times*, lieutenant governor of New York

Winfield Scott, General of the Army

William H. Seward, Governor of New York, senator

Alexander Stephens, Congressman from Georgia

Nicholas Trist, Diplomat, negotiator of the Treaty of Guadalupe Hidalgo

Daniel Webster, Congressman, senator from Massachusetts, secretary of state

Thurlow Weed, Editor, the *Albany Evening Journal*, Whig Party political leader

ABOLITIONISTS AND ANTISLAVERY ADVOCATES

Gamaliel Bailey, Editor, *The National Era* newspaper in Washington

James G. Birney, Liberty Party presidential candidate

Salmon P. Chase, Liberty Party and Free Soil leader, senator from Ohio

William Lloyd Garrison, Editor, *The Liberator*

Joshua Giddings, Congressman from Ohio, Lincoln's boardinghouse mate

John P. Hale, Congressman, senator from New Hampshire

Elijah Lovejoy, Minister, editor, *Alton Observer*

Owen Lovejoy, Brother of Elijah Lovejoy, Illinois legislator, Republican Party founder

Horace Mann, Congressman from Massachusetts

John G. Palfrey, Conscience Whig congressman

Theodore Parker, Boston Unitarian minister

Charles Sumner, Conscience Whig leader, senator from Massachusetts

Theodore Weld, Anti-Slavery Society editor and orator; assistant to John Quincy Adams

PRESIDENTS

James Madison, 4th President

James Monroe, 5th President

John Quincy Adams, 6th President, congressman from Massachusetts

Andrew Jackson, 7th President

Martin Van Buren, 8th President, Free Soil Party candidate

William Henry Harrison, 9th President

John Tyler, 10th President

James K. Polk, 11th President

Zachary Taylor, 12th President

Millard Fillmore, 13th President

Franklin Pierce, 14th President

James Buchanan, 15th President

A SELF-MADE MAN

THE SLAVE

———————•◦•———————

"I used to be a slave."

The first time Abraham Lincoln spoke openly about his origins was the year he assumed his new identity as a Republican. Until then he had been remarkably reticent about the facts of his personal life. He was one of the best-known political figures in Illinois, yet he kept an essential part of himself mysterious. By 1856 he had been a professional politician on public view for twenty-four years, more than half his lifetime a stalwart member of the Whig Party, and it was as a Whig that he had climbed rapidly in its ranks. At the age of twenty-seven he was elected to his second term in the legislature and his peers chose him as the Whig floor leader. He was dubbed the "Sangamon chieftain," head of the so-called Springfield Junto that directed the state party and de facto coeditor of the leading Whig newspaper, the *Sangamo* (later the *Illinois*) *Journal*, writing many of its editorials anonymously. He was the manager of Whig presidential campaigns in the state and a presidential elector to the Electoral College. He was the prime mover behind installing the convention system that selected candidates, enforcing party discipline, and using that system to drive out a competitor and make himself congressman. He had always campaigned on the Whig platform for economic development: internal improvements—federal and state financing of massive infrastructure projects—and the tariff to protect and encourage manufactures. He emphasized that he was one of "the people," not "the aristocracy," and felt hurt that he was once accused of being part of the upper class because of his marriage to Mary Todd, who belonged to the Edwards-Todd family, the most distinguished in Springfield, living on Aristocracy Hill. Projecting himself as a self-made man, he believed himself to be and wanted to be seen as rising from the common clay. He was also determined to leave his past behind, even to bury it, as if hiding his humiliation. His impulse was to protect himself from revelations about his origins. As for the actual details of his early existence, he had been stone silent.

By 1856 he was out of office for the biblical length of seven years since his obscure one-term congressional term, wandering on a horse named Bob from county courthouse to courthouse in the Eighth Judicial District of Illinois. While he sharpened his skills as a lawyer before juries and read Euclid late into the night to deepen his understanding of logical argumentation, he also unsuspectingly gathered around him the network of political men who would help lift him to the presidency, his team of loyalists. In the meantime, the party of his lifelong attachment shattered. This shipwreck, leaving him adrift as a political Ishmael, was his miraculous chance. His political career had capsized before his party went under, but he discovered himself suddenly afloat.

Emerging from the Whig crack-up, which he observed from a distance like a great natural disaster, he was a more mature man who had absorbed the experience of his wilderness years. "It is a fact that Mr. Lincoln was a peculiar man, a wonderful, marvelous, and mysterious man to the world generally," recalled William Henry Herndon, his law partner. On the one hand, "He was a marginal man, always leaving a blank on his paper, so that the future might write the future lessons thereon." On the other hand, "Lincoln's man"—Lincoln's own platonic ideal—"was purely logical, and he followed his conclusions to the ultimate end, though the world perished." He seemed paradoxical, but was of a piece. "While I say that Mr. Lincoln was ambitious, secretive, and somewhat selfish, do not infer from these words that he was a dishonest man, nor an insincere man, nor a hypocrite, nor a mean man, nor a base man. He was, on the contrary, full of honesty, integrity, sincerity; open, fair, and candid when speaking or acting. He was for Lincoln always, but with Lincoln's intense honesty." He learned the political values of time and patience, but often aroused criticism that he was too slow or too fast, vacillating or rash, on everything from the Emancipation Proclamation to military strategy. "He was self-reliant, self-poised, self-helping, and self-assertive, but not dogmatic by any means. He clung like gravity to his own opinions. He was the most continuous and severest thinker in America." But he was not always this way, not in the beginning, and it took decades for Lincoln to develop and realize his self-conception as "Lincoln's man."

Lincoln's phoenix-like ascent was made possible in constant friction with Stephen A. Douglas. From his earliest days until the presidency Lincoln measured himself against his rival and obsessive object of envy, the "Little Giant," flying toward the sun far above him, the most influential figure in Illinois, a power in the Senate, presidential hopeful, and wealthy from his real estate investments in Chicago and a Mississippi plantation. For nearly a quarter century, long before they would face off for the U.S. Senate in 1858, Lincoln and Douglas were fierce combatants in a contest that began with street brawls and a knife fight between their partisans in the muddy streets of Springfield. Douglas had already tried once, in 1852, to gain the Democratic presidential nomination, and he would try again and again. If any man from Illinois would be president, it was Douglas. Lincoln's forward movement was always in pursuit of Douglas.

It was at one of those campaign events that the man who had been extraordinarily reluctant about discussing his past, sensitive about his social inferiority, blurted out a startling confession. "I used to be a slave," said Lincoln. He did not explain what prompted him to make this incredible statement, why he branded himself as belonging to the most oppressed, stigmatized, and untouchable caste, far worse than being accused of being an abolitionist. Illinois, while a free state, had a draconian Black Code. Why would Lincoln announce that he was a former "slave"? The bare facts he did not disclose to his audience were these: Until he was twenty-one years old, Lincoln's father had rented him out to neighbors in rural Indiana at a price of ten to thirty-one cents a day, to labor as a rail splitter, farmhand, hog butcher, and ferry operator. The father collected the son's wages. Lincoln was in effect an indentured servant, a slave. He regarded his semiliterate father as domineering and himself without rights. Thomas Lincoln, who had led a harsh and unfair life, wanted his son to learn an honest trade as a laborer, perhaps trained as a carpenter like himself, considered formal education a waste of time, and sought to suppress any larger ambition as useless dreaminess. It was only when the self-made man finally identified himself as a Republican that he felt free to reveal himself as "a slave." And then Lincoln completed his story, "And now I am so free that they let me practice law."

Lincoln's wry humor drove home his point about his getaway, but masked the scar. Calling himself "a slave" was not a slip of the tongue, hyperbole, or metaphor. It was not just another of his funny stories, though he made it into a joke. He truly considered himself to have been held in bondage and escaped. Lincoln rarely if ever talked about his feelings, even to his closest friends, who tried to discern the signs. He hid his depths behind his simplicity. His authenticity was not deceptive but a veneer nonetheless. "He was simple in his dress, manners, simple in his approach and his presence," recalled Herndon. "Though this be true, he was a man of quite infinite silences and was thoroughly and deeply secretive, uncommunicative, and close-minded as to his plans, wishes, hopes, and fears. . . . I venture to say that he never wholly opened himself to mortal creature." It was no wonder. His captivity as a boy, he felt, was humiliating and degrading, imprisonment in a world of neglect, poverty, fecklessness, and ignorance. It was at the root of his fierce desire to rise. If he was angry with his father, he also knew that his father had been reduced to a dirt farmer and compelled to flee Kentucky to escape from slavery. "Slave States are places for poor white people to remove FROM; not to remove TO," Lincoln said in 1854 in opposition to Douglas's Nebraska Act. "New free States are the places for poor people to go to and better their condition." Lincoln had been oppressed by a man who himself was oppressed. By crossing the Ohio River into Indiana, his father had made his own escape. Lincoln was a fugitive's son—and a fugitive himself.

Even more startling than Lincoln's self-description as chattel was his subsequent self-identification as a particular kind of slave—a fugitive slave, a runaway. In one of only two brief autobiographical interviews he ever granted, this one intended for circulation in support of his Senate candidacy in 1858, and given to his friend Jesse W. Fell, an Illinois lawyer and businessman who had advised him to challenge Douglas to debate, Lincoln offered this physical description of himself: "If any personal description of me is thought desirable, it may be said, I am, in height, six feet, four inches, nearly; lean in flesh, weighing on an average one hundred and eighty pounds; dark complexion, with coarse black hair, and grey eyes—no other marks or brands recollected." Many, perhaps even at the time, might have missed Lincoln's allusion at the end of his seemingly bland self-portrayal, though the politician and lawyer who had learned to wield words with surgical precision certainly knew his own intent and had undoubtedly ruminated on it. "No other marks or brands recollected" was not another of his amusing jokes, but the exact language slave owners used to describe runaway slaves in newspaper ads. Lincoln had therefore identified himself not only as one of the fugitives but also mocked their owners. This was more than sympathetic projection; he believed he had his own fugitive experience and emancipated himself. He was an oppressed and stunted boy who achieved his freedom. If, with his disadvantages, he could do it, it could be done.

When he became a Republican and identified himself as "a slave," he had begun emerging as the Abraham Lincoln identifiable in history. Four years later, at the Illinois state Republican convention nominating him for president, he would be given another identity, the "Rail Splitter," the legendary ax-wielding laborer, common man of the people, establishing one of the most enduring icons in American history, though to the private Lincoln, who chuckled at the contrived image making by party handlers, it was a picture of himself from the time when he thought of himself as "a slave." Like other runaways, he had remade his identity and never took it for granted.

Despite his standing for years among the Illinois Whigs, few people spotted him for greater things other than as a provincial figure except perhaps his wife. When a Sangamon County abolitionist, Samuel Willard, and his father were indicted for helping a fugitive slave escape in 1843 and sought an attorney, another conductor of the Springfield area Underground Railroad, Luther Ransom, advised, "There's Lincoln; he always helps me when I call upon him for a man that is arrested as a runaway. He is too little known; you want one that is popular and has made a name." "And so," recalled Willard, "we failed to employ Lincoln and make acquaintance with him." But he stumbled across him in the courthouse, a "gaunt-faced, awkward, long-limbed man, who took a law book from a case and sat down on a chair rather too low for him. I noticed the long leg thrown back and doubled up under the long thigh, like that of a grasshopper I wondered at his make-up. Someone called him Lincoln, and he smilingly replied. I had not heard the name before and remembered the man for his notable physical peculiarities." Later Willard remarked that "no one could have guessed, even with the wildest imagination enlisted for the task," at Lincoln's future. Of the young lawyers Willard met in Springfield then, he seemed the least likely to become a national leader. "Lincoln will do for Sangamon County, or to go to Congress from this district; but if the lightning of a presidential nomination hits him, it will hit the wrong man; he has more risk of being hit by the real article."

One of Lincoln's fellow boardinghouse mates from his congressional days, Nathan Sargent, a journalist and at the same time sergeant-at-arms of the House of Representatives, recalled that none of those who knew him imagined great things for the backbencher. "A future President was a member of that House, yet no one surmised the fact, and perhaps the last one to suspect such a thing was the individual himself. . . . He was genial and liked; but no one would have pointed him out as the future President, if called upon to select the man who was to be from among the members. Nor do I believe that he, if told to point out the future President then in that body, would have thought it possible that the lot was to fall to him."

Lincoln's marriage was indispensable to his rise, his sense of destiny, and his equilibrium. He was an almost comically awkward suitor who had a nervous breakdown over his inability to deal with the opposite sex. One socially superior woman to whom he proposed rejected him for having the manners of a bumpkin. Mary Todd, daughter of Henry Clay's business partner and political ally, from Lexington, Kentucky, was a rare woman of the Southern upper class who loved politics, and was described as a child as "a violent little Whig." She did not hesitate to offer her strong opinions at a time when women were supposed to remain silent and deferential on the subject. If anything, she was more ambitious for her ambitious husband than he was. His alliance with her gave him more than the social standing he desired. She steadied him, pushed him forward, defended him, and never lost faith in his star. She referred to their union as "our Lincoln party." Mary was high-strung, threw temper tantrums, and made embarrassing scenes. But she also gave Lincoln a family, respectability, a proper home, and passionately believed in him. Herndon hated her, calling her a "she wolf," and she would never invite him into the Lincoln home in Springfield, calling him "a dirty dog." Lincoln's young private secretaries John Hay and John Nicolay referred to her as the "Hellcat." But there would have been no Lincoln without Mary, and he knew it. He remained smitten and in wonder that she had selected "a poor nobody."

Lincoln had a deep private life about which he was reserved, but which he drew upon as a public man. His losses—the deaths of his mother, sister, and two sons—profoundly affected him. As the burden of Lincoln's mortality grew heavier, he learned to carry on despite it. The man who had suffered breakdowns was often famously melancholy, but never alienated, though even among his closest friends he kept a distance. "I knew the man so well: he was the most reticent, secretive man I ever saw or expect to see," recalled David Davis, the Illinois circuit court judge with whom Lincoln spent countless hours, was his campaign manager for president, and whom Lincoln appointed associate justice of the Supreme Court. Lincoln withdrew into himself, but his tragedies created reservoirs of compassion and resolution. In the darkest days of the war when nearly all around him lost heart, Ulysses Grant, his commanding general, would say, "The President has more nerve than any of his advisers."

When he stepped onto the national stage in 1860, many of Lincoln's contemporaries viewed him as little more than a simple provincial hack—"an uneducated man—a vulgar village politician, without any experience worth mentioning in the practical duties of statesmanship . . . this illiterate Western boor," as James Gordon Bennett's *New York Herald* put it in 1860. But they learned in time not to underestimate his political abilities. "He has proved himself, in a quiet way, the keenest of politicians, and more than a match for his wily antagonists in the arts of diplomacy," Bennett would concede four years later. "He was the deepest, the closest, the cutest, and the most ambitious man American politics has produced," observed Gustavus Fox, his assistant secretary of the navy. "Lincoln was a supreme politician," wrote Charles Dana, his assistant secretary of war. "He understood politics because he understood human nature." His timing and patience were governed by that understanding. "He never stepped too soon, and he never stepped too late." Dana returned time and again in his memoir to Lincoln's grasp of people. "He knew human nature; he knew what chord to strike, and was never afraid to strike it when he believed that the time had arrived."

Before the eyes of those who dismissed him, even if they did not see it, the self-made man was constantly transforming himself through self-education and relentless political aspiration. "Politics were his Heaven, and his Hades metaphysics," wrote Herndon. Lincoln was a new kind of man on the American scene, not just a self-made man, but the self-made man as politician, a new profession, the partisan regular in a newly competitive and disciplined two-party system. Lincoln was one of the first men in the first generation of professional politicians. He was not landed gentry, like most of the founders; nor was he successful as a merchant. In fact, he was a dismal failure as co-owner of a general store in New Salem and spent years digging out of debt.

If being a successful businessman were the prerequisite for office he would have been disqualified before his first race for the state legislature. He became a lawyer to advance himself as a politician. His law practice thrived in the 1850s by taking on every sort of client and case that walked through the door, through referrals of friends and riding the circuit for nearly half the year. His great skill was before juries in central Illinois, where more often than not he knew many of them personally. He had little ability at business, did not accumulate real estate holdings like some of his affluent friends, and never achieved rank near the tier of top-flight attorneys like Edwin Stanton, who inflicted his greatest professional humiliation by refusing to let the ungainly provincial hired as a co-counsel speak at a trial involving a major corporation.

Politics was not for Lincoln a grudging necessity, as a number of the most distinguished Lincoln scholars of the twentieth century insisted. The preeminent historian of the "golden age" of Lincoln scholarship, from the 1930s through the post–World War II period, James G. Randall, established the long accepted split theme of Lincoln as political but only out of obligation, operating on an elevated plane above grubby politicians, holding party politics beneath him, and defining statesmanship and partisanship as opposites. How could the Great Emancipator be reconciled with the politician? Randall's resolution was that Lincoln wasn't really a politician. "It was, of course, with parties and politicians that Lincoln had to work," he wrote. "That in so doing he kept his record clear is an achievement whose full value is not perceived. . . . It cannot be denied that Lincoln was a party man; he had to be if he wanted a political career. He worked by and through party organization; he engaged in party maneuvers; it was as party candidate that he obtained elective office. But it is also worth noting that he saw the evils of party politics and that the worst party excesses never had his approval." This was, to put a fine and polite point on it, sheer fiction. If it were true, to begin with he never would have become president and in the end would never have enacted the Thirteenth Amendment abolishing slavery. Lincoln the politician and Lincoln the Great Emancipator were not antithetical sides of the same person or antithetical stages in the same life, but one man. If it were not for Lincoln the politician, Lincoln the Great Emancipator would never have existed.

The mythology of Lincoln as too noble for politics long obscured the reality of Lincoln. Lincoln above politics was not Lincoln. "What! This a simple-minded man?" exclaimed Herndon. "This a politically 'innocent dear' man? This a mere thing, without ideas and policies? Away with all such opinions!" Lincoln did not believe that politicians were unsavory creatures he felt compelled to associate with out of duty. He did not hold himself above the political give-and-take or dismiss the deal making, or "log-rolling," as it was called, as repugnant to his higher calling. He did not see politics as the enemy of his principles or an unpleasant process that might pollute them. These notions were wholly alien to him. He never believed politics corrupted him. He always believed that politics offered the only way to achieve his principles. And he never thought of politics as separate from who he was. He discovered the promise of American life—and created the man who became Abraham Lincoln—through politics itself.

In Lincoln's youth, partisanship evolved into the expression of commitment to American democracy after the inchoate pre-party period of the 1820s. Yet antiparty sentiment had remained even within Whig ranks as a powerful form of anti–Democratic Party feeling with an edge against popular participation. Lincoln appeared in politics at the start of a new phase. He was the partisan as democrat who gloried in two-party competition. He completely embraced party politics, the rise of political professionals like himself, and partisan organization, including partisan newspapers, as fundamental to mass involvement in politics. His idea of politics was not separate from his idea of democracy.

The historical truth reveals one of the most astute professional politicians the country has produced. For this self-made man of the nineteenth century, striving was the emblem of his political authenticity, not only central to his self-conception but self-presentation. From the moment he first ran for the state legislature, at the age of twenty-three, he never ceased to aim for higher office. He made himself into a political being to the marrow of his bones, a politician through and through. In any room he was to be found at the center of a crowd of politicians, debating issues, trading gossip, and telling jokes, some off-color. He gained a reputation as a young man as a "slasher," who delighted to "take down" rivals, even as he was learning subtler arts to seduce or outmaneuver them. He deployed his repertoire not just to win elections, but also to guide passage of legislation, from "the System" of far-reaching internal improvements in the Illinois of 1837 to the Thirteenth

Amendment. Once he reached the White House his survival and that of the nation depended upon those political arts. As a lawyer on the circuit, he studied Euclid, mastering the art of "demonstrating" a proposition. Lincoln's presidency demonstrated the use of political acumen to advance "the proposition" he would state in the Gettysburg Address.

Lincoln's education was hardly finished when he arrived in Washington as president, not least his education about the presidency. His experience in government had been legislative, not executive. The traditional Whig view was that the presidency should defer to the congressional leadership—the self-interested doctrine of the Whig titans and rivals in the Congress, Henry Clay and Daniel Webster, who saw themselves as the puppeteers of figure-head chief executives who were nominated for their iconic images as military heroes. Above the exalted nonpolitical presidents would supposedly lurk the political string pullers, until one or the other gained center stage, though it never worked out that way. Both Whig presidents died early in office with their successors betraying their intentions. In the case of John Tyler, a states' rights Democrat, Clay and Webster were shunted aside. In the case of Zachary Taylor, they sought to undermine him once he asserted himself as his own man, relying upon Senator William Seward as his confidential counselor. Each still clung to the dream he would become president. But even Millard Fillmore proved less than malleable in the end. The Whig model of the presidency was nasty, brutish, and short.

For a self-described "Old Whig" who was the first Republican in the office, Lincoln had no ingrained party tradition of the executive to restore. In the secession crisis, he reached for guidance to Andrew Jackson's Proclamation Against Nullification and with that began his swift and rough education. His battles for control over his military commanders, his struggles with his ambitious cabinet members, and his policy toward emancipation defined presidential powers. These conflicts ran parallel to each other, but the outcome of each as they played out depended on the outcome of all—and through their consequences Lincoln maneuvered his way to a new understanding of the presidency and the Constitution.

Lincoln's words were among his greatest weapons. But his oratory, even at its most poetic, was always tactical and strategic. Deliberate, methodical, and meticulous, he crafted every line for political impact. He never spoke to hear the sound of his own high-pitched, rather shrill voice, or for the aesthetic experience of seeing his words in print. In his eulogy of Henry Clay, his early "beau ideal," Lincoln stated his own view of speechmaking, "All his efforts were made for practical effect. He never spoke merely to be heard." Lincoln always wanted to win. The prairie politician and forensic lawyer closely followed his adversaries' arguments and concentrated his mental energies on turning their language and ideas against them. These rhetorical jumping jacks were inimitably Lincolnian. What he practiced before county courthouse juries he performed as a politician. His antislavery "House Divided" speech borrowed the scriptural phrase from Daniel Webster's defense of the Fugitive Slave Act. His "new birth of freedom" in the succinct Gettysburg Address was the culmination of a series of lengthy speeches given over previous months rebutting the Copperhead and Confederate cant about "liberty." And his argument in the Second Inaugural on how "the war came" was a point-by-point refutation of Jefferson Davis's recent statements on its origin and meaning. The lawyer was a politician, and the politician was a lawyer.

Lincoln knew from his practical experience that great change required a thousand political acts, many small, some difficult and a few grand, beginning in the Illinois legislature field marshaling passage as the Whig floor leader of "the System" of modern infrastructure, of canals, bridges, and roads, the largest project ever to be enacted in the state, lifting it from a frontier wilderness into a commercial center. He understood that defeat could be the father of victory and that mere victory was often not the goal in itself but the means to higher ends. He knew that indirection had a direction and men often heard what they wanted to hear. He knew that little jokes could be serious and orotund orations could be jokes. His contemporaries learned that his rustic drollery was usually his cover for political subtlety. His high and low rhetoric, inspirational and banal, had its own symphonic uses.

Lincoln's political mind and sinuous methods, however, confounded some of the most perspicacious academic historians of the late twentieth century. Richard Hofstadter, the most brilliant historian of the post-Randall generation, famously dismissed the Emancipation Proclamation as having "all the moral grandeur of a bill of lading" and no purpose "beyond its propaganda value"—his witticism ignoring the Proclamation's thunderous impact, not least in authorizing the recruitment of black soldiers. Hofstadter was also seemingly unaware of the contradiction of his own cleverness. If Lincoln had intended the Proclamation merely as "propaganda," why would he have been so prosaic, so lacking in demagogic rhetoric, so utterly official? David Herbert Donald, the greatest Lincoln biographer of the late twentieth century, notably asserted that Lincoln's "basic trait of character" was his "essential passivity," flourishing as his decisive proof and using as the frontispiece of his biography Lincoln's statement on April 4, 1864, "I claim not to have controlled events, but confess plainly that events have controlled me." Hofstadter, too, cited this sentence to prove that Lincoln had "turned liberator in spite of himself." Lincoln's statement was, in fact, from a letter composed as a result of urgent advice from his panicked supporters in slave-owning Kentucky, his worst state during his reelection campaign, as a gesture to attempt to subdue controversy over precisely his enlistment of black troops. It was, in short, politically crafted. That Lincoln would adopt workmanlike language in a government document and feint in politics did not, however, make him fundamentally unprincipled or passive. These were simply some of his methods. Ultimately, Lincoln became the master of events because he was the master of politics.

If politics was Lincoln's "Heaven" it was also because it was his school. With less than a year of formal education in a backcountry "blab" school, reciting doggerel from memory, he gathered information from everyone he met, debating their ideas and considering their motives. He entered every legislative chamber and saloon, every political gathering and social party, every back room and courtroom as a potentially invaluable learning experience. He called them his "public opinion baths." It was how he gained his bearings in the invisible and shifting currents of politics he would navigate. His circuit riding around Illinois was more than the peripatetic ramblings of a country lawyer. His travels on behalf of clients advanced his political network. In every town and courthouse, he made friends and allies of lawyers and judges, the nucleus of his campaigns for the Senate and the presidential nomination. He loved the relationships of politics, the fraternity, friendship, and humor. There was little he liked more, especially in the White House, than a late night conversation with a group of politicians, except perhaps a night at the theater.

Lincoln sought to know who everybody was, their histories personal and political, their public speeches and private conversations. Politics, after all, is about relationships. As a wild boy he rambled far and wide throughout the counties of central Illinois introducing himself to all sorts of people of every class and description he found interesting or could advance his intellectual inquisitiveness. He especially fixed on the most important local lawyers, all politically connected. In New Salem, he befriended every soul and converted the local gang, Clary's Grove Boys, into his first political machine. He knew everyone, legislators and log-rollers, in Vandalia, the rickety early state capital, and everyone in Springfield down to the clerks in every minor office. As he widened his orbit as a congressman in Washington, he engaged everyone he could, from the leading abolitionist leader of the House of Representatives to the future vice president of the Confederacy.

He had devoured newspapers as a primary source for his education since he was a boy, memorizing the major speeches of the great statesmen in the Congress, avidly following every twist and turn of national debates from harbors to slavery. He closely studied the rhetoric of the greatest speakers, especially Henry Clay, his idol, and Daniel Webster, borrowing their language and adapting them into some of his most famous phrases—Webster's "Second Reply to Hayne" for "of the people, by the people, for the people."

After the parties disintegrated and reorganized in the Civil War, Lincoln studied each and every significant man's odyssey, just who had been what, where, and when, their alliances and conflicts, their remarks public and private, and to whom, the gossip about them, what was true and half true, and the underlying motives for their complex political patterns over decades. He knew the great and their traces to the Jacksonian era; the good and their fierce sectarian battles against each other in the abolitionist movement; and the eccentric but influential lords of the press. Without his granular knowledge, he simply would not have thrived and survived. But he did not accumulate his encyclopedic intimate knowledge as mere necessity. He didn't think of politics as a calling, like a revelation as might dawn on a religious figure summoned to serve, or as a businessman with an instinct for the ledger sheet of assets and debits, but as his human endeavor, his life, and ultimately inextricable from his struggle to preserve democracy.

Lincoln surrounded himself throughout his career with journalists, who were to him a species of politician, which they were. Newspapers were universally partisan organs, attached to one party or faction. He was in all but name the coeditor of the leading Whig newspaper in Springfield, the *Sangamo Journal*, later the *Illinois Journal*, and wrote hundreds of articles and editorials, most unsigned. He was the secret owner of a German language newspaper, the Illinois *Staats-Anzeiger*, published to promote his candidacy for the Republican nomination among German Americans. Journalism was critical to his continuing education, constantly refreshing his understanding of fast-moving events. And he enjoyed the company of journalists in the same way he enjoyed that of other politicians. They were part of the political life he loved. In many cases, there were no distinctions between newspapermen and politicians, the roles merging—Henry Jarvis Raymond, founder and editor of the *New York Times*, was at the same time chairman of the Republican National Committee. Lincoln received a constant stream of strident and often hysterical urgings from Horace Greeley, editor of the most influential Republican newspaper, the *New York Tribune*, who hated Raymond, but with whom Lincoln had been involved since he sent him political advice during the Whig campaign of 1848 and for whose correspondence he kept a separate slot marked "Greeley" in the desk of his presidential office. Throughout his presidency, Lincoln's relationships with journalists were central to his politics. He used them to gain insight and information, sometimes from the front lines of battle before dispatches had arrived from his generals. He leaked to favored reporters, played newspaper editors against each other, and even offered the post of minister to France to "His Satanic Majesty," James Gordon Bennett, editor of the *New York Herald*, a vicious critic, to help win his support for reelection. Both of his personal secretaries were journalists—John Hay and John Nicolay—and so was his assistant secretary of war, Charles A. Dana, the former managing editor of the *New York Tribune*, whom he used as an independent set of eyes and ears and for discreet political tasks, like evaluating his new general, Ulysses S. Grant. Lincoln advanced his ideas through his intimate journalist friends, sent them on diplomatic missions, sometimes edited their copy, and even wrote articles for august journals such as the *Atlantic Monthly* under their bylines. And he badgered journalists for gossip they didn't report. But, most importantly, he saw them as part of the elaborate machinery of public opinion.

Lincoln thought of politics as both a vast theater and an intimate society. He was stagestruck from an early age. After politics, the theater and especially Shakespeare was his greatest passion. In his drama, the audience was not a random gathering of strangers. Its members were not paying customers who had come for an evening of entertainment. They were citizens, not spectators. Lincoln had a keen knowledge of who they were. Before every jury and crowd in Illinois, he could name friends and neighbors. But the rest were familiar to him as well. He grew up among them, spoke their language, and hoped to give voice to their aspirations. Standing onstage, he sensed which words connected. Nor did he make an artificial distinction between campaigning among voters and working among politicians. Politics itself was always seamless for Lincoln. Collective and individual action was of a piece, community and man inseparable. In every group of politicians and before every audience the theater of politics was his natural environment.

Lincoln was a striver who never thought of himself as an imperial individual whose rise could only occur severing the restraining ties of society. He never conceived himself above other men, holding self-regarding contempt for the rest as a mediocre mass of envious failures using government or politics as their instruments to pull down the successful. He saw individual opportunity on a coherent continuum of government, public policy, and democracy. When his original party fell apart beneath him, he imported into the Republican Party his policies on the economy as a Henry Clay Old Whig who believed in the "American System," modernizing it to create the transcontinental railroad and land grant colleges. His destruction of the "slave power" was the culmination of his logic of a "people's contest."

Throughout the war, Copperheads, the Northern Peace Democrats, and Confederates flung the word "liberty" at him as the tyrannical ruler of an authoritarian government. Lincoln rebutted them in a series of speeches in 1863 and 1864 whose most memorable was the Gettysburg Address. He finally defined "liberty" directly in a speech on April 18, 1864, amidst his reelection campaign. This was the fully developed Lincoln in control of his powers cutting to the heart of the matter. "The world has never had a good definition of the word liberty, and the American people, just now, are much in want of one," he said. "We all declare for liberty; but in using the same *word* we do not all mean the same *thing*. With some the word liberty may mean for each man to do as he pleases with himself, and the product of his labor; while with others the same word may mean for some men to do as they please with other men, and the product of other men's labor." He used a metaphor to illustrate how those claiming to be its defenders twisted the word "liberty": "The shepherd drives the wolf from the sheep's throat, for which the sheep thanks the shepherd as a *liberator*, while the wolf denounces him for the same act as the destroyer of liberty, especially as the sheep was a black one. Plainly the sheep and the wolf are not agreed upon a definition of the word liberty; and precisely the same difference prevails today among us human creatures, even in the North, and all professing to love liberty. Hence we behold the processes by which thousands are daily passing from under the yoke of bondage, hailed by some as the advance of liberty, and bewailed by others as the destruction of all liberty."

Just as he would use Aesopian stories to make his points, Lincoln could also be the most humorous and entertaining man late at night in a room filled with boisterous and opinionated men talking politics and freely drinking whiskey, a drop of which he would not touch. It was in the role of droll comedian that he met his first president. When former president Martin Van Buren toured Illinois in 1842, the stalwart Whig state legislator who had viciously campaigned against him was invited as the best local raconteur to keep him laughing with his storytelling. Lincoln often used humor to illustrate his political points or subtly control the atmosphere around him, especially in the presence of serious men. His most memorable digression occurred on September 22, 1862, summoning the cabinet to the White House after the Battle of Antietam, the bloodiest so far in the war. He began reading a ridiculous story in frontier dialect entitled "Outrage in Utiky" by one of his favorite humor writers, Artemus Ward, editor of *Vanity Fair*. "It seemed to me like buffoonery," recalled Secretary of War Edwin Stanton. "Having finished, he laughed heartily without a member of the Cabinet joining in the laughter. 'Well,' he said, 'let's have another chapter,' and he read another chapter, to our great astonishment. I was considering whether I should rise and leave the meeting abruptly, when he threw his book down, heaved a long sigh, and said: 'Gentlemen, why don't you laugh? With the fearful strain that is upon me night and day, if I did not laugh I should die, and you need this medicine as much as I do.'" Then, to their further astonishment, he read them the Emancipation Proclamation. "I have always tried to be calm," Stanton continued, "but I think I lost my calmness for a moment, and with great enthusiasm I arose, approached the President, extended my hand and said: 'Mr. President, if the reading of chapters of Artemus Ward is a prelude to such a deed as this, the book should be filed among the archives of the nation, and the author should be canonized. Henceforth I see the light and the country is saved.' And all said 'Amen.' And Lincoln said to me in a droll way, just as I was leaving, 'Stanton, it would have been too early last spring.' And as I look back upon it I think the President was right."

Lincoln's politics altered and sharpened with changing circumstances, and though never an abolitionist, he was, as he insisted, "naturally antislavery." He grew up in an atmosphere far more suffused with antislavery sentiment than has been generally understood, in his father's cabin, the churches, newspapers, and books, the men he chose as his mentors, conversations and debates he joined in country stores, and the politics of Indiana pitting the party of "the People" against the party of "the Virginia Aristocrats."

Lincoln's deepening understanding of slavery in its full complexity as a moral, political, and constitutional dilemma began in his childhood among the Primitive Baptist antislavery dissidents in backwoods Kentucky and Indiana, whose churches his parents attended. As a boy he rode down the Mississippi River to New Orleans, where the open-air emporium of slaves on gaudy display shocked him. His development was hardly a straight line, but he was caught up in the currents of the time. His self-education, which started with his immersion in the Bible, Shakespeare, and the freethinking works of Thomas Paine and French philosophes, was the intellectual foundation for his profoundly felt condemnation of Southern Christian pro-slavery theology that surfaced first in his eulogy for Henry Clay and was shaped to diamond hardness in his Second Inaugural. His 1837 Springfield Lyceum address protested the murder by a pro-slavery mob in Alton, Illinois, of the abolitionist editor, Elijah Lovejoy, though he did not mention him by name. Lincoln was one of only two Illinois state legislators who performed the unheard of act of proposing a bill in favor of emancipation in the District of Columbia. As a congressman, he lived in a boardinghouse known as "Abolition House." He experienced the appalling invasion of slave catchers coming to seize one of the waiters as a fugitive slave. Undoubtedly, he knew the secret of the house where he lived, that it was a station in the Underground Railroad. He denounced the Mexican War as fraudulently started and voted numerous times for the Wilmot Proviso against the expansion of slavery. With the quiet assistance of the leading abolitionists in the Congress, his fellow messmate Joshua Giddings of Ohio and Horace Mann of Massachusetts, he drafted a bill for emancipation in the District, for which none other than John C. Calhoun, of South Carolina, the former vice president, U.S. senator, and tribune of the master class, rebuked him.

Lincoln's definition of freedom was neither abstract nor indivisible, but began with his autobiography. The "slave" who became the freeman was more than Lincoln's odyssey—it was the root of his creed. His political insight rested on his own escape, the beginning of his rise. From the dawning of his consciousness as a boy and awakening sense of himself as an American, he viewed the positive actions of government on every level from the town to the nation as essential to the opening of opportunity and advancement of democracy. "As I would not be a slave, so I would not be a master," he said in 1858. "This expresses my idea of democracy. Whatever differs from this, to the extent of the difference, is no democracy." He equated freedom, as he understood it, with the American government as he understood it. "This is essentially a people's contest," he said in his message to the Congress on July 4th in the first year of the war. "On the side of the Union it is a struggle for maintaining in the world that form and substance of government whose leading object is to elevate the condition of men; to lift artificial weights from all shoulders; to clear the paths of laudable pursuit for all; to afford all an unfettered start and a fair chance in the race of life. Yielding to partial and temporary departures, from necessity, this is the leading object of the Government for whose existence we contend." And the self-made man who hated slavery was the embodiment of the social and political democracy that the Southern aristocracy despised and whose election as president itself precipitated secession and war.

Visions of the coming apocalypse had filled the minds of John Quincy Adams, the former president and as a member of the Congress relentless antagonist of the "slave power," and John C. Calhoun. In the civil war they prophesied, Calhoun believed the South would be unconquerable, but Adams described how the president of the future would be compelled to use his constitutionally mandated war power for emancipation in order to triumph. On Adams's insight, Lincoln would finally find solid ground and his power as president. Only the imperatives of the war lifted the fog of peace and led him under the doctrine of military necessity to the Emancipation Proclamation.

When the war came, Lincoln grasped its universal significance. So did Jefferson Davis, president of the Confederate States of America. After democratic revolutions across Europe in 1848 had been crushed by a conservative alliance of emperors, aristocrats, and pope, Lincoln had chaired a meeting in Springfield to denounce the repression and hail the visit to America of the Hungarian revolutionary exile leader, Louis Kossuth. In the war, Lincoln's foreign policy was aimed against those European powers that sought to support and ultimately gain recognition of the Confederacy as an independent nation, and smash the United States, the only example of republican government, "the last best hope of Earth." That is what Lincoln meant when he made that remark, and, to that extent, the Civil War and the vindication of the United States had global stakes, revolutionary not only within its borders.

Lincoln would decide finally on a policy of "hard war," to extirpate the Southern system root and branch. After years of conflict, he concluded that only this form of revolutionary warfare would succeed. His open remarks in this period about slavery had a razor-sharp edge, differing in tone from the high-flown moral preachments of the abolitionists. When it came to dramatization, the abolitionists had recited the stories of escaped slaves, slave narratives like that of Solomon Northup or Frederick Douglass, or read *Uncle Tom's Cabin*, a fictional slave narrative. They appealed to pity, sympathy, and outrage. But the man who had thought of himself as "a slave" turned more personal. "I have always thought that all men should be free; but if any should be slaves it should be first those who desire it for themselves, and secondly those who desire it for others," Lincoln said near the end of the war, on March 17, 1865, to a group of soldiers from Indiana, one of his home states, at Willard's Hotel in Washington. Having made this severe statement, he was not satisfied to stop. "Whenever I hear any one arguing for slavery I feel a strong impulse to see it tried on him personally," he went on. And, about "those white persons who argue in favor of making other people slaves," he continued, "I am in favor of giving an opportunity to such white men to try it on for themselves." It was a rare occasion in which the emotionally reticent Lincoln stated exactly what "I feel." The former "slave" declared slavery a form of justice for slave owners. It was his new proclamation, the inverse of the Proclamation. Of course, it was one of his jokes, and it drew laughter from the soldiers. But it was also not a joke. It was a sarcastic twist on his Second Inaugural Address, given less than two weeks earlier, placing the guilt for the war's "blood" on slavery and the rebellion in its name. (Among those present at Willard's Hotel, where Lincoln delivered these remarks, was John Wilkes Booth, having just missed kidnapping him that afternoon.)

The coming of the Civil War was the making of Lincoln. Of course, he did not anticipate that it was coming even as events were preparing him for it. That did not make him passive, just living in history. It was through his self-education that he developed himself intellectually for the task he could not imagine. The war was a political struggle by other means, a politics for dominance over the United States lasting decades in which secession was provoked finally by his election. It was through his life in politics, beginning in the back rooms of post offices and general stores, that he slowly learned the elements of leadership, became president, and then waged the war, transforming it into a revolution, remaking the Constitution, ending slavery—the greatest expropriation of property in human history—and establishing the framework of a new American nation that is still at issue.

In 1860, John Locke Scripps, an editor of the *Chicago Tribune*, came to interview Lincoln in order to provide a campaign biography. "Why Scripps," said Lincoln, "it is a great piece of folly to attempt to make anything out of my early life. It can all be condensed into a single sentence, and that sentence you will find in Gray's Elegy, 'The short and simple annals of the poor.' That's my life and that's all you or anyone else can make of it." But it was hardly so simple, as he well knew better than anyone.

CHAPTER ONE

THE READER

A braham Lincoln was of the seventh generation of Lincolns in America, descended from a weaver from Norfolk, England, Samuel Lincoln, who became a modestly successful merchant in Hingham, Massachusetts, whose eleven children dispersed to Pennsylvania, New Jersey, and Virginia, and a number of whose descendants became distinguished and affluent. Amos Lincoln, participant in the Boston Tea Party, lieutenant colonel of the Massachusetts artillery in the Revolutionary War, and who married successively two of Paul Revere's daughters, was the father of Levi Lincoln, the leading Jeffersonian of Massachusetts, member of Congress, U.S. senator, Thomas Jefferson's attorney general and secretary of state, and then governor. As a lawyer he argued the case in 1783 in which slavery was ruled illegal in Massachusetts. His son, Levi Jr., became governor, too, and Abraham Lincoln would eventually meet him in 1848, introducing himself to his illustrious and distant relative, "I *hope* we both belong, as the Scotch say, to the same clan; but I *know* one thing, and that is, that we are both good Whigs."

Thomas Lincoln

John Lincoln, a great-grandson of Samuel, left his well-to-do family in New Jersey, where his father, Mordecai, owned land and foundries, for Pennsylvania and then Virginia, buying a large expanse in the fertile Shenandoah Valley. He deeded his son, Abraham Lincoln, a tract of 210 acres of the rich Valley land. A captain in the Virginia militia during the Revolution, Abraham appeared to have been inspired by the adventure stories of his distant relative by marriage, Daniel Boone, and trekked through the Cumberland Gap to stake a claim to even more extensive farmland. (The genealogical web linking the Lincoln and Boone families was tightly woven, with four intermarriages between them.) Abraham was well positioned to establish himself among the most prosperous first families of Kentucky, securing 3,200 acres of the best land. But he was ambushed by Indians and killed in 1786. His youngest son, eight-year-old Thomas, barely escaped being snatched as a captive when his older brother, Mordecai, shot the Indian. According to the law of primogeniture still in effect, Mordecai inherited Abraham's entire estate and was elevated into the Kentucky gentry—slave owner, racehorse breeder, and member of the legislature. Nothing was left to Thomas or his other brother Josiah.

Thomas's two older brothers were in fact half brothers, offspring of an earlier marriage. After his father's murder, his stepmother abandoned him, his dead mother's relatives reluctantly took him in, and he was left to fend for himself as "a wandering labor boy," as his son would later put it. Working for an uncle in Tennessee, Isaac Lincoln, a planter who owned dozens of slaves, Thomas picked up tradecrafts as a carpenter, mechanic, and farmer, working side by side with his uncle's slaves. He accumulated enough money, some of it possibly a loan from his half brother Mordecai, to purchase 238 acres in Hardin County, Kentucky, which he leased to a sister's husband.

Apprenticed at the carpenter's shop of Joseph Hanks, he spent much of his time at the home of Hanks's aunt and uncle, Rachel Shipley and Richard Berry, who were the guardians of Hanks's sister, Nancy. Berry was a fairly well-to-do farmer, with six hundred acres, thirty-four cattle, and three slaves. Rachel was the sister of Nancy's mother, Lucy Shipley, who had run off with her second husband, Henry Sparrow. Nancy's father, said to be one James Hanks, or Joseph Hanks, has never conclusively been identified. Some have claimed that Thomas Lincoln and Nancy Hanks were cousins, his mother the older sister of her mother.

Stories of Nancy's illegitimacy were widespread in the area and by several accounts Lincoln believed it. He once referred to his grandmother as "a half-way prostitute" and admitted "that his relations were lascivious, lecherous, not to be trusted." Rumors were rife that Nancy was "loose," even that she had an illegitimate child.

"Billy, I'll tell you something, but keep it a secret while I live," Lincoln confessed, riding on the legal circuit with his law partner, William Herndon. "My mother was a bastard, was the daughter of a nobleman, so called, of Virginia. My mother's mother was poor and credulous, and she was shamefully taken advantage of by the man. My mother inherited his qualities and I hers. All that I am or hope ever to be I get from my mother. God bless her. Did you never notice that bastards are generally smarter, shrewder and more intellectual than others? Is it because it is stolen?" Lincoln's story as he told it contained the themes of a classic fairy tale, an Old World tale of a pauper who is really a prince, a romance substituting for squalor. The poor boy is unrecognized as the natural-born offspring of aristocracy, possessing not only nobility of lineage but also of mind. But the point of the story was more than compensation for shame or revelation of true aristocracy as a happy ending. The bastard's child, it turns out, must survive by his wits, what he naturally possesses, not what he's lost, somehow "stolen." The would-be fairy tale ends with a twist, the boy creating his past out of dim recollections he has heard about a far-off place he can never regain, as he is inventing himself.

Thomas Lincoln and Nancy Hanks were married in 1806 in a ceremony conducted by a friend of the groom, Jesse Head, a Methodist circuit rider, man of God, and jack-of-all-trades—assistant county judge, local newspaper editor, and cabinetmaker. According to the testimony of a neighbor, the local doctor, Christopher Columbus Graham, the Lincolns were "just steeped full of Jesse Head's notions about the wrong of slavery and the rights of man as explained by Thomas Jefferson and Thomas Paine." Neither of them could write, though they might have been able to read a little, but it is improbable that they read anything by Jefferson or Paine, and instead were likely influenced by what they heard from Head. He was vehemently and vociferously antislavery, later breaking away from the regular Methodist Church over the issue to join the Radical Methodists.

Antislavery agitation had roiled Hardin County, especially its churches, since settlers poured through the Cumberland Gap into Kentucky after the

Revolution. Slavery was not incidental but central to its life and economy. In 1811, there were nearly as many slaves in the county as white men—1,007 slaves, compared to 1,627 white males older than sixteen. Living in Elizabethtown, young Thomas Lincoln in 1787 was hired as a laborer constructing a mill, working alongside slaves, whose wages were collected by their masters. The price of free labor competed directly with that of slave labor, driving his wages down.

At the mill he was paid no more than the slaves. Like other white men, he was inducted into the local slave patrol to catch runaways, presumably the men he worked with, serving a three-month stint.

The year Thomas helped build the mill a new preacher, Reverend Joshua Carman, appeared at the Elizabethtown Baptist Church, "an enthusiastic Emancipationist," according to a chronicler of the Kentucky Baptists. The next year Carman founded the South Fork Church, pressing the local Baptist association to stand against slavery. "Is it lawful in the sight of God for a member of Christ's church to keep his fellow-creatures in perpetual slavery?" he demanded. Failing to receive a satisfactory answer, "fanatical on the subject of slavery, he induced Rolling [South] Fork Church to withdraw from the association and declare non-fellowship with all slave holders." Though the congregation decided to return to the association in 1802, Carman was hardly discouraged from evangelizing against slavery. Finally, he and another pastor, Josiah Dodge, split off to form a new "Emancipationist" church in nearby Bardstown, "the first organization of the kind in Kentucky."

In 1807, eleven "Emancipationist" ministers and nine churches in Kentucky created their own antislavery organization, the Baptist Licking-Locust Association Friends of Humanity, which soon organized an Abolition Society. The new preacher in the pulpit at the South Fork Church, William Downs, "was one of the most brilliant and fascinating orators in the Kentucky pulpit in his day," and he was every bit as antislavery as his predecessor. In 1808, Downs, an "Emancipationist," was expelled by the pro-slavery majority of the church, which passed a resolution "not to invite him to preach" and branded him "to be in disorder." Downs was only one of a number of antislavery ministers in Kentucky expelled from their pulpits. He led a group of dissidents to form the Little Mount Separate Baptist Church. David Elkins, another strong antislavery preacher, was also a pastor there. Thomas and Nancy Lincoln, who had belonged to the South Fork Church, left with

Downs and joined the new church. Their Knob Creek farm ran close to the Old Cumberland Trail, a principal transportation route between Louisville and Nashville, regularly used by slave dealers moving their human cargo to markets west and south. Undoubtedly, the Lincolns observed the never-ending coffles of enchained blacks marched near their cabin.

The Lincolns' first child, Sarah, was born in 1807, Abraham on February 12, 1809, and a second son, Thomas, soon after, but who died in infancy. The parents brought Sarah and Abraham regularly to church services, where they almost certainly heard, along with Primitive Baptist preaching, hollering, and hymn singing, vigorous sermons against the wickedness of slavery. Parson Elkins especially befriended the bright little boy. Young Abraham was taught to read and write at what he called an "ABC school." One of his teachers, Caleb Hazel, was the Lincolns' next-door neighbor, and a member of the antislavery Little Mount Church. Thomas Lincoln was the groomsman at Hazel's wedding, a service performed by Reverend Downs. Lincoln described the formation of his views on slavery as among his earliest memories in a letter to A. G. Hodges, a newspaper editor in Frankfort, Kentucky, on April 4, 1864. "I am naturally antislavery," he said. "If slavery is not wrong, nothing is wrong. I cannot remember when I did not so think and feel."

On January 1, 1815, a suit was filed to evict Thomas Lincoln from his farm. Claims, surveys, and deeds in Kentucky were remarkably hazy at the time. He had a written contract, paid a fair price and taxes, but lacked a proper deed. A wealthy Philadelphia-based absentee landlord asserted ownership of 10,000 acres of Kentucky real estate, including the tiny Knob Creek property, citing Lincoln as defendant and attaching his income for years of supposed back rent. In June 1816, the trial was postponed for two years. Thomas continued to contest and would even win the case, but he did not know that he would. So he decided to cross the Ohio River into Indiana, admitted that year into the Union as a free state. He had felt under attack from all sides. "This removal," Lincoln recounted to Scripps, "was partly on account of slavery, but chiefly on account of the difficulty in land titles in Kentucky." Before leaving, Nancy brought her son to pray at the grave of his lost brother, Thomas.

Thomas Lincoln had to hack his way through dense forests and brush to enter the land of promise. For two months, the family huddled in a half-enclosed tent open on one side to wind, rain, and cold, spooked at night by the cries of wild animals, before moving into a rough one-room cabin they built. A year later, they were joined by Nancy's aunt and uncle Thomas and Elizabeth Sparrow, who had been ejected from their Hardin County farm by the same sort of lawsuit that bedeviled the Lincolns. They brought with them Elizabeth's nephew, Dennis Hanks, a cast-off child, born illegitimate, whose real last name was Friend but which he changed to his mother's maiden name; she, too, was named Nancy Hanks. He was ten years older than Abraham, shared the cabin loft with him, and became his constant companion.

About forty families, most of them migrants from Kentucky, lived within five miles of the Lincolns around a town they called Little Pigeon Creek. In the autumn of 1818, the small community was stricken with "milk sickness," an epidemic that claimed thousands of lives in the region. Thomas Sparrow caught the illness first, and then Elizabeth, and finally Nancy, who tended them before their deaths. She died on October 5. Nine-year-old Abraham helped his father build the plain wooden coffins. "O Lord, O Lord," recalled Dennis Hanks, "I'll never forget the misery in that little green log cabin when Nancy died!" In his old age, he told an interviewer about Lincoln, "He never got over the miserable way his mother died. I reckon she didn't have no

Sarah Bush Johnston Lincoln

sort of care—poor Nancy!" Abraham, the most literate member of his family, wrote a letter to Pastor Elkins requesting that he travel to perform a funeral service, and he came some months later, perhaps even a year later, preaching at her grave.

Eleven-year-old Sarah was now in charge of the household duties, including care of her brother. "He tried to interest little Sairy in learning to read, but she never took to it," recalled Dennis Hanks. "Sairy was a little gal, only eleven, and she'd get so lonesome, missing her mother, she'd set by the fire and cry. . . . Tom, he moped 'round." Thomas left twice for long periods of time, abandoning the children to forage for food in the wilderness. The first time he went to sell pork down the Ohio River; the second to bring back a new wife. He had proposed to Sarah Bush Johnston years before in Kentucky, but she rejected him for the Hardin County jailer, a better catch. Now a widow, she accepted him, a strategic domestic alliance, and in another trek from Kentucky he brought her and her three children to the dirt floor cabin in Little Pigeon Creek. She discovered Abraham and Sarah "wild—ragged and dirty," and immediately washed them so they "looked more human." One chronicler who spoke with eyewitnesses recalled, "Mr. L does not appear to have cared for home after the death of his mother." But his stepmother brought order and affection to his life. "Abe was the best boy I ever saw or ever expect to see," she said. And he described her as his "kind, tender, loving mother," to whom he was "indebted more than all the world for his kindness."

Sarah Bush Lincoln brought civility and domesticity to the rough existence of Thomas Lincoln. She filled a wagon for her new life with her belongings— pots and pans, pewter dishes, pillows, and blankets. Then she made him put in a wooden floor and build beds and chairs. She made everyone wash before dinner. And, according to Dennis Hanks, she made her husband join a church.

Thomas helped construct the new church in the village, the Little Pigeon Creek Baptist Church, affiliated with the United Baptist Association, bridging the Regular Baptists and the Separate Baptists, which refused to have any written articles of faith and to which Thomas adhered. He would not join the Little Pigeon Creek Church, the only one in the town, for seven years, until the theological schism was resolved—and his new wife insisted.

The pastor of the church, Thomas Downs, was the brother of William Downs, also undoubtedly sharing his antislavery creed. Thomas Lincoln became a church trustee and young Abe served as sexton. Two other preachers at the Little Pigeon Creek Church were "Emancipationists," Alexander Devin and Charles Polke, who had been members of the Indiana constitutional convention that wrote a section going beyond the prohibition on slavery in the Northwest Ordinance of 1787 to ban "the indenture of any negro or mulatto" made in another state, effectively preventing slave states from extending their reach over black freemen into Indiana. Thus the figures of moral authority of the tiny rural community where Lincoln experienced his earliest formative shaping were antislavery.

Sarah Bush Lincoln could not help noticing that "Abe read all the books he could lay his hands on . . . he read diligently . . . he didn't like physical labor—was diligent for knowledge—wished to know and if pains and labor would get it he was sure to get it." John Hanks, Dennis's brother, who came to live with the Lincolns in 1823, called him "a constant and voracious reader." He was sent to school for less than a year, the most extended period of formal education he ever received, a "blab" school where pupils were made to recite lessons in unison. "There was absolutely nothing to excite ambition for education," Lincoln wrote in his 1858 autobiography. But Dennis Hanks pointed to the memory of Nancy Lincoln as the initial spark for Abe's education. "I reckon it was thinking of Nancy and things she'd done said to him that started Abe to studying that next winter. He could read and write. Me and Nancy'd learned him that much, and he'd gone to school a spell; but it was nine miles there and back, and a poor make-out for a school, anyhow. Tom said it was a waste of time, and I reckon he was right. But Nancy kept urging Abe to study. 'Abe,' she'd say, 'you learn all you can, and be some account,' and she'd tell him stories about George Washington, and say that Abe had just as good Virginny blood in him as Washington. Maybe she stretched things some, but it done Abe good." But it was his stepmother who was the guardian of his education. "She didn't have no education herself, but she knowed what learning could do for folks." Unlike her husband, she valued ambition and invested it in her stepson.

Lincoln read whatever books he could find and whenever he could. He read Weems's *Life of George Washington*, John Bunyan's *Pilgrim's Progress*, *Robinson Crusoe*, *The Arabian Nights*, and *Aesop's Fables*. He studied Noah Webster's *American Spelling Book*, among other standard schoolbooks. He read Lindley Murray's *English Reader*, containing an antislavery poem by William Cowper, "I would not have a slave to till my ground,/to carry me, to fan me while I sleep,/And tremble when I wake, for all the wealth/that sinews bought and sold have ever earn'd./I had much rather be myself the slave,/And wear the bonds, than fasten them on him."

"I induced my husband to permit Abe to read and study at home, as well as at school," recalled Sarah Bush Lincoln. "At first he was not easily reconciled to it, but finally he too seemed willing to encourage him to a certain extent. Abe was a dutiful son to me always, and we took particular care when he was reading not to disturb him—would let him read on and on till he quit of his own accord."

Most people thought of reading as indolence. "Lincoln was lazy—a very lazy man," said Dennis Hanks. "He was always reading—scribbling—writing—ciphering—writing poetry." "Abe was not energetic except in one thing—he was active and persistent in learning—read everything he could," said his stepsister Matilda Johnston Moore. John Romine, a neighbor, who hired him as a day laborer, said, "Abe was awful lazy: he worked for me—was always reading and thinking—used to get mad at him." Thomas Lincoln believed his son's reading was willful shirking and he punished him for it. "He was a constant and I may say stubborn reader, his father having sometimes to slash him for neglecting his work by reading," recalled Dennis Hanks.

Thomas Lincoln was not naturally an angry or harsh man. "He was a man who took the world easy—did not possess much envy," said Dennis Hanks. "He loved his relatives do anything for them. . . . No better man then old Tom Lincoln." But he could be severe and was unsympathetic with his son's unusual temperament. Abe was lively, unusually clever, staging mock religious services with other children, delivering his own hellfire sermons, writing doggerel and poems, and curious about strangers, asking questions. "Often," recalled Matilda Johnston Moore, his stepsister, "Abe would make political speeches such as he had heard spoken or seen written." "Abe was then a rude and forward boy," said Dennis Hanks. "Abe when whipped by his father never bawled but dropped a kind of silent unwelcome tear, as evidence of his sensations—or other feelings." Hanks recalled Abe's small gestures provoking his father's abrupt hostility. "I have seen his father knock him down off the fence when a stranger would call for information to neighbor house. Abe always would have the first word." Though Thomas Lincoln wanted Abe to acquire the rudiments of reading and writing, he was not "easily reconciled" to his son's voracious reading. "I suppose that Abe is still fooling hisself with eddication," Thomas Lincoln remarked later to a friend. "I tried to stop it, but he has got that fool idea in his head, and it can't be got out."

Life had been starkly unfair to Thomas Lincoln—his father murdered, deprived of patrimony, abandoned, forced to compete with slaves and slave owners, driven from his farm by wealthy absentee landlords into the wilderness, his wife suddenly dead of a mysterious sickness. He also had another disability—he was apparently nearly blind, completely blind in one eye and weak in the other, "so he felt his way in the work much of the time: his sense of touch was keen," according to a neighbor, Elizabeth Crawford, for whom he made furniture. His craft enabled him to operate by feel. He depended on his hands even more than other workmen. And he never complained about his condition, expressed self-pity, demanding sympathy or help. He simply bore his blurred one-eyed vision of the world as he did his other burdens. But it must have frustrated him—and he sometimes lashed out at his son. He had no idea how to handle his gifted child and seemed to resent any sign of his brightness. No matter how desolate the circumstances that Abe had to contend with, they were not as wretched as those his father experienced. Thomas did his best to provide for his family, even getting a new mother for his children. He expected his son to suffer adversity silently like he had, to learn physical skills and a trade. He seemed to respond to Abe's intelligence as though it was the boy's conscious insult to make him feel inadequate. He took Abe's cleverness as pointed humiliation, somehow trying to show him up by acting smart. Sarah Bush Lincoln, however, recognized that he was unusually intelligent and tried to nurture him. "Mrs. Lincoln soon discovered that young Abe was a boy of uncommon natural talents and if rightly trained that a bright future was before him and she done all in her power to develop those talents," recalled Augustus H. Chapman, Dennis Hanks's son-in-law. But Thomas's life allowed no space for acknowledging intellectual pursuits. It was more than a waste of time, but also a distraction from the struggle for survival. The frontier was limitless, but wherever he went he found himself confined. "Thomas Lincoln never showed by his actions that he thought much of his son Abraham when a boy," said Chapman. "He treated him rather unkind than otherwise, always appeared to think much more of his stepson John D. Johnston than he did of his own son, Abraham." Knocking Abe off a fence for speaking or "slashing" him for reading was his instinctive way of keeping him in his place, where he needed to bear down. Thomas Lincoln did not want his son to rise above him; nor could he imagine how that might be possible. He thought of ambition as dangerous.

"I never could tell whether Abe loved his father very well or not. I don't think he did," said Dennis Hanks. In his two brief autobiographies, Lincoln's description of his father was of an ignorant man who "grew up literally without education. He never did more in the way of writing than to bunglingly write his own name." The key word was "bunglingly." Lincoln defined education as the main distinction between himself and his father, and essential to his rise and respectability. "What he has in the way of education he has picked up," Lincoln said about himself. "After he was twenty-three and had separated from his father, he studied English grammar—imperfectly, of course, but so as to speak and write as well as he now does. He studied and nearly mastered the six books of Euclid since he was a member of Congress. He regrets his want of education, and does what he can to supply the want." Lincoln never wanted to do anything "bunglingly."

In his mid-teens, the hireling Lincoln, "slave" to his father, lived a peripatetic existence, wandering from neighbor house to house, often staying with those for whom he worked, beyond parental control. He and his sister went as a team, Sarah as the kitchen maid and Abe as the field hand, for Josiah and Elizabeth Crawford. "She was a good, kind, amiable girl, resembling Abe," recalled Elizabeth Crawford about Sarah. Abe split rails, filled the cracks in the cabin, and harvested crops. "Abe was a moral and a model boy, and while other boys were out hooking watermelons and trifling away their time, he was studying his books—thinking and reflecting." Once, at the Crawfords', Sarah scolded her younger brother for teasing girls. "Abe you ought to be ashamed of yourself—what do you expect will become of you?" "Be President of the U.S.," he replied instantly. "He said that he would be President of the U.S., told my husband so often," said Elizabeth Crawford. "Said it jokingly—yet with a smack of deep earnestness in his eye and tone, he evidently had an idea. . . . No doubt that in his boyish days he dreamed it would be so. Abe was ambitious—sought to outstrip and override others." A neighbor boy, Joseph C. Richardson, remembered Lincoln as "the best penman in the neighborhood" and asked him to write copy so he could practice imitating him. "One of them I have never forgotten, although a boy at the time, it was this, 'Good boys who to their books apply; will all be great men by and by.'"

Lincoln borrowed Weems's *Washington* from Josiah Crawford, left it in a field, where it got soaked in the rain, and had to work three extra days to repay him. He read through the Crawford library of more than a dozen books, including *The Kentucky Preceptor,* "which we brought from Kentucky and in which and from which Abe learned his school orations, speeches and pieces to recite." The volume included Jefferson's First Inaugural Address and Thomas Gray's "Elegy Written in a Country Churchyard," which he recited decades later to Scripps. It also contained two striking antislavery stories. In "The Desperate Negro," a young slave, whipped by the master with whom he grew up, rebels, holds the master hostage, but after vindicating himself against the injustice, commits suicide. The moral of the story is that the slave, not the master, is the man of honor. In "Liberty and Slavery," decrying "millions of my fellow creatures born to no inheritance by slavery," the narrator described the life of one slave, manacled in a cell for thirty years, representative of oppression without end.

Lincoln's sister, Sarah, married Aaron Grigsby, son of a well-to-do farmer, in a wedding on August 1826 at which Abe recited a light poem, "Adam and Eve's Wedding Song." He spent much of his time at his sister's home. In January 1828, Sarah gave birth to her first child. The doctor summoned was drunk. The baby was stillborn and Sarah died of complications. She was twenty years old. When told the news, waiting in the smokehouse, aware that things were going badly, Abe "hid his face in his hands while the tears rolled down through his long bony fingers," according to Redmond Grigsby, Aaron's brother. "Those present turned away in pity and left him to his grief." "What do I have to live for?" he moaned repeatedly.

"Tom owned Abe's time till he was twenty-one and didn't want him to go," recalled Dennis Hanks. "He was too valuable for chores. When Abe was on the farm Tom had more time to hunt and fish, and he'd always rather do that than grub roots or hoe corn. Yes, Tom was kind of shiftless."

Lincoln's family had grown into a clan. His stepsisters had married his cousins—Matilda paired with Dennis Hanks and Sarah Johnston with a second cousin, Levi Hall. But even as the family expanded, his immediate family dissolved, with his father the only living link. His stepbrother, John D. Johnston, favored by Thomas, remained in the house, sharing Abe's love of fun, but was dull-witted and lacked ambition.

In 1827, the two teenagers went down to Louisville to work on the Louisville and Portland Canal. The backbreaking job was hardly a lark; for Lincoln, it was part of his political and economic education, where he earned some of his first silver dollars. The building of the canal to bypass the falls of the Ohio River was prolonged by years of state and national debate. Chartered by Indiana and partially funded by the federal government, the canal was subject to intense controversy as a chief example of internal improvement. In 1829, President Jackson vetoed funds as a subsidy to private corporations, while others argued that by blocking the necessary construction of infrastructure he was retarding economic progress. Lincoln's position in favor of internal improvements was rooted partly in his early work experience, and he would launch his political career on the issue, remaining an unwavering advocate through the creation of the transcontinental railroad.

Just over the horizon, about thirty miles to the west, a New Jerusalem was being built on the banks of the Wabash River. Robert Owen, the wealthy cotton mill owner and reformer, whose plant in New Lanark in Scotland had banished child labor and established an eight-hour day, decided to construct an ideal community in Indiana. He purchased in its entirety the village of Harmonie and its thirty thousand acres, where a German religious sect, followers of the Lutheran Pietist George Rapp, had created the "Harmony Society," a pre-millennial commune based on celibacy, pacifism, industry, and the imminent second coming of Christ. Landing in America, Owen expounded his utopian socialist vision before a sympathetic audience assembled on March 7, 1825, in the House of Representatives, consisting of President James Monroe, Secretary of State John Quincy Adams, and leaders of the Congress. In his community of equality, property would be held in common, nobody would be poor, everyone educated, and there would be free love, with music and dancing every night. Hundreds of colonists volunteered for the experiment, notable scientists from all over the world flocked to the far corner of Indiana, and Owen himself appeared to direct the enterprise.

New Harmony featured a school called "the Education Society" that was open to a limited number of outside students for tuition of one hundred dollars a year. "So when this foreign feller spoke in Congress about that Garden of Eden he was going to fence in on the Wabash, we soon heard about it," said Dennis Hanks. "Abe'd a broke his back to go, and it nigh about broke his heart when he couldn't." "'Denny,'" Hanks remembered Lincoln saying, "'there's a school and thousands of books there, and fellers that know everything in creation,' . . . his eyes as big and hungry as a hoot-owl's . . . but Abe might just as well have wished for a hundred moons to shine at night. . . . Tom didn't set no store by them things. . . . Well, I reckon Abe put it out of his mind, after awhile. If he couldn't get a thing he wanted he knowed how to do without it, and maybe he looked at it different afterwards. But things'd been easier for him if he could have gone to that school."

Abe was tethered to his father, "a slave." Mary Lincoln later recalled him saying on the subject of paternal authority, "It is my pleasure that my children are free, happy, and unrestrained by parental tyranny. Love is the chain whereby to lock a child to its parent." Though he was bound as a contract laborer, giving his wages to his father, he used his work to stay away from home, rarely returning, and roamed within a thirty-mile radius to discover new connections. He adopted a series of mentors to open unexplored vistas. They did not choose him as a protégé, but rather he selected them.

Lincoln had attended the "blab" school with a neighbor, David Turnham, six years older, who, after elected justice of the peace, came to possess a copy of the *Revised Statutes of Indiana*. Lincoln was riveted by it. But his friend would not let him borrow the book essential to his position, so Abe spent long periods at Turnham's home reading and rereading it. The volume contained the Declaration of Independence and the Constitution, probably the first time Lincoln encountered them. It would also have been his introduction to the legal basis of slavery.

After studying the *Revised Statutes*, Lincoln not only closely observed the proceedings before his friend's informal civil court—misdemeanors, landlord and tenant disputes, debts, and the like—but also stepped forward to represent clients who were his neighbors. "This both amused and interested him very much," recalled Augustus H. Chapman. Practicing law without a license, with rudimentary knowledge, and entirely on a pro bono basis, the budding attorney, at the age of seventeen and eighteen years old, attired in rough homespun clothes, discovered the power of argument through these long forgotten, unrecorded obscure cases, "in most of which he was successful."

While working as a ferryman on the Anderson River near the Ohio, Abe transported passengers to steamboats. "I could scarcely credit that I, a poor boy, had earned a dollar in less than a day," he later recounted to Seward. But the regular licensed ferry operators, the Dill brothers, filed a lawsuit against him for infringing on their business. Arguing his own case before a Kentucky justice of the peace, Lincoln claimed he was innocent because he never ferried passengers across the river but only to the boat in the middle of it. He won the case and began attending trials at that civil court, too.

Lincoln also wandered to Boonville, attending trials at the county court, and "paid strict attention to what was said and done," according to an eyewitness. At a murder trial in 1828, "the shabby boy" approached the prosecuting attorney, John Brackenridge, telling him his presentation was "a clear, logical and powerful effort." Thirty-four years later, when Brackenridge went to Washington, Lincoln "instantly recognized" him and remembered the trial. "It was the best speech that I, up to that time, ever heard," he told Brackenridge, and as a result he had "formed a fixed determination to study the law and make that his profession."

Lincoln on his own composed articles that he showed to one of the neighbors he worked for, William Wood, who also shared his newspapers with him. Abe called him "Uncle Wood." In 1827, Wood recalled, Lincoln gave him "a piece on national politics—saying that the American government was the best form of government in the world for an intelligent people—that it ought to be kept sound and preserved forever: that general education should be fostered and carried all over the country: that the Constitution—should be saved—the Union perpetuated and the laws revered." Wood was so impressed he showed it to a friend, John Pitcher, perhaps the leading lawyer in the county. Pitcher didn't believe that a "neighbor boy" had written it, but Wood insisted it was so. "The world can't beat it," declared Pitcher, who arranged its publication in a local newspaper. Soon Lincoln appeared at Pitcher's office in Rockport and began reading through his library. He told him he wished he could study law with him but that his parents needed him to work on the farm. (Pitcher was antislavery. His sons became generals in the Civil War, and one of them, Thomas Pitcher, was appointed superintendent of West Point in 1866.) Another "neighbor boy," twelve years younger than Lincoln, Alvin P. Hovey, did study law with Pitcher, became a prominent antislavery Democrat, switched parties after President James Buchanan removed him as U.S. attorney for Indiana, rose to become a Civil War major general, serving closely with Grant at Vicksburg, and was later elected governor of Indiana. President Lincoln was well aware of him, helping direct his counterespionage in Indiana against the Confederate secret service and pro-Confederate Copperheads.

Lincoln's true schoolhouse was a general store in the crossroads village of Gentryville, located about a mile and a half from his family's cabin. The hamlet's founder was James Gentry, the richest man in the immediate area, owning more than a thousand acres and opening his store in 1826. His chief clerk, William Jones, was appointed postmaster and started a little store of his own. Lincoln was hired as his clerk and often slept there. Jones was a graduate of Vincennes University, the first public institution of higher learning in Indiana, had a library, subscribed to newspapers, and as postmaster had access to all the papers that came through.

Jones's store became the debating society for a host of men before whom Abe learned to make his points and hold an audience enthralled. "The sessions were held in Jones's store, where the auditors and disputants sat on the counter, on inverted nail kegs, or lolled upon barrels or bags, while the wordy contest raged," wrote Henry Clay Whitney, an Illinois friend of Lincoln to whom he told stories of his early days. "The questions selected for discussion were not concrete. At one time there would be a debate upon the relative forces of wind and water; at another, upon the comparative wrongs of the Indian and the negro; the relative merits of the ant and the bee; also of water and fire."

"Lincoln would frequently make political speeches to the boys; he was always calm, logical, and clear," said Dennis Hanks. "His jokes and stories were so odd, original, and witty all the people in town would gather around him. He would keep them till midnight. Abe was a good talker, a good reasoner, and a kind of newsboy." "We had political discussions from 1825 to 1830, the year Lincoln left for Illinois," recalled Nathaniel Grigsby, one of Lincoln's friends, brother of his sister's husband, and a regular participant in the rustic salon. "We attended them—heard questions discussed—talked everything over and over and in fact wore it out. We learned much in this way. . . . His mind and the ambition of the man soared above us. He naturally assumed the leadership of the boys. He read and thoroughly read his books whilst we played. . . . Lincoln was figurative in his speeches, talks and conversations. He argued much from analogy and explained things hard for us to understand by stories, maxims, tales, and figures. He would almost always point his lesson or idea by some story that was plain and near as that we might instantly see the force and bearing of what he said."

The emergence of the "newsboy" was a new phenomenon of American democracy. Reading newspapers to keep up with current events suddenly became a widespread activity in the 1820s. The population had grown from 3.9 million in 1790 (Thomas Lincoln was born in 1788), to 12.9 million in 1830, matched by an explosion in the number and proliferation of newspapers. Like Rip Van Winkle (written by Washington Irving in 1819), the country awoke surrounded by a "rising generation." By the time Lincoln was holding forth in Jones's store, there were more than fifty newspaper subscriptions for every one hundred households, spread by the most comprehension postal system in the world. Newspaper circulation in the United States was three times greater than in Britain by 1835. Almost all the American papers were filled with national and international news, with little local information, which editors assumed people received by word of mouth. Entire speeches by politicians were a regular feature. Reading was becoming a necessity of modern life, especially for the younger generation; but for those who were semiliterate and mired in old rural customs like Thomas Lincoln it just seemed a mystifying distraction.

"Colonel Jones was Lincoln's guide and teacher in politics," said Nat Grigsby. Jones was also a ready source of newspapers and books. "Jones told me that Lincoln read all his books and I remember History of the U.S. as one," said John R. Dougherty, a friend of Jones.

William Grimshaw's *History of the United States*, published in 1821, a particular volume Lincoln studied, concluded with an account of how Northern states established laws for emancipation and prohibited slavery. "Since the middle of the last century, expanded minds have been, with slow gradation, promoting the decrease of human slavery in North America," wrote Grimshaw. "The progress of truth is slow; but it will in the end prevail." His history looked forward to a new dawn of enlightenment. "Virginia, as well as every other American republic that still sanctions domestic bondage, will, we confidently anticipate, at no distant period, make arrangements to unloosen, by degrees, the fetters, which are no less alarming to the master, than galling to the slave. Let us not only declare by words, but demonstrate by our actions, 'That all men are created equal, that they are endowed, by their Creator, with the same unalienable rights; that, amongst these, are life, liberty, and the pursuit of happiness.' " (The historian's son, Jackson Grimshaw, would become a lawyer in Quincy, Illinois, a founder with Lincoln of the Republican Party, and a member of the inner circle of Lincoln's political intimates who attended the crucial meeting with him in February 1860 that decided to launch his run for president. Lincoln would appoint him a collector of internal revenue for Quincy.)

The history of antislavery politics was hardly remote or theoretical to the cracker-barrel talkers in Jones's store. It was central to the emergence of the state of Indiana, whose political divisions were drawn by the antislavery struggle. That battle had been going on for more than twenty years before Lincoln began to voice his opinions. He had to have been informed about its background in order to have confidence in speaking about politics.

Thomas Lincoln, fleeing the slave system, brought his family into Indiana just as it was admitted into the Union as a free state, the culmination of a bitter clash between the powerful forces in favor of slavery and the insurgency against it. William Henry Harrison, the territorial governor, the dominant political figure in Indiana, tried for years to abrogate the prohibition of slavery in the Sixth Clause of the Ordinance of 1787 that created the Northwest Territory, the vast region north of the Ohio River lying between Pennsylvania and the Mississippi River that would become six distinct states. Framed by Thomas Jefferson and enacted as one of the first acts of the Congress, the Ordinance was the first antislavery charter. The ruling elite of Indiana clustered around Harrison, known as the Vincennes Junto, was becoming outnumbered by the influx of antislavery immigrants, both from the North and South, adamantly opposed to slavery as a system to oppress poor whites. Only by legalizing slavery could the elite attract slave owners into the territory and secure a majority to sustain themselves in power. At Harrison's direction, the territorial legislature circumvented the refusal of the Congress to suspend the Sixth Clause, passing "An Act to Introduce Negroes and Mulattoes" as slaves in 1806.

Harrison, the son of a wealthy Virginia planter, was a classic case of the upward mobility of the upper class, ratcheting up from position to position through his social and political connections. Starting as aide-de-camp to General "Mad" Anthony Wayne, victor of the Battle of Fallen Timbers against the Western Confederacy of Indian tribes that wrested control of the Ohio territory in 1794, Harrison used his family connections through the Federalist Party to secure appointment as territorial governor of the Indiana Territory. President Thomas Jefferson reappointed him in order to clear Indians from the region; yet Jefferson opposed the extension of slavery. He was, after all, the inspiration of the Ordinance of 1787 as author of the Report of Government for Western Territory of 1784 that excluded slavery. In 1808, a legislative commission headed by Harrison's adjutant, General Washington

Johnston, presumed to be pro-slavery, filed a surprisingly eloquent antislavery report, whose ringing conclusion cited to great effect Jefferson's prophetic line against it from his *Notes on Virginia*: "At the very moment that the progress of reason and general benevolence is consigning slavery to its merited destination; that England, sordid England, is blushing at the practice; that all good men of the Southern States repeat in one common response 'I tremble for my country when I reflect that God is just'; must the Territory of Indiana take a retrograde step into barbarism and assimilate itself with Algiers and Morocco?"

On the defensive, Harrison's junto was delivered yet another blow when the Illinois Territory, where its support was strong, was separated from Indiana in 1809, a division Harrison desperately opposed. The separation triggered an election for a territorial delegate to the House of Representatives in anticipation of statehood, a contest that crystallized the antislavery movement. Its leader, twenty-five-year-old Jonathan Jennings, a New Jersey migrant, son of a Presbyterian minister who had learned the law, was a rising man with a popular touch, who campaigned under the slogan "No slavery in Indiana." The junto's candidate, Thomas Randolph, a native Virginian of the aristocratic Randolph family, cousin of Jefferson and ally of Harrison, was soundly defeated. In 1816, Jennings triumphed again, and was elected president of the constitutional convention that established the new state, outlawed slavery, and upheld the Ordinance's Sixth Clause. The constitution was adopted in June 1816 and the state admitted in December. Jennings was elected Indiana's first governor and then to nine terms in the Congress, where he promoted internal improvements, ultimately drifting away from the Jacksonian Democrats into a new alignment. Harrison was appointed general of the Army of the Northwest for the war against Indian tribes led by Tecumseh, and would become the first elected Whig president in 1840.

Out of the decisive battles over statehood and slavery the two political parties in Indiana were defined until the emergence of the Whigs in the 1830s. One side was called "the Virginia Aristocrats" and the other simply "the People." For two decades after the first territorial election, those remained the prevailing sides of the political world of Lincoln's youth.

Thomas Lincoln undoubtedly voted for Jennings. Abe had more than a passing acquaintance with members of the constitutional convention, Alexander Devin and Charles Polke, Emancipationist preachers at the Little

Pigeon Creek Church that he and his family attended. And he regularly read the *Western Register*, published in Terre Haute and edited by John W. Osborn, an antislavery crusader, to which William Jones subscribed. Osborne was a central character in the drama for abolition in Indiana. Osborn had initiated the lawsuit on behalf of a mulatto woman named Polly, held as a slave by Hyacinthe Lasselle, one of the mainstays of the Vincennes Junto and the town's biggest innkeeper. The circuit court ruled there was "no reason" she should not be bound as a slave because she was "born a slave." But the Indiana Supreme Court decided in 1820 that according to the antislavery provision of the state constitution of 1816 "the framers of our constitution intended a total and entire prohibition of slavery in this State." It was slavery's death knell in Indiana. (Osborn continued as a crusading journalist, during the Civil War founding a pro-Lincoln newspaper called *The Stars and Stripes*.)

Even as the slavery issue was closed in Indiana, it raged across the state line in Illinois. The tumultuous battle, at last ending slavery throughout the whole of the Northwest Territory, captivated Indiana, filling its newspapers with passionate articles and drawing antislavery activists into the fray. Osborn, for one, railed against slavery in Illinois, influencing his readers there. News of this contest would have been Lincoln's earliest introduction to the politics of Illinois, an incipient civil war, subsuming them into his own career. They occurred at the very inception of Illinois as a state, but would settle like a geological layer in Lincoln's mind. The politics of Illinois would become his arena and its history his history.

Illinois was admitted to the Union in 1818 and the next year adopted a constitution forbidding slavery. But pro-slavery forces in control of the state legislature adopted a harsh Black Code restricting the presence and activities of blacks, and slavery actually continued to exist. At about the same time, Edward Coles arrived, appointed the federal land registrar by Secretary of the Treasury William Harris Crawford, who was planning to run for the presidency in 1824 and sought to place a political agent in Illinois to counter its U.S. senator, Ninian Edwards, who was backing the prospective candidacy of his rival, Secretary of War John C. Calhoun. Edwards and Calhoun would loom as shadows over Lincoln's life in very different ways.

Edward Coles was the son of a wealthy Virginia aristocrat, John Coles, brother-in-law of Patrick Henry and uncle of Dolley Payne Todd Madison. Thomas Jefferson was a neighbor and special friend of the family. Under the tutelage of Bishop James Madison, president of the College of William and Mary, Coles read the classic texts of Enlightenment thinkers and concluded that slavery violated the spirit of the Declaration of Independence—a document that in its original draft included a lengthy paragraph written by Jefferson condemning the slave trade, "this execrable commerce." A protégé of Jefferson, Coles urged him after his presidency to assume leadership of the antislavery movement; but while Jefferson favored gradual emancipation, at least in theory, he wrote that the task must fall to a younger generation. In his reply to Coles, Jefferson wrote on August 25, 1814, "Your solitary but welcome voice is the first which has brought this sound to my ear, and I have considered the general silence which prevails on this subject as indicating an apathy unfavorable to every hope, yet the hour of emancipation is advancing in the march of time. It will come." President James Madison appointed Coles his private secretary and then plenipotentiary to Russia. Coles held lengthy conversations with Madison pressing him on slavery. In 1819, he sold his plantation and took his slaves with him to Illinois. On the voyage down the Ohio River, before reaching his destination, he gathered them on the deck of his flatboats and declared them freed, and gave each family 160 acres of fertile Illinois farmland.

Coles ran for governor in 1822 against three pro-slavery opponents, whose split votes enabled him to win with a plurality. In his inaugural address, he called in the name of "justice and humanity" for the end of slavery and reform of the Black Code, including a law to thwart slave owners from kidnapping free blacks they claimed as fugitives. His speech triggered an explosion. Pro-slavery feeling in Illinois was reaching fever pitch as a result of the Missouri Compromise of 1820, which permitted slavery south of the Mason-Dixon Line, but allowed Missouri as the exclusion. Prosperous immigrants from Virginia and Kentucky streamed to the promised land of Missouri across Illinois, trailing wagons, cattle, and slaves, and creating an impression

Edward Coles, Second Governor of Illinois

stoked by pro-slavery advocates that if slavery were legal Illinois would be a boom state. But legalization required a convention that would adopt a new constitution to erase its antislavery provision. In order to reach the two-thirds legislative majority for a referendum on a convention, the pro-slavery faction in a coup removed a representative who was an obstacle and replaced him with one in favor. The night after the resolution passed, pro-slavery leaders marched at the head of a mob to Coles's residence, according to a contemporary account, "a wild and indecorous procession by torchlight and liquor," shouting threats: "Convention or death!" "Their object was to intimidate, and crush all opposition at once," wrote Thomas Ford, a Democratic governor of Illinois in the 1840s, who knew Lincoln as a state legislator. Opponents also filed a malicious lawsuit against Coles for supposedly violating the Black Code, claiming his emancipation of his slaves was illegal. Then he was persecuted with a frivolous suit charging him with libel of his antagonists. All the suits drained his resources, but were eventually dismissed years afterward.

Coles, however, was not intimidated. He organized a movement, even bought a newspaper, spent his entire salary in the cause, and was supported by antislavery journalists and preachers. His chief aide was Colonel William S. Hamilton, Alexander Hamilton's son—the protégé of Jefferson and the son of his rival united on the frontier against slavery. For eighteen months, "a long, excited, angry, bitter, and indignant contest" was waged until the conclusive vote in August 1824 banishing slavery from Illinois forever. The county with the greatest vote against the convention, the most antislavery, was Sangamon County.

Antislavery Baptist preachers were at the heart of the movement, forming an anti-convention group of thirty ministers in St. Clair County that spread through fourteen counties blanketing the state. Pro-convention forces, while counting many of the most important political figures, depended more on clamor and invective, lacking the effective organization of the evangelical abolitionists. Lincoln was familiar with at least one of these influential preachers, Reverend James Lemen Sr., who had helped write the original antislavery constitution of Illinois and was later elected to the state legislature while Lincoln served there. In Springfield, Lincoln befriended Lemen's son, James Jr., pastor of a large Baptist church, and was especially close to Lemen cousins, James Matheny, one of Lincoln's earliest political allies, and Ward Hill Lamon, who would become his law partner in Danville, utterly devoted follower, and self-designated bodyguard. The Lemen family later disclosed sketchy diaries of the patriarch and letters claiming to prove he had been originally sent to Illinois by Jefferson on a secret mission to wrest it from the grip of slavery, referred to as "The Jefferson-Lemen Antislavery Compact." Among the letters was one Lincoln supposedly wrote in 1857 to James Lemen, Jr., describing the father as "Jefferson's antislavery agent in Illinois," and praising him for having "set in motion the forces which finally made Illinois a free state." But the historian James A. Edstrom exposed the letter as almost certainly fraudulent and declared the "compact" with Jefferson a "myth." Whether the document was fabricated or not, Lemen did, in fact, play a pivotal role in the antislavery movement in Illinois, and Lincoln was aware of it. More generally, he understood that the North itself was not born free; that the state of his youth and the state he made his own had to struggle to abolish slavery despite the Ordinance of 1787; and that the battles against the extension of slavery in Indiana and Illinois were precursors of "Bleeding Kansas."

Almost at the moment of the 1824 vote in Illinois against a new constitutional convention, the Marquis de Lafayette, the great French general of the American Revolution, Washington's comrade-in-arms, landed in New York for his final tour of America and to pay his last respects to his old revolutionary compatriot Jefferson. It was the most celebrated and widely publicized event of the time, from his grand reception by President James Monroe to his travels through twenty-four states. Lafayette had known Coles in Paris, and Coles accompanied him for a portion of his trip in the Western states, bringing him to Illinois in April 1825, where together they toasted the universal rights of man. Lafayette's personal secretary, Auguste Levasseur, in his account of the tour, reported at length on Coles's political fight in Illinois against men "led astray by ancient prejudices" and how "justice and humanity triumphed." Lafayette's trip would have fired the imagination of the Illinois teenager who worshipped Washington and read everything he could on the American Revolution.

But, above all, especially after the death of his sister, Lincoln wanted to flee, to "light out for the territory ahead." He began clerking at James Gentry's store about a month after she died and a month after that Gentry asked him if he would join his son Allen on a flatboat trip to New Orleans. Lincoln jumped at the chance to explore the wide world. Allen, a few years older, was his friend, and Gentry offered eight dollars a month. It took them weeks to build the boat, but they did not leave until December 1828, shoving off from Gentry's Landing at Rockport on the Ohio River. Lincoln acted as cook, navigator, and crew, the real boy rafting down the Mississippi before the fictional one, steering past shoals, waving lights at twilight to avoid being rammed by steamboats, keeping the small craft from being capsized in storms that turned the mighty river into an angry sea, and guiding the boat at night to the bank, where he and his shipmate slept on deck. Along the way, in the towns on the river, they traded bacon, potatoes, and apples for cotton, tobacco, and the prized commodity of sugar.

One night, on the Sugar Coast of Louisiana, six miles south of Baton Rouge, Gentry and Lincoln were attacked by a gang of blacks armed with hickory clubs, slaves from a nearby plantation, seeking to rob and, according to Lincoln, "kill them." "Lincoln," shouted Gentry, "get the guns and shoot!" But they had no guns; it was a ruse to scare off the intruders. "They were hurt some in the mêlée," Lincoln recalled, speaking in the third person to Scripps, "but succeeded in driving the negroes from the boat, and then 'cut cable,' 'weighed anchor,' and left." Lincoln bore a scar on his head as a memento of the nighttime fight.

New Orleans was the third largest and most cosmopolitan city in the country, about half its residents French speaking, and half black, those divided almost equally between slaves and freemen. The provincial boy must have been dazzled by the public dance halls and theaters, and was appalled by whole streets filled with slave pens and auction blocks. Slaves were paraded before buyers, who inspected them like livestock, purchasing a son but not the mother, a father but not the wife—"a mournful scene indeed," wrote one slave sold at a New Orleans auction house, who later escaped to tell the tale. "I would have cried myself if I had dared." The prohibition of the transatlantic slave trade in 1808 had created a boom in the domestic market, with New Orleans as its most thriving center, providing an endless supply of fresh labor for the new plantations of Alabama, Mississippi, and Louisiana. In the year Lincoln landed in New Orleans, ten thousand slaves were bought and sold there, a more lucrative business than any other, profits sweeter than in sugar. Wandering the teeming city, Lincoln and Gentry were stunned to see barely clothed mulatto women their own age being sold, brazen human trafficking, the sexual subtext as little disguised as the scanty attire. "Allen," said

Lincoln, "that's a disgrace." "We stood and watched the slaves sold in New Orleans," recalled Allen Gentry, "and Abraham was very angry." "When a boy I went to New Orleans on a flatboat," Lincoln wrote in a letter on January 9, 1860, "and there I saw slavery and slave markets as I have never seen them in Kentucky, and I heard worse of the Red River plantations." His letter disclosed that he already had firsthand familiarity with slavery, had seen it as a young boy, and at least once in Louisiana held conversations about its scope. "Why, Abe always was against slavery!" exclaimed James Gentry when later asked about it.

Selling their cargo and the boat, the boys stayed in New Orleans an indeterminate amount of time before boarding a steamer heading north up the Mississippi. Decades later, the battles in the towns and cities along the river would not have been mere names to Lincoln, but distinct places he had seen. Having demonstrated that he could handle himself as a river man, a trader, beating off bandits, and as a buckskin boulevardier, Lincoln returned from his adventures to the grinding life of a contract laborer in an isolated hamlet. He begged William Wood to find him another job on the river. "Abe," he replied, "your age is against you. You are not twenty-one yet." "I know that," he said, "but I want a start."

While Lincoln was hammering together the flatboat and waiting to glide it downriver, he would have been paying close attention to the raucous political campaign of 1828 that marked the advent of the second party system splintering out of the old Jeffersonian Republican-Democrats. Four years earlier, Andrew Jackson won a plurality for president, winning in Indiana, but the election was decided in the House of Representatives, where Henry Clay threw his backing behind John Quincy Adams, an alliance denounced by Jacksonians as "the corrupt bargain." Politics in Indiana still remained organized around personalities and the lingering split between "the Virginia Aristocrats" and "the People." Lincoln memorized Clay's speeches, studying them in the Louisville newspapers, reciting them for friends. "Harry of the West," eloquent and canny, apostle of the "self-made man," advocate of internal improvements and tariff protection of manufactures, the "American System" financed by the federal government, was his hero. The contest of 1828 pitted Adams against Jackson again. Two of the towns near Gentryville were named Jackson and Clay, illustrating the argument. According to Dennis Hanks, he and Abe "went to political and other speeches and gatherings as you do now. We would hear all sides and opinions, talk them over, discuss them, agreeing or disagreeing." Undoubtedly, Lincoln also heard the speeches of the congressman representing his district, Ratliff Boon, who had been Jonathan Jennings's lieutenant governor and succeeded him as governor. He was a Jackson supporter, who campaigned by proudly declaring, "I have nothing to claim through my ancestors." Lincoln, Hanks said, "was originally a Democrat after the order of Jackson—so was his father—so we all were." But he could not fix precisely when Lincoln became a Whig, a party that did not emerge under that label until 1834. "I opposed Abe in politics when he became Whig—was till 20 years of age a Jackson Democrat—turned Whig or Whiggish about 1828—think Col. Jones made him a Whig—don't know."

"I think when the Lincolns left here, they were Jackson men," recalled David Turnham. "I think that Jackson's opposition to the U.S. Bank and the crisis that followed caused them to turn." He was fairly certain that Abe "turned Whig in Illinois." John Hanks, who was not present in Indiana in 1828, offered that Lincoln "could not hear Jackson wrongfully abused, especially where a lie and malice did the abuse." But he added confusedly and almost certainly wrongly, particularly about Thomas Lincoln, "I can say that Abe never was a Democrat: he was always a Whig—so was his father before him."

Lincoln's mentors—the store owner Jones, Justice of the Peace Turnham, and neighbor Wood—were Adams men. But Elizabeth Crawford remembered Abe singing a Jackson campaign jingle ridiculing Adams: "Let auld acquaintance be forgot, And never brought to mind, And Jackson be our President, And Adams left behind." Indiana went overwhelmingly for Jackson. It was possible Lincoln supported him, too, but turned to the new Whigs after Jackson was elected and opposed internal improvements. President Jackson's Maysville Road veto against using federal funds to build a highway in Kentucky in May 1830, a direct rebuff of Clay, did not come until several months after the Lincolns left Indiana. Yet it is also possible that Lincoln was for Adams. (Jones, Lincoln's "guide," was elected a Whig member of the Indiana legislature from 1838 to 1841, and remained a friend. In 1844, when Lincoln returned to Gentryville to deliver a campaign speech for Clay's presidential candidacy, he stayed with Jones. During the war, though in his sixties, Jones joined the Union army, became a colonel, and was killed at the Battle of Atlanta.)

Upon his return to Little Pigeon Creek from New Orleans, Lincoln would have been absorbed reading the newspapers covering the great debate in Washington over states' rights and the authority of the federal government. The conflict had been sparked by a bill to place a moratorium on the sale of Western lands until the current stock was mostly sold, seized as an occasion to forge an alliance of Southern slave owners with the Western states, isolating the nonslaveholding North, protecting and extending slavery. Senator Robert Y. Hayne of South Carolina rose first to defend what he called "the Carolina doctrine"—the right of a state to nullify federal law. As colonel in the state militia he had commanded the suppression of the Denmark Vesey slave revolt conspiracy of 1822 in Charleston, a "conspiracy" undoubtedly inflated by forced confessions obtained through torture, and in 1826 denounced the American Colonization Society, the philanthropy of moderate antislavery elites that sought to reestablish blacks in Africa, for casting aspersions on slavery. Hayne was the protégé of Vice President John C. Calhoun, ideologue of slavery and states' rights, who, sitting as president of the Senate, coached him from the sidelines as he spoke, passing notes. Hayne argued that only the states had true sovereignty, that the federal government was their mere contrivance, and that the policies on public land and tariffs were "grievance oppression." He sarcastically derided the Ordinance of 1787, which banished slavery from the Northwest Territory (including Illinois), declaring that if the states were deprived of the right to nullify federal law the United States would have "a Government without limitation of powers." He finished with a ringing call for "a firm, manly and steady resistance against usurpation" that if not overthrown "will soon involve the whole South in irretrievable ruin."

Then, on January 26 and 27, 1830, Senator Daniel Webster of New Hampshire, "the Godlike Daniel," took the floor. "This," he said, "leads us to inquire into the origin of this government and the source of its power." The idea that "this general government is the creature of the States," was an "absurdity" that "arises from a misconception as to the origin of this government and its true character. It is, Sir, the people's Constitution, the people's government, made for the people, made by the people, and answerable to the people." His conclusion distilled in a phrase the credo of American nationalism: "Liberty and Union, now and forever, one and inseparable!"

Webster's "Second Reply to Hayne" was the most famous speech ever delivered in the Senate, published in full in the newspapers, and reproduced in a pamphlet with an unprecedented circulation of 100,000. (In preparing his First Inaugural Address, Lincoln asked his law partner, William H. Herndon, to bring him a copy of Jackson's proclamation against nullification of 1832 and Clay's oration in favor of the Compromise of 1850, but he did not need the pages of Webster's speech, "the very best speech that was ever delivered," he told Herndon, because he had long ago committed it to memory, paraphrasing it in many speeches of his own, including the Inaugural Address, and later at the dedication of the Gettysburg cemetery.)

In the fall of 1829 and early winter of 1830, Lincoln helped his father build a new house out of wooden planks, a finer and larger structure than the original log cabin. But after an aunt and uncle died in a new epidemic of the milk sickness, the family in a panic decided to leave Indiana. John Hanks had gone to Illinois a year earlier, reporting that it was good territory for starting a farm—and healthier. Thomas sold his corn and hogs, his cabin and new house, and loaded up a wagon pulled by oxen. "I well remember the day when the Lincolns started for Illinois," said James Gentry. "Nearly all the neighbors was there to see them leave." On March 1, 1829, fifteen Lincolns, Johnstons, and Hankses set off. "I reckon we was like one of them tribes of Israel that you can't break up, no-how," said Dennis Hanks. "And Tom was always looking for the land of Canaan. There was five families of us, then, and Abe. It took us two weeks to get there, rafting over the Wabash, cutting our way through the woods, fording rivers, prying wagons and steers out of sloughs with fence rails, and making camp. Abe cracked a joke every time he cracked a whip, and he found a way out of every tight place while the rest of us was standing around scratching our fool heads."

The Lincolns settled outside Decatur in a cabin they built overlooking the Sangamon River. Abe labored as a farmhand, plowman, and mauler of wood, which John Hanks would later recall at a propitious moment during the 1860 campaign to create the indelible image of the "Rail Splitter." Lincoln did, indeed, split many rails, "three thousand rails," according to John Hanks. In the summer of 1830, working to clear a field on the farm near Springfield of William Butler, who was well connected in what would become the state Whig Party, Lincoln attended a political speech delivered by Reverend Peter Cartwright. Cartwright, a Jacksonian Democrat, who represented the district off and on in the state legislature, was one of the most prominent preachers in Illinois, a hellfire-and-brimstone Methodist saver of born-again souls at camp meetings, and once proclaimed, "I have waged an incessant warfare against the world, the flesh, the devil, and all the other enemies of the Democratic Party!" Lincoln, Butler recalled, "was as rough a specimen of humanity as could be found. His legs were bare for six inches between bottom of pants and top of socks," while Cartwright "dressed as became his station." The preacher, according to Butler, "laid down his doctrines in a way which undoubtedly seemed to Lincoln a little too dogmatical. A discussion soon arose between him and Cartwright, and my first special attention was attracted to Lincoln by the way in which he met the great preacher in his arguments, and the extensive acquaintance he showed with the politics of the state—in fact he quite beat him in the argument." It was Lincoln's initial clash with the pastor, whom he would run against twice for public office.

At yet another political meeting that summer, in Decatur, Lincoln heard two Democratic candidates running for the state legislature, one named Ewing and the other Posey. John Hanks thought Posey's speech "was a bad one and I said Abe could beat it." Hanks turned over a box, which Lincoln mounted. "Abe beat him to death—his subject being the navigation of the Sangamon River. The man after the speech was through took Abe aside and asked him where he had learned so much and what he did so well. Abe explained, stating his manner and method of reading and what he had read: the man encouraged Lincoln to persevere." In another account of the incident, George Close, who split rails with Lincoln, recalled that he was at first "frightened but got warmed up and made the best speech of the day. This was L first speech. Did not abuse Posey but spoke well of both men—pictured out the future of Ill[inois]. When he got through Ewing said, 'He was a bright one!' "

Escaping the milk sickness in Indiana, Thomas Lincoln, his wife, and her daughter were afflicted in Illinois in the fall of 1830 with chills and fever, probably malaria. Then what became known as the Deep Snow fell, endless blizzards and subzero temperatures, the bitterest winter in living memory. Abe suffered frostbite while foraging for food. Thomas determined to "git out o' thar" when it was warm again, to return to Indiana.

But John Hanks approached Abe with a proposition to take a flatboat to New Orleans. Hanks had been down the Mississippi several times and a friend of his would stake them. Lincoln, his stepbrother, and Hanks canoed down the Sangamon to Springfield to rendezvous with the middleman. Entering the Buckhorn Tavern, under the sign riddled with bullet holes, they discovered their sponsor sleeping off a drunken night. Denton Offutt, speculator and confidence man, "a wild, harum-scarum kind of a man," "a gassy—windy—brain rattling man," according to those who knew him, was filled with constant schemes, and had unusual talents of persuasion with men and animals. He was probably the first renowned horse whisperer, his skill so unusual that no less than Henry Clay, a fellow Kentuckian, provided him with a letter to proffer touting his ability. "Such is the extraordinary effect of his system in the management of the horse, that he will, in a very short time, render the wildest animal gentle and docile, insomuch that he will subject it to his easy control and direction," Clay wrote. But a sheriff in Vincennes, Indiana, from whose jail Offutt miraculously escaped in 1834, described him as "very talkative and wishes to pass for a gentleman."

Offutt had plied the Mississippi to New Orleans himself and had the notion that he could operate a thriving flatboat trade. He confessed to Hanks, Lincoln, and Johnston that all he lacked was a flatboat. For six weeks, they built one, eighty feet long. Lincoln passed the time playing cards and visiting a magic show in Sangamon Town, his introduction to the theater that would become his lifelong obsession. When the magician asked for his hat as a prop for cooking eggs, Lincoln initially hesitated. "The reason why I didn't give you my hat before was out of respect to your eggs, not care for my hat," he said. Caleb Carman, who met Lincoln as he built the flatboat and would know him later at New Salem, originally thought from his ragged, "very odd" appearance that he was a "Green horn," but changed his mind as soon as Lincoln spoke. "He was funny, jokey, humorous, full of yarns, stories . . . he was frequently quoting poetry, reciting prose like orations. . . . He was a good reader rather than a 'much reader' as the Indian would say: what he read he read thoroughly and well and never forgot it." Lincoln also "talked about politics considerable. He seemed to have the run of politics very well. He was a John Q. Adams man and went his length on that side of politics. He was opposed to slavery and said he thought it a curse to the Land."

The boat's voyage almost ended in disaster near its start. After Lincoln pried loose the boat, which had gotten stuck on a dam at New Salem, while the whole town turned out to watch the spectacle, the first time the people there caught a glimpse of him, he guided the craft down to the Illinois

River and then into the rushing Mississippi, past Cairo and Memphis, Vicksburg and Natchez. The sight of slaves being sold on the streets of New Orleans and in auction houses was not a surprise anymore but still an offense. His anger was hardly softened by familiarity, but instead intensified. "There it was," said John Hanks, "we saw Negroes chained, maltreated, whipped, and scourged. Lincoln saw it—his heart bled—said nothing much—was silent from feeling—was sad—looked bad—felt bad—was thoughtful and abstracted. I can say knowingly that it was on this trip that he formed his opinions of slavery: it ran its iron in him then and there." Lincoln's hostility to slavery, according to John Hanks, was so vociferous that it worried him. "His talk against slavery right down there amongst it reminded me of our good old deacon, back in Indiana, accusing the people of their wickedness afore their face, and backing it up reading from Scripture as he went along. By them days he could talk as well as anybody, not excepting the biggest preachers, and we had some good ones. We were afeared of getting into trouble about his talking so much, and we coaxed him with all our might to be quieter-like down there, for it wouldn't do any good no-how."

Herndon later vaguely remembered hearing from John Hanks an implausible story he would not confirm that in New Orleans "they visited an old fortune teller, a Voudou negress. Tradition says that during the interview she became very much excited, and after various predictions exclaimed: 'You will be President, and all the negroes will be free.'" But Herndon did assert positively to Isaac Arnold, an Illinois friend and biographer of Lincoln, that Hanks told him they observed "a slave, a beautiful mulatto girl, sold at auction. She was *felt over, pinched, trotted* around to show to bidders that said article was sound, etc. Lincoln walked away from the sad, inhuman scene with a deep feeling of *unsmotherable* hate." It was then, according to Hanks, that he declared, "By God! If I ever get a chance to hit that institution I'll hit it hard, John."

When Abe arrived home in June, Thomas Lincoln packed up yet another family caravan. Lincoln was already twenty-one years old, no longer bound to his father, but had stayed to help the family settle into its new home. Now Thomas cut the cord, leaving Abe behind. Intending to return to Indiana, he stopped in Coles County, Illinois, at the home of his sister-in-law, where he built a cabin in Buck Grove. Three years later, he moved again, to Muddy Point, and three years after that to Goosenest Prairie. "They moved so often," said Sarah Bush Lincoln, "that it reminded her of the children of Israel try-ing to find the Promised Land." Abe rarely saw his father again, but when he was a prosperous lawyer gave him money so that he and his stepmother could live comfortably. He never permitted him to visit his family in Spring-field. When Thomas was dying in 1851, Lincoln refused to come, writing his stepbrother, John D. Johnston, "Say to him that if we could meet now, it is doubtful whether it would not be more painful than pleasant." Lincoln did not attend the funeral.

"Lincoln can do anything," declared Offutt, after the successful venture to New Orleans. "I really believe he could take the flatboat back again up the river." But Offutt had another plan in mind for his new discovery. As Lincoln told Scripps, "he conceived a liking for Abraham, and believing he could turn him to account, he contracted with him to act as clerk for him." Offutt would open a general store and mill in New Salem with Lincoln run-ning it. In July Lincoln set off for the town walking through the tall prairie grass and riding down the Sangamon. "He assured those with whom he came in contact that he was a piece of floating driftwood," wrote Herndon, "that after the winter of deep snow, he had come down the river with the freshet; borne along by the swelling waters, and aimlessly floating about, he had accidentally lodged at New Salem."

CHAPTER TWO

THE AGE OF REASON

—————◆———————

Can you write?" "Yes, I can make a few rabbit tracks," replied Lincoln. Mentor Graham, the schoolteacher in New Salem, was also the town's election clerk. National, state, and local offices were on the ballot that August. Lincoln had spent about two months leisurely waiting for Offutt's supplies for the general store to arrive. As usual, Offutt's promises exceeded his performance. Hanging around the polling place, the lanky young man found himself recruited by Graham as his assistant. It was Lincoln's first official position and his first vote. He cast his ballot for Congress for James Turney, the former Illinois attorney general and a follower of Henry Clay, who was defeated. (Edward Coles also lost a race for the Congress in the neighboring district.) Passing the time while the voters sauntered in, Lincoln entertained a gaggle of men with a comical story about a preacher, who after declaring to his congregation, "I am the Christ, whom I will represent today," discovered a lizard had

Thomas Paine

crawled into his pants, which he threw off, and then into his shirt, which he also tossed aside, provoking a church lady to announce, "Well! If you represent the Christ then I am done with the Bible."

New Salem was a market town with great expectations, founded only three years before in 1828 by John Camron, a Cumberland Presbyterian preacher, and his uncle, James Rutledge. (Camron's first cousin, Simon Cameron, would become Lincoln's first secretary of war. Rutledge was related to the South Carolina Rutledges that included a signer of the Declaration of Independence and the second chief justice of the Supreme Court.) Offutt's investment banked on New Salem becoming a boomtown. He rented Rutledge's mill, built a store and a hog pen, and announced he would sell corn and cotton seed. A few months later, the store opened, with chief clerk Lincoln behind the counter. He was paid $25 a month, assisted by two even younger clerks, William E. "Slicky Bill" Greene and Charles Maltby. "The store was usually closed at 7 P.M.," recalled Maltby, "when occasionally an evening would be spent with some family or young people in the village, and those occasional visits or calls were seasons of mutual pleasure and gratification. Lincoln's humorous fund of anecdotes and stories made him a welcome visitor at all times. The most of the evenings, however, after closing the store, were, from 8 to 11 o'clock, employed by Lincoln in reading and study; a short time then was spent in reviewing the reading of the evening, and then blankets were spread upon the counter and the inmates retired to rest on their hard couch, which prepared them for the labors and duties of the coming day."

"There lived at this time in and around New Salem, a band of rollicking, roistering fellows, known throughout all this region as the 'Clary's Grove Boys,'" recalled John Todd Stuart, who would soon serve as one of Lincoln's mentors. "These rowdies, although they included among their number many of the most influential men of the central region of Illinois, were emphatically wild and rough, and were the terror of all those who did not belong to the company. These 'Boys' in connection with the duty of regulating the neighborhood took it upon themselves to try the mettle of every new comer and ascertain what sort of stuff he was made of by appointing some one of their number to wrestle, fight or run a foot race with him, as the case might be." Offutt boasted to Bill Clary that his clerk, six foot four inches tall and weighing about two hundred pounds, could best in a wrestling match their toughest champion, Jack Armstrong, who, incidentally, Lincoln had voted for sheriff. Lincoln did not want to fight, but failing to pass this hazing would lead to being accused of cowardice, "social death, in fact," wrote Whitney. In any case, Offutt and Clary had gambled ten dollars on the outcome. When Lincoln seemed to be winning, the "Boys" intervened to help Armstrong throw Lincoln, but according to various garbled versions the match ended in a kind of draw. "Lincoln however took all this in perfect good humor," said Stuart, "and by laughing and joking displayed such an excellent disposition that he at once won their hearts and was invited to become one of the company." Lincoln did more than prevent further trouble or even make new friends. According to Stuart, *"This was the turning point in Lincoln's life."* Lincoln, of course, had many turning points, but the wrestling match was the origin of his political rise. The Clary's Grove Boys, a rough-and-tumble gang, became his personally devoted boosters, advocates, and organizers—the core of a political operation.

In the winter of 1832, James Rutledge organized a debating society, the town's intellectual center. Robert B. Rutledge, his son, recalled Lincoln's appearance—"as he arose to speak his tall form towered above the little assembly." The meeting was "in an underground room of a rude log cabin," said Jason Duncan, a physician, who had befriended Lincoln and was present. "Both hands were thrust down deep in the pockets of his pantaloons," said R. B. Rutledge, describing Lincoln as he prepared to deliver his first speech. "A perceptible smile at once lit up the faces of the audience for all anticipated the relation of some humorous story. But he opened up the discussion in splendid style to the infinite astonishment of his friends. As he warmed with his subject his hands would forsake his pockets and would enforce his ideas by awkward gestures; but would very soon seek their easy resting place."

One subject of debate, according to Charles Maltby, was: "Are the principles and policy of African slavery so unjust, and the evils thereof of such magnitude as to make the colonization and emancipation of the enslaved colored race in the United States necessary and desirable for the welfare of the American people?" He claimed that it was Lincoln who suggested the question. The best men of the town were there—the schoolteacher, doctors, and preachers—and women were invited, too. But Dr. John Allen, who was present, stated, "With but a rare exception, clubs were composed of men of no education whatever." Lincoln began by citing the Declaration of Independence, recalled Maltby. In his account, Lincoln declared:

The object and aim of our Government is and should be to elevate and dignify free labor, to make the laboring man a peer of any employed in the different avocations and pursuits of life. We see and know that the effects and results of slavery are to degrade labor and to make it despicable and to bring it into contempt. Those of us who came from the slave States know from observation and experience that the condition of the poor white man there is a hopeless one, and that by the side of slavery, which brands labor with degradation and disgrace, the condition of the poor white laborer and his family is without hope in the present as well as for the future. Society there takes the form of an aristocracy instead of an equality, and caste, which is inimical to our republican institutions, becomes a fixed and deleterious principle in our body politic.

If these were not Lincoln's exact words, it is likely they were a recollection of them, even if improved in retrospect. Yet this rhetoric was informed by the political experiences of Indiana and Illinois, and made the common points of antislavery Whigs.

The New Salem club was one of many that proliferated in the vicinity, discussing a host of topics: slavery, women's rights, and the urgency of internal improvement that would make the Sangamon River navigable. Lincoln, according to Dr. Allen, "used to walk six miles to attend another debating society, and 'practice polemics' as they said." It was a revelation to one and all that the shabbily dressed, gangly village character that wrestled and told uproarious, often off-color stories, when he was not strangely reading compulsively, could also make a cogent argument. He suddenly appeared in a new light, a raw talent that could represent the river town in the legislature, where it had no spokesman. James Rutledge and a group of respectable figures, undoubtedly those who had heard Lincoln speak at the debating society, suggested that he should run for office, "claiming that they had a right to a member from that part of the county," according to John Rowan Herndon, a storeowner married to Mentor Graham's sister. At first, Lincoln resisted, telling his would-be backers "that it was impossible to be elected," recalled John B. Rutledge. But they replied that the campaign would make him prominent in the district and lay the groundwork for his future election in 1834—"in time would do him good."

Lincoln launched his political career on March 9, 1832, with an "address to the people of Sangamon County." His platform was for extensive internal improvements, clearing the Sangamon River, of course, and building railroads and supporting public education. In his first effort at self-presentation, he committed himself to the political vocation. "Every man is said to have his peculiar ambition. . . . How far I shall succeed in gratifying this ambition is yet to be developed. . . . I am young and unknown to many of you. I was born, have ever remained, in the most humble walks of life. I have no wealthy or popular relations or friends to recommend me."

Just at that moment a heroic effort to navigate the Sangamon offered a chance to raise his profile. Vincent Bogue, who owned mills along the Sangamon, secured the financial backing of leading citizens to take a steamship, the *Talisman*, up the river to Springfield. (One of the supporters was Dr. John Todd, whose niece Lincoln would soon meet.) The *Talisman* nearly spanned the river, and in the freezing weather ax-men, including Lincoln, hacked through the tangle of trees blocking the boat's path, until it docked at Springfield, greeted by the townspeople as the herald of a new era. "The people then believed that the Sangamon would always be navigable for steamboats and they were wild with excitement with the outlook for Springfield's prosperity," wrote one resident. They staged a ball at the courthouse and held a round of parties. Lincoln attended a celebration at a tavern called the Indian Queen. He had the forethought to bring along handbills of his "address to the people" for distribution. "It was my first sight of a steamboat, and also the first time I ever saw Mr. Lincoln," wrote thirteen-year-old William H. Herndon, who would become Lincoln's law partner. His cousin, John Rowan Herndon, and Lincoln piloted the steamship back down the river, but the river level had dropped and it had to be brought back to Springfield. Lincoln was paid forty dollars. The voyage of the *Talisman* was the last time a large boat attempted to navigate the river. Bogue, who had been hailed as a conqueror in poetic verses in the *Sangamo Journal*, went bust, leaving his creditors in the lurch. But his ill-fated enterprise had provided Lincoln his public entrance into Springfield.

About the time of Lincoln's return to New Salem, Offutt's house of cards collapsed and he skipped town, leaving his creditors with unpaid bills and Lincoln without his job. (Years later, Offutt was spotted passing himself off as a veterinarian and working his magic as a horse whisperer.) At the same time, an Indian war broke out on the Illinois frontier. Black Hawk, chief of the Sac and Fox tribes, expelled from Illinois to the Iowa Territory under terms of a bogus treaty, brought hundreds of warriors across the Mississippi to the Rock River Valley to stake land and plant corn. Governor John Reynolds issued a ringing call for volunteers to repel the invasion. Lincoln promptly answered it.

The first order of business of the 4th Illinois Regiment of Mounted Volunteers from New Salem was the election of their captain. It was expected that they would select William Kirkpatrick, a sawmill owner, one of the most affluent men from the town. Lincoln had labored for him cutting logs, "but had fallen out with him and left him because he was so tyrannical," according to Dr. Allen. So Lincoln decided he would stand as a candidate for captain against Kirkpatrick. The voting was conducted in the open with the men lining up behind the one they wanted as their officer. "Slicky Bill" Greene began by moving behind Lincoln. Then the Clary's Grove Boys joined him. Kirkpatrick was left standing alone. Jack Armstrong served as Lincoln's sergeant. "Lincoln informed me in general terms of this, his first candidacy," wrote Whitney, "and observed that no event of his life ever gave him such a thrill of happiness as this triumph."

Lincoln saw no combat in the Black Hawk War and later spoke humorously of his duty: "I had a good many bloody struggles with the mosquitoes." But, in fact, he witnessed the ghastly consequences of warfare, burying five soldiers killed and scalped by Indians in the Battle of Stillman's Run at Kellogg's Grove. "I remember just how those men looked as we rode up the little hill where their camp was," he told the journalist Noah Brooks. "The red light of the morning sun was streaming upon them as they lay head towards us on the ground. And every man had a round red spot on top of his head, about as big as a dollar where the redskins had taken his scalp. It was frightful, but it was grotesque, and the red sunlight seemed to paint everything all over." Lincoln did not know the victims, but the shock must not have been anonymous. The mutilated bodies were bloody reminders of how his grandfather, his namesake, Abraham Lincoln, had been murdered.

Late in the war, an old Indian named "Jack" entered Lincoln's company's camp bearing a safe conduct letter from Secretary of War Lewis Cass. The easily aroused men held him prisoner and wanted to kill him on the grounds that they were there to kill Indians. "Barbarians would not kill a prisoner," said Lincoln. But some replied to their captain that he was "cowardly." "Try me," he said, and, according to "Slicky Bill," "swore if Indian was slaughtered must be done over his dead body. Asked them to come out and fight *him*, if they thought he was cowardly." Undoubtedly, the Clary's Grove Boys stood behind him. The Indian was saved.

William Cullen Bryant, the poet and editor of the *New York Post*, who traveled to Illinois to observe the war, encountered Lincoln's company. "They were a hard-looking set of men," he wrote, "unkempt and unshaved, wearing shirts of dark calico, and sometimes calico capotes." Bryant also had a "quaint and pleasant talk" with their young captain, whose identity he learned only decades later after he had introduced him to speak at Cooper Union.

John Dixon, the operator of the ferry on the Rock River and founder of the town aptly named Dixon, a center of the war's action, insisted that he had met there Lieutenant Colonel Zachary Taylor, Lieutenant Jefferson Davis, and Private Abraham Lincoln. (Dixon would become the boyhood home of another future president, Ronald Reagan.) Most of Lincoln's company had mustered out in May, but he reenlisted, assigned as a private to a unit called "the spy company." Dixon claimed also to have met Lieutenant Robert Anderson, who would become commander at Fort Sumter. For this assertion, there is corroboration from Lincoln himself and his captain, who both recalled that it was Anderson who mustered out the company, on July 16, 1832. During the war Lincoln made even more valuable contacts: John Todd Stuart, a major in another company, and Elijah Iles, captain of "the spy company," who was perhaps the largest real estate developer in Springfield, and a state senator, both of whom would figure in Lincoln's career.

After three months in the militia, Lincoln immediately resumed electioneering. He had only about two weeks before the election in August. "Gentlemen," he announced at one public gathering, "I have just returned from the campaign. My personal appearance is rather shabby and dark. I am almost as red as those men I have been chasing through the prairies and forests on the rivers of Illinois." Before another crowd, he declared himself a thoroughgoing Whig: "My politics are short and sweet, like the old woman's dance. I am in favor of a national bank. I am in favor of the internal improvement system and a high protective tariff. These are my sentiments and political principles. If elected, I shall be thankful; if not, it will be all the same." Wherever he went he was accompanied by the Clary's Grove Boys, having served under him in the Black Hawk War, now his soldiers in politics, whipping up enthusiasm and roughly dispatching any hecklers, though Lincoln didn't require their physical intervention, jumping into a fight at a public sale where he was speaking and tossing the combatants ten feet. "I know that it made him many friends," remarked Rowan Herndon about the thrashing he delivered to the roustabouts.

The *Sangamo Journal* mistakenly left Lincoln, still obscure beyond New Salem, off the list of candidates. But his obscurity and inexperience did not prevent him from asserting himself as the equal of the best-known politicians. Quietly, he established a relationship with John Todd Stuart, the leader of the anti-Jackson, pro-Clay party in Springfield. Two days before the election, on August 4, all the candidates were invited to address the public at the Old Court House at Springfield. "I never saw Lincoln until he came up here to make a speech," observed Stephen T. Logan, an attorney who would later become his law partner. "I saw Lincoln before he went up into the stand to make his speech. He was a very tall and gawky and rough looking fellow then—his pantaloons didn't meet his shoes by six inches. But after he began speaking I became very much interested in him. He made a very sensible speech."

Just days earlier the pro-Clay *Sangamo Journal* had published the news about President Jackson's veto of the Bank of the United States, a titanic collision over economic policy and political power. Lincoln, the avid and assiduous newspaper reader, devoured the details, and spoke for a half hour without hesitation on the subject. Then he wheeled on Reverend Peter Cartwright, the most prominent Democratic candidate in the field, who was sharing the stage with him. Two years earlier he had taunted the preacher on the stump. Now he demanded that Cartwright explain his position on the bank veto. When the usually intimidating Cartwright stammered an indecisive answer, Lincoln unsheathed his rhetorical scalpel for the first time in a political setting. "I heard him debate with Peter Cartwright, who was the terror of every local orator, as his opponent," recalled one of his New Salem supporters. "He asked Cartwright if General Jackson did right. . . . Cartwright evaded the question and gave a very indefinite answer. Lincoln remarked that Cartwright reminded him of a hunter he once knew who recognized the fact that in summer the deer were red and in winter gray, and at one season therefore a deer might resemble a calf. The hunter had brought down one at long range when it was hard to see the difference, and boasting of his own marksmanship had said: 'I shot at it so as to hit it if it was a deer and miss it if it was a calf.' This convulsed the audience, and carried them with Lincoln."

Voters could cast their ballots for four candidates to fill the slots. Three Jackson men won, including Cartwright, and one Clay man, Stuart. Lincoln finished in the second tier of thirteen candidates, with 657 votes, 205 coming from New Salem, where he only lost three votes. He was more than encouraged—he had invisibly crossed the line into committing himself to politics. In a field of old hands, he had proven he had a core of loyal supporters, held his own against a fabled orator, and impressed leading political men with his ability to develop rapport with voters. "Everybody who became acquainted with him in this campaign of 1832," said Stuart, "learned to rely on him with the most implicit confidence."

In distant Washington, the crisis over nullification moved toward its climax. The South Carolina legislature had passed a measure nullifying the tariff, Vice President Calhoun had quit to be elected U.S. senator, where he acted as tribune for nullification, taking the seat of Hayne, who became governor, where he mobilized an army to defend states' rights and seize the forts around Charleston. On December 8, Jackson drew a line in the sand with his Proclamation Against Nullification, asserting that it was the Union that preceded the states, the central question that would later arise over secession: "I consider, then, the power to annul a law of the United States, assumed by one State, incompatible with the existence of the Union, contradicted expressly by the letter of the Constitution, unauthorized by its spirit, inconsistent with every principle on which It was founded, and destructive of the great object for which it was formed." In Illinois, Democratic governor John Reynolds issued his own supporting proclamation, declaring nullification "treasonable." Calhoun backed down, the tariff was negotiated downward, but the groundwork was laid for secession.

In New Salem, Clary's Grove Boys, back from their splendid little war without a scratch and their raucous campaigning for their captain, ran amok. Reuben Radford had a grocery store that sold liquor, as nearly every store did, but had decreed that he would not serve more than two drinks to a customer. Taking the rule as a personal insult, the Boys "got roaring drunk and went to work to smash everything in the store," recalled townsman Thompson G. Onstot. Radford sold out to Reverend John Berry, a well-to-do property holder and Cumberland Presbyterian preacher, who bought it for a proper business to set up his wild son, William, in a partnership with Lincoln. Berry & Lincoln's took on too much inventory, gave too much credit, and Berry drank too much. "Of course," Lincoln told Scripps, "they did nothing but get deeper and deeper in debt." Lincoln was pleasant to customers, when he bothered to work behind the counter, leaving the business side to his dissolute partner. Inevitably, as Lincoln put it, "The store winked out." Lincoln was left with what he called "the national debt" and was hounded for years by creditors.

Lincoln was much happier with his appointment as postmaster, which he ran out of his hat and Samuel Hill's store. Despite being a Clay man, the patronage job was so insignificant that his Democratic supporters in the town swung it for him. "Never saw a man better pleased," recalled Dr. Allen. ". . . Was because, as he said, he would then have access to all the newspapers, never yet being able to get the half that he wanted before." "His favorite paper was the *Louisville Journal*, which he for many years studied—and paid for when he had not money enough to dress decently," said his friend George Close. Rowan Herndon recalled him reading the *Louisville Journal*, *Sangamo Journal*, *Missouri Republican*, and the *Congressional Globe*, the nineteenth-century version of the *Congressional Record*, which published all the debates in Washington. "His text book," said Mentor Graham, "was the *Louisville Journal*. He was a regular subscriber to the Journal." That paper was the voice of Henry Clay.

Lincoln also was appointed to an even better paying position, allowing him to continue as postmaster at the same time. The county surveyor, John Calhoun, a leading local Democrat, who had voted in 1832 for Clay because of Jackson's bank veto and served in the Black Hawk War, hired him as his deputy. Lincoln laid out new towns throughout Sangamon County and gained firsthand knowledge of nearly every inch. He would have been aware, of course, that George Washington had been a surveyor. More importantly, the commercial men of the town who were now his political backers had an interest in his work setting the parameters of real estate in a county larger than Rhode Island. (Calhoun would later move to Kansas, becoming a leader of the pro-slavery forces and president of their Lecompton Constitution Convention.)

Mentor Graham, the schoolteacher, with whom Lincoln was boarding, instructed him in the craft of surveying. Graham also got a copy of *Kirkham's Grammar* and drilled him. "If you ever expect to go before the public in any capacity I think it the best thing you can do," Graham told him. "I have taught in my life four or six thousand people as school master and no one ever surpassed him in rapidly, quickly and well acquiring the rudiments and rules of English grammar." Like others in the town, Graham was helping to prepare Lincoln for the rigors of public life.

Lincoln's assistants in surveying were Hugh Armstrong, Jack's brother, who had served with Lincoln in the militia, and Jack Kelso, jack-of-all-trades and amateur literary scholar, who rambled along with Lincoln discussing the finer points of the poetry of Robert Burns and the plays of Shakespeare. "Kelso and Lincoln were great friends—always together—always talking and arguing," recalled Hardin Bale, who ran the mill. Kelso loved the Bard and fishing. "Abe loved Shakespeare but not fishing," said Caleb Carman. ". . . they used to sit on the bank of the river and quote Shakespeare—criticize one another." "Slicky Bill" recalled that Lincoln "was always reading Burns and Shakespeare. Knew all of Burns by heart." "He could very nearly quote all of Burn's poems from memory. . . . He had acquired the Scotch accent, and could render Burns perfectly," said Milton Hay, who studied law under Lincoln in his Springfield office, became a prominent lawyer, and was the uncle of John Hay, who became Lincoln's White House private secretary.

Lincoln would certainly have known Burns's poem on slavery, "The Slave's Lament":

> *It was in sweet Senegal*
> *That my foes did me enthral*
> *For the lands of Virginia, 'ginia, O!*
> *Torn from that lovely shore*
> *And must never see it more*
> *and alas! I am weary, weary, O!*
> *The burden I must bear,*
> *While the cruel scourge I fear,*
> *In the lands of Virginia, Oginia, O!*
> *With the bitter, bitter tear,*
> *And alas! I am weary, weary, O!*

Milton Hay remembered Lincoln reciting various Burns poems, especially "Holy Willie's Prayer," a savage satire of a Calvinist calling down bolts of heavenly vengeance on those he hated but dispensation for himself, a poem that lampooned piety, predestination, and God's retribution. Lincoln's close friend James Matheny, the assistant postmaster in Springfield, who would become the best man at his wedding, an attorney, and a Whig politician, "often" heard him "quote Burns—quoted 'Holy Willie's Prayer' with great pleasure: That it was L[incoln's] religion. . . . Burns helped Lincoln to be an infidel as I think—at least he found in Burns a like thinker and feeler."

Burns, the bard of the Scottish Enlightenment, elevated skepticism and individual rights against Calvinist dogmatism and hierarchical authority, "the science of man," as David Hume put it, a paramount belief in "toleration and liberty." It was a broad movement that influenced its English, French, and American counterparts, not least Benjamin Franklin, who corresponded with its learned members. Lincoln would have paid special attention to Burns's personal story, "the heaven-taught ploughman," son of a tenant farmer, a failed farmer himself, who taught himself grammar.

In the period between the elections of 1832 and 1834, Lincoln applied himself as a student of Enlightenment literature. Burns's verses were not Lincoln's sole sources of skepticism. He devoured the works of the era's preeminent freethinkers and debunkers of Scripture, Thomas Paine's *The Age of Reason* and Constantine de Volney's *The Ruins: Meditations on the Revolutions of Empires*. "Lincoln read both these books and thus assimilated them into his own being," wrote Herndon.

Paine, the English radical, was a man for all revolutions. His friend Benjamin Franklin had encouraged Paine to emigrate to America. Whether Paine wrote an early pamphlet against slavery in 1775, "African Slavery in America," remains uncertain, but a short time after its publication he helped found in Philadelphia the first abolitionist society in the country, the Society for the Relief of Free Negroes Unlawfully Held in Bondage, to which, after its further organization, Franklin was elected its president. During the American Revolution, Paine wrote *Common Sense*, its trumpet call, and then plunged himself into the French Revolution, got elected to the National Convention, and was nearly executed in the Reign of Terror. Defending the Revolution of 1787 in *The Rights of Man* against Edmund Burke's conservative polemics, Paine completed his demolition of the old regime with *The Age of*

Reason, reducing organized religion to rubble. "All national institutions of churches," he wrote, "whether Jewish, Christian or Turkish, appear to me no other than human inventions, set up to terrify and enslave mankind, and monopolize power and profit." Paine deconstructed the mythologies of the Bible, stripping them of mystery and miracles, from the Garden of Eden to Jesus' virgin birth, revealing merely "impositions and forgeries." In place of "the general wreck of superstition," he upheld "morality," "humanity," and "theology" rooted in free thought. "I believe the equality of man; and I believe that religious duties consist in doing justice, loving mercy, and endeavoring to make our fellow creatures happy. . . . My own mind is my own church." The Federalists especially excoriated Paine for his impiety, President John Adams denouncing him as a "Blackguard," and Paine was marked as notorious until his impecunious death.

Volney is a forgotten philosophe, yet probably was the closest to the Americans, not only to Paine, but also especially to Jefferson. One of the younger members of Madame Helvétius's fabled intellectual Parisian salon that included Voltaire, Diderot, and Benjamin Franklin, he was an ally of Lafayette in the Revolution and with him founded La Société des Amis des Noirs, the first French abolitionist group in 1788, distributing antislavery tracts. Like Paine, he was imprisoned during the Terror, and upon his release traveled to America. This friend of Lafayette stayed with Washington at Mount Vernon, who was astounded by his precise predictions of Napoleon's military strategies, only to learn that Volney had been his tutor. Volney moved on to Monticello, where he began a literary project with Jefferson. Volney was displeased with various English translations of his book, *The Ruins*, so Jefferson stepped in to translate it himself. In 1798, Adams and the Federalists enacted the repressive Alien and Sedition Acts to quash political opposition from Jefferson's party. Volney was singled out as an "infidel" for his religious iconoclasm. "Volney has in truth been the principal object aimed at by the [Alien] law," Jefferson wrote Madison. The freethinker fled back to France, where he refused Napoleon's offer to make him minister of the interior, but nonetheless accepted designation as a senator. Jefferson, who had already translated twenty chapters of *The Ruins*, turned the task over to Joel Barlow, the poet and diplomat to whom Paine had vouchsafed his manuscript of *The Age of Reason* for publication. The Jefferson-Barlow translation was published in 1802.

Volney had lived for years in the Middle East, mastered Arabic, and studied Islam. His work was a sweeping anthropological survey of world religions as "dogma . . . that in every instance, the means and the causes of propagating and establishing systems have exhibited the same scenes of passion and the same events everywhere, disputes about words, pretexts for zeal, revolutions and wars excited by the ambition of princes, the knavery of apostles, the credulity of proselytes, the ignorance of the vulgar, the exclusive cupidity and intolerant arrogance of all: in fine, you will see that the whole history of the spirit of religion is only the history of the errors of the human mind."

In *The Ruins*, Volney mounted an assault on slavery as barbarism, "this inequality" of the strong over the weak, "taken for the law of nature"— might makes right—and yet, he argued, "individual slavery prepared the way for the slavery of nations." He categorized forms of "political despotism" and "sacred imposters" that manipulated religion—aristocracy, monarchy, theocracy, and all distinct versions of "tyranny" contemptuous of "the inconveniences of democracy." Drawing on his experience with the Terror, he also described a new kind of tyranny: "Then the factions, taking advantage of the general discontent, flattered the people with the hope of a better master; they scattered gifts and promises, dethroned the despot to substitute themselves in his stead; and disputes for the succession or the division of power have tormented the state with the disorders and devastations of civil war." And then he charted Napoleon's rise, how "one individual more artful or more fortunate than the rest, gaining the ascendancy, concentrated the whole power in himself." With this analysis, Volney was perhaps the first political writer to begin outlining the emergence of modern dictatorship.

"Volney and Paine became a part of Mr. Lincoln from 1834 to the end of his life," wrote Herndon. Others who knew Lincoln well also commented on his attachment to their ideas. James Tuttle, an Illinois lawyer and friend, remarked, "He was one of the most ardent admirers of Thomas Paine I ever met. He was continually quoting from the 'Age of Reason.' Said he, 'I never tire of reading Paine.'" The works of Paine and Volney, both Deists, argued that God exercised no rule over reason and liberal secular democracy should prevail against dogmas of all sorts but especially the influence of church authorities. Lincoln echoed their religion when he declared his own pithy credo, according to Herndon, "When I do good, I feel good; when I do bad, I feel bad, and that is my religion." The influence of Paine can also be detected in Lincoln's logical, pointed, unadorned, and lapidary writing style. And the influence of Volney might be reflected in Lincoln's Cooper Union address, refuting the idea that "might makes right."

Inspired by Paine and Volney, Lincoln wrote his own theological tract, "Lincoln's little book on infidelity," as James Matheny called it. "The book was an attack upon the whole grounds of Christianity, and especially was it an attack upon the idea that Jesus was *the Christ,* the true and only-begotten Son of God, as the Christian world contends," recounted Herndon. Lincoln showed his work to the shopkeeper Samuel Hill, who apparently shared his skepticism, but took an avuncular, protective approach to the reckless Deist. "Hill at that time saw in Mr. Lincoln a rising man, and wished him success." He urged Lincoln to destroy his manuscript, Lincoln refused, and Hill simply tossed it into the stove, "and so Lincoln's book went up to the clouds in smoke."

The book burning did not brand him with the caution that he should stifle his views on organized religion. It was only later that he learned to speak with politic respect for it. The evidence from his close friends through the decades of what was called his "infidelity," but what was in reality his skepticism, is overwhelming. Testimony that Herndon collected through extensive interviews piled one confirming anecdote upon another. Ward H. Lamon's biography includes an entire section of such statements. To wit: One of Lincoln's White House assistants, John G. Nicolay, said, "Mr. Lincoln did not, to my knowledge, in any way, change his religious ideas, opinions or beliefs, from the time he left Springfield till the day of his death." David Davis, one of Lincoln's closest associates, an Illinois circuit court judge who became his presidential campaign manager and was appointed a justice of the Supreme Court, remarked: "He had no faith, in the Christian sense of the term."

Lincoln regarded the primitive evangelical churches as part of a world, his father's world, which he was rising beyond. But, more than that, he was repulsed by heartlessness justified by claims of scriptural surety, damning sinners to hell, fostering fear and guilt. He had observed preachers and cliques punish ordinary people with harsh condemnations, ostracizing them from their little congregations, branding them as outcasts, sowing bitterness, ruining reputations, and curdling lives. Reverend Berry, the father of his partner in the misbegotten store venture, for example, had disowned his teenaged daughter for a youthful marriage and shunned the funeral of her stillborn child. For Lincoln, the hurtful consequences of religion, especially intolerant versions of Calvinism, were entwined with its irrationalism. The appeal to ecstatic fervor also ran against his grain. His encounter with Paine and Volney came just as he sought to develop himself through logic, law, and grammar, following the clear lines of the surveyor, beginning to chart his career. He rejected the authority of divines he thought ignorant, cruel, and emotionally exploitative, relying instead on his own emerging age of reason, which he thought reflected not a more indifferent, fatalistic outlook but a kinder and more humane one.

Jesse Fell, an Illinois friend, explained Lincoln's rejection of specific religious doctrines widely held to be eternal truths. "On the innate depravity of man, the character and office of the great Head of the Church, the atonement, the infallibility of the written revelation, the performance of miracles, the nature and design of present and future rewards and punishments (as they are popularly called), and many other subjects, he held opinions utterly at variance with what are usually taught in the Church. I should say that his expressed views on these and kindred topics were such as, in the estimation of most believers, would place him entirely outside the Christian pale." That said, Fell defensively added, "Yet, to my mind, such was not the true position, since his principles and practices and the spirit of his whole life were of the very kind we universally agree to call Christian; and I think this conclusion is in no wise affected by the circumstance that he never attached himself to any religious society whatever." "All this is no evidence of a want of religion in Mr. Lincoln," Herndon, his fellow skeptic, concluded. "It is rather an evidence that he had his own religion."

There is no record, reminiscence, or report of Lincoln attending a camp meeting, though he must have witnessed more than one. But there is an account of his attendance at the first circus ever to visit Springfield in 1833, featuring a frightening eighteen-foot-long anaconda that had the audience "transfixed with terror" and a daredevil woman riding a horse at full speed around a ring that "took people's breath away." Lincoln traveled from New Salem to watch the parade and the performance, attired in a new suit, necktie, and fancy hat for the occasion. The circus was said by one longtime resident to have caused the most excitement since Lincoln helped land the *Talisman*.

Lincoln's study of the law was pursued under the watchful eye of the man whom he adopted as a kind of surrogate father, Bowling Green, the mirthful, storytelling justice of the peace. Lincoln "loved Mr. Green . . . as he did his father," recalled Abner Y. Ellis, a friend of Lincoln, "and Mr. Green looked on him with pride and pleasure. I have heard Mr. Green say that there was good material in Abe and he only wanted education." (Lincoln, by the way, pressed Ellis if he had read Paine and Volney.) Green had a special connection to Lincoln, having "some little acquaintance with Mr. Lincoln's mother's family." He was also Jack Armstrong's half brother, in effect, the political leader of Clary's Grove Boys. The older Green had held a host of positions from sheriff to canal commissioner to State House doorkeeper, and Lincoln told Ellis "he owed more to Mr. Green for his advancement than any other man." Green even allowed the unlicensed Lincoln to try law cases in his court, preparing him for the future the older man envisioned for him.

Green recruited Lincoln as his assistant at "a respectable meeting of the citizens of new Salem," a gathering of local Whigs on March 1, 1834, to endorse and promote a candidate for governor, General James Henry, a Springfield merchant and hero of the Black Hawk War. Green served as chairman, Lincoln as secretary. The meeting not only endorsed a candidate but also passed a resolution calling for a governor "free from and above party and sectarian influence." That statement was aimed at the two Democratic contenders, Congressman Joseph Duncan, who had used his position to become one of the richest men in the state, and Reverend William C. Kinney, a Baptist minister and former lieutenant governor, who became wealthy trading whiskey, hogs, and slaves. The New Salem resolution proposing that preachers should not hold public office—"sectarian influence"—helped undermine Kinney. Unfortunately, General Henry died of consumption shortly after the endorsement, and Duncan became governor, keeping his Democratic label but embracing Whig policies.

Lincoln's duties as surveyor and postmaster sent him to Springfield, where he cultivated the local Whigs. His friend Ellis, who had a job in a store there, introduced him to political people. Matheny, who worked in Springfield, delivered his anonymously bylined articles for the *Sangamo Journal*—"took hundreds of such editorials from Lincoln to the *Journal* office," he said.

By the spring of 1834, Lincoln was already campaigning, running again for the state legislature, and making the rounds of public gatherings accompanied by his bodyguard of Clary's Grove Boys. But word was around that he was a religious skeptic. Matheny recalled that his father, a Methodist minister, "loving Lincoln with all his soul, hated to vote for him because he heard that Lincoln was an infidel." Another Lincoln friend, Russell Godbey, said his brother-in-law told him "Abe was a deist," but Godbey voted for him anyway.

Lincoln had the approval of the Whigs in Springfield, but it was his supporters in New Salem that found the pressure point. Many of them were Democrats, but "very mad" that in the last election "their chosen candidate did not receive votes elsewhere in the county," according to Stephen T. Logan, and "they told their democratic brethren in the other parts of the county that they must help elect Lincoln, or else they wouldn't support the other democratic candidates. This they did purely out of their personal regard for him, and through that influence he was elected in 1834. That was the general understanding of the matter here at the time. In this he made no concession of principle—whatever. He was as stiff as a man could be in his Whig doctrines. They did this for him simply because he was popular—because he was Lincoln."

Before the gambit went into effect, Lincoln quietly pulled John Todd Stuart aside at a campaign event to inform him that the Democrats "would drop two of their men and take him up and vote for him for the purpose of beating me." Stuart was grateful to Lincoln for telling him and in doing so Lincoln had revealed to him that he was more than fair; he was politically shrewd. Stuart said he "had great confidence in my strength," and he "told Lincoln to go and tell them he would take their votes. . . . I and my friends knowing their tactics, then concentrated our fight against one of their men . . . and in this way . . . elected Lincoln and myself."

Lincoln's relationship with Stuart, the leader of the Whigs in the legislature, soon to make him his law partner, was cemented. "During the canvass, in a private conversation he encouraged Abraham [to] study law," Lincoln told Scripps. "After the election he borrowed books of Stuart, took them home with him, and went at it in good earnest. He studied with nobody."

With his first election, Lincoln, the self-made man in his first vindication, viewed himself in the image of Henry Clay. "Henry Clay was his favorite of all the great men of the nation. He all but worshiped his name," recalled John Rowan Herndon. If any book was his bible, it was the *Biography of Clay*, written by George D. Prentice, the editor of the *Louisville Journal*. According to the first full-scale life of Lincoln, a campaign biography published in 1860, based on materials provided by Lincoln himself, entitled *The Pioneer Boy*, by William Makepeace Thayer, "He was particularly taken with the discouraging surroundings of Clay in his boyhood and youth, when he was known as the 'mill-boy of the slashes,' because those surroundings were so much like those of his own boyhood. Some of his friends believe that reading the Life of Clay turned his thoughts or aims, perhaps unconsciously to himself, in the direction of a public career." Clay's path provided a map. Lincoln studied the life as well as the politics of his "beau ideal."

"I inherited infancy, ignorance and indigence," said Clay, the son of a Baptist pastor and middling Virginia planter, a father who died when Henry was four, leaving him and his mother to be terrorized by British soldiers during the Revolution. Educated in a common school, Clay's brilliance attracted the attention of powerful public men in Virginia, studying the law under George Wythe, a signer of the Declaration of Independence and mentor of Thomas Jefferson and John Marshall. After moving to Lexington, Kentucky, Clay made his initial impression through his first speech at the local debating society, surprising listeners with his eloquence. Clay then made his political entrance at the age of twenty-one with an essay in 1798 about the Kentucky constitutional convention, arguing against slavery and for gradual emancipation. "All America," he wrote, "acknowledges the existence of slavery to be an evil. The sooner we attempt its destruction the better." But unlike those states covered in the Northwest Ordinance that entered later and prohibited slavery, Kentucky came into the Union as a slave state. In 1803, Clay began his ascent up the political ladder by running for the state legislature, where he unsuccessfully proposed moving the state capital from Frankfort to Lexington. His social status was secured by marrying the well-connected Lucretia Hart, daughter of Colonel Thomas Hart, a wealthy merchant and landowner. As U.S. senator, congressman, speaker of the house, secretary of state, and presidential candidate he became "Prince Hal," "Harry of the West," and "The Great Compromiser." "If any man wants the key to my heart," he would say in 1844, "let him take the key of the Union, and that is the key to my heart."

Lincoln's early career closely followed the stations of Clay—the debating society, the state legislature, the law, and the upward marriage. He memorized and cited his speeches, quoting him forty-one times in his 1858 debates with Stephen A. Douglas. When Lincoln was edged out for a congressional nomination, feeling deserted, he wrote in a letter on February 13, 1843, to a friend, "It would astonish if not amuse the older citizens to learn that I (a strange, friendless, uneducated, penniless boy, working on a flat-boat at ten dollars per month) have been put down here as the candidate of pride, wealth, and aristocratic family distinction." His self-description was nothing less than a direct paraphrase of Clay's emotional speech of May 16, 1829, upon his return to Lexington after four years as secretary of state, for a lengthy enforced political retirement, securing his home base, before running for president against Andrew Jackson in 1832. "I came among you, now more than thirty years ago," said Clay, "an orphan boy, penniless, a stranger to you all, without friends, without the favor of the great." Even in a private letter, Lincoln echoed Clay, whose words he had absorbed and whose model he sought to emulate.

In December 1834, Lincoln prepared for his new career by asking his friend Coleman Smoot for a loan of $200 to buy a new suit. "I want to make a decent appearance in the legislature," he explained. "He was then dressed in a very respectable looking suit of jeans," said his friend Jesse K. Dubois. "Henry Clay once went to Congress in a suit of jeans, and it had become a sort of Whig dress."

CHAPTER THREE

THE SLASHER

———◆————

L incoln, the political apprentice, put himself in the service of John Todd
Stuart, only two years older, but already Springfield's leading attorney,
a college-educated gentleman, the Whig minority floor leader, known to his
peers as "Jerry Sly" for his sinuous arts and "Sleepy Johnny" for his somnambulant speaking style. Stuart recalled, "He frequently traded Lincoln off.
He was the author of no special or general act—had no organizing power.
When he learned in 1838 and '40 more of the tricks, etc.,
of men he refused to be sold. *He never had a price.*"
Lincoln learned log-rolling by first being a log
rolled by the log-rollers, the term for the lobbyists before they were called lobbyists, though
he was apparently unusual in not receiving
any monetary reward. Members of the legislature were commonly said to be "greased
and swallowed" by log-rollers, as well as lubricated with "soft soap."

Lincoln did not deliver a single speech
in his first session as a legislator. "If Lincoln
at this time felt the divine afflatus of greatness
stir within him I have never heard of it. . . . The
impression that Mr. Lincoln made upon me

John Todd Stuart

when I first saw him . . . was very slight," wrote a fellow state representative, Usher F. Linder, a native Kentuckian who happened also to know Lincoln's well-to-do Uncle Mordecai. "He had the appearance of a good-natured, easy, unambitious man, of plain good sense, and unobtrusive in his manners," Linder wrote of Lincoln. "At that time he told me no stories and perpetrated no jokes." Linder must have missed a couple of Lincoln's jokes, which amounted to the sum and substance of his remarks before the legislature.

Lincoln arrived duded up in his new suit at the state capital, Vandalia, located on the Kaskaskia River, eighty-two miles southeast from St. Louis, hardly the gleaming Emerald City, containing about eight hundred people, one hundred houses, half a dozen taverns and inns (where nearly all the legislators lodged), two churches, and a school. There were no sidewalks and the main street either swirled with dust or was mired in mud. Beyond the village lay hundreds of unbroken square miles of prairies whose tall grasses rolled like the ocean, described as "the most extensive tract of rich land in the world," by an awestruck visitor, James Stuart, the Scottish politician (who after an argument over supposedly libelous articles had killed James Boswell in a duel). If Stuart liked coming to blows he had come to the right town.

Vandalia's nightlife mainly consisted of drunken sprees and wild fights. A special area called "the Bull Pen" was designated for bare-knuckle battling, but hardly restricted there. Stores kept an open barrel of whiskey with a dipper at the door. Physical brawls and political brawls were frequently indistinguishable. The distinguished gentlemen of the legislature regularly threatened each other with physical harm, occasionally wrestling on the floor, with biting not unknown. These representatives were not far removed from their constituents—"the half-horse, half-alligator men," "the butcher-knife boys," "the huge-pawed boys"—names catalogued by Governor Thomas Ford in his memoir—like Clary's Grove Boys. The usually alcohol-fueled violence among men who were almost all of Southern origin was justified according to a debased and vernacular version of the Southern code of honor. Manhood was at stake, as in the wrestling match posed to Lincoln when he first appeared at New Salem. Debates often took on the aspect of duels with legislators daring to "take down" their opponents. Refusal to engage a challenge was seen as cowardice. Winning elevated social status. Careers rose and fell on these fights and duels.

Illinois was a Northern state without a north, the most Southern of the free states, populated largely from the upper South, with the most draconian Black Code of any state without slavery. The Yankee migration to northern Illinois was just trickling in. Chicago barely existed. It was not incorporated as a formal city until 1837. Its population in 1830 was an estimated 100 people, in 1840, 4,470. By 1860, it had become one of the fastest growing cities in the world, its population exploding to 112,172. But when Lincoln appeared at Vandalia, there was not yet even a Cook County.

Kaskaskia was the original capital of the Illinois Territory, a bustling river town on the Mississippi, located deep in southern Illinois, an area so southern it was called Upper Louisiana, founded by French settlers who traded slaves for labor in Missouri's lead mines. This was the northern-most reach of the culture and economy of slavery rooted at New Orleans. Kaskaskia, however, was constantly flooded, prompting the U.S. Congress in 1819 to donate a patch of land in the wilderness for the new state's capital. In time, Kaskaskia was swallowed by the Mississippi waters and became a tiny island. The 2010 census recorded a population of fourteen.

The first State House at Vandalia burned to the ground in 1823. The floors of the hastily constructed second one buckled and its walls bulged. It was so ramshackle a structure that legislators refused to enter fearful it would collapse on them. About the time Lincoln arrived, a third State House was being built.

Vandalia attempted a veneer of respectability with a distinctly Southern cast. "The brilliant modes of the *elite* of Kentucky society were initiated," wrote Henry Clay Whitney, a lawyer and friend of Lincoln's who had attended college in Kentucky, "and young lady graduates from the Kentucky seminaries were 'introduced' into Illinois society here. Local statesmen affected the lofty airs of Kentucky politics, and Vandalia, during a legislative session, was a reflex of Frankfort during a similar period. The Yankees had made no perceptible impression as yet."

Political parties were yet to tighten their ranks. New issues meant new alliances, opportunities for shifting positions, and plunder. "Personal politics, intrigue, and a disregard of the public welfare, were carried from the primary elections into the legislature," wrote Thomas Ford, governor of Illinois in the early 1840s. "Almost everything there was done from personal motives. Special legislation for the benefit of friends occupied members, and diverted their attention from such measures as were for the general benefit. The man of the most tact and address, who could make the most friends and the most skillful combinations of individual interests, was always the most successful in accomplishing his purposes."

The concept of very limited government played out in the provincial state capital to the advantage of the log-rollers. "During this period of twelve years," wrote Ford, "neither the people nor their public servants ever dreamed that government might be made the instrument to accomplish a higher destiny for the people. . . . The people asked nothing and claimed nothing but to be let alone, and the politicians usually went to work to divide out the benefits and advantages of government amongst themselves; that is, amongst the active men, who sought them with most tact and diligence. Offices and jobs were created, and special laws of all kinds for individual, not general benefit, were passed, and these good things were divided out by bargains, intrigues, and log-rolling combinations, and were mostly obtained by fraud, deceit, and tact."

Vandalia was the early lyceum of Lincoln's political education, where he began his study of its arts and science. The first session of the legislature he attended in early 1835 was similar to the "blab school" where he said and did as he was told, and recited his lessons.

Before he departed for the capital, he put his life in order, quietly becoming engaged to marry Ann Rutledge, according to numerous people. "I loved the woman dearly and sacredly," he told his old friend from New Salem, Isaac Cogdal, shortly after he was elected president in 1860. "She was a handsome girl, would have made a good loving wife, was natural and quite intellectual, though not highly educated. I did honestly and truly love the girl and think often—often of her now."

Lincoln had known Ann since he arrived in New Salem, when she was the seventeen-year-old daughter of James Rutledge, one of the town founders. Lincoln boarded with the Rutledges sporadically in 1834–35. The red-haired, blue-eyed Ann was engaged to a man named John McNamar, who departed for his native New York to see his family sometime in 1832, while Lincoln enlisted in the Black Hawk War. McNamar had not returned for two years when the courtship between Abe and Ann began. They sang songs together, studied *Kirkham's Grammar*, both writing their names in the book, and planned to marry. The engagement was kept private, though generally known to her relatives and other close friends, because she sought

English Grammar Book signed by Lincoln and Ann Rutledge

"the propriety of seeing McNamar, inform him of the change in her feelings and seek an honorable release, before consummating the engagement with Mr. L. by marriage," her brother Robert B. Rutledge recalled. She confided in her cousin, James McGrady Rutledge, "that engagements made too far ahead sometimes failed, that one had failed [meaning her engagement with McNamar] Ann gave me to understand, that as soon as certain studies were completed she and Lincoln would be married." He believed she was "contented to wait a year for their marriage after their engagement until Abraham Lincoln was admitted to the bar."

After an unusually rainy spring and summer of 1835, Ann was stricken with what was commonly described as "brain fever," almost certainly typhus, and died on August 25. Lincoln, who hovered over her deathbed, suffered the first of his depressive mental breakdowns. The death of his fiancée summoned his grief from the earlier deaths of his mother and sister. "The effect upon Mr. Lincoln's mind was terrible; he became plunged in despair, and many of his friends feared that reason would desert her throne," said Robert B. Rutledge. No less than eighteen eyewitnesses offered descriptions of his anguish, many fearing not just for his sanity but also that he might commit suicide. "Mr. Lincoln's friends after this sudden death of one whom his soul and heart dearly and loved were compelled to keep watch and ward

over Mr. Lincoln, he being from the sudden shock somewhat temporarily de-
ranged," said "Slicky Bill" Greene. "We watched during storms, fogs, damp
gloomy weather Mr. Lincoln for fear of an accident. He said, 'I can never be
reconciled to have the snow, rains and storms to beat on her grave.'"

"Lincoln and she was engaged—Lincoln told me so. She intimated to me
the same," recalled Mentor Graham. "He, Lincoln, told me that he felt like
committing suicide often." A fellow state legislator from Sangamon County,
Robert L. Wilson, remembered, "In a conversation with him about that
time, he told me that although he appeared to enjoy life rapturously, still he
was the victim of terrible melancholy. He sought company, and indulged in
fun and hilarity without restraint, or stint as to time. Still when by himself,
he told me that he was so overcome with mental depression, that he never
dare carry a knife in his pocket. And as long as I was intimately acquainted
with him, previous to his commencement of the practice of the law, he never
carried a pocket knife."

Lincoln's surrogate father, Bowling Green, took him in for weeks until he
recovered his equilibrium. Then he immersed himself in the study of the law
so obsessively that his friends worried for his health. "The continued thought
and study of the man caused—with the death of one whom he dearly and
sincerely loved, a momentary—only partial and momentary derangement,"
observed Mentor Graham. (Some months after Ann's death, John McNamar
suddenly reappeared at New Salem, carting furniture in preparation for his
marriage, startled to learn of Ann's death.)

Everyone who knew Ann Rutledge eulogized her as attractive, bright,
and kind. The daughter of a prosperous member of a town father, she undoubtedly gave Lincoln a sense of rootedness. Without his own family, she
would be the center of his new one. She was apparently interested in self-
improvement and to her he must have represented an exciting new life of
discovery that would carry her beyond the little world of New Salem. It is
impossible to know how Lincoln would have developed if he had been completely content, married to a pleasant wife, but who, while lending him support, still lacked a keen political upbringing and preternatural ambition that
would spur him to reach for the highest rewards in politics. There would be
only one woman he would ever meet like that.

The death of Ann Rutledge marked the beginning of the end of Lincoln's
relationship to New Salem. He would soon relocate to Springfield, establish-

ing it as his new political base, running as a candidate from a district there. New Salem was already starting to unravel in any case. Its residents were moving two miles away, often carting their houses and stores with them, to the better-sited new town on the Sangamon of Petersburg, which Lincoln had surveyed and whose incorporation he had helped sponsor. The clear sign of New Salem's decline came when its post office closed in May 1836. By 1840, after Sam Hill literally carried his store to Petersburg, leaving his abandoned house as the sole building standing, New Salem had become a ghost town, winking out like Berry & Lincoln's store.

When the second session of the legislature was called on December 7, 1835, Lincoln was untethered to any particular place by personal ties; his dream of marriage and family had been shattered. He had no life except politics. In the legislature he was an enthusiastic proponent of internal improvements, voting for the Illinois and Michigan Canal Act that would favor northern Illinois, and which was opposed by representatives from the southern part of the state. Lincoln also successfully sponsored the Beardstown and Sangamon Canal Act, purchasing stock himself in the B&S Canal Company, one dollar down and four dollars on margin. The bill was heavily promoted by a close Lincoln ally, Francis Arnez, editor of the *Beardstown Chronicle*, a newspaper in which Lincoln often published pseudonymous political articles. The early Whigs were a tightly bound community of interests. Arnez became the B&S Canal Company president, and a number of its executives, including Ninian W. Edwards, Lincoln's future brother-in-law, also purchased real estate in the new town of Huron, which was surveyed by Lincoln and would be the terminus of the canal. Lincoln himself bought forty-seven riverfront acres in Huron at the minimum government price of $1.25 an acre.

Beneath the debate over the Illinois and Michigan Canal flowed a deeper conflict. "The old settlers were convinced that *negro* slavery was the normal condition of all civilized life, and they believed that it existed here as well as in 'Old Kaintuck,'" said Joseph Gillespie, one of Lincoln's closest friends, a Whig legislator who also served in the Black Hawk War. The Black Code was as near to legalizing slavery as could be enacted. "They were, however, afraid that an influx of Yankees might interfere with their sacred rights, and hence they hated the 'Down-Easters' with the most intense feelings. It was no uncommon thing to hear some of them declare that it would have been a God's blessing if the *May Flower* had gone to the bottom of the ocean with all her crew and passengers. They opposed the construction of the Illinois and Michigan canal, because 'it would open up a way for the Yankees to get here.'"

Among the articles Lincoln published in the *Beardstown Chronicle* one was particularly notable, an ad hominem attack, appearing in November 1834, written under the byline of "Samuel Hill," aimed at one of Lincoln's favorite targets, Reverend Peter Cartwright. Hill and Cartwright had a long-standing acrimonious relationship. Holding forth to a crowd gathered in front of Hill's store, Cartwright had declared, "He said he had some doubts whether he had a soul till one day he put a quarter and dollar on Hill's lips, when his soul came guggling up to get the piece of silver." Hill undoubtedly paid Lincoln to write the piece assailing his enemy in the pages of the *Chronicle*. Lincoln, the brazen freethinker, flayed Cartwright's congregants as "priest ridden" three times, and claimed falsely that the pastor had bilked them to maintain "one of the largest and best improved farms in Sangamon County. . . . For a church or community to be priest ridden by a man who will take their money and treat them kindly in return is bad enough in all conscience; but to be ridden by one who is continually exposing them to ridicule by making a public boast of his power to hoodwink them, is insufferable." For good measure he called Cartwright a "hypocrite" and "fool or knave."

Hill knew that alongside the studious, diligent, and melancholy Lincoln there existed another Lincoln, gleefully wielding sarcasm and ridicule like a stiletto. He had honed his satirical derision at an early age. Embittered at the Grigsby family after the death of his sister, and after he was not invited to the double wedding of two of the brothers, Reuben and Charles, he composed a ribald spoof in mock biblical verse. In this backwoods burlesque the brothers bedded the wrong brides while the third brother, William, "has married a boy." After Ann Rutledge's death, the pattern of mourning and aggression seemed to repeat itself. Politics now allowed Lincoln free play for his aggressive invective.

Returned to Vandalia, he plunged into the tempest of the election campaign, with every office from his own up to the presidency at stake. Through his cutting style he emerged as a brilliant revelation to his fellow Whigs and vaulted almost overnight to the front rank of leadership in his party. No longer circumscribed by his own district, he roamed from town to town debating in public, leaving a trail of prominent Democrats tattered and humiliated. He deployed the tricks of the trade with forensic skill that was unrestrained and yet subtle—combining logic and illogic, innuendo, invidious comparison, and accusations of hypocrisy. He hurled opponents' words back at them and exploited divisive issues. Lincoln was unleashed at a propitious moment for the Whigs. The Democrats had begun enforcing strict party discipline to restrain factionalism, triggering an equal and opposite reaction among the Whigs. Lincoln was an exemplar of this new partisanship.

President Jackson was a commanding figure, but he was retiring. He bequeathed the rancor stirred up during his tumultuous administration to his vice president, Martin Van Buren, "The Little Magician," a smooth political operator who spent his career trying to avoid making enemies. The ingenious wirepuller of the Democratic machine of New York state, the Albany Regency, he had been central in assembling the diverse national Jackson coalition. He was the man behind the curtain, but stumbling as he was thrust center stage, a classic case of bureaucratic leadership succeeding the charismatic. Jackson's golden blessing ironically made the glittering prize unsteady in his hand. Fearful of offending any person or faction, Van Buren had privately counseled Jackson not to issue his proclamation against nullification—"caution—caution"—yet it was that clash that allowed him to supersede John C. Calhoun as vice president and as the favored one to follow Jackson. But Van Buren was infinitely nervous that he was the first Democratic presidential candidate not from the South. His early nomination in May 1835, moreover, made him a stationary target a year and a half before the election. Trying to solve his Southern problem with his choice of a running mate—the number two trying to demonstrate his cunning in picking his own number two—he disastrously selected Congressman and former senator Richard Mentor Johnson of Kentucky, lionized as the killer of the great Indian chief Tecumseh. Jackson had been a military hero, so the idea was to add a military hero to his ticket. The Southern aristocracy, however, held Johnson in contempt for his unspeakable vulgarity, in particular flaunting liaisons with three of his female slaves and openly acknowledging two mulatto daughters. The appalled Virginia delegation to the Democratic convention, already disenchanted with Van Buren, whom they suspected without evidence of antislavery sympathies, attempted to derail Johnson's nomination, proposing instead a sterling member of the Richmond Junto,

Senator William C. Rives. After tamping down their rebellion, Van Buren tried to calm Southerners by rallying support in the Congress for the "Gag Rule" that automatically tabled abolitionist petitions to end slavery in the District of Columbia. "Since I was a boy I have been stigmatized as the apologist of Southern institutions," Van Buren protested, "and now forsooth you good people will have it that I am an abolitionist." But his reflexive reactions only made him seem, forsooth, like a weathervane in a windstorm.

One of the most widely circulated Whig campaign documents, *The Life of Martin Van Buren,* published in 1835, bore the authorship of David "Davy" Crockett, a Whig congressman from Tennessee defeated the year before, already a folk legend, the result of his trail-blazing self-promotion, but who was absent for the rest of the campaign, departed to Texas, where he was killed at the Battle of the Alamo on March 6, 1836. "Van Buren," he wrote, "is as opposite to General Jackson as dung is to a diamond. Jackson is open, bold, warm-hearted, confiding, and passionate to a fault. Van Buren is secret, sly, selfish, cold, calculating, distrustful, treacherous; and if he could gain an object just as well by openness as intrigue, he would choose the latter." But even more nefarious, Crockett accused Van Buren of harboring a secret agenda—"his support of abolition"—intending to subvert the Constitution. The backroom politician had a backroom conspiracy. "Can Mr. Van Buren say he is not one of these *agitators* for *a political purpose?*" Thus Crockett pioneered the line of attack that the quintessential Northern man with Southern sympathies was really a Northern man with abolitionist plans.

The Whig strategy lacked central focus and consistent principles, its haziness characteristic of the whole history of the party, not simply its rough beginnings. Four Whig candidates were supported for president with the idea that they would accumulate enough votes to throw the election into the House of Representatives, where Van Buren would be denied just as Jackson had been in 1824. Lincoln and the Illinois Whigs backed the Western candidate, Senator Hugh Lawson White, a wealthy Tennessee slave owner, whose father had founded the town of Knoxville, and been one of Jackson's closest allies, "known to have been opposed to all the leading measures and policy of the Whigs of the Northern States," according to his daughter's account. White, however, had bitterly turned against Jackson, claiming that certain of his executive actions violated states' rights and especially objecting to the anointment of the Northerner Van Buren as his successor. For Illinois

Whigs, the White candidacy was intended to play upon dissatisfaction with Van Buren of Southern-minded Democrats, who were called "White Democrats," and among the most active of them Bowling Green.

Daniel Webster ran as the Whig candidate from New England while his ideological opposite, Senator Willie Person Mangum, a nullifier from North Carolina, was the Southern Whig addition. William Henry Harrison, now living in Ohio, was a late entry, filling out the Whig slate of candidates from each region of the country, sometimes jostling each other and without any common platform. (That Mangum would win South Carolina's electoral votes was not any sign of Whig strength but of the tight control of Calhoun, who was his own party.)

In Vandalia, the Democrats took advantage of the first day of the legislative session to stage a novel process, a statewide party convention of county delegates to endorse candidates and lift up the beleaguered Van Buren under the slogan "Unite and Conquer." The tactic was partly an effort to counter the Whigs' "White Democrats" gambit. Two days later the Whig minority in the state House of Representatives, including Lincoln, introduced a symbolic resolution: "That we believe the establishment of the convention system in this state, for the purpose of nominating all state and county officers, to be anti-republican, and ought not to be tolerated in a republican government."

This set off a rapid-fire game of tit-for-tat. The Whigs proposed a bill in the state Senate endorsing the candidacy of White and denouncing the "Van Buren party" for calling itself the "Democracy." With several "White Democrats" joining the Whigs, the measure passed by 13 to 12. In a spirit of retaliation, the Democrats in the House introduced a resolution endorsing Van Buren and decrying that "the false and arrogant claims of the Webster, White, and Harrison party, to the exclusive use of the ancient and honorable name of *Whig* was grossly unjust."

Finally, the Whigs rallied behind a resolution intended to affix onto the Democrats the issue of Van Buren as a covert abolitionist: "Resolved, that the elective franchise should be kept pure from contamination by the admission of colored voters." Van Buren, in fact, had supported a provision in the New York state constitution of 1821 that would sustain the existing qualification for free blacks who owned $250 in property to vote in state Senate elections. "Mr. Van Buren is an abolitionist," the *Sangamo Journal* proclaimed. "We have long been apprised that Mr. Van Buren is the candidate through whose election the Northern fanatics hope to consummate their schemes of amalgamation"—introducing the theme of racial sexual panic.

Lincoln maneuvered on behalf of these resolutions and chided Democrats in an anonymous letter published in the *Journal* for not passing the one prohibiting black voting. The *Journal*'s editor, Simeon Francis, was Lincoln's close friend, and its pages were always open to his pseudonymous articles and editorials subject to his influence. Lincoln was named a Whig presidential elector pledged to White and coordinated the statewide campaign on the Illinois Whig Central Committee. On the stump, he became the foremost practitioner from his party of the "slasher-gaff" style, a local term that a Whig state senator had coined to describe the scornful style of Democrats but that gained general currency.

Lincoln was likely the author of a series of letters published in the *Journal* assailing Democrats for "their votes in favor of negro suffrage," according to the historian Michael Burlingame. One letter in black dialect, appearing under the name of its supposed black author, "Sees-Her" (Caesar), likely written by Lincoln, stated, "Wanjuren [Van Buren] says de nigger all shall vote, and dat oder man in Kentucky state [Richard Mentor Johnson], is goin to make all the nigger women's children white."

Lincoln was also likely the author, according to Burlingame, of letters in rustic dialect in the *Journal* under the byline "Johnny Blubberhead," intended to present the mangled thoughts of George R. Weber, coeditor of the leading Democratic newspaper, the *Springfield Republican*, maligning a host of Democrats, including Congressman William "Big Red" May, against whom John Todd Stuart was running. In another letter, under the pseudonym "Spoon River," Lincoln praised Stuart for his "untiring zeal" in passing the Illinois and Michigan Canal Act, while labeling the Democrats the "Monster party." "Spoon River" also cast the presidential election as a contest between "ruffle-shirted Vannies" for Van Buren and "the people" for White.

"Lincoln was by common consent looked up to and relied on as the leading Whig exponent," said fellow legislator Robert L. Wilson, who explained "that he was the best versed and most captivating and trenchant speaker on their side; that he preserved his temper nearly always, and when extremely provoked, he did not respond with the illogical proposal to fight about it, but used the weapons of sarcasm and ridicule, and always prevailed." Ninian W. Edwards would occasionally campaign with Lincoln, "although the former was a scion of wealth and aristocracy, while the latter was of the poorest of his class." Lincoln would slice up an opponent, always maintaining cool composure, but "Edwards would get mad, and propose to fight it out then and there." In a heated debate with his Democratic opponent, Achilles Morris, Edwards resorted to waving a pistol at him.

Lincoln's sudden surfacing as an effective figure attracted the immediate attention of Democrats anxious to diminish and destroy him. Rumors of an unnamed but damaging Lincoln scandal began circulating. One traceable source was a prominent Democrat, Robert Allen, who had been a colonel in the Black Hawk War and owned the largest stagecoach company in Springfield. Lincoln wrote him on June 21 an audacious letter in a tone of high sarcasm:

> I am told that during my absence last week, you passed through this place, and stated publicly, that you were in possession of a fact or facts, which, if known to the public, would entirely destroy the prospects of N. W. Edwards and myself at the ensuing election; but that, through favor to us, you should forbear to divulge them. No one has needed favors more than I, and generally, few have been less unwilling to accept them; but in this case, favor to me, would be injustice to the public, and therefore I must beg your pardon for declining it. That I once had the confidence of the people of Sangamon, is sufficiently evident, and if I have since done anything, either by design or misadventure, which if known, would subject me to a forfeiture of that confidence, he that knows of that thing, and conceals it, is a traitor to his country's interest. I find myself wholly unable to form any conjecture of what fact or facts, real or supposed, you spoke; but my opinion of your veracity, will not permit me, for a moment, to doubt, that you at least believed what you said. I am flattered with the personal regard you manifested for me, but I do hope that, on more mature reflection, you will view the public interest as a paramount consideration, and, therefore, determine to let the worst come.

Allen backed down from Lincoln's challenge and the rumors, if they were ever more than that, never materialized as public accusations.

The formal campaign was launched on July 11 at the Springfield courthouse with rival teams of legislators debating. The first speaker, Ninian W. Edwards, assailed Van Buren's support for black suffrage. Jacob M. Early, a physician and Methodist minister, known as "The Fighting Parson," replied that Andrew Jackson himself had taken the same position as a delegate to the Tennessee constitutional convention. Early attempted to turn the knife by claiming "that one of the principal writers on the question of free negro suffrage, here, would sooner see his daughter married to a negro than a poor white man." Presumably, he meant the wealthy Edwards. It was probably at this point that Edwards climbed onto a table to accuse Early of lying. "The excitement that followed was intense, so much so, that fighting men thought a duel must settle the difficulty," wrote Robert L. Wilson. Then Lincoln got his chance to speak. He had served under Captain Early in "the spy company" during the Black Hawk War. He started in a "slow and deliberate manner," according to his first biographer, John Locke Scripps. Then "some well-aimed shaft of ridicule penetrated and disclosed a weak place in his opponent's argument," and "he laid bare the sophisms and misrepresentations. . . . When he sat down, his reputation was made. Not only had he achieved a signal victory over the acknowledged champion of Democracy, but also he had placed himself, by a single effort, in the very front rank of able and eloquent debaters. The surprise of his audience was only equaled by their enthusiasm; and of all the surprised people on that memorable occasion, perhaps no one was more profoundly astonished than Lincoln himself." For the first time, recalled Wilson, Lincoln "spoke in that tenor intonation of voice that ultimately settled down into that clear shrill monotone style of speaking that enabled his audience, however large, to hear distinctly the lowest sound of his voice."

The *Sangamo Journal* editorialized after the debate with a transparent double entendre referring to candidate Hugh Lawson White: "Let every WHITE man do his duty." The newspaper extravagantly praised Lincoln for his speech: "A girl might be born and become a mother before the Van Buren men will forget Mr. Lincoln." In the aftermath of his clash with Reverend Dr. Early, Lincoln likely wrote a letter on one of his favorite themes, published in the *Journal* on July 16, excoriating the Democrats, which, "as it now stands can in truth be called the PREACHER TICKET—there being no less than three preachers out of seven candidates, a pretty heavy load, I think."

After the Springfield opening debate opposing partisans rode in a caravan through the prairies, staging performances in towns throughout vast

Sangamon County. At one debate, Lincoln was said to have "skinned" an opponent and at another to have "peeled" him. The traveling road show returned for a grand finale back at the Springfield courthouse on July 31, the day before the legislative election. In the sequence of speakers, Lincoln finished last "in a most masterly style," according to Joshua Speed, who witnessed the event. As the crowd began to disperse, George Forquer, who was not one of the scheduled speakers, stepped forward. "This young man will have to be taken down, and I am truly sorry that the task devolves upon me," he announced. Forquer, one of the most influential politicians in the state, had obviously been tasked by the Democrats with the job of cutting down the new Whig champion. He had been an ally of the territorial governor, Ninian Edwards, an Illinois Supreme Court judge, and was the older brother of Thomas Ford, guiding him from office to office until Ford was elected governor in 1842. The most salient political fact about Forquer was that he had been a stalwart Whig until his recent conversion to Democrat, his apostasy miraculously accompanied by appointment as head of the lucrative General Land Office. He also resided in the largest house in Springfield, the first to be topped with a newfangled lightning rod. In the pages of the *Sangamo Journal*, Lincoln had scoffed at him as "King George" and "the royal George." Undoubtedly, Forquer was well aware of the identity of the anonymous editorial writer. "He then proceeded in a vein of irony, sarcasm, and wit, to ridicule Lincoln in every way that he could," recalled Speed. Lincoln stood ten feet away on the podium, his arms folded. "The gentleman commenced his speech by saying that this young man would have to be taken down, alluding to me," Lincoln replied. "I am not so young in years as I am in the tricks and trades of a politician; but live long, or die young, I would rather die now, than, like the gentleman change my politics, and simultaneous with the change, receive an office worth three thousand dollars per year, and then have to erect a lightning rod over my house, to protect a guilty conscience from an offended God." Lincoln's feigned deference was a brilliant rhetorical tactic that turned his opponent into a worn political hack; his inclusion of a wrathful deity was intended to rankle because he knew that, like him, Forquer was a freethinker. With these quick but deep thrusts, Forquer was left for politically dead.

Lincoln was the biggest vote getter in Sangamon County, first among seventeen candidates. Yet Van Buren eked out a victory in reliably Democratic Illinois. Stuart, for his part, was defeated for the Congress. Lincoln became Stuart's law partner on April 12, 1837, their office located on the second floor off the main square in Springfield, directly above a courtroom, with a trapdoor opened to listen to the trials below. It was where Lincoln "slept—and lounged—talked—joked," according to Stuart. After losing his campaign, Stuart, who "had the reputation of being the ablest and most efficient jury lawyer in the state," wrote Usher Linder, became a lobbyist, a log-roller, while preparing for another run for the seat.

Setting up his new residence in Springfield, Lincoln went to buy a bed at the store of Joshua Speed, but balked at the price of seventeen dollars. Speed suggested he simply share his room upstairs. "Well, Speed," replied Lincoln, "I'm moved." Speed was the scion of a wealthy Kentucky plantation owner, related to the various branches of the Clay family. Cassius Clay, the aristocratic politician and iconoclastic abolitionist newspaper editor, Henry Clay's second cousin, was brother-in-law to Speed's father's uncle. Just as Speed was aware that Lincoln was a rising man in the Whig Party, Lincoln would have known that Speed came from bluegrass aristocracy and linked to the family of his idol. Speed, "my most intimate friend," charged Lincoln no rent. Lincoln ate for free at the home of William Butler, who had served in the Black Hawk War with him, a Whig political operator working as clerk of the Sangamon Circuit Court. Lincoln, said Herndon, "always had influential and financial friends to help him; they almost fought each other for the privilege of assisting."

Three quarters of the members of the legislature were new members. Not one had been born in Illinois, which twenty years earlier had been a howling wilderness populated by a scattering of French fur and slave traders. The vast majority was from the South. "The years 1836 and '37 were a sort of formation period; the starting point of many great men who distinguished themselves in the subsequent history of Illinois," wrote Linder. Among the class of 1836 were one future president,

Joshua Speed

another presidential candidate, a cabinet member, six U.S. senators, eight congressmen, three governors, and a number of generals.

In Stuart's place the second-term Lincoln became the Whig floor leader in the House and was appointed to the powerful Finance Committee. "He seemed to be a born politician," said Robert L. Wilson. "We followed his lead, but he followed nobody's lead; he hewed the way for us to follow, and we gladly did so. He could grasp and concentrate the matters under discussion, and his clear statement of an intricate or obscure subject was better than an ordinary argument. It may almost be said that he did our thinking for us, but he had no arrogance, nothing of the dictatorial; it seemed the right thing to do as he did. He excited no envy or jealousy. He was felt to be so much greater than the rest of us that we were glad to abridge our intellectual labors by letting him do the general thinking for the crowd. He inspired absolute respect, although he was utterly careless and negligent."

The new legislature opened with a Democratic trap—a resolution to investigate the alleged corruption of the State Bank, most of whose directors were Whigs. Pulling the strings was an Illinois Supreme Court justice, Theophilus Smith, whose career began as a junior law partner and protégé of Aaron Burr, the subversive founding father, and in the Burr tradition of disgrace was the first official in Illinois to be impeached, for the corrupt sale of court clerkships, though he was not convicted. "He had for a long time aimed to be elected to the United States Senate; his devices and intrigues to this end had been innumerable," wrote Thomas Ford. "In fact, he never lacked a plot to advance himself, or to blow up some other person. He was a laborious and ingenious schemer in politics; but his plans were always too complex and ramified for his power to execute them. Being always unsuccessful himself, he was delighted with the mishaps alike of friends and enemies; and was ever chuckling over the defeat or the blasted hopes of someone." Smith had once drawn a pistol on Governor Edwards, who grabbed it, smashed his assailant, and broke his jaw.

For his instrument Smith chose a freshman Democratic legislator sharing the same boardinghouse in Vandalia. Usher Linder wrote, "one night the judge asked me if I would not like to be a great man. I told him I certainly would not object to be such. 'Well,' said he, 'I will put you on the high road to become such, if you will follow my advice and instructions.'" Smith drew up the resolution, which "fell like a bombshell in the House," and during the raucous debate Smith "stood behind me, furnishing me with facts and arguments and keeping me thoroughly posted." Lincoln's new rival was the same age, born in the same part of Kentucky, an attorney, already renowned for his oratory, but dressed stylishly unlike the carelessly attired Lincoln.

Lincoln led the debate from the Whig side, making his first major floor speech on January 11, 1837. He criticized the resolution as a transparent political scheme, explaining his ability to see through it by identifying himself as a politician himself. "This movement is exclusively the work of politicians; a set of men who have interests aside from the interests of the people, and who, to say the most of them, are, taken as a mass, at least one long step removed from honest men. I say this with the greater freedom because, being a politician myself, none can regard it as personal." Then, after disdaining any interest in making "personal" charges, he launched an ad hominem attack on Linder, accusing him of being alternatively "too ignorant to be placed at the head of the committee which his resolution proposes" and "too uncandid to merit the respect or confidence of anyone."

"Mr. Lincoln's remarks on Mr. Linder's bank resolution . . . are quite to the point," editorialized the *Sangamo Journal*. "Our friend carries the true Kentucky rifle, and when he fires seldom fails of sending the shot home." The newspaper, meanwhile, in a piece perhaps written by Lincoln, censured Linder for "little else than dirty appeals to party feeling, in which he attempted to skin his opponents; and in turn, for which he got himself very handsomely skinned." The Democratic majority, however, passed the resolution, the investigation discovered no wrongdoing, and Linder was handsomely rewarded, elevated to attorney general by his fellow Democrats.

Lincoln now took charge in the freshly constructed state capitol, its plaster still damp, of the effort to abandon the state government at Vandalia. "Lincoln was at the head of the project to remove the seat of government to Springfield; it was entirely entrusted to him to manage," said Stephen Trigg Logan, who would become Lincoln's second law partner. Sangamon County had the biggest delegation in the legislature, seven representatives and two senators, and because of their height of over six feet, called the "Long Nine," after a type of naval cannon. They "looked to Lincoln as the head," according to Logan, even as Stuart returned to Vandalia as a log-roller for the Springfield interests. "The delegation from Sangamon were a unit, acting in concert in favor of the permanent location at Springfield," recalled Wilson. Lincoln first maneuvered to set the issue on the agenda and then put the matter in the hands of the legislature, overturning the 1834 plebiscite deciding that Alton would be the new capital.

Many towns scrambled to claim the prize, including one virtually un-inhabited burg called Illiopolis, a spot on the map laid out by real estate speculators (including Governor Duncan). But the "Long Nine" remained firmly united. "Amongst them were some dexterous jugglers and manag-ers in politics, whose whole object was to obtain the seat of government for Springfield," wrote Ford. "This delegation, from the beginning of the ses-sion, threw itself as a unit in support of, or opposition to, every local measure of interest, but never without a bargain for votes in return on the seat of government question. Most of the other counties were small, having but one representative, and many of them with but one for a whole district; and this gave Sangamon County a decided preponderance in the log-rolling system of those days."

When, at one point, the move to Springfield appeared lost, Lincoln rallied the pro-Springfield group. "In these dark hours," recalled Wilson, "when our bill to all appearance was beyond resuscitation, and all our opponents were jubilant over our defeat, and when friends could see no hope, Mr. Lincoln never for one moment despaired, but collected his colleagues to his room for consultation, his practical common sense, his thorough knowledge of human nature then, made him an overmatch for his compeers and for any man that I have ever known."

But at a low point in the effort Lincoln unburdened himself to his friend, fellow legislator Jesse Dubois, "and told me that he was whipped—that he had traded off everything he could dispose of, and still had not got strength enough to locate the seat of government at Springfield." At the same time that the shifting of the capital was under consideration so was the internal improvements bill. It was referred to as "the System," after Clay's "Ameri-can System." "Roads and improvements were proposed everywhere, to enlist every section of the State," wrote Ford. "Three or four efforts were made to pass a smaller system, and when defeated, the bill would be amended by the addition of other roads, until a majority was obtained for it." The number of projects grew exponentially, finally to encompass forty-four of sixty counties, with the other sixteen receiving $200,000 flat grants. The town of Alton, once designated by a statewide vote to be the new capital, extracted lucrative concessions. "Three roads were appointed to terminate at Alton, before the Alton interest would agree to the system." The final bill authorized $14 million to lay 1,300 miles of railroad track, clear five rivers, construct bridges, and build the canal connecting the Illinois River to Lake Michigan, among many other projects. Four newspapers published stories on the quid pro quos involved. "Removal of the seat of government from Vandalia to Springfield was part and parcel of the 'noble System,'" stated the *Vandalia Free Press*, a Whig paper.

Lincoln confided to Joshua Speed "his highest ambition was to become the De Witt Clinton of Illinois," an ambition that would begin as the political architect of the new capital and "the System." Clinton had been the governor of New York who built the Erie Canal, the model internal improvement that made him the most popular politician in the state.

On February 28, at Ebenezer Capp's Tavern, the Sangamon delegation celebrated the final passage of the bill, with Ninian W. Edwards picking up the tab for oysters, cigars, and eighty-one bottles of champagne. That summer, at a dinner in the district to honor the "Long Nine," Lincoln was toasted as "Abraham Lincoln, one of nature's noblemen." "I have often thought," recalled Wilson, who was present, "that if any man was entitled to that compliment it was he." At a festive dinner at Springfield, another toast went: "Abraham Lincoln: he has fulfilled the expectations of his friends, and disappointed the hopes of his enemies." Lincoln replied: "All our friends: they are too numerous to mention now individually, while there is no one of them who is not too dear to be forgotten or neglected."

Twenty-eight years old, just a little more than two years in the legislature, Lincoln had become leader of his party in the House, partner to one of Springfield's most prominent lawyers, and successful in moving the capital to his district and enacting "the System," seemingly fulfilling his aspiration to follow in the footsteps of Clay and Clinton. There was only one slight matter left on the day before the first session adjourned. That residual issue was slavery. "His intimate friends, those whom he loved and honored," wrote John Nicolay and John Hay, were "Kentuckians all, and strongly averse to any discussion of the question of slavery. The public opinion of his county, which was then little less than the breath of his life, was all the same way." Abolitionism carried such a taint that it had made any position other than harsh condemnation of emancipation followed by oaths to enforce the Black

Code "dangerous to the popularity of politicians," according to Thomas Ford. In Illinois politics, black rights were an issue to wield symbolically as a cudgel to beat opponents, as Lincoln had done against Van Buren; otherwise, slavery was a diversion and distraction to be avoided. It was not central, like internal improvements, but could be menacing. The Missouri Compromise of 1820, drawing the line between North and South, free and slave states, was intended to have insulated politics from contention over slavery. But now the inflammatory question threatened to singe the reluctant politicians of Illinois. For the first time, Lincoln was forced to vote as a public official on slavery.

CHAPTER FOUR

PARADISE LOST

O n his deathbed, Andrew Jackson, reflecting on the dramatic episodes
of his presidency, expressed his greatest regret. It was that he had not
had John C. Calhoun hung for treason. "My country," he said, "would have
sustained me in the act, and his fate would have been a warning to traitors
in all time to come." Jackson had
once considered him a friend, just
as Henry Clay regarded him as
a political comrade-in-arms and
John Quincy Adams thought of
him as an intellectual companion,
but they each independently came
to the same conclusion that he
was a brooding Mephistophelian
figure of rancor, vengeance, and
dark designs driven by a thwarted
and raging mania to be president.

In an egalitarian age Calhoun was the most nuanced
class-conscious politician of his
generation. He was once the most
promising, the golden young man

John C. Calhoun

of American politics, and the most liberal nationalist from the South. He regarded himself the best man above all other leading men, whom he felt were beneath him. His spectacular rise imbued him with a belief in his own inevitable destiny. To the extent that others stood in his way they were squalid representatives of a corrupt system. Party politics was for them "a game," in which "those who are engaged in it but act a part," speak "not from honest conviction," but only "as the means of deluding the people, and through that delusion to acquire power." But he practiced the same tactics, if less adroitly, pretending he did not. His judgment of many of the gamesters he encountered was not wrong, but what truly unsettled him were the raucous uncertainty of popular democracy and his own uncertainty in handling it. His fall from grace was as stunning as his ascent, but the consequences were far more alarming.

After Calhoun failed to attain the presidency in his initial sputtering attempts, his politics turned to intricate plots to undermine everyone else and somehow edge himself on top, provoking national crisis after crisis over the decades. He justified his actions through ever elaborate variations on the theme that majority rule must be stymied in the name of sovereign states' rights, a projection of his sovereign self, a party unto himself, a majority of one. He wore his austerity and isolation as emblems of his tragic nobility. Among intimate friends and colleagues he was said to be charming, and he was unfailingly polite to those like Senate pages he met in his official roles. "It was only his equals and rivals, Clay, Jackson, Crawford, and the rest, who hated him; and they did hate him most cordially," wrote Jackson's biographer James Parton. After his traumatic conflict with Jackson he retreated into glowering condescension. He was calm, composed, and contemptuous. For a politician he strangely combined intellectual formidability with an almost complete inability to read human nature. He could only have been sustained in the hothouse political culture of oligarchic South Carolina. He was worshipped as fervently as he was hated. His aristocratic disdain made him "a Demi-God" to his followers, "my Statesman," as one wrote. "No vice, no folly, no frailty has soiled his nature." He was beyond "the sordid intrigue of partisanship." Only "the weak, the dull, and the unfeeling alone are insensible to its instincts." Though he had ambition, "the ephemeral glories of the Presidency can add no luster to his virtue, no honor to his name." Behind his steely veneer he seethed with a sense of having been wronged by a conspiracy of lesser lights. He assumed the self-sacrificing air of a knight for a just lost cause. On the Senate floor his severe debating style was withering, and his Senate colleagues raptly listened, but he lacked the slightest capacity to move an audience of ordinary folk. His punishing orations were declaimed with precise mechanical order, emphasized with hand-chopping motions, utterly devoid of any gesture to the popular mind. He would never lower himself.

His speeches and writings gave the impression of airtight logic that upon close inspection were often not logical arguments at all. They were a series of assertions that he demanded must be accepted on the imprimatur of his own implacable authority. His tone was dogmatic, relentless, and opaque, "arid as a desert, no pretensions to genuine eloquence," observed Rufus Choate, the renowned lawyer and senator from Massachusetts. There is no recorded case of his wit. "Mr. Calhoun," recalled Harriet Martineau, the celebrated English writer, upon meeting him,

> the cast-iron man, who looks as if he had never been born, and never could be extinguished. . . . It is at first extremely interesting to hear Mr. Calhoun talk; and there is a never-failing evidence of power in all he says and does, which commands intellectual reverence: but the admiration is too soon turned into regret—into absolute melancholy. It is impossible to resist the conviction that all this force can be at best but useless, and is but too likely to be very mischievous. His mind has long lost all power of communicating with any other. I know no man who lives in such utter intellectual solitude. He meets men and harangues them, by the fire-side, as in the Senate . . . he either passes by what you say, or twists it into a suitability with what is in his head, and begins to lecture again. . . . There is no hope that an intellect so cast in narrow theories will accommodate itself to varying circumstances: and there is every danger that it will break up all that it can, in order to remould the materials in its own way.

But one friend described the "intense look" of his "piercing" blue eyes, "I believe they give out light in the dark."

Calhoun's aggressive politics were wholly defensive, nurtured from his vulnerabilities personal and political. He stood on the principles with which he became thoroughly identified only after his setbacks, searching for firm ground after losing his balance. Adamant and imperious, he was unusually sensitive for a man in public life. He took political defeats as insults, but fought only intellectual duels, channeling his grievances into developing a determinist theory of a tyrannical central government, a leviathan lacking constitutional legitimacy—an originalist theory adapted from his early critics who had assailed him as treacherous to the cause of states' rights. Once considered among the nation's most liberal men, he became the leader of "the Carolina doctrine" only after he succumbed to it. But irony was as alien to him as humor.

Calhoun the young champion of nationalism became Calhoun the forefather of secession. After his transformation from one thing into its opposite he proclaimed he was guided by enduring principles: the United States was not a nation-state but a loose confederation of states, each of which had primacy over the federal government that could be dissolved on a moment's notice; democracy was a menace to order; security and freedom belonged only to the privileged few who deserved it; and slavery was the true basis of enlightened civilization, morality, and liberty. He believed in driven racial theories, too, that "blood in their veins" explained the level of civilization of a people, that Anglo-Saxon whites were superior, while "impure races" and "mixed blood equally ignorant and unfit for liberty," and that it was "a great mistake in supposing all people are capable of self-government." He insisted his constitutional doctrine was the one true original interpretation of a perversely distorted document plagued by the "general welfare" clause, but his static view yielded an audacious novelty, adducing nullification from checks and balances. He was for preserving the Union only by means that if adopted would destroy it. Those who disagreed were always unprincipled, though he had once held their very principles. He came to despise everything he once stood for. He would embrace the poisonous notions of Jefferson's harshest enemy, John Randolph, who had once been Calhoun's nemesis before he had become the prisoner of his curdled ambition.

Henry Clay openly ridiculed him in a Senate speech in 1841 as "tall, careworn, with furrowed brow, haggard, and intensely gazing, looking as if he were dissecting the last and newest abstraction which sprung from metaphysician's brain, and muttering to himself, in half-uttered sounds, 'This is indeed a real crisis!'" "A man of infinite address in his intercourse with individuals, but utterly without tact when he comes to deal with men in masses," wrote Beverley Tucker, the Virginia jurist and early proponent of secession, whose distinguished family of anti-Jefferson Southern nationalists was closely linked with Calhoun and who had worried about his liberal tendencies. Tucker described Calhoun as a self-defeating character, "eager for public favor, he always finds out the most unpopular side of every question," changing his positions to demonstrate his "consistency," yet "always setting his face against the wind." He was, lamented Tucker, "the most unskilled leader of a party that ever wielded a truncheon." "Mr. Calhoun was pure of all vices but the vice of ambition which grew stronger by the virtues that restrained him from other indulgencies," wrote William J. Grayson, his political ally, a congressman from South Carolina, and the poet who coined the term "the master-race" to describe its mission to make the slave "tamed, enlightened, and refined."

"But Mr. Calhoun had no youth, to our knowledge," eulogized one of his followers, Senator James Henry Hammond of South Carolina. "He sprang into the arena like Minerva from the head of Jove, fully grown and clothed in armor." But Mr. Calhoun indeed had a youth, to the full knowledge of his contemporaries, and their experience informed their understanding of the "cast-iron man" as a dangerous changeling.

Calhoun's father, Patrick Calhoun, a rudely educated immigrant from northern Ireland, who fought Cherokees in hand-to-hand combat in the French and Indian War, became the political leader of his corner of up-country South Carolina, serving for thirty years in the colonial and state assemblies, and as a judge. He imbued in his son an intense political interest, according to his earliest memory. Patrick Calhoun was the owner of a plantation with thirty-one slaves, a quintessential Piedmont man who resented the low-country gentry of Charleston for their superior manner. An anti-federalist radical, he opposed ratification of the Constitution because it provided taxation for purposes outside South Carolina, which he claimed was nothing less than taxation without representation in violation of the revolutionary cause. When the father died, an older brother who lived in Charleston convinced the eighteen-year-old Calhoun that he was not destined to be a planter. His family had other resources and avenues available for him. He attended the famous preparatory academy for the elites of South Carolina and Georgia, founded by Dr. Moses Waddel, who was married to Calhoun's sister, and then attended Yale and the Litchfield Law School in Connecticut, graduating with distinction.

When he returned as the only Eastern-educated man of Abbeville County, Calhoun was promptly elected to the legislature. Over the course of two sessions over two years, he spent a total of nine weeks there, after which he was overwhelmingly elected to the Congress in 1810, succeeding his cousin Joseph Calhoun, who had retired in favor of the brilliant twenty-eight-year-old. The following year he married his second cousin, Floride Bonneau Colhoun, heiress to a rice plantation and real estate around Charleston, and whose father, John Ewing Colhoun, Patrick Calhoun's nephew, had been a U.S. senator. A Southern belle from the highest level of society, she spent half her year in Newport, and was a censorious Calvinist who was shocked when she attended the theater, "not at all pleased," which she subsequently avoided as the devil's workshop.

With his excellent marriage, Calhoun vaulted into South Carolina's oligarchy. But he never adopted the affectations of Charleston. He was not a fashion plate, did not assume old English pretensions, and would not play the absentee landlord surrounded by waiting servants. He was never the squire. He was the opposite of indolent, complacent, and self-satisfied. Instead he was industrious, inventive, and incisive. He carried not a scent of moonlight and magnolia, hummed not a bar of camptown races and the old folks at home. His South was without a twig of romance or nostalgia. He was the ultimate New England–educated man as the ultimate Southern man. When he was denied the place of head of the nation he summoned the South to become the nation he would head. He transmuted the secession-flirting and class-conscious federalism of Yale into secession-flirting anti-federalism, turning the early politics of the Republic upside down, from the aristocratic North against the democratic South to the aristocratic South against the democratic North. He deployed the intellectual presumption of New England to galvanize a new South. His Southern Confederacy existed first and last in his own mind, created in his detached study furnished in a spare New England style at his Fort Hill plantation in the far corner of upcountry South Carolina.

Calhoun arrived in Washington on the crest of a political tidal wave. After years of futility the country rejected Jefferson's and Madison's policies of treating the British impressment of American seamen with neutrality and an embargo that had only damaged American commerce. Fully half of the Congress was swept out in the election of 1810, bringing in a new post-revolutionary generation of political leadership demanding military action. Its epicenter was Mrs. Dawson's boardinghouse on Capitol Hill, dubbed the "war mess," where Henry Clay presided at the table of young hotspurs with Calhoun as the most brilliant. On the first day of the Congress, Clay was elected speaker, overwhelmingly defeating the peace candidate. He had left his safe seat in the Senate for the House precisely to raise the banner of war and subdue its opposition, particularly John Randolph. Among his first acts was to appoint Calhoun to the Foreign Relations Committee. On the first day of its meeting, he became its chairman, at that moment the second most important place in the House of Representatives.

Calhoun's maiden speech was a missile hurled at the administration's most hostile and influential antagonist, John Randolph of Roanoke, who patronized the new men with the sobriquet of "war hawks" and had dominated the floor of the House through his eloquence and sharp wit. "Sir," replied Calhoun, "I only know of one principle to make a nation great, to produce in this country not the form but real spirit of Union." For challenging Randolph, Thomas Ritchie in the *Richmond Enquirer* hailed Calhoun as "one of the master-spirits who stamp their names upon the age in which they live." Working hand in glove with Clay, Calhoun outmaneuvered Randolph time and again, ultimately compelling his unnatural silence through a point of order. Then Calhoun reported from his committee a call for "an immediate appeal to arms." With Clay, he led in passing the declaration of war, making his "national reputation," according to Thomas Hart Benton, who as senator from Missouri and member of Jackson's Kitchen Cabinet would become one of his fiercest enemies.

In the aftermath of the War of 1812, Calhoun stood in the front rank of the new nationalists that had dispersed war opponents North and South, Old Federalists and Old Republicans, and superseded the politics rooted in the conflict between the parties of Jefferson and John Adams. The war made Calhoun and shaped his views. He was enthusiastically in favor of an activist, well-funded government devoted to unifying the country through the most liberal policies. He was for a national bank, a splendid navy, a permanent professional army, federally financed internal improvements of all kinds from canals to "great permanent roads," and, above all, the tariff. The war had created a barrier to foreign imports that had generated burgeoning domestic manufacturing. Calhoun wanted a tariff, an external tax, to provide

a constant and increasing flow of revenues to finance the growing government, and to protect and build up nascent American industry. For Calhoun,
prosperity and activist government went hand in hand. He warned against
"sectional feeling," and in a speech arguing for protectionism against Randolph he declared, "The liberty and the union of the country were insepara-
bly united." Protectionism was nothing less than "the duty of this country,"
"a means of defense," and above "the claims of manufacturers" a question
of "general principles." It was nothing less than a matter of "the security
and permanent prosperity of our country." The tariff's greater purpose was
"calculated to bind together more closely our widely spread republic," and to
"outweigh any political objections that be urged against the system." In his
last major speech as a member of the House, he delivered his summation
against the strict construction of the Constitution that "urged that the Congress can only apply the public money in execution of the enumerated power.
I am no advocate for refined arguments on the Constitution. The instrument
was not intended as a thesis for the logician to exercise his ingenuity on." But
his advanced program was vetoed as overreaching in one of Madison's last
acts as president. Even Madison would not embrace Calhoun's liberal interpretation of the Constitution.

President James Monroe appointed Calhoun, at the age of thirty-five, the
secretary of war, a position Monroe himself had held. Calhoun was his favorite cabinet secretary, something of a protégé. Four other prominent men
had been offered the post, including Andrew Jackson, but turned it down
at least partly because the department was a shambles. As much as anyone
could manage, Calhoun transformed it. He used his position to advocate the
construction of extensive public works in the name of national defense, the
full system of internal improvements. John Quincy Adams, Monroe's secretary of state, not only admired Calhoun but also regarded him an intellectual companion. "Calhoun," he wrote in his diaries in 1821, "is a man of fair
and candid mind, of honorable principles, of clear and quick understanding,
of cool self-possession, of enlarged philosophical views, and of ardent patriotism. He is above all sectional and factious prejudices more than any other
statesman of this Union with whom I have ever acted."

But Calhoun's far-reaching projects, his earnest efforts to reform his department and modernize the country, were constantly under attack. Randolph
attempted to undermine him at every turn within the Congress, sabotaging

funding for forts, the navy, and anything else Calhoun proposed. Calhoun confided to Adams that he was "dispirited by the results of the attacks systematically carried on through the whole Congress," and by the repeal of the internal tax, which deprived the government of necessary revenues. Calhoun traced the most pernicious subversion to the secretary of the treasury, William Harris Crawford. Crawford, of Georgia, was a physically gargantuan man whose presence seemed to radiate his political force. The former president pro tempore of the Senate, "acting vice president" upon Vice President George Clinton's death, and Madison's secretary of war before Monroe was of Old Republican convictions except when they were effortlessly discarded out of inconvenience. He presumed he should be president. He had after all been next in line. He had clawed his way up and it was his turn. His campaign was based on thwarting the administration in which he served in order to curry favor with the congressional caucus he was certain would lift him into the office. "Crawford has no talents as a financier," wrote Adams. "He is just, and barely, equal to the current routine of the business of his office. His talent is intrigue." Adams agreed with Calhoun about Crawford's strategy of internal ruin. "His position is a bad one. Having been a caucus candidate for the Presidency against Mr. Monroe, he feels as if his very existence was staked upon his being his successor. And, although himself a member of the Administration, he perceives every day more clearly that his only prospect of success hereafter depends upon the failure of the Administration, by measures of which he must take care to make known his disapprobation." Crawford targeted Calhoun as Monroe's pet, resenting the younger man as a presumptuous upstart from an entitled class, lacking proper deference to his elder and far too liberal. Crawford stirred up congressional investigations of alleged corruption in granting defense contracts, falsely accusing Calhoun of benefiting friends, charges that were widely circulated in newspapers partisan to Crawford's candidacy, especially in the *City Gazette*, his Washington organ. He was also behind the Senate's rejection of appointments to the War Department and drastic cuts to the military budget.

In the party-less "Era of Good Feelings," quasi-parties of shifting coalitions formed around personalities, and politics became viciously personal, descending into an "Era of Bad Feelings." Clay, Adams, Jackson, and Crawford contended against each other to succeed Monroe. Crawford was the candidate of the "Radicals" of the South, the Old Republicans, in alliance with the new-style New York political machine run by Martin Van Buren, who as Crawford's campaign manager saw himself in the role of re-creating the Jeffersonian regional alliance. Calhoun promised both Crawford and Adams he would not run. It was not his turn; he had all the time in the world. But Crawford's smears injured his pride and spurred his ambition. He would be barely forty in 1824, untarnished by failure, obviously capable, intelligent, and incorruptible, rising and rising.

On December 28, a delegation of congressmen crowded into Calhoun's boardinghouse to implore him to run for president. Many were anti-Crawford Southerners and many were from Pennsylvania, where Calhoun was popular as the champion of protection for manufactures. Calhoun saw his alliance of Southerners and Pennsylvanians as a counter to the Crawford–Van Buren combination. "As Calhoun stands now most in his way," wrote Adams about Crawford, "the great burden of his exertions this session and the last has been against the War Department; while Calhoun, by his haste to get at the Presidency, has made a cabal in his favor in Congress to counteract Crawford's cabal, and the session has been little more than a violent struggle between them."

Calhoun launched his own newspaper, the *Washington Republican*, subsidizing it and hiring one of his former War Department clerks as editor. In 1823, it published a series of articles signed "A.B." accusing Crawford of malfeasance in the Treasury Department. An outraged Crawford demanded a congressional investigation to clear his name. The inquiry into the "A.B. plot" exposed the identity of its author—Ninian Edwards, the first territorial governor of Illinois. Newly appointed as minister to Mexico, he resigned in disgrace.

Crawford struck back at Calhoun in South Carolina. In this wrinkle of the campaign can be located the origins of Calhoun's metamorphosis, "from a protectionist to a free trader, from a liberal to a conservative, from a liberal constructionist to a strict constructionist, from a progressionist to an obstructionist," according to the historian David Franklin Houston. When support for Crawford was joined to opposition to the tariff passed in 1824 a new conservatism was synthesized. Calhoun's local enemies, remnants of Old Republicanism, who hated him as the embodiment of liberal nationalism, forged a movement around the new cause. The tariff, it was said, was a violation of states' rights, a mockery of the strict construction of the Constitution, and a tyrannical imposition of federal authority. The leader of the pro-Crawford forces within South Carolina was the longtime foe of Calhoun, William Smith. Like Crawford, his friend since boyhood, Smith was an older man, twenty years older, who resented Calhoun's sophistication, Eastern education, and meteoric rise. Smith was an unreconstructed pro-slavery states' rights advocate, who as a U.S. senator had argued against the Missouri Compromise because it limited slavery from flowing into the North. Slavery, he argued on the Senate floor from biblical citations, was divinely inspired. From 1821 through 1824, Smith helped organize protests against the tariff and Calhoun in nearly every county. Calhoun managed to oust him from his Senate seat in 1824, but Smith was immediately elected to the state legislature on an anti-Calhoun platform. His resolutions enacted the next year established the basis for resistance to the federal government. They declared that the official policy of the state of South Carolina was that the U.S. Congress had no constitutional power to enact internal improvements or tax its citizens for national purposes (echoing his enemy's father Patrick Calhoun), and that the tariff was unconstitutional. Calhoun was defied and repudiated. "By the passage of these resolutions," wrote Houston, "the State deliberately entered upon that course of opposition to the general government which ended only with the surrender at Appomattox."

While Smith galvanized the political movement, Dr. Thomas Cooper provided the intellectual patina. "A learned, ingenious, scientific, and talented mad-cap is Dr. Cooper," wrote John Quincy Adams. Cooper, the president of South Carolina College (now the University of South Carolina), taught chemistry and political economy. Born in England, educated at Oxford, and a participant in the French Revolution, he was both scholar and agitator, jailed and fined under the Alien and Sedition Acts of 1798 for protesting against them. In 1823, he published a manifesto entitled "Consolidation," arguing that the states were independent and sovereign, the Constitution itself could be annulled by any of them at will, and that a political party he called the "National" or the "Consolidation" party had as its object "to abolish and annihilate all state governments, and to bring forward one general government over this extensive continent, of a monarchial nature." Under President Monroe, the evil influences of this "monster" party were J. Q. Adams and Calhoun. "He was the adviser of that fool Monroe," wrote Cooper. "He is a national internal improvements man. . . . He is active, shewy, fluent, superficial, and conceited." But he wondered, "Is South Carolina destined to be a federal state?"

"For the first time," John Randolph wrote sarcastically about Calhoun, "we have presented to the people the army candidate for the presidency." Randolph loathed all the candidates but particularly Clay and Calhoun, the "war hawks." On the eve of the War of 1812, he remarked to a friend, "They have entered this House with their eye on the Presidency, and mark my words, sir, we shall have war before the end of the session!" Looming over all the Old Republicans was Randolph's shadow, Calhoun's most caustic critic and his preceptor, whose eccentricities Calhoun would turn into orthodoxy.

Randolph descended from bloodlines of various First Families of Virginia, a Jefferson cousin, sometimes living with him as a boy, and could trace his lineage back to no less than John Rolfe and Pocahontas. His first cause was to oppose the Constitution as "a danger to our liberties." After witnessing George Washington take the oath of office as president, he remarked about the Constitution, "I saw what Washington did not see . . . the poison under its wings." Yet Randolph faithfully supported President Jefferson as his floor leader in the House of Representatives until 1806, when he suddenly denounced him for having betrayed states' rights principles by expanding the powers of the federal government, which, like the Louisiana Purchase, Ran-

John Randolph

dolph had previously promoted. He felt betrayed and humiliated when, instigated by Jefferson, he led the impeachment of Supreme Court justice Samuel Chase and failed to remove him, and was disgusted that Jefferson anointed James Madison as his political successor. Blocking Jefferson's purchase of West Florida, he declared the "issue" was "whether this nation is to be governed by a secret Machiavellian, invisible, irresponsible Cabinet." He also decided retrospectively that he loathed Jefferson's abolition of primogeniture in Virginia, believing he had destroyed the hereditary basis of aristocracy. "I am an aristocrat," Randolph said. "I love liberty, I hate equality." Liberty was the rightful property of the aristocracy and the more a man had liberty the more it reflected his status.

Randolph asserted himself as the leader of a third force, the country Southern conservatives, Old Republicans, styled as the Quids, after the Latin, *tertium quid*, or third thing, which he was himself. He suffered from a hormonal deficiency that left him without facial hair and a falsetto voice. Unknown to have had a relationship with a woman, he dressed as an English dandy, wore a blue riding coat and hip-length black boots, smoked opium at least partly to deal with the tuberculosis that eventually killed him, and when not in Washington resided on his plantation on the Appomattox River he named Bizarre, surrounded by his slaves and dogs (which he would bring onto the floor of the Congress until forbidden by Speaker of the House Clay). He named one of his favorite horses "Radical" and another "Jacobin." His erudite orations were considered astounding performances worthy of the finest actors of the stage. Appearing like a well-dressed scarecrow on storklike legs, with jet-black hair flopping over his boyish head, his shrill voice, according to an observer, "pierced every nook and corner of the hall," and "his elvish fore-finger—like an exclamation-point, punctuating his bitter thought—showed the skill of a master." During dramatic pauses in his speeches he would refresh himself with draughts of beer and whiskey.

Randolph despised the industrial world coming into being, a dystopia threatening to engulf his Southern paradise. The manufacturers of the North were "Egyptian taskmasters," and he refused to buy even a penknife made in New England. He hated modernity and everyone he believed responsible for it. Those who supported John Quincy Adams and Henry Clay "deserve to be slaves, with no other music to soothe them but the clank of the chains which they have put on themselves and given to their offspring." He saved his special scorn for the most ardent young nationalist, John C. Calhoun. "I say," said Randolph, "that these doctrines go to prostrate the State governments at the feet of the General Government."

"When I speak of my country," Randolph said, "I mean the Commonwealth of Virginia." Out of his romantic fetish for localism he conjured up a phantom Southern Confederacy existing captive within the United States, which he considered a loose league of sovereign states, not a nation itself. He exalted states' rights above all else, but finally as a bulwark of slavery. "We must preserve the rights of the States, as guaranteed by the Constitution, or the negroes are at our throats," he explained. "The question of slavery, as it is called, is to us a question of life and death. Remember, it is a necessity imposed on the South; not a Utopia of our own seeking. You will find no instance in history where two distinct races have occupied the soil except in the relation of master and slave."

On slavery, he was a case study of contradictions, which he felt were thoroughly consistent because of his unwavering opposition to federal power. When South Carolina repealed its ban on the African slave trade in 1803, the only state to do so, he denounced "her indelible disgrace" and "horrid thirst for African blood." Yet he opposed a proposed ten-dollar tax on each imported slave to discourage the trade. When Jefferson called for banning the African slave trade as of January 1, 1808, and the Senate attempted to prohibit transportation of slaves by sea from one place to another within the United States, Randolph warned "it might be made the pretext of universal emancipation," "laid the axes at the root of all property in the southern states," and he threatened that if it passed "let us secede and go home." Despite his dire warnings Jefferson signed the enacted law.

Opposing the War of 1812, Randolph claimed it would be the signal for slave revolts. In a speech on December 10, 1811, he told the House that the "poor slaves" of Haiti had been "polluted" by the French Revolution, and "similar doctrines were disseminated by peddlers from New England," causing "repeated alarms of insurrection among the slaves," and with "the spreading of this infernal doctrine, the whole Southern country had been thrown into a state of insecurity." Fear of slave revolts was a recurrent theme of Randolph's rhetoric, which he raised on frequent occasions and on a wide range of issues when his other arguments faltered.

Yet Randolph was one of the founders with Clay of the American Colonization Society, and yet again he turned against it for having "done mischief instead of good." He opposed the Missouri Compromise restricting slavery as nothing more than cynical Northern aggression to impose centralized federal power on the rights of slaveholders. Yet he oversaw a congressional report documenting the slave trade within the District of Columbia that abolitionists referenced. In a speech in 1824 against internal improvements, Randolph warned that the Congress "might emancipate every slave in the United

States" through "the war-making power"—"the most dangerous doctrine." During the nullification crisis he declared, "I am no nullifier," called nullification "sheer nonsense," and yet urged South Carolina to wage war against the United States, to "put down this wretched old man," Andrew Jackson, whose stand against it, he said, was "good and sufficient cause to secede." He held long conversations with his enslaved valet and said, "both agreed it was wrong." Meanwhile, as opium fumes wafted over Bizarre, he became more abusive toward his slaves, crossed out an emancipation clause from his will, blaming his slaves for "ingratitude," before reinstating it in a deathbed conversion.

Later, in 1838, Calhoun held forth on the Senate floor on Randolph's virtues, in the context of regretting passage of the Missouri Compromise of 1820, which limited slavery north of the Mason-Dixon Line. "Had it then been met with uncompromising opposition, such as a then distinguished and sagacious member from Virginia [Mr. Randolph], now no more, opposed to it, abolition might have been crushed forever in its birth. He then thought of Mr. Randolph, as, he doubts not, many think of him now, who have not fully looked into this subject, that he was too unyielding, too uncompromising, too impracticable; but he had been taught his error, and took pleasure in acknowledging it." In Calhoun's lexicon "abolition" meant any objection to slavery and its extension.

"John Randolph," wrote Henry Adams, "stands in history as the legitimate and natural precursor of Calhoun. Randolph sketched out and partly filled in the outlines of that political scheme over which Calhoun labored so long, and against which Clay strove successfully while he lived—the identification of slavery with states' rights. All that was ablest and most masterly, all except what was mere metaphysical rubbish, in Calhoun's statesmanship had been suggested by Randolph years before Calhoun began his states'-rights career."

Calhoun would make coherent what was confused in Randolph's weirdness. To the peculiarities of Randolph, Calhoun added not only the invention of nullification but also an unapologetic defense of "the peculiar institution." But without the master of Bizarre there would have been no tribune of the master class.

In the contest of 1824, Calhoun's presumed chief rival, the perennially sturdy Crawford, suddenly fell gravely ill and was nearly killed by quack doctors who bled him. Van Buren still pulled the wires to win Crawford the congressional caucus, but it only tainted him as not the people's choice. That figure would be Senator Andrew Jackson of Tennessee, the charismatic war hero of the most humble origins, whose campaign rapidly drained support from Calhoun. Calhoun was a national man with a national reputation, but he was not a hero. He had fought the War of 1812 in the Senate chamber, Jackson at the Battle of New Orleans. Yet he was an overwhelming second choice. When the votes were counted he was elected vice president, sweeping every region, including New England. His position as the coming man was secured, placing him in line for the succession to the presidency in the next election or at the latest the one after that, when he would not even be fifty.

The presidential contenders, however, were divided. Jackson had won a plurality of the popular vote, closely followed by Adams. Clay threw his support to Adams, about whom he was unenthusiastic but thought most qualified, not a "military chieftain" like Jackson. Daniel Webster and John Randolph counted the ballots in the Senate and announced the result. Adams offered Clay the post of secretary of state, from which he and others before him regularly had ascended to the presidency. Jackson angrily called Clay "the Judas of the West," and his followers assailed Adams's election as a "corrupt bargain." The atmosphere at the beginning of the new administration was embittered. In the new Congress, Jackson's men joined with the strict constructionists led by Randolph to demonize and bedevil Adams, whom Randolph called "John II" and spoke freely in the House of "this old animosity rankling in my heart."

Calhoun made public statements as late as 1825 in favor of internal improvements and for the tariff, but he was already shifting. He had not backed Adams for president, instead slyly suggesting he had achieved the office corruptly. "I am with the people, and will remain so," Calhoun wrote, drawing an invidious comparison between himself and the deal-making Clay. Calhoun saw the drift to Jackson, felt the undercurrent in South Carolina running against him, and understood that the means of Adams's election would be lethal to his presidency. Adams and Clay, his former friends, stood in his way. He could not patiently bide his time, just as he could not wait to run in 1824. He chafed at the vice presidency, calling it "a post of dignified inaction."

Now he hated Clay, hated him with visceral intensity, hated his charm, his ambition frustrating his own ambition, and would hate his policies, which he had previously advocated. As vice president, Calhoun deviously pulled strings on the Senate Foreign Relations Committee to try to thwart Clay's confirmation as secretary of state. Then he sought to damage Adams and his administration from within. "Mr. Clay governs the President," he explained. "The latter is in his power. He has thought proper to consider me as his rival." So he was the victim justified in retaliation.

Calhoun began a sub rosa courtship of Randolph. "The VP has actually made love to me," Randolph boasted in a letter on February 27, 1826. He was referring in particular to Calhoun's connivance in embarrassing Adams and Clay in the appointment of representatives to a conference with Latin American republics, which Adams considered the proper advancement of the Monroe Doctrine that he had framed as secretary of state. Randolph smeared the conference as a covert attempt to promote emancipation in league with Chile and Haiti, which had abolished slavery, and spread innuendo that the U.S. delegates would have sex with black and mulatto diplomats. With Calhoun's tacit encouragement, presiding as president of the Senate, Randolph unleashed a stream of invective that concluded with denunciation of the "combination, unheard of till then" of Adams and Clay, "the puritan and the blackleg," an allusion to comic characters from Henry Fielding's novel *Tom Jones*. Clay felt compelled to defend his honor, challenging Randolph to a duel. Randolph had merely wanted to destroy Clay's ability to function as secretary of state and his possibility for the presidency, not actually to murder him, but he could not refuse the challenge "without losing caste," observed Henry Adams. Randolph and Clay fired twice at each other and missed, and walked off the field shaking hands. But the incident damaged Clay's reputation and Calhoun gloated. "Had either man fallen I should have considered, not the survivor, but Calhoun as the murderer," remarked Congressman Edward Everett of Massachusetts. When a pseudonymous written article appearing in the pro-Adams newspaper criticized Calhoun for offending the dignity of the Senate for his collusion with Randolph, Calhoun counterattacked with a transparently pseudonymously written article of his own, claiming that Adams himself had composed the original article (it was, in fact, a State Department clerk), calling Adams "despotic and dangerous," and "imbecile and absurd."

Clay struck back at Calhoun, reviving the old false scandals that had been raised by Crawford against him as secretary of war. He was charged with profiting from a contract to build a fort, dubbed "Castle Calhoun." Behind the scenes Clay encouraged two congressional investigations, both of which wound up acquitting Calhoun, though they besmirched his reputation. His sense of victimization fueled his desire for revenge.

Calhoun thought of himself as part of a new national coalition, informally called "the Combination," whose unifying theme was overthrowing Adams. Calhoun had once called Adams "that great and good man." Now in the sanctum of his vice presidential retreat within the Capitol he confided to a political visitor in late 1825 or early 1826 about the administration "that such was the manner in which it came into power that it must be defeated at all hazards, regardless of its measures." Calhoun allied himself with Jackson, who had declared before running in 1828 he would only serve one term. By electing Jackson he would make himself his successor. "Here, then, was Mr. Calhoun's short road to the Presidency," wrote the well-informed journalist Nathan Sargent. To promote a Jackson-Calhoun ticket and tear down Adams and Clay, Calhoun helped create a new newspaper in the capital, the *United States Telegraph*. Founding a newspaper took money. "Very true," said Calhoun, "but if the play is worth the candle, buy the candle. If not, let us give up the play." Its editor was Duff Green, a native Kentuckian, St. Louis editor, and speculator. He was married to Ninian Edwards's sister and his daughter would marry Calhoun's son. Calhoun was always his master's voice. "The malevolence of the assaults upon and misrepresentations of the administration at this time has no precedent," recalled Sargent. "The 'Telegraph' daily teemed with falsehoods, uttered with the most positive asseveration, as if they were gospel truths. . . . To contradict them was useless, as the contradiction could never overtake the falsehood, and this no one knew better than the editor himself."

After the passage of a new tariff in 1828 during the election year, denounced as the "Tariff of Abominations" in South Carolina, the leading men of the state privately came to Calhoun to ask him to write a report to the legislature laying out the constitutional grounds for opposition. Calhoun agreed, but insisted on keeping his authorship secret. In the South Carolina Exposition and Protest Calhoun expounded the novel doctrine of nullification, to be known as "the Carolina doctrine." The state, according to Calhoun, had the power of "interposition" to overrule "unconstitutional" federal policy. Abandoning his liberal interpretation of the Constitution and embracing the rigi shibboleths of strict construction, he went even further in his rejection of majority rule. "No government based on the naked principle, that the majority ought to govern, however true the maxim in its proper sense and under proper restrictions, ever preserved its liberty, even for a single generation. The history of all has been the same, injustice, violence and anarchy, succeeded by the government of one, or a few, under which the people seek refuge, from the more oppressive despotism of the majority. . . . Constitutional government and the government of a majority are utterly incompatible." Now he had undergone his transformation, but he was still unready to reveal himself. His Exposition, unsigned, was adopted by the legislature, which ordered four thousand copies printed. South Carolina was not the Cartesian image of Calhoun: he thought, therefore it was. Rather it was South Carolina that moved Calhoun, even when his movement was invisible.

Calhoun's defenders retrospectively argued that he had supported Jackson out of principle in order to win a tariff reduction, while they claimed the Jacksonians used him out of expediency to silence the South and "to lend respectability to what conservatives held to be an uneducated rabble," according to Calhoun's exculpatory biographer Charles M. Wiltse. For their part the Jacksonians held him in suspicion from the start. "The truth is," wrote Major William B. Lewis, Jackson's longtime military aide and political confidant, "that many of General Jackson's friends believed that the support of him by the friends of Mr. Calhoun was, from the first, a secondary consideration with them. That they were using his popularity and strength with which to break down Adams and Clay; and then at the close of the General's first term, to set him aside (Adams and Clay having been previously put out of the way), and elevate Mr. Calhoun to the presidency."

During the transition between administrations Calhoun attempted to control the key appointments to the cabinet and through them the succession to the presidency. The secretary of state portfolio had been the royal road to the executive office. Calhoun urged Jackson to name one of his South Carolina followers, either Governor James Hamilton or Senator Robert Y. Hayne. Instead, Jackson nominated his campaign manager, who had been Crawford's former manager, and had brought into Jackson's fold the Southern Radicals and the New Yorkers—Martin Van Buren. Calhoun simmered, too, at the appointment as secretary of war of John Eaton, the childless Jackson's "almost adopted son," according to Margaret Bayard Smith, a doyenne of Washington society. Eaton was also Major Lewis's brother-in-law. As senator from Tennessee he had voted for the tariff, along with Senator Van Buren. Only Congressman Samuel D. Ingham, a low-tariff Pennsylvanian, who had been Jackson's campaign manager in the state, appointed secretary of the treasury, counted as a true Calhoun ally.

Calhoun's self-destruction started even before Jackson's inauguration. His actions were a series of miscalculations leading from a personal affront to a political schism to a constitutional crisis. He misjudged Jackson's character, the strength of his own position, and blundered in every political situation, which he would blame on infernal plots against him. He regarded the new president as intellectually and socially inferior, ill-suited for the job, while he thought of himself as the preeminent statesman through two decades in the Congress and the cabinet. He believed he should be the premier of the administration with the president serving like a constitutional monarch. His hubris began with hauteur.

Jackson's beloved wife, Rachel, died shortly after the election, on December 22, 1828. During the campaign the couple had been smeared in newspapers claiming they had committed bigamy while Rachel was still married to another man. Jackson blamed Clay and Adams for publication of the innuendo, threatened a "day of retribution," and after her death from a weak heart held his political enemies responsible.

Eleven days later, on January 1, 1829, John Eaton married Margaret "Peggy" O'Neale Timberlake, a union on which Jackson bestowed his blessing. Peggy was the attractive, flirty daughter of an innkeeper in Washington. Her first husband, John Timberlake, had been an alcoholic naval purser who ran up a large debt. Senator Eaton, a widower, boarded at the inn. He helped pay off Timberlake's debt and secured him a posting to the Mediterranean, where he died. It was rumored he had committed suicide, possibly because of his wife's illicit affair with Eaton. The wedding took place less than a year after his death.

While Jackson was considering his cabinet, Floride Calhoun decided that as the vice president's wife and leader of society in Washington the adulterous tavern keeper's daughter was unfit to be received. Calhoun approved of her staunch defense of "the purity and dignity of the female character." Following her lead the proper ladies of the capital shunned the fallen woman, marking her with an invisible scarlet letter, and organized her exclusion from respectable company. The battles raged from parties, balls, and even to embassy invitations. The Dutch ambassador, swayed by the ladies' brigade, blackballed Mrs. Eaton, while the British ambassador made a point of escorting her. Behind this snobbery lay political calculation. Pressure mounted on Jackson not to appoint Eaton to the cabinet. The "public opinion" of Washington, according to Margaret Bayard Smith, "will not allow of Genl. Eton holding a place which would bring his wife into society—(for this is the difficulty). Every one acknowledges Genl. Eton's talents and virtues—but his late unfortunate connection is an obstacle to his receiving a place of honour."

The campaign against Mrs. Eaton through the drawing rooms of Lafayette Square incited Jackson to a wrathful rage. He regarded the spite against her the extension of the smear of his wife. By defending Peggy he sought posthumous vindication for Rachel. He defiantly named Eaton to the cabinet, announced Mrs. Eaton "chaste as a virgin," and wrote voluminous letters to notable people around Washington, especially certain clergymen who were supporting the ladies' boycott, pleading her case and citing his late wife as the final authority on Mrs. Eaton's innocence. At first, Jackson blamed Clay and "satellites of Clay" for "the Eaton malaria." Then, after three cabinet members' families most closely associated with the Calhouns refused to accept Mrs. Eaton socially even after Jackson ordered them to open their French doors to her, he concluded the source of the trouble was Calhoun.

Martin Van Buren, a widower, nimbly befriended and championed Mrs. Eaton, winning the heart of the president. With Van Buren's strategic civility the cabinet was irreconcilably split and paralyzed through Jackson's first year. "Calhoun heads the moral party, Van Buren that of the frail sisterhood," observed John Quincy Adams, "and he is notoriously engaged in canvassing for the Presidency by paying his court to Mrs. Eaton." This was more than frivolous "petticoat politics," a comedy of manners. For Jackson the affair was nothing less than raw class conflict, the scorn of elites intended to demean him, and through the scandal to attempt a political coup. Sex dominated the gossip, but the true subject was power. The "persecution" of the Eatons, Jackson wrote in a letter on November 24, 1829, "was founded in political views, looking to the future. Jealousy arose that Eaton might not be a willing instrument to those particular views, that his popularity was growing and it was necessary to put him out of the Cabinet and destroy him regardless what injury it might do me or my administration."

His feeling toward Calhoun turned rancid. On December 31, 1829, Jackson wrote a friend about Calhoun, "You know the confidence I once had in that gentleman. I, however, of him desire not to speak; but I have a right to believe that most of the troubles, vexations, and difficulties I have had to encounter, since my arrival in this city, have been occasioned by his friends." In the same letter he designated Van Buren as his "well qualified" successor, but his anointment remained secret.

In January 1830 Calhoun sent out Senator Hayne of South Carolina, whom he had proposed for secretary of state, to use the issue of federal control of public lands to make the complete case for "the Carolina doctrine": for sovereign states' rights and nullification, against "consolidation" and "despotism," and a defense of slavery in the name of "freedom." Hayne quoted John Randolph, Edmund Burke, and Shakespeare in flourishes of erudition. Daniel Webster rose to answer for the national idea, and to rebut each and every one of Hayne's and Calhoun's propositions. In his first reply, Webster mischievously went out of his way to praise Calhoun by name as the author of early federal internal improvements. Then looking directly at the vice president perched at the podium, Webster artfully took issue with Hayne's interpretation of Shakespeare, citing Macbeth to allude to Calhoun's betrayals of Adams and Jackson. "Those who murdered Banquo, what did they win by it?" asked Webster. "Substantial good? Permanent power? Or disappointment, rather, and sore mortification,—dust and ashes, the common fate of vaulting ambition overleaping itself? Did not even-handed justice erelong commend the poisoned chalice to their own lips? Did they not soon find that for another they had lo 'filed their mind,' that their ambition, though apparently for the moment successful, had but put a barren scepter in their grasp?" Then, in his second reply, Webster struck down "the South Carolina doctrine" that the states were sovereign with thunderous phrases. "It is, Sir, the people's Constitution, the people's government, made for the people, made by the people, and answerable to the people."

By now Jackson firmly believed Calhoun was trying to usurp his place. Major Smith, Jackson's close adviser and member of his Kitchen Cabinet, arranged in March 1830 for members of the legislatures of Pennsylvania, Ohio, and New York to sign letters urging him to seek a second term, "as the most effectual, if not the only means of defeating the machinations of Mr. Calhoun and his friends, who were resolved on forcing General Jackson from the presidential chair after one term," according to Smith.

Jackson was scheduled to appear at the gala event of Democrats in the capital, the Jefferson Day dinner on April 13. Van Buren convinced him that it was premeditated to lend support to "the Carolina doctrine" and advance Calhoun's shadow candidacy for president, an elaborate trap to exploit Jackson's presence against himself. Nearly two dozen toasts were delivered to the eternal memory of Jefferson followed by tributes to states' rights, each accompanied by trumpeting from the Marine Band, when Jackson at last stood to offer his toast. He raised his glass and gazed sternly at Calhoun as though standing at ten paces. "Our Federal Union—it must be preserved." All fell silent. Calhoun promptly stood to reply to Jackson. "The Union—next to our liberty most dear." He had lost the duel.

Despite everything, Jackson still thought that his relationship with Calhoun remained based on the solidity of an old friendship. He believed as certain as he believed anything that Calhoun alone had stood by him during one of his greatest crises, alone had believed in his rightness and integrity, and alone had saved his reputation. In 1818, General Jackson in his war against the Seminole Indians in Spanish-held Florida had seized forts without authorization, creating an international incident. The Monroe cabinet deliberated about whether to investigate and reprimand him. Jackson believed that Crawford was the one who had called his conduct into question and urged the inquiry, and that only Calhoun had defended him and was responsible for Monroe deciding against an investigation. For Jackson a man's good faith about his motives was everything. So he always viewed Calhoun with special fondness as having protected his name against the entire cabinet with nothing to gain personally. A year or two later, in 1819 or 1820, at a large public dinner, Jackson delivered a toast to "John C. Calhoun—an honest man, the noblest work of God," and in 1825 he wrote, "Calhoun was the only friend I had in the cabinet."

In November 1829, Jackson attended a dinner with former President Monroe in Richmond. Monroe's confidant, Tench Ringold, regaled Jackson's confidant, Major Lewis, with the story of how it was Monroe who had defended Jackson at that cabinet meeting and Adams had written a formal letter to Spain justifying Jackson's action. In fact, Lewis had already heard an account communicated through intermediaries from Crawford during the 1828 campaign in which he wrote a letter stating that it was Calhoun who "urged upon the President the propriety of arresting and trying Gen. Jackson." But Lewis withheld that information from Jackson until now and waited until the Monroe dinner's end to inform him. Jackson was "incredulous," insisted the story "must be mistaken" and demanded that the Crawford letter be produced.

After he read it, thoroughly convinced, Jackson sent Crawford's letter to Calhoun on May 13, 1830, requesting an explanation. Calhoun responded with "indignation" at the attempt "for political purposes, to injure my character." Characteristically, he wrote at length. "I should be blind not to see that this whole affair is a political maneuver, in which the design is that you should be the instrument and myself the victim, but in which the real actors are carefully concealed by an artful movement." Over and over again, he called the story "a plot," but tellingly he did not deny its substance. When Jackson finished reading Calhoun's reply, he told Major Lewis "he had never been so much deceived in any man as he had been in Mr. Calhoun."

Jackson's reply to Calhoun captured the Shakespearean drama of a friendship sustained on years of misperception between men who became president and vice president. "I had a right to believe that you were my sincere friend," wrote Jackson on May 30, "and, until now, never expected to have occasion to say of you, in the language of Caesar, *Et tu, Brute?*" Calhoun was an assassin who had presented himself in the guise of Jackson's noble defender. Calhoun's reply was received as proof of his deception. He did not admit that he was the one who sought to set in motion the machinery that would destroy Jackson, but he also did not deny it. Instead, he cast aspersions on a host of conspirators against him. But his reply confirmed for Jackson that he alone was the conspirator, that Calhoun was Brutus.

Calhoun desperately pled with William Wirt, attorney general serving in the administrations of John Quincy Adams and Monroe, to speak with Adams and for both to somehow rescue him by attacking Crawford. Both of them knew that Crawford had argued in the cabinet along with Calhoun that Jackson had violated his orders in Florida. Wirt felt Calhoun "had blasted his prospects of future advancement forever," but discussed the matter with Adams. "Wirt concurred entirely with me in opinion that this was a snare deliberately spread by Crawford to accomplish the utter ruin of

Calhoun," wrote Adams. He could not help feel sympathy for Calhoun, who was "a drowning man," and he wrote, "Upon mere principles of humanity I would save Mr. Calhoun—extricate him from the deep into which he is sinking, and let him run, to live upon his reflections." But he and Wirt agreed "we would furnish no statement for the private portfolio of Mr. Calhoun." Adams thought both Crawford and Calhoun "treated me with base and gratuitous ingratitude." But Adams would later allow his letters on the matter to be published, a drop of pity. Calhoun called the whole controversy "a conspiracy for my destruction."

The feud between the president and vice president was completely hidden from public view, a war to the knife conducted behind the curtain. Major Lewis and others of Jackson's Kitchen Cabinet felt that the ultimate loyalty of Duff Green, editor of the *U.S. Telegraph*, lay with Calhoun and that he would defect. In anticipation of the reelection campaign, they quietly recruited an editor to found a new newspaper in the capital that would serve as Jackson's voice. Francis Preston Blair, a clerk in the Kentucky state court, local banker, and farmer, was an occasional contributor to the *Frankfort Argus* newspaper, owned by Amos Kendall, one of Jackson's inner circle. Blair appeared cadaverous, on the verge of dying of starvation, but socially animated and charming, and, more surprisingly, wrote with rapier-like ferocity, cutting his opponents to ribbons. His particular enemy of the moment was nullification. The first issue of the *Washington Globe* was published on December 7, 1830, without any prior notice or advertising. Its sudden emergence had the impact of a grenade exploding. It was the first sign of the secret conflict. Every politically appointed federal employee was required to subscribe.

Calhoun refused to make the customary call to greet the president at the White House on New Year's Day. He was determined to publish the correspondence surrounding the Seminole affair, foolishly giving the material beforehand to Eaton, who he thought would show it to Jackson, who he thought with equal naïveté would forgive him. Eaton returned it with a few markings, told him nothing about Jackson, and Calhoun convinced himself through extraordinary powers of self-delusion that Jackson had given it his personal stamp of approval. Duff Green published a fifty-two-page pamphlet entitled *The Correspondence Between General Andrew Jackson and John C. Calhoun* through the *Telegraph* on February 17, 1831. It was a folly revealing an inconceivable lack of political common sense. Webster told Clay that Calhoun's pamphlet was "so ambitious . . . so factious . . . that it creates no small degree of disgust." Blair wasted no time wielding the stiletto of his pen to draw blood. Calhoun and Green, said Jackson, "have cut their own throats, and destroyed themselves in a shorter space of time than any two men I ever knew."

But Calhoun was persuaded that it was Jackson who was irretrievably damaged and his own prospects for the presidency brighter than ever. In Richmond he was the guest of honor at a dinner on March 10 hosted by Governor John Floyd, an enthusiast for nullification, and more than sixty others, mostly members of the Virginia legislature and editors of influential newspapers. Floyd declared, "He has won upon all and I think nineteen twentieths will support him for the presidency." Arriving in South Carolina, he held forth expansively on March 18 to his acolyte, James Henry Hammond, an influential newspaper editor, relating his misconceptions with perfect certainty. Jackson "was losing the confidence of the Republican party everywhere," "three fourths of the members of Congress were with him agt. the President," and "for himself, he had dissolved all ties, political or otherwise, with him and forever." He was optimistic about his own chances. "He then hinted pretty strongly that if things went right, he might be placed in nomination for the Presidency next fall. . . . He said his object was to throw himself entirely upon the South and if possible to be more Southern if possible."

The next month his allies were purged from the cabinet, the only dissolution of a cabinet to occur before a change of administrations, achieved through a brilliantly contrived scenario. Van Buren offered to resign and be nominated as minister to England, while Eaton exchanged his job with the senator from Tennessee, thereby removing that source of friction through the appearance of self-sacrifice, enabling Jackson to demand the resignations of the other cabinet members, removing Calhoun's influence. Shortly after being forced to quit, Secretary of the Treasury Ingham wrote in a letter on May 7, 1831, about Jackson: "I am persuaded that the objects nearest his heart are 1. His reelection 2. to avenge Mrs. E 3. To destroy Mr. Calhoun 4. To have Mr. V.B. for a successor."

Days after the cabinet's dissolution the *Telegraph* published a full-scale biography of Calhoun that could only be read as a campaign document. Then Calhoun wrote a disastrous "reply" to Eaton, praising the exclusion of Mrs. Eaton as "the great victory that has been achieved, in favor of the morals of the country, by the high-minded independence and virtue of the ladies of Washington," which should not "be lost by perverted and false representations of the real question at issue."

Calhoun was greeted home with a laudatory dinner on March 28, 1831, at which he praised his friends for "my vindication against the unprincipled and artful attempts to destroy my private and public character." He offered a toast: "*The union*—May the period he indefinitely postponed when we may be compelled to choose between its dissolution, and submission to a government of unlimited powers."

In South Carolina politics divided between a new party for nullification, the State Rights and Free Trade Party, encouraged behind the scenes by Calhoun, and the Union Party. On May 19, 1831, in reaction to the cabinet shake-up in Washington and purging of the Calhoun faction, Governor James Hamilton of the State Rights Party held a dinner in honor of Congressman George McDuffie, the silver voice of nullifiers, who in private was railing about "revolution" and delivered a stem-winding oration defying accusations of treason. "Shall we be terrified by mere phantoms of blood, when our ancestors, for less cause, encountered the dreadful reality?" One observer thought his gesticulating fists would "fly off and hit somebody."

McDuffie was more than Calhoun's follower. He was a virtual family member, taken in as an orphan boy by Calhoun's older brother James, apprenticed as a law clerk in the Calhoun firm, educated at Calhoun brother-in-law Moses Waddel's academy, built his lucrative law practice on an account with Calhoun's mother, a large plantation owner, elevated with Calhoun backing to the legislature and the Congress. McDuffie's role was to stake the most radical rhetorical position among Calhoun loyalists, even in advance of Calhoun's own. "When I hear the shout of 'glorious Union,'" he said, "methinks I hear the shout of a robber gang." A "spare, grim looking man," who spoke in "tempests" and "whirlwinds of passion," he was impulsive to the degree of fighting a duel for Calhoun's honor that would leave him maimed.

On the wall behind the podium at the State Rights dinner were hung portraits of Calhoun and Randolph. The incendiary event was partly intended to force Calhoun out in the open as the State Rights champion, as Hamilton admitted to Hammond afterward. "Mr. Calhoun," he wrote, "has too much sense not to see the essential weakness of his occupying a double position, Janus faced, with one expression of countenance for one side of the Potomac and another expression for the other." Calhoun was displeased at the "imprudent" display. He still thought he was a candidate for president. His strategy was to win Virginia, triggering the other Southern states to fall into line, depriving Jackson of victory by deadlocking the election and throwing it into the House. Duff Green, acting as Calhoun's manager, wrote Hamilton asking if they "were all crazy at McDuffie's dinner" and whether they "intended to start into open rebellion and insure the empire of the whore of Washington."

On July 4th at Charleston the State Rights and Union parties held competing celebrations. At the Union dinner a letter from President Jackson was read four times, from each corner of the hall, each time to tumultuous cheers, intended as a warning to the nullifiers that he would answer his "high and sacred duties" against "any plan of disorganizations, by whatever patriotic name it may be decorated, or whatever high feelings may be arrayed for its support." At the same hour Hayne, acting as Calhoun's surrogate, addressed the State Rights dinner. "When nullification shall be our only means of deliverance from this oppression, who is there that would not be a *nullifier?* . . . We will take any remedy that may be proposed to us, short of disunion . . . call it Nullification or call it what you will." The next day the State Rights controlled legislature expressed its fury at Jackson, passing a resolution denouncing him and upholding nullification. "The Executive of a most limited government, the agent of an agency, but a part of a creature of the States, undertakes to prescribe the line of conduct to a free and sovereign State under denunciation of pains and penalties!"

Calhoun finally stepped from behind the curtain as the chief nullifier with the publication on July 26 of a manifesto that made the same arguments as his anonymously written South Carolina Exposition. He wrote that the country should not "be subjected to the unchecked will of the majority," denigrated the whole federal government as a mere "agent" of the "sovereign states," and proposed nullification as the remedy to restore "justice." Blair's *Globe* eviscerated Calhoun's tract as "treason." Calhoun printed three thousand for distribution as a campaign document and mailed it to the new members of Jackson's cabinet.

Duff Green traveled throughout New England and New York trying to convince the Anti-Mason Party to nominate Calhoun for president at the first party convention ever staged on September 26, 1831. The party's young leaders, little known New York politicos named William Seward and Thurlow Weed, were Adams men hostile to Calhoun, and arranged the nomination of William Wirt. Calhoun quietly made it known in letters that he was still for internal improvements, contrary to Jackson; he was also in favor of a federal income tax to replace the tariff.

That summer a house slave at Fort Hill had run away after Floride Calhoun threatened to whip him. Aleck, as he was called, was caught hiding in the woods. Calhoun wrote specific instructions to the man who captured him for Aleck's punishment: "have him lodged in Jail for one week, to be fed on bread and water and to employ some one for me to give him 30 lashes well laid on, at the end of the time."

Van Buren's diplomatic nomination, meanwhile, could not have worked out better for him. On January 24, 1832, Calhoun cast the tie-breaking vote against it, blaming him for dissolution of the cabinet. "It will kill him, sir, kill him dead. He will never kick, sir, never kick," Calhoun gloated, according to Thomas Hart Benton, who overheard him. Benton remarked, "You have broken a minister and made a vice president." The Jacksonians planned at this point two terms for Jackson, two for Van Buren, and two for Benton.

At the start of the campaign, in July 1832, the Congress cut the tariff in half, which Jackson believed would deflate the nullifiers. Duff Green's *Telegraph* mercilessly attacked him for the rest of the campaign. "You may rest assured Duff Green, Calhoun & Co. are politically dead," Jackson wrote Van Buren. He wrote again: "What must a moral world or community think of a man so perversely prone to secret lying as John C. Calhoun is proven to be?" Jackson was reelected in a landslide against Clay.

Events in South Carolina cascaded in reaction. Its presidential electors announced they would vote for Governor Floyd of Virginia, Calhoun's friend, who was not a candidate. Even before Jackson's election, the State Rights Party swept the legislative elections, winning such an overwhelming majority that when the state legislature convened on October 26 its first order of business was to call for a convention to take up nullification. The State Rights men, representing the economic and political elite, ratified the Ordinance of Nullification on November 24, the honor of first signing given to six ancient Revolutionary War soldiers. Three days later, the legislature endorsed it. Tariffs were declared "null, void and no law," state courts were forbidden from questioning the authority of the Ordinance, nor could it be appealed to the U.S. Supreme Court, and all state officials civil and military were required to take a loyalty oath to the Ordinance or be removed. If the federal government were to attempt to enforce its laws "the people of this State will henceforth hold themselves absolved from all further obligation to maintain or preserve their political connection with the people of the other States; and will forthwith proceed to organize a separate government, and do all other acts and things which sovereign and independent States may of right do." In short, the Ordinance of Nullification encoded the suppression of the civil liberties of Unionists, created a one-party state with no minority rights, and, far from shunning secession, upheld it. As Calhoun's ideas went from theory into action abstract pretenses dropped.

The state also authorized money for an arsenal of weapons and mustering twenty thousand militia volunteers. Governor Hamilton resigned in anticipation that he would lead the armed conflict. Hayne was elected governor. Calhoun resigned as vice president and was elected senator to fill Hayne's place. Medals were struck: "John C. Calhoun, First President of the Southern Confederacy."

Days before this shuffling of leadership in preparation for war Jackson produced a conciliatory annual message on December 4 calling for a further reduction in the tariff. Then on December 10 he issued his Proclamation Against Nullification, written with Edward Livingston, his secretary of state. The eagle turned from facing the olive branch to the arrows. Defining the presidency "invested" with the power "for preserving the Union," he declared South Carolina's "strange position" as "palpably contrary to the Constitution." There was no originalist basis to it. "If this doctrine had been established at an earlier day, the Union would have been dissolved in its infancy." In a line clearly aimed at Calhoun, he stated, "Metaphysical subtlety, in pursuit of an impracticable theory, could alone have devised one that is calculated to destroy it." In the next sentence Jackson cast nullification into the abyss as "incompatible with the existence of the Union, contradicted expressly by the letter of the Constitution, unauthorized by its spirit, inconsistent with every principle on which it was founded, and destructive of the great object for which it was formed." Calhoun's notion, Jackson went on, would transform the Constitution into a "wretched, inefficient, clumsy contrivance." He mocked Calhoun, contrasting "the most zealous opposers of federal authority" to George Washington and "the sages." "Was this self-destroying, visionary theory the work of the profound statesmen, the exalted patriots, to whom the task of constitutional reform was intrusted?" Jackson contemptuously dismissed nullification. "Miserable mockery of legislation!" He threw aside the claim that it was not about disunion, describing it as asserting "the right of secession." But there was no such "constitutional right." Instead this "fallacious" notion was contrary to the very existence of the United States. Then for thousands of words Jackson explained that the states were not sovereign, the Union created the states, there was no "undivided sovereignty," and that those who argued otherwise were guilty of "radical error." He warned South Carolina to draw back from "the brink of insurrection and treason," from "the mad project of disunion." He did not use the word "treason" casually. Seven times he repeated it. He spared no scorn for Calhoun and his "instigators," men of "dishonor." "Look back to the arts which have brought you to this state—look forward to the consequences to which it must inevitably lead!" Jackson did not hesitate to spell them out: civil war, "deluge with blood" and "bloody conflicts." It was up to those "who have produced this crisis to see the folly, before they feel the misery, of civil strife." Jackson announced his duty to execute his office as president, but the "necessity of a recourse to force" was up to South Carolina: "if it be the will of Heaven that the recurrence of its primeval curse on man for the shedding of a brother's blood should fall upon our land, that it be not called down by any offensive act on the part of the United States."

Jackson dispatched General Winfield Scott to Charleston, two navy cutters to its harbor, ordered the forts' garrisons strengthened, and artillery units mobilized. He spoke of enlisting an army to march into South Carolina. "The President was resolved, and avowed his resolve," wrote Jackson's biographer James Parton, "that the hour which brought the news of one act of violence on the part of the nullifiers, should find Mr. Calhoun a prisoner of state upon a charge of high treason. And not Calhoun only, but every member of Congress from South Carolina who had taken part in the proceedings which had caused the conflict between South Carolina and the general government."

South Carolina sought to win other Southern states to its cause. But while there was strong support for nullification in Georgia and Virginia, all the legislatures rejected or condemned its course. The effort to rally the South was a belated version of Calhoun's presidential campaign strategy. But South Carolina was left standing alone.

In a rage against Jackson, the South Carolina legislature passed a resolution denouncing him for "threatening them with military coercion," and Governor Hayne called his proclamation "specious and false." Jackson would "destroy the liberties of the citizen" and build in its place "a great, consolidated empire, one and indivisible, the worst of all despotisms." Militias drilled in the streets. John Randolph wrote of his wish to "be borne . . . in a litter to the field of battle and die in your ranks."

But February 1, the feared deadline for South Carolina to enact nullification, came and went. The State Rights men held a brave gathering affirming it, as well as secession, but they urged that the "collision" be avoided to await the end of the congressional session on March 4, 1833, Inauguration Day—a "pause with honor." Eyeball-to-eyeball with Jackson, the nullifiers blinked.

Van Buren had advised Jackson against issuing his proclamation and was against enforcing it. Looking forward to his campaign for the presidency in 1836, he anxiously wanted to accommodate Southern opinion. There had been no Northern president who was not named Adams, and no Northern Democrat, and Van Buren was filled with worry. His ally, Congressman Gulian Verplanck of New York, proposed a bill that would effectively eliminate the tariff, lending political credit to Van Buren. But the Verplanck bill was doomed, strenuously opposed by the leading representative of New England mill owners, Daniel Webster. Just trounced at the polls, Clay stepped into the vacuum. "It is mortifying, inexpressibly disgusting," he wrote, "to find that considerations affecting an election now four years distant," and observed, "if it passes, its passage may be attributed to the desire of those same friends of Mr. Van Buren to secure Southern votes."

Clay killed the Verplanck bill and substituted his own, proposing gradual reductions of the tariff until 1842, satisfying the demands of the South Carolinians, to the extent that they were attached to a policy resolution, while still preserving elements of his "American System." Senator Calhoun arrived in Washington to discover Clay scripting the play. Cornered, he worked with Clay behind the scenes and then attempted to prevent being recorded on the record voting for it. When the crucial moment came on a key amendment he frantically conferred with his followers behind the vice president's podium in the Senate and sent out word that he wished to abstain, but Senator John Clayton of Delaware, Clay's man, informed him his vote was indispensable. "This union of Mr. Calhoun and Mr. Clay," wrote Benton, ". . . afforded a strong instance of the fallibility of political opinions."

Clay's bill liberated Calhoun from his self-created peril. Jackson was prevailing, but he sought symbolic victory. He was displeased with the "Compromise of 1833," though he signed it. He did not want Calhoun to escape obloquy. So he proposed a measure to justify executive powers to enforce tariffs, dubbed by the nullifiers the "Force Bill." The debate gave Webster and Calhoun yet another chance to expound their views of the Constitution and Union. "The constitution," Webster warned, "does not provide for events which must be preceded by its own destruction. Secession, therefore, since it must bring these consequences with it, is revolutionary. And nullification is equally revolutionary." It was nothing less than the doctrine of disunion. "It strikes a deadly blow at the vital principle of the whole Union," he said. "Sir, the constitution of the United States was received as a whole, and for the whole country. If it cannot stand altogether, it cannot stand in parts." Calhoun then held forth on how the bill forged "a consolidated government in which the States have no rights" and "utterly overthrows and prostrates the constitution; and that it leaves the government under the control of the will of an absolute majority." While Calhoun made his reply to Webster, John Randolph took a seat in the Senate near him. A man in front of him wore a hat that partially blocked his view. "Take away that hat," he said, "I want to see Webster die, muscle by muscle." But the "Force Bill" passed with only one senator present voting against it—Senator John Tyler of Virginia, an ally of nullification.

Calhoun had already left the Senate chamber when the vote was taken, and he departed for home the day before Jackson's second inauguration. On March 4, Inauguration Day, the *Telegraph* printed the text of the "Force Bill" on its front page within black mourning borders, accompanied by an editorial calling it the death of "all that is valuable in our institutions" and echoing Calhoun's rhetoric that it would "subvert the sovereignty of the States of this Union, to establish a consolidated Government without limitation of powers, and to make the civil subordinate to the military power."

Calhoun hurried to South Carolina to calm his excited followers who might repudiate the tariff compromise and to claim he had won the war against all enemies. After conferring with him the legislature repealed the Ordinance of Nullification. That November, the State Rights Party completely swept the elections and the Unionists were shattered. Calhoun came to Charleston to celebrate the triumph as the guest of honor at a dinner where his entrance was greeted by "bursts of applause." He declared that the tariff compromise had delivered "a mortal wound" to Clay. There was, he declared to "prolonged peals of applause," "magic in nullification."

Calhoun had succeeded in turning the tariff into a fundamental question of the Constitution, producing a national crisis. "If you should ask me the word that I would wish engraven on my tombstone, it is Nullification," he told one of his worshipful admirers. But he confessed in a letter to his friend Virgil Maxcy, the solicitor of the Treasury, "I consider the Tariff, but as the occasion, rather than the real cause of the present unhappy state of things." The true underlying question, he wrote, which "can no longer be disguised," was "the peculiar domestick institution of the Southern States"—slavery.

Jackson felt all along that Calhoun had used the tariff as a ploy. "The tariff was only the pretext, and disunion and a Southern Confederacy the real object," he wrote after the nullification crisis. "The next pretext will be the negro or slavery question." James Petigru, the leader of the Unionists of South Carolina, the former state attorney general, believed that nullification was the first step toward a conflict over slavery and secession. "It is clear," he wrote, "that our nullifiers mean to pick a quarrel with the north about negroes. . . . Nullification has done its work. It has prepared the minds of men for a separation of the States—and when the question is moved again it will be distinctly union or disunion." (In December 1861, after South Carolina enacted its Ordinance of Secession, Petigru, who, according to Mary Chesnut, the intimate chronicler of the Confederate elite, "alone in South Carolina has not seceded," remarked, "South Carolina is too small for a republic and too large for an insane asylum.")

After nullification, fuming at Jackson, Calhoun did whatever he could to weaken him, swerving to work with Clay's newly organized Whig Party, yet in fundamental opposition to it, too. His politics were calculatingly corrosive. He pitted the parties against each other, sometimes aligning himself with the Whigs, but only to undermine the Democrats, or vice versa. He despised them when they failed to do his bidding, which exposed their foolish arrogance, and when they did, which exposed their hollow vassalage. He projected himself the embodiment of South Carolina, therefore living embodiment of the South, therefore of the nation as it should be. "For many years Mr. Calhoun was absolute in South Carolina, and all who sought promotion in the State had to follow him and swear by him. He thought for the State and crushed out all independence of thought in those below him," wrote Benjamin Franklin Perry, a Unionist newspaper editor there. Southerners who differed with him, Calhoun believed, dangerously fragmented Southern unity, therefore thwarted Southern control of the federal government, therefore objectively aided and abetted abolitionism, therefore destroyed the Union. He believed the South should be controlled by the federal government, which would fall under its sway when the South was unified, which would occur when it was led by South Carolina, which would be under Calhoun. Only to the degree that he associated the Union with his Ptolemaic conception revolving around himself was he a Unionist. This spiraling logic concluded inevitably with his repeated threats of secession that he insisted he wished to prevent. Those who failed to heed him, he demonized. They did not need to be sworn enemies; they only had to object.

"I cannot describe to you," Calhoun remarked to a friend, "I cannot express the indifference with which I regard the presidential chair, compared to the honor and the usefulness of establishing this great measure of free trade." But, above all, he still desperately wanted to be president. "He lived two lives," recalled Rufus Choate, "for, being Monroe's Secretary of War, he expected to succeed J. Q. Adams as President. At that time he was altogether the first young man in the nation. But when Jackson came up, he saw—for he had perfect sagacity, and could see a great way into the future—that his day was over, his chance was gone. From that time he became one-sided, mischievous, and making good evil, always. He had no generous joys; was of a saturnine cast. He was not, perhaps, willfully wicked; but he was disappointed to death."

Calhoun would not have to wait long for what Jackson predicted would be his "pretext."

CHAPTER FIVE

OLD MAN ELOQUENT

William Lloyd Garrison, the son of poor English immigrants who landed first in Canada, was born in Newburyport, Massachusetts, apprenticed as a printer, campaigned for temperance, and then joined Benjamin Lundy, a Quaker, as coeditor of the early abolitionist newspaper, *The Genius of Universal Emancipation.* Jailed for seven weeks for alleged libel for publishing the name of a slave trader, Garrison split with his mentor, disagreeing with his gradualism, and launched his own sheet in 1831. *The Liberator,* with only a few hundred subscribers, proclaimed, "I *will be* as harsh as truth, and as uncompromising as justice. On this subject, I do not wish to think, or speak, or write, with moderation. No! no! Tell a man whose house is on fire to give a moderate alarm; tell him to moderately rescue his wife from the hands of the ravisher;

John Quincy Adams

tell the mother to gradually extricate her babe from the fire into which it has fallen;—but urge me not to use moderation in a cause like the present. I am in earnest—I will not equivocate—I will not excuse—I will not retreat a single inch—AND I WILL BE HEARD."

On a trip to Britain in 1833 to establish transatlantic linkage, he befriended George Thompson, chief agent of the Anti-Slavery Society, met with Thomas Clarkson, the now blind founder of the abolitionist movement in England, and William Wilberforce, who had led the fight for emancipation in Parliament. Garrison secured a "Protest" signed by Wilberforce and other eminences criticizing efforts at colonization as an alternative to emancipation as "delusive." From the gallery in the House of Commons, Garrison witnessed the historic passage of the emancipation bill in July 1833, followed days later by Wilberforce's death and stately funeral in Westminster Abbey, an apotheosis. In a London newspaper, Garrison published a letter denouncing the Constitution: "A sacred pact! A sacred pact! What then is wicked and ignominious?"

Upon Garrison's return he founded the American Anti-Slavery Society in Philadelphia, an assembly attended by fifty-six delegates, many clergymen, almost all motivated by profound religious conviction that slavery was immoral, in violation of higher law than the Constitution, and disdaining politics with its compromises and equivocations.

Its "Declaration of Sentiments," written by Garrison, stated: "With entire confidence in the overruling justice of God, we plant ourselves upon the Declaration of our Independence and the truths of Divine Revelation as upon the Everlasting Rock."

But Garrison's invocation of the Declaration did not align him with those abolitionists who took it as an inspiration for political action. He preached perfectionism, spurning politics in all of its forms as immoral compromise with evil, urged rejection of the ballot box, and was censorious of antislavery politics and poli-

William Lloyd Garrison

ticians. Unswerving in his belief in moral suasion, he opposed abolitionists who proposed any practical political tactics, disdained support for antislavery candidates, condemned the formation of the Liberty and Free Soil parties, and denounced those opposing the extension of slavery to Kansas and fighting to make it a free state. His fervor was stoked by the moral glamour of virtuous protest, which confirmed for him the wickedness of the enemy. It intensified his absolute conviction that the Constitution was "born of hell" and "a work of the devil." Garrison's slogan was even more extreme than its absolutist rejection of politics suggested; it was the inverse complement of the most radical secession-minded Southerners: "No Union With Slaveholders!" He was as opposed to Unionism as any Southern fire-eater. Not until the middle of the Civil War, after he personally befriended President Lincoln, would he abandon his perfectionism and begin to grasp politics, his own potential influence in the process, and break with his closest and most brilliant protégé, Wendell Phillips, who still adhered to the strictures of Garrisonian moral purity and sought to defeat Lincoln for reelection in 1864.

The American Anti-Slavery Society at once began its fervent evangelical work, establishing branch societies and helping to fund newspapers to publish abolitionist speeches and sermons, accounts of slavery, and news of antislavery events. In May 1835 the AASS began a postal campaign to send more than one million pieces of abolitionist literature to religious and community leaders throughout the South appealing to their Christian conscience. The intent was to shame slaveholders out of slavery. Naive goodwill was greeted with violence.

On July 29, a mob raided the Charleston post office to seize copies of newspapers named *The Emancipator* and *Human Rights*, and the next night two thousand gathered to burn the confiscated papers, illuminating makeshift gallows from which swung effigies of Garrison and Arthur Tappan, who with his brother Lewis, New York merchants and publishers of the *Journal of Commerce*, were the chief funders of the movement. Robert Y. Hayne, the former U.S. senator, governor, and now mayor, chaired a city council meeting, attended by the town's clergymen, who all supported his letter to Postmaster General Amos Kendall demanding that abolitionist literature be banned. Kendall declared his sympathy for its destruction and pledged he would not enforce the law to protect it. "On this subject, therefore, if this view be correct," he declared, "the States are still independent, and may fence round and protect their interest in slaves, by such laws and regulations as in their sovereign will they may deem expedient."

In Washington, Dr. Reuben Crandall, found possessing an abolitionist newspaper on August 11, was jailed, charged with seditious libel and attempting to incite slave revolts, before he was finally acquitted eight months later. The U.S. Attorney prosecuting him was Francis Scott Key, a slaveholder and author of "The Star-Spangled Banner"—"land of the free, home of the brave." Crandall died two years later of tuberculosis contracted in prison.

From July to October 1835, in the North and the South, there were thirty-five riots against abolitionists, eleven mobs rampaging against supposed slave insurrections, and eleven riots against blacks. These outbreaks were not unprompted responses, however misguided, to hard economic times, because the times were prosperous. Nor were these populist insurgencies against entrenched elites of wealth and power, extensions of Jackson's polarizing bank wars. To be sure, there were random riots at the same time aroused by other issues: riots both against and by Irish immigrants, riots against election laws, riots against a local bank in Maryland, and riots over steamship races. But these disturbances were not spontaneous, but all organized by local authorities and traceable to a panic over the menace of abolitionism.

One after another, Southern state legislatures enacted resolutions calling upon Northern ones to "effectively suppress . . . abolitionist societies," according to those of both South Carolina and Virginia; "penal laws as will finally put an end to the malignant deeds of the Abolitionists," according to Alabama; "to crush the traitorous designs of the Abolitionists," according to Georgia. Senator John Forsyth of Georgia wrote Van Buren "unless the most decided steps are taken in New York, the present seat of the conspirators, to break them up, I should not be at all surprised at a decisive renewed movement to establish the Southern Confederacy." He urged "a little more mob discipline of the white incendiaries would be wholesome at home and abroad. . . . A portion of the magician's skill is required in this matter be assured and the sooner you set the imps to work the better." (As president, Van Buren would appoint Forsyth his secretary of state.) In New York, the postmaster promptly banned abolitionist mail. "These men can be silenced in only one way—Terror—Death. . . . This is the only remedy," wrote James Henry Hammond, Calhoun's protégé, now a congressman.

On August 21, 1835, the elite of Boston filled Faneuil Hall, historic cradle of the Revolution, to rally against abolition. More than 1,500 eminent citizens, many with commercial interests in the cotton trade—the beginning of the Cotton Whigs—had signed their names to a newspaper advertisement calling for the meeting. The most distinguished public men accused the abolitionists of fomenting servile insurrection, being directed by foreign agitators, who were supposedly responsible for the riots, and while inspired by foreign influences (namely George Thompson) were guilty of treason. Describing the Boston meeting "to soothe and conciliate the temper of the Southern slaveholders," John Quincy Adams scathingly wrote in his diary, "All this is democracy and the rights of man." Yet Adams was also opposed to the abolitionist mailings, believing they might well kindle slave insurrections. Northern Whig papers uniformly condemned abolitionists over the mailings, many echoing the call for censorship. Abolitionists were utterly rejected, socially stigmatized, and politically isolated.

A few weeks later, a gallows was constructed in front of Garrison's home in Boston with two ropes hanging down, one for him, and another for George Thompson, then on a speaking tour of the United States. Thompson wrote Garrison on September 15 that "a recent Southern paper has stated that if the prominent fanatics were not put down by the strong arm of the Law in the North, ASSASSINATION *would cease to be reprehensible or dishonorable.* Such writing must do good. Let the South go the whole length of the rope, and let there henceforth be no mistake about the meaning of the words 'Southern chivalry,' 'highmindedness,' 'nobility,' 'bravery,' 'generosity.'"

On October 21, 1835, the Boston Female Anti-Slavery Society met for the first time to hear the announced speaker, George Thompson, but he had been mobbed at an earlier appearance at Plymouth and had fled the country for the safety of a ship back to England. Garrison showed up in his place. A mob assembled outside the gathering. Mayor Theodore Lyman, who had presided at the Faneuil Hall anti-abolitionist meeting, entered to request that the thirty women disperse and Garrison leave. When Garrison attempted to walk home the mob grabbed him, tied him up, and dragged him down the streets. The mayor intervened, harboring Garrison overnight for protection in the city jail, where he inscribed on the wall: "William Lloyd Garrison was put into this cell on Monday afternoon, October 21st, 1835, to save him from the violence of a respectable and influential mob, who sought to destroy him for preaching the abominable and dangerous doctrine that all men are created equal, and that all oppression is odious in the sight of God."

The same day as the Boston riot, a mob attacked the founding convention of the New York Anti-Slavery Society in Utica. It was led by Democratic congressman Samuel Beardsley, Van Buren's closest ally in the House of Representatives, who insisted that if the group were allowed to meet it would transform Utica into "Sodom and Gomorrah." The rioters, with the congressman at their head, stampeded into the church where the delegates gathered, breaking up the session. In Montpelier, Vermont, a mob led by the town's notables—the bank president, the postmaster, and merchants— busted up the founding meeting of the Vermont Anti-Slavery Society. But the efforts at intimidation had an opposite effect than intended. Instead of discouraging abolitionism, they galvanized it. Within a year, the number of abolitionist societies proliferated to 527.

In December, stoking the furor, the new governor of South Carolina, George McDuffie, Calhoun's acolyte, proclaimed slavery "the cornerstone of the republican edifice"—the metaphor that Alexander Stephens as vice president of the Confederacy would use in his famous 1861 "cornerstone" speech justifying secession and slavery. The stakes were raised: to attack slavery was to threaten the whole constitutional American order. With this turn, the nullifiers were able to fling back the charge of treason and any who refused to repress the abolitionists.

President Jackson, in his annual message to the Congress, on December 7, 1835, called for a federal law against the "unconstitutional and wicked" abolitionists for circulating "incendiary publications, intended to instigate the slaves to insurrection." Amid this uproar, John C. Calhoun, stranded on his own island within the Senate, saw his opportunity for a triumphant return from internal political exile. He seized upon the issue of abolitionist literature, grabbing authority away from the post office committee to claim it for a select committee he chaired.

On February 4, 1836, Calhoun submitted his report on abolitionist literature in the mail, a classic Calhoun production, rebuking Jackson for executive arrogance and asserting states' rights. Jackson's proposal, he argued, was unconstitutional, as Calhoun had argued that much of what Jackson did was unlawful. He claimed Jackson's policy would violate free speech and could be equally applied to censor any opinion, even pro-slavery opinion. Calhoun asserted that the matter was not for Congress to decide, but must be reserved to the states, which alone had the right to supersede federal authority, ruling what was permissible in the U.S. mail. Decrying that Jackson would suppress free speech, he wanted that power of suppression invested only in the states in the interest of "domestic tranquility." But both Jackson's and Calhoun's measures languished and died, at odds with each other and superfluous in any case. Southern states simply destroyed abolitionist mail when it arrived, virtual nullification on the spot, receiving the approval of the postmaster general. By then the issue of "incendiary" mail had already been replaced by an even more inflammatory one.

After the Charleston bonfire the abolitionists recognized that the South would not be converted through newspapers and pamphlets. In December 1835, they adopted a new tactic, submitting petitions to the Congress to emancipate the slaves held in Washington, over which the Congress had complete constitutional authority as the only federal territory. As early as March 24, 1828, more than 1,100 of the most influential citizens of the District, owning much of its property, had signed a petition calling for the abolition of slavery. Now the abolitionists devoted their full energy to making this movement national.

As early as 1834, Calhoun had been on alert against petitions against slavery in the District of Columbia. "This is no time for discord in our ranks," he wrote Congressman Francis W. Pickens of South Carolina, one of his satellites. When he had heard a rumor that a petition for abolition in the District would be presented, he warned that it "can only be considered as the commencement of the work of immediate emancipation over the whole [of] the South, to which event it will certainly lead, if not promptly met by the entire slave holding states, with the fixed determination to resist at any hazard." He instructed Pickens to remain neutral in the coming presidential contest. "We are on our guard . . . we are determined to preserve our separate existence on our basis. If there is to be Union against the administration, it must be Union on our own ground."

The idea of submitting petitions en masse to the Congress sprang fully formed from the brain of Theodore Dwight Weld, son of a Connecticut Congregationalist minister, inspired by the Second Great Awakening, and cofounder of the Lane Theological Seminary in Ohio, where he spearheaded a split over abolition in 1834, before becoming secretary of the AASS. Weld wrote the original petition that was copied in the hundreds, signed by thousands, then tens of thousands, and first introduced by Congressman Thomas Morris of Ohio on January 7, 1836. (Morris was friendly with a local tan-

Theodore Dwight Weld

ner and abolitionist in George-town, Ohio, Jesse Grant, who later wrote him a letter seeking an appointment to West Point for his son, Ulysses.) Calhoun was instantly on his feet in the Senate against the "gross, false, and mali-cious slander" against slave states. "Nothing can, nothing will, stop these petitions but a prompt and stern rejection of them. We must turn them away from our doors, regardless of what may be done or said."

The surfacing of abolitionist petitions was the signal of a clear and present danger that Calhoun and his cohort had awaited since the quell-ing of the nullification crisis. Calhoun lived in a boardinghouse on Capitol Hill, Mrs. Lindenberger's, cloistered with his entourage. The Lindenberger mess was the nexus of Calhoun's operation. His fellow boarder, newly elected Congressman Hammond, was now his chief lieutenant in the House. A par-venu climber of humble origins from Massachusetts married into upcountry plantation wealth, he was a self-adopted ultra-Southerner, more ultra than the ultras. (There are few people who hate high-minded Bostonians more than swamp Yankees.) His floor speech in the House on February 1, 1836, his first appearance, following Calhoun's instructions, laid the markers of a new politics of loyalty tests, ultimatums, scorn for compromise, threats of violence, contempt for party politics, and derision of democracy itself.

Declaring that the Congress had "no constitutional power" over the Dis-trict, Hammond insisted the petitions must not be received at all. They were sent by "persons who are pursuing a systematic plan of operations, intended to subvert the institutions of the South . . . a disciplined corps." He waved ab-olitionist newspapers. "Here, Sir, is a number of the paper entitled 'Human Rights'—a neat, well-printed sheet. Here are several numbers of the 'Anti-Slavery Record,' on the outside of each of which is a picture representing a master flogging naked slaves, and each of which contains within pictures equally revolting. I hold also in my hand, that most powerful engine in party warfare, an 'Anti-Slavery Almanac for 1836.'"

Those who failed to resist the subversive abolitionist cadres were guilty of treason. "He who falters here or elsewhere, he who shrinks from taking the highest and the strongest ground at once, is a traitor!" Three more times Hammond shouted, "Traitor! Traitor! Traitor!" He was tossing back the charge thrown at the nullifiers. Then he defended slavery as a natural state for blacks. "The camel loves the desert; the reindeer seeks the everlasting snows; the wild fowl gather to the waters; and the eagle wings his flight above the mountains. It is equally the order of Providence that slavery should exist among a planting people, beneath a southern sun. Slavery is said to be an evil; that it impoverishes the people, and destroys their morals. . . . But it is no evil. On the contrary, I believe it to be the greatest of all the great blessings which a kind Providence has bestowed upon our favored region."

If slavery was the rightful condition for the slaves it was also the rightful basis for the American nation. "*It is a government of the best,* combining all the advantages, and possessing but few of the disadvantages of the aristocracy of the old world. . . . In a slave country *every freeman* is an aristocrat." In the "war" and "crusade" against "this institution" the banner carries "that visionary and disastrous sentiment, 'Equality to all mankind'"—a foreign-born notion from the French Revolution. "The sans-culottes are moving."

Suppressing petitions and "incendiary pamphlets" was the first line of defense of "our institutions." "We may have to adopt an entire non-intercourse with the free states, and finally, sir, we may have to dissolve this Union." Southerners were prepared to "maintain" slavery or "die." "And," Hammond concluded, "I warn the abolitionists, ignorant, infatuated barbarians as they are, that if chance shall throw any of them into our hands he may expect a *Felon's Death.*" Hammond's fiery speech set the stage for Calhoun.

Five days later, on February 5, Calhoun took to the floor in the Senate, delivering his most famous oration, setting out his maximum strategy in defense of slavery, "the peculiar institution." "I do not belong," said Calhoun, "to the school which holds that aggression is to be met by concession. Mine is the opposite creed, which teaches that encroachments must be met at the beginning, and that those who act on the opposite principle are prepared to become slaves. In this case, in particular, I hold concession or compromise to be fatal. If we concede an inch, concession would follow concession—

compromise would follow compromise, until our ranks would be so broken that effectual resistance would be impossible. We must meet the enemy on the frontier, with a fixed determination of maintaining our position at every hazard." The battle was "our Thermopylae."

Every petition must be refused, every effort to "reason it down" rejected. Congress had no authority over the matter and assuming it did would lead to civil war. "As widely as this incendiary spirit has spread, it has not yet infected this body, or the great mass of the intelligent and business portion of the North; but unless it be speedily stopped, it will spread and work upwards till it brings the two great sections of the Union into deadly conflict." Unless abolitionism was suppressed, civil war was inevitable. Just as abolitionists warned that slavery and the Union were incompatible, Calhoun cautioned that abolitionism and Union were irreconcilable. "By the necessary course of events, if left to themselves, we must become, finally, two people. It is impossible under the deadly hatred which must spring up between the two great sections, if the present causes are permitted to operate unchecked, that we should continue under the same political system. The conflicting elements would burst the Union asunder, powerful as are the links which hold it together. Abolition and the Union cannot co-exist."

The slaves were not only naturally inferior, suited to slavery, but benefited from it. They had arrived in a "low, degraded, and savage condition," but "in the course of a few generations" risen to a "comparatively civilized condition." Slavery was for the slaves not "an evil, a good—a positive good." Southern "civilization," rooted in slavery, was superior to European and Northern societies, where free labor was nothing but the source of turmoil. The South had resolved the vexing question of class conflict by establishing a master class and a slave one that lived in harmony. "There is and always has been in an advanced stage of wealth and civilization, a conflict between labor and capital. The condition of society in the South exempts us from the disorders and dangers resulting from this conflict; and which explains why it is that the political condition of the slaveholding States has been so much more stable and quiet than that of the North." If he were unheeded in suppressing every abolitionist "fanatic," then the South would have no resort. "Surrounded as the slaveholding States are with such imminent perils, I rejoice to think that our means of defense are ample, if we shall prove to have the intelligence and spirit to see and apply them before it is too late."

The day before his defiant speech Calhoun had filed his committee report on "incendiary pamphlets." But rather than glorying in his exercise of authority, he glowered at a defection in his ranks. Without advance warning, on February 4, Congressman Henry Laurens Pinckney, a nullifier from Charleston, had proposed an alternative approach—not to reject the petitions, but instead to refer them to a select committee, which would table them. This clever legerdemain, consigning them to oblivion, enraged Calhoun. It was the "reason" he reproached, the "compromise" he reproved, breaching the "frontier" he guarded. By not rejecting the petitions outright, Pinckney's bill implicitly recognized the constitutional authority of the Congress to abolish slavery in the District. In Calhoun's eyes, this was apostasy, disloyalty, even treason. Of course, the constitutional right was plain and ever broader—that Congress had the power to abolish slavery beyond the District—it had, after all, eliminated the transatlantic slave trade in 1808. But Calhoun was furious over more than this doctrinal deviance. His true target was the presidential ambition of Martin Van Buren. Through the petitions issue Calhoun intended to shatter Van Buren's unsteady national support North and South, creating an opening for his own continuing influence and potential rise to the presidency, and to wreak revenge on Jackson. Pinckney's measure, introduced to ease Van Buren's election by removing the question, literally tabling it, would confound Calhoun's settling of scores, his plan for vengeance and vindication.

No Carolinian had a more illustrious lineage than Henry Laurens Pinckney. His father, Charles Pinckney, was the state's signer of the Declaration of Independence, his mother's father, Henry Laurens, president of the Continental Congress. Founder and editor of the *Charleston Mercury*, he had served as Calhoun's messenger on nullification. Brother-in-law to Hayne, speaker of the legislature, and elected to the Congress as candidate of the State Rights Party, he was Calhoun's most refined voice. Now, one after another, Calhoun's acolytes poured anathema on Pinckney. Congressman Henry A. Wise of Virginia "hissed and spurned" him "as a deserter" and "traitor." Hammond condemned him for his "treachery." (Suffering fits of nervousness and gastrointestinal disorders, Hammond quit the House within three weeks. He would return, first as an intransigent governor of South Carolina and then a secessionist U.S. senator, notorious as much for his flagrant liaisons with the teenage daughters of plantation aristocrats and his female slaves as renowned for coining the phrase "Cotton is King" in an 1858 speech.)

Two future Democratic presidents blocked Calhoun, isolating him among the Southern members of the Congress, to enact the Pinckney Rule: Speaker of the House James K. Polk of Tennessee, a Jacksonian heir who controlled regular order, and Senator James Buchanan of Pennsylvania, early practicing his politics of Southern appeasement for his own advancement. Polk appointed Pinckney to chair the committee to report on his own resolution. Joining him was a third future Democratic president: Congressman Franklin Pierce of New Hampshire, beginning to burnish his credentials as a Northern man of Southern sympathies. (That fall, in retribution against Pinckney, Calhoun recruited a willing Unionist to run against the renegade, purged him, and further tightened his grip over South Carolina as though it were his satrapy.)

On the day the Pinckney Report was brought up for a vote in the House, May 25, 1836, when the third section was read, the part on the Gag Rule, John Quincy Adams arose from his seat seeking recognition. Speaker Polk refused to acknowledge him, instead calling on a member of the Pinckney Committee. Once again Adams asked to be heard. "The question is not debatable," replied Polk. "I will appeal when the decision is made," said Adams. "I am aware that there is a slaveholder in the chair." Polk attempted to cut him off. "Am I gagged or not?" demanded Adams. Polk ruled that he was.

Adams was thwarted from speaking, but he found a later time that day, rising on the issue of providing food rations to refugees from the Seminole War in Florida and Georgia to decry the annexation of Texas as a slave state, prophesying civil war and inevitable emancipation.

Are you ready for all these wars? A Mexican war? . . . And, as an inevitable consequence of them all, a civil war? For it must ultimately terminate in a war of colors as well as of races. And do you imagine, that while, with your eyes open, you are willfully kindling, and then closing your eyes, and blindly rushing into them, do you imagine, that while, in the very nature of things, your own southern and southwestern states must be the Flanders of these complicated wars—the battle field upon which the last great conflict must be fought, between slavery and emancipation—do you imagine that your Congress will have no constitutional authority to interfere with the institution of slavery, *in any way*, in the states of this confederacy? Sir, they must and will interfere with it—perhaps to sustain it by war; perhaps to abolish it by treaties of peace; and they will not only possess the constitutional power so to interfere, but they will be bound in duty to do it by the express provisions of the Constitution itself. From the instant that your slaveholding states become the theatre of war—civil, servile, or foreign—from that instant, the war powers of Congress extend to interference with the institution of slavery in every way in which it can be interfered with.

Adams would return again to elaborating the constitutional legitimacy of the war power to emancipate slaves six years later, in a speech on April 14 and 15, 1842, on the consequences of extending slavery and the prospect of war with Mexico.

I say it is a war power; and when your country is actually in war, whether it be a war of invasion or a war of insurrection, Congress has power to carry on the war, and must carry it on, according to the laws of war; and by the laws of war, an invaded country has all its laws and municipal institutions swept by the board, and martial law takes the place of them. This power in Congress has, perhaps, never been called into exercise under the present constitution of the United States. But when the laws of war are in force, what, I ask, is one of those laws? It is this: that when a country is invaded, and two hostile armies are set in martial array, *the commanders of both armies have power to emancipate all the slaves in the invaded territory*. Nor is this a mere theoretic statement.

The sixth President of the United States, son of the second president, ambassador to Britain and six other European nations, U.S. senator, former secretary of state, nominated and confirmed as a justice of the Supreme Court (an honor he declined), professor of rhetoric at Harvard, fluent in seven languages, John Quincy Adams had been elected to the House of Representatives in 1830, choosing to hold an office far beneath the presidency from an overwhelming sense of duty and sense that without public service his life was aimless. The most cosmopolitan man of his generation was ill adapted to democratic politics, adhering to his dignity and disdaining vulgar appeals. He believed that disinterested men, "the most able and the most worthy," should settle national affairs, the rule of "talents and virtue alone." His program of internal improvements was both physical and moral. "The spirit of improvement is abroad upon the earth," he proclaimed in his first annual message to the Congress on December 6, 1825. "Let us not be unmindful that liberty is power; that the nation blessed with the largest portion of liberty must in proportion to its numbers be the most powerful nation upon earth." He envisioned extensive highways and canals, a national university, and an astronomical observatory, all ridiculed as fanciful. "A politician in this country must be the man of a party. I would fain be the man of my whole country," he had written in his diary years earlier in 1802. True to his self-demanding creed, preserving himself from "temptation," he had not descended to become a mere politician and was ousted after one term by Jackson.

Afflicted with a host of ailments, rheumatism, sciatica nerve pain, eye infections, and skin diseases, he scribbled endlessly in the diary he had kept since he was young, often describing the merry-go-round of politicians swirling around him ("universal mediocrity"), an acidic sketch journalist writing for an audience only of himself and posterity. "In the multitudinous whimsies of a disabled mind and body," he recorded on September 9, 1833, "the thick-coming fancies often occur to me that the events which affect my life and adventures are specially shaped to disappoint my purposes. My whole life has been a succession of disappointments. I can scarcely recollect a single instance of success to anything that I ever undertook." His time in the House seemed a sentence to Purgatory to test his forbearance—until he stood against the Gag Rule.

After his speech on May 25 predicting civil war, the day he had been prevented from speaking about the Gag Rule, he wrote in his diary that while the South greeted his statement with "echoes of thundering vituperation" the North had given "one universal shout of applause." He now committed himself to the fight for the right of petition. "This is a cause upon which I am entering at the last stage of life, and with the certainty that I cannot advance in it far; my career must close, leaving the cause at the threshold. To open the way for others is all that I can do. The cause is good and great."

Adams had held private conversations with Calhoun about slavery when they were both in Monroe's cabinet, during the debate over the Missouri Compromise. At a party at Calhoun's house in Washington, on the evening of February 4, 1820, Adams was shocked at the vehemence expressed against even the slightest comments opposed to the extension of slavery. "The slave-holders cannot hear of them without being seized with cramps," he wrote in his diary. "They call them seditious and inflammatory, when their greatest real defect is their timidity. Never since human sentiments and human conduct were influenced by human speech was there a theme for eloquence like the free side of this question now before the Congress of this Union. By what fatality does it happen that all the most eloquent orators of the body are on its slavish side? There is a great mass of cool judgment and plain sense on the side of freedom and humanity, but the ardent spirits and passions are on the side of oppression." One month later, walking home with Calhoun from a cabinet meeting, Calhoun patiently explained that the rights Adams spoke of applied only to whites, and that if he, Calhoun, had a white servant in his house "his character and reputation would be irretrievably ruined," and only slaves, never white men, should perform manual labor. "It is, in truth, all perverted sentiment—mistaking labor for slavery, and dominion for freedom," Adams wrote in his diary. "The discussion of this Missouri question has betrayed the secret of their souls . . . they show at the bottom of their souls pride and vainglory in their condition of masterdom." Years later, after noting in his diary on January 1843 that Calhoun intended to run again for the presidency, Adams cast him as satanic: "Calhoun is the high-priest of Moloch—the embodied spirit of slavery."

Adams was naturally inclined to be antislavery, a belief he inherited from his extraordinary parents, reinforced by his encounter with the appalling conditions of serfdom in 1781 in Russia and Poland. But when he initially opposed the Gag Rule his premise was that slavery was legally sacrosanct and could be altered only by and within the various states. His speeches were for free speech and the right to petition—civil liberties. Through his eight-year-long crusade he evolved from carefully distancing himself from abolitionists who would "ruin me and weaken and not strengthen their cause" into a "Conscience Whig" and avowed antislavery man.

Adams deployed every wile and tactic against the Gag Rule, and delighted in demonstrating its absurdity. He introduced as many petitions as he could, read them until he was gagged, even introducing one from nine free black women, and tricking Speaker Polk into reading one aloud thinking it was about something else, dramatically presented one petition from twenty-two slaves, provoking a censure motion that collapsed into farce when he revealed the slaves asked "that slavery not be abolished"—and then was charged with having "trifled with the House." Southern congressmen regularly condemned his "continued assault upon the South," called for a grand jury to indict him for inciting insurrection, and demanded his expulsion. The *Congressional Globe* reported that he "wantonly tortured the feelings" of Southern members, while the *Democratic Review* described him "growling and sneering . . . lashing the members into the wildest state of enthusiasm by his indignant and emphatic eloquence." The 24th Congress overwhelmingly voted in favor of the passage of a resolution: "Resolved, That slaves do not possess the right of petition secured to the people of the United States by the Constitution."

The Gag Rule perfectly played into the hands of the American Anti-Slavery Society, whose tiny membership suddenly exploded to 100,000. Its leaders decided to turn the stream of petitions into a flood, which poured onto Adams's wooden desk. "Order! Order!" shouted Southern members to stifle Adams. The more he was castigated, the more he was determined to make his adversaries appear ridiculous. "Mr. Adams persisted in holding the floor, and in affirming that he was not out of order," the *Congressional Globe* reported about just one of these confrontations. He gleefully recorded another episode in his diary, on February 4, 1841: "I then took my turn for an hour, and arraigned before the committee, the nation, and the world, the principles avowed by Henry A. Wise, and his three-colored standard, of overseer, black, dueling, blood-red, and dirty, cadaverous, nullification, white. Of its effect I will not now speak. I have discharged what I believe to be a solemn and sacred duty. At the close of his reply, his gang of duelists clapped their hands, and the gallery hissed."

Wise was the chief proponent of and expert on the Code Duello, or the Code of Honor, within the Congress, and the instigator and arranger of a duel on February 24, 1838, between two members, Jonathan Cilley, a Democrat of Maine, and William Graves, Whig of Kentucky, over an obscure matter of "honor"—an anonymous article in a New York newspaper for which neither man held any responsibility alleging a senator of corruption. Wise interjected himself as Graves's "second," and after the initial shots missed and the duelists declared the affair concluded he insisted on a second round, which killed Cilley. In the shock that followed Adams sponsored a bill to prohibit dueling in the District, which passed. He considered dueling, its Code, and the Southern concept of "honor," nothing but "an appendage of slavery." His success with the anti-dueling act was universally understood as part of his crusade.

"He is no literary old gentleman, but a bruiser, and loves the melee," Ralph Waldo Emerson wrote of Adams in his *Journals*. "When they talk about his age and venerableness and nearness to the grave, he knows better, he is like one of those old cardinals, who, as quick as he is chosen Pope, throws away his crutches and his crookedness, and is as straight as a boy. He is an old roue who cannot live on slops, but must have sulphuric acid in his tea." His supporters took to calling him "Old Man Eloquent."

By 1838 the abolitionist movement was an organizational shambles. The House of Tappan, which had been the main source of funding, collapsed in the Panic of 1837. Garrison's rigidities, eccentricities, and heresies created fissures and splits with just about everyone from virtually the whole of the New England clergy to Arthur Tappan. State committees broke off from the central office, which kept trying to dun them for uncollected dues. Garrison's insistence on moral suasion as the only legitimate approach, condemnation of politics as inherent compromise with evil, personal jealousies with other leaders, and factional dogmatism reduced the movement to tatters. William Ellery Channing, the leading Unitarian minister, conferred with Adams about launching a rival to the AASS, but nothing came of it except that the attempt so angered some of the Garrisonians that they ran a candidate against him in 1838. In the aftermath of this fracas, Adams turned the full blast of his ridicule in an address "to the Abolitionists of the North" on the doctrine of immediate emancipation as politically ludicrous and dangerous, concluding by invoking Jonathan Swift's *Gulliver's Travels*: "What then is the meaning of that immediate abolition which the Anti-Slavery Society has made the test of orthodoxy to their political church? A moral and physical impossibility . . . as far beyond the regions of possibility as any project of the philosophers of Laputa."

A year later, when abolitionists sought the most distinguished representative for their cause, they turned to Adams. In 1839, slaves captured in Sierra Leone were transported in a Portuguese ship named the *Amistad* to Cuba and sold to labor on Spanish plantations. On the voyage to their owners in the Caribbean the slaves revolted and ordered the surviving crew to navigate back to Africa. Instead, they sailed northward until the ship was caught off Long Island, New York, and the slaves imprisoned in New Haven, Connecticut. President Van Buren attempted to return the slaves to Cuba and their Spanish claimants at the demand of the Spanish government. In the *Amistad* issue he saw an opportunity to appeal to Southern voters in the 1840 presidential campaign. His position only succeeded in elevating the *Amistad* case to a cause. Abolitionists at a local church in Connecticut raised funds for the slaves' defense on the grounds that they were free once they touched U.S. soil because the slave trade was illegal under the law, an interpretation of the British Somerset ruling of 1772, which held that a slave on British territory was by definition emancipated. After initially turning down their insistent requests, Adams agreed to represent the case before the Supreme Court. On February 20, 1840, he spoke for four and a half hours. Pointing to the copy of the Declaration of Independence hanging in the courtroom, he connected the Africans to the values of the Revolution, "I will not recur to the Declaration of Independence—your Honors have it implanted in your hearts—but one of the grievous charges brought against George III was that he had made laws for sending men beyond seas for trial. That was one of the most odious of those acts of tyranny which occasioned the American Revolution. The whole of the reasoning is not applicable to this case, but I submit to your Honors that, if the President has the power to do it in the case of Africans, and send them beyond seas for trial, he could do it by the same authority in the case of American citizens." His argument incomplete, he continued on another day for four more hours. Finally, he finished by noting that he had first been admitted to appear before the Supreme Court in 1804. He called the roll of all the members of that court beginning with John Marshall. "Where are they all? Gone! Gone! All gone!" Adams commended the members of the sitting court to achieve the virtue of "those illustrious dead." On March 9, Justice Joseph Story, in his majority opinion, ruled that the slaves were indeed free and had the "ultimate right . . . to resist oppression, and to apply force against ruinous injustice." Thirty-five ultimately returned to Africa.

By 1840, despite the *Amistad* victory, the AASS had become little more than a shell controlled by Garrison and his most devoted sectarian followers. That year antislavery men who embraced political solutions broke with the Garrisonians' perfectionism and immediatism to form the Liberty Party.

Meanwhile, the pile of petitions landing on Adams's desk towered higher than ever. Now he became the center of the cause.

When a Whig majority swept into the Congress with the 1840 election a small but critical mass of antislavery advocates formed around the nucleus of Adams. Led by Joshua Giddings, a lawyer from the Western Reserve of Ohio, newly elected to the House, they created an unofficial "Select Committee on Slavery" to force the issue despite the Gag Rule. This band of brothers lived together in Mrs. Sprigg's boardinghouse facing the East Portico of the Capitol where today sits the Library of Congress, soon known notoriously as "Abolition House," and where in a few years Lincoln would lodge. To help present their case they decided to hire an assistant for eight dollars a day—Theodore Weld.

Since the battle had begun against the Gag Rule, Weld had written four seminal books, systematically making the legal, theological, moral, and economic arguments against slavery. The opening sentence of *The Power of Congress over the District of Columbia*, published in 1837, read: "A CIVILIZED community presupposes a government of law." *The Bible Against Slavery* appeared the same year. *American Slavery as It Is: Testimony of a Thousand Witnesses* was a compilation of stories from many sources documenting slavery's cruelties. (His co-writers were his extraordinary wife, Angelina Grimké and her sister, Sarah Grimké, born and raised within the South Carolina plantation elite, and passionate abolitionists. This particular book would have a profound impact on Harriet Beecher Stowe and serve as a major source of documentary material in her writing of *Uncle Tom's Cabin*.) Finally, Weld's *Slavery and the Internal Slave Trade in the United States*, published in 1841, provided facts and figures on the profiteering in human property in the South.

Weld was, in effect, the first congressional staffer. (The Congress created its professional staff in 1893, each member then allocated a single aide.) Upon his arrival in Washington in January 1842, he was invited to dinner by Adams—Reverend Ezra Weld, Theodore's grandfather, had been John Adams's pastor and baptized his son John Quincy—and would immediately find himself acting as his aide in his congressional trial charged with nothing less than treason.

Adams began the second session of the 27th Congress renewing his perennial assault on the Gag Rule, reading petition after petition. On January 21, 1841, he read one from Georgia that demanded he be removed as chairman of the House Foreign Affairs Committee for being a "monomaniac," enabling him to claim a point of personal privilege to defend himself from the charge, gaining control of the floor, reading more petitions, and thwarting an effort to remove him. The next day he decided to turn the tables on the Calhounites by reading a petition from fifty-six citizens of Massachusetts praying for a "peaceful dissolution of the Union" because "the resources of one section of the Union is annually drained to sustain the views and course of another section" and "will overwhelm the nation in utter destruction." Southerners shouted for attention. At last, they imagined they had the cause for evicting Adams. Wise asked the speaker whether "a move to censure" Adams could proceed. "Good!" said Adams. A censure motion was promptly introduced. But the next day the designated speaker for the Southerners, Congressman Thomas F. Marshall of Kentucky, nephew of Chief Justice John Marshall, offered a substitute to try the former president for "the crime of *high treason*," for which, if guilty, he would be expelled.

"I call for the reading of the first paragraph in the Declaration of Independence," replied Adams—"*the first paragraph in the Declaration of Independence*"—proclaiming the duty of the people to abolish a government destructive of their rights. Adams declared that if put on trial he would "show there is a persistent intention to destroy the right of the free states and to force slavery upon them." It would be a show trial, but not as those against him contrived. Wise accused Adams of conspiracy with "foreign influence"—British abolitionists. "Break down slavery and you would with the same blow break down the great democratic principle of equality among men," Wise said. "One portion of the House," according to the *Congressional Globe*, burst into laughter. Adams reminded the chamber of Wise's culpability in the duel, that he was "a man with his hands and face dripping with the blood of murder." Wise rose to cast blame for the duel on Clay, who was blameless.

Marshall had been standing imperiously with his arms folded throughout the debate when Adams turned to address him next. After praising his uncle, Adams rebuked him for failing to understand the meaning of treason. "Now," said Adams, "thank God the Constitution of the United States has defined high treason, and it was not left for the gentleman of Kentucky, nor for his puny mind, to define that crime, which consists solely in levying war against the United States, or lending aid and comfort to their enemies." His tongue-lashing of the whippersnapper went on. "Were I the father of that young man I could feel no more anxiety for his welfare than I do now; but if I were his father I would advise him to return to Kentucky and take his place in some law school, and commence the study of that profession which he has so long disgraced." Marshall felt utterly humiliated. "I wish I were dead," he confided to a friend. "I would rather die a thousand deaths than again to encounter that old man."

For six years, Adams had been gagged. "Mr. Adams now began to arraign the slave power," wrote Giddings, "no longer attempting to defend himself, he boldly stood forth as the accuser and prosecutor of the slave interests." The trial had become his platform. For two weeks, provided with research from Weld, his condemnation of slavery could not be stopped. He was, he wrote in his diary, "in the midst of that fiery ordeal." On the House floor, he waved one of the many letters threatening him with assassination, "the engraved portrait of me with the mark of a rifle-ball on the forehead." "I reviewed my relations with the Virginian Presidents of the United States heretofore—Washington, Jefferson, Madison, Monroe—and contrasted them with this base conspiracy of three Virginians, banded here, together with numerous accomplices in and out of the House, for my destruction." Hoping, he said, "better things of Virginians," he recited lines from the Irish poet Thomas Moore's "Loves of the Angels": "That holy shame which ne'er forgets/What clear renown it used to wear."

When Adams proposed that his defense might last three months, his tormentors knew they were vanquished. They sued for peace, abruptly ending the trial, tabling the matter that had stopped all other business. Enraged that Adams outwitted them, they censured Giddings. He was formally punished for arguing that the mutinous slaves on a ship that forced it to sail to Nassau, which was British territory, should not be pursued, but his true crime was that he was a vulnerable surrogate target. Giddings resigned, put the judgment in the hands of his district, and was overwhelmingly returned to office. For all intents and purposes, the Gag Rule was shredded. Adams went on slashing at it until it was conclusively defeated two years later, in 1844.

"Old Man Eloquent" as he was now called hardly rested on his laurels. Instead, he heightened his rhetoric, further inciting Southern reactions. In 1848, during a House debate, Congressman James Dellet of Alabama read a statement Adams had made to a group of free blacks in Pittsburgh, intending by exposure of the offensive passage to rebuke him. "We know," Dellet said, reading Adams's words, "that the day of your redemption must come. The time and the manner of its coming we know not: It may come in peace, or it may come in blood; but, whether in peace or in blood, let it come." Then he read it again with emphasis to shame Adams. But Adams spoke up unapologetically, "I say now, let it come." "Yes," said Dellet, as though he had clinched his case, "the gentleman now says 'let it come,' though it cost the blood of thousands of white men." But Adams replied, "Though it cost the blood of millions of white men, let it come. Let justice be done though the heavens fall." "A sensation of horror ran through the ranks of the slaveholders," recalled Giddings. "Dellet stood apparently lost in astonishment, and all were silent and solemn until the Speaker awoke members to the subject before them by declaring the gentleman from Massachusetts was out of order." Once again, Adams had won.

Adams had started against the Gag Rule as a singular voice—"I stand in the House of Representatives, as I did in the last Congress—alone"— but quelled it leading a growing chorus. The son of a founding father was founder of an emergent North, the antiparty man forerunner of the Republican Party, the Puritan moralist a forerunner of practical antislavery politics, his evolution foreshadowing Lincoln, Adams's "fiery ordeal" anticipating the nation's "fiery trial," the failed president providing legal authority for the Emancipation Proclamation. Adams's speeches on emancipation and the war power of the president would be cited at length by William Whiting, solicitor general of the Department of War, in his seminal report of 1862, plainly entitled *War Powers of the President*, which provided the legal arguments that President Lincoln would use to underpin the Emancipation Proclamation and the recruitment of black soldiers.

Calhoun would anoint as his political successor a rising young man who in 1847 took the seat next to him in the Senate, looked to him for guidance, and whom he came to know and trust—Jefferson Davis. Two years later Calhoun took contemptuous passing notice of "the member from Illinois" who had introduced an aborted bill for emancipation in the District of Columbia. But Calhoun would not lower himself to mention the name of Abraham Lincoln.

In Calhoun's dreams began Lincoln's responsibilities. Calhoun's frustrated ambition inspired ever more grandiose notions to counter his enemies—and those of slavery and the South. Embittered rivals who never reconciled, Jackson and Adams shared at least a common hostility to Calhoun. Their struggles with him charted Lincoln's future battlefields, laying out the arguments that would be used against secession and the policies against slavery. During the secession crisis Lincoln kept a copy of Jackson's Proclamation Against Nullification close at hand for constant reference. In his White House study he hung Jackson's portrait.

Adams likely barely perceived and never acknowledged the presence of the freshman congressman from Illinois taking his seat in the back row of the House to listen to his orations, and who was present as a witness on the day when he was stricken with his fatal stroke.

CHAPTER SIX

THE SPRINGFIELD LYCEUM

The struggle over the Gag Rule at its beginning resonated in Vandalia as distant rumbling over the horizon. Here people were scrambling for the move to Springfield. But even in Illinois the near universal opinion of the tempest in Washington was incontestably on the side of the Southerners. Southern legislatures had passed resolutions condemning the "dark, deep and malignant design of the abolitionists" (Alabama), their "prostitution of the freedom of the press" (Kentucky), their incitement of "insurrection and revolt" (Virginia), and "plotting" against "the harmony and safety of the Union" (Mississippi)—all sent to Northern states appealing for solidarity. Connecticut's legislature proclaimed "sympathy" for the "slaveholding states," censured abolitionists as "dangerous," and reproved the suggestion of emancipation in the District of Columbia as "unjust and impolitic." New York's legislature endorsed the message of Governor William L. Marcy, a Jacksonian Democrat,

Elijah Parish Lovejoy

expressing "unanimity" of disapproval of "the whole system" of the abolition-ists and "affection for their brethren of the south."

The Illinois General Assembly voted, January 20, 1837, on a resolu-tion that reproached the abolitionists, who "have aroused the turbulent passions of the monster mob, whose actings are marked by every deed of atrocity," and promised "our brethren of the South" that to suppress insurrection the people of Illinois "would fly to their assistance." The state-ment concluded: "That we highly disapprove of the formation of abolition societies, and of the doctrines promulgated by them. That the right of property in slaves, is sacred to the slave-holding States by the Federal Con-stitution, and that they cannot be deprived of that right without their con-sent. That the General Government cannot abolish slavery in the District of Columbia, against the consent of the citizens of said District without a manifest breach of good faith." Seventy-one members voted in favor, only six against. Voting for the resolution was politically safe and sound, an easy symbolic gesture.

Only one protest was lodged, on March 3, by two members, both from Sangamon County, Dan Stone, already appointed a circuit court judge and politically secure, and Abraham Lincoln. "They believe," they wrote, "that the institution of slavery is founded on both injustice and bad policy; but that the promulgation of abolition doctrines tends rather to increase than to abate its evils." Their protest made two more points: "They believe that the Congress of the United States has no power, under the Constitution, to in-terfere with the institution of slavery in the different states. They believe that the Congress of the United States has the power, under the Constitution to abolish slavery in the District of Columbia; but that that power ought not to be exercised unless at the request of the people of said District."

Lincoln and Stone waited to register their dissent five days after the pas-sage of the Springfield bill, though their votes against the main resolution were taken before the all-important measure for removal of the capital. Lincoln's protest might in retrospect have appeared cautious, narrow, and hedged, but it was the only one, marking the furthest edge of dissent while still remaining within the strict boundaries of viable politics in Illinois. "It is not surprising, I think, that Lincoln should have viewed this New England importation with mingled suspicion and alarm," Herndon observed about his early attitude toward abolitionism. "Abstractly, and from the standpoint of conscience, he abhorred slavery. But born in Kentucky, and surrounded as he was by slave-holding influences, absorbing their prejudices and following in their line of thought, it is not strange, I repeat, that he should fail to estimate properly the righteous indignation and unrestrained zeal of a Yankee Abolitionist." And yet Lincoln's position was little different, even in his criticism of abolitionists or in seeing slavery as a state matter, from where John Quincy Adams stood at that moment.

The day after Lincoln's protest, which went unnoticed beyond tiny Vandalia, Martin Van Buren was sworn in as president. In his Inaugural Address, he warned "the least deviation from this spirit of forbearance" toward slavery "is injurious to every interest." He affirmed he would be "the inflexible and uncompromising opponent of every attempt on the part of Congress to abolish slavery in the District of Columbia against the wishes of the slaveholding states, and also with a determination equally decided to resist the slightest interference with it in the states where it exists." He denounced "the agitation of this subject" for "terrifying instances of local violence." And he appealed to the people "to resist and control every effort, foreign or domestic, which aims or would lead to overthrow our institutions."

Five weeks after Van Buren's inauguration the speculative bubble inflated by highly leveraged private debt began to burst. By April, 250 New York mercantile houses failed, and on May 10 the New York banks refused to accept paper money, in effect declaring it worthless; all debts were immediately called, triggering bankruptcies and cascading collapse. The Panic of 1837 set off an economic depression that lasted about six years. Lacking any understanding of business cycles and the governmental capacity for stimulating the economy to achieve recovery, Van Buren attributed the crisis to unmanly weakness, "a sickly appetite for effeminate indulgence," announced the government had no responsibility to "relieve embarrassments," and prescribed "strict economy and frugality." He acquired the nickname "Martin Van Ruin." The Whigs blamed the catastrophe on a chain reaction stemming from Jackson's policies, his war on the Second Bank of the United States, removing its ability to manage national credit, in turn inciting inflationary speculation, stoked by his substitute "pet banks," which issued unsupported banknotes and multiplied unsecured loans, prompting his Species Circular, which imposed hard currency payments for soaring federal land transactions, which prompted deflationary contraction. The Democrats, for their part, blamed the Whigs and the Whig-oriented business community for, on the one hand, not supporting the shaky house of cards that Jackson had constructed and, on the other hand, for supporting internal improvements that Jackson had vetoed. Partisanship became even more embittered than during the polarizing Jacksonian era. But no one had a program that actually addressed the underlying economic problems.

The roots of the crisis went deeper than the terms of the partisan debate and exposed the corrosive effects of slavery. The United States was enmeshed in a new global economy, its imports dependent on credit from British banks. After a bad harvest Britain had to import wheat from Europe. The Bank of England began closing credit and demanding payment on loans. As a result, some suggested that the Panic was little more than an episode in the history of British banking in which the Americans were collateral damage. But even this partial analysis failed to grasp the nature of the American sources of the crisis. Mortgage-backed securities, zombie banks, and toxic debt were not unique to the crash of 2008, but were also at the bottom of the Panic of 1837. One principal difference was the monetization of slaves.

Brilliant financial innovation had transformed slaves into securities, packaged and repackaged, marketed and sold. "For everyone who drew profit in the system, enslaved human beings were the ultimate hedge," wrote historian Edward E. Baptist. "Cotton merchants, bankers, slave traders—everybody whose money the planter borrowed and could not pay until the time the cotton was sold at a high enough price to pay off his or her debts—all could expect that eventually enslaved people would either 1) make enough cotton to enable the planter to get clear or 2) be sold in order to generate the liquidity to pay off the debt."

This scheme was pioneered by a New Orleans bank called the Consolidated Association of the Planters of Louisiana, which built a towering but rickety economic structure based on manipulations of the price of slaves. Slaveholders mortgaged their slaves in exchange for bank loans, in turn backed by the state legislature, which issued bonds on its "faith and credit," providing confidence to the Baring Brothers bank of London, which sold them on the European financial markets as securities and dizzyingly accelerated the entire leveraged process. "The sale of the bonds created a pool of high-quality credit to be lent back to the planters at a rate significantly lower than the rate of return that they could expect that money to produce. That pool could be used for all sorts of income-generating purposes: buying more slaves (to produce more cotton and sugar and hence more income) or lending to other enslavers. Clever borrowers could pyramid their leverage even higher—by borrowing on the same collateral from multiple lenders, by also getting unsecured short-term commercial loans from the C.A.P.L., by purchasing new slaves with the money they borrowed and borrowing on them too." The price of slaves and plantation land skyrocketed; the false euphoria of a boom mentality fueled the wild spinning of the markets. Speculators scrambled to get in on the windfall profits. The CAPL innovation was copied by banks across the South, supported by state legislatures, and drawing in investors from Wall Street, Broad Street, and Lombard Street, including the Rothschild bank, which plunged in deeply in Alabama. "Using the C.A.P.L. model, slave-owners were now able to monetize their slaves by securitizing them and then leveraging them multiple times on the international financial market." Soon New Orleans held the greatest concentration of bank capital in the country.

Cotton production had almost doubled, from 300 million to more than 600 million pounds in the six years from 1831 to 1837, flooding the British market, which bought more than 80 percent to weave into cloth in its vast mills. But the bubble expanded to its breaking point. With supply glutting the market, prices began to fall, and as early as the summer of 1836 the Bank of England, anxious about the overinvestment in U.S. securities, sharply curtailed credit, forcing British banks to call in loans from American debtors, nearly all heavily leveraged far more than the value of their slaves and land. Three big British banks collapsed by late 1836. By March 1837, the ten largest cotton-trading firms in New Orleans went under. The toxic debt could not be repaid. Planters, banks, and states themselves went bust. New Orleans collapsed as a banking center, ceding primacy to Wall Street. But slavery as a source of the disaster was simply not discussed. The slave owners sought to recover by revving up another boom: increasing cotton production, which rose to two billion pounds by 1859, and claiming new territory for the endless expansion of the slave economy. "Cotton is King," James Henry Hammond of South Carolina famously proclaimed. Even as the paralytic effects of the Panic spread through the economy, the South was already fixed on the annexation of Texas, and John Quincy Adams had been for two years decrying a possible war with Mexico.

The shock from the New York bank closings in May 1837 rapidly rolled across the country. By June 1, the State Bank of Illinois suddenly stopped making species payments. The Democrats in the state tried to pin the blame on the Whigs, claiming that extravagant government spending for internal improvements caused the crisis, though many Democrats had voted for "the System" and it had not yet gone into effect. At a special session of the legislature called for July 10, Democrats attempted to rescind the internal improvements bill, a political commotion to shift the burden from the incumbent Democratic administration to the Whigs.

Hard times swiftly ended the Jackson period of Democratic dominance. The advent of a political opening for the Whigs quickly became apparent to them, especially to the new breed of politicos like Lincoln, who understood the novel methods of party organization, popular appeal, and tactical exploitation of issues for partisan gain. Lincoln thrust himself into these harsh politics of austerity, into the middle of vicious charges and counter-charges, provocations of violence, and a malicious lawsuit filed transparently for partisan purposes. The imbroglio was notable as his first if indirect collision with the rival who would obsess him and become his target of every major speech for nearly a quarter century to come.

Stephen A. Douglas's rise as a self-made man ran parallel to Lincoln's. He was born in Vermont, an unusual Yankee in the frontier state of Illinois filled with migrants from the upper South. His father was not a dirt farmer, but a physician who died young. Douglas dropped out of school for lack of funds and was apprenticed as a cabinetmaker. He arrived penniless in Illinois, in 1833, studied the law, and within months established himself as the young star of the Democratic Party after delivering an impassioned speech defending Jackson in the bank wars, earning him the sobriquet "The Little Giant." "I have become a Western man," he wrote home. Douglas was dwarflike, barely five feet tall, weighed about 110 pounds, had striking blue eyes, and an oversized leonine head. He was elected to the legislature as a Democrat in 1834, the same year as Lincoln, and in 1835 appointed state's attorney in Illinois' sprawling First Judicial District. Another member of the legislature, Usher Linder, wrote that Douglas "looked like a boy, with his smooth face and diminutive proportions, but when he spoke in the House of Representatives, as he often did in 1836 and '37, he spoke like a man, and loomed up into the proportions of an intellectual giant, and it was at that session he got the name of the 'Little Giant.'" But upon encountering the character he would shadow for decades, Lincoln remarked he was "the least man I ever saw."

Douglas was as single-minded and unvarnished in his ambition as Lincoln. Unlike Lincoln, he had no interests whatsoever other than politics. He did not bother with Shakespeare, Burns, or Paine. "He had no avocations," wrote an early admiring biographer, "he had no private life, no esoteric tastes which invite a prying curiosity; he had no subtle aspects of character and temperament which sometimes make even commonplace lives dramatic." He spent nearly every hour among men who might advance him, his haunts circumscribed by Springfield's American Tavern and the State House, the office of the *Springfield Republican* newspaper and the backrooms of general stores. He was as ruthless as he was relentless, as coldblooded toward members of his party who might stand in his way as to any opponent.

In 1836, Douglas replaced George Forquer, who had been humiliated by Lincoln, as head of the General Land Office at Springfield. Forquer, in any case, was dying of tuberculosis. The newly elected Democratic U.S. senator Richard M. Young and Congressman William L. "Big Red" May installed Douglas, prompting the *Sangamo Journal* sarcastically to editorialize, "We are told the *little man* from Morgan was perfectly astonished, at finding himself making money at the rate of from one to two hundred dollars a day!" It is likely the author of the accusatory article was that frequent anonymous contributor, Abraham Lincoln.

After Young's election the senator hosted a celebration at a Vandalia hotel, where Douglas staged a demonstration as a "Western man." "After the company had gotten pretty noisy and mellow from their imbibitions of Yellow Seal and 'corn juice,'" wrote an eyewitness, "Mr. Douglas and General [James] Shields, to the consternation of the host and intense merriment of the guests, climbed up on the table, at one end, encircled each other's waists, and to the tune of a rollicking song, pirouetted down the whole length of the table, shouting, singing, and kicking dishes, glasses, and everything right and left, helter skelter. For this night of entertainment to his constituents, the successful candidate was presented with a bill, in the morning, for supper, wines, liquors, and damages, which amounted to six hundred dollars." (The witness to this raucous event, John H. Bryant, the brother of the poet and abolitionist William Cullen Bryant, and a poet in his own right, had settled in Princeton, Illinois, and come to the capital to lobby Douglas to help create a new county in the northern part of the state. Bryant, at the time a Democrat, eventually became a leader in the antislavery Liberty Party, a congressional candidate of the Free Soil Party, his house a station of the Underground Railroad for fugitive slaves, and a founder of the Illinois Republican Party. He became a friend of Lincoln, a delegate to the 1860 convention, and was appointed collector of internal revenue in Illinois.)

Shortly after the Panic hit, the Democrats, with Douglas at their forefront, launched an attack on the Whig official they believed was most politically vulnerable. Dr. Anson Henry, a close friend of Lincoln, was the chief commissioner in charge of building the new State House in Springfield. He had informed Governor Duncan that the appropriation of $50,000 might not be sufficient and the governor suggested that he proceed without worry because the legislature would certainly make up the cost. Henry was at the time a candidate for probate justice of the peace in Springfield. Soon an article appeared on June 14 in the *Springfield Republican*, the Democratic newspaper, smearing both him and the *Sangamo Journal*: "He was selected by our representation in the legislature on account of the dirty work he had done for their party, writing corrupt articles for the *Journal*. . . . The people are paying dear for the services of a desperate reckless adventurer to write for the *Journal*."

Douglas himself was the anonymous author of the attack piece. He was, in fact, one of the new owners of the *Springfield Republican*. The dying Forquer had sold his control of the paper to a syndicate consisting of Douglas, John Calhoun, Thomas Ford, and Dr. Jacob Early (who had been Lincoln's commanding officer during the Black Hawk War in "the spy company"). Angered by the offending editorial, Dr. Henry gathered a posse armed with guns and clubs on June 14 and invaded the *Republican* office, demanding that its editor, George Weber, disclose the name of the writer of the article defaming him. Weber refused. On June 17, the *Journal* fired back with a piece claiming that the true writer of the libel against Henry was none other than his Democratic opponent, James Adams. "He must know that his own house stands upon disputed ground," the *Journal* concluded cryptically. The article was signed, "Sampson's Ghost." Adams, however, replied in the *Republican* that he was not the author of the original article.

On June 22, Lincoln lifted the veil of mystery about the "disputed ground" when he filed a lawsuit against Adams on behalf of a widow, Mary Anderson, and her son, claiming that Adams had forged a land title that rightfully belonged to them as heirs of her late husband. The charge went to the heart of the office at stake in the election—the probate justice of the peace had the authority to decide wills. The ethereal "Sampson's Ghost" was a reference to one Andrew Sampson, who had contested another piece of land with Adams. Lincoln had filed the "Sampson's Ghost" article into the newspaper before filing his suit before the court, and then wrote a whole series of pieces accusing Adams of drunkenness and "Toryism." (Adams had a long record of misdeeds, but had in fact served as a soldier in the War of 1812.) One of Lincoln's "Ghost" articles opened with a quotation from Hamlet: "Art thou some spirit or goblin damn'd/Bringst with thee airs from heaven or blasts from hell?" In the small world of Springfield, Lincoln's authorship was ill disguised.

The day before Lincoln filed the suit the *Springfield Republican* published another anonymous article, this one written by Douglas, attacking Henry and Dr. Garret Elkin, the Springfield sheriff, who had been a member of the posse. The next evening, June 22, at the head of a mob of twenty men, Elkin broke down the door of the newspaper and tried to smash the printing press. Douglas and other defenders fought back and ejected them. The following day Elkin and his men confronted the editor, George Weber, and his brother on the street. He knocked Weber unconscious with a truncheon, and Weber's brother stabbed him and two others. Eventually, the various charges arising from the fracas were resolved through fines, but the bitterness between the two camps simmered.

While besmirching Adams, Lincoln defended Henry. On June 24, at a public meeting called by Henry and under the chairmanship of John Todd Stuart, Lincoln introduced a resolution that was unanimously passed creating a committee to report on Henry's stewardship. A week later the pro-Henry committee unsurprisingly announced that Henry was innocent of the serious charges published in the *Republican*. On July 4th, the exonerated Anson led a procession of military companies starting at the steps of the First Presbyterian Church to lay the cornerstone of the new state capitol and to be hailed for overseeing its construction. A salute was fired and an all-day celebration commenced.

On Election Day, however, Henry was badly beaten. But Lincoln continued his campaign, writing "Sampson's Ghost" articles assailing Adams's integrity for months. Adams, represented by Douglas as his attorney, fended off the lawsuit for six years, unresolved at his death, when it was finally dismissed. Lincoln's clients were left with nothing but his bills. (Before his demise Adams would reemerge in a mysterious political role to confound the Whigs again—as the closest counselor to Mormon prophet Joseph Smith.)

The Whigs and Lincoln had better luck with the special legislative election to fill the seat of Dan Stone. Lincoln was almost certainly the author of an anonymous article in the *Journal* accusing the Democratic candidate, John Calhoun, his former superior as surveyor, of corruption and betrayal. The piece charged Calhoun and his Democratic supporters with having real estate interests in towns seeking to be the new capital other than Springfield, trying to dilute the political clout of Sangamon County in the legislature by dividing it and calling for rescinding the grant to Springfield. "With the fact that the *Illinois Republican* is now used by Calhoun and his friends, to cause the removal of the seat of government from this place, can anyone doubt what services he is to perform if elected?"

Calhoun lost by a decisive margin to a newcomer, who would soon become one of Lincoln's best friends—Edward Dickinson Baker. An immigrant from England, raised and educated for a time in the utopian community of New

Edward Dickinson Baker

Harmony, Indiana, he moved to Illinois, where as a teenager he was an active Whig and became a protégé of Governor Ninian Edwards. Two years younger than Lincoln, tall and handsome, he could recite English poetry and literature at length in a musical voice that sometimes verged into blustery grandiloquence, and was known as "Silver Tongued Ned." Stephen T. Logan took him as his first junior partner for his ability to sway juries with his florid Shakespearean performances delivered in his perfect English accent. His orations "produced what no logic can," recalled Herndon. "Baker roused . . . made one yell." At the July 4th laying of the State House cornerstone, Baker stood on it to deliver an oration, ending with recitation of his own poetry: "If with the firm resolve to wear no chain, They dare all peril, and endure all pain. . . . So long, my country, shall thy banner fly, Till years shall cease, and time itself shall die."

For the special two-week legislative session in July devoted to the motion to repeal removal of the capital to Springfield the Democrats assigned leadership to their most formidable figure, William L. D. Ewing. A former governor and U.S. senator, he had a history of mayhem—indictments and a conviction for assault and battery, drunken brawls, and a barroom stabbing, among other highlights. He bellowed that "the arrogance of Springfield—its presumption in claiming the seat of government—was not to be endured; that the law had been passed by chicanery and trickery; that the Springfield delegation had sold out to the internal improvement men." "Lincoln was chosen by his colleagues as their champion, to reply to him," wrote Usher Linder, "and I want to say here that this was the first time that I began to conceive a very high opinion of the talents and personal courage of Abraham Lincoln. He retorted upon Ewing with great severity; denouncing his insinuations imputing corruption to him and his colleagues, and paying back with usury all that Ewing had said." Ewing replied to Lincoln with scorn: "Gentlemen, have you no other champion than this coarse and vulgar fellow to bring into the lists against me? Do you suppose that I will condescend to break a lance with your low and obscure colleague?" Some members feared Ewing was attempting to provoke a duel. By the session's end, however, the effort to reverse the Springfield move was defeated and Lincoln returned to Sangamon County, where he was acclaimed as savior. Campaigning for his friends was foremost on his mind.

A year earlier, on July 30, 1836, the *Sangamo Journal* had published an editorial about a commotion in Alton, about seventy miles away. The *Journal* condemned a mob's destruction of the press of the relocated *St. Louis Observer* and defended the right of its editor to publish his antislavery views. Almost certainly Lincoln would have discussed and perhaps even co-written the editorial with his constant co-conspirator, Simeon Francis, whose brothers were abolitionists.

The editor of the *Observer* was Elijah P. Lovejoy. Just as abolitionist literature was being burned in Charleston and John Quincy Adams mounted his crusade against the Gag Rule, Lovejoy's refusal to yield to challenges to his right to publish his views on slavery elevated him in Missouri and Illinois into the symbol of all that was despised about "fanatical" abolitionists. Lovejoy's murder was a harbinger, "the approach of danger," as Lincoln would put it in his first major speech.

Lovejoy was a pure distillation of high-minded, right-thinking, and stiff-necked New England attitudes transplanted to the borderlands of the frontier and slavery. Born in Albion, Maine, his father was a Congregation-alist minister, and after graduating from Colby College he wandered west to St. Louis, where he became the editor of an anti-Jackson, pro-Clay newspaper, the *St. Louis Times*. Feeling the call of religion, he attended Princeton Theological Seminary, and, ordained as a Presbyterian minister, returned to St. Louis to edit the local Presbyterian newspaper, the *St. Louis Observer*.

At once Lovejoy courted trouble, publishing an article in 1834 condemn-ing "the curse of slavery" and sermonizing that it was contrary to Christian-ity. Slavery was not his sole topic, but he cast anathema on it in issue after issue. To be sure, he separated himself from Garrison and the demand for immediate abolition. "Gradual emancipation is the remedy we propose," he wrote in 1835. For his enemies, however, it was a distinction without a dif-ference. A mob threatened to destroy his press. While he briefly attended a religious conference, his anxious board announced in his absence "an entire suspension of all controversy upon the exciting subject of Slavery" and "being one and all opposed to the mad schemes of the Abolitionists." A committee of prominent St. Louis men signed a proclamation insisting on the suppression of any antislavery expression, directly rebuking Lovejoy's theological state-ments: "We consider Slavery as it now exists in the United States, as sanc-tioned by the sacred Scriptures." Fierce opposition only inspired in Lovejoy a fiercer resistance. "We have slaves, it is true, but *I* am not one," he replied. "Is this the land of Freedom or Despotism?" Threatened with vigilante violence if he did not relent, he declared, "I can die at my post, but I cannot desert it." He refused to veer from his stations of the cross, the way of the martyr. "And let me entreat my brothers and sisters to pray for me, that I may pass through this 'fiery trial,' without denying my Lord and Master," he wrote his brother, Owen, on November 2, 1835.

In April 1836, a free black worker on the docks of St. Louis, Francis McIn-tosh, obstructed the arrest of two fighting boatmen, stabbing a policeman to death and wounding another. A mob led by a city alderman invaded the jail, brushed aside the sheriff, seized McIntosh, chained him to a tree, and set him on fire. "We may all see, (and be warned in time,) the legitimate result of the spirit of *mobism*," Lovejoy editorialized. He deplored other instances of "mobism," including the hanging of gamblers in Vicksburg, Mississippi, "and in St. Louis it forces a man—a hardened wretch certainly, and one that deserved to die, but not *thus* to die—it forces him from beneath the aegis of our constitution and laws, hurries him to the stake and burns him alive!"

Judge Luke Lawless, appropriately named, convened a grand jury to determine indictments in the McIntosh matter. Lawless's reappointment to the bench by the governor had just been challenged by most of the lawyers in St. Louis, citing his "prejudice" and "imperious, overbearing, and disrespectful" behavior. Lawless was an intimate friend of Senator Thomas Hart Benton, his second in a duel in which Benton killed an opposing attorney in a case in 1817. Lawless claimed, undoubtedly falsely, to have been a graduate of Dublin University and a colonel in Napoleon's army. He was certainly a highly partisan pro-slavery Democrat, notorious for his ill temper. On May 16, Lawless instructed the grand jury that if the murderers of McIntosh had acted as a mob they could not be indicted. If they were "seized upon and impelled by that mysterious metaphysical and almost electrical frenzy which in all ages and nations has hurried on the infuriated multitude to deeds of death and destruction—then, I say, act not at all in the matter. The case then transcends your jurisdiction; it is beyond the reach of human law." Then he spun a story in which McIntosh became Nat Turner, the leader of a Virginia slave revolt, with Lovejoy as his instigator. Lovejoy, he said, was possessed with "a sort of religious hallucination—a monomania. . . . They seem to consider themselves as special agents . . . in fact, of Divine Providence. They seem to have their eyes fixed on some mystic vision, some Zion, as they term it, within whose holy walls they would impound us all, or condemn us to perish on the outside. . . . Are we to be victims of those sanctimonious madmen?" Lovejoy's writings, he charged, were "calculated to fanaticize the Negro and excite him against the white man." Lawless held up a copy of the *Observer* before the grand jurors. "It seems to me impossible that while such language is used and published as that which I have cited from the *St. Louis Observer*, there can be any safety in a slaveholding state." The grand jury did not issue any indictments.

On July 21, Lovejoy editorialized in the *Observer* against Lawless's "monstrous doctrine," "so absurd and so wicked," a product of "ignorance and prejudice." A mob descended on his office and wrecked it. Lovejoy had already made plans to move across the river to Alton, where he had sent his printing press, but an organized gang destroyed it the next day on the dock. He ordered another one and promptly began publishing again, assuring the wary citizens of Alton that he was not an abolitionist and "did not come here to establish an abolitionist newspaper." Alton's prosperity, after all, rested on its trade with New Orleans and the town fathers were as pro-slavery as those in St. Louis.

Lovejoy continued to write occasional antislavery articles and then committed the truly unpardonable act in June 1837 of publishing Theodore Weld's request for petitions on emancipation in the District of Columbia. A month later, on July 6, Lovejoy issued the call for the formation of the Illinois Anti-Slavery Society. "We would do nothing rashly, but it does seem to us that the time to form such a society has fully come. With many, we are already a 'fanatic' and an 'incendiary,' as it regards this matter, and we feel that we must become more and more vile in their eyes. We have never felt enough, nor prayed enough, nor done enough, in behalf of the perishing slave. This day [the 4th] reproaches our sloth and inactivity. It is the day of our nation's birth."

Within days a committee of town notables signed a statement calling for "the suppression of abolitionism," and visited Lovejoy, demanding that he cease publishing antislavery articles at once. Lovejoy responded by printing a piece entitled, "What Are the Doctrines of Antislavery Men," quoting as its first doctrine the preamble of the Declaration of Independence. On August 21, about a dozen men armed with clubs, the most influential citizens of Alton, stopped Lovejoy on the road at night as he was bringing medicine from the apothecary to his ill wife. They planned to kidnap, tar and feather him, and launch him on a boat down the Mississippi, never to be heard from again. But when he asked them to deliver the medicine to his wife and maintained an utterly cool composure, they let him go, after which they went to his newspaper office and smashed the press. On September 21, a new press arrived, was stored in a warehouse, which was invaded that night by the mob, breaking it and throwing the pieces into the Mississippi. Ten days later, the mob broke into Lovejoy's house at night, trying to terrify him and his sick wife.

Lovejoy traveled to Springfield in October, where he conferred with one of his network of antislavery pastors, Reverend Jeremiah Porter, who mounted the pulpit at the First Presbyterian Church on the 19th to deliver a well-advertised abolitionist sermon. A mob swarming the church to shout him down was suddenly silenced by the large presence of Lincoln's friend Edward D. Baker, insisting they respect Porter's right to speak. A public meeting led a few days later by an Illinois Supreme Court justice, Thomas C. Browne, passed resolutions denouncing abolitionists as "dangerous members of society" who "should be shunned by all good citizens" and blaming them for creating "contention, broils and mobs."

Lovejoy had planned strategy over the summer for the founding meeting of the Illinois Anti-Slavery Society with Reverend Edward Beecher, president of Illinois College at Jacksonville. They gathered the key leaders of the embryonic group, mostly clergymen, at his house. Beecher belonged to one of the most extraordinary families of nineteenth-century America and carried the mantle of his lineage. His father, Lyman Beecher, descendant of Connecticut Puritans, was the most renowned minister of New England, a Presbyterian evangelical and an inspiration of the Second Great Awakening, who had condemned the Missouri Compromise for permitting the extension of slavery, attributing the sins and vices of the South, an odious region, to the accursed institution of slavery. He founded the Lane Theological Seminary, where his student, Theodore Weld, took a more radical position in favor of immediate emancipation and split off an abolitionist vanguard. Edward's sister was Harriet Beecher, who married Calvin Stowe, cofounder of the Lane Seminary with her father, and she would write the most influential book of the century, *Uncle Tom's Cabin*. Edward's younger brother, Henry Ward Beecher, was just beginning his career as a preacher that would make him the most famous in the nation, at Brooklyn's Plymouth Church a champion of the antislavery movement, shipping rifles to Kansas—"Beecher's Bibles"—and during the war serving as an important envoy to England for President Lincoln.

In order to diffuse the growing hostility to the coming meeting, Beecher suggested to Lovejoy that the Anti-Slavery Society advertise itself as a group devoted to "free inquiry" on the subject. Lovejoy happily agreed. On October 26, antislavery delegates from across the state congregated at the Presbyterian Church at Alton. (Among them was Josiah Francis, co-owner of the *Sangamo Journal* and brother of Simeon Francis, Lincoln's close friend.) They found themselves overwhelmed by a mob, determined to bust up the meeting. The leader of that mob was a resident of Alton, the Illinois attorney general, Usher Linder, who had been a sponsor of the pro-slavery resolution in the legislature from which Lincoln had dissented. At the close of the legislative session, Linder had become embroiled in a personal argument with a state senator, John Reilly, leading to the challenge for a duel that was only stopped by the intervention of cooler heads. Dueling was illegal in Illinois, but the state attorney general decided not to indict himself. Now he led the mob to intimidate the abolitionists into appointing him to write a report denouncing them. The abolitionists reconvened separately at a supporter's house, urging Lovejoy to continue publishing. When Beecher arose to speak at another meeting at the Presbyterian Church on October 30, a stone was thrown through the window.

On November 2, notable citizens of Alton called a meeting to resolve the conflict. Beecher presented his statement to the assembly in favor of free speech. Linder accused the abolitionists of being "foreigners," shook his fist in Lovejoy's face, and introduced a resolution acclaimed by the crowd packing the hall: "That the discussion of the doctrines of immediate Abolitionism, as they have been discussed in the columns of the 'Alton Observer,' would be destructive of the peace and harmony of the citizens of Alton, and that, therefore, we cannot recommend the re-establishment of that paper, or any other of a similar character, and conducted with a like spirit."

Lovejoy answered that he would "never" yield to "the demand of a mob." "Why should I flee from Alton? Is not this a free state? When assailed by a mob at St. Louis, I came hither, as to the home of freedom and of the laws. The mob has pursued me here, and why should I retreat again? Where can I be safe if not here? Have not I a right to claim the protection of the laws?" And if he were not defended, he announced he was prepared to meet his fate. The judgment would not fall on him, but on his crucifiers. "You may hang me up, as the mob hung up the individuals of Vicksburg! You may burn me at the stake, as they did McIntosh at St. Louis: or, you may tar and feather me, or throw me into the Mississippi, as you have often threatened to do; but you cannot disgrace me. I, and I alone, can disgrace myself; and the deepest of all disgrace would be, at a time like this, to deny my Master by forsaking his cause. He died for me; and I were most unworthy to bear his name, should I refuse, if need be, to die for him."

Linder emerged from the meeting triumphant, his edict for the shuttering of the newspaper forced through. He led the crowd outside, where he mounted a woodpile and, according to an eyewitness, "began a furious tirade against the Yankees, meaning Northern and Eastern people, generally. He spoke of the new things they were introducing, their home-missionaries, their sunday-schools, their Abolitionism, their temperance societies—and just at that moment he remembered that within a few days, just after a notably disgraceful fit of drunkenness, he had been induced to sign the total-abstinence pledge. Instantly correcting himself, he changed his tone and said, 'But, by the way, gentlemen, temperance is a very good thing;' and for two or three minutes he made, to his rowdies, a fair temperance speech; and then he resumed his abuse of Yankees in general, Abolitionists in particular, and Mr. Lovejoy specially."

The new press for the *Observer* arrived on November 6 at a warehouse on the Mississippi. About thirty men waited with Lovejoy to guard it. The next night, the mob surrounded the warehouse. Both sides were armed with muskets and pistols. The mob stoned the defenders and attempted to storm their fortress. Shots were fired, a member of the mob killed. "Burn them out!" the crowd shouted. A ladder was leaned against the building and a man climbed to the roof to set it on fire. Lovejoy and several others stepped out of the main door to shoot at the arsonist. He was met with a hail of bullets hitting him in the chest. "I am shot!" he exclaimed, and died. With their leader fallen, the defenders surrendered. Cheering and cursing, the mob surged into the warehouse, dragged out the press and dumped it in the Mississippi. Lovejoy's body was left behind, lying bleeding in the doorway, not retrieved until the morning.

The city attorney of Alton indicted the defenders for "resisting an attack made by certain persons unknown to destroy a printing press" and "unlawfully defending a certain ware-house." Linder joined the prosecution team, but when the warehouse owner was acquitted the case collapsed. Then Linder leaped into the fray as the defense counsel for the members of the mob. In his closing argument to the jury, he retailed a version of Judge Lawless's doctrine that mob violence may be vindicated as a popular act. "Are you to select these eight out of the hundred men who entered that building with them, and say that these, and these only, are guilty?" he asked. The brazenness of the mob, he insisted, was exonerating. "The person who sets himself about the commission of such a crime works in the dark. . . . But this act was not done in a corner." Finally, he praised the mob as the triumph of "genuine democracy."

A distinguished and influential attorney, Alfred Cowles, presented the case for the defense. As a member of the constitutional convention of 1824 he had joined with Governor Edward Coles to defeat the pro-slavery resolution. He became the close friend of Ninian Edwards, who, upon election as governor designated him as the state's lawyer in matters before the court. Now, in the case against members of the mob, he represented the state again. "Your verdict," said Cowles, "is to determine, whether law or licentiousness is to prevail; whether we are to live under the rule of law, or the 'reign of terror.'" He knew that the jury sympathized with the defendants. "You may be infected with that spirit, which by the sanction it has given to the violent, illegal, and murderous acts, of the 7th of November last, has made the name of this city a byword of reproach to all coming generations. Your verdict may legalize riot, may legalize arson, may legalize murder. If your verdict sanctions those acts, it will sanction any and every dishonor, which can disgrace civilized society." To be sure, Cowles made clear that he was not a follower of Lovejoy. "I am no abolitionist. I have no sympathy for the party; no communion with their creed. But I am a friend to law; an enemy to mobs; and an advocate for good order. I am opposed to the lawless acts of an unprincipled, an infuriated, a licentious mob. I am opposed to any resort to brute force, much more when it is resorted to break down the barriers which the Constitution has thrown around us all. Put down the freedom of thought! Suppress the freedom of speech! Restrain the freedom of the press! Lawless force cannot do it." The jury deliberated ten minutes before returning a verdict of not guilty.

The transfiguration of Lovejoy into a martyr galvanized the movement against the Gag Rule and for abolition. His killing became an allegory for the cause, a contemporary story in the image of *Foxe's Book of Martyrs*, the 1563 account of Protestant martyrs during the reign of the Catholic Queen Mary. Meetings to mourn and protest Lovejoy's murder were held across the north. At the Faneuil Hall gathering, the youthful Wendell Phillips, scion of Boston Brahmins, emerged as the "Golden Trumpet" for the movement, rebuking Massachusetts attorney general James T. Austin for defending the mob action at Alton. At a prayer meeting at the Presbyterian Church in Hudson, Ohio, Laurens P. Hickok, a theology professor at Western Reserve College, who had been recruited by Weld, proclaimed, "The crisis has come. The question before the American citizens is no longer alone, 'Can the slaves be made free?' but are we free, or are we slaves under Southern mob law?" Owen Brown, a trustee of Oberlin and Western Reserve colleges, both founded by abolitionists, appealed "to the Court of Heaven for a decision." His son, John Brown, stood up at the back of the church, lifted his right arm and announced, "I pledge myself, with God's help, that I will devote my life to increasing hostility to slavery."

In Illinois, the common opinion was to blame Lovejoy's killing on Lovejoy: he had brought his assassination on himself. Even sixteen years later, Thomas Ford wrote that "no language can be loaded with sufficient severity for the fanatical leaders who, by their violence, by their utter disregard of honest prejudices, drove a peaceful community to a temporary insanity, and to the commission of enormous crimes."

The trial acquitting the mob leaders at Alton concluded on January 19. Eight days later, on the 27th, Lincoln mounted the podium to address the Springfield Young Men's Lyceum, located in the Baptist Church. In contrast to the rowdy legislature, the Lyceum was designated as a center of dispassionate intellectual discussion and cultural uplift. Speakers lectured on subjects such as whether capital punishment should be abolished. Its genteel tone was secured by opening its sessions to women. Open partisanship was forbidden by the rules for Lyceum lectures, but the audience, closely attuned to current events, would have understood every inference, allusion, and nuance of Lincoln's pointedly political talk.

Lincoln composed his first important speech in a style different from his usual sarcastic debating style. He aspired to make a more elevated impression. Appearing at the Lyceum lent a speaker the aura of a gentleman and a scholar. Holding forth at that refined venue would help erase Ewing's characterization of him as "coarse and vulgar." "No other speech by Abraham Lincoln has been more closely scrutinized by psychobiographers," observed the historian Thomas F. Schwartz—and no speech of his has been more misinterpreted.

His style at the Lyceum was modeled on Webster's carefully staged magnificence, unlike Lincoln's later plain style, much more devastating to his opponents, which seemed less deliberate though it was the product of years of concentrated experience. The twenty-nine-year-old Lincoln had met Webster eight months earlier, in mid-June of 1837, the first of his heroes he ever encountered, on the great man's visit to Illinois during his sweeping tour of the West. Webster came mainly for private motives, to inspect his investments in Western lands, but he delivered stem-winding orations at every stop. (Webster's godson, William Pitt Fessenden, who would become a U.S. senator from Maine and Lincoln's secretary of the treasury, accompanied him.) Lincoln was one of the sponsors of the Whig host committee, which held a barbecue for him at a grove outside Springfield. Webster did not disappoint the Illinois Whigs, holding forth for an hour and a half against Van Buren's economic policies and urging adherence to the Constitution. Lincoln would hang an engraving of Webster in his law office alongside those of Clay and Jefferson. During the war, he recalled to his friend Henry Clay Whitney a speech he had heard Webster deliver, perhaps the one in Illinois, and quoted him: "Politicians are not sun-flowers, they do not turn to their God when he sets, the same look which they turned when he rose."

Lincoln awkwardly entitled his talk "The Perpetuation of Our Political Institutions," and began by clearing his throat seemingly endlessly. "In the great journal of things happening under the sun, we, the American People, find our account running, under date of the nineteenth century of the Christian era. We find ourselves in the peaceful possession, of the fairest portion of the earth, as regards extent of territory, fertility of soil, and salubrity of climate. We find ourselves under the government of a system of political institutions, conducing more essentially to the ends of civil and religious liberty, than any of which the history of former times tells us." It was this sort of orotund purple language that prompted one of Lincoln's friends, Albert Taylor Bledsoe, a Springfield lawyer, to remark that he was "most woefully given to sesquipedalian words, or, in Western phrase, highfalutin bombast."

The founding generation, Lincoln went on, "a *once* hardy, brave, and patriotic, but *now* lamented and departed race of ancestors," had "nobly" given the "legacy" of "a political edifice of liberty and equal rights; 'tis ours only, to transmit these. . . ." He rambled on about "the lapse of time" and "duty to posterity," and on. Then he snapped to attention, posing his main question and beginning to provide an answer:

> At what point shall we expect the approach of danger? By what means shall
> we fortify against it? Shall we expect some transatlantic military giant, to
> step the Ocean, and crush us at a blow? Never! All the armies of Europe,

Asia and Africa combined, with all the treasure of the earth (our own excepted) in their military chest; with a Buonaparte for a commander, could
not by force, take a drink from the Ohio, or make a track on the Blue Ridge,
in a trial of a thousand years. At what point then is the approach of danger
to be expected? I answer, if it ever reach us, it must spring up amongst us. It
cannot come from abroad. If destruction be our lot, we must ourselves be its
author and finisher. As a nation of freemen, we must live through all time,
or die by suicide.

Insisting that the source of conflict was internal—"it must spring up
amongst us"—Lincoln rejected out of hand the popular conservative argument that foreign ideas imported from French revolutionaries and English emancipationists had infected fanatical American abolitionists, whose
disturbance was the root of all trouble. This was the argument introduced
to suppress abolitionist literature made by James Henry Hammond and
John C. Calhoun—echoed by Martin Van Buren in his inaugural address
in which he pledged his "inflexible and uncompromising" opposition to any
effort of Congress to abolish slavery in the District of Columbia, claiming for
his "constitutional sanction . . . the spirit that actuated the venerated fathers
of the Republic," to resist the "dangerous agitation" of "foreign or domestic"
origin, "which aims or would lead to overthrow our institutions."

If there were any doubt that Lincoln was refuting the political justifica-
tions and legal rationales for mob actions, he went directly at them. "I hope
I am over wary; but if I am not, there is, even now, something of ill-omen,
amongst us," he said. "I mean the increasing disregard for law which per-
vades the country; the growing disposition to substitute the wild and furious
passions, in lieu of the sober judgment of Courts; and the worse than savage mobs, for the executive ministers of justice. This disposition is awfully
fearful in any community; and that it now exists in ours, though grating to
our feelings to admit, it would be a violation of truth, and an insult to our
intelligence, to deny."

With that, Lincoln confronted the "monstrous doctrine" of Judge Lawless, the protector of the mob at St. Louis, and Usher Linder, who had stirred
up the mob at Alton and whose summation in defense of Lovejoy's murderers reiterated Lawless's contempt for the law. Linder's statement delivered
just a little more than a week before Lincoln's speech was fresh in everyone's

minds. Taking down Linder's argument, Lincoln was taking on one of his chief antagonists, who had forced the investigation of the State Bank to attempt to prove the Whigs' corruption, tried to divide Sangamon County to dilute its political influence, and been behind the pro-slavery resolution from which Lincoln dissented. Lincoln had already publicly called him "too ignorant" and "too uncandid." Now he attacked Linder's behavior at Alton, though not by name, as "worse than savage mobs."

"Accounts of outrages committed by mobs form the every-day news of the times," said Lincoln. "They have pervaded the country, from New England to Louisiana." But he chose to focus his attention on two cases, one involving the cascade of violence of slaveholders and the other the burning of McIntosh, before bringing himself to the killing of Lovejoy. These examples were precisely the ones that Lovejoy had cited in his offending editorial in the *St. Louis Observer* that Lawless excoriated. Now Lincoln went further than Lovejoy in pinpointing the paranoia of slave insurrection as the psychosis behind the frenzy of lynching at Vicksburg, Mississippi. "Those happening in the State of Mississippi, and at St. Louis, are, perhaps, the most dangerous in example and revolting to humanity," he said.

> In the Mississippi case, they first commenced by hanging the regular gamblers; a set of men, certainly not following for a livelihood, a very useful, or very honest occupation; but one which, so far from being forbidden by the laws, was actually licensed by an act of the Legislature, passed but a single year before. Next, negroes, suspected of conspiring to raise an insurrection, were caught up and hanged in all parts of the State: then, white men, supposed to be leagued with the negroes; and finally, strangers, from neighboring States, going thither on business, were, in many instances subjected to the same fate. Thus went on this process of hanging, from gamblers to negroes, from negroes to white citizens, and from these to strangers; till, dead men were seen literally dangling from the boughs of trees upon every road side; and in numbers almost sufficient, to rival the native Spanish moss of the country, as a drapery of the forest.

Then he turned to "that horror-striking scene at St. Louis." Before mentioning McIntosh's crime, Lincoln made a point of emphasizing that he had been a freeman. "A single victim was only sacrificed there. His story is very short; and is, perhaps, the most highly tragic, if anything of its length, that has ever been witnessed in real life. A mulatto man, by the name of McIntosh, was seized in the street, dragged to the suburbs of the city, chained to a tree, and actually burned to death; and all within a single hour from the time he had been a freeman, attending to his own business, and at peace with the world."

These, he explained, were "the effects of mob law." "But you are, perhaps, ready to ask, 'What has this to do with the perpetuation of our political institutions?' I answer, it has much to do with it." As isolated incidents, hanging gamblers was "but little consequence" and McIntosh the murderer would have been executed in any case. "When men take it in their heads to day, to hang gamblers, or burn murderers, they should recollect, that, in the confusion usually attending such transactions, they will be as likely to hang or burn someone who is neither a gambler nor a murderer as one who is; and that, acting upon the example they set, the mob of tomorrow, may, and probably will, hang or burn some of them by the very same mistake."

Lawlessness, he argued, inspired contempt for government. "Having ever regarded Government as their deadliest bane, they make a jubilee of the suspension of its operations; and pray for nothing so much, as its total annihilation. . . . Thus, then, by the operation of this mobocractic spirit, which all must admit, is now abroad in the land, the strongest bulwark of any Government, and particularly of those constituted like ours, may effectually be broken down and destroyed." When "good men" see a government unable to protect the law, "the attachment of the People" will be lost.

He drew the curtain back on the ultimate scene of depravity, "the full extent of the evil." "Whenever this effect shall be produced among us; whenever the vicious portion of population shall be permitted to gather in bands of hundreds and thousands, and burn churches, ravage and rob provision-stores, throw printing presses into rivers, shoot editors, and hang and burn obnoxious persons at pleasure, and with impunity; depend on it, this Government cannot last."

At a time when the overwhelming view in Illinois was that Lovejoy had brought his catastrophe upon himself and deserved his fate, Lincoln stood apart. Judiciously, carefully but deliberately, he turned the conventional wisdom on its head. Lovejoy did not, after all, bring about his own death. On the contrary, he was wholly innocent, victim of "the vicious." Those who "shoot editors" were not simply committing a crime, but also overthrowing the foundation of government. By extension of Lincoln's implicit logic, the murder of Lovejoy was a form of treason.

Deploring mobs and "mobocracy" was classic Whig rhetoric about Andrew Jackson—"The reign of King Mob," as Supreme Court Justice Joseph Story had remarked at the start of his administration. Anson Henry, in a talk before the Sangamon County Lyceum in 1835, had declared that those who enjoyed "the benefits of our free institutions" should "show it by putting down every symptom of mobocracy and lawless violence by enforcing the laws. The blood of our fathers, let it not have been shed in vain." But while Lincoln's theme and language were familiar, the circumstances had shifted. Jackson was gone, Van Buren discredited, the Gag Rule controversy raging, and Lovejoy's blood fresh.

Having presented the problem, Lincoln offered his answer. While Van Buren in his inaugural address had summoned the founders in defense of slavery, Lincoln arrayed them against the mob. "The question recurs, 'how shall we fortify against it?'" he asked. "The answer is simple. Let every American, every lover of liberty, every well-wisher to his posterity, swear by the blood of the Revolution, never to violate in the least particular, the laws of the country; and never to tolerate their violation by others. As the patriots of seventy-six did to the support of the Declaration of Independence, so to the support of the Constitution and Laws, let every American pledge his life, his property, and his sacred honor—let every man remember that to violate the law, is to trample on the blood of his father, and to tear the character of his own, and his children's liberty." So it was, by inference, the pro-slavery mobs violating the spirit of '76, not as Van Buren had it the petitioners for emancipation in the District of Columbia, or the martyred antislavery editor.

Here, for the first time, Lincoln used the image of "blood." It would become one of his recurrent motifs. "Blood" dripped from Shakespeare's works, especially Macbeth, Lincoln's favorite, and it would drip endlessly from Lincoln's speeches. At the Lyceum, "blood" stood for authority, the price paid by the revolutionary fathers, an indelible line not to be crossed. "Blood" would take on many meanings for Lincoln—blood for innocence, blood for guilt, until he reached the conclusion of his Second Inaugural, blood for justice, "until every drop of blood drawn with the lash shall be paid by another drawn with the sword."

Lincoln turned his admonition for law and order into a kind of secular prayer. "Let reverence for the laws, be breathed by every American mother, to the lisping babe, that prattles on her lap—let it be taught in schools, in seminaries, and in colleges; let it be written in Primers, spelling books, and in Almanacs—let it be preached from the pulpit, proclaimed in legislative halls, and enforced in courts of justice. And, in short, let it become the *political religion* of the nation." But his solemnity in adopting the literary form of prayer was not, of course, a summons from heaven. His point was not about religion—neither attaching religious faith to civic republicanism nor anything to do with his understanding of the separation of church and state. At the Lyceum, he demanded respect for the rule of law, cast scorn on the mob and those justifying and exploiting those mobs for their own purposes. He had specific instances in mind, especially the recent murder of Lovejoy— and, though these went unmentioned by name, he had specific demagogues in mind, too. In his speech advocating self-control, Lincoln exercised it himself in masking his own controversial beliefs. The freethinker's antagonism to organized religion remained restrained here, but not for long; if there were any doubts about his long-held views, in four years he would finally unleash his rejection of the tenets, methods, and effects of Calvinist theology to the detriment of his political career.

Reaching his political conclusion, Lincoln demonstrated his ability at legalistic parsing. "There is no grievance that is a fit object of redress by mob law," he said. "In any case that arises, as for instance, the promulgation of abolitionism, one of two positions is necessarily true; that is, the thing is right within itself, and therefore deserves the protection of all law and all good citizens; or, it is wrong, and therefore proper to be prohibited by legal enactments; and in neither case, is the interposition of mob law, either necessary, justifiable, or excusable." On the one hand, abolitionism was legal; on the other hand, perhaps it could be forbidden. But Lincoln did not believe it should be made illegal. In fact, he defended Lovejoy's right to free speech and disdained the mob that murdered him. His proposition on the one hand was obviously the rational one, while the other he equated with the mob. Not even the Illinois legislature in its resolution criticizing abolitionism, from which he dissented, had called for censorship. Lincoln was plainly arguing for the first position and, in any case, was against the mob. Against slavery, he made his target the mobs.

Lincoln identified yet another "danger to our political institutions." It was a source of peril discussed at length by James Madison's Federalist Paper Number 51, the threat of ambition in a republic. "Ambition must be made to counteract ambition," Madison famously wrote.

> The interest of the man must be connected with the constitutional rights of the place. It may be a reflection on human nature, that such devices should be necessary to control the abuses of government. But what is government itself, but the greatest of all reflections on human nature? If men were angels, no government would be necessary. If angels were to govern men, neither external nor internal controls on government would be necessary. In framing a government which is to be administered by men over men, the great difficulty lies in this: you must first enable the government to control the governed; and in the next place oblige it to control itself.

Lincoln's commentary did not refer to the Madisonian system of checks and balances, but focused instead on the potential emergence of a great man consumed with "celebrity and fame, and distinction." The old generation of the Revolution had passed. "This field of glory is harvested, and the crop is already appropriated." An unscrupulous figure might seek to stamp his imprint over their legacy for his own glory.

> But new reapers will arise, and *they*, too, will seek a field. It is to deny, what the history of the world tells us is true, to suppose that men of ambition and talents will not continue to spring up amongst us. And, when they do, they will as naturally seek the gratification of their ruling passion, as others have so done before them. The question then, is, can that gratification be found in supporting and maintaining an edifice that has been erected by others? Most certainly it cannot. Many great and good men sufficiently qualified for any task they should undertake, may ever be found, whose ambition would inspire to nothing beyond a seat in Congress, a gubernatorial or a presidential chair; *but such belong not to the family of the lion, or the tribe of the eagle.* What! think you these places would satisfy an Alexander, a Caesar, or a Napoleon? Never! Towering genius disdains a beaten path. It seeks regions hitherto unexplored. It sees *no distinction* in adding story to story, upon the monuments of fame, erected to the memory of others. It *denies* that it is

glory enough to serve under any chief. It *scorns* to tread in the footsteps of *any* predecessor, however illustrious. It thirsts and burns for distinction; and, if possible, it will have it, whether at the expense of emancipating slaves, or enslaving freemen. Is it unreasonable then to expect, that some man possessed of the loftiest genius, coupled with ambition sufficient to push it to its utmost stretch, will at some time, spring up among us? And when such a one does, it will require the people to be united with each other, attached to the government and laws, and generally intelligent, to successfully frustrate his designs. Distinction will be his paramount object, and although he would as willingly, perhaps more so, acquire it by doing good as harm; yet, that opportunity being past, and nothing left to be done in the way of building up, he would set boldly to the task of pulling down.

Lincoln's forewarning against the will to power joined to the exploitation of "celebrity and fame" was his most modern caution. But was he portentously advising against the advent of a genius politician that had not yet revealed himself? Edmund Wilson, the literary critic, in his *Patriotic Gore*, published in 1962, claimed that Lincoln was obviously speaking about himself: "It is evident that Lincoln has projected himself into the role against which he is warning them." Thus Wilson provided the sort of brilliantly intuitive literary insight that only lacks political comprehension, historical reference, and facts, and inspired a school of psychobabble. This conjecture became so unconditionally accepted that even the judicious historian David Herbert Donald wrote in his biography of Lincoln, "Few could have realized that he was unconsciously describing himself."

Once again, Lincoln's description of the dictator in the wings was in the line of standard Whig jeremiads decrying "King Andrew." But he had a candidate to insert into this empty but exalted place left by Jackson in the Whig cosmology, hardly filled by the wreckage of Van Buren. Instead, he had in mind a new figure on the scene, someone he had identified as his rival. Readers of the *Sangamo Journal* would have known the identity of the nemesis. Beginning with a series of articles under the pseudonym "A Conservative," Lincoln lambasted none other than Stephen A. Douglas. The first of the pieces appeared on November 25, 1837, then one on January 13, another on the 27th, the morning of his Lyceum speech, and two more in February. In early November, Douglas had organized the first political party convention in Illinois, in the Third District, rigging the vote, with only thirteen of thirty-five counties represented, to anoint himself the Democratic nominee for the Congress, even though he would not reach the constitutional age to take the oath of office for six months. His Whig opponent would be John T. Stuart, Lincoln's law partner.

The initial article by "A Conservative" accused Douglas of striking a corrupt bargain to gain the nomination. Douglas, in fact, had betrayed one of his early sponsors, the incumbent congressman he had ousted, William "Big Red" May, aligning himself with a more powerful sponsor, Senator Young. In revenge, May challenged Young for his seat. Douglas published anonymous editorials in the *Illinois State Register* attacking May for being a party turncoat, insufficiently supporting Van Buren, and instead embracing "the principles of the Federal party." When the blast by "A Conservative" was printed, Douglas demanded that the *Journal* disclose the name of the "infamous, villainous liar" and "cowardly scoundrel" who had written it. "My acts have been misrepresented," he said, "my opinions perverted, my motives impugned, and my character traduced in language as unkind and ungentlemanly as it was unjust and untrue." (The *Register*, a Democratic newspaper, was absorbed by the *Springfield Republican*; George Weber remained editor and Douglas co-owner.)

On the day of the Lyceum lecture, Lincoln responded with a new anonymous piece in the *Journal*, featuring a raucous cast of characters in his personal political theater. According to his satire, Douglas was persuaded to leave the General Land Office so that a panting John Calhoun could have his heart's desire. "You may be President of these United States just as well as not," Calhoun flatteringly told Douglas in Lincoln's fiction. "History gives no account of a man of your age occupying such high ground as you now do." "A Conservative" sarcastically described Douglas as a "towering genius," a slighting reference to his diminutive height, exactly the phrase Lincoln would use in his Lyceum speech to describe the shadowy dictator in the wings.

Shortly after Lincoln's first pseudonymous article, on December 7, 1837, he wrote a letter to a Whig activist, "I write this to say that it is Stuart's intention to be a candidate for congress again; and that he will be publicly announced before long. I would suggest to you the propriety of your letting our friends in your parts know, that he is to be the candidate. . . . P.S. We have adopted it as part of our policy here, to never speak of Douglas at all. Isn't that the best mode of treating so small a matter?"

Then, in the article of January 27, "A Conservative" compared Douglas to Napoleon, just as Lincoln repeated a warning against a new Napoleon that evening. "History," he wrote in the *Journal*, "gives no account of a man of your age occupying such high ground as you do now. At twenty-four Bonaparte was unheard of, . . . There is no doubt of a seat in Congress being within your reach. The only question is whether you will condescend to occupy it." The would-be Caesar, the presumptive Napoleon, the aspiring Alexander the Great, who "disdains a beaten path," was obviously the "Little Giant."

For his peroration, Lincoln wondered how the "faded" revolutionary generation would find its successor. "They *were* the pillars of the temple of liberty; and now, that they have crumbled away, that temple must fall, unless we, their descendants, supply their places with other pillars, hewn from the solid quarry of sober reason. Passion has helped us; but can do so no more. It will in future be our enemy. Reason, cold, calculating, unimpassioned reason, must furnish all the materials for our future support and defense."

Lincoln's appeal to reason would have seemed to be generic. Who could object to "reason"? But there may have been a subtext. "We are now told," declared John C. Calhoun in his famous speech a year earlier defending "the peculiar institution," "that the most effectual mode of arresting the progress of abolition is, to reason it down." For insidious "reason" Calhoun the logician had little but contempt. "Reason" was nothing less than "absurd." "Reason" would not stop aggression against slavery. "I do not belong," said Calhoun, "to the school which holds that aggression is to be met by concession." "Reason" would not quell the "incendiary spirit." "Reason" was a feeble instrument in an existential struggle against abolitionists, where the front line was the Gag Rule. "Reason" was the wretched method of "compromise."

Through his intensive reading of newspapers and journals, which reprinted whole speeches delivered in the Congress, Lincoln would have likely read this notorious denunciation of "reason." In his speech before the nonpartisan Lyceum, Lincoln did not identify Douglas, or Linder, Lawless, or Calhoun. Nor did he mention Lovejoy by name. But anyone in the audience who read the *Sangamo Journal*, followed the news from Washington, which had washed back to Vandalia with the resolution against the petition drive to abolish slavery in the District of Columbia, or was familiar with the well reported chain of events that led to Lovejoy's killing, would have recognized the silhouettes looming behind Lincoln's gauzy rhetoric.

Lincoln's lament of the passing of the generation of the Revolution might also have seemed as trite as his call for "reason." His closing, like those of innumerable patriotic speeches, including Anson Henry's, paraphrased Webster's famous oration delivered on the commencement of the construction of the Bunker Hill Monument at Charlestown in 1825 on the fiftieth anniversary of the battle. "And let the sacred obligations which have devolved on this generation, and on us, sink deep into our hearts," said Webster. "Those who established our liberty and our government are daily dropping from among us. The great trust now descends to new hands."

The difference between Lincoln's peroration and previous speakers who had also liberally paraphrased Webster was the moment it was delivered. The revolutionary generation had "faded," but one indissoluble link vividly remained. While Lincoln gave his speech, John Quincy Adams was emphatically insisting on the right of petition, free speech, and open debate, and standing against Calhoun's Gag Rule. On the floor of the House, time and again, Adams summoned the spirits of Washington and Madison, men he had known well, just as Calhoun claimed the founders for his own. By early 1837, a battle of titans over the revolutionary legacy had been joined.

On December 23, 1837, a month before the Lyceum address, Adams arose on the floor of the House to oppose annexation of Texas as a slave state. Admitting Texas as a slave state, he said, invoked "all the other means and arguments by which the institution of slavery is wont to be sustained on this floor—the same means and arguments, in spirit, which in another place have produced murder and arson. Yes, sir, the same spirit which led to the inhuman murder of Lovejoy at Alton." He was instantly gaveled out of order. Texas could be openly debated, but Lovejoy was a forbidden subject. When, months later, Lovejoy's brothers published *Memoir of the Rev. Elijah P. Lovejoy: Who Was Murdered in Defence of the Liberty of the Press*, Adams contributed the introduction. "The incidents which preceded and accompanied, and followed the catastrophe of Mr. Lovejoy's death, point it out as an epoch in the annals of human liberty," he wrote. "They have given a shock as of an earthquake throughout this continent, which will be felt in the most distant regions of the earth." The widely circulated book would have been readily accessible and of great interest to Lincoln, and he might have encountered Lovejoy's description of his ordeal as a "fiery trial" there, a phrase Adams also used in his diary to describe his fight against the Gag Rule, and which Lincoln would appropriate in his second annual message to the Congress in 1862.

Lincoln's Lyceum address was the earliest template for the method of nearly all his future major speeches. He built his logic slowly, point by point. He worked from an opposing argument he was deconstructing, a narrative he was shaping, and language he was defining, against rivals named and unnamed. He never delivered a speech that did not have political intent. Behind his lacey phrases at the Lyceum he had a sharply honed agenda he would soon unsheathe against the Democrats. It would be Lincoln's first speech debating Douglas, the launching of a contest that would last twenty-two years.

CHAPTER SEVEN

THE RIVALS

Stephen A. Douglas's frantic climb up the political ladder, quickly stepping over others in his own party like rungs, soon provoked a murder, the most notorious in the history of Springfield, that pit Lincoln and Douglas on opposite sides of the courtroom. Douglas rose as the chief force behind a group of upstart young Democrats organizing the novel instrument of a party convention to slate candidates, enforce discipline, and oust those in Douglas's way. The incumbent congressman, William "Big Red" May, had been the patron who had made Douglas the Register of the Land Office and complacently assumed his enduring gratitude. But at the Democratic convention of only forty delegates controlled by Douglas, he pushed May aside to grab the nomination for himself. The convention also passed a resolution requesting that President Van Buren remove May's son-

Stephen Arnold Douglas

in-law, Henry Truett, as the Register of the Land Office in Galena, a vindictive act intended to eliminate every vestige of May's potential influence. That resolution was offered by one of Douglas's staunchest supporters, Jacob Early, a medical doctor and preacher, "The Fighting Parson," Lincoln's former "spy company" commander.

On March 7, 1838, Truett, a lawyer, arrived in Springfield to represent clients before the Sangamon Circuit Court and checked into the Spottswood Hotel, where he found Early in the sitting room. He demanded to know whether Early was the author of the resolution, but Early refused to admit it. Truett unleashed a stream of epithets—"liar, scoundrel, coward, and hypocrite"—calculated to incite a duel. When Early stood up, Truett pulled out a pistol. Early lifted his chair and Truett shot him dead. Truett hired a team of attorneys: Stephen Logan, who was his former law partner, John T. Stuart, Edward D. "Ned" Baker, and Lincoln. Lincoln assumed responsibility as his lead attorney, his first big case. The state's attorney, John Urquhart, had witnessed the shooting and was therefore disqualified, so he named his law partner to take charge of the prosecution—Stephen A. Douglas. Political and legal tracks ran parallel. For seven months, while Douglas campaigned against Stuart for the Congress, the Truett trial served as a homicidal surrogate contest. Douglas expected to win both.

Stuart's prospects, however, seemed bright. He had narrowly lost to May two years before, when Jackson's prestige carried into office Democrats down the ticket. Now with the Democrats blamed for the economic depression and Van Buren a liability, Whigs had momentum. Stuart's campaign was tightly organized, run by the group of about a dozen influential Whig politicos dubbed the Springfield Junto that included Baker, Logan, Anson Henry, Simeon Francis, Joshua Speed, and Lincoln. The Junto had already launched a poison-pen campaign against Douglas with the letters by Lincoln written as "A Conservative." According to the chief Democratic paper, the *Register* (Douglas, co-owner), the Junto's "members deliberate in secret, write in secret, and work in darkness—men who dare not let the light of day in upon their acts—who seek to rule a free people by their edicts passed in midnight secrecy. . . . The mask is on them in all their acts."

Douglas and Stuart traveled together around the district debating, sometimes staying together in local inns. Once, when told they would have to share beds, Douglas inquired about the party affiliation of other guests. "I will sleep with the Democrat," he insisted, "and Stuart may sleep with the Whig." Their debates became so heated that they turned into a wrestling match. At Archie Herndon's grocery store, "they both fought till exhausted," rolling on the "floor slippery with slop," according to James Gourley, a friend of Lincoln who was present.

The Little Giant's fulminating speaking style, often fueled by alcohol, resembled that of a frontier fighter, spitting, shouting, and gouging. His aim was not merely to beat an opponent in argument, but to humiliate him. He relied on ranting, illogic, and invective, peppered with frequent use of the word "nigger," regularly accusing opponents of being their lovers. Lincoln observed, in 1854, about coping with Douglas's method, "A neatly varnished sophism would be readily penetrated, but a great, rough non-sequitur was sometimes twice as dangerous as a well polished fallacy."

John Quincy Adams, in 1844, was startled to encounter Douglas's technique on the floor of the House of Representatives, tearing off his tie, unbuttoning his shirt, like a "half-naked pugilist," "raved out," spewing "abusive invectives" and "slanders," his face "convulsed, his gesticulation frantic, and he lashed himself into such a heat that if his body had been made of combustible matter it would have burnt out." "He is a model demagogue," wrote E. L. Godkin, later editor of *The Nation*, of the Douglas style. "He is vulgar in his habits and vulgar in his appearance, 'takes his drink,' chews his quid, and discharges his saliva with as much constancy and energy as the least pretentious of his constituents, but enters into the popular feelings with a tact and zest rarely equaled, and assails the heads and hearts of the multitude in a style of manly and vigorous eloquence such as few men can command. There lies in his bullet head and thick neck enough combativeness, courage, and ability for three men of his dimensions. The slightest touch of what genteel people would call improvement would spoil him. If he were one degree more refined he would be many degrees less popular."

In the climactic Stuart-Douglas clash, in the large square before the Market House in Springfield, Douglas's insults provoked Stuart to grab him in a headlock and carry him around the stage like a trophy until Douglas bit his thumb, leaving a scar. On Election Day, Douglas believed he had narrowly won on the basis of an overwhelming vote from several thousand Irish laborers on the Illinois and Michigan Canal (who happened not to be citizens). He rode home triumphantly atop a stagecoach smoking a victory cigar.

"Douglas is elected," glumly reported the *Journal*. But many of the county returns were late and a number of Douglas's were tossed out. Stuart eked out a fourteen-vote margin out of the 36,495 cast in the August election. The Whigs held a gigantic barbecue to celebrate, officially hosted by members of the Springfield Junto. "Big Red" May leapt onstage to crow over Douglas's defeat. "May, the apostate and former successful opponent of Stuart, was the bitterest of all," reported a Democratic newspaper. After Stuart exhausted the crowd with a ninety-minute oration, Lincoln awoke them with his shout about Van Buren: "Crucify him!"

Lincoln closely monitored vote totals for Stuart for more than a year afterward, guarding his razor-thin margin. He never truly believed that Douglas would concede and thought he still might do something to overturn the result. On November 14, 1839, Lincoln wrote Stuart, "Though, speaking of authenticity, you know that if we had heard Douglas say that he had abandoned the contest, it would not be very authentic."

The 1838 elections created a new set of complications both political and personal for the Whigs and Lincoln. Yet another Junto target, John Calhoun, survived the assault, winning a legislative seat, and would immediately stir up trouble. The Whig candidate for governor, the conservative state senator Cyrus Edwards, uncle of Ninian Edwards, a "refined and cultivated aristocrat," but "made more for social than political life," according to Linder, was narrowly defeated after Democrats circulated pamphlets claiming he had attended an abolitionist meeting at Alton with Lovejoy. In fact, he had tried to no avail to negotiate a peaceful truce at Alton. During the campaign, Democrats across Illinois used the tactic of falsely tagging their Whig opponents as secret financial supporters of Lovejoy's newspaper.

One Democrat, however, received the Junto's backing, Archie Herndon, who had supported them against dividing Sangamon County and thereby diluting their influence. They endorsed him for the legislature against a proponent of the county's division, Bowling Green, Lincoln's surrogate father. Maintaining the sanctity of the county was essential to the Junto's power and anyone against it must be opposed. After Green's defeat, Lincoln felt compelled to half apologize in an anonymous article in the *Journal*: "To see our old friend, Bowling Green, beaten, and to have been under the necessity of aiding in defeating him, we confess is, and has been, extremely painful to us. Under other circumstances, we would have been glad to do battle for him; but as it was, he threw himself in the ranks of our enemies, and there we COULD do no less than we did."

But there was soon another verdict more to Lincoln's satisfaction—a second defeat of Douglas. In October, to add insult to Douglas's injury, Truett was acquitted. The jury had been swayed by Lincoln's "short but strong and sensible speech," claiming self-defense, according to Logan. And Truett went on to become mayor of Galena.

When the legislature assembled in December, Lincoln was the Whig candidate for speaker of the house against his archenemy William L. D. Ewing. More was at stake than the speakership. If the Whigs gained control of the House, they could replace the Democratic U.S. senators. But the Whigs could not maintain unity—two defected to vote for Ewing, three were strangely absent, and four voted for others who stood no chance. Ewing won by one vote on the third ballot. A Whig newspaper attributed Lincoln's loss to pressure exercised by a Democratic congressman, "a certain judicial officer of the state" and "local influence," undoubtedly traced to Douglas. Patronage and favors were likely dispensed to defeat Lincoln. Still, his party preeminence guaranteed his appointment to key committees that would enable him to protect Springfield as the capital and Sangamon to remain undivided.

One of the first matters before the legislature was a resolution to condemn the governor of Maine for refusal to extradite two abolitionists who carried a fugitive slave on a ship from Georgia. The Georgia legislature demanded solidarity from Northern states, just as Southern states had asked for support in suppressing abolitionist literature. The Illinois legislature's judiciary committee voted in favor of censuring the Maine governor as "dangerous to the rights of the people," "clearly and directly in violation of the letter of the Constitution," and deplored abolitionists as "misguided philanthropists." Lincoln declared at first he was "inclined to vote in favor," but wasn't sure about a section that stated free states must not "interfere with property of slave-holding states," and moved to table the motion "indefinitely." His motion, however, lost. Drawn to the fray, the new Democratic member, the pro-slavery John Calhoun, introduced a resolution declaring that the Congress "ought not to 'abolish slavery in the District of Columbia,' or in 'the several Territories of this Union,' or 'prohibit the slave trade between the several States,'" and another one proclaiming that Illinois would not "protest" the admission of new slave states. These overreaching statements enabled a majority, including

Lincoln, to table them, cutting off the controversy. With that, in March 1839, the assembly adjourned until December.

The Whigs had great expectations after big wins in the 1838 midterm elections, sweeping in a tide of new-school Whigs like the antislavery William H. Seward, elected governor of New York. In Illinois, the organization for the 1840 campaign began a year early, in January 1839, with the meeting of the "Whig Young Men" in Springfield, adopting a platform criticizing "the daring contempt of law and order" and blaming "the rottenness which seems to have tainted the whole system of the present administration." At a meeting a month later of the Whig members of the legislature, Lincoln introduced a resolution calling for party unity against "the present administration." The *Sangamo Journal* had been publishing for months a series of editorials, likely written by Lincoln, favoring William Henry Harrison over Clay on the basis of his electability. One, on May 26, 1838, under the pseudonym "A Voice from Southern Illinois," argued that "the people are for Gen. Harrison, and be it whim or not—they must be humored or the Vannites [Van Buren Democrats] will take advantage of the deep toned feeling of the public mind in his favor, and a victory which is properly ours will be theirs."

On October 7, 1839, delegates gathered in Springfield for the first statewide Whig convention ever held, where they enthusiastically upbraided Van Buren and named five delegates to the national convention, commissioned to vote for one or the other of the "Harries of the West," either Henry Clay or William Henry Harrison.

The political consequences of the Panic of 1837 for Van Buren were dire. He had inherited Jackson's enemies and now lost most of his friends. Fatally damaged by the economic depression, already weakened with the South, he threw himself into the arms of his mortal enemy, John C. Calhoun, becoming a dependent of the nullifiers. Van Buren, reported the fire-eating *Charleston Mercury*, "had become a Calhoun man." Midterm election losses in 1838, bringing into power the first Whig-controlled Senate as well as the first open abolitionists, shocked the Democrats. Within his party, Van Buren floundered, clinging like a life raft to Calhoun, who hated him and was always his own party. Calhoun effectively controlled the balance of power within the House through his followers, and with administration support elected a sympathetic speaker and gained control of key committees. "I belong to the smaller party of the country," Calhoun declared. "I am simply an honest nullifier." "He considers Mr. Van Buren as actually defunct—altogether past resuscitation—and that his party is without a head, and under the necessity of having one," observed Senator William C. Preston of South Carolina. "He is in the engine car! The rest, all passengers," said Webster. On January 3, 1840, Calhoun quietly met with Van Buren in the White House ending their decade-long estrangement. "He supported my administration for the residue of my term," wrote Van Buren. Calhoun endorsed him for another term, "now the logical man to succeed Van Buren in 1844," according to Calhoun's biographer Charles M. Wiltse. "Let events turn as they may, the prospect will not be bad for us," Calhoun wrote on April 29, 1840. "Should the party in power keep their place we would be able to control events, and if their opponents (consisting of every hue and colour) come in, their expulsion from power will not be difficult."

Van Buren's long fall from grace was breaking apart the old alignments. As the Democrats disintegrated, the Whigs encompassed incongruous elements without a center or leader and whose only coherence was the overwhelming desire for victory. Desperate to seize the nomination in a year when whoever possessed it was likely to become president, Clay decided to parse the confused politics as he had in the past, achieving a great compromise that would put himself on top. On the record against the annexation of Texas, labeled an abolitionist by nullifiers, yet alienating the abolitionists by spurning them, Clay made a convoluted play for the Southern Whigs. On February 7, 1839, he took the floor of the Senate to urge that petitions against slavery in the District of Columbia be accepted, read, and rejected. He denounced the "ultra-abolitionists," "alien" as "if they lived in Africa or Asia," and disavowed that "either of the two great parties in this country has any designs or aim at abolition." Clay also upheld slavery in the District, in the Florida Territory, and the slave trade across the whole country, declaring it as constitutionally protected as "the transportation of livestock." "That is property," he said, "which the law declares to be property"—including property in people.

Clay warned that the "ultra-abolitionists" would precipitate a civil war, a war they might not win, but even if they did would have won a Pyrrhic victory.

Abolitionists themselves would shrink back in dismay and horror at the contemplation of desolated fields, conflagrated cities, murdered inhabitants, and the overthrow of the fairest fabric of human government that ever rose to animate the hopes of civilized man. Nor should these abolitionists flatter themselves that, if they can succeed in their object of uniting the people of the free States, they will enter the contest with a numerical superiority that must insure victory. All history and experience proves the hazard and uncertainty of war. And we are admonished by holy writ, that the race is not to the swift, nor the battle to the strong. But if they were to conquer, whom should they conquer? A foreign foe; one who had insulted our flag, invaded our shores, and laid our country waste? No, sir; no, sir. It would be a conquest without laurels, without glory; a self, a suicidal conquest; a conquest of brothers over brothers.

Rather than civil war, Clay preferred the peace of white supremacy. "I am, Mr. President, no friend of slavery. . . . But I prefer the liberty of my own country to that of any other people; and the liberty of my own race to that of any other race."

Listening on the floor of the Senate, John C. Calhoun grasped immediately the spectacularly self-destructive act his rival had just committed. He rushed over to throw his arms around Clay in a deathly embrace, praising him for delivering "the finishing stroke" against the antislavery cause. "This is," he stated, "a great epoch in our political history." Throughout the North, Clay was excoriated. "I had rather be right than be president," he replied with irritation. He set off on a national tour to prove he could be both, drawing larger crowds than he had ever attracted before, but he had lost control of the levers of party power.

The new-school Whig power broker, Thurlow Weed of New York, Seward's alter ego, promoted the candidacy of General Winfield Scott, a Whig version of a proto-Jackson figure. William Henry Harrison, once the territorial governor of Indiana, but now residing in Ohio, was also touted as a military hero, a Jackson manqué, a man on horseback, and victor of the skirmish of Tippecanoe, an icon floating above politics. His background from a wealthy Virginia family and as a pro-slavery politician in Indiana where he was characterized as leader of the "aristocracy" was shunted aside and forgotten in favor of the image of a log cabin, as though he had miraculously risen from humble origins.

At the first national Whig convention, on December 4, 1839, held in Harrisburg, Pennsylvania, the balance was held by the Virginia delegation. Thaddeus Stevens, a state legislator and abolitionist, who controlled the Pennsylvania delegation and backed Harrison, having extracted a promise that he would be appointed to his cabinet, physically dropped a letter from Scott at the Virginia headquarters hotel expressing antislavery sentiments to Congressman Francis Granger of New York, who had been a Whig vice presidential candidate in 1836. Granger, in league with Stevens for Harrison, had given him the damaging letter. It did the trick, turning the Virginians to Harrison. The politically attuned Weed and Seward instantly dumped Scott and herded the New York delegation on the bandwagon. As its price Virginia obtained the vice presidency for former senator John Tyler, a strict states' rights advocate and Calhoun man. (Stevens awaited his reward, but received nothing.) Tippecanoe and Tyler, too!

In the chess game for the nomination Scott had been the rook to knock Clay off the board, and then Scott was eliminated for Harrison. The Whigs relentlessly descended into sheer insubstantiality in pursuit of an unblemished hero who could deliver victory. Webster and others determined to topple Clay had pulled strings behind the screen. "My friends are not worth the powder and shot it would take to kill them!" exclaimed Clay upon learning of his loss. He rattled off the names of the intriguers. "I am the most unfortunate man in the history of parties: always run by my friends when sure to be defeated, and now betrayed for a nomination when I, or any one, would be sure of an election."

For more than a year, "a kind of Poetical Society" met at Joshua Speed's store, according to James Matheny, including Lincoln, reciting, composing, and discussing poetry and literature, and conducting debates. Around the fireplace in the rear of the store, Lincoln, Baker, and Douglas

William Henry Harrison

turned to politics and the discussion "got warm—hot—angry," recalled Speed. "Douglas, I recollect," wrote Herndon, who was Speed's clerk, "was leading on the Democratic side. He had already learned the art of dodging in debate, but still he was subtle, fiery, and impetuous. He charged the Whigs with every blunder and political crime he could imagine." "Gentlemen," Douglas finally announced, "this is no place to talk politics. We will discuss the questions publicly with you."

So the "Poetical Society" members decided they would conduct a series of joint debates on the principal issue of the day—not slavery, not the Gag Rule, but the sub-treasury. Van Buren had proposed a new federal department, a central depository for federal funds, removing them even from state banks—a sub-treasury. Rather than restoring credit, Van Buren's radically deflationary policy of restricting credit would dismantle the remaining ability to maintain economic equilibrium, further deepen the depression, bankrupt the states, and destroy investments in internal improvements, the chief program of the Whigs. "All communities are apt to look to government for too much," he lectured in his special message of September 1837. And he was as good as his word.

John C. Calhoun, sensing his opening, to nearly everyone's surprise but his own, leaped to sponsor the Senate bill, enchaining Van Buren to him. "Van Buren has been forced by his situation and the terror of Jackson to play directly into our hands," Calhoun gloated, "and I am determined, that he shall not escape us." Meanwhile, Democrats attempted to shift the blame for the economy onto the Whigs' big government spending. Across Illinois, as state revenue dried up, the construction of canals and railroads stopped, and bridges were built to nowhere. Thomas Ford accused the Whigs, especially the "Long Nine," of bankrupting the state by creating "the System" of internal improvements and moving the capital to Springfield, the means by which "the whole State" was "bought up and bribed, to approve the most senseless and disastrous policy which ever crippled the energies of a growing country."

The "Poetical Society" debates on the economic crisis drew large, attentive crowds, but soon slipped into threats of violence and then an act of violence, less poetry than pummeling. Tensions had not abated since the Anson Henry candidacy, the James Adams affair, and the scuffles at the *Register*. Douglas's conviction that his election to the Congress had been stolen turned the flame higher. Both he and Lincoln were at the center of the action while inciting others behind the scenes.

The first debate, on November 19, in the Presbyterian church, began in the afternoon, with Cyrus Walker, a lawyer and Whig presidential elector, leading off, followed by Douglas, and, after a dinner break, by Lincoln, another elector. The speeches went unrecorded, but the *Register* reported, "Between the two Whig speakers, our Democratic 'little giant' . . . had a rough time of it." The paper conceded about Lincoln, "His argument was truly ingenious." But it dismissed his sarcastic, mocking style. "He has, however, a sort of assumed clownishness in his manner which does not become him, and which does not truly belong to him. It is assumed—assumed for effect. Mr. L. will sometimes make his language correspond with this clownish manner, and he can thus frequently raise a loud laugh among his Whig hearers, but this entire game of buffoonery convinces the mind of no man, and is utterly lost on the majority of his audience."

Round two, on the next night, went to Douglas, who, according to the *Register* "literally swamped his adversaries. . . . Mr. Lincoln, was, however, again put forward; but he commenced with embarrassment and continued without making the slightest impression. . . . He could only meet the arguments of Mr. Douglas by relating stale anecdotes and left the stump literally whipped off of it, even in the estimation of his own friends." His performance proved that his cause was "rotten to the core." Lincoln knew he had botched his reply to Douglas. "He was very sensitive where he thought he had to come up to the expectations of his friends," recalled Joseph Gillespie, his fellow Whig legislator. "Lincoln did not come up to the requirements of the occasion. He was conscious of his failure and I never saw any man so much distressed."

Round three, the next night, took place at the courthouse, on the floor below the law office of Stuart & Lincoln, featuring Edward D. Baker for the Whigs and John Calhoun for the Democrats. Baker's speech was a screed accusing the Democrats of sustaining their party through graft. "Wherever there is a land office there is a paper to defend the corruptions of office," he charged. "Pull him down!" shouted John Weber, who later explained, "This was a personal attack on my brother George Weber"—editor of the *Register*. Suddenly, a noise was heard through the trapdoor in the ceiling. "A shuffling of feet, a forward movement of the crowd, and great confusion followed," recalled Herndon.

Just then a long pair of legs were seen dangling from the aperture above, and instantly the figure of Lincoln dropped on the platform. Motioning with his hands for silence and not succeeding, he seized a stone water-pitcher standing nearby, threatening to break it over the head of the first man who laid hands on Baker. "Hold on, gentlemen," he shouted, "this is the land of free speech. Mr. Baker has a right to speak and ought to be heard. I am here to protect him, and no man shall take him from this stand if I can prevent it." His interference had the desired effect. Quiet was soon restored, and the valiant Baker was allowed to proceed. I was in the back part of the crowd that night, and an enthusiastic Baker man myself. I knew he was a brave man, and even if Lincoln had not interposed, I felt sure he wouldn't have been pulled from the platform without a bitter struggle.

Lincoln's adversary, Usher Linder, persecutor of Lovejoy and defender of his murderers, had not politically profited from the controversy and decided suddenly to switch parties, turning his vituperation on the Democrats, who were enraged at his betrayal. Linder delivered a speech "that incensed Democrats," he recalled, and "some ruffian in the galleries flung at me a gross personal insult, accompanied with a threat." Lincoln and Baker marched out of the audience onto the stage and flanked him, each taking an arm. "We both think we can do a little fighting," Lincoln told him, "so we want you to walk between us until we get you to your hotel; your quarrel is our quarrel."

Even while jumping through a trapdoor and playing bodyguard Lincoln warily kept his eye cocked on Douglas. In a letter to his law partner, Stuart, detailing business affairs of the firm, he added, "P.S. The Democratic giant is here; but he is not now worth talking about." But Lincoln was obsessed with him.

The debates had seemingly concluded with Lincoln ranked least effective among the speakers.

"He begged to be permitted to try it again and was reluctantly indulged," wrote Gillespie. On the day after Christmas, with the temperature below zero, the Whigs put him back on the platform but without any debating opponent. "It is peculiarly embarrassing to me to attempt a continuance of the discussion, on this evening," he began humbly. ". . . I am, indeed, apprehensive, that the few who have attended, have done so, more to spare me of mortification, than in the hope of being interested in anything I may be able to say. This circumstance casts a damp upon my spirits, which I am sure I shall be unable to overcome during the evening. But enough of preface."

His speech, a brief against Van Buren's economic policies, rounded to attack his true but absent rival. Ten times he mentioned Douglas. "Those who heard Mr. Douglas, recollect that he indulged himself in a contemptuous expression of pity for me. 'Now he's got me,' thought I." Systematically, he exposed Douglas's factual errors, repeating each time, "I knew to be untrue." After carefully working his way through his argument, he finished with a trope of astounding bloviation: "I know that the great volcano at Washington, aroused and directed by the evil spirit that reigns there, is belching forth the lava of political corruption, in a current broad and deep, which is sweeping with frightful velocity over the whole length and breadth of the land, bidding fair to leave unscathed no green spot or living thing, while on its bosom are riding like demons on the waves of Hell, the imps of that evil spirit, and fiendishly taunting all those who dare resist its destroying course, with the hopelessness of their effort; and knowing this, I cannot deny that all may be swept away." More rhetorical lava flowed: "I swear eternal fidelity to the just cause, as I deem it, of the land of my life, my liberty and my love." And there was more. Lincoln's inferno was conjured from the depths of Whig desperation for power at last nearly in its grasp.

"He transcended our highest expectations," said Gillespie. "I never heard and never expect to hear such a triumphant vindication as he then gave of Whig measures or policy. He never after to my knowledge fell below himself." Lincoln's address was a hit among Whigs, if Lincoln said so himself. "Well," he wrote Stuart, "I made a big speech, which is in progress of printing in pamphlet form. To enlighten you and the rest of the world, I shall send you a copy when it is finished." As a member of the Whig Central Committee for Illinois (mostly the Springfield Junto in a new guise), Lincoln had ordered the printing. "Lincoln's Speech, and 'Tippecanoe's Almanacks,' to be disposed of, in quantities, at this office," read a notice in the *Sangamo Journal*.

On behalf of the Whig Central Committee, Lincoln wrote a battle plan of campaign organization from top to bottom: lists of reliable and doubtful voters, timetables for reports to the Central Committee, and subscriptions to the campaign newspaper. Whig workers were instructed: "To divide their county into small districts, and to appoint in each a sub-committee, whose duty it shall be to make a perfect list of all the voters in their respective districts, and to ascertain with certainty for whom they will vote. . . . In each of your letters to us, you will state the number of certain votes, both for and against us, as well as the number of doubtful votes, with your opinion of the manner in which they will be cast. . . . When we hear from all the counties, we shall be able to tell with similar accuracy, the political complexion of the State." Lincoln strictly instructed: "Plan of operations will of course be CONCEALED FROM EVERY ONE except OUR GOOD FRIENDS."

The war between the *Journal* and the *Register* grew fiercer when they respectively published campaign newspapers, the *Journal* launching *The Old Soldier* and the *Register* launching *Old Hickory*. These publications were yet another face-off between Lincoln, coeditor of the sheet named for Harrison, and Douglas, Democratic state chairman and coeditor of *Old Hickory*. When *Old Hickory* surreptitiously obtained and printed Lincoln's campaign document it charged that one Harrison campaign supporter in league with Simeon Francis, editor of the *Journal*, was an abolitionist, while the *Journal* accused the *Old Hickory* editors of theft and named Douglas and John Calhoun as the culprits. In response, *Old Hickory* declared that it would "hold up the authors personally to public scorn and contempt. We shall conduct the 'war to the knife and the knife to the hilt.'"

Douglas plotted a surprise attack—he would cane Francis. According to the Code Duello, only a gentleman could be challenged to a duel. Caning was reserved for a slave or equally low person. Firing pistols at ten paces recognized high social rank, but whipping with a stick marked dishonor. On a Springfield street, on February 29, 1840, Douglas leapt, his eyes "glared like live coals, his frame dilated into grand and gigantic proportions, and with like seven-toned thunder he bellowed forth his ire," recalled Francis. "He got a stick bigger than himself . . . big words fell from his lips, his mighty hand raised the stick—it fell and we received the blow upon an unoffending apple, which was as we thought secure from the chances of war—in our left hand coat pocket."

Old Hickory replied to Francis's ridicule by calling him a "compound of goose fat and sheep's wool." In a letter to Stuart, Lincoln described the farcical assault of the pint-sized Douglas on the bearish Francis. "Francis caught him by the hair and jammed him back against a market-cart, where the matter ended by Francis being pulled away from him. The whole affair was so ludicrous that Francis and everybody else (Douglas excepted) have been laughing about it ever since." After again diminishing his rival, Lincoln called Stuart's attention to the all-important etiquette of politics. "Evan Butler"—the deputy circuit court clerk in Sangamon County and a member of the "Poetical Society"—"is jealous that you never send your compliments to him. You must not neglect him next time."

In early June, from the 2nd through the 4th, the Whig Central Committee staged the largest extravaganza ever seen in Springfield, a rally drawing more than fifteen thousand people from every county, and Indiana, Iowa, and Missouri. The pilgrims camped on grounds north of the city provided by Elijah Iles, an old Lincoln backer, owner of about one quarter of the real estate of Springfield and the American House hotel, and a major Whig funder. They paraded into town led by 250 Revolutionary War and War of 1812 veterans, a float of a ship drawn by six white horses, and a log cabin pulled by twenty-six oxen with a delegation from Sangamon County perched on its roof. They heard orators, sang songs, and chanted slogans while holding a vast barbecue. Then they repeated the whole event the next day, ending with the presentation of an eagle to the Whig leaders at the *Journal* office, which, according to Francis, "reared its head, expanded its eyes, and gave a loud cry."

"It seemed as if Pandemonium had been let loose upon earth. Reason was everywhere reeling in the storm, and madness ruled the masses," recalled Albert Taylor Bledsoe, a Whig lawyer in Springfield. "But Mr. Lincoln was merry. He entered into the very soul of the contest with a glee which seemed perfectly assured of 'the glad success.' Hence, when we ventured to express our intense mortification that the Whig Party, which had claimed a monopoly of all the intelligence and decency of the country, should descend to the use of such means, Mr. Lincoln replied: 'It is all right; *we must fight the devil with fire; we must beat the Democrats, or the country will be ruined.'* "

Bledsoe, a Kentucky native, who had attended West Point with Jefferson Davis and Robert E. Lee, was ordained as an Episcopal minister, trained as a lawyer, would teach mathematics at the University of Mississippi and the University of Virginia, and be appointed assistant secretary of war for the Confederacy—the future Confederate leader with the most intimate relationship with Lincoln, "almost daily intercourse with him at the Bar." After the war, he became an influential Southern apologist of the Lost Cause as editor for the *Southern Review* and author of a defense of secession entitled "Is Davis a Traitor?" "We all look to you for our vindication," Lee told him.

Bledsoe remained unreconstructed to the end, arguing, "The Southern states constitute no part of the United States." He portrayed Lincoln as a conniving politician driven solely by the desire for fame and unscrupulous in manipulating the unwashed masses of the North. "No man fitter than he, indeed, to represent the Northern Demos. . . . For if, as we believe, that was the cause of brute force, blind passion, fanatical hate, lust of power, and the greed of gain, against the cause of constitutional law and human rights, then who was better fitted to represent it than the talented, but the low, ignorant and vulgar, rail-splitter of Illinois?"

And yet Bledsoe still regarded Lincoln as impenetrable. "He was, take him all in all, one of the most incomprehensible personages we have ever known." Lincoln had "a powerful intellect" of a unique kind. "His education was radically deficient, never going beyond the barest elements of reading, writing, and arithmetic. But he possessed the power of patient thought; he could distinguish, analyse, and *meditate*—a very rare quality now-a-days—and these alone made him a formidable antagonist, both at the Bar and on the hustings." Bledsoe dismissed the rumor that Lincoln's speeches in his debates with Douglas were prepared by others as "slander." "No other man in Illinois could have done that work for him. . . . He was a full match for Mr. Douglas, or for any other man of the day, on the stump or before the people." Whatever Bledsoe's demonizing, bafflement, or acknowledgment of Lincoln, his account of their conversations about the "Hurrah and Hallelujah" campaign of 1840 was probably more or less accurate.

During that campaign, Lincoln indeed set out to "fight the devil with fire." "He was always very independent and had generally a very good nature. Though he had at times, when he was roused, a very high temper," recalled Stephen T. Logan. "He controlled it then in a general way, though it would break out sometimes—and at those times it didn't take much to make him whip a man."

When a Democratic newspaper in Baltimore derided Harrison as the candidate of "log cabin and hard cider" the Whigs wielded the symbols to demonstrate that the aristocrat was a man of the people. The Whig campaign became a din of songs, slogans, and pageants, lubricated by free hard cider. "Van, Van, the used up man" was rumored to guzzle champagne. The Democrats answered the hoopla with a negative attack intended to tar the vapid image of Harrison. He was not a hero above politics, after all, but a secret abolitionist—"the abolition candidate," declared Thomas Ritchie, editor of the *Richmond Enquirer* and chief of the Richmond Junto. From his retirement at the Hermitage, Andrew Jackson denounced "Harrison with his abolition principles." Democratic newspapers across the country picked up the accusation. The *Washington Globe*, the capital's Democratic organ, edited by Francis P. Blair, the pluperfect Jacksonian politico, published a special campaign paper called *The Extra Globe*, filled with stories exposing Harrison's supposed abolitionist past and agenda. "PEOPLE OF THE SOUTH" screamed the headline in the *Richmond Enquirer.* "You will find out (will it be too late?) that Whiggery and Abolition are BOTH ONE."

In Illinois, the Democrats, led by Douglas, waged an unremitting race-baiting campaign. Harrison, proclaimed the *Register*, was an "Abolitionist of the first water," who would "make slaves of White men" while making "free men of black slaves." *Old Hickory* declared that the goal of the Whigs was "TO MAKE THE NEGRO THE EQUAL OF THE WHITE MAN!" And, wherever "an abolitionist is found, he is loud and warm in support of Harrison." At yet another debate between Lincoln and Douglas in Jacksonville before a crowd of about one thousand, after Lincoln assailed the Van Buren administration for corruption, Douglas deflected the charges with an attack on Harrison's alleged abolitionism. According to the *Register*, he "proved Abolitionism upon Harrison so strong, that many of his friends declared that they would not support him until he . . . denounces the Abolitionists."

As a young man in Virginia, Harrison had once followed Washington and Jefferson in expressing a tepid, abstract sentiment in favor of eventual emancipation, but as territorial governor of Indiana had fought to override the Ordinance of 1787 to make it a slave state. In his most recent statement, in 1835, he had condemned the efforts of abolitionists as "weak, injudicious, presumptuous, and unconstitutional." But the clamor put the Whigs on the defensive. Democrats insisted that Harrison's silence on the issues was proof he was hiding his true position. After Anson Henry, a member of the Whig Central Committee with Lincoln, exchanged private correspondence with Harrison on the subject, his letter's existence was somehow leaked and became a national sensation. Blair's *Extra Globe* hyped the alleged scandal and Illinois Democrats led by Speaker Ewing passed a resolution taunting "that the leaders of the Whig Party in this place dare not lay said letter before the public." Though Harrison had requested Henry keep his correspondence "confidential," the *Sangamo Journal* printed his letter. In it, Harrison announced himself "safe," reiterating the sentiments of his 1835 anti-abolition statement. "One of the strongest reasons against my publishing any further opinions upon the abolition, or any other political question," he wrote, 'is the vile course of my opponents, in mutilating and perverting everything that I have heretofore spoken or written."

Archie Herndon, the Democratic state senator from Sangamo County, one of the most vociferous demanding that Henry release the letter, assailed "the British-Negro-Indian-Sympathy-and-Anti-Republican-Bloodhound Party . . . calling themselves Whigs, but more familiarly known as the Federal-Abolition Party." Soon an article appeared in the *Journal* under the pseudonym of "Sam Slick," likely Lincoln, humorously writing, "It don't seem to me that the Senitor ort to make such a noise about private letters," and threatening to divulge not only Herndon's letters from the 1836 campaign "denouncing Van Buren and his followers," proving he was not a loyal Democrat, but also his illicit sexual affairs, "Showin how he—an innocent youth of five and forty was seduced from the path of chastity, and became a blind worshiper at the shrine of Cupid. O these women—these women!" "Sam Slick" even identified by name one of his mistresses. Then an article appeared under the byline of "A Citizen," also likely Lincoln, calling Archie Herndon a "traitor" for his "bowing and scraping to the powers that be."

Traveling by horse from town to town throughout central and southern Illinois as a party missionary, sometimes accompanied by Ned Baker, Lincoln spoke and debated as often as he could. At Petersburg, when Archie Herndon confronted Lincoln in debate, calling him "an interloper," Lincoln "cut Herndon off at the knees," recalled "Slicky Bill" Green, declaring that "when he had been a candidate as often as Herndon he would quit."

Another of the Democratic orators Lincoln encountered was Colonel E. D. "Dick" Taylor, a former state representative, who had defeated Lincoln in 1832, and a state senator, Virginia born, a wealthy merchant with far-flung interests, who had earned his colonelcy in the Black Hawk War serving with Captain Jefferson Davis. Now he was running for reelection to the state Senate against Baker. The *Journal* challenged Taylor to account for the funds he handled as head of the Land Office in Chicago. Taylor's stump speech routinely berated the Whigs as "aristocrats." As he spoke, Lincoln "nudged up" to him on the platform, "inch by inch," then quickly jerked on his vest, out of which spilled his ruffled shirt, gold chains, and gold watches. The crowd, recalled James Matheny, "burst forth in a furious and uproarious laughter," while the object of ridicule suddenly fell silent. Taylor "saw that it killed him—was vexed and quit and never much afterwards said even to himself 'Aristocracy.'"

Lincoln's opponent for the state legislature was Illinois Supreme Court justice Jesse B. Thomas, whom he was also suing on behalf of Ninian W. Edwards for an unpaid debt. On July 20, 1840, Thomas appeared before a crowd at the Springfield courthouse to expose once and for all the true authorship of the scurrilous articles written by "A Conservative" in the *Journal* trashing Douglas that had triggered the street brawl and stabbings, the caning of Francis, and the near "take down" of Baker. "It was demonstrated in the course of the controversy on Monday that the gang who control the *Sangamo Journal* wrote the articles which appeared in that paper over the signature of 'A Conservative,' and privately impressed it upon the minds of the friends of the administration that the Judge was the author," reported the *Register*. "The Junto resorted to this foul stratagem to render the Judge obnoxious to the friends of Van Buren, hoping that thereby he would be driven to become a Federalist [Whig]."

While Thomas spoke, an alert Whig rushed to bring forward Lincoln, who jumped onto the platform just as Thomas finished. "The excitement of the crowd was intense," recalled Bledsoe. "Mr. Lincoln's effort was absolutely overwhelming and withering." "He imitated Thomas in gesture and voice, at times caricaturing his walk and the very motion of his body," wrote William Herndon. "Thomas, like everybody else, had some peculiarities of expression and gesture, and these Lincoln succeeded in rendering more prominent than ever. The crowd yelled and cheered as he continued. Encouraged by these demonstrations, the ludicrous features of the speaker's performance gave way to intense and scathing ridicule." "He had not proceeded far, indeed, before Judge Thomas began to blubber like a baby, and left the assembly," wrote Bledsoe, who described Lincoln's relentless deconstruction in "minute accuracy" of Thomas's inconsistent political history and his "various somersaults." "His manner was easy, natural, and self-possessed, and his language was simple, direct, and plain Anglo-Saxon English, delivered in a conversational, rather than an oratorical, style and tone. But every word was a real 'railsplitter.'"

Herndon immortalized Lincoln's performance as "The Skinning of

Thomas." The *Register* condemned him: "He has fallen into the ditch which he dug for his neighbor." After the event, Thomas was a broken man. "He cried all the rest of the day," wrote Bledsoe. "He came to our office for sympathy, and we should have sincerely pitied the poor fellow, if every feeling of compassion had not been swallowed up in contempt." Bledsoe, in fact, was Thomas's law partner, an association he ended within months, forming a new partnership with Ned Baker.

Though Lincoln won the August contest against Thomas, he came in fifth and last among those elected in the county. Yet, he was only fifteen votes short of the number one winner, which was accounted for as the result of the elimination of the already atrophied New Salem township from the district. The Whigs, however, lost the legislature, increasing pressure to carry the state for Harrison. Weakest in the southern part of Illinois, populated by Southerners, Lincoln got back on his horse to debate there.

For months, Lincoln had attempted to counter the Democratic attack on Harrison as an abolitionist with the story that had been retailed with little effect from the 1836 campaign of Van Buren's support for enfranchisement of free blacks at the 1821 New York state constitutional convention. Lincoln always cited as his authority a pro–Van Buren campaign biography written by William M. Holland, referring to it in a debate with Douglas on April 30 in the town of Tremont. In fact, Holland chronicled how Van Buren did and said absolutely nothing in favor of black rights, but simply voted with the majority to extend the vote to free blacks who owned at least $250 in property and paid a tax on it—a restriction over the old constitution, in which, wrote Holland, "no distinction was made with regard to color in the qualifications of electors."

Seeking another element for his accusation, Lincoln got his friend Dr. William H. Fithian, a Whig state legislator and Black Hawk War veteran, to write an innocent-sounding letter to Van Buren, asking him to verify the credibility of the Holland hagiography. The Little Magician let down his guard, and was gulled into replying that it was "substantially correct."

Douglas, who was familiar with Lincoln's inventory of gimmicks, called out his bluff in a debate probably held in early September. "Lincoln used to read the facts out of the Life of Van Buren by Holland in his joint debates with Douglas or in his presence," recalled Herndon. But Douglas charged him with "using a fraudulent and forged Life of Van Buren in order to swindle the democracy. . . . This broad and bold charge somewhat took the wind out of the Whigs." "I understand," said Lincoln, "that Mr. Douglas asserts, more or less directly, that Holland's Life of Van Buren is a swindle and a forgery. I would ask the Democracy if this is not so." "Yes!" shouted the Democrats in the crowd. "Fraud, swindling, forgery!" "You say, gentlemen," Lincoln continued, "that this book is a fraud, a swindle, and a forgery?" "Yes, yes!" "Well," said Lincoln, "I have a letter in my hands which will settle that little matter forever." With that, he triumphantly flourished the Van Buren letter to Fithian. According to Matheny, Douglas "snatched up the book and slung it into the crowd." "Any man who would write such a Life and send it out to the great West expecting that it would advance his hero's interest was a damned fool," he declared. Quick and brash, Douglas refused to be cornered, blaming the author. But, wrote Herndon, "the charge of Whig fraud, Whig swindle, and Whig forgery was never heard of any more"—at least about that book.

To the end of the campaign the Whigs were filled with anxiety about the impact of the attack against Harrison as an abolitionist. In order to combat the impression, the Whig central campaign office in Washington published a pamphlet circulated far and wide entitled *The Northern Man with Southern Principles and the Southern Man with American Principles*. Van Buren, of course, was the former, Harrison the latter. In the section on Van Buren's support in 1821 for granting free blacks the franchise, the pamphleteers wrote: "And we are asked to believe that these are 'Southern principles'!"

Harrison trounced Van Buren, winning a national mandate, but lost Illinois by less than two thousand votes. He had run on no platform whatsoever, but his program was clear. The Whig economic plan, Clay's "American System," was at last to be enacted—a new Bank of the United States to restore financial credit, protective tariffs to encourage manufactures, and internal improvements. From the Senate, Clay, commanding the Whig caucus, prepared for the moment of truth. Webster was appointed secretary of state, poised to become the virtual prime minister of the administration, with Harrison as a figurehead president. In his Inaugural Address, Harrison announced he would defer to the Congress and remain in office only one term. In four years, both Webster and Clay calculated they would rise to the presidency.

Unfortunately, Harrison's calculation was off by three years and eleven months. Neglecting to wear an overcoat during his hour-and-a-half speech, the Old Soldier caught pneumonia and within a month was a corpse in a coffin mounted in the White House East Room. "General Harrison himself got to the capital some months before his inauguration, and it cost him his life," wrote Congressman Henry A. Wise. "He was very infirm, and the excitement was too great for him. He yielded to the 'vulgar crowd,' was elated by their pressure upon him, and literally sank under a total derangement of his nervous system. . . . We witnessed scenes at and before the inauguration of 1841 which it is to be hoped will never be described by either biography or history." It seems apparent that Harrison drank himself to death.

Tyler, the states' rights Virginian, became president. His ally, Congressman Wise, wrote, "Immediately the victorious party became dismembered. It had in itself the seeds of destruction."

Clay dismissed Tyler as "His Accidency," acting as though he were a supernumerary, and passed the bill for incorporating a new Bank of the United States. Tyler vetoed it in the fall of 1841. Every member of the cabinet resigned, except Webster. "A president without a party, and parties without a president!" exclaimed Clay. Tyler filled the cabinet with states' rights advocates as unyielding as he was. Its leading member was Secretary of the Navy Abel P. Upshur, a nullifier from Virginia, under the influence of Calhoun. When Webster finally quit, Upshur was named to replace him as secretary of state. Tyler's focus became the annexation of Texas and the expansion of slavery. Calhoun's influence was the ironic result of the great Whig landslide of 1840.

In Illinois, after the Harrison victory, the euphoria of the Whigs swiftly deflated. The special session of the legislature called for the last week in November and first of December cast them into purgatory. Once again, Lincoln lost the vote to become speaker to Ewing. He remained a staunch defender of "the System," whose scope he had thought would make him the DeWitt Clinton of Illinois, though the state was bankrupt. He engineered new land taxes, but they were insufficient to cover the debt. While he tried to negotiate the floating of new state bonds, the Democrats, in the majority, literally sprang a trap on him. They proposed a *sine die* adjournment that would force the Illinois State Bank to stop payments in notes, thereby exhausting its reserves of specie or hard currency and destroy itself. The Whigs believed they could thwart this maneuver by withholding a quorum. Lincoln and Gillespie remained to count heads, but when they decided to leave they discovered that the doors had been locked. So they lifted the window on the second floor of the Presbyterian church where the session was taking place and jumped out. Their escape came too late—they were counted for the quorum anyway and the bank was wrecked, closed in 1842. Lincoln was subjected to merciless ridicule in the *Register*, which wondered whether the State House should be raised "one story higher, in order to have the House sit in the third story! So as to prevent members from jumping out of the windows? Mr. Lincoln will in the future have to climb down the spout." He was deeply embarrassed about the incident, "always regretted that he entered into the arrangement," said Gillespie, and never wanted to talk about it.

His rival rose and rose. First, the Democratic governor appointed Douglas secretary of state. Then the Democratic legislature expanded the state Supreme Court by five seats because the Whigs on it had blocked approval of aliens voting. (Aliens with six months residence could vote in Illinois without becoming citizens.) The ten thousand Irish workmen who were not citizens but nonetheless cast ballots, about ninety percent for the Democrats, provided the crucial margin not only in the presidential election but also state races. When the court-packing bill passed, known as the "Douglas bill" after its chief lobbyist, Governor Thomas Carlin appointed Douglas a judge on the Illinois Supreme Court.

Lincoln signed a statement with other Whig legislators criticizing the court bill as "a party measure for party purposes . . . a party judiciary, made by one party, and for one party, and of one party"—of, by, and for the party—demonstrating "supreme contempt for the popular will."

From the opening of the special session on November 23, 1840, until New Year's Day 1841, Lincoln played his role fully as Whig floor leader. Then he appeared at the legislature only sporadically, and then he abandoned it. "Lincoln in his conflicts of duty—honor and his love," said Ninian W. Edwards, "went as crazy as a *Loon*."

CHAPTER EIGHT

THE ROMANCE

I often heard Mr. Edwards speak of Mr. Lincoln, and one time I told him: 'You are always talking of this Mr. Lincoln. I wish you would bring him down some time and let me see him.' So Mr. Edwards had him come down, and that is the way I met him," explained Frances Todd, sister-in-law to Ninian W. Edwards, visiting in 1837 from Lexington, Kentucky. Edwards was married to the oldest Todd sister, Elizabeth. Lincoln, often accompanied by Joshua Speed, made a habit of dropping in nearly every Sunday.

"Yes," Frances admitted, "he took me out once or twice, but he was not much for society. He would go where they took him, but he was never very much for company. I don't think he could be called bashful. He was never embarrassed, that I saw, and he seemed to enjoy ladies' company.

Mary Todd

But he did not go much, as some of the other young men did." Yet another woman remembered Lincoln on Springfield's party scene. "We liked Lincoln though he was not gay. He rarely danced, he was never very attentive to ladies, but he was always a welcome guest everywhere, and the center of a circle of animated talkers. Indeed, I think the only thing we girls had against Lincoln was that he always attracted all the men around him."

The Todd-Stuart-Edwards family, the most politically influential in Springfield, was also the most socially prominent. The Edwards house on Aristocracy Hill was the pinnacle of the town's social life, its spacious rooms hosting exclusive parties and, at least once every year, the entire state legislature. Speed, scion of a wealthy Kentucky family, brought along Lincoln, who was also connected as the junior law partner of Stuart, first cousin of Elizabeth Todd Edwards. Ninian Edwards had secured the Springfield dynasty by marrying Elizabeth Todd in 1832 when he was a student at Transylvania University at Lexington. Her cousin, John Todd Stuart, son of Robert Stuart, a Presbyterian minister, and Hannah Todd, her father's sister, was already established in Springfield as a lawyer in 1828, moving there after graduating from Centre College near Lexington. Stephen Trigg Logan, another cousin, arrived shortly after the Edwards-Todd marriage, becoming one of the most important lawyers and a circuit court judge. Over the next decade, one by one, Elizabeth's sisters were welcomed into her gracious home and introduced to the most eligible and rising young men.

The lineage of the extended family was renowned, unrivaled, and translated into unparalleled status in Springfield. Family was power—political, social, and cultural. While Illinois was an open frontier, Southerners, mainly Kentuckians, whose finely gradated sense of class derived from kinship networks, as they did throughout the South, dominated. The Todd-Stuart-Edwards clans were all First Families of Kentucky. In the land of opportunity ancestry counted, just as in the South.

Ninian W. Edwards's grandfather, Benjamin Edwards, was a Maryland landowner who was a member of the state constitutional convention and the U.S. Congress, and his son, Ninian Edwards, moved to Kentucky to handle family-owned property, and rose to chief justice of the Kentucky Court of Appeals before President Madison appointed him the first and only territorial governor of Illinois, an office he held for three terms until the state was admitted to the Union in 1818 and he was elected the first U.S. senator. In 1826 he was elected the third Illinois governor.

The Todd family line properly began with Levi Todd, who served in the Revolutionary War as a lieutenant with the legendary Rangers commanded by Colonel George Rogers Clark that fought in the Indiana and Illinois Territory—and he fought in battles with Indians alongside Daniel Boone. Todd was a lawyer, surveyor, and appointed Fayette County clerk, a lucrative position from which he made his fortune in land speculation, becoming a large slaveholder. One of the early settlers of Lexington, he succeeded Boone as general of the Kentucky militia and was a member of the state's constitutional convention. His son was Robert Smith Todd.

Robert Smith Todd, the third of six sons, graduated from Transylvania University, apprenticed as a lawyer, served without hearing a shot fired in the War of 1812, and married eighteen-year-old Eliza Parker, also from one of the First Families of Kentucky. Her grandfather, General Andrew Porter, was a Revolutionary War hero who was at Valley Forge and was personally commended by Washington. His sons were David Rittenhouse Porter, who became governor of Pennsylvania (whose son, General Horace Porter, would serve as General Grant's aide-de-camp), George Bryan Porter, appointed by President Jackson governor of the Michigan Territory, and James Madison Porter, a federal judge who became secretary of war under President Tyler. His son Andrew Porter, after graduating from West Point, became a general. And his daughter, Elizabeth Rittenhouse Porter, married Major Robert Porter Parker, a cousin, who served in the Revolutionary War, built the first brick building in Lexington, and became a lawyer. Their daughter Eliza married Robert Smith Todd and their fourth daughter was named Mary.

Eliza died in childbirth in 1825 after bearing five children. Mary, six years old, was bereft. Within six months of his wife's death, Todd remarried. His new wife was Elizabeth Humphreys, from another First Family of Kentucky. One of her uncles, James Brown, was a U.S. senator, while another, John Brown, was a U.S. senator from Louisiana. John Crittenden was the best man at the wedding. (Crittenden, then a state legislator, would become a U.S. senator, U.S. attorney general, and governor, the most influential figure in Kentucky after Clay.) Betsy Todd had nine children. She resented her husband's offspring from his first family, neglected and mistreated them, was exhausted by relentless child bearing and rearing, and became withdrawn, nervous, and mean-spirited, leaving her stepchildren to be raised by a slave, "Mammy Sally." Todd, a state legislator powerful on the banking committee, was also a cotton broker, owner of a dry goods store, landowner, and president of Lexington's Branch Bank of Kentucky. He was a friend and business partner of Henry Clay. Gone much of the time from Lexington on business trips, he was often neglectful of the bright and needy Mary, who constantly sought his attention, missed her mother, and felt abandoned by her stepmother.

Lexington in the early nineteenth century was the largest town west of the Alleghenies, except for New Orleans, boasting Transylvania University and a host of other schools, and claimed the mantle of the "Athens of the West." The formal style, manners, and culture of its elite were a point of pride. But its aspiration to aristocratic pretension was as great as its veneer was thin. As Louisville and Cincinnati flourished on the Ohio River, Lexington, distant from a major river, languished and assumed an air of moldy decay as the imperative for affected and compensatory refinement among its elite became even more pronounced. Lexington was the chief slave-trading center of the upper South, where more than two dozen dealers operated openly. Slave auctions were held on a block next to the courthouse. Around the corner from the Todd house, one of the grandest homes in Lexington, stood the cavernous slave pens of Lewis C. Robards, who profited from kidnapping and selling free blacks, and was notorious for his brazen selection of mulatto "fancy girls" sold as concubines. The woman who lived across the street from the Todds was locally infamous for torturing her slaves until one strangled her and was hung.

Just on the outskirts of town, Henry Clay resided at his eighteen-room mansion called Ashland, whose Greek Revival wings were designed by Benjamin Latrobe, architect of the U.S. Capitol.

In 1832, a thirteen-year-old girl rode up to the door on a white pony to show it off to Clay, but was informed by the butler, "Mr. Clay is entertaining five or six fine gentlemens." "You go right back," she replied, "and tell him that Mary Todd would like him to step out here for a moment." The amused Clay promptly appeared. "My father says you are the best judge of horse-flesh in Fayette County," Mary said. "What do you think about this pony?" He praised the pony "as spirited as [its] jockey." And he invited the girl to be one of the guests for dinner. "Mr. Clay," she announced at the table, "my father says you will be the next President of the United States. I wish I could go to Washington and live in the White House. I begged my father to be President but he only laughed and said he would rather see you there than be President himself. He must like you more than he does himself. My father is a very, very peculiar man, Mr. Clay. I don't think he really wants to be President." "Well," said the charmed Clay, "if I am ever President I shall expect Mary Todd to be one of my first guests. Will you come?" "If you were not already married," she announced, "I would wait for you." Finally, she excused herself, "I've been gone a long time. Mammy will be wild! When I put salt in her coffee this morning she called me a limb of Satan and said I was loping down the broad road . . . to destruction."

Frances Todd, the second-born sister, was the second one to come to Springfield, taking up residence at Elizabeth's house. After swiftly dismissing Lincoln as a potential suitor, she married William Smith Wallace, a doctor, who had graduated from the University of Pennsylvania School of Medicine, in a large formal wedding at the Edwardses' in 1839. "And after we were married," she recalled, "my sister Mary came out from Lexington to stay with Mrs. Edwards, just the same as I had done before I was married."

Mary had visited briefly in 1835, but came to live at her sister's in the ritual Todd search for a husband in 1839 or early 1840, to her stepmother's relief. "If she thought any of us were on her hands again," Mary wrote Lincoln later, "I believe she would be worse than ever." Mary was unusually well educated for a young woman, sent to the Shelby Female Academy, a new school for daughters of the bluegrass elite, and then to Madame Mentelle's, where she learned science, history, geography, spoke only in French, and was taught to dance. Madame Charlotte Victorie Leclere Mentelle and her husband, Augustas Waldemare Mentelle, had been royalists who fled the French Revolution and spoke of the guillotined king and queen tearfully. They attained high social status in Lexington through the marriage of their daughter Marie to Henry Clay's son, Thomas, in 1837. Mary was unusually politically attuned at a time when politics was not considered a proper subject for women. At fourteen, a family member described her as a "violent little Whig," a political interest that came naturally in one of Kentucky's most influential families that was in the inner Clay circle.

The romantic history of Lincoln was the first-time tragedy with Ann Rutledge and the second-time farce with Mary Owens. After Ann died, Lincoln stayed at the cabin of Bennett and Elizabeth Abell, old settlers of New Salem from Kentucky. Mrs. Abell held Lincoln in high regard, "always social and lively," "good natured," and "never heard him use a profane word, drink a drop of spirits or chew tobacco in my life." She decided to play matchmaker for her sister, Mary Owens, who had visited the town briefly in 1833, and persuaded Lincoln to marry her if she were to return. Mrs. Abell, according to Mrs. Samuel Hill, was "a great talker." Mary Owens, from a wealthy Kentucky family, was well-educated, well-dressed, and well-regarded—"a handsome woman—a fine looking woman," recalled Caleb Carman, "sharp—shrewd and intellectual I assure you. Miss Rutledge was a pretty woman—good natured—kind—wasn't as smart as Miss Owens by a heap."

Lincoln's courtship technique consisted of treating her as a backwoods frontier woman expected "to care for herself." He would not help her cross a deep stream, leaving her on the riverbank to fend for herself. Yet he avidly pursued her, writing letters and seeking her company, while she avoided him. Not only clumsy he was also clueless. Unable to take the hint, he proposed. When she failed to give him an answer, trying to evade him, he pressed the point in a strange letter on May 7, 1837, written as a kind of legal brief laying out the reasons she would be unhappy with him. "I am often thinking about what we said of your coming to live at Springfield. I am afraid you would not be satisfied. There is a great deal of flourishing about in carriages here, which it would be your doom to see without sharing in it. You would have to be poor without the means of hiding your poverty. Do you believe you could bear that patiently?" Having explained why she should not marry him because of his lowly station in life, he reiterated his proposal, adding that she should refuse. "For my part I have already decided. What I have said I will most positively abide by, provided you wish it. My opinion is that you had better not do it. You have not been accustomed to hardship, and it may be more severe than you now imagine." Yet he was perplexed by her rejection and kept pressing the point in another letter on August 17, 1837. "Perhaps any other man would know enough without further information; but I consider it my peculiar right to plead ignorance, and your bounden duty to allow the plea." She never replied.

Later, Owens explained to Herndon, "I thought Mr. Lincoln was deficient in those little links which make up the great chain of woman's happiness, at least it was so in my case; not that I believed it proceeded from a lack of goodness of heart, but his training had been different from mine, hence there was not that congeniality which would have otherwise existed."

Spurned after revealing his deep-seated feelings of social inadequacy,

Lincoln defended his bruised self-esteem in a letter on April 1, 1838, to Eliza Browning, the wife of O. H. Browning, an Illinois state senator and close friend. The letter, written partly in his slashing polemical style and partly in a reflective personal tone, began with self-justification and ended with self-defeat. He justified his obsessive pursuit of Owens as merely passivity, seeing "no good objection to plodding life through hand in hand with her." He underscored his good intentions, but protected himself from her rejection by casting her as shockingly ugly. "I knew she was over-size, but she now appeared a fair match for Falstaff; I knew she was called an 'old maid' . . . but now, when I beheld her, I could not for my life avoid thinking of my mother; and this, not from withered features, for her skin was too full of fat, to permit its contracting in to wrinkles; but from her want of teeth, weather-beaten appearance in general." Yet he claimed he was committed to carrying through his part of the supposed bargain, his good-faith effort already pointless. "But what could I do? I had told her sister that I would take her for better or for worse; and I made a point of honor and conscience in all things, to stick to my word, especially if others had been induced to act on it."

He quickly described the denouement, surprising only to him after repeated rebuffs. "I now want to know, if you can guess how I got out of it. Out clear in every sense of the term; no violation of word, honor or conscience. I don't believe you can guess, and so I may as well tell you at once. As the lawyers say, it was done in the manner following, to wit. After I had delayed the matter as long as I thought I could in honor do, which by the way had brought me round into the last fall, I concluded I might as well bring it to a consummation without further delay; and so I mustered my resolution, and made the proposal to her direct; but, shocking to relate, she answered, No."

Poor Lincoln lamented his failed romantic method and reconciled himself to sad acceptance of loneliness.

> I tried it again and again, but with the same success, or rather with the same want of success. I finally was forced to give it up, at which I very unexpectedly found myself mortified almost beyond endurance. I was mortified, it seemed to me, in a hundred different ways. My vanity was deeply wounded by the reflection, that I had so long been too stupid to discover her intentions, and at the same time never doubting that I understood them perfectly; and also, that she whom I had taught myself to believe nobody else would

have, had actually rejected me with all my fancied greatness; and to cap the whole, I then, for the first time, began to suspect that I was really a little in love with her. But let it all go. I'll try and outlive it. Others have been made fools of by the girls; but this can never be with truth said of me. I most emphatically, in this instance, made a fool of myself. I have now come to the conclusion never again to think of marrying; and for this reason; I can never be satisfied with anyone who would be block-head enough to have me.

Despite his protests in the letter to Mrs. Browning, Lincoln had divulged that he had wanted to marry Mary Owens and thought of her affectionately, but the notion produced feelings of inferiority that he felt compelled to parade before her, which, combined with his rustic manners, prompted her to reject him. He declared he had behaved as a "fool," but his mortification and wounding came from the exposure of his greatest vulnerability, his lowliness. Her rejection cut one of the last threads that might have held him to New Salem, just about to disappear into the mist in any case. Abandoned by Ann Rutledge's death and Mary Owens's dumping he was unencumbered to advance his political career.

Two years after his breakup with Owens he found himself in the Edwards parlor mesmerized by another Kentucky belle, better educated and more cultivated, a class above, and who could talk circles around him. She was unlike any other young woman he had met, unhesitating to offer sharp political opinions. "L. could not hold a lengthy conversation with a lady— was not sufficiently educated and intelligent in the female line to do so," recalled Elizabeth Todd Edwards. "He was charmed with Mary's wit and fascinated with her quick sagacity—her will—her nature—and culture. I have happened in the room where they were sitting often . . . and Mary led the conversation. Lincoln would listen and gaze on her as if drawn by some superior power, irresistibly so. He listened—never scarcely said a word."

Mary flourished as a center of attention within the lively set of young people that designated themselves "the coterie." "Springfield society contained some of the brightest young men that any state could produce" and "a galaxy of beautiful girls, with vivacity and intelligence and propriety of deportment," wrote a local chronicler. Their social life was a movable feast of parties, picnics, and nightly promenades up and down Springfield's dimly lit streets. Mary was "the very creature of excitement you know and never enjoys herself more than when in society and surrounded by a company of merry friends," wrote James C. Conkling, a young lawyer who was part of the coterie and would later become chairman of the Illinois Republican Party. "In our little coterie in Springfield in the days of my girlhood," Mary recalled, "we had a society of gentlemen, who have since, been distinguished, in a greater or less degree, in the political world." "Mary Todd had naturally a fine mind and a cultivated taste," recalled Mrs. Benjamin S. Edwards, her sister-in-law. "She was a thinker and possessed a remarkable memory. Her brilliant conversation often embellished with apt quotations made her society much sought after by all the young people of the town. She was also quick at repartee and when occasion seemed to require it, was sarcastic and severe." The description of her as "sarcastic and severe" was meant as a compliment for her skill at raillery and ability to hold her own. "Mary Todd," remarked her cousin and friend, Margaret Stuart Woodrow, "was very highly strung, nervous, impulsive, excitable, having an emotional temperament much like an April day, sunning up all over with laughter one moment, the next crying as though her heart would break."

One week before Election Day in 1840 the Whigs built a large log cabin to represent Harrison's imaginary humble origins and where they held raucous nightly rallies filled with speeches and singing. On the cabin's opening night sixty women came to listen to the Tippecanoe Singing Club. Mary Todd was likely one of them. "This fall," she wrote a friend, "I became quite a politician, rather an unladylike profession, yet at such a crisis, whose heart could remain untouched while the energies of all were called in question."

Mary's romance with Lincoln began during the exhilaration of the campaign. Exactly when it was sparked and how it warmed is mostly unknown. She was possibly present at the formal cotillion held at the American House on December 16, 1839, where Lincoln served as a manager to welcome new members of the legislature and celebrate the finishing of the new State House. But Mary spent much of the summer visiting her uncle David Todd in Missouri, and Lincoln traveled around the state for the Whigs for months. "Mary was quick, lively, gay—frivolous it may be, social and loved glitter, show and pomp and power," said Elizabeth Todd Edwards. "She was an extremely ambitious woman and in Kentucky often . . . contended that she was destined to be the wife of some future President—said it in my presence in Springfield and said it in earnest." Other rising young men paid her attention, including Stephen A. Douglas and his friend James Shields, the state auditor, but she preferred the socially ungainly Lincoln. "Mr. Douglas used to come to see Mary," recalled Mrs. Edwards. "Probably it is quite likely that his intentions were true and sincere. Mary was asked one day by some of her friends which she intended to have. 'Him who has the best prospects of being President,' said Miss Todd." "All thought that Mr. Douglas was more assiduous in his attentions than Mr. Lincoln," wrote a local observer. Lincoln, according to Speed, was the pursued. "She darted after him," he said. Mary's ambition to marry a future president would have been highly unusual. Women were not supposed to show open interest in politics and especially not to voice their own aspirations in relation to it. But Mary's elite background had exposed her to the inside workings of politics and even a man who might be president. She was used to stating her frank opinions and liked to startle men as a form of flirtation and entertainment. But did she dream that Lincoln could offer her the White House? He was gifted, honest, and self-disciplined, had worthy personal habits, was growing into a good lawyer, but also was sometimes boorish and remarkably inept with women.

The last scene of the first act of the romance has always been somewhat obscure, but the conclusion was definite: boy loses girl. Lincoln had courted Mary and made some sort of commitment, possibly an engagement. Elizabeth Todd Edwards even insisted "everything was ready and prepared for the marriage—even to the supper," a scene resembling Miss Havisham's abandonment at the altar in Dickens's *Great Expectations*, almost certainly a faulty memory, possibly confusion about the grand wedding she held for her other sister, Frances; all the weight of other witnesses was that there was no planned wedding. "I heard a rumor of an engagement between Mr. Lincoln and Mary Todd," recalled Helen Edwards, married to Benjamin Edwards, Ninian's brother, "yet I considered it one of those unfounded reports always floating in society."

Sometime during the special legislative session, between November 23 and December 5, Lincoln decided to break off his relationship. He wrote Mary a letter and showed it to Speed, asking him to serve as his messenger. "I shall not deliver it nor give it to you to be delivered," Speed told him. "Words are forgotten—misunderstood—passed by—not noticed in a private conversation—but once put your words in writing and they stand as a living and eternal monument against you. If you think you have will and manhood enough to go and see her and speak to her what you say in that letter, you may do that." Lincoln summoned his courage and "told her that he did not love her. She rose and said, 'The deceiver shall be deceived, woe is me,' alluding to a young man she fooled"—the deceived swain either Douglas or Gillespie, possibly encouraged to inspire Lincoln's jealousy. Then, perhaps out of guilt, regret, or pity, "Lincoln drew her down on his knee—kissed her—and parted." "The last thing is a bad lick," reproved Speed, "but it cannot now be helped."

Lincoln's "bad lick" was not his most damaging behavior. Before kissing Mary, he apparently told her he was in love with another woman. She was Matilda Edwards, the eighteen-year-old daughter of Cyrus Edwards, Ninian's cousin, who had come from Alton to live in the Edwardses' Springfield house, likely sharing a room with Mary, during the special legislative session. "A most interesting young lady, her fascinations, have drawn a concourse of beaux and company round us," Mary wrote a friend. Lincoln had become suddenly infatuated with her. Complicating the plot, Speed had fallen under her spell as well, waxing poetic in a letter to his sister about her charms: "Lips so fresh, fair, and lovely that I am jealous even of the minds that kiss them. A form as perfect as that of the Venus de Medici." The swooning Speed was in the throes of his own personal crisis. His father had died in March, leaving him responsibility for the well-being of his mother and sister and the management of the economically precarious Farmington plantation at Louisville with its fifty slaves. He had sold his interest in the Springfield store, a transaction that would go into effect on January 1, 1841, a date that Lincoln designated in a later letter on March 27, 1842, as "that fatal first of Jany. '41," referring undoubtedly to Speed's sale, not to Lincoln's breakup with Mary which had occurred earlier.

Unfortunately for the two roommate suitors, the object of their desire was utterly indifferent. In Lincoln's case, despite his moonstruck infatuation, Matilda Edwards had no idea of his obsession. When Elizabeth Todd Edwards later asked her about it, she said, "On my word he never mentioned such a subject to me: he never even stooped to pay me a compliment." Just as curiously, Speed was giving advice to the lovelorn Lincoln while they were both fixated on the same "Venus." After "that fatal first," the rejected and dejected Speed left Springfield for Farmington, another trauma for Lincoln, losing his closest friend.

Lincoln's star-crossed romance collided with political disappointment. Exhausting himself riding far and wide for Harrison, debating Douglas and the Democrats, the state still went for the discredited loser Van Buren. Lincoln's patronage requests to the incoming national administration were ignored. His dream of becoming the DeWitt Clinton of Illinois was in tatters. In the wake of the Panic, "the System" collapsed, he could not stop the Democrats from destroying the State Bank, his bill to increase taxes could not close the gap, and after he jumped out the window of the legislature he had become a laughingstock.

Ninian W. Edwards later said he hoped that Lincoln would marry Mary and Speed would marry Matilda—for "policy reasons," he later said. Then the core of the Springfield Junto would have been bonded as family. But Lincoln had confounded those plans by becoming bewitched with Matilda, though he "did not ever by act or deed directly or indirectly hint or speak of it to Miss Edwards." Instead of Edwards's plan being realized, "The Lincoln and Todd engagement was broken off in consequence of it." That was why, he explained, Lincoln "went as crazy as a *Loon.*"

Elizabeth Todd Edwards offered a more paradoxical theory. "In his lunacy," she said, "he declared he hated Mary and loved Miss Edwards. This is true, yet it was not his real feelings. A crazy man hates those he loves when at himself . . . often is this the case. Mr. Lincoln loved Mary—he went crazy in my own opinion—not because he loved Miss Edwards as said, but because he wanted to marry and doubted his ability and capacity to please and support a wife." In other words, his insecurity blurred his vision, divided his heart, and he wounded the one he truly loved.

But these theories of Lincoln's social ineptitude offered after he had become a national martyr concealed the Edwardses' true feelings at the time even as they hinted at them. They were decidedly not in favor of the match, regarding Lincoln beneath Mary. Their actual view, as Mary's grandniece Katherine Helm wrote, was that "his future was nebulous, his family relations were on a different social plane. His education had been desultory. He had no culture, and he was ignorant of social forms and customs." Not even his nomination as the Republican candidate for president really altered their condescension, at least in private. "It seemed impossible that this should ever be," clucked Helen Edwards, married to Benjamin Edwards, Ninian's brother. "There were so many others that we could name who seemed so much better fitted for this position than he."

Lincoln's private and public humiliations were complete. His foolish behavior was the chief topic of gossip in town. His maladroit handling of his love life was thoroughly exposed for amusement, censure, and ridicule. He had stumbled, moreover, with two young ladies of the Edwards family, the cynosure of social prestige. His sensitivity about his inferiority must have spiraled into panic. Self-conscious that his oafishness cut to the core of his identity, revealing his low origins, he suffered a crisis of respectability and reputation.

In early January, Lincoln had a nervous breakdown. "Lincoln went crazy," said Speed, "had to remove razors from his room—take away all knives and other such dangerous things, etc., it was terrible." For about a week, Lincoln confined himself to his room or at the home of his friend William Butler, whose wife ministered to him. Sixty-six years later, in 1907, her sister, Sarah Rickard Barret, gave a version to a St. Louis newspaper reporter: "Suffering under the thought that he had treated Mary badly, knowing that she loved him and that he did not love her, Mr. Lincoln was wearing his very life away in an agony of remorse. He made no excuse for breaking with Mary, but said, sadly, to my sister: 'Mrs. Butler, it would just kill me to marry Mary Todd.'" Sarah Rickard also contended later to Herndon that when she was sixteen years old, sometime in 1840, Lincoln had proposed to her and she had turned him down, a claim for which there is no corroboration; but just because it seems bizarre does not make it inconceivable.

Despite Speed's dramatic talk about suicide, Lincoln never made the slightest gesture to hurt himself. He missed only a few days at the legislature. Hiram Thornton, a Whig legislator who boarded at Dr. Anson Henry's house, dismissed the later reports of Lincoln's supposedly suicidal state of mind. "The missing days, from January 13th to 19th, Mr. Lincoln spent several hours each day at Dr. Henry's; a part of these days I remained with Mr. Lincoln," he recalled. "His most intimate friends had no fears of his injuring himself. He was very sad and melancholy, but being subject to these spells, nothing serious was apprehended."

Lincoln's isolation may well have been prescribed by Dr. Henry, who likely administered a regime of bleeding, vomiting, blue mass pills (dosed with poisonous levels of mercury), and frigid water plunges. Subjected to this gruesome treatment, standard for the era, which Henry was known to apply enthusiastically, it would be little wonder that Lincoln was wretched. Henry also suggested he consult with Dr. Daniel Drake of Cincinnati, one of the leading physicians in the West, considered to be an early expert in treating depression and whose method involved opium, "the medicine of the mind." Lincoln wrote him a lengthy letter, but Drake replied that he would only treat him in person. (Lincoln's letter has never been recovered.)

The cure, worse than the disease, was a severe penalty for social embarrassment. "We have been very much distressed, on Mr. Lincoln's account; hearing he had two cat fits, and a duck fit since we left," wrote Martinette Hardin, who had been part of the Springfield whirl around New Year's, on January 16, to her brother, John J. Hardin, a Whig member of the legislature from Jacksonville, both third cousins of the Todd sisters. "Is it true? Do let us hear soon?" Hardin's wife, Sarah, wrote him on January 26, after receiving his news that Lincoln seemed to be better. "I am glad to hear Lincoln has got over his cat fits. We have concluded it was a very unsatisfactory way of terminating his romance. He ought to have died or gone crazy. We are very much disappointed."

Lincoln's plight set the coterie's tongues wagging. "Poor L! how are the mighty fallen!" wrote James C. Conkling to his fiancée, Mercy Ann Levering, a friend of Mary. "He was confined about a week, but he now appears again he is reduced and emaciated in appearance and seems scarcely to possess strength enough to speak above a whisper. His case at present is truly deplorable but what prospect there may be for ultimate relief I cannot pretend to say. I doubt not but he can declare that loving is a painful thrill, And not to love more painful still but would not like to intimate that he has experienced 'That surely 'tis the worst of pain To love and not be loved again.'"

On January 20, Lincoln was restored enough to send a request to Stuart in Washington, seeking a patronage plum for Henry as Springfield postmaster. "You know I desired Dr. Henry to have that place when you left; I now desire it more than ever. I have, within the last few days, been making a most discreditable exhibition of myself in the way of hypochondriasm and thereby got an impression that Dr. Henry is necessary to my existence. Unless he gets that place he leaves Springfield." (Henry did not get the job and he did not leave.)

Three days later, Lincoln wrote Stuart in a histrionic tone: "I am now the most miserable man living. If what I feel were equally distributed to the whole human family, there would not be one cheerful face on the earth. Whether I shall ever be any better I cannot tell; I awfully forebode I shall not.

To remain as I am is impossible; I must die or be better, it appears to me." But rather than fading into an early grave, Lincoln was already attending the legislature. With Stuart at Washington, he also began his new legal partnership with Stephen T. Logan.

Logan was exacting, precise, and more knowledgeable than Stuart, despite his shambling dress and drooling tobacco chewing. He did not allow his new junior partner to coast on his wit, but insisted that he fully prepare for each case. Logan had quarreled with his previous partner, Edward Dickinson Baker, over his casual handling of fees. "Baker was a brilliant man but very negligent, while Lincoln was growing all the time, from the time I first knew him," Logan said. Lincoln rapidly developed into an adept case lawyer. "Lincoln's knowledge of law was very small when I took him in," said Logan. At first, Logan used him to cajole juries, but he soon expanded his range. "After a while he began to pick up a considerable ambition in the law. He didn't have confidence enough at first." Logan observed that Lincoln was a quick learner, whose initial slowness masked his methodical depth. "So far as his reading and knowledge of law went he had a quite unusual grasp of the principles involved. When he was with me I have seen him get a case and seem to be bewildered at first, but he would go at it and after a while he would master it. He was very tenacious in his grasp of a thing that he once got hold of." Under the discipline of the law and the watchful eye of Logan, Lincoln regained his balance. Not taking Dr. Henry's cure might have helped, too.

Despite Lincoln's rejection, Mary appeared to be thriving. "Miss Todd and cousin Miss Edwards seemed to form the grand centre of attraction," Conkling wrote to his fiancée on March 7. "Swarms of strangers who had little else to engage their attention hovered around them, to catch a passing smile." But Lincoln walked under a cloud of gloom. "And L., poor hapless simple swain who loved most true but was not loved again. I suppose he will now endeavor to drown his cares among the intricacies and perplexities of the law. No more will the merry peal of laughter ascend high in the air, to greet his listening and delighted ears. . . . Alas! I fear his shrine will now be deserted and that he will withdraw himself from the society of us inferior mortals."

Yet Mary still had thoughts about Lincoln. "His worthy friend deems me unworthy of notice, as I have not met him in the gay world for months," she wrote Mercy Levering on June 17. "With the usual comfort of misery, I imagine that others were as seldom gladdened by his presence as my humble self, yet I would that the case were different, that he would once more resume his station in Society, that 'Richard should be himself again,' much, much happiness would it afford me." Mary wished for Lincoln's feeling for her to be restored, casting him as Richard III, at least by becoming himself again, not the tyrant but her regal suitor. After he had clumsily broken their engagement and suffered his collapse, something she would have certainly heard about, she had not put him out of her mind.

Lincoln was famously subject to melancholy spells, but over the next twenty months he did more than plod on. He was immersed in productive legal work at Logan & Lincoln, trying dozens of cases, including one of the most significant of his entire career, freeing his first slave; delivered the most important speech of his pre-congressional years, far more consequential for his political fate than his Lyceum address; engaged in the tumultuous politics of the Illinois Mormon War, which consumed state politics for years and was the latest chapter of his rivalry with Douglas; and staged a cloaked partisan attack on one of Douglas's closest allies of which the denouement was his marriage to his co-conspirator.

For thirteen years, since 1828, a black woman, Nance Legins-Costley, had the audacity to maintain her suit for her freedom. She was an orphan sold at auction for $150 with her sister to Sangamon County sheriff John Taylor in July 1827 and held in chains after she refused to be conveyed as a servant to Nathan Cromwell, a wealthy landowner in Tazewell County. The court ruled that as property she had no rights whatsoever. "A servant is a possession and CAN BE SOLD," read the decision. Her persistent challenge to the legacy of slavery in Illinois had elements of the Dred Scott case—her own pursuit of emancipation, the intervention of an abolitionist benefactor, and appearance of an antislavery lawyer.

Traveling to Texas on business, Cromwell left the pregnant Nance as a servant with David Bailey for a promissory note of $400. Cromwell and Bailey were both early settlers of the county. Cromwell promptly died in St. Louis, leaving a chaotic estate. His son, Dr. William Cromwell, sued Bailey for the $400. Nathan Cromwell's lawyer had been John Todd Stuart, but he was busy running for the Congress so William Cromwell hired Stephen T. Logan. In *Cromwell v. Bailey*, the court ruled in October 1839 in favor of

Cromwell simply on the basis of Bailey's acknowledgment he had signed the promissory note. Lincoln happened to have been present in the courthouse that day and on his own composed a "bill of exceptions" in the case. Bailey decided to appeal to the Illinois Supreme Court and hired Lincoln.

Lincoln and Bailey had known each other during the Black Hawk War. Major Bailey's men were those massacred and mutilated in the Battle of Stillman's Run that Captain Lincoln was ordered to bury. Bailey was a descendant of Pilgrims on the *Mayflower*, grew up in New Hampshire, and was a founder of the town of Pekin, Illinois. He was more than prominent—he was also an avowed abolitionist. Bailey had signed Elijah Lovejoy's call for the convention of the Illinois Anti-Slavery Society and was possibly present in Alton for the clashes that climaxed in Lovejoy's killing. The reason Bailey filed his appeal was not the cash, but the principle. He shouldered the lawyer's fee in order to free Nance.

On July 9, 1841, Lincoln argued that the promissory note was invalid because Nance was already emancipated and therefore selling her was an illegal attempt to "introduce slavery" into Illinois. Three times he quoted the phrase, "Neither slavery nor involuntary servitude," invoking the prohibition from the Northwest Ordinance of 1787 and the state constitution of 1818. The court issued its decision on July 23: "It is a presumption of law, in the State of Illinois, that every person is free, without regard to color. . . . The sale of a free person is illegal." Concurring in the decision was Judge Stephen A. Douglas.

Lincoln had taken on a leading abolitionist as a client, not merely representing him in an ordinary transaction but a controversy over the power of slavery in a free state. *Bailey v. Cromwell* established a precedent cited in antislavery briefs to come. Nance was declared free, Lincoln's "first freed slave." Though the practice of holding slaves and indentured servants still continued in Illinois, protected under the U.S. Constitution, the sale of human beings was ended. Both the Wilmot Proviso intended to prohibit slavery in the territory annexed after the Mexican War, which he would vote for futilely in the Congress, and the Thirteenth Amendment contained the salient words of the Northwest Ordinance that he cited in his summation on behalf of the slave Nance: "Neither slavery nor involuntary servitude . . ."

"I stick to my promise to come to Louisville," Lincoln wrote Speed on June 20. After wrapping up eighteen cases in a single day at the court, the last day of the summer term, August 5, he set out for Farmington, the Speed plantation with its classical fourteen-room mansion said to be based on a design by Thomas Jefferson, who had been a neighbor of Speed's mother's family. At this Old Kentucky Home, Lincoln was treated as a member of the family. He romped with Speed's younger sister Mary, was fretted over by his mother, Lucy, and rode into Louisville to borrow books from his brother James with whom he discussed "his life, his reading, his studies, his aspirations." He also found himself in the position of counseling his friend, who was enamored with a young woman named Fanny Hennings. Speed and Lincoln reversed roles of afflicted and comforter with Lincoln drawing on his ragged romantic experience for guidance.

He left his idyll with the Speeds after about three tranquil weeks, on September 8, boarding a steamboat down the Ohio to St. Louis, accompanied by Speed, who journeyed to Springfield to clear up his remaining business at the store. Lincoln related an account on September 27 to Mary Speed, whom he wrote he could trust now as one of his "cronies." After discussing a toothache and a painful extraction, "being unable to eat, I am living upon the remembrance of the delicious dishes of peaches and cream we used to have at your house," he gossiped about Fanny, "one of the sweetest girls in the world," adding that she had "a tendency to melancholy," Lincoln's own burden. "This, let it be observed," he wrote, "is a misfortune not a fault." He asked Mary to thank her mother for giving him a Bible. "I doubt not that it is really, as she says, the best cure for the 'Blues' could one but take it according to the truth." He could not help hedging his gratitude with freethinking skepticism.

The longest passage in his chatty letter was a description of slaves on the steamer. "By the way," he wrote,

> a fine example was presented on board the boat for contemplating the effect of condition upon human happiness. A gentleman had purchased twelve negroes in different parts of Kentucky and was taking them to a farm in the South. They were chained six and six together. A small iron clevis was around the left wrist of each, and this fastened to the main chain by a shorter one at a convenient distance from, the others; so that the negroes were strung together precisely like so many fish upon a trot-line. In this condition they were being separated forever from the scenes of their childhood,

their friends, their fathers and mothers, and brothers and sisters, and many of them, from their wives and children, and going into perpetual slavery where the lash of the master is proverbially more ruthless and unrelenting than any other where; and yet amid all these distressing circumstances, as we would think them, they were the most cheerful and apparently happy creatures on board. One, whose offense for which he had been sold was an over-fondness for his wife, played the fiddle almost continually; and the others danced, sung, cracked jokes, and played various games with cards from day to day.

Appealing to the Speed women's piety, he concluded, "How true it is that 'God tempers the wind to the shorn lamb,' or in other words, that He renders the worst of human conditions tolerable, while He permits the best, to be nothing better than tolerable."

Nearly fourteen years later, on August 24, 1855, Lincoln recollected this episode in a letter to Speed with a wholly different emphasis: "That sight was a continual torment to me; and I see something like it every time I touch the Ohio, or any other slave-border. It is hardly fair for you to assume, that I have no interest in a thing which has, and continually exercises, the power of making me miserable. You ought rather to appreciate how much the great body of the Northern people do crucify their feelings, in order to maintain their loyalty to the constitution and the Union." By then he was passionately arguing with Speed about "Bleeding Kansas." And in making his case he demonstrated that on his Kentucky sojourn of 1841 and on a later visit in 1849 to his wife's home in Lexington, he had closely observed the slaveholders' society. "The slave-breeders and slave-traders, are a small, odious and detested class, among you," he wrote, "and yet in politics, they dictate the course of all of you, and are as completely your masters, as you are the masters of your own negroes."

When Lincoln arrived back at Springfield in mid-September he at once took up a host of new cases before the courts. His status as a leader of the Junto remained unaffected, remaining on the Whig Central Committee, and he declined a push to nominate him as the party's gubernatorial candidate.

After Speed returned to Kentucky, he wrote Lincoln expressing his ambivalence about marrying Fanny. They were already engaged, but he raised fear of her health to justify his hesitation. On January 3, 1842, Lincoln replied with lawyerly exactitude, enumerated in three points how he could understand and overcome "a nervous temperament." First, Lincoln explained that "your exposure to bad weather on your journey, which my experience clearly proves to be very severe on defective nerves." Second, he told Speed he was guilty of "the absence of all business and conversation of friends, which might divert your mind, and give it occasional rest from that intensity of thought." In conclusion, Lincoln wrote, "The third is, the rapid and near approach of that crisis on which all your thoughts and feelings concentrate." In case Speed might dismiss Lincoln's clinical approach, he advised him that he spoke from personal experience: ". . . let me, who have some reason to speak with judgment on such a subject, beseech you, to ascribe it to the causes I have mentioned; and not to some false and ruinous suggestion of the Devil."

One month later, on February 3, Lincoln gave more advice: "I hope and believe, that your present anxiety and distress about her health and her life, must and will forever banish those horrid doubts, which I know you sometimes felt, as to the truth of your affection for her." He underscored his own fear of death to lift it from Speed's mind. "You know the Hell I have suffered on that point, and how tender I am upon it. You know I do not mean wrong." He reported his own improvement as encouragement. "I have been quite clear of hypo since you left—even better than I was along in the fall." On the 13th, in anticipation of Speed's wedding, Lincoln sent another letter: "If you went through the ceremony calmly, or even with sufficient composure not to excite alarm in any present, you are safe, beyond question, and in two or three months, to say the most, will be the happiest of men." Speed's courtship and marriage was Lincoln's dress rehearsal wedding. Counseling Speed, Lincoln walked himself down the aisle of his anxieties.

On the day of Speed's wedding, Lincoln attended Bowling Green's funeral. When he arose to deliver his eulogy of the man who nurtured his early political career and yet whom Lincoln had denied an endorsement for his partisan irregularity he broke down. "He only uttered a few words and commenced choking and sobbing," recalled Abner Y. Ellis. "He told the listeners that he was unmanned and could not proceed."

Unable to compose his emotions at the death of his surrogate father, just months earlier he had carefully arranged the security of his actual father. The previous October, Lincoln traveled to Goosenest Prairie in Coles County, where Thomas was once again at risk of financial failure. He had bought forty acres of land from his stepson, John Johnston, for fifty dollars, but was in trouble. Lincoln simply bought the same property from Thomas for $200, giving him a large profit, and by transferring the title to himself shielded his father from potential creditors. Thomas and Sarah were now taken care of. Lincoln, who had renounced his father's way of life, provided him with the security Thomas could not provide for himself.

One week after Speed's wedding and Green's funeral, on February 22, Washington's Birthday, following a parade of the Sangamo Guards, "under the command of Captain E. D. Baker," the Washingtonian Society of Springfield crowded into the Second Presbyterian Church to hear Lincoln speak. Several confirmed drunkards had founded the society in Baltimore only two years earlier, a precursor to Alcoholics Anonymous a century later. In contrast to the dominant evangelical temperance groups, the Washingtonians were not only devoted to self-help but also pointedly secular. They did not pray to the deity for salvation, but were instead dependent on each other's moral support for a cure. Lincoln's friends had organized the Springfield lodge just three months earlier—Herndon was president and James Matheny corresponding secretary.

Lincoln's freethinking was no secret, but he had felt restrained from voicing it publicly since Sam Hill burned his tract disputing the divinity of Jesus. Among his friends, he did not hesitate to "ridicule" religious orthodoxy—the notion of the Virgin Mary, divine "inspiration" and "revelation"—according to Matheny. Now standing before the association of town drunks, Lincoln unleashed an unreserved attack on the self-righteous. "The warfare heretofore waged against the demon of Intemperance, has, somehow or other, been erroneous," he began. "Either the champions engaged, or the tactics they adopted, have not been the most proper. These champions for the most part, have been preachers, lawyers, and hired agents"—a trinity of sanctimony, deception, and corruption. "The preacher, it is said, advocates temperance because he is a fanatic, and desires a union of Church and State; the lawyer, from his pride and vanity of hearing himself speak; and the hired agent, for his salary." When a drunkard freed himself from his addiction through his own volition, Lincoln continued, he also proved the falsity of his would-be redeemers and exposed their ulterior motives. "They cannot say that he desires a union of church and state, for he is not a church member; they cannot say he is vain of hearing himself speak, for his whole demeanor shows, he would gladly avoid speaking at all; they cannot say he speaks for pay for he receives none, and asks for none."

Lincoln used his speech to eviscerate the Calvinism he had instinctively hated as a boy and intellectually rejected through his reading of Paine and Volney. He did not believe that people were naturally sinful, fallen creatures, who must concede their depravity in order to achieve redemption. Instead, he openly condemned the moral coercion and social cruelty of the evangelical enterprise and the "system of tactics" of forcing alcoholics to submit and confess their sins.

> When the dram-seller and drinker, were incessantly told, not in the accents of entreaty and persuasion diffidently addressed by erring man to an erring brother; but in the thundering tones of anathema and denunciation, with which the lordly Judge often groups together all the crimes of the felon's life, and thrusts them in his face just ere he passes sentence of death upon him, that they were the authors of all the vice and misery and crime in the land; that they were the manufacturers and material of all the thieves and robbers and murderers that infested the earth; that their houses were the workshops of the devil; and that their persons should be shunned by all the good and virtuous, as moral pestilences—I say, when they were told all this, and in this way, it is not wonderful that they were slow, very slow, to acknowledge the truth of such denunciations, and to join the ranks of their denouncers, in a hue and cry against themselves.

Then Lincoln offered his own little history of drink, "just as old as the world itself," its production an "honorable livelihood," liquor prescribed by physicians, and ladled out by the government to soldiers and sailors. Just twenty years ago, he argued, "none seemed to think the injury arose from the use of a bad thing, but from the abuse of a very good thing. The victims to it were pitied, and compassionated, just as now are, the heirs of consumptions, and other hereditary diseases. Their failing was treated as a misfortune, and not as a crime, or even as a disgrace." But the preachers and their agents had taken over the issue with an approach contrary to "human nature"—"so repugnant to humanity, so uncharitable, so cold-blooded and feelingless."

His peroration, like that of his Lyceum address, was a purple call to reason, comparing the bondage of drunkenness to that of slavery, linking the movements of reform to the spirit of the American Revolution. "Happy day, when, all appetites controlled, all passions subdued, all matters subjected, mind, all conquering mind, shall live and move the monarch of the world. Glorious consummation! Hail fall of Fury! Reign of Reason, all hail! And when the victory shall be complete—when there shall be neither a slave nor a drunkard on the earth—how proud the title of that Land, which may truly claim to be the birth-place and the cradle of both those revolutions, that shall have ended in that victory."

Unsurprisingly, the *Sangamo Journal* editorialized that Lincoln's speech was "excellent." The *Journal* also reprinted the speech on behalf of the Washingtonians. Lincoln sent a copy to Speed. "You will see by the last *Sangamo Journal* that I made a Temperance speech on the 22. of Feb. which I claim that Fanny you shall read as an act of charity to me," he wrote on March 27, "for I cannot learn that anybody else has read it, or is likely to."

Unfortunately, he was quite wrong that his talk to the Washingtonians was ignored. The devout either heard or read his speech, and were deeply offended. "The professing Christians regarded the suspicion" he had cast on them as "a reflection on the sincerity of their belief," wrote Herndon. "I was at the door of the church as the people passed out, and heard them discussing the speech. Many of them were open in the expression of their displeasure. 'It's a shame,' I heard one man say, 'that he should be permitted to abuse us so in the house of the Lord.' . . . The whole thing, I repeat, was damaging to Lincoln, and gave rise to the opposition on the part of the churches which confronted him several years afterwards when he became a candidate against the noted Peter [Cartwright] for Congress."

Even before Lincoln delivered his speech, but knowing it was scheduled, in an effort to preempt it, Douglas's newspaper, the *Register*, accused Simeon Francis, the editor of the *Journal*, Douglas's caning target, of drunkenness. "It is quite unnecessary for us to join the society," the paper wrote, "because we do not indulge in ardent spirits; but we do not censure the editor of the *Journal* for joining, because he doubtless had good reasons for doing so." (The pose of the conspicuously alcoholic Douglas and friends as teetotalers was plainly risible.) Then the *Register* slashed Lincoln for "attempting to turn the Washington Temperance Society into a political engine. . . . Does any rational man believe for a moment that Abraham Lincoln, William L. May . . . and Edward D. Baker have joined the Washington society from any other than political motives?"

Now known as the "Sangamon Chief," Lincoln deliberated with the

Springfield Junto in slating the list of Whig candidates from top to bottom for the fall elections. He was in favor of former Democrat turned Whig Joseph Duncan for governor, whose switch allowed hope he might have broad appeal, but in fact was regarded skeptically by Democrats and Whigs alike, and vulnerable to the repeated charge of "turncoat." For the legislature, Lincoln gave up his spot to his senior law partner, Logan, who also bumped aside Ninian W. Edwards. Lincoln assuaged his disappointment at losing the nomination, writing Speed that Edwards "is a little mortified though he is quite quiet, and has permitted no one but me to know his feelings." Lincoln's role as confidant indicated that after the Mary Todd breakup he had patched up his relationship with Edwards.

For the first time, in mid-June, Lincoln met a president, by that time an ex-president, the one he had sought to "crucify," Martin Van Buren, who arrived near Springfield and gathered a little party that invited the fabled storyteller Lincoln, "pressed into service to entertain Mr. Van Buren," recalled Gillespie. The evening was filled with the telling of humorous political stories. "Van Buren himself entertained the crowd with reminiscences of politics in New York, going back to the days of Hamilton and Burr," related Herndon. Then, said Gillespie, Lincoln provided stories and jokes, "a constant supply, one following another in rapid succession, each more irresistible than its predecessor. The fun continued until after midnight, and until the distinguished traveler insisted that his sides were sore from laughing." "The yarns which Lincoln gravely spun out, Van Buren assured the crowd, he never would forget," wrote Herndon. But Van Buren's visit had a transparently ulterior motive—he was lining up support for the Democratic nomination in 1844. This was the start of his revenge tour. And even as Lincoln was regaling him with funny stories he was organizing the Henry Clay for president campaign in the state with Baker and Logan.

The outcome of the main contest of 1842 in Illinois, for governor, twisted and turned on assigning blame for the continuing economic depression, the state deficit, collapse of "the System," the State Bank, and a surprising issue that would soon overwhelm all the others—a new constituency that suddenly held the balance of political power and had emerged as a power unto itself—the Mormons.

CHAPTER NINE

THE PROPHET

Anticipating his campaign against Stephen A. Douglas for the Senate, Lincoln spoke on June 26, 1857, for the first time publicly about Mormonism in order to bait his opponent on his doctrine of "popular sovereignty" as he applied it to "Bleeding Kansas." "If the people of Utah shall peacefully form a State Constitution toler-ating polygamy, will the Democ-racy admit them into the Union?" asked Lincoln.

The founding platform of the Republican Party in 1856 equated Mormonism with slavery, declar-ing "the right and the imperative duty of Congress to prohibit in the Territories those twin relics of barbarism—Polygamy, and Slavery." Polygamy was a form of slavery—slavery of women—and Mormonism was almost univer-sally regarded as a tyrannical and fanatical cult inimical to democ-racy. In Lincoln's hands, Mor-

Joseph Smith as General of the Nauvoo Legion

monism became a cudgel to beat his perennial rival—so beyond decency that it was inarguable. Though he did not mention it then, Lincoln was well aware of Douglas's early and close alliance with the Mormons and his role in their rise—and Douglas knew Lincoln knew it, too. Lincoln, after an initially benign view of the Mormons, accepting at face value their claims of persecution, and hoping to win them for the Whigs, had turned against them. From the Mormons' colonization of Illinois to build their New Jerusalem on the Mississippi through their armed clashes with old settlers that escalated into the Illinois Mormon War of 1844 and 1845, Mormonism dominated Illinois politics, drawing Douglas and Lincoln into a new phase, a little examined chapter of their rivalry that would carry larger lessons for the future.

Joseph Smith, Jr., was the semiliterate son of drifting squatters, moving nineteen times in ten years from his birth in 1805 in Vermont until settling in Palmyra, New York, epicenter of the Second Great Awakening. There, according to a letter signed by sixty-two prominent citizens of Palmyra in 1833: "Joseph Smith, Sr., and his son Joseph were, in particular, considered entirely destitute of moral character, and addicted to vicious habits." These were among the kinder words from those who considered them grifters and confidence men. "Joe was the most ragged, lazy fellow in the place, and that is saying a good deal," recalled Daniel Hendrix, who helped Smith publish the Book of Mormon as its typesetter. "I never knew so ignorant a man as Joe was to have such a fertile imagination." Another resident of Palmyra who knew him well and collected dozens of interviews with townsfolk about him, Pomeroy Tucker, wrote, "From the age of twelve to twenty years he is distinctly remembered as a dull-eyed, flaxen-haired, prevaricating boy—noted only for his indolent and vagabondish character, and his habits of exaggeration and untruthfulness . . . by reason of his extravagancies of statement, his word was received with the least confidence by those who knew him best. He could utter the most palpable exaggeration or marvelous absurdity with the utmost apparent gravity. He nevertheless evidenced the rapid development of a thinking, plodding, evil-brewing mental composition—largely given to inventions of low cunning, schemes of mischief and deception, and false and mysterious pretensions."

Joe Smith briefly joined a Methodist church but dropped out, dismissing the Bible as "a fable." Father and son, according to Tucker, were "unqualified atheists." For years, they plied neighbors with a crystal they carried in a felt hat, declaring it to be a magic or seer stone, claimed to locate buried treasure, cajoling money from the gullible to dig it up "at a dead hour of night," and would invariably announce that the devil had intervened at the last moment to hide it. The Smiths also brandished a divining rod that they said could discover wells for a price. In 1826, a neighbor swore out a complaint against Joe Smith for disorderly conduct as an impostor, tricking people into paying for searches for "hidden treasures," "gold mines," and "lost property." The county court found him guilty, though the punishment went unrecorded.

Within months, Smith announced that he had discovered buried ancient golden plates engraved with hieroglyphics. Soon he said that he had translated them by gazing through thick crystals called the Urim and Thummim, mentioned in the Book of Exodus, which were miraculously recovered in Wayne County, New York, and that an angel had vouchsafed him this new holy document superseding the Bible. Two neighbors insisted on seeing the golden plates that Smith had safely deposited in a wooden chest—"Egad, I'll see the critter alive or dead!" shouted one—and pushing past Smith unwrapped the canvas covering the glorious object only to find a brick.

While farming on land given him by his father-in-law, Smith haltingly dictated the Book of Mormon over two years, the divine revelation later amended more than one thousand times, some of these revised sections likely composed by a zealous Campbellite preacher, Sidney Rigdon, who attached himself to the new religion. Rigdon's authorship or coauthorship has been a constant subject of contention. From nearly the beginning, various witnesses stated that Rigdon had read the manuscript of an early sort of science fiction novel by a Congregationalist minister, Solomon Spalding, and plagiarized its essential elements and mythical characters for the composition of the Book of Mormon. A team of scholars at Stanford University using computer text analysis concluded in 2008 that "multiple" authors had written it, and "we find strong support for the Spalding-Rigdon theory of authorship. In all the data, we find Rigdon as the unifying force." (The chief scribe who recorded Smith's visions, Martin Harris, a serial religious enthusiast and unwavering believer in the power of seer stones, mortgaged his farm to enable publication of the Book of Mormon, and signed testimony as one of three witnesses "that we beheld and saw the plates," yet was later excommunicated by Smith after squealing that Smith "drank too much liquor while translating" the Golden

Bible and for joining the Shakers, though he later wandered to Utah to rejoin the Mormons.)

Putting aside the volume's thousands of pseudo-biblical inflections of "and it came to pass," "thereof," and "therefore"—"chloroform in print," as Mark Twain quipped—it would take an exegesis twice the epic length of the Book of Mormon to untangle its mumbo jumbo, hocus-pocus, and topsy-turvy—a mishmash of plagiarism, anachronism, and contrivance, composed of wholesale quotations as well as distorted and error-filled transposition of parts of the Old Testament and the New, invention of a multitude of imaginary heroes, villains, and prophets with supposedly biblical-sounding names, folklore about the origins of the Indians, Christ's post-resurrection visit to America, laced with anti-Catholic prejudice (the church as "whore"), Jews as Christ killers, and the Deist framers of the Constitution as divinely inspired (like Smith as "translator" of the Book of Mormon), along with a lurid fictionalization in faux biblical tropes of anti-Masonic themes then pulsating through upstate New York politics. At the heart of the narrative is the voyage from the Middle East to America of the dark-skinned, cursed, and evil Lamanites, who in a racial Armageddon nearly exterminated the virtuous white-skinned Nephites. The surviving Lamanites, according to Smith's revelation, became the American Indians, who were also the lost tribes of Israel. Mormon, a Nephite general, last survivor of the final battle with the Lamanites, dictated the whole story to his son Moroni, an angel, who inscribed it on the golden plates hidden in a hill to be dug up centuries later by Joe Smith.

The original version of the book concluded with Smith identifying himself as "Author and Proprietor." Two weeks later, he proclaimed himself "Seer, a Translator, a Prophet, an Apostle of Jesus Christ, and Elder of the Church through the will of God the Father, and the grace of your Lord Jesus Christ." "I considered the whole of it a delusion, and advised them to abandon it," Smith's father-in law, Isaac Hale, stated in a legal affidavit. "The manner in which he pretended to read and interpret was the same as when he looked for the moneydiggers, with the stone in his hat and his hat over his face, while the book of plates was at the same time hid in the woods. . . . I conscientiously believe . . . that the whole Book of Mormon (so-called) is a silly fabrication of falsehood and wickedness, got up for speculation, and with a design to dupe the credulous and unwary."

The Mormon Church, like other pre-millennial sects whose prophecy of the impending end of the world failed to materialize, might have dwindled away had Smith not merged with Rigdon's evangelical colony in Kirtland, Ohio, outside Cleveland, the United Order, based on communist ideals, upon which Smith overlaid with predatory self-aggrandizing enterprises—a unique mixture of collectivism and cronyism. The settlement began a pattern of scandal, apostasy, and political manipulation, breaking out into warfare with the "Gentiles," inevitably depicted by Smith as persecution.

At Kirtland, "the New Jerusalem," Smith staged miraculous faith healings, including supposedly raising the dead, to attract converts, speculated in land (a "Stake in Zion"), and through "revelation" founded a bank that Smith said "would swallow up all the other banks." After the state of Ohio refused a charter to the Kirtland Safety Society Bank, Smith redubbed it the "Anti-Bank," claimed $4 million in nonexisting capital, and issued $200,000 in worthless banknotes, stamped "Anti-Bank" over "Bank." It shuttered during the Panic of 1837, paid none of its obligations, and Smith and Rigdon were arrested for swindling, trailed by angry former followers, but escaped to another New Jerusalem in Independence and then Far West, Missouri, which Smith proclaimed the exact spot Adam and Eve inhabited after leaving the Garden of Eden. In the aftermath of the Ohio debacle, the earliest accusations of polygamy surfaced.

"God is my right-hand man," Smith revealed, staking his claim to the New Zion. He announced he would buy up all the land around his holy cities, displacing the local residents. Unsurprisingly, friction immediately developed with people in the surrounding towns, suspicious of the Mormons' strange rites, including their refusal to own slaves and seeking to evangelize Indians, presumably the lost tribes of Israel that must be converted to Mormonism as precondition of the Second Coming of Christ—in Missouri. The Mormons were also accused of cattle rustling, fraudulent land deals, and counterfeiting, habits transported from Kirtland. Smith organized a militia, the Army of Zion, and an elite band of enforcers and killers, first called the Destructives, then Avenging Angels, then the Sons of Dan, or Danites, after the Book of Daniel. At a large public meeting on July 4, 1838, Rigdon delivered a sermon calling for "a war of extermination" if Mormons were not allowed complete autonomy. "Armed Mormon parties patrolled the country, robbing and plundering the inhabitants; all the plunder being deposited in one place, called 'the Lord's treasury,'" according to Thomas

Ford, the Illinois governor, in his memoir. With Democrats in control of the state, Mormons had been ordered to vote uniformly for the Democrats and after an Election Day melee with Whigs at a county polling station appealed for protection from the incumbent Democratic governor in Missouri, Lilburn Boggs, who replied that they were on their own. Smith announced he would destroy all enemies and march to St. Louis. "If they come on us to molest us, we will establish our religion by the sword," he said. "I will be to this generation a second Mohammed." The state militia, summoned to quell conflict, instead committed a massacre, murdering eighteen Mormons. In response, Mormons burned two towns. Boggs issued an order, echoing Rigdon's sermon, that the Mormons "must be exterminated or driven from the state." About forty Mormon leaders were captured and Smith charged with treason, but in April 1839 he fled across the Mississippi to join the Saints in establishing another New Jerusalem in Illinois.

Seizing on the chance to secure a new voting bloc for the Whigs to counter the Irish that voted almost uniformly for the Democrats, John Todd Stuart made a statement in the Congress decrying the Mormons' persecution in Missouri and welcoming them to Illinois. Henry Clay, looking toward the next presidency election when he might be the candidate, joined in. Smith responded by moving the Mormon votes in 1840 behind Whig candidates for the legislature and for Harrison, and in 1841 for Stuart. "And the leaders of both parties believed that the Mormons would soon hold the balance of power, and exerted themselves on both sides, by professions, and kindness and devotion to their interest, to win their support," wrote Ford. Both parties fell over each other in the legislature supporting the incorporation of the new Mormon city of Nauvoo (the name based on an imaginary Hebrew word for "The Beautiful"), investing Smith with extraordinary, unlimited powers, including the power to raise his own militia called the Nauvoo Legion to which he promoted himself to George Washington's rank of lieutenant-general.

Lincoln joined in the unanimous voice vote in favor of the Nauvoo City Charter and kept track of the Mormons on Stuart's behalf. "Speed says he wrote you what Jo. Smith said about you as he passed here," he wrote him on March 1, 1840. "We will procure the names of some of his people here and send them to you before long." Strangely, Lincoln's name as a Whig presidential elector in 1840 was erased from the ballot in Nauvoo—the only elector in the state whose name was wiped out—replaced with that of Democratic state senator James Ralston, who would run against Stuart the next year. It was a deliberate act. "We desired to show our friendship to the Democratic Party," later wrote Dr. John C. Bennett, the chief log-roller for the Mormons in Springfield and ally of Stephen A. Douglas. Bennett, soon installed as mayor and major general of the Nauvoo Legion, was also the president of Nauvoo University, which had no students but granted honorary degrees to helpful politicians and newspaper editors.

Through the Nauvoo Charter, wrote Ford, Smith established "a government within a government, a legislature with power to pass ordinances at war with the laws of the State; courts to execute them with but little dependence upon the constitutional judiciary; and a military force at their own command, to be governed by its own by-laws and ordinances, and subject to no State authority but that of the Governor. It must be acknowledged that these charters were unheard-of, and anti-republican in many particulars; and capable of infinite abuse by a people disposed to abuse them. The powers conferred were expressed in language at once ambiguous and undefined; as if on purpose to allow of misconstruction." But both parties were tolerant. "Each party was afraid to object to them for fear of losing the Mormon vote, and each believed that it had secured their favor."

With Joseph Smith's endorsement of Stuart, the *Journal* defended the Mormons while the *Register* assailed their partisanship. On January 1, 1841, the *Journal* editorialized against the *Register*: "That paper says, 'Let Mr. Stuart beware that he does not dig a pit for himself to fall into.' Is Mr. Stuart to dig a pit for himself by doing a simple act of justice to a portion of his constituents?"

Douglas, now a judge on the state Supreme Court, wooed the Mormons for the Democrats, making a pilgrimage in May 1841 to Nauvoo, where he delivered a flattering speech, followed by his ruling that the Nauvoo Legion was not subject to the state militia, and then appointing Nauvoo mayor Bennett master-in-chancery for Hancock County. "Judge Douglas," Smith wrote in a statement, "has ever proved himself friendly to this people; and interested himself to obtain for us our several charters."

For more than a year, Governor Thomas Carlin, a Democrat, refused to act on Missouri's extradition order for Smith, but when Smith would not withdraw his support for Stuart's reelection Carlin had him arrested. The *Journal* accused Carlin of "a concerted movement with the *Register* and its friends to get up another Mormon war, in order to make political capital." And the *Register* returned the fire: "The intention of the *Journal* is obvious. It is attempting to induce the Mormons in a body to vote for John T. Stuart, regardless of the public good, which demands that no religious sect should become a political faction." Douglas claimed authority over the case, ruling on June 10 that the extradition order was invalid and freeing Smith. Behind the scenes Douglas used his influence to equip the Nauvoo Legion with arms from state arsenals.

On December 20, 1841, Smith issued a proclamation: "Douglas is a *Master Spirit,* and *his friends are our friends,*" exhorting support for Douglas's handpicked candidate for governor, nominated just weeks before, state senator Adam W. Snyder, chairman of the Judiciary Committee that had approved the Nauvoo Charter. "Such men we love. . . . They have served us and we will serve them," Smith proclaimed. Double-crossed, despite having placated Smith, the Whigs turned on him. The Whig candidate Joseph Duncan made the Mormon issue paramount in the campaign, accusing Douglas of "having corruptly sustained" Smith, while the *Journal* conjectured that Douglas would soon be baptized a Mormon, "go into the water with Joe Smith before the election." The *Register* replied, "Every man has a right to worship God as he pleases."

The Democrats were almost completely unified in defending the Mormons with the notable exception of the Methodist preacher and Democratic politico Peter Cartwright, who had a stormy meeting with Smith. "I found him," he wrote, "to be a very illiterate and impudent desperado in morals, but, at the same time, he had a vast fund of low cunning." When Smith invited him to visit Nauvoo to witness faith healing, speaking in tongues, and physical immunity to poisons, Cartwright told him of an old Mormon woman who tried to take over one of his revivals by speaking in tongues, and that he had exposed her ruse and threatened her and any other Mormon with "Lynch's law." "I will show you, sir," replied Smith, "that I will raise up a government in these United States which will overturn the present government, and I will raise up a new religion that will overturn every other form of religion in this country!" To which Cartwright cited "my Bible": "The bloody and deceitful man shall not live out half his days."

The Mormon factor grew in divisiveness directly in proportion to the exploding population of Nauvoo, almost overnight becoming one of the largest towns in the state. Mormon missionaries were shipping thousands of converts recruited from the slums of England to the Promised Land, often after entrancing them with staged miracles, especially raising the dead. Nearly all the immigrants were poverty stricken, illiterate, and had their passage paid by the Mormon agency headquartered in Liverpool. Once they arrived, they turned over their meager personal possessions to the Prophet as "consecration" to the Lord, labored to purchase houses and land from him (Smith was the head of the Land Office), purchased goods at the general store (owned by Smith), and "devotedly attached to the Prophet's will, and obey his dictates as they would those of God himself . . . they consequently go blindly to the polls, and cast their ballots for whoever is in favor with Joe Smith, and has the expressed approbation of that holy personage," according to John C. Bennett. The young women became prey for Smith and his inner circle.

Smith reigned as an autocrat giving bombastic orders for Nauvoo's religious, political, and economic life. The "old citizens" of Hancock County not only resented losing total control to an eccentric despot but were also angered that the holy city had become a teeming clearinghouse of crime. Fugitives from justice, thieves, and smugglers on the Mississippi discovered, especially if they converted, that the local court protected residents from outside arrest warrants. Once stolen non-Mormon property disappeared into Nauvoo there was no chance it would emerge again.

After Smith hailed Douglas as the "master spirit," Duncan criticized his emergence as a dictator. "All extraordinary, anti-republican, and arbitrary powers, which the corruption of a legislature granted them solely for the purpose of obtaining their political support, he unhesitatingly proclaimed he was for taking from them," Duncan said in a speech, adding that Smith was attempting to create "an established religion by legal enactment . . . an arbitrary and monarchial form of government." The Whig candidate for lieutenant governor, William Henderson, weighed in with an attack on "religious fanatics . . . all of whom believe that this republican government must, and will be destroyed, and be succeeded by a new government, the principles of which are set forth in the Mormon bible." But the *Register* mocked Duncan in an editorial headlined "A House Divided Against Itself," and pointed out that Henderson had voted in the legislature for the Nauvoo Charter: "Such a house cannot stand."

On May 4, 1842, former governor Boggs of Missouri was shot three times in the head while sitting in his house and barely survived. "Boggs is undoubtedly killed according to report," stated Smith's newspaper, the *Nauvoo Wasp*, "but who did the noble deed remains to be found out." While Smith's organ hailed the murder, he protested that his heart was pure and hands clean. Several witnesses later claimed that Smith had sought Boggs's death and had commissioned Smith's zealous bodyguard, O. Porter Rockwell, to kill him. The most reliable of them, William Law, second counselor to Smith, "a man of integrity," according to Smith's biographer Fawn M. Brodie, later signed an affidavit stating, "Joseph told me that he sent a man to kill Governor Boggs of Missouri. The fellow shot the Governor in his own house, shot him through a window, wounding him severely, but failed to kill him." The state of Missouri issued an arrest warrant for Smith and Rockwell, who had mysteriously been in Missouri during the attempted assassination and probably committed dozens of murders later as a Mormon enforcer. One reliable Mormon witness later stated that Rockwell had told him: "I shot through the window and thought I had killed him, but I had only wounded him; I was damned sorry that I had not killed the son of a bitch!"

The day after the assassination attempt Douglas stood next to Smith, attired in his military uniform with gold braid, before an assembly of the entire population of Nauvoo as the Nauvoo Legion marched in review. Douglas's candidate for governor, Adam W. Snyder, suddenly died a week later, a fortuitous tragedy. From around the state Democrats crowded into the *Register*'s office to nominate Thomas Ford, a state Supreme Court judge without any public record of supporting the Mormons, while Douglas still promised Smith his interests would be protected.

But the Mormon issue could not be neatly contained. Within the sacred precincts of Nauvoo, the Prophet and the mayor vied for the sexual favors of nineteen-year-old Nancy, the daughter of the stern Sidney Rigdon. For years, Smith and a number of his closest counselors had been secretly practicing polygamy, or what he called "spiritual wifery," or "celestial marriage." By this time, he had been "sealed" in eternity with sixteen wives, eight already married; within two years, he would have at least forty-nine wives. The polygamy practice had threatened to become public weeks before when Smith tried to coerce an eighteen-year-old girl named Martha Brotherton, an English immigrant, into submission as one of the "spiritual wives" of Brigham Young, one of Smith's earliest recruits and a member of his inner Quorum of the Twelve Apostles, by insisting it was a "revelation from God." She and her parents fled from the colony to St. Louis and soon her account was published in a newspaper there.

Major General Bennett, the president of the Nauvoo University without any students, meanwhile, had been seducing young women without the benefit of Smith's benediction of "spiritual wifery." He also served Smith as his personal abortionist to dispense with "the celestial consequences" of his plural wives, according to the eyewitness testimony of Sarah Pratt, wife of Orson Pratt, one of the original Mormon apostles who practiced polygamy himself. (Sarah Pratt had resisted Smith's demand that she become one of his "spiritual wives.")

Smith's next target was Nancy Rigdon, also an object of Bennett's unrequited affection, offering, Bennett said, $500 and prime real estate for procuring her for his harem. Instead, Bennett warned her of the impending charm offensive. Smith cornered her alone, she threatened to scream, and he retreated to write her a letter justifying polygamy, comparing himself to King Solomon, which she showed to her father. A shocked Sidney Rigdon, excluded from the inner circle of "spiritual wifery," confronted Smith, who explained he was testing Nancy's purity. It was the beginning of Rigdon's personal disenchantment with the Prophet.

Smith collected statements about Bennett's promiscuous affairs with which he was already intimately familiar in order to blame him for any scandal. After vowing before the city council that Smith had never given him "authority to hold illicit intercourse with women," Bennett hoped he could return to good grace. But Smith decided he needed the scapegoat and excommunicated Bennett on June 23.

"EXTRA. The Mormon Plot and League" screamed the headline across the front page of the *Sangamo Journal* on July 8, running above a story exposing "the Mormon seraglio" and "the pollutions and corruptions and enormities of Joe Smith." Its source was expellee John C. Bennett, who provided startling details of the sex cult: the three orders of "Mormon ladies of pleasure" available to Mormon leaders—Cyprian, Chambered, and Cloistered Saints—and the "amours and attempted seductions" of Smith, "Prince of the Seraglio" and "Lord of the Harem."

The *Register* cast the exposé as nothing but a Whig plot, reporting that Bennett had been spotted beforehand in Springfield. "He was seen in conversation with several of the leaders of the Junto, who made arrangements with him to make sundry awful disclosures about the Mormons." It was likely that among those Junto leaders was Lincoln. He was initially disappointed about the muted reaction to the *Journal*'s story. "Bennett's Mormon disclosures are making some little stir here, but not very great," Lincoln wrote a few days after publication, on July 14, to his friend Samuel D. Marshall, publisher of the *Illinois Republican*, a Whig newspaper in Shawneetown, and justice of the peace, who was notarizing Bennett's affidavits against Smith. The language of Lincoln's letter was echoed the next day in the *Journal*. "We cannot say that *all* have partaken of the indignation which these disclosures should have produced," it editorialized, lambasting Democrats for decrying Bennett and sustaining Smith, and slamming the *Register* as "the faithful mirror of their sentiments and wishes." But Lincoln's frustration that the *Journal* story wasn't getting picked up was premature. It swiftly turned into a national sensation, the biggest story in the *Journal*'s history. Not only would Whig newspapers across Illinois reprint it—the *Peoria Register* published it as a pamphlet—but it would be widely serialized by major papers across the country. "The whole thing," the *New York Herald* declared on July 24, "is full of philosophy, fun, roguery, religion, truth, falsehood, fanaticism, and philosophy. Read the following extracts, put your trust in the Lord, and learn how to restrain your passions."

After Bennett's exposure, Lincoln's enemy and Douglas's ally James Adams, the target of Lincoln's anonymous "Sampson's Ghost" articles and lawsuit, stepped forward to replace Bennett as Smith's lobbyist and defender in Springfield. Adams had met Smith in Springfield upon his arrival there in November 1839. According to Smith, Adams "sought me out, took me home with him, and treated me like a father." Adams was soon baptized a Mormon and placed at the head of the Springfield branch of the church. Smith anointed him a High Priest and Patriarch, while Adams, the Deputy Grand Master of the Masonic Grand Lodge of Illinois, established a Masonic lodge at Nauvoo and installed Smith as its chief, despite the Book of Mormon's condemnation of Masons as an evil secret society. Smith adopted Masonic symbols for the Mormons as well as special clothes and passwords. Then he staged an "endowment ceremony," playing the role of God casting out Adam and Eve from the Garden of Eden, concluding with bestowal of secret names for initiates by which they would be known in heaven. The ceremony at the Nauvoo Masonic House became the basis for Mormon temple rites. It was about this time that Smith also began another basic Mormon ritual—baptizing the dead, granting Mormons the power over all past humankind to release the tortured souls to Mormon nirvana. "Smith was a poor judge of character who repeatedly surrounded himself with fawners, by whom he was easily influenced and who often ended up his enemies," wrote the historian Kent L. Walgren. "The Nauvoo introduction of Freemasonry, which flew in the face of clear Book of Mormon proscription of secret societies, illustrates the extremes to which Smith could be swayed." His induction into the Masonic order was entangled with his sexual affairs. High Priest Adams would, in 1843, conduct the ceremony marrying two young sisters at the same time to Smith, who returned the favor by sealing Adams to his first plural wife. Soon afterward, Adams died of cholera.

There was a further Adams wrinkle in the plot: the witness in Adams's defense against Lincoln's lawsuit, a Democratic mainstay and Douglas friend, James W. Keys, Springfield's postmaster and director of the State Bank, arranged, after Lincoln dropped his suit in March 1841, for Stephen T. Logan, his partner, to be fired as the bank's attorney, a loss of a well-paying client. Logan's replacement was a double insult to Lincoln—Jesse Thomas, whom Lincoln had humiliated in his famous "skinning."

Lincoln, the virtual coeditor of the *Journal*, for which he had written hundreds of articles, was never closer to Simeon Francis, its editor, than during the summer of 1842. It was then that the childless Francis and his wife played matchmaker for Lincoln and Mary Todd, bringing them secretly together at their house to rekindle the romance. At the same time, Lincoln was paying close attention to the gubernatorial race and the *Journal*'s coverage, likely contributing to it as he usually did.

The Bennett scoop seemed to be vindication for the Junto and the *Journal*, which had been on the attack against the Mormons since Smith had tilted to the Democrats after his pronouncement of Douglas as the "master spirit." Months before the exposé, on January 21, the *Journal* had published an anonymous article that was a parable of the Mormon betrayal of the Whigs written in what appears to be Lincoln's inimitable style. "A countryman, upon a cold winter day saw an asp, a very poisonous snake, lying torpid with cold, by the road side, and in the simple kindness of his heart, he lifted it up and took it home—where he laid it before the fire to recover; and with his wife and children kindly rejoiced in seeing life returning to the snake. After the heat had sufficiently acted upon the asp, it raised its head, and instead of thanks to its benefactor, began hissing and curling itself up preparatory to a deadly attack upon the former; who, seeing its *intent and aim, destroyed it!*"

The possible author of that passage spoke eighteen years later during his 1860 campaign repeatedly using the same metaphor about a snake:

> If the Republicans, who think slavery is wrong, get possession of the general government, we may not root out the evil at once, but may at least prevent its extension. If I find a venomous snake lying on the open prairie, I seize the first stick and kill him at once. But if that snake is in bed with my children, I must be more cautious. I shall, in striking the snake, also strike the children, or arouse the reptile to bite the children. Slavery is the venomous snake in bed with the children. But if the question is whether to kill it on the prairie or put it in bed with other children, I think we'd kill it!

On July 29, the *Journal* assailed Adams, "long known as a political Mormon," for being "busy with the editors of the *Register* and other leading Ford men in this city" in planting stories in the *Register* and the *Nauvoo Wasp* claiming that the Bennett exposé was a "Whig plot." The *Journal* poured ridicule on Douglas: "Judge Douglas is not expected to appoint a successor to his esteemed friend, Gen. Bennett, as Master in Chancery of Hancock Co. until after the election."

Despite the scandal Duncan lost the election to Ford by a decisive margin. (The vote in Nauvoo went 1,037 for Ford, six for Duncan.) And the *Register* mockingly reported that when Lincoln learned of the result, "The tears fairly came into Lincoln's eyes when the news arrived." "We are again beaten in Illinois," the *Journal* mourned, "not so much for want of numbers, as from local divisions and apathy on the part of the Whigs." The paper blamed Tyler and the Mormons, comparing them to a biblical plague, but anticipated victory for Whigs in 1844: "The treachery of John Tyler, has temporarily scattered and disorganized our forces; but with Henry Clay for their leader, they will soon rally in sufficient strength to bid defiance to Joe Smith's Loco Foco Legion that are now in possession of the land, and devouring its substance like a hungry swarm of Egyptian locusts."

Immediately after the Democrats won the governor's race, Bennett provided evidence to the Missouri authorities about Smith's alleged involvement in the Boggs assassination attempt and sheriffs arrived in Nauvoo on August 8 to arrest him. The Nauvoo city council passed a bill that the Nauvoo court had supremacy over all warrants. Smith disappeared into hiding for four months. Thomas Ford, the new governor, announced he believed the warrant was illegal, so Smith was persuaded to submit to a trial. He marched into Springfield at the head of forty uniformed soldiers of the Nauvoo Legion carrying rifles mounted with gleaming bayonets. James Adams posted his bail and he stayed at Adams's house. On New Year's Eve, Smith attended a grand ball, "a splendid blow-out," at the American House given by U.S. senator Sidney Breese to celebrate his election, narrowly won over Douglas, with whom he likely made a deal to back for the Senate next time, in 1846. Douglas, reported a correspondent on the scene for the *New York Herald*, "took an active part in the dancing," while another guest, Lincoln, undoubtedly did not dance but told stories to a cluster of politicians and friends.

Smith hired an accomplished Whig attorney, Justin Butterfield, to argue his case. The presiding judge was Nathaniel Pope, who had been the original territorial secretary of Illinois and cousin of Ninian Edwards, instrumental in having him named the first territorial governor through the influence of Pope's brother, a U.S. senator from Kentucky. Pope had originally drawn the boundaries of the state to include Chicago and was an important ally of Governor Edward Coles in thwarting the introduction of slavery into Illinois at the 1824 constitutional convention. (Pope's son, John, would become a general in the Civil War, a Lincoln favorite, a Radical Republican rival of George McClellan, who was defeated at the Second Battle of Bull Run.) Smith spent the evening before the hearing at Adams's house dining with Douglas. Judge Pope flanked himself on the bench with a half dozen fashionable Springfield ladies, his own lighthearted mockery of Smith's polygamy—"all anxious to see the man of a plurality of wives," according to attorney Gustave Koerner, a Douglas ally who would later become a Lincoln friend. (Next to him Pope sat the two months pregnant Mary Todd Lincoln.) Butterfield opened his remarks saying, "Here on his right was the prophet, to be tried by the pope, surrounded by a chorus of angels." On January 5, 1843, Pope ruled the writ invalid and discharged Smith.

"Smith was too ignorant of law to know whether he owed his discharge to the law, or to the favor of the court and the Whig party," wrote Thomas

Ford. "Such was the ignorance and stupidity of the Mormons generally, that they deemed anything to be law which they judged to be expedient." Euphoric after his release, Smith announced that the laws of Illinois were subject to his rule of Nauvoo. "We stand in the same relation to the state as the state does to the union," he declared on February 25. "Shall we be such fools as to be governed by its laws, which are unconstitutional?" Outdoing Calhoun, he was promulgating a doctrine of municipal nullification—holy city rights above state rights.

On May 18, Smith hosted Douglas for a dinner at which the judge, currying favor, "spoke warmly in depreciation of Governor Boggs and the authorities in Missouri," according to one of the Mormon apostles present. Smith then entranced his guests with a series of divinely inspired prophesies: the U.S. government would be "utterly overthrown and wasted" unless officials in Missouri were punished for their crimes, and Douglas would seek the presidency but would achieve it only on the sufferance of "the saints." "Judge," Smith intoned gravely, "you will aspire to the presidency of the United States; and if ever you turn your hand against me or the Latter-day Saints, you will feel the weight of the hand of Almighty upon you; and you will live to see and know that I have testified the truth to you; for the conversation of this day will stick to you through life." Douglas "appeared very friendly, and acknowledged the truth and propriety of President Smith's remarks." (In 1981, Ezra Taft Benson, president of the Mormon Quorum of the Twelve Apostles, and former secretary of agriculture under President Dwight Eisenhower, published an article, "Joseph Smith: Prophet to Our Generation," citing Smith's warning to Douglas, noting that Douglas in 1857 "viciously attacked the Church as 'a loathsome, disgusting ulcer in the body politic,'" and then lost the presidency to "an obscure backwoodsman," and "died a broken man in the prime of life." The officially sanctioned history of the Mormons stated, "The prediction concerning Stephen A. Douglas . . . is one of the most remarkable prophecies either in ancient or modern times.")

Seeking revenge, John C. Bennett crossed into Missouri to meet with Boggs, still nursing his wounds. It took very little persuasion to secure a new extradition order from Missouri governor Thomas Reynolds to try the Prophet for treason and assassination and to which Governor Ford was compelled to issue a warrant. Disguised as Mormon elders, a Missouri posse captured Smith in Dixon, Illinois, where he was evangelizing. But units of the Nauvoo Legion dashed to his rescue. Cyrus Walker, a prominent lawyer and the Whig candidate for the Congress from that district, whose previous attempt to gain Smith's support had been rebuffed at Nauvoo, immediately offered his services for a $10,000 fee and political endorsement. "I am now sure of my election," he said, "as Joseph Smith has promised me his vote, and I am going to defend him." After consulting with Walker, Smith decided not to bring his case before the court in Quincy, where Douglas was waiting to preside, but to return to the sanctuary of Nauvoo. By that detour the Whig candidate cut out the Democratic chieftain who had been his protector.

Smith's grand entrance was greeted with the firing of guns and cannon and a band playing "Hail, Columbia!" Walker's Democratic opponent, Joseph P. Hoge, rushed to the Nauvoo courthouse to second Walker's argument that the city had the authority to override a state warrant. At once, Smith's court ruled in Smith's favor. "All the power there was in Illinois she gave to Nauvoo; and any man that says to the contrary is a fool," Smith declared on June 30. Pointing to Walker, he said, "I have converted this candidate for Congress that the right of habeas corpus is included in our charter. If he continues converted, I will vote for him." "Thus," wrote Ford, "the Mormons were deluded and deceived by men who ought to have known and did know better."

Smith's grandiosity led him into temptation. His original wife Emma was increasingly moody about his growing collection of multiple spouses. "If you will write the revelation on celestial marriage," offered his brother Hyrum, "I will take and read it to Emma, and I believe I can convince her of its truth, and you will hereafter have peace." "You do not know Emma as well as I do," Smith replied, feeling henpecked over the small matter of polygamy. Nonetheless, he wrote out his revelation, and his brother showed it to Emma, who was unsurprisingly infuriated and threatened to leave him. Never, she made clear, would she acknowledge her husband's other wives. As she put her foot down he announced a lightning bolt from heaven had struck. On August 12, 1843, the Prophet disclosed to his High Council his "Revelation on Celestial Marriage": "Verily, thus saith the Lord unto you, my servant Joseph, that inasmuch as you have enquired of my hand, to know and understand wherein I, the Lord, justified my servants Abraham, Isaac and Jacob; as also Moses, David and Solomon, my servants, as touching the principle and doctrine of their having many wives and concubines." The provisions of this inspiration entitled "any man," if he were to "have ten virgins given unto him by this law," for example, "he cannot commit adultery, for they belong to him, and they are given unto him, therefore is he justified." Section 24 was devoted solely to Emma Smith, "to abide and cleave unto my servant Joseph, and to none else. But if she will not abide this commandment, she shall be destroyed, saith the Lord." Thus, polygamy became a Mormon sacred sacrament carried into the eternal life. "Then shall they be gods, because they have all power, and the angels are subject unto them." And Emma should shut up.

More than any other of Smith's acts, this revelation crystallized the antagonism of the general population to Mormonism as a cult of perversity, vice, and crime, especially in the neighboring country around its citadel. Smith's designs were viewed as more than a moral disgrace, but an imminent political danger, "an intolerable tyranny which he had established over his people," according to Ford. "But the great cause of popular fury was, that the Mormons at several preceding elections, had cast their vote as a unit." Worse than swindling, counterfeiting, shielding thieves, and polygamy was Smith's political dictatorship.

"I will make war," Smith pledged, if he were pursued. Governor Ford dithered. Instead of calling out the militia, he let the illegal Nauvoo order overriding the state warrant stand. The *Register* published a lengthy article in July claiming the events surrounding Smith's latest discharge were "a Whig conspiracy" to defeat Democratic congressional candidates—Bennett "a mere tool in the hands of the Whig junto at Springfield" and "a great pet of both the *Journal* and the junto," Lincoln and his friends. Governor Ford, editorialized the *Register*, was forced to issue a writ "so as to incense the Mormons, create a necessity for Walker's and perhaps Browning's professional services in favor of Smith, to get him delivered out of a net of their own weaving, and thereby get the everlasting gratitude of the Mormons and their support for the Whig cause." This editorial revealed Douglas's nervousness about the Mormons' political support. He had quit the Supreme Court to run for a congressional seat in a new district against Orville Browning, a Whig lawyer who was one of Lincoln's friends.

In a ploy to trump Smith's endorsement of Walker, the Democrats in Hancock County sent an agent to Springfield, Jacob B. Backenstos, whom Douglas had installed as a circuit court judge in Carthage, the town adjacent to Nauvoo, to serve as a political emissary to the Mormons. (Backenstos's brother was also married to Smith's niece.) On his return, Backenstos falsely stated that Ford had promised he would not call out troops against Nauvoo if the Mormons voted for the Democrat, Joe Hoge. Ford, in fact, happened not to be in Springfield, but in St. Louis. Hyrum Smith, who had earlier pledged a straight Mormon vote for the Democrats in exchange for a seat in the legislature, announced after Backenstos's Springfield mission that he had a divine revelation to switch to Hoge. On the eve of the election, Joseph Smith spoke: "Brother Hyrum tells me this morning that he has had a testimony to the effect it would be better for the people to vote for Hoge; and I never knew Hyrum to say he ever had a revelation and it failed. . . . When the Lord speaks, let all the earth be silent."

Verily, Hoge received more than two thousand Mormon votes cast as a bloc, winning by 455. Douglas, in the neighboring district, barely won, with Mormons voting overwhelmingly for the Whig on the basis of the old revelation, news of the new one failing to reach them by Election Day. Now triple-crossed, Whigs were enraged. "From this time forth," wrote Ford, "the Whigs generally, and a part of the Democrats, determined upon driving the Mormons out of the State; and everything connected with the Mormons became political, and was considered almost entirely with reference to party."

Smith's grandiosity rapidly rose to stratospheric heights. In December 1843 he petitioned the Congress to declare Nauvoo an independent territory and its mayor, himself, empowered to command the U.S. army. He prophesied "by virtue of the holy Priesthood vested in me, and in the name of the Lord Jesus Christ, that, if Congress will not hear our petition and grant us protection, they shall be broken up as a government and God shall damn them, and there shall be nothing left of them—not even a grease spot!" Secretly, he formed a Council of Fifty "princes" to crown him as King of his own Kingdom of God.

Having pitted the Democrats and the Whigs against each other in Illinois, he vaulted onto the national stage to play the game there. He began the year 1844 announcing, "My feelings revolt at the idea of having anything to do with politics." But on April 4 he declared his candidacy for the presidency. "It is now time to have a President of the United States," announced Brigham Young, president of the Quorum. "Elders will be sent to preach the Gospel and electioneer. The government belongs to God. No man can draw the dividing line between the government of God and the government of the children of men." "Damn the system of splitting up the nation into opposite belligerent parties," cursed Hyrum Smith. The Prophet proclaimed that he would campaign to acknowledge God as "lawgiver," establishing a "Theo-democracy" that would "conduct the affairs of men in righteousness." Joe Smith would dismiss most members of the Congress as no longer necessary, release all prisoners, and annex Texas. Then, he said, "I would liberate the slaves in two or three states, indemnifying their owners, and send the negroes to Texas, and from Texas to Mexico, where all colors are alike. And if that was not sufficient, I would call upon Canada, and annex it."

Seized by Texas fever, Smith's Council of Fifty sent a "minister to Texas" to negotiate with the Mexicans to secure most of it for the Mormons. Then Smith petitioned the Congress on April 26 for the authority to raise an army of 100,000 men under his command "to extend the arm of deliverance to Texas" and "to supersede the necessity of a standing army." Anyone interfer-ing with him would be fined and sentenced to hard labor. That day, Smith's agent in Washington, Orson Hyde, wrote him that he had "a long conver-sation" with Congressman Douglas in which he said "he would resign his seat in Congress if he could command the force" that Smith requested and "would be on the march to the country in a month," shades of Aaron Burr. (Hyde was an apostle, who, after a bout of apostasy, had returned to good grace, his wife "sealed" to Smith as one of his celestial marriages.)

Preparing for his presidential campaign, Smith plotted a purge. He in-tended to eliminate any murmur of dissent. In an address to the Nauvoo police on December 29, 1843, he warned against "traitors" and "assassins," comparing himself to Caesar and Christ. "If I can escape from the ungrate-ful treachery of assassins, I can live as Caesar might have lived, were it not for a right-hand Brutus. I have had pretended friends betray me . . . and we *have a Judas in our midst.*"

William Law, second counselor, upright and enterprising, was a well-to-do Canadian convert, the most capable businessman in Nauvoo, its chief builder and industrialist, real estate developer, constructing houses and stores, lumber supplier, and mill owner. His brother, Wilson Law, was his partner and a major general of the Nauvoo Legion. But Smith ordered Law to invest in his hotel, the Nauvoo House, declared his own monopoly over real estate, and expropriated the funds raised through missions as his personal treasury. While Law paid wages in dollars, Smith offered barter and worthless scrip, and when the workers protested he attacked Law for undermining the church "for personal interest and aggrandizement." When Hyrum Smith received his revelation to vote for the Democrat Hoge for Congress, Law raised an objection. The Prophet retaliated by claiming Law's wife, Jane, as one of his plural spiritual wives, the ultimate property grab.

Law confronted him, demanding that he renounce polygamy, which Smith angrily refused to acknowledge. "I'll be damned before I do!" Demanding a public investigation of Smith's corruption and debauchery, Law gained adherents from other Nauvoo businessmen whose wives Smith had attempted to seduce and whose businesses he threatened to ruin. On April 20, Smith excommunicated Law, his brother, and their small band of dissidents. Law went to the nearby town of Carthage to testify before a grand jury, which issued an indictment of Smith for polygamy. The others also filed suits against him for defamation. Smith launched a manic defense, assembling the faithful in the Nauvoo town square to hear his sermon on May 16 declaring himself greater than Jesus. "I glory in persecution," he said. ". . . Come on! ye prosecutors! ye false swearers! All hell, boil over! Ye burning mountains, roll down your lava! for I will come out on the top at last. I have more to boast of than ever any man had. I am the only man that has been able to keep a whole church together since the days of Adam. . . . Neither Paul, John, Peter, nor Jesus ever did it. I boast that no man ever did such a work as I. The followers of Jesus ran away from Him; but the Latter-day Saints never ran away from me yet."

"The Truth, the whole Truth, and nothing but the Truth" read the motto of the *Nauvoo Expositor*, the newspaper published on June 7 by Law and his "seceders." It proclaimed its intention to "explode the vicious principles of Joseph Smith" and expose "whoredoms and all manner of abominations are practiced under the cloak of religion." The *Expositor*'s lead article detailed Smith's method of wooing a procession of poor immigrant girls, thinking they were to receive a "blessing" as they were led to a room marked "Positively NO Admittance," where he would force himself on them. "She is thunder-struck, faints recovers, and refuses. The Prophet damns her if she rejects." Law's description of the exploitation of these young immigrant women's sordid experience, enticed into sexual slavery, was an early account of human trafficking. (John Hay, then a boy living in Warsaw, whose father was the doctor for its militia, and of course later Lincoln's personal secretary in the White House, wrote, "the flocks were sheep, but the keepers were wolves. This doctrine of spiritual wives was the result, not the cause, of the lewd lives of Smith, Young, and their fellow-blackguards.")

As proof, the *Expositor* printed the affidavits of Law and the other heretics of their firsthand knowledge of Smith's "doctrine of a plurality of wives." Then it listed fifteen resolutions condemning Smith, from his financial swindling ("humbug practiced upon the saints") to his political ambitions. "We do not believe that God ever raised up a Prophet to Christianize a world by political schemes and intrigue." Finally the editors declared: "That we disapprobate and discountenance every attempt to unite church and state; and that we further believe the effort now being made by Joseph Smith for political power and influence, is not commendable in the sight of God."

Smith summoned an emergency meeting of the city council, which he conducted as an inquisitorial star chamber. Without evidence, Law was accused of plotting murder and the others charged with a host of crimes, including counterfeiting. "Is it not treasonable against all chartered rights and privileges, and against the peace and happiness of the city?" Smith asked. Hyrum moved that the paper be branded "a nuisance" and "destroyed." The vote was unanimous. That night, the Nauvoo Legion dragged the *Expositor* press into the street, demolished it with sledgehammers, and set it on fire.

The *Expositor*'s editors fled to the nearby towns of Carthage and Warsaw, securing a warrant for Smith's arrest for riot. The day after smashing the press, Smith poured out his wrath on those who "were not willing to wade knee-deep in blood to do his bidding," reported the *Signal*, the Warsaw newspaper, which detailed the destruction of the *Expositor* and added that Hyrum promised legal immunity to anyone who might silence the *Signal*'s editor and called for breaking its press "with a sledgehammer." "CITIZENS ARISE, ONE and ALL!!!" was emblazoned across the *Signal*. "Can you stand by, and suffer such INFERNAL DEVILS! to ROB men of their property and RIGHTS, without avenging them? We have no time for comment: every man will make his own. LET IT BE made with POWDER AND BALL!!!" The frenzied townspeople throughout the county were of one mind: Smith was about to impose a political dictatorship abolishing the separation of church and state. "Public meetings were held in every precinct. Volunteer companies sprang up everywhere at the tap of a drum. There was drilling on every common, and hoarse eloquence in all the schoolhouses," wrote John Hay.

Judge Jesse Thomas, Douglas's ally and Lincoln's enemy, immediately traveled to Nauvoo, discreetly advising Smith to have the case fixed in the Nauvoo city court, which would "cut off all legal pretext," and Thomas would then "be bound to order them to keep the peace." On June 17, the Nauvoo court discharged Smith. But officials in Carthage demanded that the governor arrest him. Ford came to the scene to discover it an armed camp, interviewed Law and his apostates, ordered the disbanding of the Nauvoo Legion, and called upon Smith to submit to arrest. Through his own sources, Ford was convinced of Smith's abuse of the municipal court that "frequently discharged individuals accused of high crimes and offences against the laws of the state," and that he had sent his Danites "to Missouri, to kidnap two men, who were witnesses against a member of his church, then in jail, and about to be tried on a charge of larceny."

Smith's council denounced the *Signal*'s report as slander and his own newspaper justified wrecking the *Expositor* as necessary to save Nauvoo, claiming that "when the paper came, the course and the plan to destroy the city was marked out." Smith now declared martial law. On June 18, he appeared in his full-dress uniform before the Legion, raising his sword to heaven. "I call God and angels to witness that I have unsheathed my sword with a firm and unalterable determination that this people shall have their legal rights, and be protected from mob violence, or my blood shall be spilt upon the ground like water, and my body consigned to the silent tomb." He summoned his friends and cursed his enemies. "I call upon all friends of truth and liberty to come to our assistance; and may the thunders of the Almighty and the forked lightnings of heaven and pestilence, and war and bloodshed come down on those ungodly." After depicting himself as the martyr for "our liberties," he fled at night to Iowa, but returned in response to Ford's promise of a fair trial, his counselors' fear that Nauvoo would be destroyed if he did not, and his wife Emma's plea.

In the jail at Carthage, Ford tried to reason with him, explaining the importance of a free press and why the destruction of the *Expositor* had antagonized people. "The press in the United States is looked upon as the great bulwark of American freedom," he said, "and its destruction in Nauvoo was represented and looked upon as a high-handed measure, and manifests to the people a disposition on your part to suppress the liberty of speech and of the press." But Smith insisted that he was the victim. He held forth on "the persecutions that I have endured," "every conceivable indignity and lawless outrage perpetrated upon me," that charging him was "contrary to law," and damned the editors of the *Expositor*, "that infamous and filthy sheet," as "a set of worthless vagabonds," and their accusations as "base rumors." When Ford told him he would travel to Nauvoo to calm the Mormons, Smith asked to join him. Despite promising to bring him along, Ford left without him, believing his authority guaranteed Smith's safety.

But on the night of June 27, members of the local militia company assigned to guard Smith stormed the jail, killing his brother, and after Smith fired two pistols shot him dead as he jumped out the window.

In a struggle for power an imperious Brigham Young seized control of the Saints at a meeting of the council, comparing his rival Sidney Rigdon to the renegade William Law. Young spoke "with the voice of the Prophet Joseph," considered the voice of God, according to one of the apostles. The alleged murderers of Smith, including the editor of the *Warsaw Signal* and the state senator, were tried but acquitted by a local jury. In 1845, the Mormons elected as Hancock County sheriff their trusted agent Jacob B. Backenstos, who organized the remnant of the Nauvoo Legion into a posse and rode into Carthage, asserting his authority in a little coup d'état. Open warfare broke out: house burnings, lootings, ambushes, and murders. Ford sent in the state militia under the command of General John J. Hardin, routing Backenstos's force. Then the governor dispatched Douglas to join Hardin in negotiating the Mormons' evacuation to the Rocky Mountains under a general amnesty. "They had now become convinced," Ford wrote, "that the kind of Mahometanism which they sought to establish could never be established in the near vicinity of a people whose morals and prejudices were all outraged and shocked by it, unless indeed they were prepared to establish it by force of arms." That winter, Brigham Young began the exodus to the Valley of the Great Salt Lake—and, John Hay wrote, "there was not in all the slavish East a despot more absolute than he when at last he started, with his wives and his servants and his cattle, to lead his people into the vast tolerant wilderness."

Smith had dominated and distracted Illinois politics for about half the decade, swaying many of the most powerful politicians to do his bidding, putting any number from both parties on his payroll, while he created an enclave where his ecclesiastical authority reigned supreme, suborned the law, and subjected women to sexual servility, a perverse analogue to the slave power. The major figure most closely aligned with Smith and whose allies were indispensable to extending his influence, Stephen A. Douglas, paid no price for the Prophet's downfall. From adoration of the messiah to washing his hands of the martyr, Douglas escaped being tainted, though Lincoln would try to remind voters in Illinois of his history.

While the new Republican Party in 1856 condemned Mormonism alongside slavery, asserting "the right and the imperative duty of Congress to prohibit in the Territories those twin relics of barbarism—Polygamy, and Slavery," Democrats considered it a singular anathema, not linking it to slavery. In 1857, when President James Buchanan sent federal troops to the Utah Territory to attempt to topple Brigham Young's theocracy, Douglas supported Young's removal, calling on the Congress "to apply the knife and cut out this loathsome, disgusting ulcer." At the same time, rather than firmly opposing slavery's extension into Kansas, Douglas advocated "popular sovereignty," letting the territory's settlers vote on whether it should be free or slave, the practical effect of which was to intensify the conflict. The Mormons issued a statement supporting Douglas's doctrine, declaring that "the doctrines of sovereignty apply to us in the desert as well as to the settlers in Kansas and Nebraska." Young offered a new revelation: "The Democratic party is the instrument, in God's hand, by which is to be effected our recognition as a sovereign State, with the democratic institution of slavery and polygamy, as established by the patriarchs and renewed to the saints of latter days, through God's chosen leaders and prophets."

In Springfield, looking forward to running against Douglas for the Senate, Lincoln sensed an opening. On June 26, 1857, he used Mormonism as a rhetorical device to expose the illogic, hypocrisy, and rank opportunism of "popular sovereignty." "It is very plain the Judge evades the only question the Republicans have ever pressed upon the Democracy in regard to Utah," said Lincoln. "That question the Judge well knows to be this: 'If the people of Utah shall peacefully form a State Constitution tolerating polygamy, will the Democracy admit them into the Union?' There is nothing in the United States Constitution or law against polygamy; and why is it not a part of the Judge's 'sacred right of self-government' for that people to have it, or rather to keep it, if they choose? These questions, so far as I know, the Judge never answers. It might involve the Democracy to answer them either way, and they go unanswered." Douglas never answered Lincoln on Mormonism, for it would have dredged up his long and intimate association with the Prophet.

A week after Lincoln's election as president, on November 14, 1860, the *Deseret News*, the official Mormon organ, published an editorial that was not quite a revelation but a prophesy: "The day is not far distant, when the United States Government will cease to be, and that the Union, about which the politicians have harped and poets sung, will be no more." Brigham Young privately derided the new president as "Abel Lincoln" and recalled that he had not been an ally during the Illinois Mormon War. "Abel Lincoln was no friend of Christ, particularly," he said on March 15, 1861. "He had never raised his voice in our favor when he was aware that we were being persecuted." A few months later, in a burst of bitter nostalgia, Young remarked that Douglas, who had recently died, was "a far better man than President Abel Lincoln, for he knew his feelings were hostile to this people." Yet Young pledged his loyalty, telegraphing Washington: "Utah has not seceded but is firm for the constitution and laws of our once happy country." Lincoln refused to federalize the local militia, still called the Nauvoo Legion, because he considered it untrustworthy; initially, he sent in internal revenue agents before dispatching the 3rd California Infantry to ensure passage of the overland trail. "I will see them in hell before I will raise an army for them," railed Young on December 11, 1861. "Abe Lincoln has sent these men here to prepare the way for an Army. . . . I will see the day when those wicked rulers are wiped out. . . . I am not in league with such cursed scoundrels as Abe Lincoln and his minions. They have sought our destruction from the beginning."

On July 2, 1862, Lincoln signed the Morrill Anti-Bigamy Act, outlawing a central tenet of Mormonism, which he regarded as slavery of women. Before he acted he studied the issue in depth, taking out from the Library of Congress the Book of Mormon and several accounts of Mormon life. The most informative of the books he read, *Mormonism: Its Leaders and Designs*, published in 1857, was written by John Hyde, an apostate elder, who provided a detailed, firsthand description of the practice and psychology of polygamy, which he referred to as "their 'peculiar institution,'" quoting John C. Calhoun on slavery. Hyde's reference was not a mere allusion; he meant precisely that. Mormon women were forced into polygamy, he testified—"slavery." "Degraded into slavery by this Mormon stepback into barbarism, they are almost as submissive and as miserable as the Indian squaws around them." Yet the coercion was not necessarily physical. "The engine of Mormon power is not brute force; not attempted or threatened violence, but the lever of a skillfully combined and ably-handled system of religious machinery, operating on duped and bewildered fanatics." The conflicts leading to the Mormon expulsions from one state after another were not driven by persecution as their chieftains claimed, but by their leaders' "political wire-working." "It has been their constant anxiety and incessant truckling for political ascendancy that has induced much of their sufferings already. . . . It is themselves who have divested their system of its religious character, and, therefore, subjected themselves to political interference." But the Mormons, according to Hyde, were about more than "political jugglery." They were "an autocracy in the center of the republic." Lincoln had closely observed the manipulations in Illinois that had spiraled into disaster—the exploitation of religion, creation of an authoritarian regime based on "slavery," abuse of military power, suppression of free speech, and virtual secession. His reading of Hyde on Mormonism and the phantasmagorical Book of Mormon occurred at the same moment he was working through his thinking for the Emancipation Proclamation, which he would disclose to members of his cabinet two weeks after signing the Anti-Bigamy Act. With that measure and the Proclamation, Lincoln fulfilled the pledge of the original Republican platform against "the twin relics of barbarism."

But Lincoln did not enforce the law against polygamy. He could not afford another Mormon War amid the Civil War. "Occasionally we would come to a log that had fallen down," the rail splitter explained. "It was too hard to split, too wet to burn, and too heavy to move, so we ploughed around it. That's what I intend to do with the Mormons. Tell Brigham Young that if he will let me alone, I will let him alone." And he did. It was not until 1896 when Utah was admitted to the Union as a state that Lincoln's law began to be applied.

By then, the Saints routinely extolled Lincoln as a godly man. The political history of the Mormons in Illinois was forgiven, if not forgotten. In a show of respect, on Lincoln's one hundredth birthday in 1909, former Apostle Matthias Cowley performed a sealing ceremony marrying him to both Mary Todd and Ann Rutledge. Through this Mormon rite established by Joseph Smith the Prophet, the president who had abolished polygamy was consecrated for eternity as a polygamist.

CHAPTER TEN

THE DUELIST

Immediately after sweeping the statewide contests of 1842, two weeks after the election, on August 15, the Democratic victors—the governor, treasurer, and auditor—issued a proclamation against that "degrading" Whig institution—the State Bank—prohibiting payment of taxes with its paper,

instead demanding hard currency. The *Register* editorialized that "the Democratic Party will not tolerate worthless rags to usurp the place of a sound currency any longer" while the *Journal* raged that "the order has been issued without authority of law." At a debate at the Springfield State House, Dr. Anson Henry accused the Democrats of "arbitrary and tyrannical usurpations of power," while James Shields, the state auditor, charged Henry with "an attempt to excite a spirit of rebellion." This partisan sniping of Democrats and Whigs try-

James Shields

ing to blame each other for the economic problems of the state would soon escalate into a confrontation potentially lethal to Lincoln, which he would later look back on as the most embarrassing of his career, and yet that led incongruously to one of the most important events of his life—his marriage.

James Shields was Douglas's indispensable political ally, not only his rowdy dancing partner on tavern tables but also the most prominent Irish Catholic in Illinois politics, reliable deliverer of its decisive vote to the Democrats. Douglas had promoted his career from the state legislature to the auditor's office and together in 1841 they had launched the investigation into the alleged malfeasance of Whig commissioners in the construction of the new State House, notably Dr. Anson Henry. Shields was a capable lawyer with a gift for reciting fluent Latin, smatterings of French, and passages of English poetry. But he was as ill tempered as he was sociable, as volatile as he was vain. As a boy in County Tyrone, he had struck a British veteran of the Battle of Waterloo, challenged his bravery, and provoked a duel. "He was exceedingly vain and very ambitious, and like most ambitious men, on occasions, quite egotistical," wrote his law partner, Gustave Koerner. Lincoln found the pomposity of the Irishman "an irresistible mark for satire," according to Nicolay and Hay.

"Shields is a fool as well as a liar. With him truth is out of the question," read an odd article in the *Sangamo Journal*, appearing on September 2, entitled "Letter from the Lost Townships," an imaginary location, bylined "Rebecca," a make-believe old woman, and written in rustic dialect. "If I was deaf and blind I could tell him by the smell," wrote "Rebecca," a fragrant hint of whiskey, describing Shields at a party of "the ladies," "floatin about on the air, without heft or earthly substance, just like a lock of cat-fur where cats had been fightin," and "in the exstatic agony of his soul, spoke audibly and distinctly—'Dear girls, it is distressing, but I cannot marry you all. Too well I know how much you suffer; but do, do remember, it is not my fault that I am so handsome and so interesting.'"

Two more letters from "Rebecca" followed in the *Journal* on September 9, piling ridicule on Shields and the Democrats. "A pretty mess they have made of it. . . . This State Bank of Illinois will never become prosperous until the Whig party are in power." These letters also added the element that the Democrats had been able to play their tricks because of the Mormons— "Democratic pets"—a direct riposte to the *Register*'s calling John C. Bennett, the Mormon turncoat, "a great pet of both the *Journal* and the junto" just two months earlier. One of the telltale characteristics of Lincoln's writings and speeches throughout his career was his appropriation of the rhetoric of his opponents to turn against them.

If the Democratic plan had been known before the election, "Rebecca" wrote, even "the Mormon votes could not have saved the party." (That month, the *Journal* was filled with stories of efforts to arrest Smith for the assassination of Governor Boggs of Missouri and other accounts of his "villainies," probably some written by Lincoln.) Finally, "Rebecca" wrote that her sister suggested a happy ending: "You needn't be surprised if at the next presidential election you should see a clean vote for HENRY CLAY here." Soon the *Journal* published a poem by "Cathleen" announcing the marriage of "Rebecca" and Shields: "Ye Jew's harps awake! The Auditor's won./ Rebecca the widow has gained Erin's son." The poets behind "Cathleen" were Mary Todd and her friend Julia Jayne. And they likely collaborated on the latter two "Rebecca" articles in literary partnership with Francis and Lincoln. "The poor Genl [Shields], in our little gay circle, was oftentimes, the subject of mirth and even song," Mary confessed later. "The Genl was very impulsive and on the occasion referred to, had placed himself before us, in so ridiculous a light, that the love of the ludicrous, had been excited, within me and I presume, I gave vent to it, in some *very* silly lines."

Feeling his honor wounded, the excitable Shields was intent on a duel. He had cause to feel personally insulted. The "Rebecca" articles cruelly played on the ethnic stereotype of the blarney-babbling, conceited, and socially absurd Irishman. He sent his second, John D. Whitehead, the state fund commissioner, to Simeon Francis at the *Journal* to demand the identity of the author of the offensive articles. After delaying for a day, Francis admitted that it was Lincoln.

"I have become the object of slander, vituperation and personal abuse," Shields wrote him, insisting on an "absolute retraction of all offensive allusions used by you" as the only remedy to "prevent consequences." Lincoln declined to apologize. Shields issued the challenge. Under the Code Duello, Lincoln chose the weapons: "Cavalry broadswords of the largest size, precisely equal in all respects, and such as are now used by the cavalry company at Jacksonville." He stipulated that a ten-foot plank would be the line between them that neither could cross. At six feet four inches, Lincoln figured the broadswords gave him an advantage over the five feet nine inches Shields. He practiced with his fellow lawyer Albert T. Bledsoe, whom he brought along as one of his seconds. "To tell you the truth, Linder," Lincoln later confessed to Usher Linder, "I did not want to kill Shields and felt sure that I could disarm him, having had about a month to learn the broadsword exercise; and furthermore, I didn't want the damned fellow to kill me, which I rather think he would have done if we had selected pistols." Lincoln was said to have first suggested another choice of weapons: "How about cow dung at five paces?" His reach was longer than Shields, but he seemed to discount that the smaller man had learned fencing as a boy from a British war veteran and was expert enough to have taught it himself in Toronto. "I heard the General, himself say at one time he was afraid of no man in America with a sword," wrote Shields's biographer. "The duel, if it had come off, would have ended differently from what Lincoln's biographers prophesied."

Escalated into a matter of honor the partisan feud over the State Bank elevated the status of the Irish immigrant and the provincial politician into gentlemen. Each brought his contingent of seconds about a hundred miles from Springfield to the field of honor, a large sandbar in the Mississippi, near St. Louis and Alton, claimed by neither Illinois nor Missouri, which both outlawed dueling, a no-man's-land receiving its name "Bloody Island" after Thomas Hart Benton shot dead a political opponent in a duel there in 1817.

On September 22, 1842, a crowd of hundreds congregated to watch the spectacle. Lincoln arrived on the scene first, trimmed brush swinging his broadsword and hummed "Yankee Doodle." Suddenly, Congressman John J. Hardin, Mary Todd's cousin, rode up to end the nonsense, proposing that the two men submit their differences to a disinterested panel. With that Shields's friends withdrew his initial note and Lincoln promptly apologized. The gladiators sheathed their swords. But Lincoln's friend, William Butler, one of his seconds, wrote an account in the *Journal* that Shields read as a further insult requiring satisfaction and challenged him to a duel. Butler chose rifles as the weapons. Preparing for the shootout in Missouri, Butler's seconds, who included Lincoln, somehow failed to connect with Shields's and the series of duels ended as farces without ever being fought.

Under Illinois law, dueling was a crime carrying a one-to-five-year sentence. But no one in this case was prosecuted. Shields's political career was unaffected. He was reelected state auditor within weeks, appointed a justice of the state Supreme Court within a year, commissioner of the General Land Office within three years, and U.S. senator by 1849. Wounded in the Mexican War, he would serve as a brigadier general in the Civil War, a position approved by Lincoln. Astonishingly, he was the only person ever to serve as a U.S. senator from three states—Illinois, Minnesota, and Missouri.

Lincoln, however, returned from Bloody Island to a torrent of criticism that would trail him for years. Not only did the *Register* ridicule him as "Aunt Becca," tossing his female pseudonym at him, but to his astonishment he also found himself chastised by the Whig press. For Southerners and a Democratic Party dominated by a Southern ethos dueling was the mark of a gentleman, but for Northern Whigs it was a disgrace, an atavistic ritual associated with slave owners that should be harshly suppressed. The *Alton Telegraph* rebuked Lincoln for participating in "the calmest, most deliberate and malicious species of murder—a relic of the most cruel barbarism that ever disgraced the darkest periods of the world—and one which every principle of religion, virtue and good order, loudly demands should be put a stop to." The *Jacksonville Illinoisan* editorialized that any future "knights of chivalry" on their way to a duel should be "unceremoniously arrested and taken to the first hog-hole and there cooled off." An early historian of Illinois observed that "the newspapers of the day commented widely upon them [Lincoln and Shields], and thus they helped greatly to bring dueling into disrepute."

The *Alton Telegraph* also disclosed on October 15 the most scandalous news of all, that the provocateurs of the now infamous duel were two young women. "The name of the author of the 'lines' on the marriage of Rebecca and the auditor was demanded. Miss M.T. wrote them in the parlor of her friend, Miss J.J. for fun. The latter snatched them and sent them to the printer. No challenge will be sent in this case, the author being a female—the code does not require it."

Lincoln, for his part, never wanted to be reminded again of the incident, though it kept surfacing to his embarrassment. "The occasion was so silly, that my husband, was always so ashamed of it, that months before our marriage, we mutually agreed—never to speak of it, ourselves," Mary wrote a friend later. When Herndon toured the Eastern states for Lincoln in 1858, he informed Lincoln that the duel had been raised. "If all the good things I have ever done are remembered as long and well as my scrape with Shields," he replied, "it is plain I shall not soon be forgotten." In February 1865, a "distinguished officer of the army" asked whether he had indeed fought a duel. "I do not deny it," Lincoln said, "but if you desire my friendship you will never mention the circumstance again!" An eyewitness described his face as "flushed."

Twenty months before, Lincoln's political and social embarrassments had precipitated his nervous breakdown. This latest humiliation of the duel prompted his marriage. The sequence of events remains hazy and historians offer alternative scenarios. "I should have been entirely happy, but for the never-absent idea, that there is one still unhappy whom I have contributed to make so," Lincoln wrote Speed on March 27, referring to his broken engagement. "That still kills my soul. I cannot but reproach myself, for even wishing to be happy while she is otherwise." "Mrs. Francis shrewdly got them together," recalled Elizabeth Todd Edwards. Anson Henry, she noted, also played Cupid. "Doctor Henry who admired and loved Mr. Lincoln had much to do in getting Mary and Lincoln together again." According to Mrs. Edwards, "All at once we heard that Mr. L and Mary had secret meetings at Mr. S. Francis'—Editor of the *Springfield Journal*. Mary said the reason this was so—the Cause why it was—that the world—woman and man were uncertain and slippery and that it was best to keep the secret Courtship from all eyes and ears."

Yet according to Sarah Rickard, William Butler's sister-in-law, Lincoln and Mary did not resume their relationship until September 27, five days after the duel, when they encountered each other at the wedding of Martinette Hardin in Jacksonville. "I sat next to Mr. Lincoln at the wedding dinner," said Rickard. "He was going with me quite a good deal then. Mary Todd sat just across. Of course, rather than bring constraint upon the company, they spoke to each other, and that was the beginning of the reconciliation." But Rickard's impressions, given to a St. Louis newspaperman in 1907 sixty-five years after the events occurred, might be somewhat unreliable as well as self-serving, though it was a fact that Lincoln and Mary were at the wedding party. In that interview Rickard also claimed without corroboration that Lincoln had proposed to her and that he said it would "kill me" to marry Mary.

According to Mary's account, "Mr. Lincoln, thought, he had some right, to assume to be *my* champion, even on frivolous occasions. . . . Genl Shields, called upon the Editor, and demanded the author. The Editor, requested a day, to reflect upon it—The latter called upon Mr. Lincoln, to whom he knew I was engaged and explained to him, that he was certain, that I was the Author—Mr. L. then replied, say to Shields, that 'I am responsible.'" Thus, in her version, she and Lincoln were already engaged and he gallantly protected her honor.

That Mary would leap into the fray against Shields without Lincoln's knowledge of her participation is extremely implausible. As the coeditor of the *Journal* in all but title he would have known everything going on there. It would have been virtually inconceivable that he would have been in the dark about the identity of another writer at the newspaper using the voice of his fictional creation, the gossipy widow "Rebecca." The sequence strongly suggests that Lincoln and Mary were already meeting at the Francis house. The "violent little Whig" had cleverly figured out the way to her man's heart—politics. Playfully joining him in the political affair sparked the love affair. She won the duel.

There is one other tantalizing artifact, a souvenir—vote tallies of Lincoln's victories in 1832, 1834, and 1836, carefully handwritten himself, which he had notarized on September 9, and wrapped with a pink ribbon, a present to his fiancée.

About two weeks after the duel and a week after the wedding party at Jacksonville, Lincoln wrote Speed, asking a question that in retrospect seems transparently a request for his own reassurance: "Are you now, in *feeling* as well as *judgement*, glad you are married as you are? From anybody but me, this would be an impudent question not to be tolerated; but I know you will pardon it in me. Please answer it quickly as I feel impatient to know."

Mary had first come to Springfield for the elaborate wedding on May 12, 1839, of her sister Frances to Dr. William S. Wallace, in the parlor of her other sister Elizabeth's home, the Edwards mansion atop Aristocracy Hill. Neither Mary nor Lincoln wanted a large affair under the domineering social control of her older sister. The Edwardses had not approved of the match and their reservations were almost certainly why the couple clandestinely renewed their relationship at the Frances house. They wanted the wedding to establish their independence and autonomy separate from her overbearing family. When Mary informed them over breakfast on November 4, 1842, that she and Lincoln would marry that evening, the news set off the conflict she sought to evade. "Our aristocratic sister, with an outburst, gave Mary a good scolding," recalled Frances Wallace. "Do not forget that you are a Todd," Elizabeth lectured. "But, Mary, if you insist on being married today, we will make merry, and have the wedding here this evening. I will not permit you to be married out of my house. Mr. Lincoln should ask the Reverend Dr. Dresser to officiate at the ceremony." She added, "Mary Todd even a free negro would give her family time to bake a ginger cake."

Apparently, Mary made a spirited case for her marriage to Lincoln. "Mary, I agree with you," said Ninian W. Edwards. "Mr. Lincoln is talented and will be an influential man, a leader among men. And now, ask all of your friends to be present at your wedding." According to the account offered by Albert S. Edwards, the son of Ninian and Elizabeth, "Mr. Lincoln met my father on the street and said they were going to be married that evening at the residence of Simeon Francis. My father said to Mr. Lincoln: 'That will never do. Mary Todd is my ward. If the marriage is going to take place, it must be at my house.' There was an immediate change of plans."

"As soon as Mrs. Edwards knew they were engaged, she wanted to give them a big wedding just the same as she had me, but they were both opposed to it," said Frances Wallace. "They both wanted a simple, private wedding. So they wouldn't tell anyone when they were to be married."

But once Elizabeth Edwards knew, the preparations were hurriedly made. Lincoln went to the rectory of the Episcopal Church to see Reverend Dresser. "I want to get hitched tonight," he said. Elizabeth sent for her sister Frances. "She was terribly disappointed, for she could not get up a dinner in that short time," Frances recalled. ". . . and she hardly knew what to do. But they would not have it any other way, so she wrote a note to me, and told me they were to be married that night, and asked me if I could help her. So I worked all day. I never worked harder all day in my life. And in the evening they were married, and we had a very nice little supper, but not what we would have had if they had given Mrs. Edwards time." The tension, not far below the surface, broke through. "Someone had spoken of Mr. Lincoln as a plebian," wrote Thompson G. Onstot, an old friend of Lincoln from New Salem days. "This rankled in the heart of Miss Todd sorely, so when about noon on the wedding day Mrs. Edwards' feelings were sufficiently calmed to talk to her sister of the affair, she said: 'Mary, you have not given me much time to prepare for our guests this evening.' Then she added, 'I guess I will have to send to Old Dickey's'—a tavern—'for some of the gingerbread and beer.'" "Well," Mary replied tartly, "that will be good enough for plebians I suppose."

Lincoln dressed for the wedding at the home of William Butler. "The night Mr. Lincoln and Mary Todd were married," wrote Eugenia Jones Hunt, Butler's daughter, "I thought my mother was very handsome in her yellow satin evening gown, as she walked down the hall to Mr. Lincoln's room to see if he was dressed properly for his marriage. As usual, my brothers and I trooped in behind her. As my mother tied Mr. Lincoln's necktie on him, little Speed [Butler] called out: 'Where are you going, Mr. Lincoln?' Mr. Lincoln jokingly replied: 'to the devil!'" Many chroniclers depict Lincoln's remark, often conveyed as "To hell, I suppose," as sarcastic fatalism, darkly foreboding, based on Herndon's unattributed rendering, but the eyewitness, the only one, contradicts the sense of that interpretation. Lincoln was almost certainly making a joke.

One of the distinguished guests provided the merriment at the ceremony—"one of the funniest things to have witnessed imaginable—no description on paper can possibly do it justice," recalled James Matheny, Lincoln's best man. Circuit Court judge Thomas C. Browne stood directly behind the groom—"the Falstaff of the bench," as Usher Linder dubbed him, "full of wit and humor," mostly unintentional, who "never refused to take a horn when invited, but very rarely invited others to take a horn with him." "If he ever read a law book it was so long ago that he must have forgotten it," wrote one of his fellow justices. "There was of course a perfect hush in the room as the ceremony progressed," said Matheny. Reverend Dresser, attired in his black "clerical robes," had intoned the words of the Episcopal service: "With this ring I thee endow with all my goods and chattels, lands and tenements," when Browne, "who had never witnessed such a proceeding, was struck with its utter absurdity and spoke out." "Lord Jesus Christ, God Almighty, Lincoln, the statute fixes all that," he declared. "This was too much for the Old Parson—he broke down under it—an almost irresistible desire to laugh out, checked his proceeding for a minute or so—but finally recovered and pronounced them husband and wife." (A year later, Lincoln would successfully defend Browne, a Whig, against a Democratic effort to impeach him and pack the court further with one of their own.)

Lincoln had bought the ring he put on Mary's finger at Chatterton's jewelry shop and thoughtfully had it engraved: "A.L. to Mary, Nov. 4, 1842.

Love is Eternal." Yet Matheny's later account portrayed a panicked, miserable Lincoln, compelled to commit an act against his will. "That Lincoln came to him one evening and said—Jim—'I shall have to marry that girl.' Matheny says that on the same evening Mr. and Mrs. Lincoln were married—That Lincoln looked and acted as if he was going to the slaughter—That Lincoln often told him directly and indirectly that he was driven into the marriage— Said it was concocted and planned by the Edwards family—That Miss Todd—afterwards Mrs. Lincoln told L. that he was in honor bound to marry her." The fundamental confusion of this jumbled version is apparent in that it seamlessly runs into Matheny's story of Lincoln's infatuation with Matilda Edwards as though he were offering a reliable chronology. It is likely that he was describing a garbled recollection of Lincoln's agitated state of mind from the earlier broken engagement. His misunderstanding might be similar to Herndon's tale of the earlier wedding party preparations gone awry that might well have been blurred into his memory of Frances Todd's wedding.

"I certainly saw him the night he was married," Frances recalled, "and he was not distracted with grief, or anything else. He was cheerful as he ever had been, for all we could see. He acted just as he always had in company." "Be assured, Eugenia, it was a hurly-burly day," she told the Butler daughter. "How we hustled! I had a whole boiled ham which I took over for the wedding supper, and made the bride's and groom's cake. It was a very pretty and gay wedding. The ladies were in lovely evening gowns. Sister Mary was handsome in her beautiful bridal dress of white satin, with her pearl necklace, earrings, and brooch. Miss Lina Lamb and Julia Jayne were Mary's bridesmaids. After the ceremony, congratulations, and the wedding supper, we danced until midnight in those spacious parlors of the Ninian Edwards home."

A week after the wedding, Lincoln wrote his friend Samuel D. Marshall, editor of the *Shawneetown Republican* newspaper, "Nothing new here, except my marrying, which to me, is a matter of profound wonder." It was the start of a close, productive, and sometimes difficult marriage between two people who nonetheless loved each other.

The Lincolns moved into the same room that Mary's sister Frances had occupied immediately after her marriage at the Globe Tavern. Shortly after the birth nine months later of their first son, Robert, they rented a three-bedroom cottage, and in 1844 bought Reverend Dresser's house, where they lived until they left for Washington.

Stories of Mary's uncontrolled temper and Lincoln's miseries were legion. Herndon called her the "tigress" and "she-wolf." Lincoln's White House private secretaries nicknamed her "the Hell-cat." "Lincoln and his wife got along tolerably well, unless Mrs. L got the devil in her," recalled James Gourley, a Springfield neighbor and friend of Lincoln. "Lincoln paid no attention— would pick up one of his children and walked off—would laugh at her— pay no earthly attention to her when in that wild furious condition." "Mrs. Lincoln often gave L hell in general," said Matheny. "*Ferocity*—describes Mrs. L's conduct to L." He recounted to Herndon "one of her insane mad spells," hitting a maid. There were also stories of various rages against her husband, striking him with firewood, chasing him with a kitchen knife, swatting him with a broom, throwing a teacup, pelting him with potatoes—and stories of Lincoln escaping for a few days onto the county court circuit. "Poor Lincoln!" lamented Herndon, whose hostility to Mary never abated. "He is domestically a desolate man—has been for years to my own knowledge," married to "a very curious—eccentric—wicked woman," and argued that in marrying her he "saved his honor and threw away domestic happiness." One contemporary Lincoln scholar has conjectured on the basis of accumulating comments about Lincoln being "honor bound" that Mary seduced him and rushed him to the altar the next day.

There is another more plausible theory, beginning with the historian Ruth Painter Randall's plain observation that the Lincoln marriage was "the triumph of romantic love over family opposition and snobbery." In important ways it was an unusual relationship. His interest in her opinions was part of her attraction to him. Respectable women were not supposed to have any interest in politics and certainly not to speak about it. Yet he was remarkably egalitarian for the standards of the time. He accepted her speaking on subjects that other men would actively disapprove of any woman voicing. His first political statement, his announcement of his candidacy for the state legislature in 1832, included his eccentric support for the right of women to vote. Mary's publication of harsh political polemics, even anonymously, was unheard of, much less brazenly offering political opinions, a sphere reserved to men. Not only was it daring for a young woman to venture into that realm, it was as equally daring for a man to accept it. Coming from a political family, she was not naive about the lines she was crossing. Lincoln did not always follow her advice, but he listened. She had turned down a series of appropriate suitors whose social background was loftier than Lincoln's, including a descendant of Patrick Henry living in Columbia, Missouri. "I love him not, and my hand will never be given, where my heart is not," she wrote. By contrast, Lincoln "had the most congenial mind she had ever met," wrote Katherine Helm. Mary, for her part, was probably the best-educated woman he had ever met, opening a whole new world to him. They had other serious links: both shared a love of poetry and had each lost their mother at a young age. But their love of politics was unquestionably a major reason they married. Mary would never be the typical political wife of the era, the little lady with no opinions beyond the management of the household and children. That alone made their relationship unique. Mary also gave him something else, completing the void at the center of his life. "Mr. L. has neither brother nor sister, aunt or uncle, and only a few third cousins," she remarked. Mary gave the man who had severed his ties to his family, who had renounced his father, a sense of place, a home, a family of his own.

Mary constantly sought to improve him. She wanted him to appear to be what he was becoming, a successful politician and attorney. But he remained rough around the edges, often oblivious to proper dress and conduct. "I do not think he knew pink from blue when I married him," she said. She took upon herself the task of his makeover. "Why don't you dress up and try to look like somebody?" she admonished. And he accepted her criticism. "His manners," she said, "got quite polished." But he remained a complicated and demanding man to live with, often emotionally remote, occasionally depressed, disappearing onto the court circuit for weeks at a time, and leaving her to raise their boys alone. It's likely that any marriage he would have made would have been troubled.

"That Lincoln did not observe the conventionalities of society alternately amused and irritated Mary," recalled her niece, Katherine Helm,

> although she realized that many things he did not know or do must be ingrained and carefully taught in childhood, by precept and example, and that if merely conformed to later in life is only an artificial veneer more easily peeled off than put on. When Mary slyly poked fun at him for committing some faux pas he would look at her quizzically, his gray eyes twinkling, as if to say, "How can you attach such great importance to matters so trivial?" and Mary's color would deepen as though caught in a petty meanness, or if she spoke sharply in reproof, the hurt look in his eyes made her repentant

and almost ready to weep. "Mary could make a bishop forget his prayers," chuckled Ninian Edwards one day when Mary mimicked the mannerisms of some of her beaux with unflattering fidelity, although her imitation of Lincoln was never so full of spice.

"In her domestic troubles I have always sympathized with her," the harshly critical Herndon conceded. "The world does not know what she bore and the history of the bearing. I will write it out some time. This domestic hell of Lincoln's life is not all on one side." In another of his recollections, he wrote, 'I have always sympathized with Mrs. Lincoln. Remember that Every Effect must have its Cause. Mrs. Lincoln was not a she wolf—wild Cat without a Cause."

For all the difficulties she caused him, plaguing him with her fits to the end, their devotion to each other was apparent. "Anyone could see that Mr. Lincoln admired Mary and was very proud of her," recalled Emilie Helm, her half sister. "She took infinite pains to fascinate him again and again with pretty coquettish clothes and dainty little airs and graces. She was gay and light-hearted, hopeful and happy. She had a high temper and perhaps did not always have it under complete control, but what did it matter? Her little temper was soon over, and her husband loved her none the less, perhaps all the more, for this human frailty which needed his love and patience to pet and coax the sunny smile to replace the sarcasm and tears—and, oh, how she did love this man!"

"It was always, music in my ears, both before and after our marriage, when my husband, told me, that I was the only one, he had ever thought of, or cared for," Mary wrote a friend in 1865 after Lincoln's assassination. "It will solace me to the grave and when I again rest by his side, I will be comforted."

In 1864, at a party at the White House, Lincoln turned to a friend and spontaneously remarked, "My wife is as handsome as when she was a girl, and I, a poor nobody then, fell in love with her; and what is more, I have never fallen out."

Despite his "plebian" background and manners that needed constant attention, she was certain that he was suited for the highest office. She married for love, but she married a man she thought had a destiny because of his special character that transcended wealth. Joe Gillespie recalled a conversation between Matilda Edwards, the young woman who once compelled Lincoln's fascination but who chose to marry an older man, Newton D. Strong, a prosperous lawyer in Alton, and Mary. "Miss Edwards one day was asked why she married such an old dried up husband—such a withered up old Buck. She replied: 'He had lots of houses and gold.' Mary was present at this question and answer and she then remarked—'Is that true—I would rather marry a good man—a man of mind—with a hope and bright prospects ahead for position—fame and power than to marry all the houses—gold and bones in the world.'"

Lincoln's own ambition was burning. "His ambition was a little engine that knew no rest," wrote Herndon. Before he married, he had derailed himself, suffered a nervous breakdown, sometimes acted clownishly, and opened himself to ridicule. He would always remain subject to spells of morose introspection, his famous melancholy, withdrawing into himself as a form of self-defense to the point of immobilization. Mary may not have had firm control over her own temper, but she tempered Lincoln. She was the manager of his emotional life. She had seen him collapse and would never allow him to disintegrate again. Her belief in him, demonstrated at the beginning with their wedding, overcoming the objections of her family, was unwavering and unreserved. Lincoln and Mary had won each other and he would never lack for a champion.

"Miss Todd's ambition was colossal," wrote Thompson Onstot, the old settler. "She had from early girlhood said she expected to marry a man who would someday be president of the United States, and she seemed to have a prophetic vision that this ambition would be realized. But what was there in Mr. Lincoln to encourage such ambition and expectation? Apparently nothing." "Lincoln is a gloomy man—a sad man," observed John Todd Stuart. "His wife made him President. She had the fire—will and ambition—Lincoln's talent and his wife's ambition did the deed." Stuart recalled that Joshua Speed had told him that "if Mr. Lincoln had married another woman—for instance Speed's wife he Lincoln would have been a devoted husband and a very—*very* domestic man. That Lincoln needed driving." And Stuart added: "Well he got that."

Together, Lincoln and Mary would be devoted to each other and to their great cause, their marriage and mission, one and the same—as she called it, "our Lincoln party."

CHAPTER ELEVEN

COUP D'ÉTAT

———————◆•◆———————

E ncouraged by his wife, Lincoln readied himself to succeed Stuart, who
had decided not to run for reelection to the Congress in 1843. "Now if
you should hear anyone say that Lincoln don't want to go to Congress, I wish
you as a personal friend of mine, would tell him you have reason to believe he
is mistaken," he wrote Richard S. Thomas, a Whig lawyer, on February 14.
"The truth is, I would like to go very much."

Illinois' rapid population growth had gained the state three additional
districts, raising the number to seven, but the Democratic-controlled legislature gerrymandered them so that much of the Whig vote was concentrated
in only one, the Seventh District centered in Sangamon County and the city
of Springfield. Douglas's *Register* even floated a short-lived scheme for an
at-large statewide canvas that would deprive the Whigs of its sole representation. The Democrats' redistricting ploy was of a piece with the packing of the
state Supreme Court and the wrecking of the State Bank, and it forced the
rising young Whigs into a cockpit where they might tear each other apart.

Lincoln proposed adoption of the convention system to nominate candidates, packing a five-man party committee to recommend his plan with
three supporters (his new brother-in-law Ninian W. Edwards, Dr. Anson
Henry, and James Conkling), who in turn appointed a committee consisting
of himself, Logan, and Bledsoe to compose an "Address to the People of
Illinois" to justify it. He was its author. "That 'union is strength,'" Lincoln's

manifesto argued, "is a truth that has been known, illustrated and declared, in various ways and forms in all ages of the world. That great fabulist and philosopher, Aesop, illustrated it by his fable of the bundle of sticks; and he whose wisdom surpasses that of all philosophers, has declared that 'a house divided against itself cannot stand.'" He ended with an explanation of how the great Whig victory of 1840 was undone after Harrison's death. "By the course of Mr. Tyler the policy of our opponents has continued in operation; still leaving them with the advantage of charging all its evils upon us as the results of a Whig administration." If only the Whigs would turn out to vote, "always a majority of this Nation," then "surely will a Whig be elected President of the United States."

Lincoln faced a field of Ned Baker, his close friend, and John J. Hardin, his cousin by marriage, well-born, college-educated, and personally attractive. At the Sangamon County Whig convention, Lincoln was surprised to discover his own political liabilities. His marriage into the toney Todd-Edwards clan, high-handed speech to the Washington Society chastising the clergy for their sanctimony, and unspeakable dueling were held against him. "It would astonish if not amuse, the older citizens of your county who twelve years ago knew me a stranger, friendless, uneducated, penniless boy,

Henry Clay

working on a flat boat—at ten dollars per month to learn that I have been put down here as the candidate of pride, wealth, and aristocratic family distinction," he wrote a friend in a letter. "Yet so chiefly it was. There was too the strangest combination of church influence against me. Baker is a Campbellite, and therefore as I suppose, with few exceptions got all that church. My wife has some relatives in the Presbyterian and some in the Episcopal Churches, and therefore, wherever it would tell, I was set down as either the one or the other, whilst it was everywhere contended that no Christian ought to go for me, because I belonged to no church, was suspected of being a deist, and had talked about fighting a duel."

Lincoln's problem was that the accusations against him rang true. Baker carried the county and Lincoln's reward was designation as a Baker delegate. "We had a meeting of the Whigs of the county here on last Monday to appoint delegates to a district convention, and Baker beat me and got the delegation instructed to go for him," Lincoln wrote Speed on March 24. "The meeting, in spite of my attempt to decline it, appointed me one of the delegates; so that in getting Baker the nomination, I shall be 'fixed' a good deal like a fellow who is made groomsman to the man what has cut him out, and is marrying his own dear 'gal.'" But he still had won two delegates from Menard County, his old New Salem stomping grounds, and it was to one of those delegates, Martin Sims Martin, that he addressed his letter enumerating the causes for his loss. He went to the district convention working for Baker, but with a contingency plan to use his Menard delegates in order to emerge as the alternative should Baker and Hardin deadlock. Each had fifteen delegates. The outcome rested on a single delegate, J. M. Ruggles, pledged to Hardin but favoring Baker. "As soon as I arrived Baker hurried to me, saying: 'How is it? It all depends on you.' On being told that notwithstanding my partiality for him, the people I represented expected me to vote for Hardin, and that I would have to do so, Baker at once replied: 'You are right—there is no other way.' The convention was organized, and I was elected secretary. Baker immediately arose, and made a most thrilling address, thoroughly arousing the sympathies of the convention, and ended by declining his candidacy. Hardin was nominated by acclamation; and then came the episode."

"Immediately after the nomination," Ruggles explained, "Mr. Lincoln walked across the room to my table, and asked if I would favor a resolution recommending Baker for the next term. On being answered in the affirmative, he said: 'You prepare the resolution, I will support it, and I think we can pass it.' The resolution created a profound sensation, especially with the friends of Hardin. After an excited and angry discussion, the resolution passed by a majority of one." That deciding vote was Ruggles himself. His defection from Hardin's camp instantly established a rule of rotation in the congressional seat. The quick-witted Lincoln had limited Hardin to one term before he had even been elected to the office. Baker would follow him—and by inference the third candidate, Lincoln, would succeed Baker. Thus Lincoln put himself in line for the nomination, though he had lost. But he still brooded about his defeat. "He took his friend James Matheny out into the woods with him one day," wrote Herndon, "and, calling up the bitter features of the canvass, protested 'vehemently and with great emphasis' that he was anything but aristocratic and proud. 'Why, Jim,' he said, 'I am now and always shall be the same Abe Lincoln I was when you first saw me.'"

This time Lincoln did not retreat from his setback into his gloom. He threw himself into the 1844 campaign for his idol Henry Clay, disappointed since he first ran twenty years earlier, but finally given an unencumbered nomination and seemingly straight path to his ultimate goal of the White House. The Whig program of economic nationalism, vetoed by His Accidency, John Tyler, was more salient and popular than even four years earlier. And Clay's opponent was expected to be none other than Van Buren—"Van, Van, the used up man"—more tarnished than ever, but seemingly as inevitable for the Democratic nomination as he was unappealing.

Whigs behaved as though the magic of 1840 would work again by repeating the same incantations and parading with the same symbols. Nostalgia was the strategy. The Springfield campaign headquarters was called "the Cabin" after the "log cabin and hard cider" campaign of "Tippecanoe and Tyler, Too." Energy focused on hammering and sawing the tallest flagpole ever seen, which crashed, killing a worker. Finally, the Whigs raised a skyscraper of a pole measuring two hundred fourteen and a half feet tall, atop which an American flag and Clay banner were proudly displayed. Clay Clubs sang "Harry of the West" and shouted "Restore Prosperity." "We sing good old songs for 'Gallant Harry,' and this with eloquent speaking from Logan, Lincoln, and Baker, you may well imagine the effect," Herndon reported in a letter to Hardin.

Lincoln was designated a statewide presidential elector and rode tirelessly around central Illinois as a Whig missionary as he had done in 1840. From every platform he spoke in favor of the national bank, the State Bank, and tariffs, just as he had done before. When he failed to rouse a crowd with these dry subjects, he would simply assail Van Buren. Lincoln's chief debating partner was his old boss, John Calhoun, cooler and more logical than Douglas, and running as the Democratic candidate for the Seventh District against Baker. "Calhoun in 1844 was a strong, very strong, and clear-headed man, Lincoln's equal and the superior of Douglas," Herndon wrote Lamon later. "Frequent contact and conflict with such an opponent must have had its educational influence on Mr. Lincoln," wrote Milton Hay. "It habituated the sententious, precise and guarded statements of political propositions for which Mr. Lincoln became so remarkable."

They debated almost exclusively about economics, leaving unmentioned the most inflammatory issue consuming the state—the Mormons. None of Lincoln's speeches or debates from this political season was preserved, except a snippet of one. "Big Red" May, after switching from Democrat to Whig, had reversed course once again and ridiculed the Whig flagpole as "hollow at the butt end." To which, according to a newspaper report, Lincoln replied that "was where the Col. had crawled out of the Whig Party! He proposed to stop up the hole so that he couldn't get back again!" May sputtered a challenge of a duel, but having tried that a few months earlier to his embarrassment Lincoln chose to apologize, already having rhetorically shot his opponent clean through and left him for politically dead.

Lincoln's preparation for his debates left a more lasting impression on him than his one-liners suggested. He carefully studied the economic issue, adopting a method of concentrated focus, intensive reading, and long cogitation that he would later employ in mastering the constitutional and political quandaries of slavery's extension, *Dred Scott*, and secession. From Herndon's library he read *Elements of Political Economy* by Francis Wayland, a Baptist preacher who was the president of Brown University, considered the most distinguished man of Rhode Island, his treatise the classic American free market work of its time: against government regulation, internal improvements, and intervention of elected politicians, whom he called "peculiarly disqualified" from "directing the manner in which labor or capital shall be employed." Lincoln emphatically and fundamentally rejected these views.

Casting aside Wayland, he enthusiastically embraced Henry C. Carey's *Essay on the Rate of Wages*, which resonated with his most basic beliefs and sense of himself. Lincoln thoroughly assimilated Carey's book, read his subsequent works, and as president would turn to him for advice. Carey's *Essay* was a missile aimed against the political economy of austerity. He argued forcefully against the ideas that scarcity was a natural condition produced by impersonal laws of the market, that profits required driving down wages, and that government properly could and should do nothing. Carey had no

nostalgia for rustic life, but instead advocated policies for a dynamic society that invested through government in transportation, public education,
and technology. He openly castigated laissez-faire economics, the Manchester School, as the ideology intended to justify the British monopoly of the
world market—"'free trade,' or the British system," he called it. He was as
opposed to the false premise of the "iron law of wages," that low wages best
served high profits, as he was to the idolization of economic man, that society
didn't really exist but was merely an appendage of the market. He proposed
protective tariffs and an expansive monetary policy to build up American
manufacturing for the general good. He believed in a free society, not an
idealized free market; a central economic role for government as essential
for progress; and a market economy that broadened opportunity for all. At
a time of rising nativist suspicion he encouraged immigration, seeing immigrants as consumers and "are therefore employers to nearly the same extent
that they are competitors."

Carey had special contempt for Robert Malthus's fashionable views of inevitable scarcity and austerity. "I am not aware of a fact in his book in regard
to man in a state of civilization, that goes to support his theory," Carey wrote,
"or that is not much better evidence that man has been misgoverned, and
his increase repressed thereby, than that it has been repressed by inability
of the earth to afford him support." Rather than condemning the masses to
increased misery in the grip of a heartless world, he believed in their democratic capacity to produce progress. "Highest, therefore, amongst the tests
of civilization, is that continuity . . . which enables all to find demand for
their whole physical and mental powers." Rather than low wages necessary
for high profits, he argued "that high wages . . . are an infallible evidence
of prosperity." And anticipating John Maynard Keynes's theory of priming
the fiscal pump of demand, Carey wrote, "The less promptly the demand
follows the supply the greater, therefore, must be the waste. The more instant
the demand the greater must be the economy of power, and the amount of
force."

Carey addressed slavery in *The Slave Trade*, published in 1853, which
Lincoln would certainly have read. Carey's contribution was to understand
slavery as a global system fostered by the British Empire and to which the
American South was intrinsic. "The system to which the world is indebted
for these results is called 'free trade'; but there can be no freedom of trade

where there is no freedom of man, for the first of all commodities to be exchanged is labour, and the freedom of man consists only in the exercise of the right to determine for himself in what manner his labour shall be employed, and how he will dispose of its products. . . . It is the most gigantic system of slavery the world has yet seen." Thus Carey saw laissez-faire economics and slavery as links in the same chain.

Carey was the first internationally recognized American economist, his name synonymous with the American School posed against the "free trade," or British School. He was as much a social thinker as economist, a branch of what was commonly called political economy. His prestige was burnished by his lineage, wealth, and political influence. Mathew Carey, his father, was a Dublin publisher (an early pamphleteer against dueling), whose anti-British activity propelled him to exile in Paris, where he was drawn into the circle of Lafayette and Benjamin Franklin, becoming Franklin's assistant and political heir. Establishing a publishing house in Philadelphia, he uniquely promoted Hamiltonian economics and Jeffersonian politics. He bequeathed both his business and politics to his son. Henry C. Carey was literary mentor to the American School, publishing Washington Irving, James Fennimore Cooper, Edgar Allan Poe—and the *Encyclopedia Americana*. He also expanded his business holdings, founding the Franklin Insurance Company and investing in the Pennsylvania coal and steel industry. As a political economist, after brushing off an early infatuation with free market doctrine, he emerged as the towering intellectual figure of Whig and then Republican policies, becoming Lincoln's personal economic adviser.

Lincoln's diligent study of the political economy of the tariff provided him with an intellectual foundation for larger convictions. Carey's work articulated Lincoln's belief in the harmony of the self-made man and governmental activism, that the ability to take advantage of opportunity rested on more than the enterprising individual alone, that policies for progress must be national, and that behind the rhetoric of "free trade" and "liberty" lay vested interests, particularly British monopolists and slaveholders. Carey appealed to Lincoln's sense of the modern world, his utter lack of rural nostalgia, and fascination with technological innovation. Unlike Wayland, who defined separate realms of economic man and religious man, Carey saw society as a whole. Secular in his sensibility, his ideas had moral basis.

From 1844 onward, Lincoln spent years plumbing economic issues along the lines of Carey's thought. In one unpublished "Fragment of a Tariff Discussion," likely from 1847, he wrote, "In the early days of the world, the Almighty said to the first of our race 'In the sweat of thy face shalt thou eat bread.' . . . And, inasmuch [as] most good things are produced by labour, it follows that [all] such things of right belong to those whose labour has produced them. But it has so happened in all ages of the world, that some have laboured, and others have, without labour, enjoyed a large proportion of the fruits. This is wrong, and should not continue. To [secure] to each labourer the whole product of his labour, or as nearly as possible, is a most worthy object of any good government." Labor must be rightly rewarded and not dependent upon the beneficence of "free trade" but rise through the concerted action of "any good government."

As Lincoln relentlessly hammered his points on the tariff in debates, a spreading shadow loomed that he did his best to avoid. The *Journal* reported Lincoln's succinct opinion that Texas annexation was "altogether inexpedient," the most elaborate notice of his position. He continued with his discussion of the tariff as though politics would proceed as usual. But in Springfield the Democrats staged a rally on May 30, 1844, raising an American flag in which the "lone star" representing Texas was stitched in, larger than all the others. "The true question," read a statement signed by Governor Ford and a host of Democrats including John Calhoun and Archie Herndon, "is whether England, aided by the American abolitionists, shall have Texas, or whether it shall become a portion of this republic."

Through most of the Tyler administration Texas was a sleeping question, and when John C. Calhoun suddenly vaulted again to the center of power it became a stark imperative. With the election of the first Whig president, William Henry Harrison, in 1840, Henry Clay had expected to rule. He controlled the House and the Senate, was chairman of a Select Committee that controlled all the rest of the key committees, and took chairmanship of the Senate Finance Committee. Daniel Webster was appointed secretary of state, already jostling with Clay over the succession to Harrison. His Inaugural Address was a rebuke to Jackson, blaming the country's troubles on excessive executive power and conceding responsibility instead to the Congress even to the point of disclaiming almost all uses of the veto. "If you don't like anything in my administration, put it to Clay and Webster, but don't harpoon me," Harrison told Benton. Clay called for a special session to pass his whole program in one swoop, to expunge Van Buren's miserable sub-treasury, to charter a federal bank, sell Western public lands, and secure the tariff to raise revenue, and forge his system. When Harrison dithered Clay wrote him a strict note admonishing him for his "vacillating course." Harrison complained, "You are too impetuous," and informed Clay, his would-be master, he would never meet with him again. Before he could vacillate further, after a month in office Harrison was dead of pneumonia caught at his inauguration.

Clay had inserted John Tyler of Virginia into the vice presidential slot because Tyler had taken his side against Jackson after the United States Bank veto and resigned his Senate seat on principle. He was a states' rights Democrat who had favored nullification and wound up on the Whig ticket through Clay's casting because his hostility to Jackson at one point happened to coincide with Clay's. Tyler was not only in a secondary role but also an incidental character expected to fade into the woodwork. While Clay elevated him, he was anything but a Clay man; he gazed at Calhoun like a sun god. Once in the White House, Tyler cloistered himself with a coterie of advisers who were Calhoun's friends in Virginia such as Henry A. Wise. Clay, meanwhile, whipped his bills through the Congress. His critics lambasted the Great Compromiser as the Great Dictator. Calhoun, who had imposed the Gag Rule against antislavery petitions, accused Clay of attempting to impose "a gag system" on the Senate. Tyler met the passage of Clay's policies with veto after veto. On the eve of the first veto, Clay denounced Tyler as a traitor. "Tyler is on his way to the Democratic camp," he said. "They will give him lodgings in some outhouse, but they will never trust him. He will stand here, like [Benedict] Arnold in England, a monument of his own perfidy and disgrace." On September 11, 1841, the entire cabinet resigned in protest, except for one. Only Webster remained, half out of rivalry with Clay. When he told Tyler he would stay, Tyler offered a handshake, "Give me your hand on that, and now I am willing to say that Henry Clay is a doomed man from this hour." Clay delivered another speech tracing the source of trouble to Tyler's Calhounite entourage: "There is a rumor abroad, that a cabal exists—a new sort of kitchen cabinet—whose object is the dissolution of the regular cabinet, the dissolution of the Whig Party, the dispersion of Congress without accomplishing any of the great purposes of the extra session, and a total change, in fact, in the whole face of our political affairs." He had now taken to calling the president derisively "Captain Tyler." This "cabal," he charged, was "endeavoring to form a third party, with materials so scanty as to be wholly insufficient to compose a decent corporal's guard."

On March 31, 1842, Clay retired from the Senate, the hero of his party, "the Civil Hero of our country," according to Horace Greeley's *New York Tribune*, its inevitable nominee for president. He was in complete control of the Congress, but powerless. He had made the deals, even tried to make his bills acceptable to Tyler through amendments proposed by his supporters, and passed the programs, but was stymied by this minor actor he had plucked from obscurity. On the day of his resignation, he sent a letter to the Whig convention in North Carolina casting anathema on Tyler and his friends: "A president without a party, and parties without a president! A president denouncing his friends and courting his political opponents, who, in their turn, without entertaining for him the least respect or confidence, give him flattery and praise! enough just to deceive and delude him. A president who, affecting to soar in an atmosphere above that of all parties, and to place himself upon the broad and patriotic foundation of the whole nation, is vainly seeking, by a culpable administration of the patronage of the government, to create a third party!" Clay's frustration was not only confounding but also paradoxical. It had now brought him near to the edge of the presidency. If all things were equal, he had only to await the inexorable ticking of events. But he was suffering under the weight of disappointment. He had lost the presidency and now he lost everything again. He played the game as neatly as anyone, and he knew that the game went on and on, but in the end it was not just a game. His ambition was blocked, but his ambition was not merely about the offices and honor he sought. He had ambition for his ideas, choked just as they were finally about to come to life. Three days after his retirement, he suffered a minor heart attack, "great pain."

Tyler surrounded himself with Calhoun's followers, but Calhoun did not think of Tyler as one of them, even though he had been during the nullification crisis. "The course of Mr. Tyler is doubtful," he wrote on June 13, 1841. "He is no doubt deeply opposed to Clay, but he is essentially a man for the middle ground, and will attempt to take a middle position now when there is none. Such is my fears. If he should he will be lost." By August, Calhoun saw that the split between Tyler and Clay "cannot be healed." By November, he believed that the Whigs "are thoroughly defeated, and will dissolve, as a party, never to rise again under the same name and form." There "will be no foe to dread." He was ready to discuss "the next presidency." That, he thought, should and would be him. "It is my own impression, that, if it is ever intended, now is the time." He foresaw "an important epocha in our political History," in which "federalism and consolidation" may be "entirely overthrown, and the old State rights Republican principles and policy established in their place"—"now is the time." His issue again would be the tariff.

Calhoun's campaign handlers immediately began organizing supporters in the states. Quietly, they held out the prospect of the vice presidency to Senator Silas Wright of New York and Senator Levi Woodbury of New Hampshire, who might balance the ticket. Calhoun retired from the Senate at the end of 1842, and the *Charleston Mercury* announced he was a presidential candidate. But Calhoun's campaign had more ideological certainty than organizational finesse. In Virginia, the pro–Van Buren forces led by Ritchie of the Richmond Junto gerrymandered congressional districts to oust Calhoun's campaign chairman, the complacent aristocrat of the "Virginia Chivalry" faction, Congressman Robert M. T. Hunter. In New York and Massachusetts Democratic state conventions passed resolutions upholding the tariff. Calhoun's premise as a sectional leader demolished his standing as a national candidate. The tariff was not an issue that would carry him to the White House, but instead a self-destructive mechanism. Even his followers understood that he could not win. Webster, who quit the cabinet, decided to back Clay. The dynamic among Democrats quickly moved toward Van Buren. When the new Democratic majority of the 28th Congress held its first caucus on December 2, 1843, the Calhoun group tried to control election of the new speaker through a two-thirds rule change, but simply lost outright. The little attempted coup was interpreted within the party as the end of Calhoun's hopes. Van Buren seemed certain to be the party's next nominee. On December 22, Calhoun sent a letter to Hunter with his "address" to his "political friends and supporters" announcing the withdrawal of his candidacy. "The object now is, not victory, but to preserve our position and principles," he wrote. He had no use for Van Buren, "a doomed man . . . whose defeat is necessary to save the party." Within days he raised a new issue to "keep the flag flying"—Texas. It had already eclipsed the tariff months earlier.

John Quincy Adams's opposition to Texas annexation was early, adamant, and intransigent. He glimpsed past the sloganeering for "Manifest Destiny," the militant editorials of the jingoist *Democratic Review*, and the political grouping around it calling itself Young America to see a portentous future. Along with Joshua Giddings and eleven other members of the House Foreign Affairs Committee he issued "An Address to the People of the Free States" on March 3, 1843, decrying the annexation of Texas and the extension of slavery—an act that would be "identical with dissolution . . . a violation of our national compact, its objects, designs, and the great elementary principles which entered into its formation . . . so injurious to the interests and abhorrent to the feelings of the people of the free states, as, in our opinion, not only inevitably to result in a dissolution of the Union, but fully to justify it; and we not only assert that the people of the free states 'ought not to submit to it,' but we say, with confidence, they would not submit to it."

Adams's "Address" was a response to a choreographed propaganda campaign directed by the Tyler administration. On January 23, 1844, Congressman Thomas W. Gilmer of Virginia, one of Tyler's inner circle, whom he would name secretary of the navy a month later, launched the agitation in favor of annexation in *The Madisonian*, the Tyler paper in the capital.

The election of 1844 was the turning point, if not of a critical realignment of voters identified by modern political scientists, then the fatal undermining of the two-party system that had emerged under Jackson. Its consequences fundamentally upset the balance of power between the slave states and the free, opening the irreconcilable issue of slavery's extension that had supposedly been closed by the Missouri Compromise, and began the disintegration of the parties that led to the Civil War.

In June 1843, Tyler appointed Abel P. Upshur to replace Daniel Webster as secretary of state. (Tyler's first replacement, Hugh Swinton Legaré of South Carolina, a states' rights Unionist, whom he shifted from attorney general, died after two months in the job.) Upshur had been Tyler's secretary of the navy, a veteran Virginia politician and planter, an old ally of both Tyler and Calhoun, and fervent nullifier. As recently as 1840 he had written a lengthy book denouncing the Constitution for counting slaves only as three fifths of a person for political representation. "The truth is, the slave-holding States have always contributed more than their just proportion to the wealth and strength of the country. . . . This is the only perfectly just measure of political influence. . . . The slave-holding States, therefore, had a right to demand that *all* their slaves should be represented; they yielded too much in agreeing that only three-fifths of them should possess that right." Upshur's constitutional treatise was not so much a squire's leisurely foray into history as a politician's anxiety that the political balance of power was tipping against the South. His remedy was annexation of Texas, which he believed would incidentally undermine the candidacies of both Van Buren and Clay.

As soon as he was sworn in, Upshur began receiving letters from Tyler's private agent roaming through London, Calhoun's devoted operative and in-law, Duff Green, "the ambassador of slavery," as Adams dubbed him. When Green, a lifelong Democrat, joined the Whigs in 1840 and pledged his backing to Harrison's candidacy, his motive was to gain the federal printing contract and secure the vice presidency for Calhoun. Calhoun, however, would have nothing to do with Harrison. "I would rather," he wrote Green, "to use your own expression, stand alone in my glory, seeing what is coming, raising an honest and fearless voice of forewarning, untainted and untouched by the times, than to be President of these States." But Calhoun's distant equipoise was hardly his true stance. His gestures of humility always signaled ambition.

Green reported personally to Tyler that the British government intended to make a loan to Texas in exchange for the emancipation of its slaves. Gallivanting through London's drawing rooms and meeting with Prime Minister Robert Peel, Green superseded the U.S. minister to the Court of St. James, the dignified and capable Edward Everett, Webster's friend and former governor of Massachusetts. In a letter to Upshur adorned with ornate politeness, Everett described Green's "mind being preoccupied with certain unfounded impressions"—a letter marked "Not sent." Green's confidential intelligence, in fact, was based on erroneous rumor as well as wild hearsay about the intentions of delegates to the British and Foreign Anti-Slavery Society convention. Every distortion led to a self-serving political conclusion. Green advised Tyler in one letter, on July 3, 1843, that if he would "meet this crisis" it would "greatly advance your own fame and popularity" and "you will control events." Green explained how by exploiting the issue he could defeat each of his political rivals. "Rely on what I tell you," he wrote. "It is to become the question which will absorb all other questions."

Upshur, as well as Tyler, accepted Green's unreliable reporting at face value because it was what they wished to believe. Upshur had other reasons, which he spelled out in a letter on August 14 to Calhoun. If not annexed Texas would fall under British influence, become an economic rival and haven for fugitive slaves. "To the South, it is a question of safety." Based on an appeal to the Northern profit motive, "I think it will not be difficult to convince them that their interest required the admission of Texas into the Union as a slaveholding state." He added, "The history of the world does not present an example of such insult, contempt, and multiplied wrongs and outrages from one nation to another as we have received and are daily receiving from our Northern brethren!!" He begged Calhoun for his views. "What then ought we to do?" Calhoun agreed that the "danger is great and menacing," threatening "the very existence of the South."

Calhoun composed for the president a "master plan," according to the historian Frederick Merk, precise in tactics on how to blame the British for being provocative: demanding a formal "explanation," diplomatically drawing in France and Prussia to criticize Britain, and mounting a domestic propaganda campaign stemming from Virginia, not South Carolina, beginning in the *Richmond Enquirer* that would be "copied and followed up in the Southern papers." Calhoun's plan would be executed to a fine point, but in a sequence staggered by unpredictable events.

By the fall of 1843 Calhoun's candidacy was already undone, defeated by Van Buren, still the Little Magician of organization, in nearly all the state party conventions, which endorsed him. "Unless some explosion should take place in Congress to arouse the South I fear that V B will get the nomination from a convention constituted on his own terms and I suppose the resistance which he will experience in the party will be rather passive than active," Hunter wrote Calhoun. "Such seems to me to be the present tendency of events. In this view of the case I look to the probable future course of public affairs with deep despondency." "Some explosion" would literally soon come.

By January 20, 1844, Upshur, following Calhoun's blueprint, authorized a message to Texas that there would be a treaty of annexation to be followed by the dispatch of "a large naval force" and "Military force." A month later, on February 28, President Tyler took his cabinet and other notables for a scenic cruise down the Potomac on the navy's largest battleship, the USS *Princeton*, to celebrate the first firing of its enormous new cannon, dubbed "the Peacemaker." When it came time for the demonstration, the gun blew up on deck, killing Upshur and Gilmer, Tyler's two closest cabinet members. Congressman Henry Wise of Virginia, one of Tyler's intimate advisers, wrote, "as long as Upshur or Legare was alive, the Southwestern question was in safe Southern hands, but now that they were both taken away, there was one man left who was necessary above all others to the South in settling and obtaining the annexation of Texas. We need hardly say that man was John C. Calhoun, of South Carolina. But we knew that, for some reason of which we were never informed, the President was opposed to calling him to his Cabinet."

Carpe diem. Acting without any authority but that provided by his own audacity, Wise informed George McDuffie of South Carolina, who replaced Calhoun in the Senate and was his agent, that the president had already offered the position of secretary of state to Calhoun. Then Wise scurried to the White House, where he found Tyler weeping over the *Princeton* disaster. Wise explained that if he didn't nominate Calhoun he would face an extraordinary break with the influential Senator McDuffie, who, Wise insisted, had already informed Calhoun of the decision, and that Wise himself, Tyler's indispensable counselor, would never again speak to him. The emotionally distraught Tyler collapsed and promptly announced Calhoun's appointment. "But 'the policy of rashness' saved us, as it had often done before and has often done since, and sent in Mr. Calhoun's nomination," wrote the triumphant Wise, ". . . and neither Mr. Calhoun nor Mr. McDuffie ever knew, so far as we are informed, how it was procured."

Now secretary of state, Calhoun, on April 18, electrified politics, following the "master plan" he had laid out to Upshur. He issued what was called the Pakenham Letter, his feverishly written but coolly calculated reply to a proper and regular communiqué from the British ambassador, Richard Pakenham, in which Pakenham had reiterated his country's well-known views as the mediator of the Texas-Mexican conflict that Britain wished for Texas independence and while generally favorable to abolition would apply no pressure to that end. Calhoun, however, twisted his statement to transform the whole issue of Texas annexation into a question of the sanctity of slavery. "Great Britain desires and is constantly exerting herself to procure, the general abolition of slavery throughout the world," Calhoun charged, and he launched into a defense of slavery as the essential foundation of the United States: "what is called slavery is in reality a political institution, essential to the peace, safety, and prosperity of those States of the Union in which it exists." He underpinned his argument with bogus census statistics supposedly proving that emancipated blacks suffered compared to slaves. "They have been invariably sunk into vice and pauperism, accompanied by the bodily and mental inflictions incident thereto—deafness, blindness, insanity, and idiocy—to a degree without example; while, in all other States which have retained the ancient relation between them, they have improved greatly in every respect—in number, comfort, intelligence, and morals." Massachusetts, he claimed, presented the worst case, where "the greatest zeal has been exhibited in their behalf," but where "the condition of the African is amongst the most wretched." Britain's supposed abolitionism lurking behind its Texas diplomacy would "involve in the greatest calamity the whole country, and especially the race which it is the avowed object of her exertions to benefit."

On the same day as the release of Calhoun's Pakenham Letter, Clay and Van Buren coincidentally issued statements opposing the annexation of Texas. Van Buren's letter, written a month earlier and published in the *Washington Globe*, contrasted "aggression and conquest" to "reason and justice," promising that if the majority of public opinion was in favor of annexation sometime in the future he might then be favorable. Van Buren complacently expected to be nominated, anticipated that Clay would not run on annexation, and calculated that he would take the issue off the table, "this Texas mania," as Senator Silas Wright of New York, his close adviser, put it. Van Buren's letter, framed cautiously, seeking to capture the middle ground, in retrospect appeared either the most courageous or foolish act of his careful career. He had angled characteristically along what he thought was the safest course. At the moment Van Buren released his letter, annexation was not particularly popular and he was advised that he would not offend those Democrats for whom it was. He did not know that he was walking blindly into a trap set by those plotting to deprive him of the nomination, hoping to open the door for either Senator Lewis Cass of Michigan or Senator James Buchanan of Pennsylvania. The combination of Calhoun's Pakenham Letter and Van Buren's own letter ravaged him among Democrats in the South and finally convinced those Democrats already privately worried about his viability that he was finished. Van Buren's letter sent Calhoun into a self-described "extacy of delight." One of Van Buren's friends, Congressman Job Pierson of New York, who would back him to the bitter end, wrote Polk after the Democratic convention that while he considered Van Buren's letter the act of "a statesman," he had "on the Texas question committed as Talleyrand said, 'more than a crime. It was a blunder.'" But it was more than "a blunder"—it was an ambush.

Just as Van Buren expected to face Clay, Clay expected to face Van Buren.

He planned a contest waged around economic issues that would give him the decided advantage as demonstrated by the Southern Whig support for the Tariff of 1842. Van Buren still carried the taint of the Panic of 1837. Clay dismissed the Texas issue as having "no other than the wicked purpose of producing discord and distraction in the nation." In his so-called Raleigh Letter, he wrote, "Annexation and war with Mexico are identical." He was against both. With that, he thought he had disposed of the issue. Instead, like Van Buren, he opened fissures in his support on every side.

"Texas is all now—tariff is nothing," declared Senator Thomas Hart Benton of Missouri. "Van Buren and his friends are kicked off. Tyler and Texas is the word—and all the rest may go to the devil."

Andrew Jackson's letter in favor of annexation, calling it a "golden moment," was at last published in *The Madisonian* on April 3. It had been held in reserve for a year in order for the moment that would stoke the campaign to fever pitch. Old Hickory had hesitated in the past to plunge into the cauldron. His statement not only caused maximum damage to Van Buren, but signaled at once the apotheosis and imminent dissolution of the Jacksonian political world.

Senator Robert J. Walker of Mississippi, acting as Tyler's political agent, took on the assignment of setting Jackson against his loyal successor, "to blow Van out of the water." Walker told Jackson that annexation would be his "crowning act." Jackson needed little convincing. He was passionately in favor of annexation. The spark of his excitement was his usual highly flammable combination of nationalism and Anglophobia. Hatred of the British never left him since a British soldier gashed his skull during the Revolutionary War. He bore the scar and hostility for life. The hero of the Battle of New Orleans still tightly held to his conviction that the British were plotting to seize Texas to establish their own empire in the American West. It was a grand paranoid theory with a corollary about thwarting "that arch fiend, J.Q Adams" and "the abolition and Eastern Federal papers." At a meeting at the Hermitage, Jackson's home, on May 10, Old Hickory pronounced his successor Van Buren "ruined" and anointed former speaker of the house James K. Polk of Tennessee, dubbed Young Hickory, as his new protégé. He had traded protégés before, Calhoun for Van Buren, and now he dumped "the used up man" for a bright shiny object. Jackson said that Van Buren's letter against annexation "mortified" him and made him "shed tears of regret."

He wrote Van Buren that "the die was cast" and "it was impossible to elect him," pronouncing a political death sentence. Jackson's adviser, Francis P. Blair, who published Van Buren's letter against annexation in the *Globe*, pled with Jackson not to abandon Van Buren and reminded him not to enable his ancient enemy Calhoun, who was promoting "dissolution of the Union, and a Southern Confederacy." Jackson conceded that Blair was right about Calhoun, but that he was determined on "annexation regardless of the consequences." It would be, after all, his legacy.

Adams always understood Calhoun's game and homed in on the weakness he found in his Pakenham Letter, his false census statistics about slaves and free blacks, turning the issue in a merry little replay of the Gag Rule drama. He submitted a letter to be read by the speaker deriding Calhoun for his errors, which was tabled and went unread. So he walked over to the State Department to confront Calhoun personally. Calhoun "answered like a true slavemonger," Adams wrote in his diary. "He writhed like a trodden rattlesnake on the exposure of his false report to the House . . . and finally said that where there were so many errors they balanced one another, and led to the same conclusion as if they were all correct." Adams's ruthless humiliation of Calhoun, exposing his intellectual and political squalor before an audience consisting mainly of himself, was personally gratifying, recorded in his diary (doubly gratifying), but had no public resonance.

On April 22, four days after the release of Pakenham Letter, Tyler sent the treaty for annexation to the Senate with Calhoun's letter appended, "to explode the Texas bomb," in a popular phrase of the day. It was lit on a long fuse a month before the Democratic convention, timed to "explode" under Van Buren.

At the convention at Baltimore opening on May 27 Van Buren arrived with a substantial but soft majority, which he could not hold after a procedural vote on a rule change that radically altered the process for nomination. Senator Walker, Tyler's agent, steered a resolution for a two-thirds majority requirement. Calhoun's man at the convention, Congressman Francis W. Pickens, worked hand in glove with Walker. "Walker I have been with much—he fights nobly, but does not see the end of his own moves," Pickens reported to Calhoun from Baltimore. "If they dispute all points, as they will do I think, it will end in confusion, and blowing up of the convention. All the members begin to see the nomination is in fact the election, and therefore they will contend for every inch." Van Buren's enemies coalesced to destroy him through the torpedo of the rule change. Once it passed, his fate was sealed. On the first ballot, his large majority fell short of two-thirds. In any previous convention he would have received the nomination. For seven ballots his delegate strength steadily eroded until he collapsed on the ninth. James K. Polk emerged as nominee, the first dark horse ever to win at a party convention. He offered the vice presidential place to Silas Wright, Van Buren's New York ally, to heal the party rift, but Wright rejected it, too embittered and opposed to annexation. George M. Dallas, former U.S. senator from Pennsylvania and Walker's brother-in-law, one of the anti–Van Buren plotters, was slated instead. "V. B. dead forever," Pickens gleefully wrote Calhoun. (The two-thirds rule, which remained in effect until Franklin D. Roosevelt removed it in 1936, gave the South a virtual veto over the nomination.) Polk's surprising nomination completely altered the dynamics of the race, removed the burden of Van Buren and his past baggage, guaranteed that Texas would be the sole issue, and threw Clay on the defensive.

The rejection of the Texas treaty by the Senate under Whig control, on June 8, did not put an end to the issue. Instead, it raised it as the paramount question of the campaign and lifted Polk's candidacy. Dissident Jacksonians were enraged at what they considered Calhoun's coup. It was the realization of their worst nightmare. Thomas Hart Benton and Francis P. Blair, titans of the Jackson era, both Jackson's intimates, bore the past as more than distant memory but had it encoded in their frontal lobes. They knew what everyone had really done, with whom and to whom, recalled what had been printed in public and what had been said in private, which promises were broken and which kept, and, most importantly, who was loyal and who had betrayed. Calhoun hated them as irredeemable Jackson men and they returned his hatred.

As a young Tennessee lawyer and state senator Benton had attached his star to Jackson, who appointed him aide-de-camp at the start of the War of 1812. During a ferocious quarrel the next year, Benton shot Jackson in a tavern brawl in which Jackson almost died, his blood soaking two mattresses. "General Jackson was a very great man, sir. I shot him, sir," remarked Benton. Moving to St. Louis, Benton became the first citizen of the Missouri Territory, its most prominent attorney, owner of its biggest newspaper, the *Missouri Enquirer*, and elected its first U.S. senator. By the time of Jackson's election as president in 1828, he and Benton had reconciled as the closest of political allies, and Benton emerged as the Democratic leader in the Senate and a member of Jackson's "Kitchen Cabinet." Benton's great cause was Western expansion and he had been among the earliest and most strenuous advocates of adding Texas to the Union, but not this way, not through these tactics, not through Calhoun's and Tyler's scheming. A wealthy slave owner and self-proclaimed Southerner, who brought slaves with him to Washington, Benton turned decisively against the expansion of slavery.

Like Benton, Blair remained true to ingrained Jacksonian loyalties and animosities, even as the world of Jacksonian politics came apart. Within the "Kitchen Cabinet" Blair was a shrewd adviser on how to navigate the currents of Northern and Southern opinion within the party. Blair and Benton, in fact, were distant cousins and raised their families almost as one—Benton's daughter Jesse Hart Benton like a sister to Blair's sons Montgomery and Frank Blair. Benton and Blair embodied the crisis of Jacksonianism as politics entered a new, tumultuous period whose worst-case scenario of Southern secession and Civil War they could both envision.

Like Benton, Blair clearly recalled why he was hostile to Calhoun and why that hostility endured. During the nullification crisis, Blair had written in the *Globe* that "the right of nullification" appealed to "certain men, who, like Caesar, would rather reign in a village, than be second in Rome"—an allusion to John Milton's Lucifer, the fallen angel from *Paradise Lost* who would prefer "to reign in Hell than to serve in Heaven." Those words still clung to Calhoun and stung him. In the Senate, his agent McDuffie threw a reference back at Benton, comparing his opposition to the Texas treaty to Brutus assassinating Caesar. Everyone would have remembered that it was Jackson who had accused Calhoun of being an assassin with the famous words: "Et tu, Brute?"

Two weeks after the Democratic convention, on June 15, Benton rose on the Senate floor, pounded his desk, and pointed at McDuffie. His startling accusation about the inner politics of Texas annexation was emblazoned across Whig newspapers—and Blair's *Globe*. "Disunion is at the bottom of this long-concealed Texas machination. Intrigue and speculation co-operate; but disunion is at the bottom, and I denounce it to the American people," Benton charged. "Under the pretext of getting Texas into the Union, the scheme is to get the South out of it. A separate confederacy, stretching from the Atlantic to the Californias (and hence the secret of the Rio Grande del Norte frontier), is the cherished vision of disappointed ambition; and for this consummation every circumstance has been carefully and artfully contrived. A secret and intriguing negotiation, concealed from Congress and the people; an abolition quarrel picked with Great Britain to father an abolition quarrel at home." And he predicted the method of dissolution. "I mention secession as the more cunning method of dissolving the Union. It is disunion, and the more dangerous because less palpable. Nullification begat it, and if allowed there is an end to the Union." When he finished, Adams, who had come from the House to observe, walked across the floor to shake Benton's hand. Jackson, who had cast Van Buren to the wolves and rebuffed Blair, who had worshipped him, wrote that "Benton's position is inexplicable" and wondered whether he had been unhinged by the explosion on the *Princeton*. Throughout the South, Benton was reviled as a traitor. But to him these politics were the triumph of nullification by other means. He wrote that the nomination of Polk was the result of an "intrigue," beginning with the Gilmer letter and ending with the two-thirds rule change at the convention, "the power of the minority to govern the majority," which "nullified the choice of the people" and put the presidency into the hands of a "cabal."

Tyler still wished to be president, elected in his own right, and arranged his nomination at a rump convention of his own contrivance, the vanity affair of a man without a party attempting to conjure the illusion of one. If he gathered any momentum, he would split the South and elect Clay. But Polk solidified Southern support by cutting a deal with Calhoun through his emissary Pickens. At a meeting at Polk's Nashville home on August 15, the candidate agreed to all of Calhoun's demands, not least eliminating Blair's government printing contract. "He and Mr. Calhoun thoroughly understood each other," wrote Pickens, who composed a letter in Polk's library to Calhoun with the final details of the deal, wrapping up his comprehensive revenge. "Everything is completely satisfactory," Pickens wrote Calhoun, who replied that with Polk's imminent ascension they could "throw off the burden, which has been weighing down the South, exhausting her means and debasing her spirit . . . since 1828"—that is, since Jackson trumped Calhoun in the nullification crisis. With the agreement between Polk and Calhoun, Tyler withdrew his candidacy.

In July, Clay tried to appeal to the South through his so-called Alabama

Letters. "As to the idea of my courting the abolitionists, it is perfectly absurd," he protested. On the contrary, he proudly trumpeted that he had been "abused by them more than any other public man in the United States." As to Texas, that was "a bubble blown up by Mr. Tyler." Clay's previous letter from April against annexation was to be forgotten. Now, he declared, he wasn't against annexation, or against slavery in Texas, but only against war with Mexico, and he would be "governed" by "the state of public opinion existing at the time I may be called upon to act." With that, he echoed Van Buren's blundering statement on Texas, seeming to validate the worst criticism of himself as little more than a gamester. Disaffection spread through the North. "I feel tolerably angry," wrote a gloomy Webster. "Things look blue," wrote Thurlow Weed, the New York political boss. "Ugly letter, that to Alabama."

The Alabama Letters did Clay little good in the South. His wet position was a sop that simply slid off the table. Southern Whigs deserted him wholesale. "The Coalition Between the Clay Party and the Abolitionists of the North and Northwest" ran a typical screaming headline in a Southern newspaper. Senator Walker, who had engineered Jackson's letter on Texas and the convention's two-thirds rule, was busy again, publishing a pamphlet entitled *The South in Danger* that was widely circulated as the chief Democratic campaign document. "The object is to taboo the South, to render us infamous, to put the mark of Cain upon our forehead, and to deprive us of character first, as the means of despoiling us of our property afterwards. Men of the South, the effort is to disgrace and degrade you and your children forever." The Whig Party's secret agenda, he claimed, was abolition, "only using different means to accomplish the same object" as the abolitionists, and that "the abolition of slavery will be more certainly effected by the election of Clay" than by the openly abolitionist candidate of the Liberty Party.

Clay's running mate was a paragon of virtue, Theodore J. Freylinghuysen, one of the most prominent evangelical Christians in public life, the former U.S. senator from New Jersey and president of the American Bible Society, descended from his namesake, the Dutch Reform preacher who had launched the First Great Awakening in 1720. But his presence on the ticket did not inoculate Clay from character attacks. "No Duellist or Gambler" read a Democratic banner featuring Clay holding a pack of cards and a pistol. "Christian Voters! Read, Pause and Reflect! Mr. Clay's Moral Character" read the title of one widely circulated Democratic pamphlet. "I believe," Clay complained, "I have been charged with every crime enumerated in the Decalogue."

Lashed as an abolitionist by Southern Democrats, Clay was flayed by abolitionists as a slave owner. The Liberty Party was the first party devoted to abolition, moving beyond Garrison's moral suasion into the political arena, taking the Declaration of Independence as its credo. Its candidate, James Birney, a former Alabama slaveholder converted to the cause by Theodore Weld, had freed his slaves, and published an antislavery newspaper in Cincinnati, *The Philanthropist*, destroyed by a mob in 1836. The Liberty Party did not focus its attack on Polk, the candidate who would extend slavery, but on Clay, who would restrict it. Its newspapers published cartoons depicting him whipping slaves and circulated a quotation falsely attributed to him: "If gentlemen will not allow us to have black slaves, they must let us have white ones." Birney coauthored one pamphlet, *The Great Duelist*, and another, *Headlands in the Life of Henry Clay*, that portrayed him as a dissolute, murderous Southern oppressor. These documents perfectly complemented the negative Democratic campaign.

Clay lost the entire Deep South and barely held on to his own border region. He lost New York by 5,106 votes and Michigan by 3,422 where Birney held the decisive margins by 15,812 and 3,632. Clay also lost Northern voters who simply stayed home, unenthusiastic after his Alabama Letters. If Clay had won both states he would have handily won the election. Whigs firmly believed that the Liberty Party cost Clay the election. But New York was lost for the Whigs as a result of more than the razor-thin vote for the Liberty Party; the Democrats also won it as a result of Van Buren. Deprived, discarded, and debased, he remained a man of the party. He had pride of authorship, as it were, in creating the Democratic Party that had elected Jackson twice and elevated him to the presidency. He would not abandon it, just because he did not get a nomination. Polk appealed to him that he would revive his sub-treasury plan. With Silas Wright on the ticket for New York governor, there was the crucial incentive to turn out the party line vote. Wright and his followers were opposed to annexation—but their efforts elected Polk and made annexation possible. Van Buren felt his long political career was at a close. But after he and his New York faction delivered the presidency to Polk, they would be rewarded with cold betrayal, excluded from the spoils, and setting the stage for a schism in the next presidential election. Van Buren's good-faith support for his party was the prelude to his rupture with it.

In Illinois the election was foretold in the August legislative results in which the Democrats swamped the Whigs and swept every congressional seat except for the Seventh District. The *Quincy Whig* newspaper blamed the landslide on the "foreign vote . . . the abolition vote, and the Mormon vote," leaving Texas unmentioned. Toward the close of the campaign Lincoln gave up on Clay winning Illinois and rode into Indiana, to "the neighborhood in that State in which I was raised, where my mother and only sister were buried," he wrote. At Gentryville he had an emotional homecoming with his old friends—Josiah Crawford, the Gentrys, Nat Grigsby, and the others. "That part of the country is, within itself, as unpoetical as any spot of the earth," Lincoln wrote, "but still, seeing it and its objects and inhabitants aroused feelings in me which were certainly poetry; though whether my expression of those feelings is poetry is quite another question." Nonetheless, he composed a melancholy little poem: "My childhood's home I see again/ And sadden with the view; And still, as memory crowds the brain,/ There's pleasure in it too./ Ah, Memory! thou midway world,/ 'Twixt earth and Paradise,/ Where things decayed and loved ones lost/ In dreamy shadows rise. And freed from all that's earthy, vile,/ Seems hallowed, pure and bright,/ Like scenes in some enchanted isle/ All bathed in liquid light." Clay lost Indiana, too.

The motley array of political forces that collectively rained invective on Clay had set the country veering onto a disastrous course, Adams wrote in his diary with inimitably vigorous pessimism, beginning his entry with a description of a total eclipse of the moon. "The partial associations of Native Americans, Irish Catholics, abolition societies, Liberty party, the Pope of Rome, the Democracy of the sword, and the dotage of a ruffian, are sealing the fate of this nation, which nothing less than the interposition of Omnipotence can save." By "Native Americans" he didn't mean Indians but anti-immigrant nativists—and the "ruffian," of course, referred to Andrew Jackson. So far as he was concerned the election in any case was illegitimate, based on the clause of the Constitution for counting slaves as three-fifths of a person for electoral representation. "It has been accomplished by fraud through the slave-representation."

After the election Tyler repackaged the defeated Texas treaty as a joint resolution of the Congress, requiring a simple majority vote, not two thirds of the Senate. Along with a sheaf of supporting documents Tyler sent the Congress a letter from Secretary of State Calhoun to the U.S. minister to France, William R. King, from August 12, 1844, making clear that his principal concern must be the protection and extension of slavery. Calhoun emphasized repeatedly the canard that British diplomacy was aimed at "abolishing it in Texas, with the view of its abolition in the United States"—and that this "scheme" had "originated with the prominent members of the party in the United States, and was first broached by them in the so-called world's convention, held in London in the year 1840, and through its agency brought to the notice of the British Government." Thus, in consummate exploitation of the paranoid style, Calhoun exposed a supposed conspiracy of the British government allegedly directed by abolitionist delegates to the British and Foreign Anti-Slavery Society four years earlier. But his frightful analysis delved further into the depths of conspiracy: Britain's emancipation of its slaves in the West Indies had been "disastrous," a "suicidal policy," bringing investments there to "the brink of ruin," and was its "motive" behind "abolition of slavery in Texas as a most important step toward this great object of policy"—"a fatal blow" against slavery in the United States, giving Britain "a monopoly in the productions of the whole continent, and the command of the commerce, navigation, and manufactures of the world." Acting at Calhoun's direction, following his original scenario laid out for Upshur, Ambassador King secured the assurance of King Louis Philippe of France, which still maintained slavery in its West Indies colonies, that he would support the U.S. position. (King, former U.S. senator from Alabama, was one of the state's largest slaveholders, owner of a massive plantation near Selma, a town he named. He was also the intimate friend of Senator James Buchanan of Pennsylvania, his longtime housemate, "a gentle slave-monger, called by Jackson 'Miss Nancy,'" as Adams noted piquantly in his diary. King would become Franklin Pierce's vice president, and die after little more than a month in office.)

Visions of Texas divided into five new slave states danced in the heads of Southerners—memorialized in an amendment to the resolution offered by Congressman Milton Brown of Tennessee. Brown was a Whig, a symptom of the faltering Southern Whig Party over the question of slavery extension. After McDuffie introduced Tyler's resolution in the Senate, Benton proposed a mischievous amendment that would split Texas into two states, one slave and one free, "but for none of the negro reasons—or as it ought to be pronounced on this occasion, nigger reasons." But Benton soon dropped his derisive gesture. Just a week before Polk's inauguration, the joint resolution passed with the majority provided by defecting Southern Whigs. "Such a victory was never obtained by a President without a party," exulted Wise of Virginia.

As one of his first acts, true to his agreement with Calhoun, President Polk purged Blair, handing his lucrative government-printing contract to Thomas Ritchie, editor of the *Richmond Enquirer* and leader of the Richmond Junto. During the campaign Ritchie had been "Van Buren's Secretary of the Southern Department," but had abandoned him on the eve of the Democratic convention, where he threw Virginia's delegation, last on the roll call, behind the two-thirds rule, and coined the slogan: "Polk and Texas." Blair was pressured to sell the *Globe*, with even Jackson weighing in against his ultimate loyalist, the age of Jackson culminating in an act of pettiness, as Young Hickory, heir apparent, assumed office.

Calhoun had once again failed to gain the presidency, but he had succeeded in forcing the issue of Texas annexation, transforming it into a litmus test on slavery, crushing Van Buren and Clay, and escorting Tyler offstage. A month after the election, Calhoun came to Richmond to dine with Ritchie, celebrating the new era they would usher in, but was still wary of him as Jackson's old ally. Ritchie soon arrived in Washington to edit a new paper to provide the artillery of opinion for the Polk administration. It was entitled, without any irony, *The Union*. Calhoun contemplated a reign as the power behind the throne. But Polk, regarding himself the second coming of Jackson, wrote in December 1844, "I intend to be myself President of the U.S." Calhoun soon bitterly fell out with Polk, as he bitterly fell out with anyone occupying the presidency he always cherished for himself.

CHAPTER TWELVE

INFIDELS

If the Whig abolitionists of New York had voted with us last fall, Mr. Clay would now be president, Whig principles in the ascendant, and Texas not annexed; whereas by the division, all that either had at stake in the contest, was lost," Lincoln lamented a year after the defeat. He found the politics of moral absolutism irrational and counterproductive, achieving unintended tragic consequences. The Liberty Party's undermining of Clay was as clear a case as he had ever seen of the perfect as the enemy of the good. "What was their process of reasoning, I can only judge from what a single one of them told me. It was this: 'We are not to do evil that good may come.' This general, proposition is doubtless correct; but did it apply? If by your votes you could have prevented the extention, &c. of slavery, would it not have been good and not evil so to have used

Salmon P. Chase

your votes, even though it involved the casting of them for a slaveholder? By the fruit the tree is to be known. An evil tree cannot bring forth good fruit. If the fruit of electing Mr. Clay would have been to prevent the extension of slavery, could the act of electing have been evil?"

But Lincoln confessed that he had not taken the Texas issue seriously—and still misjudged its gravity. Unlike Adams or Calhoun, Benton or Blair, he did not have a premonition that it would transform politics. "I perhaps ought to say that individually I never was much interested in the Texas question," he wrote. "I never could see much good to come of annexation; inasmuch, as they were already a free republican people on our own model; on the other hand, I never could very clearly see how the annexation would augment the evil of slavery." On the other hand, he argued, if annexation meant the spread of slavery, he would be opposed. "To whatever extent this may be true, I think annexation an evil. I hold it to be a paramount duty of us in the free states, due to the Union of the states, and perhaps to liberty itself (paradox though it may seem) to let the slavery of the other states alone; while, on the other hand, I hold it to be equally clear, that we should never knowingly lend ourselves directly or indirectly, to prevent that slavery from dying a natural death—to find new places for it to live in, when it can no longer exist in the old."

Lincoln's correspondent was Williamson Durley, "a Liberty-man" whose support he was cultivating for future elections. "I was glad to hear you say that you intend to attempt to bring about, at the next election in Putnam [County], a union of the Whigs proper, and such of the liberty men, as are Whigs in principle on all questions save only that of slavery," Lincoln wrote. "So far as I can perceive, by such union, neither party need yield anything, on the point in difference between them." This gesture, in his letter of October 3, 1845, was an early indication of the fusion of political forces that Lincoln did not then foresee—the emergence a decade later of the Republican Party of Illinois.

The Liberty Party of Illinois won a grand total of 157 votes in 1840. Though the party was listed on the ballot it was not formally organized in the state. It was the product of a bitter national split between two abolitionist factions, one that by 1839 had concluded that political action was necessary to achieve its ends and the other led by William Lloyd Garrison that insisted on the utter corruption of the electoral process and the moral imperatives of "perfectionism" and "nonresistance." "Mr. Garrison! Do you or do you not believe it a sin to go to the polls?" demanded Henry B. Stanton, secretary of the American Anti-Slavery Society. "Sin for me!" Garrison replied. At a meeting of the Massachusetts chapter on January 23, 1839, where this confrontation took place, Garrison crushed a resolution stating that it was the "duty of every abolitionist who could conscientiously do so, to go to the polls." "The Society hauled down its flag and run up the crazy banner of the non-government heresy, and we had to rally around or be ostracized," Stanton wrote. "The split is wide, and can never be closed up."

Only 121 delegates from six Eastern states gathered at Albany in early April 1840 to create the Liberty Party and nominate James Birney as its candidate; no Westerners were present—none from Ohio, Indiana, Michigan, or Illinois. The Garrisonians ridiculed the assemblage as the "April Fools" convention. In the election, most abolitionists cast ballots for Harrison, encouraged by Congressman Giddings, who exhorted them that the Whig candidate would restrict slavery and lead a path to eventual emancipation. Garrison, who regarded the political abolitionists as enemies, gloated at Birney's failure. "The farce," he declared, "is equally ludicrous and melancholy."

When the Liberty Party met in 1843 to nominate a presidential candidate for the upcoming election Westerners predominated. While Stanton and the New York group of abolitionists favored political action and were tarred by the Garrisonians as dangerously pragmatic for involving themselves in elections, they remained "immediatists," for immediate abolition, which the Westerners viewed as political fantasy, strategically misguided, and constitutionally suspect. What Garrison was to Stanton, a starry-eyed purist, Stanton was to the Westerners. They were as committed to abolition as the New Englanders and New Yorkers—most of them were originally from New England and New York—but living on the borderlands of the South and coping with harsh politics within their states they were tough-minded in drawing the line between moral posturing and effective political action.

The most important group controlling the message of the Liberty Party came from Ohio and the man who wrote the party platform would become the chief legal strategist of the antislavery movement, the state's most important political figure, a U.S. senator, presidential hopeful, and Lincoln's secretary of the treasury and chief justice of the United States, his most nettlesome rival within his cabinet and an indispensable ally, Salmon Portland Chase.

Chase came from a family as distinguished as Lincoln's was obscure. His father, Ithamar Chase, a prosperous manufacturer and farmer, was a member of the New Hampshire governor's council, a state legislator, and friend of Daniel Webster. His uncle Dudley Chase was the U.S. senator from Vermont. Salmon was nine when his father suddenly died, and he became the ward of another uncle, Philander Chase, the presiding bishop of the Episcopal Church and the first bishop of Ohio and Illinois, founder of Kenyon College, and president of Cincinnati College, where he enrolled his nephew. Salmon entered Dartmouth as a junior and after graduating Bishop Chase arranged for him to read the law under William Wirt, then attorney general under President John Quincy Adams. (Wirt, at the request of his former neighbor, Thomas Jefferson, had served as the prosecutor in the treason trial of Aaron Burr.) In Washington, the diligent and serious young Chase was welcomed as a guest into the parlors of Webster, Clay, and Adams.

When his apprenticeship in Washington was completed in 1830, Chase searched for a home for his ambition and talent, settling in Cincinnati, the Queen City, facing the unlimited horizon to the west, yet a place where proper people like him dominated business and society. He established himself as a commercial attorney with an expertise in banking, the biggest banks among his clients, and became renowned for compiling his three-volume *Statutes of Ohio*, the first of its kind. He voted in 1836 for his former preceptor Wirt running as the Anti-Masonic Party candidate and in 1840 unenthusiastically for Harrison, with whom he was acquainted in Cincinnati. That year he declined to participate in an antislavery meeting to which he was invited. Though he expressed distant admiration for England's emancipation movement and joined the local Colonization Society, he was more involved in temperance efforts and the Sunday School Union. Then his sedate progress as a business attorney with high-minded cultural and religious pursuits was interrupted. He discovered he was not, after all, living in a proper little world, but on a volcanic fault line.

Ohio was divided almost evenly from its beginning, geographically and demographically, its northern border shared with Canada and Michigan and its southern running the length of the Ohio River, and its settlement patterns derived from the original land grants of the northern section to Connecticut and the southern to Virginia. Northern Ohio was an extension of New England while southern Ohio was an extension of the South. This combination of North and South within a single state was combustible.

The movement to rescue and guide runaway slaves in Ohio probably dates as early as the Ordinance of 1787, declaring "there shall be neither slavery nor involuntary servitude in the said Territory," and in reaction prompted the first federal Fugitive Slave Act in 1793 giving masters the right to seize their fleeing property, the start of the rising cycles of resistance and repression. (There was already a fugitive slave clause written into the Constitution, which carefully did not mention the words "slave" or "slavery" in order not to create a national right to property in humans, and provided for no enforcement.) Though there was no organized effort to transform Ohio into a slave state as there was in Indiana and Illinois, it adopted a stringent Black Code in 1807. An antislavery society was founded at least as early as 1810 at Ripley, Ohio, on the Ohio River, a crossing point for fugitives. (The tiny abolitionist town would be formative in the early education of Ulysses Grant, whose father was part of this embattled outpost.) Benjamin Lundy organized an antislavery society in Ohio in 1817 and launched the first abolitionist newspaper, *The Genius of Universal Emancipation*, in 1821. At Lane Seminary, founded in 1829 outside Cincinnati to educate young men for the Presbyterian ministry, Theodore Weld, an instructor, and Calvin Stowe, a professor, married to Harriet Beecher, daughter of the school's founder, Lyman Beecher, the famous pastor, attempted to force a debate on slavery that was quashed, prompting their exodus. James C. Ludlow, a wealthy manufacturer and real estate owner who would serve as chairman of the executive committee of the Ohio Anti-Slavery Society, offered one of his buildings in Cincinnati for the dissidents to continue their training and receive lectures from Gamaliel Bailey, a doctor who had taught physiology at Lane and was a leading antislavery publicist, editor, and organizer. In 1834, antislavery men founded Oberlin College, based on thirty of the dismissed teachers and students from Lane, including Weld. The first school to admit free blacks to be educated along with whites, Oberlin became a beacon of abolitionism. The Western Reserve, the vast district along Lake Erie, elected the antislavery Joshua Giddings in 1838 to the Congress, where he joined Adams in the fight against the Gag Rule.

Beneath Cincinnati's veneer of propriety ran a seething undercurrent of violence. Dependent on Southern commerce and situated just across the river from Kentucky, it was strictly intolerant of blacks and abolitionists. After a mob attack on the free black community of Cincinnati in 1829, half of its 2,200 residents fled to Canada. The founding of the Ohio Anti-Slavery Society in April 1835 and of its newspaper, *The Philanthropist*, edited by James Birney, triggered another explosion. A mob smashed its press under the darkness of night on July 12, but the paper kept publishing. Twelve days later, a meeting of the most prominent citizens of Cincinnati passed resolutions to demand its closing: "*Resolved,* That we will use all lawful means to discountenance and suppress every publication in this city which advocates the modern doctrines of abolitionism." *The Philanthropist* must be put down, declared its leaders, "peaceably if it could, forcibly if it must." The chairman of the citizens committee, Jacob Burnet, a former U.S. senator and judge on the Ohio Supreme Court, issued an ultimatum: "It must also be apparent to the most careless observer, that a high degree of excitement exists in the minds of a large portion of our population, which the most prudent and discreet among us, find it difficult to restrain. It is to be feared, that this excitement cannot be kept down much longer, unless some arrangement be made for removing the cause which has produced it." When the Anti-Slavery Society refused to shutter the paper, a mob descended on July 27, wrecking it, marched to Birney's house, but discovered he had fled. "We have done enough for one night," Mayor Samuel Davies announced to the crowd.

On that terrifying night, Chase's sister, Abigail, wife of Dr. Isaac Colby, member of the Anti-Slavery Society executive committee, sought refuge from the mob at his home. "I was opposed at this time to the views of the abolitionists," Chase wrote, "but I now recognized the slave power as the great enemy of freedom of speech, freedom of the press and freedom of the person. I took an open part against the mob." He organized a meeting to denounce the violence, but it was taken over by its opponents and his resolutions voted down. On another evening the mob rushed to the Franklin House, a Cincinnati hotel, on the rumor that Birney was hiding there. Chase had gone there looking for him, too, and stood in front blocking the way. "I stood in the doorway, and told them, calmly but resolutely, no one could pass. They paused. One of them asked who I was? I gave my name. One, who seemed a ringleader, said I should answer for this. I told him I could be found at any time." The mayor emerged to declare that Birney wasn't there and the mob dispersed.

For his defense of free speech, Chase was propelled into the antislavery movement, and broke with most of his reputable friends and business associates, who were the leaders of the mob. The following year, in 1837, he took on the case of a fugitive slave, Matilda, harbored by Birney as a servant, and lost, the first of his many defenses of runaways, always assumed without fee, always losing, earning him the sobriquet "the attorney general of runaway negroes," applied as a term of opprobrium. He was soon drawn into the Liberty Party, becoming its chief political and legal strategist.

The Garrisonians had condemned the Constitution as a "devil's pact" and, citing Isaiah, "a league with death and covenant with hell." The only true moral position, Garrison insisted, was Christ-like nonresistance and separation from slavery, even secession from the corrupt Union, as the motto of *The Liberator* boldly proclaimed: "No Union with Slaveholders!" Stanton and his allies who had split over electoral politics were also "immediatists" and offered no argument about the Constitution. Like Garrison, they believed in the power of sublime morality. In his most famous speech, speaking before the Massachusetts legislature in 1837 against the congressional Gag Rule, Stanton stated, "The effects of antislavery agitation are not hemmed in by state lines, nor circumscribed by local boundaries. They are moral in their nature; obey no laws but those of the human mind; owe allegiance to no constitution but that of the immortal soul. Impalpable, but real, the truths we proclaim overleap all geographical divisions, and lay their strong grasp upon the conscience. Moral light, diffused at the North, is like the Aurora Borealis; it will travel onward to the South." Where Stanton and his faction differed with Garrison was about whether or not voting was sinful. They were for politics, but developed no actual politics.

Adams had never called himself an abolitionist even as he battled the hosts of slavery over the Gag Rule and never favored immediate emancipation. In this he was a forerunner of Chase. After meeting with his friend Benjamin Lundy in Boston in 1837, Adams wrote in his diary, "He and the abolitionists generally are constantly urging me to indiscreet movements, which would ruin me and weaken and not strengthen their cause. . . . I walk on the edge of a precipice in every step that I take." A year later, after abolitionists ran a candidate against Adams for failing to adhere to their orthodoxy, he wrote, "The result of their interposition has been hitherto mischievous, and, I believe, injurious to their own cause. . . . The moral principle of their interference to defeat elections when they cannot carry them appears to me to be vicious." Despite his lonely battle against the Gag Rule, and because he declined to convert to Garrison's strictures of purity, which would have made his position as an elected official hypocritical if not untenable, Garrison in 1839 pronounced Adams in league with Satan: "you are acting in concert with all that is despotic and inhuman in the land." Birney, in 1843, denounced Adams as "eccentric, whimsical, inconsistent, and, taken as a whole, thus far is unworthy of a statesman. . . . He has given the Abolitionists words, *words,* WORDS, and to their adversaries everything that is substantial."

The words Adams had reclaimed against slavery were those of the Declaration of Independence. As the only living public man who knew all the founders, his personal authority was unassailable. "No one attentive to the progress of our history as an independent nation," he wrote in a letter to the Rhode Island Anti-Slavery Society in 1838, "can fail to see that in the silent lapse of time slavery has been winding its cobwebthread around all our free institutions. This was not the covenant to which we pledged our faith in the Declaration of Independence." Of the founders' belief in abolition, only the "time and mode" were left to the not-so-distant future. "George Washington was an Abolitionist; so was Thomas Jefferson," he wrote. "But were they alive, and should dare to show their faces and to utter the self-evident truth of the Declaration within the State of South Carolina, they would be hanged."

The break between Garrisonian abolitionism and antislavery politics was fundamental. In the 1837 Matilda case, Chase made the novel argument that the Constitution "contains no recognition whatever, of any right of property in man" and that therefore it was "impossible, in Ohio, to commit the offense of harboring, or secreting a person being the property of another person." According to Chase's reasoning, slavery was limited to where it was expressly enacted and "can have no existence beyond the territorial limits of the state which sanctions it." His logic was "a turning point in the history of antislavery politics," according to the historian James Oakes. The next year Theodore Weld in his book *The Power of Congress over the District of Columbia* made the case that the framers of the Constitution carefully and euphemistically acknowledged slaves as "persons," not "property," and that therefore the Constitution did not recognize slavery. His argument was fortified in 1840 with the publication of James Madison's notes on the Constitutional Convention, reporting the internal debates that concluded with rejection of granting legitimacy to slavery because, as Madison wrote, it was "wrong to admit in the Constitution the idea that there could be property in men."

In 1841, taking advantage of Madison's notes, John Quincy Adams argued on the constitutionality of slavery in the *Amistad* case before the Supreme Court, "The Constitution nowhere recognizes them as property. The words slave and slavery are studiously excluded from the Constitution. Circumlocutions are the fig-leaves under which these parts of the body politic are decently concealed Slaves, therefore, in the Constitution of the United States are recognized only as persons, enjoying rights and held to the performance of duties." By 1850, Senator William Seward declared, "I deny that the Constitution recognizes property in man." By then the idea that the Constitution did not protect slavery had become a common tenet of antislavery politics, giving the movement to limit slavery its basic sense of legitimacy. It would become a central animating principle for Lincoln.

But it was not until Chase that a compelling and complex constitutional case was made as a basis for an antislavery political strategy. He had little use for the airy rhetoric of sheer morality, instead bringing the antislavery argument down from the Aurora Borealis to earth. Rather than appealing to the angels, he developed a series of logical theses: the Constitution did not protect slavery; the founders' intent was indeed eventual abolition; slavery was entirely a state matter; and the Ordinance of 1787 was the authoritative legal precedent. From this reasoning it flowed that slavery could not legally be extended beyond its current borders and that slaves once on free soil were free. On his crucial point he rested on British law antedating the existence of the United States, the Somerset case of 1772, in which a court ruled that a slave no longer in a place where slavery held "any dominion" could not be returned into bondage. Chase believed that once slavery was quarantined within Southern confines it would wither and die, first in the upper South and then in the Deep South. His slogan: "Freedom national, slavery sectional." "The general government has power to prohibit slavery everywhere outside of slave States," Chase wrote in 1856 to the Boston Unitarian and Transcendentalist minister Theodore Parker, whose congregation included Garrison, Julia Ward Howe, Louisa May Alcott, and Elizabeth Cady Stanton. "A great majority of the people now accept this idea. Comparatively few adopt the suggestion that Congress can legislate abolition within slave States. . . . I say, then, take the conceded proposition and make it practical. Make it a living, active reality. Then you have taken a great step. Slavery is denationalized."

In 1842, Chase took the case of John Van Zandt, a religiously motivated, uneducated farmer in Ohio, who was charged with hiding fugitives, which he freely admitted. (Van Zandt became the prototype for John Van Trompe, the goodhearted abolitionist of *Uncle Tom's Cabin.*) Losing in Ohio, Chase appealed to the Supreme Court, where, with his co-counsel, William Seward, he offered his fullest argument that the Ordinance of 1787 was the decisive legal authority and that the federal government "has nothing whatever, directly, to do with slavery." In a decision issued in 1847 and written by Justice Roger Taney, anticipating the *Dred Scott* decision ten years later, the court dismissed both of Chase's key points, ruling that the Fugitive Slave Act of 1793 was "not repugnant to the Constitution of the United States" and that it was also "not repugnant" to the Ordinance of 1787. Chase's constitutional theory was rejected, but antislavery politics was galvanized.

After the negligible showing of the Liberty Party in 1840, Chase searched for viable alternatives to the rigidly moralistic Birney, suggesting Adams, Seward, or William Jay, son of the first chief justice, who was a New York county judge and a founder of the Anti-Slavery Society. But they all refused, holding on to their attachment to the Whig Party. Birney's penchant for sweeping vituperation encouraged more politically minded members of the Ohio group to attempt again to dislodge him as the Liberty Party candidate for 1844. Preempting his critics, Birney accepted another nomination, in the process assailing Adams and Seward—"how can they be abolitionists?"— while decrying the rapid degeneration of the whole American people in whom, he declared, he had "faint hope." "Slavery," he wailed, "has corrupted the whole nation." Again Chase and Gamaliel Bailey tried to push the apocalyptic Birney aside. "I have had doubts, as to your being the most eligible candidate," Bailey wrote Birney. "You have always appeared in the character of a Moralist, a reformer, rather than a Politician or Statesman. Your letter of acceptance, I remember, so was written in the spirit of a prophet." After Birney's success in defeating Clay and throwing the election to Polk, they again renewed their effort to remove him. Bailey wrote to Liberty Party members that "he has no personal claim upon our future support." But in 1845, when Birney fell from his horse and suffered a stroke that left him partially paralyzed and speechless, the matter of succession was settled. The political figure who would take the reins in Ohio would be Chase.

Tall, erect, with a high forehead and square jaw, Chase appeared the model of what a statesman should look like, or an Episcopal bishop. He was dignified, unflappable, intelligent, logical, and utterly certain of his opinions.

He was also ponderous, humorless, and dry, except in a parlor with men who shared his classical education, social background, and politics, especially Charles Sumner. "One defect in this eminent statesman was his ignorance of human nature," wrote one of his protégés, Donn Piatt, an Ohio journalist and politician. Chase could not move a crowd with a joke, a phrase, or a sentiment, all the natural arts of political speech beyond his grasp. It was up to the crowd itself to acknowledge his unswerving high-mindedness and thereby prove its worthiness to him. "With few gestures he spoke in an even, unemotional way, as if addressing a court. He got little aid from the expression of his fine face, for being extremely nearsighted, he had a way of contracting his eyelids, as if he were turning his sight in on himself."

Chase was driven by an overriding sense of duty. His solemnity was reinforced by his personal tragedies, losing two beloved wives and three children within ten years. By 1845, his only surviving family member was a five-year-old daughter, Kate, whom he admonished at the age of eleven for her lack of religiosity: "You may die soon." She chose to pay little attention to his censorious gloom, and became the most vivacious, stylish, and sought after young woman in Washington, the capital's most fashionable hostess, and her father's political adviser and chief booster. Chase's third wife, Sarah Ludlow, whom he married in 1846, was the granddaughter of a city founder, who laid out the city plan of Cincinnati. Her father, James C. Ludlow, a wealthy manufacturer and real estate owner, was chairman of the executive committee of the Ohio Anti-Slavery Society, who had provided one of his buildings to the students and faculty that broke from Lane Seminary. When Sarah Ludlow Chase died in 1852, Chase's grave manner seemed set in stone like a marble statue, only cracked by the sparkling presence of his daughter.

In any given situation Chase profoundly believed that he was the best man. His conviction that he should be president was unwavering. From 1860 through 1876 he pursued the top prize, but was never once truly a serious contender. He never understood his own lack of appeal and received his rejections as judgments of those who had failed to recognize and measure up to his virtues. His confidence that he should be president and his constant machinations would disrupt Lincoln's administration and threaten his re-election, forcing him to assuage, balance, dismiss, and finally elevate Chase to his best suited role, chief justice, donning the bishop's black robe at last, which did not quell his ultimate ambition.

But Chase was central to the political movement that would eventually emerge as the Republican Party. As the principal author of the Liberty Party platform and prime mover behind the Free Soil Party, he established the basis for the program and political cohesion that under the stress of events at last led to the rise of the new party formation. Garrison's cries for moral purity within the church of abolitionism had forced the collapse of the American Anti-Slavery Society. His isolation, self-inflicted or not, created a vacuum within the antislavery movement, enabling the emergence of those committed to the practical workings of politics, even if they were not particularly adept at it.

The plausibility of Chase's constitutional theory and his appeal to the authority of the Constitution lent the force of reason and political momentum to the movement to stop the extension of slavery, which would become the paramount issue after the Mexican War. Chase was solidly grounded in his claim that the founders—Washington, Jefferson, and Franklin—favored the ultimate abolition of slavery. In the 1844 Liberty Party platform, most of which Chase wrote, Article 6 read: "That it was understood in the times of the Declaration and the Constitution, that the existence of slavery in some of the States, was in derogation of the principles of American Liberty, and a deep stain upon the character of the country, and the implied faith of the States and the Nation was pledged, that slavery should never be extended beyond its then existing limits, but should be gradually, and yet, at no distant day, wholly abolished by State authority." Chase's Article 6 would serve as a template for the Republican Party's platform and would be at the heart of the address that Lincoln delivered at Cooper Union in 1860.

Chase saw his mission as the vindication of the Constitution. He consistently refused to call himself an "abolitionist" and urged the Liberty Party to drop the label. He associated "abolitionism" with Garrison's fanatical repudiation of the Constitution and politics itself. As a result he drew a sharp distinction between abolitionism and antislavery politics, not simply as a matter of nomenclature or expedience but principle. Abolitionism was of a "moral nature" that "cannot be effected by political power," he wrote Thaddeus Stevens in 1842, and while "abolitionism is not properly a political object, antislavery is." To be antislavery meant to Chase that one could not be an abolitionist.

Chase clarified his views on the other parties in a speech before two thousand delegates to the Southern and Western Liberty Convention at Cincinnati in June 1845. While upholding "the maxims of True Democracy," he disdained the Democratic Party's "hypocrisy." "Its professed principles have been the same for nearly half a century," he said, "and yet the subjection of the party to the Slave power is, at this moment, as complete as ever. There is no prospect of any change for the better." The Whig Party, for its part, had no antislavery position. "There are, doubtless, zealous opponents of slavery, who are also zealous Whigs," Chase said, "but they have not the general confidence of their party; they are under the ban of the slaveholders." Waiting for the Whig Party to change was hopeless—"all expectation of efficient anti-slavery action from the Whig party, as now organized, will prove delusive." It is important to note that as early as 1845 Chase and Lincoln, one a member of a marginal group and the other a stalwart of a major party, were not really distant on what would become the crucial unifying political principle for a new coalition, opposition to the extension of slavery, as Lincoln suggested in his letter to the Illinois Liberty man Williamson Durley. But it would take a decade before the two men converged. Chase in 1845 was already consumed with "the question of slavery as the paramount question of our day and nation," while Lincoln admitted he was not that "interested" in "the Texas question," which was about to explode into war.

The Illinois abolitionists were thrilled to attend the Liberty Party convention in August 1843 at Buffalo. They tended to think of the Ohio people as more politically advanced; after all, they had already elected a congressman and developed a theory of the case, a sense of how to argue about the Constitution and slavery. The Illinoisans were largely transplanted New Englanders, like the Ohioans, but Illinois was an even harsher political environment, more Western, rougher, and largely Southern in influence until the burgeoning of Chicago in the 1850s created a north and began to shift the balance of political power. Within the Liberty Party, the Illinois group was more naturally aligned with the Ohio men than those from New England or New York. But they had their own distinct idea of themselves, bearing the burden of their state's more difficult history, illustrated by the triumph and tragedy of Edward Coles, who saved Illinois from slavery and was tainted and harassed for years, and the martyr of the whole movement—Elijah Lovejoy.

The Illinois leader was Owen Lovejoy, Elijah's younger brother, who had knelt by his coffin and vowed, "I shall never forsake the cause that has been sprinkled with my brother's blood." Like his brother, he became a minister. At the state's Liberty Party convention on May 27, 1842, held in Chicago, he coauthored its founding document, "The Usurpation of Slavery," a call "to sound the alarm and take the field for a political campaign," to warn that slavery was becoming national, a threat to "Free Labor." From the beginning, he appealed to white citizens that slavery was against their self-interest.

The Chicago meeting also approved funding for a newspaper, the *Western Citizen*, and appointed as its editor Zebina Eastman, an Amherst College graduate, who had replaced Garrison as the assistant to Benjamin Lundy in editing and publishing *The Genius of Universal Emancipation,* which Lundy had relocated to Illinois. Eastman had carried on its publication after Lundy's death in 1839 under the title of *Genius of Liberty*. Based in Chicago, the *Western Citizen* would eventually be renamed the *Free Citizen* and finally merge in 1856 into the *Chicago Tribune*. Eastman would play far-reaching roles as a publicist, organizer, strategist, and party broker, one of those who would later judge for the movement the antislavery bona fides of Lincoln. Eastman would write a history of the antislavery struggle in Illinois that was unfinished at his death, entitled *The Black Code in Illinois*, tracing the trajectory from Coles to Lincoln. It was in Illinois, he wrote, "on this consecrated soil that the moral battle was fought, and that preceded the war of emancipation. Here, in this State, was the first contest waged against slavery, which became a conquest."

Lovejoy was named as one of the five Liberty Party national secretaries at its convention, the first party gathering ever to include blacks as delegates. Lovejoy also served on the committee to nominate officers alongside Henry Highland Garnet, a former fugitive slave who had become a minister, orator, and radical abolitionist in New York City. Garnet had just delivered a firebrand speech to the Convention of the Colored Citizens calling for armed resistance: "Rather die free men than live to be slaves!" (Garnet would become the leading black pastor in Washington and probably the black leader closest to Lincoln, who would arrange for him to be the first black man to address the House of Representatives to commemorate the Emancipation Proclamation in a speech that advanced themes Lincoln would voice in his Second Inaugural.) The Liberty Party convention, Lovejoy wrote Eastman, was "a great, grand and most glorious convention. Never has there been such a political gathering since the Convention that met in Congress Hall in Philadelphia in 1776."

Shortly after the Liberty convention, Eastman heard an antislavery lecturer speak in "an old, antique meetinghouse" in Illinois, an orator of "remarkable eloquence and power"—Ichabod Codding, a Middlebury College graduate, trained by Weld as one of his "Seventy" to preach on the model of the revivals of the Second Great Awakening. Codding had founded abolitionist newspapers in Maine and Connecticut and been one of the featured speakers on the circuit for five years. Eastman persuaded him to remain in Illinois, where he became one of their most articulate voices and effective organizers, and would later prove indispensable in creating the Illinois Republican Party. During the 1844 campaign, Codding spoke in eighteen counties, accompanied by a free black, William Jones, who recounted the harrowing tale of how he had been kidnapped into slavery and escaped.

The Liberty Party was not only a political party. It was also the front office of the Underground Railroad. In Illinois, Lovejoy and the others were also the conductors of the clandestine line running from the southern part of the state up to Chicago, from where fugitive slaves were transported to Canada. As early as 1818 an informal underground of individual antislavery farmers existed in Illinois. But the Underground Railroad in Illinois as an organized network began in the fall of 1839 with its first "passenger," a "famished, terrified negro," who was accidentally discovered hiding by Eastman and helped to escape. In 1843, Owen Lovejoy and Dr. Richard Eells of Quincy were indicted for harboring and assisting fugitives in an effort to break the Underground Railroad. Lovejoy had brazenly advertised in the *Western Citizen* his services in running "ladies and gentlemen of color of the South" to "the falls of Niagara." He was acquitted, but his accomplice Eells was convicted in a court presided over by Judge Stephen A. Douglas, who fined him $400. Judge James Shields denied his appeal. Upon Douglas's sentence, the Illinois Anti-Slavery Society elected Eells its president, and he would be nominated the Liberty Party candidate for governor in 1846.

In Chicago, the chief conductors were Dr. Charles Volney Dyer and Philo Carpenter, among the earliest settlers, the first doctor and the first pharmacist when Chicago was known only as Fort Dearborn. The Chicago group rescued more than one thousand fugitives. It became an open city for the Underground Railroad after an incident in 1845 or 1846, as Eastman recalled, in which a runaway was brought before Justice of the Peace Lewis C. Kercheval, one of the town's most influential Democrats, appointed port collector through his friendship with President Jackson. Dyer led a crowd of about twenty free blacks and "quite a number of 'respectables' besides" to the court, where they physically lifted the slave, who "glided over the heads of the throng and down the staircase to the sidewalk" and disappeared into freedom. Eastman described the rescue as "the last slavery disturbance in Chicago."

Lovejoy, Codding, Dyer, Carpenter, Eastman, and the rest, after a decade of radical third party politics, would be instrumental in conceiving and organizing the fusion movement in Illinois that became the Republican Party—and in the mid-1850s they would come to know and trust Lincoln as the most influential and promising politician to advance their cause. Though they worked side by side with other abolitionists across the North and were as determined in the ultimate goal of emancipation, their experience in Illinois set them apart. Their bond with Lincoln was more than that of a moral movement gradually moving a party politician toward the light. In the crucible of Illinois, the most racially hostile of the Northern states, where a draconian Black Code was enforced, and the Democrats had long dominated, they helped develop a broad common politics in which Lincoln could emerge, and they understood the political implications when he did.

Lovejoy would be elected to the Congress and become Lincoln's unwavering defender as president against harsh criticisms from abolitionists from New York and New England, who did not have an Illinois background, lacked an intimate understanding of Lincoln, and, still attached to "perfectionism," campaigned to remove him from the White House in 1864. Lincoln would appoint Eastman the U.S. consul to Bristol, England, where he helped wage the battle for English public opinion and against Confederate blockade runners. And he would appoint Dyer as the U.S. representative to the International Court for the Suppression of the African Slave Trade. "It is a pleasant thing to remember," Eastman recalled, "as Mr. Lincoln told Dyer,—it was a great pleasure to him to appoint old abolitionists to office." But that was years away.

Lincoln's interlocutor with the Illinois abolitionists would be one of them—Lincoln's junior law partner, William Henry Herndon. Herndon had spent a year at Illinois College, the year Elijah Lovejoy was murdered, a student of Edward Beecher, the college president, Lovejoy's ally in creating the Illinois Anti-Slavery Society. When Herndon joined in the protests after Lovejoy was killed, his father, Archie Herndon, a pro-slavery Democrat, yanked his son out of the school, dismayed that he had become "a damned Abolitionist pup." "But it was too late," Herndon wrote. "My soul had absorbed too much of what my father believed was rank poison."

Stephen T. Logan had decided after the 1844 election to take his son as his partner, so Lincoln opened his own law office. He had always been the junior partner for Stuart and Logan, good at arguing cases before juries, excellent at providing a steady stream of political intelligence and gauging public opinion, and hopeless at paperwork. He did not look far for his own junior partner, hiring Herndon at once. Herndon was a Kentuckian, nine years younger, who, after his father forced him to drop out of Illinois College, became a clerk in Speed's store and shared living quarters upstairs with Speed and Lincoln. And he had apprenticed in the law at Logan & Lincoln. "Lincoln once told me that he had taken you in as a partner," Henry Clay Whitney wrote Herndon, "supposing you had system and would keep things in order, but that he found out you had no more system than he had, but that you were in reality a good lawyer, so that he was doubly disappointed." The remark was Lincoln's wry kind of joke. He had thought he was the "good lawyer" and didn't need another, while neither he nor Herndon was good at keeping the books.

Lincoln & Herndon moved into the second floor of the Tinsley Building across from the State House, beginning a partnership that lasted sixteen years until Lincoln left for Washington. They were a study in contrasts: one compulsively talkative, upbeat and impulsive, the other ruminative, moody, and logical. The younger man looked to the older one as his mentor. Herndon was the man about town, well known to just about everybody in Springfield, the high and the low, constantly attending town meetings, lectures, ceremonies, and taverns.

William H. Herndon

He was a drummer for reform, always ready to lend himself to a good cause, and so popular that he was elected mayor in 1855, though he had no real political ambition for himself. Temperance was among his great causes and he was committed to turn Springfield into a dry city, even while sneaking a drink.

The partners, "Billy" and "Lincoln" or "Mr. Lincoln," their names for each other, were more than an odd couple. Worshipful, dreamy, and often strangely effective, Herndon was useful in bridging the gap between the Whigs on Aristocracy Hill to whom Lincoln was related by marriage and the plebeian Whigs in the town below. The garrulous and sociable Herndon served as Lincoln's precinct captain, press secretary, editorial co-writer, and all-purpose aide—a one-man band. Always out and about, he was Lincoln's pulse on public opinion, his tuning fork. Herndon was deeply embedded in the Whig Party as Lincoln's utterly loyal operative even when he believed Lincoln's strategies were misbegotten if not self-destructive. Within the party, he was Lincoln's Lincoln. He presided as secretary at the convention that gave Lincoln his congressional nomination and would later help him make the leap from the collapsed Whig Party to the new Republican Party. Herndon was antislavery by conviction and Whig by allegiance. In 1840 and 1844, he would not vote for the Liberty Party candidate, but for the straight Whig ticket. Lincoln had not converted him into a Whig; Herndon was already a partisan whose ultimate partisanship was as a charter member of the "Lincoln Party."

Herndon was more than a worker bee; he buzzed with ideas, especially radical ones. When he was not researching Lincoln's legal cases, writing briefs, or making the rounds, he was a constant reader of the New England Transcendentalists and abolitionist newspapers. He subscribed to publications far and wide, giving Lincoln plenty to read—Zebina Eastman's *Western Citizen*, Horace Greeley's *New York Tribune*, William Lloyd Garrison's *Liberator*, and the conservative *Richmond Enquirer*. He purchased serious books on politics and the economy, from Henry C. Carey to Southern slavery apologists. He was Lincoln's librarian, curator of one of the best private collections in town. And he spearheaded the creation of the Springfield library association as its secretary, too. He also took it upon himself to build a network of contacts with the Illinois Liberty-men and antislavery activists around the country. "I am a southerner—born on southern soil—reared by southern parents," Herndon wrote to his friend Edward L. Pierce, a Massachusetts abolitionist, "but I have always turned New-Englandsward for my ideas—my sentiments—my education—." He corresponded with his distant heroes, including the Boston radical Theodore Parker, whose sermons and speeches he put before Lincoln. (In 1858, Parker sent him one of his lectures in which he spoke of "Direct Self-government, over all the people, for all the people, by all the people"—a paraphrase from Webster's "Second Reply to Hayne" that Lincoln had long ago committed to memory.) And Garrison would stay at Herndon's home during his pilgrimage to Springfield in 1865 just after the war's end.

Lincoln was always the indisputable senior partner in both law and politics, but Herndon offered candid advice, not hesitating to tell him when he thought he was damaging himself and constantly calling Lincoln's attention to some new article or idea. His loyalty to Lincoln's prospects did not involve shuffling deference. After Lincoln's death, Herndon would immortalize him in his *Life of Lincoln*, a compendium of anecdotes and insights, based on one of the first genuine oral history projects, an invaluable fount of information about the New Salem and Springfield years. Despite certain errors, due largely to the inevitably cloudy and confused memories of sources and Herndon himself, he tried to present a historically accurate and unsentimental portrait, "without coloring or evasion." And he was proved right about the romance with Ann Rutledge, despite the insistence of a generation of mid-twentieth-century historians that it was Herndon's myth, though he embellished parts of it. In his chronicle he depicted himself as Lincoln's amanuensis, but he came to resent his own secondary self-portrayal and the canonization of Lincoln by those who didn't know him intimately. When he was old, poor, and forgotten, he wrote that Lincoln "was a remorseless trimmer with men; they were his tools and when they were used up he threw them aside as old iron and took up new tools." Undoubtedly, Herndon's assessment contained a kernel of truth, but it was less a dark revelation than an obvious point. No one knew better than Herndon that Lincoln was a politician; few had done more to advance him. That was at the heart of their secret sharing. Herndon was hardly coerced, but avid in his labors. He believed in all of it. And Lincoln never cast Herndon aside, offered him a job in Washington, which he turned down knowing he would be beyond his depth. Then Lincoln told him to keep the shingle up while he was president, promised that he would return someday, and talked to him considerately about his drinking in the last of their innumerable conversations in the law office. Herndon's harsh words in his old age seemed less a sour complaint than a thinly disguised lament, yearning somehow for Lincoln to return to the partnership.

Lincoln recruited Herndon just as he planned his ascent to the Congress. Unfortunately, John J. Hardin didn't hold to Lincoln's plan for rotation in office leading to his turn. "To incur his displeasure was regarded by many as political suicide whether the poor victim was of the same political faith or not," wrote a contemporary journalist about Hardin. Baker had served his term, Hardin was concluding his, and Lincoln was supposedly next. But Hardin's political prestige was never greater. As the commander of the five hundred state militia troops after the murder of Mormon Prophet Joseph Smith, General Hardin had restored law and order. Wearing the military laurels of the Illinois Mormon War, he was the overwhelming Whig candidate for the U.S. Senate, easily defeating Logan and Lincoln within the Whig caucus. Throughout 1845, Lincoln and his friends Anson Henry and Simeon Francis ginned up a series of newspaper editorials pushing Hardin for governor that would not so incidentally remove him from the congressional arena. On November 24, Lincoln wrote his ally Benjamin James, editor of the *Tazewell Whig*, "You, perhaps, have noticed the *Journal*'s article of last week, upon the same subject. It was written without any consultation with me, but I was told by Francis of its purport before it was published. I chose to let it go as it was, lest it should be suspected that I was attempting to juggle Hardin out of a nomination for Congress by juggling him into one for Governor. If you, and the other papers, a little more distant from me, choose, to take the same course you have, of course I have no objection." But Hardin would not buckle under the pressure, instead announcing he would run again for the Congress. Lincoln was in a quandary, as he explained in a letter on January 7, 1846, to Dr. Robert Boal, a state legislator from Peoria, one of his supporters: "to yield to Hardin under present circumstances, seems to me as nothing else than yielding to one who would gladly sacrifice me altogether. This, I would rather not submit to. That Hardin is talented, energetic, usually generous and magnanimous, I have, before this, affirmed to you, and do not now deny. You know that my only argument is that 'turnabout is fair play.' This he, practically at least, denies."

Hardin proposed a direct primary of Whig voters in the district with candidates restricted to electioneering only in their home counties. This would have doubly disadvantaged Lincoln, thwarting him from exercising his internal party and public strengths. Lincoln stood by the convention as the means to select the candidate. "I am entirely satisfied with the old system," he wrote Hardin. In the meantime, he guided the editorial support of friendly editors and organized Whig elected officials who would be convention delegates, stressing his slogan: "Turnabout is fair play." "I shall be pleased if this strikes you as a sufficient argument," he wrote state senator M. J. Rockwell. "You understand," he wrote James of the *Tazewell Whig*, who was coordinating prospective delegates in his county. "Other particulars I leave to you." Hardin wrote Lincoln an angry letter charging him with improperly seeking the nomination through the convention, asserting that there had never been a deal for rotation, and that "my name was run up as a candidate for Governor by one of your friends under circumstances which now leave no room for doubt that the design was to keep my name out of view for congress, so that the Whigs might be more easily influenced to commit themselves to go for you." Lincoln replied coolly on February 7, claiming he had nothing to do with any campaign to force Hardin out of the race, and that Hardin's use "of the terms 'management,' 'maneuvering' and 'combination' quite freely" was an "utter injustice." Lincoln, not Hardin, was the aggrieved one. "I content myself with saying that if there is cause for mortification anywhere, it is in the readiness with which you believe, and make such charges, against one with whom you truly say you have long acted; and in whose conduct, you have heretofore marked nothing as dishonorable."

The first caucus to choose delegates for the convention held in the town of Athens went for Lincoln. When it was clear that within the next weeks he would sweep others, the sputtering Hardin withdrew. He had made the mistake of engaging Lincoln in a debate over the proper procedure of candidate selection while Lincoln wasted no time sewing up the nomination. In his statement on February 16, "To the Voters of the 7th Congressional District," Hardin grumbled that Lincoln had already "compromitted" his own friends to act as Lincoln's delegates. He struck a noble pose, throwing back Lincoln's phrases at him: "If I had cause for personal complaint, I would rather suffer real or supposed wrong, than be the means of producing dissension amongst my political friends."

On May 1, the Whig convention, with Herndon presiding as its secretary, unanimously nominated Lincoln. It adopted a platform for the tariff and left the Oregon Territory negotiation with Britain over its border and Texas unmentioned. The *Register* derided Lincoln's candidacy as the product of "the rotary system, the very worst system for the people that was ever practiced." And it challenged Lincoln to stake his ground on the issues on which the convention was so carefully silent. "No shuffling, Mr. Lincoln! Come out, square!"

For weeks, the Democrats were without a candidate in the only Whig district in the state. At last, a rump convention of ten delegates nominated Peter Cartwright, the famous Methodist preacher for whom the Jacksonian creed was the old-time religion, a paradox given that the Jacksonians were generally hostile to religion in politics while the Whigs were generally favorable. He embodied nearly everything Lincoln rejected about evangelical religion and religion in politics. From the time Lincoln first heard him speak in 1830, newly arrived in New Salem, he felt compelled to get up on a stump and challenge him. Two years after that, Lincoln ran for the legislature against him and lost, and two years later wrote an anonymous pamphlet tearing him apart as a "fool or knave." Cartwright was twenty-five years older than Lincoln, but he was as well-known as anyone in Illinois, "had at one time or

another preached to almost every Methodist congregation between Springfield and Cairo," and was "in every respect a dangerous antagonist," according to Herndon.

Cartwright, known in his youth as "Kentucky Boy," had been a circuit-riding preacher before Illinois became a state, boasting that he had "seen more than 500 persons jerking at one time in his large congregations," wrote old settler T. J. Onstot. He had once reduced a country dance to an all-night session of hymn singing, praying, and weeping. Preaching

Peter Cartwright

in a Nashville church, when informed that Andrew Jackson had entered, he shouted, "General Jackson! Who is General Jackson? If he don't repent of his sins and be a better man God Almighty will damn him as quick as a Georgia nigger." Jackson invited him the next day to the Hermitage, where he told him, "You are a brave man, just the kind of a man I have been looking for. If I had a regiment like you I could whip the whole British Nation."

Thirteen days after the Whig convention nominated Lincoln, the Congress declared war on Mexico. It was the inevitable culmination of Polk's order to General Zachary Taylor to march his 3,550-man army across the Nueces River, which Mexico considered its border, and 120 miles to the Rio Grande, claiming the territory as American soil in a ceremony at the hastily constructed Fort Texas, raising the flag and playing "The Star-Spangled Banner." When the Mexican commander facing Taylor requested that he return to the Nueces in order for negotiations between governments to resume, Taylor blockaded the Rio Grande, provoking a skirmish. In his war message to the Congress, Polk declared, "The cup of forbearance had been exhausted even before the recent information from the frontier of the Del Norte. But now, after reiterated menaces, Mexico has passed the boundary of the United States, has invaded our territory and shed American blood upon the American soil." That sentence about "American blood" would dominate Lincoln's congressional career.

The Democratic-controlled House permitted only two hours for debate on May 13. Only fourteen Whigs voted against the declaration of war in the House and two in the Senate. One of them was Adams, who, a year earlier, after Texas annexation, portentously warned of dire consequences, "firmly believing it tainted with two deadly crimes: 1, the leprous contamination of slavery; and, 2, robbery of Mexico. . . . The sequel is in the hands of Providence, and the ultimate result may signally disappoint those by whom this enterprise has been consummated. Fraud and rapine are at its foundation. They have sown the wind."

Hardin immediately enlisted as a colonel commanding one thousand volunteers. Baker, "nearly crazy with excitement," according to Whig state legislator David Davis, a friend of Lincoln, rushed back from Washington to Springfield to assume command of a regiment as a colonel, too. He and Hardin bickered over military primacy, which was decided for Hardin, the hero of the Mormon War. On May 26, Lincoln wrote Hardin requesting an appointment for a friend: "Dr. F. A. McNeil, is desirous of going the campaign to Mexico, as a surgeon, and he thinks that you, more probably than anyone else, may have the power to give him the place." Francis McNeil, in fact, had just lost nomination to the legislature at the Whig convention and Lincoln was seeking the favor as compensation. Hardin flatly turned Lincoln down and McNeil went to serve under Baker. The commander of all Illinois volunteers was none other than James Shields, whom Polk had appointed Commissioner of the General Land Office, but now was eager to go to war and designated brigadier general.

At a State House recruitment rally, Governor Ford, Baker, and other notables delivered speeches that were "warm, thrilling, effective," reported the *Journal*. But when Lincoln was summoned to speak, according to an eyewitness, Gibson W. Harris, a young law clerk in his office, he said "he would gladly make them a speech if he had anything to say. But he was not going into the war; and as he was not going himself, he did not feel like telling others to go. He would simply leave it to each individual to do as he thought his duty called for. After a few more remarks, and a story 'with a nib to it,' he bowed himself off the platform."

Baker's 4th Illinois Regiment, attired in new uniforms, marched off from Springfield on June 27 to cheering crowds. When the dust cleared, the issue of Texas suddenly seemed to depart along with the soldiers. For the moment, it was removed from local politics. The Democrats did not want to debate the tariff. So Cartwright launched a campaign against Lincoln over his religious skepticism and freethinking. "I was informed by letter from Jacksonville that Mr. Cartwright was whispering the charge of infidelity against me in that quarter," an anxious Lincoln wrote one of his key supporters, Alan N. Ford, editor of the *Lacon* (Illinois) *Gazette*.

The attack on Lincoln as an infidel was a replay of the one against Clay two years earlier. The Whig standard-bearer's immorality, from gambling to womanizing to dueling, was linked to his lack of religion. Clay had felt compelled to write a vague declaration of respect for faith, "I have a profound sense of the inappreciable value of our Religion, which has increased and strengthened." Perhaps what worked against Clay might work against Lincoln. In any case, the accusation of faithlessness was part of Cartwright's stock-in-trade.

Lincoln was swinging through nearly every town, telling humorous stories, shaking hands, and explaining the tariff. On one Sunday in Springfield he attended a revival where Cartwright was holding forth. The preacher spied him among the born-again. "If you are not going to repent and go to heaven, Mr. Lincoln," he shouted, "where are you going?" Presumably, the obvious answer was to hell. "I am going to Congress, Brother Cartwright," Lincoln answered.

But Cartwright's campaign against the unbeliever stung. "Many religious Christian Whigs hated to vote for Lincoln on that account," recalled James Matheny, who "had to argue the question with them." Lincoln's problem with the charge of infidelity was that it was basically true. In trying to find the right word to describe Lincoln's frequent discussions of religion, Matheny used "scoff" and "sneer" before settling on the phrase "an argument of ridicule." Herndon recalled that Lincoln's "slighting allusion . . . to the insincerity of the Christian people" before the Washington Temperance Society in 1842 "was not forgotten."

The week before the election, Lincoln put out a handbill reprinted in Whig papers. He adopted the Clay approach. "A charge having got into circulation in some of the neighborhoods of this District, in substance that I am an open scoffer at Christianity, I have by the advice of some friends concluded to notice the subject in this form. That I am not a member of any Christian Church, is true; but I have never denied the truth of the Scriptures; and I have never spoken with intentional disrespect of religion in general, or of any denomination of Christians in particular." His disavowal of derision of religion, however, was simply false. His freethinking was more than cracker-barrel mockery of the miracles and divine inspiration of the Bible, though he had engaged in that, too. He was a rigorous reader of Paine and Volney, a thoroughly thoughtful skeptic, and had pressed their writings on others.

Then he tried to position himself as theologically harmless. "It is true that in early life I was inclined to believe in what I understand is called the 'Doctrine of Necessity'—that is, that the human mind is impelled to action, or held in rest by some power, over which the mind itself has no control; and I have sometimes (with one, two or three, but never publicly) tried to maintain this opinion in argument. The habit of arguing thus however, I have, entirely left off for more than five years. And I add here, I have always understood this same opinion to be held by several of the Christian denominations. The foregoing, is the whole truth, briefly stated, in relation to myself, upon this subject." This entire passage was a carefully constructed distraction, an effort to substitute the noncontroversial for the controversial as though there were nothing more to it. Nobody, in fact, had raised the "Doctrine of Necessity" against him.

Finally, he ended with affirmation of the most profound respect for believers. "I do not think I could myself, be brought to support a man for office, whom I knew to be an open enemy of, and scoffer at, religion. Leaving the higher matter of eternal consequences, between him and his Maker, I still do not think any man has the right thus to insult the feelings, and injure the morals, of the community in which he may live. If, then, I was guilty of such conduct, I should blame no man who should condemn me for it; but I do blame those, whoever they may be, who falsely put such a charge in circulation against me." Not only did this argument express his willingness to defend the religious it also created the appearance that he was among them. But the veneer of piety was a finely crafted piece of lawyerly ambiguity strung together with the past conditional tense—"If, then, I was guilty . . ."—concluding with a bravura line throwing the burden of proof on his accuser.

In the future Lincoln would not stray far from his formulations about religion that he had artfully composed for his district handbill. Whatever his unknowable religious beliefs, he would never formally acknowledge them. He never joined a church or affiliated with any denomination. And he burned with indignation against those who exploited religion for their own political purposes, especially to justify slavery and the Confederacy, the subject of his Second Inaugural. "At Springfield and at Washington he was beset on the one hand by political priests, and on the other by honest and prayerful Christians," recalled Ward Hill Lamon, his close Illinois friend and frequent co-counsel, who came to Washington as part of his inner circle. "He despised the former, respected the latter, and had use for both. . . . Indefinite expressions about 'Divine Providence,' the 'justice of God,' 'the favor of the Most High,' were easy, and not inconsistent with his religious notions. In this, accordingly, he indulged freely; but never in all that time did he let fall from his lips or his pen an expression which remotely implied the slightest faith in Jesus as the Son of God and the Saviour of men."

While fending off Cartwright's infidelity charge, Lincoln quietly met with the abolitionists. Cartwright's views were well advertised. He condemned slavery and political antislavery as more or less equally "evil" and "sinful." "What has all this violent hue and cry of proscriptive abolitionism done for the emancipation of the poor degraded slaves? Just nothing at all; nay, infinitely worse than nothing." The abolitionists—"the angry and unchristian fulminating thunders of this one-eyed and one-ideaed, run-mad procedure"—were responsible for "prejudice, strife, and wrath, and every evil passion stirred up until the integrity of the Union of our happy country is in imminent danger; and what has it all amounted to?" Besides his fulminations against them, abolitionists were also hostile to Cartwright because they knew he held indentured servants, which they and others, like Lincoln, regarded as a form of slavery.

Two abolitionists, Thomas Alsop and Franklin T. King, were appointed by a committee to interview Lincoln at Springfield to "get his views on the subject of slavery," according to King. "We called on him and were so well pleased with what he said on the subject that we advised that our antislavery friends throughout the district should cast their vote for Mr. Lincoln, which was generally done."

Lincoln was already known as one of the few lawyers who would defend those accused of harboring fugitive slaves. "It is related of Edward D. Baker, Lincoln's friend and comrade, that being once asked to undertake a suit in which the rights of a fugitive slave were involved, he said that, as a public man and a politician, he did not dare to take it," wrote Noah Brooks, the journalist closest to Lincoln as president. "An antislavery friend of the man who was in trouble was next applied to for advice, and he said: 'Go to Lincoln. He's not afraid of an unpopular case. When I go for a lawyer to defend an arrested fugitive slave, other lawyers will refuse me, but if Lincoln is at home he will always take my case.'"

Brooks's story was not apocryphal. In February 1843, Samuel Willard, a student at Illinois College, and his father, Julius Willard, were indicted for transporting a fugitive. They asked for advice from Luther Ransom, whose boardinghouse was a station of the Underground Railroad, located near the Globe Tavern, where the Lincolns lived after their marriage. He suggested that the Willards hire Baker to defend them, who demurred. "I am seeking a nomination for Congress," he explained, "and my friends advise me not to take any case that can affect me injuriously, any case involving popular prejudices." He directed them to Logan, but he turned them down instantly. "After some further scrutiny of the list of Springfield's lawyers," Willard recalled, "Mr. Ransom said to my father, 'I think there is no other man here that can help you.' Hesitating a little, he added: 'There's Lincoln; he always helps me when I call upon him for a man that is arrested as a runaway. He is too little known; you want one that is popular and has made a name.' And so we failed to employ Lincoln and make acquaintance with him"—at least at that time, when they were found guilty and fined.

In 1845, as he prepared to run for the Congress, Lincoln took on the contentious case of Marvin Pond, charged with harboring a fugitive. The defendant was the son of Reverend Bilious Pond, a native New Englander who was pastor of the Presbyterian Church in Farmington on the outskirts of Springfield, a hotbed of abolitionism. Reverend Pond, Marvin, and his other son, Samuel (nicknamed "Abolition" Pond), were conductors of the Underground Railroad, part of the network that included the Willards, Luther Ransom, and others. Lincoln's old New Salem friends, Coleman Smoot and Mentor Graham, had accused Marvin Pond of the crime. Lincoln argued his case on June 11 before a jury that included another old friend, Caleb Carman, and Pond was acquitted. In September, Lincoln served as co-counsel in a defense of two conductors of the Underground Railroad, J. Randolph Scott and George Kerr, and the case was dismissed in their favor in 1847. In yet another case in 1845, Joseph Warman, possibly a fugitive or perhaps a free black, was apprehended traveling from Petersburg, Illinois, to Chicago without proof that he was free. Lincoln obtained a writ of habeas corpus securing his release.

The documentation for some of these cases is sketchy. It is likely there were others where Lincoln's role was not recorded. Later, Herndon represented a number of fugitives' cases, obviously with Lincoln's approval, tacit or otherwise. And there were other abolitionists in Springfield with whom Lincoln had close relationships. In 1846, he successfully sued the federal pension agent, Erastus Wright, on behalf of a Revolutionary War widow. Wright, who also operated a station of the Underground Railroad, was an outspoken abolitionist, well-to-do property owner, Sangamon County school commissioner, and eccentric enough to ride a pet elk. Despite the friction over the widow's pension and Wright's opposition to Lincoln's congressional candidacy, Lincoln later became his attorney and friend, certainly aware of Wright's strongly expressed beliefs and activities.

Among the Underground Railroad conductors in Springfield were four free blacks: Jamieson Jenkins, who would drive Lincoln to the train depot to leave for Washington as president-elect; William K. Donnegan, Lincoln's shoemaker; Reverend Henry Brown, who would lead Lincoln's horse in Lincoln's funeral procession; and Aaron Dyer, blacksmith and neighbor of Maria Vance, the Lincoln maid. "Lincoln must have known of the underground railroad activities of these African American friends," wrote Richard E. Hart, historian of Springfield's Underground Railroad, who identified the members of its network.

Lincoln won his congressional race by the largest margin that a Whig had ever captured in the district, 6,340 votes to Cartwright's 4,829. Elihu Walcott, the Liberty Party candidate, received 249 votes. Herndon attributed the margin to the shift of antislavery voters to Lincoln after his meeting with Alsop and King. "I have no doubt of the truth of this, none at all," Herndon wrote. "They increased Lincoln's majority greatly. This I know of my own knowledge." If so, most of the antislavery men in the district had decided not to vote for the Liberty Party but for the Whig who had received an imprimatur. At the least, Lincoln was willing to be vetted by a delegation of abolitionists, gave answers that met with their satisfaction, and in turn they demonstrated their intent on engaging in practical politics—fusion before the fact. Yet, despite his prominent position within the Illinois Whig Party, he was completely unknown to those in the northern part of the state, including to abolitionists in Chicago like Eastman. The abolitionist movement in Illinois was fragmented and fluid, partly accounting for some later suspicion of Lincoln. In the beginning, even antislavery politics was local.

While Lincoln campaigned, Congressman Stephen A. Douglas vociferously argued for the declaration of war against Mexico. Those fourteen members of the House who voted against it, he railed, were "traitors in their hearts," and that "honor and duty forbid divided counsels after our country has been invaded, and American blood has been shed on American soil by a treacherous foe." He humiliated Adams, flourishing his statement from 1819 as secretary of state that "our title" extended to the Rio Grande. When Adams protested that he was at the time simply performing "my duty" and that his dispatch had not claimed the river as the full boundary, Douglas held him to the exact spot. Lincoln in the Congress would soon hold Polk in his "Spot Resolution" to the place where the war was precipitated.

In private, Douglas debated the war with his friend Nimmo Browne, for whom he had as Illinois secretary of state secured the construction contract as builder of the new State House at Springfield. Browne, who was a Democrat and an abolitionist, said he didn't believe in the reason Polk gave for war and that his true purpose was "extending the free-labor-crushing system of slavery." Douglas, "amazed at the statement of his personal friend," replied that the Constitution protected slavery, that "slavery is not always bad as you extremists declare" and "to the African is not so bad as his wild and savage condition in his own country." The representative from Illinois, after all, was a Mississippi slaveholder.

Within the Congress, Douglas had befriended his home state colleague, John J. Hardin, both enthusiastic for the war. When Hardin enlisted, Douglas wrote, "I shall claim to be your Representative during this war." After Shields and Baker joined, Hardin wrote Douglas, "Can't you adjourn Congress and go along with us?" A delegation of Illinois congressmen visited Polk at the White House, urging his appointment as a brigade major. "I am exceedingly pleased with the expression of your determination to join my command," Hardin wrote him. But Polk did not want one of his most ardent defenders in the Congress to quit and told him he must stay. Douglas, he stated, "is a sensible man, and he received what I said to him well." The incident demonstrating Douglas's eagerness to serve in battle but restrained only by the president had a staged quality to it. Douglas was Polk's favorite young member of the Congress, whom he pushed for the speakership, a post Polk had held, and often summoned to the White House. Polk, in fact, did not like the idea of members of the Congress joining the military, which Douglas of course knew. Facing a weak Whig opponent for reelection, Douglas aimed for the U.S. Senate seat being vacated by the retiring incumbent, James Semple, whose endorsement and that of the other senator, Sidney Breese, Douglas arranged. In December, the Democratic caucus in the legislature unanimously chose Douglas for the Senate and he was overwhelmingly elected.

The 30th Congress would not convene until December 1847, sixteen months after Lincoln's election. While he was in suspended political animation the entire Mexican War was fought and won, reputations made, and the dead buried.

Shields came back a hero. He was shot through his lung and out his back in the Battle of Cerro Gordo and left for dead on the field, but miraculously recovered without even a telltale scar. In 1848, the Democratic caucus of the legislature installed him as U.S. senator, ousting Breese. "What a wonderful shot that was!" exclaimed the Whig lawyer Justin Butterfield. "The ball went clean through Shields without hurting him, or even leaving a scar, and killed Breese a thousand miles away!" Breese's friends in the exclusive club that is the Senate objected that the upstart Irishman Shields was ineligible, that he was not naturalized as a citizen for nine years and below the age of thirty-five, and his election was declared void. The fiery Shields deepened his trouble by sending Breese a threatening letter: "Let the consequences fall on your own head." Governor Augustus C. French called a special session of the legislature that after twenty-one ballots voted again for Shields. Senator Douglas intervened behind the scenes to tip the balance in his favor, but not before gaining support for his position of "non-interference" in the extension of slavery. This time the Senate seated Shields.

When Shields was wounded attacking a battery at Cerro Gordo, Ned Baker took command of the charge that routed the Mexicans and went on to participate in the siege of Vera Cruz. Upon his return to Springfield the legislature presented him with a sword and scabbard. But his health was "somewhat broken," Matheny recalled. David Davis stated that Baker had become "very dissipated in Mexico." It is likely that he suffered from what would later be called post-traumatic stress syndrome. When he recovered, he wanted to return to the Congress, but Lincoln occupied the spot, so he moved to the town of Galena in the northwest corner of the state and in 1848 won a seat from there.

John J. Hardin came home in a coffin borne by his soldiers. He was killed at the Battle of Buena Vista repulsing a superior Mexican force, a famous victory that helped propel Zachary Taylor into the White House. Taylor's battlefield order became his campaign slogan: "Give them a little more grape, Captain Bragg!" Henry Clay, Jr., also fell in the battle. Colonel Jefferson Davis, commanding the Mississippi Rifles, was wounded. A horse fell on Colonel Franklin Pierce.

On July 4, 1847, Springfield celebrated the return of its volunteers with a day of speeches, music and the firing of cannon. The constitutional convention assembled there adjourned to attend Hardin's funeral at Jacksonville and for a month afterward wore black armbands in memory of Illinois's fallen warrior-congressman. "Had Colonel Hardin, who fell at Buena Vista, lived," remarked David Davis, "he would have controlled the politics and the offices of the state."

CHAPTER THIRTEEN

GREAT EXPECTATIONS

—————•◆•—————

The newly elected congressman from Springfield was not present at the
July 4th ceremony welcoming home the troops from the war. Abraham Lincoln was on his first visit
to Chicago to attend the River
and Harbor Convention, a national gathering to protest President Polk's veto of an internal
improvements bill. In Illinois the
veto was taken as an attack on
its basic economic interests. The
Democratic Party in the state
had split, with few Democrats
willing to defend the Democratic
president. The outrage was not
confined to Illinois; Polk had enraged much of Northern opinion.
Despite the glow of victory in the
Mexican War, the veto had more
direct immediacy as a political
issue. The sandbar blocking Chicago's harbor was dubbed "Mount

Inscription to Abraham Lincoln from
Henry Clay, May 11, 1847:
"With constant regard to friendship."
The flyleaf of Lincoln's copy of "The
Life and Speeches of Henry Clay."

Polk." And as the extension of slavery in the territory acquired from Mexico became a paramount question, it was joined by critics to Polk's denial of federal resources to the North. "Are not *millions* being squandered by this same James K. Polk for the invasion of Mexico and the extension of slavery?" editorialized the *Chicago Journal*, the leading Whig newspaper in the city, predicting sectional conflict. "The North can and will be no longer hood-winked. If no measures for protection and improvement of anything North or West are to be suffered by our Southern masters, if we are to be downtrod-den, and all our cherished interests crushed by them, a signal revolution will inevitably ensue. The same spirit and energy that forced emancipation for the whole country from Great Britain will throw off the Southern yoke. The North and West will look to and take care of their own interests henceforth."

More than one thousand delegates chosen at local meetings in Illinois alone swarmed to Chicago. Lincoln was selected along with Billy Herndon, Bledsoe, Matheny, and John Calhoun. The tone was nonpartisan, drawing in discontented Democrats no longer enthralled by the Jacksonian shibbo-leth against the federal economic role, but the gathering was overwhelm-ingly Whig in orientation. At least five thousand delegates came from across the North, bringing together *New York Tribune* editor Horace Greeley, New York Whig political boss Thurlow Weed, and Edward Bates, a St. Louis lawyer and Whig, who was chosen the convention president. (Bates would become Lincoln's attorney general.) The hotels could not accommodate the immense crowd so people had to find rooms in private homes and sleep on ships.

One notable voice was heard against the din of unanimity—David Dud-ley Field, the eminent New York attorney, a Democrat, who made the case for "strict construction" of the Constitution against internal improvements. A speaker was sought to answer him. "In the afternoon, Hon. Abraham Lincoln, a tall specimen of an Illinoisan, just elected to Congress from the only Whig District in the State, was called out, and spoke briefly and happily in reply to Mr. Field," Greeley reported. Lincoln's remarks went unrecorded, but his argument was undoubtedly in line with Bates's climactic speech: "A government that has no power . . . is a poor, impotent government, and not at all such a government as our fathers thought they had made when they produced the Constitution."

The *Chicago Journal* went out of its way to report "we are happy to see"

Lincoln "is in attendance upon the Convention. This is his first visit to the commercial emporium of the State, and we have no doubt his visit will impress him more deeply, if possible, with the importance, and inspire a higher zeal for the great interest of River-and-Harbor improvements. We expect much from him as a representative in Congress, and we have no doubt our expectations will be more than realized."

Only thirty-six years old, Lincoln gained his sobriquet of "Old Abe" as he was spotted walking near the Sherman House, the main hotel, when S. Lisle Smith, the Chicago city attorney and Whig politician, called out at him. "There is Lincoln on the other side of the street. Just look at 'Old Abe.'" Elihu Washburne, a Whig lawyer who would become a congressman, recalled that "from that time we all called him 'Old Abe.' No one who saw him can forget his personal appearance at that time. Tall, angular and awkward, he had on a short-waisted, thin swallow-tail coat, a short vest of same material, thin pantaloons, scarcely coming down to his ankles, a straw hat and a pair of brogans with woolen socks."

Lincoln's reply to Field was his first speech before a national audience. The convention itself sparked Chicago's meteoric growth. Just fourteen years earlier, in 1833, known as Fort Dearborn, it had only about 350 pioneers. At the time of the meeting its population was about 16,000. In thirteen years, its population would explode to more than 112,000. Lincoln encountered Chicago over the question of its development into a metropolis at the center of national commerce and industry. Seeing Chicago in its rough, embryonic form and imagining its possibilities gave him a physical vision of an industrial North coming into being, stretching from New England and New York, across the Great Lakes to Illinois and looking westward. And the rapid expansion of Chicago would just as swiftly shift political power to the northern part of the state—lacking in Southern influence and antislavery in sentiment—fundamentally altering the political equation of Illinois that made possible the rise of the Republican Party—and Lincoln—a decade later.

While the River and Harbor Convention met, another convention was in session. The antipathy in Illinois toward the mere presence of blacks was reflected at the state constitutional convention that drew up a new article that would "effectually prohibit free persons of color from immigrating to and settling in this State." Sangamon County had four delegates—Stephen

Logan, Ninian W. Edwards, James Matheny, and a farmer, James Dawson, who employed a black indentured servant. Logan and Edwards led opposition to the restriction clause, but delegates from the southern part of the state forced a public referendum. It was approved in 1848 with more than 70 percent of the vote. Democrats overwhelmingly supported it by 92 percent—and Springfield voters backed it by 84 percent. That vote was an accurate measurement of the degree of white supremacist feeling in Illinois.

Before departing for Washington, Lincoln wrapped up his remaining law cases. On April 8, he served as co-counsel for a conductor of the Underground Railroad charged with harboring a runaway slave. He convinced the judge to quash the indictment because the accused "John Randolph Scott" was identified wrongly as "Randolph Scott." Among his last cases were several in Coles County, located southeast of Springfield, involving minor matters of real estate, debt, and slander. But in one of them Lincoln found himself in the most perplexing case of his career as the co-counsel for a slave owner attempting to recover his runaway slaves.

Robert Matson, of Bourbon County, Kentucky, bought a farm in Illinois, overseen by Anthony Bryant, a slave he carried across the state line and therefore legally free once resident in Illinois. In order to evade the Illinois law that declared slaves freed if domiciled in the state rather than being transported across it by their owners, Matson brought in slaves from Kentucky for the planting to the harvest seasons as though they were simply passing through. One of those he imported was Jane, Bryant's wife, who was likely the illegitimate daughter of Matson's brother and had six children of varying shades of skin color, one with blue eyes and red hair, from various white fathers. Bryant was the father of only one of her children. Matson was perpetually debt ridden, sued thirty-three times in Bourbon County. He lived on his Illinois farm with his mistress, Mary Corbin, and their four illegitimate children, a second family almost certainly unknown to his legitimate Kentucky family. When the Bryants heard that Jane and her children were to be taken back to Kentucky and sold to new masters they fled, taking shelter with Gideon M. Ashmore, a local innkeeper originally from Tennessee, his father a captain under General Jackson, whose shrine he worshipped. Ashmore loved nothing so much as a good fight and detested slavery. He contacted his fellow abolitionist, Dr. Hiram Rutherford, a native Pennsylvanian, and they hired the local congressman, Orlando B. Ficklin, as an attorney. Ficklin was a former Whig turned pro-slavery Democrat, married to the daughter of Senator Walter T. Colquitt of Georgia, Polk's floor leader in the Senate. He might have been retained by the abolitionists to defend slaves precisely because he was a preeminent Democratic in the county. Matson secured the services of the volatile and often effective Usher Linder, Lovejoy's antagonist who had become a Whig and was living in Charleston, the county seat.

Matson swore in his affidavit that Jane and her offspring were "on a temporary sojourn" and therefore remained his slaves, while Ficklin argued they were free once living in Illinois. The justice of the peace ruled he lacked jurisdiction, declared Jane and her children "runaway slaves," committed them to the county jail, and sent the case to the circuit court. Ashmore and Rutherford posted bond for their freedom. Then Ashmore's brother Samuel, another justice of the peace, issued a warrant for Matson's arrest for "living in an open state of fornication." He was eventually convicted and paid a thirty-dollar fine. Matson sued Ashmore and Rutherford for "harboring" blacks in Illinois without proper papers. They in turn filed a writ of habeas corpus for the blacks' release on the grounds that they were no longer slaves. William Wilson, chief justice of the Illinois Supreme Court, and Samuel E. Treat, an associate justice, impaneled themselves as the judges, indicating, as Ficklin stated, that the case was of "vital importance . . . involving as it did the question of African slavery." It seems likely that the unusual involvement of two Supreme Court judges meant that they sought to underscore the authority of a decision in favor of the Bryants. Wilson's opinion would be published in the Cincinnati-based *Western Law Journal*, probably prearranged and also unusual.

On the eve of the trial on October 16, 1847, Lincoln became Linder's co-counsel, probably secured by Linder at the last minute because Lincoln happened to be in Coles County. He appeared to regard the case as another piece of business allowing him to pick up a fee he would not have otherwise had. On the veranda of a Charleston tavern, leaning back in his chair, entertaining a gaggle of men with stories, Lincoln was approached by Rutherford. "I had known Abraham Lincoln several years, and his views and mine on the wrong of slavery being in perfect accord, I determined to employ him," he recalled. As Rutherford told him the facts of the case, Lincoln became upset. "I noticed a peculiarly troubled look came over his face now and then, his eyes appeared to be fixed in the distance beyond me, and he shook his head several times as if debating with himself some question of grave import." Lincoln informed him "with apparent reluctance" that he had already signed up to join Linder on Matson's side. "This was a grievous disappointment, and irritated me into expressions more or less 'bitter' in tone. He seemed to feel this, and even though he endeavored in his plausible way to reconcile me to the proposition that, as a lawyer, he must represent and be faithful to those who counsel with and employ him." A few hours later, Lincoln sent a message to Rutherford that he had "sent for the man who had approached him in Matson's behalf," probably Linder, and would be able to extricate himself and instead act as Rutherford's lawyer. "But it was too late; my pride was up, and I plainly indicated a disinclination to avail myself of his offer." Instead, Rutherford hired Charles H. Constable, a Whig state senator who had played a leading role at the constitutional convention in favor of the restrictive Black Code, to serve as co-counsel with Ficklin. In short, lawyers for the slave were pro-slavery, while one against, Lincoln, was antislavery.

Linder delivered a stentorian speech before the court asserting the constitutional rightness of slavery, a speech that "grated harshly," according to Jesse W. Weik, Herndon's coauthor of his *Life of Lincoln*, who interviewed Ficklin and others involved in the case. Another account, by Duncan T. McIntyre, a Charleston lawyer who recorded Rutherford's version of events, called Linder's oration "light and weak," and "out of place in that court."

Lincoln completely ignored Linder's pro-slavery argument, instead posing the matter in the most neutral terms possible, framing the question in a way that in effect required the court to rule against his client. "This then is the point on which this whole case turns: Were these Negroes passing over and crossing the State, and thus, as the law contemplates, *in transitu,* or were they actually located by consent of their master? If only crossing the State that act did not free them, but if located, even indefinitely, by the consent of their owner and master, their emancipation logically followed." "Lincoln's argument was poor too, and he gave the case away," wrote McIntyre. "He was a case lawyer but in a case where he felt that he had the right none could surpass him," Ficklin later wrote Herndon. "As a statesman, he was deeply imbued with the principles of Henry Clay, but was conscientiously opposed to slavery all his life." Stephen Logan observed that Lincoln "had this one peculiarity: he couldn't fight in a bad case."

Ficklin and Constable cited the Ordinance of 1789 and the Illinois constitution's prohibition of slavery, but "nothing helped us so much as the decisions of the English courts," Ficklin recalled.

Constable quoted the famous antislavery summation in an English court in 1772 by John Philpot Curran, an Irish orator and lawyer, defending a runaway Jamaican slave, James Somerset, a case that resulted in the judge freeing Somerset, ruling slavery "odious," and for all intents and purposes rendering it illegal in Britain. Curran's defense was as well known as almost any courtroom speech, proclaiming the natural liberty of the slave: "No matter with what solemnities he may have been devoted on the altar of slavery, the moment he touches the sacred soil of Britain, the altar and the god sink together in the dust; his soul walks abroad in her own majesty; his body swells beyond the measure of his chains which burst from around him, and he stands redeemed, regenerated, and disenthralled, by the irresistible genius of universal emancipation." That ringing conclusive phrase of the "genius of universal emancipation" inspired the name for Lundy's abolitionist newspaper, wellspring of abolitionism.

Lincoln would have been as aware as anyone in the courtroom of the resonance of the speech and familiar with the Somerset case. "I shall never forget how Lincoln winced when Constable quoted from Curran's defense," recalled Ficklin. And with that, the judges declared the slaves "free and discharged from all servitude whatever to any person or persons from henceforward and forever"—again the language of emancipation but from the Ordinance of 1787.

The American Colonization Society took charge of Anthony and Jane Bryant's emigration to Liberia, where they were miserable and longed to return to the United States. William Herndon contributed money for their passage, undoubtedly with Lincoln's knowledge and approval. Matson never paid Lincoln his fee. The Matson case was never raised as a political issue against Lincoln. Constable would become a leading Illinois Copperhead virulently against Lincoln during the Civil War, and as a circuit court judge arbitrarily freeing Union army deserters was detained, charged with treason, but finally released.

Wrapping up his legal work, Lincoln left Springfield with his family on October 25, met his old friend Speed in St. Louis, and by steamboat and rail went on to Lexington for his first visit with his wife's family there, and his first and only encounter with his "beau ideal," Henry Clay.

"It was a cold day in November, and the wide hall was chilly as the door was thrown open to receive them," Mary's half sister Emilie recalled. "The whole family stood near the front door with welcoming arms and, in true patriarchal style, the colored contingent filled the rear of the hall to shake hands with the long absent one and 'make a miration' over the babies."

At last, in Lexington, Lincoln had his chance to see Clay in person and hear his mellifluous voice. After Lincoln's campaign for the Congress, Clay had sent him an inscribed book, *The Life and Speeches of Henry Clay*: "To Abraham Lincoln: With constant regard to friendship H. Clay Ashland 11 May 1847." On November 13, Lincoln sat in the audience as Clay spoke for two and a half hours on the Mexican War. Lincoln's father-in-law, Robert Smith Todd, presided on the stage as vice chairman of the event.

The Henry Clay standing before Lincoln was a shattered seventy-year-old man attempting to put himself back together again physically, mentally, and politically. After his narrow defeat in 1844, he grieved over his loss. "I am endeavoring to separate myself as much as I can from this world," he wrote a friend. "Then indeed my heart bleeds, for the moment, for my Country and my friends." Opposed to the Mexican War—"This unhappy war" that he "foretold" and "lament," as he wrote Horace Greeley—he nonetheless gave his namesake, Henry Jr., the gift of a pair of pistols when he departed for the front lines. The news that Colonel Clay was killed at the Battle of Buena Vista devastated his father—"wounds so deep and excruciating"—and he deplored his son's sacrifice for "this most unnecessary and horrible war with Mexico." Polk sent no message of condolence.

Distressed by his son's death, Clay was further upset by the ascent of Zachary Taylor as a potential Whig presidential candidate. Just as Henry Jr. had fallen at Buena Vista, Taylor had risen. "Up to the Battle of Buena Vista," Clay wrote, "I had reason to believe that there existed a fixed determination with the mass of the Whig party, throughout the U.S., to bring me forward again. I believe that the greater portion of that mass still cling to that wish, and that the movements we have seen, in behalf of Genl Taylor, are to a considerable extent superficial and limited." Clay saw in Taylor a replay of the Harrison candidacy, "Military Chieftains" unqualified for the presidency pushing him aside. He began a tour of the East to revive his support. But he could not contain his grief, describing himself in "that theater of sadness." Once again, he was wounded, this time by the "treachery" of Senator John J. Crittenden of Kentucky, his political heir, who endorsed Taylor. Even Giddings, his staunch supporter, wrote saying he could not again back him. Clay replied that after the 1844 election he freed his manservant Charles and emancipated eight of ten slaves "during my life." "I am not surprised at the progress of the anti-slavery feeling which you describe in the Free States," he wrote. "The annexation of Texas, this most unnecessary and horrible war with Mexico, and the overthrow of the tariff of 1842, were well calculated to produce that effect." Clay reiterated his feelings against slavery and his bewilderment about what to do about it. "I regret as much as any one does the existence of slavery in our country, and wish to God there was not a single slave in the United States, or in the whole world. But here the unfortunate institution is, and a most delicate and difficult affair is it to deal with."

To frame the issues of the coming campaign and reclaim his command of Whig Party politics Clay decided to deliver a major speech. So on a cold, rainy day he mounted the podium at Lexington before a crowd of warm supporters that included Abraham Lincoln. "The day," he began, "is dark and gloomy, unsettled and uncertain, like the condition of our country, in regard to the unnatural war with Mexico." He argued that Polk had unnecessarily provoked the war and that his reason was false. "I must say that no earthly consideration would have ever tempted or provoked me to vote for a bill, with a palpable falsehood stamped on its face. Almost idolizing truth, as I do, I never, never, could have voted for that bill."

Clay described at length his failed efforts over fifty years to abolish slavery. "My opinions on the subject of slavery are well known. They have the merit, if it be one, of consistency, uniformity, and long duration. I have ever regarded slavery as a great evil, a wrong, for the present, I fear, an irremediable wrong to its unfortunate victims. I should rejoice if not a single slave breathed the air or was within the limits of our country."

And he concluded with an eight-point program, emphasizing the right and duty of the Congress to investigate the origins of the Mexican War—"to determine upon the motives, causes and objects of any war, when it commences, or at any time during the progress of its existence." Equally important, he insisted it was necessary to draw a line across the country against the extension of slavery: "Resolved, That we do, positively and emphatically, disclaim and disavow any wish or desire, on our part, to acquire any foreign territory whatever, for the purpose of propagating slavery, or of introducing slaves from the United States, into such foreign territory." His proposal was a restatement of the Wilmot Proviso, already being heatedly debated in the Congress.

After Clay's speech, Lincoln was introduced to the great man, probably by his father-in-law, and Clay invited him to dinner at Ashland. But the intimate setting did not produce a warming effect. Lincoln later confided to Linder "that though Mr. Clay was most polished in his manners, and very hospitable, he betrayed a consciousness of superiority that none could mistake. He felt that Mr. Clay did not regard him, or any other person in his presence, as, in any sense, on an equality with him. In short, he thought that Mr. Clay was overbearing and domineering, and that, while he was apparently kind, it was in that magnificent and patronizing way which made a sensitive man uncomfortable." According to one of the chroniclers of Lincoln's life, Alexander K. McClure, who as the Republican state chairman in Pennsylvania was among his most important supporters, "Clay was courteous, but cold . . . Lincoln was disenchanted; his ideal was shattered."

But Lincoln was already leaning to Taylor, just as he had backed Harrison against Clay, going with the one he thought had the best chance to win. According to one account, Whig leaders met on August 30, 1847, at the house of Ninian W. Edwards, where Lincoln "explained its object to be the selection of some other man than Henry Clay as the standard bearer of the Whig party in the coming Presidential contest. The name of General Taylor was proposed by Mr. Lincoln, and the necessity of immediate action urged, on the ground that if the Whigs did not take Taylor for their candidate, that the Democrats would. That the Whig party had fought long enough for principle, and should change its motto to success!" The source of this anecdote, John W. Singleton, claimed at that point both he and Charles Constable, the attorney in the Matson case, "immediately left the house." This story first surfaced in an anti-Lincoln pamphlet during the 1860 campaign, entitled "Opposing Principles of Henry Clay and Abraham Lincoln," written by a resentful John Hill, the son of Samuel Hill, the New Salem storeowner and friend of Lincoln. Singleton was then a Whig, who became an anti-Lincoln Copperhead like Constable, but who Lincoln permitted to go to Richmond on an unofficial peace mission in early 1865 to bring back intelligence; Singleton returned with contracts for tobacco and cotton, whose shipments General Grant ordered destroyed believing that Singleton "will sacrifice every interest of the country to succeed."

The questions that Clay raised in his speech—the origin of the Mexican War and the extension of slavery—would consume Lincoln's congressional career. And in Lexington he was surrounded by the sights and sounds of slavery—the newspapers filled with advertisements for slaves and notices about runaways, the coffles of slaves shuffling past, and the five slaves that his father-in-law and a business partner received as payment for a debt and which they had auctioned in front of the courthouse just before Clay's speech.

Lincoln spent much of his time in Robert Todd's library, reading back issues of *Niles' Register*, a weekly journal of national and international news, and marking up a poetry anthology, *Element Extracts*. He committed William Cullen Bryant's "Thanatopsis" to memory:

> *So live, that when thy summons comes to join*
> *The innumerable caravan which moves*
> *To that mysterious realm where each shall take*
> *His chamber in the silent halls of death,*
> *Thou go not, like the quarry-slave at night,*
> *Scourged by his dungeon; but, sustain'd and soothed*
> *By an unfaltering trust, approach thy grave,*
> *Like one who wraps the drapery of his couch*
> *About him, and lies down to pleasant dreams.*

And he marked Alexander Pope's line, a freethinker's credo: "Know then thyself, presume not God to scan; The Proper study of Mankind is man."

He also marked one of William Cowper's antislavery poems, "Charity." He had read one of these Cowper poems as a boy. "Charity" begins as a paean to the prosperity produced by international commerce, "Trade is the golden girdle of the globe," but it veers to the darker trade in people. Lincoln marked these lines:

> *But ah! what wish can prosper, or what prayer,*
> *For merchants rich in cargoes of despair,*
> *Who drive a loathsome traffic, gauge, and span,*
> *And buy the muscles and the bones of man?*

The tender ties of father, husband, friend,
All bonds of nature in that moment end;
And each endures, while yet he draws his breath,
A stroke as fatal as the scythe of death.

Cowper saw slavery as a crime against nature and God, "Trade in the blood of innocence," and warned "the man that treads his fellow down": "Remember, Heaven has an avenging rod."

Wait for the dawning of a brighter day,
And snap the chain the moment when you may.
Nature imprints upon whate'er we see,
That has a heart and life in it, Be free!

At these lines Lincoln turned down the page in the book to mark it.

CHAPTER FOURTEEN

RANCHERO SPOTTY

L incoln arrived at the city of his dreams, glimmering on his horizon since he had been a boy reciting the speeches of Clay and Webster. At last, he was about to enter their sanctum, Washington City's largest building, constructed of sandstone in classical Corinthian style on the highest point of land, situated by Charles L'Enfant's spectacular design, and named by Thomas Jefferson in his own handwriting on the blueprint as the "Capitol." It was built in great part by slave labor. When Charles Dickens visited the city in 1842, he was struck by the glaring disparity between the founding vision and the existing reality. "It is sometimes called the City of Magnificent Distances, but it might with greater propriety be termed the City of Magnificent Intentions," he wrote, "for it is only on taking a bird's-eye view of it from the top of the Capitol, that one can at all comprehend the vast designs of its projector, an aspiring Frenchman. Spacious avenues, that begin in nothing, and lead nowhere; streets, mile-long, that only want houses, roads, and inhabitants; public buildings that need but

The Capitol

a public to be complete; and ornaments of great thoroughfares, which only lack great thoroughfares to ornament—are its leading features." Dickens wondered whether the city was "a monument raised to a deceased project, with not even a legible inscription to record its departed greatness."

The Capitol's looming grandeur masked the squalor within. The chamber of the House was so hot and poorly ventilated in the summer that it was dubbed "the Oven," while the Senate was so cold during the winter that its members clustered around smoking stoves and wrapped themselves in overcoats and blankets. The Rotunda between the Senate and the House was the largest open indoor space in the country, adorned with John Trumbull's four mammoth triumphal murals depicting the American Revolution, and above it, a cathedral-like celestial dome of wood, rotted, cracked, and leaking. Plaster fell from the walls; dust filled the corridors; garbage piled in the corners. Wretched acoustics created an inaudible din that made it difficult if not impossible for the legislators to hear each other. The Supreme Court, vice president, commissioner of public buildings, Library of Congress, and hordes of lobbyists, so-called "claims agents," journalists, and hangers-on filled its hive.

Yet the shabbiness, noise, and filth were familiar to Lincoln. He would have been reminded of the ramshackle capital at Vandalia and the swarming corridors of Springfield. Surrounded by teeming schools of politicians, he was a proverbial fish in water. According to the Whig journalist and later clerk of the Senate, Ben Perley Poore, Lincoln "was to be found every morning in the post-office of the House charming a small audience with his quaint anecdotes." But there was reason to his humor. Lincoln joked along to get along. The Washington freshman was hardly a novice; he knew how to ingratiate himself with a crowd of politicians, entertaining them while he observed them closely, learning their motives and foibles, who was friends with whom, who hated whom, who had quiet influence, and who was a pretender.

Lincoln stepped off the train at Washington's depot on December 2, 1847, trailed by his wife and two unruly boys, four-year-old Robert and one-year-old Edward, checking first into Brown's Indian Queen Hotel, the favorite of congressmen, located on Pennsylvania Avenue between the Capitol and the White House, a garishly painted sign of Pocahontas hanging above its entrance, before settling into a boardinghouse, Mrs. Sprigg's.

On December 6, he caucused with other Whigs to elect the speaker of the house—Robert C. Winthrop of Massachusetts, Boston Brahmin of

Brahmins, direct descendant of John Winthrop, the Puritan founder of the Massachusetts Bay Colony, and protégé of Daniel Webster. Winthrop was a conservative party man who had voted for war with Mexico and considered himself the embodiment of prudence. That fall, in Boston, Winthrop had been surprised by an insurgency of antiwar, antislavery activists announcing themselves as "Conscience Whigs," suddenly challenging Winthrop and those they called "Cotton Whigs," allied with Southern interests and agenda, and foiled the upstarts when they attempted to pass an antislavery platform at the Massachusetts state party convention. To Winthrop's shock, the leader of the Conscience Whigs was his close childhood friend, who grew up on cloistered Beacon Hill and attended Harvard with him, now a Boston lawyer, Charles Sumner. Sumner assailed Winthrop for his support of the Mexican War in a series of newspaper polemics: "Blood! blood! is on the hands of the representative from Boston." These articles, whipping up the anti-Winthrop campaign, were written anonymously and published in the *Boston Whig*, edited by Charles Francis Adams, son of J. Q. Adams. Winthrop disdainfully referred to Sumner, young Adams, and their group as "a little nest of vipers." In his battle to become speaker, he was finally put across in the Whig caucus by the endorsement of the elder Adams on the basis of the ancient family bond: his father had been a friend of Winthrop's father. Following Adams, all but two of the Whig members fell into line. Joshua Giddings, adamant against Winthrop, argued with Adams, remained a holdout, and continued a bitter attack on Winthrop as a dissembler and war supporter for months, encouraged editorially by the younger Adams in the *Boston Whig*. In voting against Winthrop, Giddings was joined by John G. Palfrey, the congressman from Cambridge, formerly the dean of the Harvard Divinity School, the ultimate Conscience Whig. Lincoln voted with the rest of the Whig caucus for Winthrop, took his oath of office, and drew his seat, number 191, in the back row, where he could see John Quincy Adams, Old Man Eloquent, sitting up front.

Mary had once confided to a girlfriend that she wanted to marry a man who would take her to the theater—and Lincoln loved the theater. One of the first things he did in Washington was to take Mary to Carusi's Saloon, not a tavern at all but the finest theater in town, to a performance of the best act, the Ethiopian Serenaders, a black-faced minstrel troupe dressed in formal attire, just returned from a triumphant tour of London. The Lin-

colns' social life, however, was limited and cramped. The little known provincial was not invited to dine at the homes of the prominent, where most
of the entertaining went on, and Mary, living in a boardinghouse, could not
serve as a hostess herself as she had in Springfield as part of an influential
extended family inhabiting Aristocracy Hill. Daniel Webster, according to
Poore, "used occasionally to have Mr. Lincoln at one of his pleasant Satur-
day breakfasts, where the Western Congressman's humorous illustrations of
the events of the day, sparkling with spontaneous and unpremeditated wit,
would give great delight to 'the solid men of Boston' assembled around the
festive board." (Lincoln had once performed some legal work for Webster's
son in Illinois for a fee of ten dollars.) These were apparently not events that
included women. Mary was left alone most of the time in a confining room
with squalling boys. She learned quickly why few wives traveled with their
husbands to Washington, lasting in the forbidding environment only a few
months, until the spring, when she returned with the children to her father's
house.

Almost the instant Lincoln landed in Washington he was recruited by the
"Young Indians," a caucus of House Whigs working to nominate General
Zachary Taylor for president. In December there were only seven members,
each representing their state, but by February it had expanded from forty to
forty-five. The main organizers were Alexander Stephens of Georgia, who
had already gotten a Whig convention in his state pledged to Taylor, and
Truman Smith of Connecticut, the congressional campaign chairman. The
diminutive Stephens and giant Lincoln were an odd couple—and mutual
admiration society. Lincoln wrote Herndon that his new friend was "a little slim, pale-faced, consumptive man, with a voice like Logan's" and had
"just concluded the very best speech, of an hour's length, I ever heard. My
old, withered, dry eyes, are full of tears yet." Stephens would later recall,
"Mr. Lincoln was careful as to his manners, awkward in his speech, but was
possessed of a very strong, clear, vigorous mind." (Stephens would become
the Confederate vice president and another Young Indian, Robert Toombs,
the first Confederate secretary of state.)

The elemental attraction of Taylor for the Young Indians was his resem-
blance to Harrison, the only previous Whig president, a military hero who
could be swept into office and serve as an iconic figurehead, deferring to the
Whig congressional leaders. Taylor was more of a genuine hero than Har-

rison, winning his laurels outnumbered by a real army, not taking the scalp of an Indian chief in a fight long ago, and was far less of an actual politician, in fact a semiliterate without known opinions on any subject except a private preference for the Whigs, compared to the well-born Virginian who had been Indiana's territorial governor. An additional advantage was that, also like Harrison, Taylor was not Clay, who had been edged aside by Harrison for bearing too many political scars and now carried even more, having made emphatic and diametrically opposed statements on slavery in recent years that alienated both antislavery Northern Whigs and pro-slavery Southern Whigs. Taylor was a slave owner, but unblemished, a blank slate, and available. His image appeared in the eyes of his beholders, perceiving him to be a potential puppet. Above all, he could march to victory.

"I have to say I am in favor of General Taylor as the Whig candidate for the Presidency because I am satisfied we can elect him, that he would give us a Whig administration, and that we cannot elect any other Whig," Lincoln wrote fellow Young Indian, Thomas S. Flournoy of Virginia. (Flournoy would later become a member of Virginia's secession convention and a Confederate cavalry colonel serving with Stonewall Jackson.)

Lincoln envisioned Taylor as the best advance man for the Whigs in Illinois. "In Illinois, his being our candidate, would certainly give us one additional member of Congress, if not more; and probably would give us the electoral vote of the state," he wrote Flournoy. To his friend and former Whig state legislator Archibald Williams, he dismissed his fallen idol, "Mr. Clay's chance for an election is just no chance at all." "You should simply go for General Taylor," he advised Usher Linder, "because by this, you can take some Democrats, and lose no Whigs."

As the only Whig congressman from Illinois, Lincoln had positioned himself early as the leading Taylor man in the state. Feeling himself honor bound to a one-term pledge, he considered his time in Washington short and therefore concentrated. "I am not a candidate for re-nomination or election," he wrote a political supporter. He had no plan for a long congressional career, rising in the ranks through seniority, chairing a committee, and contending for the leadership. He also knew he could not win a Senate seat—the legislature was controlled by the Democrats—so his goal was to play an indispensable part in the campaign and win a high federal appointment. From the moment he became a Young Indian, his future was wrapped up with the outcome of the presidential election and his energy focused on securing the party victory that would be his own.

The political unraveling of Polk's presidency provided the Whigs with their opening. At the beginning of his term, Polk had confided to George Bancroft, the poet, historian, and secretary of the navy, his great ambitions for his administration—settling the Oregon question, annexing Texas and acquiring California, as well as restoring the old Jacksonian economic policies, which he believed would resolve the country's tensions far into the foreseeable future. Polk achieved all his lofty aims, expanding the territory of the country by even more than Thomas Jefferson had through the Louisiana Purchase. But the more immense his accomplishment, the more diminished his stature. Polk's destiny was anything but manifest. He was a paradox: politically dominant yet surprisingly incompetent, a successful president who was a staggeringly ineffectual chief executive. He neither knew how to wage war nor make peace. The greater his scope, the greater was his confusion. He mishandled and misjudged his generals, his chief diplomat, and his own party. Even as he climbed to higher plateaus, he became more myopic; he had no vision of the vistas that stretched before him. His eyes were turned backward. These were not the familiar politics of the Jackson era that had germi-

nated him and as Young Hickory he hoped to rejuvenate. Unable to find his way by grasping on to the signposts of the past, he stumbled through chaos. The bright lines of politics that would lead into the Civil War were emerging, but invisible to his sight as he tripped over them. He ushered in the future as yesterday's man. It was in the middle of Polk's collapse that Lincoln made his unnoticed entrance onto the Washington stage, seeking attention by taking the part of Polk's accuser.

Whigs charged that Polk had provoked the Mexican War, then

James K. Polk

didn't actually wish to fight it, and resented those Whig-aligned generals who had won it. Even before the war began, no one excoriated Polk more fiercely than Thomas Hart Benton, of his own party. "It is impossible to conceive of an administration less warlike or more intriguing than that of Mr. Polk," Senator Benton said. "They wanted a small war, just large enough to require a treaty of peace, and not large enough to make military reputations dangerous for the Presidency. Never were men at the head of a government less imbued with military spirit or more addicted to intrigue. . . . How to manage the war was a puzzle. Defeat would be ruin: to conquer vicariously [that is, by Whig generals] would be dangerous."

Polk's two main generals were Whigs: Winfield Scott and Zachary Taylor. Both fought furiously with each other and with Polk before and after they battled the Mexicans. Polk did not expect Taylor to defeat General Antonio Lopez de Santa Anna, the Mexican military dictator, with a much smaller army, and at Buena Vista, Taylor disregarded orders from Washington to fall back before he stormed Monterrey. After constant political harassment from Polk, Scott captured Mexico City in a maneuver that no less than the Duke of Wellington predicted was impossible. Polk was stunned and baffled by his generals' success.

When Scott had protested Polk's division of command between himself and Taylor in a letter to Secretary of War William Marcy, noting in passing that he was eating "a hasty plate of soup," that phrase was leaked to the partisan Democratic newspapers to hold the general up to ridicule, prompting him to write another letter complaining about having a "fire in his rear" while he met "a fire in front of the Mexicans." Polk relieved Scott, gave Taylor his command, but reversed himself, sending Scott back into the field again.

The "fire in the rear" also happened to be a "fire in front" personified by Gideon Pillow, Polk's closest friend, law partner, and manager of his convention nomination, whom he appointed a major general on Scott's staff. Pillow was an utterly inept political general, undercutting Scott and attacking Taylor every step of the way while inventing his own legend. "He was the only person I have ever known," wrote Scott, "who was wholly indifferent in the choice between truth and falsehood, honesty and dishonesty—ever as ready to attain an end by the one as the other, and habitually boastful of acts of cleverness at the total sacrifice of moral character. Procuring the nomination of Mr. Polk for the Presidency, he justly considered his greatest triumph in that way."

In September 1847, after Scott's great victories, Pillow wrote an anonymous article published in the New Orleans newspapers, claiming he was "in command of all the forces engaged," and was the true hero of the war—not Scott, who promptly had him arrested for court-martial. Taylor also burned with hatred for Polk. In November, when a false rumor of Polk's death reached Taylor in his camp, he wrote a friend, "While I regret to hear of the death of any one, I would as soon have heard of his death if true, as that of any other individual in the whole Union."

Polk's relationship with his chief diplomat dispatched to negotiate the peace treaty swiftly degenerated into mutual contempt as bitter as his relations with his generals. The man he named to deal with the Mexican government was the ablest one in the State Department. Nicholas Trist was a member of an aristocratic Virginia family, a protégé of Thomas Jefferson, studied law with him, married his granddaughter, served as his personal secretary at Monticello during his retirement, and was at his bedside at his death. A West Point graduate, he was appointed a clerk in the State Department under Clay, after which President Jackson made him his personal secretary. Then, after serving as the U.S. consul-general in Cuba, Trist was appointed the chief clerk under Polk's secretary of state, James Buchanan, equivalent today to the number two position, deputy secretary of state. Having worked intimately with Jefferson, Clay, Jackson, and Buchanan, and fluent in Spanish, he was the ideal figure to conclude the peace.

Sent in the spring of 1847, Trist overcame initial friction with the prickly Scott and they became allies, the first step in his diplomacy. Pillow, meanwhile, sent secret dispatches to Polk critical of both Scott and Trist. When Mexico City fell to Scott on September 14 and Santa Anna fled, Trist had no Mexican negotiating partner. Relying solely for information on Pillow's vilification and before receiving news of the fall of Mexico City, Polk recalled Trist on October 6, 1847, saying he "had no ability," an order Trist simply ignored and which Polk repeated, each time disregarded. By November, an interim Mexican government was constituted, led by the chief of the Supreme Court, a figure of moderate temperament amenable to making peace. On December 6, Trist sent Secretary of State Buchanan a sixty-five-page handwritten letter explaining his resumption of negotiations despite his recall. He called the opinions of the *Washington Union*, the pro-Polk newspaper, "balderdash," "stuff," and "nonsense" that no one, "however low in understanding," should give any credence; called Pillow an "intriguer" of "incomprehensible base-ness of character"; and observed that Pillow was "an individual who gives himself out as the *maker* of the President, and as the President's *other self*—a pretension which I have reason to believe but too well founded."

On December 7, the next day, Polk submitted his annual message to the Congress, the most peevish and petty ever delivered by a president, about half of it consisting of obsessive and repetitive rants about Trist for exceeding his "authority." Three days later, upon receiving a letter from Pillow falsely accusing Scott and Trist of bribing Mexican officials in order to conclude a treaty, Polk angrily aired the charge at a cabinet meeting and was deter-mined to prosecute them. On January 3, 1848, after consulting two of his key stalwarts in the Senate, Lewis Cass and Jefferson Davis (Taylor's son-in-law), Polk removed Scott from command and replaced him with a Democrat, General William O. Butler. He reduced the court-martial of Pillow and two other officers complicit with him to a court of inquiry—and charged Scott as well. In his memoirs, Scott denounced Polk's "perfidy." "I was relieved in the command, and the wronged and the wrong-doers, with stern impartiality!" (Butler would be slated as the Democratic vice presidential candidate in 1848 to provide a military aura against Taylor.)

Believing that Trist had already been relieved of his duty, Polk was shocked to discover that he was negotiating with the Mexicans, and on Janu-ary 7 declared him "a tool of Scott and his menial instrument," "destitute of honor or principle," "a very base man," and stated he would reject any treaty he made.

Trist's treaty, the Treaty of Guadalupe Hidalgo, with the Rio Grande agreed as the new boundary between the nations, arrived in Washington on February 19. Presented with the fait accompli, Polk decided he must accept its terms or destroy any hope of ever having a treaty. Buchanan, however, urged him to reject it, a gesture Polk believed was motivated by "his presi-dential aspirations, for these govern all his opinions and acts lately," he wrote in his diary. After threatening to dismiss his betraying secretary of state, Polk sent the treaty to the Senate on February 22, and ordered that Trist, his tri-umphant diplomat, not receive any further support from the U.S. army, to leave Mexico forthwith, and blocked payment of his salary. Trist referred to him as "Polk the mendacious" and to Pillow as a "reptile." On March 10, the Senate approved the treaty negotiated by the orphaned peace commissioner and rejected by the secretary of state. Three days later, a court of inquiry conducted in Mexico cleared Pillow, who was acquitted when his adjutant stepped forward as a false witness to accept the blame for his actions. Trist testified at the inquiry into Scott, which dragged on into June before the baseless charges were dropped. (After two unsuccessful bids to gain nomination as the Democratic candidate for vice president, Pillow would become a notoriously blundering Confederate general. Trist supported Lincoln for president in 1860. Impoverished, he did not receive his back pay until 1870 by an act of Congress sponsored by Senator Charles Sumner. Upon learning of Trist's plight, President Grant appointed him postmaster of Alexandria, Virginia.)

Under the stress of war and strain of peace, Polk's party came apart at the seams. Victory accelerated the centrifugal force. The vast new territory raised the tensions between North and South over the balance of political power. Would the new states admitted be slave or free? Congressman David Wilmot of Pennsylvania, a party-line Jacksonian Democrat, who had supported the war, suddenly broke with discipline, proposing a bill prohibiting slavery from any of the newly acquired territories—the Wilmot Proviso. At first, in late 1846, at Polk's urging, he withdrew the measure, but when Congressman Preston King of New York put it forward Wilmot jumped ahead of the parade. He called his measure the "White Man's Proviso," intended to "preserve for free white labor a fair country, a rich inheritance, where the sons of toil, of my own race and own color, can live without the disgrace which association with Negro slavery brings upon free labor." It passed the House several times, but never the Senate. Lincoln was one of the "Proviso Men." "I think I may venture to say I voted for it at least forty times during the short term I was there," Lincoln recalled. It may have seemed like forty times, but it was likely five and never as a stand-alone resolution but an amendment to a variety of bills.

Part of the underlying dilemma the new territory presented was that slavery had not existed under Mexican rule in California and New Mexico. Mexican law prohibited it; so American law would have to impose it. The fruits of the war therefore posed the possibility of either slavery extension—"slavery national"—or slavery restriction—"slavery sectional"—unacceptable to either the antislavery or pro-slavery forces.

Senator Cass of Michigan, Polk's floor leader, on his own demanded annexation of all of Mexico—the "All Mexico" faction—not Polk's position. A classic Northern man of Southern sympathies, Cass aspired to the Democratic presidential nomination and was playing for Southern delegate votes. Calhoun saw his opening, bluntly rejecting the "All Mexico" position as race mixing. "Ours," he sternly declared, "is the government of the white man."

Calhoun had become a rancorous enemy of Polk after being denied what he thought was his rightful position. He had hoped to be retained as secretary of state, but was jettisoned. Trying to mollify him, Polk offered him the post of minister to England, but Calhoun refused the demotion that would exile him. In May 1845, his tightly controlled inner circle in Charleston that had supported his campaign for the presidency concurred he should run again, forcing issue after issue on the president. Calhoun returned to the Senate by the end of the year, where he refused to vote for the declaration of war he had helped engineer. He attempted to block the equipping of ten new army regiments and to prevent the president from appointing commissioned officers, declaring it all an unconstitutional power grab. In his diary, Polk called him "the most mischievous man in the Senate." The *Washington Union*, the administration's mouthpiece under the editorship of Thomas Ritchie, published a column describing Calhoun's obstruction as a victory for the enemy: "the cause of Mexico is maintained with zeal and ability." Calhoun's followers in the Senate, known as "the balance of power party," joined with their most hated nemesis, the "Proviso" Whigs, to expel Ritchie from his privileged seat on the Senate floor—a swipe at Polk.

Calhoun's stem-winding speech of February 19, 1847, a week after Ritchie's expulsion and a year before the peace treaty was produced, set the stage for the postwar period of invective and division. "Sir, the day that the balance between the two sections of the country—the slaveholding States and the non-slaveholding States—is destroyed, is a day that will not be far removed from political revolution, anarchy, civil war, and widespread disaster," he stated. "The balance of this system is in the slaveholding States. They are the conservative portion—always have been the conservative portion—always will be the conservative portion; and with a due balance on their part may, for generations to come, uphold this glorious Union of ours. But if this scheme should be carried out—if we are to be reduced to a handful . . . if this is to be the result—woe! woe! I say, to this Union!" He cast a curse on compromise. Slavery must be national or it would cease to exist and with it the Union. "Let us be done with compromises. Let us go back and stand upon the constitution!"

Calhoun's speech was the most radical he had given since he courted nullification. He denied that any law was needed to legitimate slavery in territory ceded by Mexico. On the contrary, he insisted slavery was ipso facto legal, that Congress could not prohibit it, and that American citizens in those territories had no power to declare slaves free. Against the slogan of the Liberty Party—"freedom national"—he proclaimed the opposite—"slavery national." His position rejected Cass's notion of "squatter sovereignty," allowing the settlers of the new territories to decide whether they should be slave or free as a ploy designed to win Southern delegates' support for the Democratic nomination. To Calhoun, squatter sovereignty was the heart of fatal compromise itself. He took the introduction of the Wilmot Proviso, passed for the second time on February 15, as a virtual declaration of war by the North on the South. He could see clearly that the Proviso had broken down traditional barriers between Northern Whigs and Northern Democrats, creating the basis for a political realignment. The balance of power had already tipped to the North and the Proviso was its mechanism for enforcing it. And the Proviso was just the opening wedge. It was not merely an effort to limit slavery, as he saw it, but to destroy it and with it the Southern economy and society. Calhoun brushed past the contemptible Polk, who condemned the Proviso as a "mischievous and wicked agitation," and worked to strike it down, but had lost control of his party, its factions North and South battling each other. Having blown open the schism with the war, Polk could not bridge it. Calhoun, always his own party, his vision peering into an apocalyptic future, now believed that the Missouri Compromise, which he had once upheld as the linchpin of the Union, the essential agreement establishing peace between North and South, was unconstitutional. It must be abandoned with all territory and all states opened to slavery.

In the midst of the Democrats' disarray, Whigs rallied around the banner of Taylor. "General Taylor seems as formidable now as Napoleon was when expected from Egypt," William Seward wrote Thurlow Weed on January 20, 1848. Polk tottering, Democrats splintering, Whigs the ascendant majority in the House, and a messiah in the wings—this was the political scene as Lincoln joined the Young Indians.

One week after the opening of the first session of the 30th Congress, on

December 15, 1847, Polk vetoed a River and Harbor Improvement bill for the Territory of Wisconsin, issuing a statement as lengthy as his annual message to the Congress, topped by calling the measure "evil." "Where shall the exercise of power, if it be assumed, stop?" His relationship with the new Whig House rapidly descended from disdain into contempt.

Calhoun, constantly probing for Polk's vulnerability, aimed an arrow directly at the absurd "All Mexico" proposition, universally unpopular in the North and South, and at the heart of its sponsor, Senator Cass, Polk's chief defender in the Senate and aspiring Democratic presidential candidate. On December 20, Calhoun offered a resolution: "That to conquer Mexico, and to hold it, either as a province or to incorporate it into the Union, would be inconsistent with the avowed object for which the war has been prosecuted." Once again, Calhoun found a way to align with the Proviso men to damage Polk and his allies. Damaging Cass would also because of their alliance damage Polk on a position he did not hold. Outmaneuvered, Cass backed down, confessing his previous opinions were "exceedingly unwise." Calhoun condescended to praise his reversal as an acknowledgment "that there is no person in the country who thinks of the extinction of the nationality of Mexico." Cass was humiliated and left sputtering. Polk could not defend him.

The next day, Joshua Giddings, the abolitionist Quixote, petitioned that the slave trade in the District of Columbia be outlawed. The vote to table it was evenly split, 97 to 97, a tie broken by the new speaker, who voted to table. In his first vote, Lincoln had voted to accept Giddings's petition.

On December 21, Stephens launched the Young Indian offensive, taking advantage of the damage wreaked by Calhoun's successful attack on the "All Mexico" faction. He proposed a resolution that the war had not been intended for "conquest," "subjugation or dismemberment," but condemned the "invasion" of Mexico and the "storming and capturing of her towns and slaying of her people" as "acts of injustice, cruelty and wrong."

In his original speech calling for war with Mexico, Polk had stated, "American blood had been spilt upon American soil," and inserted into the preamble of the declaration of war, "Whereas, *by the act of Mexico,* a state of war exists between that government and the United States." Almost all the Whigs, even the majority that voted for it, believed that was a brazen falsehood. Crittenden voted for the war, but against the preamble, if such a thing were possible. In his most recent annual message, the one excoriating

Trist, Polk insisted on pressing his original claim about the origin of the war: "Though the United States were the aggrieved nation, Mexico commenced the war, and we were compelled in self-defense to repel the invader and to vindicate the national honor and interests by prosecuting it with vigor until we could obtain a just and honorable peace."

It was this claim about the war's source that Lincoln challenged on December 22 in his eight-point "Spot Resolution," demanding that the president disclose "all the facts which to establish whether the particular spot of soil on which the blood of our citizens was so shed was, or was not, our own soil," and whether the order for attacking Mexico was given after General Taylor had "more than once intimated to the War Department that . . . no such movement was necessary to the defense or protection of Texas."

Lincoln's "Spot Resolution" was undoubtedly coordinated with the Young Indians as an element in the strategy to discredit Polk. It would have been wholly unlike Lincoln to act as a solo operator. His contribution was duly printed in the *Congressional Globe*, buried in a list of routine resolutions, and went unremarked by friend or foe, while everyone went on Christmas holiday. The resolution was never considered by any committee, voted upon, or raised again. The controversy over the war's start resumed on January 3 with wording attached to a resolution praising General Taylor by another Whig congressman, George Ashmun of Massachusetts, that the war had been "unnecessarily and unconstitutionally begun by the President of the United States." Lincoln voted in favor, along with every Whig but one, while every Democrat voted against. The resolution passed the House by one vote, but went nowhere in the Senate, having achieved its incendiary partisan effect. (Ashmun presided as the chairman of the Republican convention in 1860 and was the last man to meet with Lincoln at the White House before he left for Ford's Theatre on April 14, 1865.)

Lincoln had not yet delivered a proper speech. "As to speech-making," he wrote Herndon on January 8, 1848, "by way of getting the hang of the House I made a little speech two or three days ago on a post-office question of no general interest. I find speaking here and elsewhere about the same thing. I was about as badly scared, and no worse, as I am when I speak in court. I expect to make one within a week or two, in which I hope to succeed well enough to wish you to see it."

On January 12, Lincoln took the floor to deliver a speech daring in its amalgam of lawyerly argument, metaphor, and ad hominem attack, calculated to vault him into the front ranks of the Young Indians. It was his explanation of his "Spot Resolution." He declared that the question of determining the spot where the war began was "the very point upon which he [Polk] should be justified, or condemned," and the war was "from beginning to end the sheerest deception." Six times in his speech he referred to "blood"—"the first blood of the war" four times—"like the blood of Abel, is crying to Heaven against him." Lincoln decried Polk as perversely ambitious and murderous in a burst of mixed metaphors gleaned from his reading of Shakespeare. "That originally having some strong motive—what, I will not stop now to give my opinion concerning—to involve the two countries in a war, and trusting to escape scrutiny, by fixing the public gaze upon the exceeding brightness of military glory—that attractive rainbow, that rises in showers of blood—that serpent's eye, that charms to destroy he plunged into it, and has swept, on and on, till, disappointed in his calculation of the ease with which Mexico might be subdued, he now finds himself, he knows not where. How like the half insane mumbling of a fever-dream, is the whole war part of his late message!"

Lincoln's maiden speech dripped with "blood" and themes of murder and guilt, drawing inspiration from Shakespeare's *Macbeth*, his favorite Shakespeare play—"I think nothing equals Macbeth," Lincoln said—in which Macbeth speaks of "blood" as the motive for "blood"—"blood in thy face," "blood will have blood," "clamorous harbingers of blood and death," "wash this blood," "bloody deed," "bloody piece of work," "mark'd with blood"—forty variations on the theme of blood. Lincoln's other metaphors— "serpent," "fever," and "dream"—were also drawn from *Macbeth*.

Reaching his peroration Lincoln described Polk, his Macbeth, as a lost soul, lacking even an "imaginary conception." "He is a bewildered, confounded, and miserably perplexed man. God grant he may be able to show, there is not something about his conscience, more painful than all his mental perplexity!"

On February 1, the new senator from Illinois, Stephen A. Douglas, took the floor to deliver his maiden speech, a rebuttal of Lincoln's, carefully not deigning to name his perennial rival, but aimed at him and other Whigs for "their unqualified denunciation of the war." Surrounded by a pile of books and documents from which he cited, Douglas took up the question of the

"precise spot." Quoting General Taylor's order to the Rio Grande, he triumphantly reached his conclusion: "But, sir, who are the men that condemn this
order, and for what purpose is the condemnation made at this time? They are
the professed advocates of the election of President Taylor to the Presidency,
and the order is condemned for the purpose of making political capital for
themselves and their candidate, against the Democratic Party." The next day,
Lincoln's fellow Young Indian Alexander Stephens delivered the speech that
brought the "tears" to his eyes, refuting Douglas point by point, and ending
by calling Polk's war "not only dishonorable, but disgraceful and infamous."

The Lincoln-Douglas debate over the Mexican War conducted through
surrogates was just beginning. Lincoln turned his speech into a pamphlet
and mailed thousands of copies under his congressional frank. Whig newspapers in Illinois reprinted it—"an able effort," the *Quincy Whig* editorialized, while the *Missouri Republican* declared it "one of great power." But
Douglas's newspaper, the *Register*, headlined one editorial "Out Damned
Spot!" and in another stated that Lincoln "will regret that he has by his
vote [on the Ashmun Amendment] stigmatized the brave men of his state."
Democrats, undoubtedly instigated by Douglas, organized meetings across
Illinois to endorse resolutions denouncing Lincoln, every one labeling him
"Spotty," and all published in the *Register*. One, adopted by Democrats in
Morgan County, cast him as a traitor: "We can but express the deep mortification inflicted upon us by our Representative in Congress, in his base,
dastardly, and treasonable assault upon President Polk, in his disgraceful
speech upon the present war, and in the resolutions offered by him against
his own government. . . . Such insulting opprobrium cast upon our citizens
and soldiers, such black odium and infamy heaped upon the living brace
and illustrious dead can but excite the indignation of every true Illinoian. . . .
Henceforth will the Benedict Arnold of our District be known here only as
the Ranchero Spotty for one term." Calling Lincoln a "ranchero" identified
him as a Mexican guerrilla fighter that U.S. troops were under orders to execute if captured. The *Peoria Democratic Press* stated that "the miserable man
of 'Spots' will pass unnoticed save in the execration that his treason will bring
upon his name." "Spotty" stuck.

From Springfield, Herndon wrote Lincoln frantic letters warning that
he was self-destructing. "I saw that Lincoln would ruin himself about the
Mexican War, and his opposition to it, and so, being his friend and not seeing

the question as he did, I tried to prevent Lincoln's destruction," he said later. "I wrote to him on the subject again and again, and tried to induce him to silence, if nothing else; but his sense of justice and his courage, made him speak, utter his thoughts, as to the war with Mexico."

"I will stake my life, that if you had been in my place, you would have voted just as I did," Lincoln replied to one of Herndon's alarms. "Would you have voted what you felt you knew to be a lie? I know you would not. Would you have gone out of the House—skulked the vote? I expect not. If you had skulked one vote, you would have had to skulk many more, before the end of the session. . . . You are compelled to speak; and your only alternative is to tell the truth or tell a lie. I cannot doubt which you would do."

He believed that it was good politics to make the point that Polk had driven the country into war on a falsehood. Herndon's concerns disclosed not only his worries but also the distance between national and local politics. Not all politics was local. From Illinois, the question of support of the war was a barometer of patriotism. But from the cockpit of Washington, where Lincoln was now immersed hour by hour in taking on a foundering president, the dimensions of the debate and the stakes appeared larger. Lincoln refused to take his partner's advice to draw back, instead continuing to mail out his speech and engage critics. He was also looking for a plum job after the election.

Months after delivering the speech that got him branded as "Spotty," Lincoln still insisted on debating the origin of the war and its morality. After reading a story in the *Belleville Advocate* of a speech given in favor of the war, he wrote the orator a letter on May 21 as someone "intelligent, right-minded, and impartial" who should reconsider his views. It appeared that Lincoln knew him. Reverend John M. Peck was a Baptist minister, an old Illinois settler, descended from New England pilgrims, founder of the Rock Spring Seminary, who had been the ally of Governor Edward Coles in the struggle to prohibit slavery in the state constitution. From his pulpit in St. Clair County, he helped organize a network of antislavery preachers, "something like the organization of the minute men in the times of the Revolution," according to a local historian, and defeated the pro-slavery forces. Therefore, Lincoln told Peck that it "disappoints me" that he would justify the Mexican War. "Now I wish to bring these facts to your notice, and to ascertain what is the result of your reflections upon them." Lincoln wrote in lawyerly fashion, reviewing the relevant evidence. "If you deny that they are facts, I think I can furnish proof which shall convince you that you are mistaken. If you admit that they are facts, then I shall be obliged for a reference to any law of language, law of states, law of nations, law of morals, law of religion,—any law human or divine, in which an authority can be found for saying those facts constitute 'no aggression.'" Then Lincoln described a Mexican village whose inhabitants were driven from their homes in the army's march to the Rio Grande. "Possibly you consider those acts too small for notice. Would you venture to so consider them, had they been committed by any nation on earth, against the humblest of our people? I know you would not." Lincoln abandoned his role as attorney and quoted from the Sermon on the Mount, Matthew 7:12: "Then I ask, is the precept 'Whatsoever ye would that men should do to you, do ye even so to them' obsolete?—of no force?—of no application?" There is no record of Peck's reply, if he made one.

One place Lincoln found reinforcement was at his boardinghouse. After his speech his messmates celebrated. "I recall with vivid pleasure the scene of merriment at the dinner after his first speech in the House of Representatives, occasioned by the descriptions, by himself and others of the Congressional mess, of the uproar in the House during its delivery," recalled Samuel Clagett Busey, a navy doctor who lived there.

Since Jefferson's day, legislators lived in boardinghouses, usually with like-minded men. Only a very few lived in their own houses. The politics of Washington could be largely charted by boardinghouse and messmate arrangements. These were not neutral or random places. Mrs. Sprigg's, also known as "Abolition House," in a row house across from the Capitol, was well known if not notorious as an antislavery center. It was there that Theodore Weld lived and his convert Giddings held forth. And it was there that Lincoln chose to live. He did not live there because it was where he could by chance get a nice room; nor did he room there because it was a convenient location, though it was. He could have lived in any number of congenial places, but he decided on Mrs. Sprigg's. He knew very well who lived there, that the association carried obvious connotations and he decided to place himself within its circle.

Those who shared the place spanned the spectrum from Giddings to Duff Green, Calhoun's pilot fish, who was the owner of the block of buildings, known as Green's Row, and took his meals there. But the range between

Giddings and Green was deceptive, if it was interpreted that Mrs. Sprigg's was a nonpartisan environment of all persuasions, a mistake nobody in Washington made at the time. Everyone knew that Mrs. Sprigg's was an antislavery Whig house—and some may have known it was also linked to the Underground Railroad. It was certainly widely known that Giddings welcomed a host of blacks there on the basis of an offensive social equality and on obviously suspicious business.

Giddings was the dominant personality at Mrs. Sprigg's, bestowed the sobriquet "Lion of Ashtabula" after his county in Ohio. He roared against the Southern code of honor as sheer hypocrisy, a false chivalric veil for slavery, regularly baiting the Southerners in the Congress into making angry gestures that he would dismiss with contempt. Through verbal duels, they sought to make themselves his masters. Every insult was like a lash of the whip to mark him as a vicious character beneath them. In 1843, one Louisiana congressman pushed him from behind onto the House floor and threatened him with a knife. Two years later, a Georgia congressman shouted he should be hanged and tried to cane him but missed his target. In 1849, during a debate on the Wilmot Proviso, a Virginia congressman grabbed him by the collar. But rather than silencing Giddings, he became more defiant. They took his resistance as "insolence" and incitement of "servile insurrection." And yet Giddings believed to the consternation of some abolitionists that the Constitution protected slavery in the states and focused his energy on slavery in the District of Columbia. He described himself as a "True Whig," and raised the Whig banner of economic nationalism as "dangerous to the interests of slavery, which must ever depend on ignorance and stupidity, and is jealous of the knowledge which teaches men to know the rights that God has given him."

Joshua Giddings

The members of the Congress residing at Mrs. Sprigg's were uniformly Whigs, most from Pennsylvania, the rest from the Middle West, with the exception of a lone Southerner—a microcosm of much of the party's tensions gathered around one long table. Giddings's closest friends were Pennsylvanians. John Strohm, the former speaker of the Pennsylvania House, one of the "Immortal Fourteen," who had joined with Adams and Giddings in voting against the declaration of war against Mexico, had also refused to vote for military appropriations. John Dickey was a gruff former sheriff from Beaver County on the Ohio River, an outpost of the Underground Railroad and antislavery societies in which he was active. A militant abolitionist, he would be succeeded by the radical Thaddeus Stevens. A. R. McIlvaine, a Quaker and abolitionist, was a harsh opponent of the Mexican War, declaring in a speech about its origins and intent on February 4, 1847: "The charge is as false in fact, and unjust to Mexico, as it is disingenuous and cowardly in its authors. It was a vile attempt to cover up the grossest act of usurpation and aggression by the President known to the history of the country. . . . I repeat, sir, this war is a war of conquest, a war for the acquisition of territory, and nothing else. With the Administration and its supporters in the South, it is a war for the extension of slavery. . . . Well, sir, I am opposed to the acquisition of another inch of slave territory."

Lincoln befriended another messmate, Elisha Embree of Indiana, like him a self-made man born in Kentucky and raised in Indiana, a lawyer and judge, and antislavery. Embree became an early Republican and his three sons served as officers in the Union army. John Blanchard, a classic stalwart Whig, a tariff man, a prominent attorney from Pennsylvania, would die on his journey home at the end of the congressional session. But the Blanchard connection continued for Lincoln through his law partner, Andrew Gregg Curtin, who became a political power in Pennsylvania, the head of its delegation at the 1860 Republican convention and at the key moment went for Lincoln, and would become the wartime governor, an unwavering organizer in 1862 of the the Loyal War Governors' Conference to endorse Lincoln and his newly issued Emancipation Proclamation.

James Pollock of Pennsylvania, another messmate, had voted for the war but became a tough critic, accusing Polk of genocide. "Extermination and acquisition must go together. Are we prepared for this? Are we prepared to make the war a war of races, and not stay our hand until every

Mexican is driven from the land of his fathers, and the Anglo-Saxon race established in the Halls of Montezuma?" As a believer in internal improvements, he was the original sponsor in this Congress of the transcontinental railroad. Temperamentally, he was the opposite of the volatile Giddings. Pollock was a strict Presbyterian, a teetotaler who denounced vices such as card playing. In a flash of anger, Giddings called him a "doughface," insulting him as a Northern man with Southern sympathies. He was elected governor of Pennsylvania in 1854 through an antislavery-nativist alliance, campaigning against the extension of slavery and the Fugitive Slave Act; became a Republican; and was appointed by Lincoln director of the U.S. Mint, where the devout Pollock had coins imprinted with the slogan: "In God We Trust."

Patrick W. Tompkins of Mississippi, the sole Whig from the Magnolia State, was something of an outlier in the group, though he was a self-made man born in Kentucky. He became a leading lawyer and judge in Mississippi, had been defeated in his first campaign for the House of Representatives by Jefferson Davis, and supported Polk in the Mexican War. He would soon lose his seat, the last Whig in Mississippi, and join the Gold Rush to California.

The other boarders included Nathan Sargent, the canny Whig journalist who wrote under the pen name of "Oliver Oldschool" as the Washington correspondent of the *United States Gazette*, author of a *Life of Henry Clay*, which Lincoln would certainly have read, and at the same time served as the sergeant-at-arms of the House of Representatives. Yet another messmate was Edmund French, a clerk in the Treasury Department, half brother of Benjamin Brown French, later Lincoln's commissioner of public buildings; Edmund would become one of the founders of the original Washington Nationals baseball team during the Civil War, a team of government clerks, for which he was also a player.

"The Wilmot Proviso was the topic of frequent conversation and the occasion of very many angry controversies," recalled fellow boarder Dr. Samuel Busey, who became a prominent physician in Washington. Dickey, "a very offensive man in manner and conversation . . . seemed to take special pleasure in ventilating his opinions and provoking unpleasant discussions," especially antagonizing Tompkins, "who held adverse opinions on the Wilmot Proviso." Sargent, "also a radical," however, was so interested in the success of the Whigs and the election of Zachary Taylor that he restrained himself and followed Mr. Lincoln, who may have been as radical as either of these gentlemen, but was so discreet in giving expression to his convictions on the slavery question as to avoid giving offence to anybody, and was so conciliatory as to create the impression, even among the proslavery advocates, that he did not wish to introduce or discuss subjects that would provoke a controversy. When such conversation would threaten angry or even unpleasant contention he would interrupt it by interposing some anecdote, thus diverting it into a hearty and general laugh, and so completely disarrange the tenor of the discussion that the parties engaged would either separate in good humor or continue conversation free from discord. This amicable disposition made him very popular with the household.

Lincoln was attempting a balancing act. He knew that Giddings was hostile to nominating Taylor, whom he disparaged as an ignorant slaveholder, yet Lincoln had also won favor with Giddings and his coterie with his speech assailing Polk. Lincoln was a party man who saw his mission as trying to prevent Whigs, even at Mrs. Sprigg's, from sliding into bitter factionalism on the eve of what he anticipated would be a great victory.

The growing band of antislavery legislators elected to serve in Washington never got over the shock of living in the heart of a slave city. Surrounded by the sights and sounds of slavery they felt like strangers in their own land. "We were in a barbarous land," said Giddings, "controlled by barbarous laws."

Washington was a Southern city, Southern in climate, Southern in its society, Southern in its brazen display of slavery. It had two principal industries—the federal government and the slave trade. Several thousand blacks, many of them free, worked as servants and laborers. But thousands more were in transit. The city was a central depot for traders acquiring slaves mostly from Virginia and Maryland and selling them to Deep South and southwestern states. Many firms flourished in this extraordinarily lucrative business. Washington newspapers were filled with advertisements for all sorts of slaves, from "prime" to children to "fancy girls." Two large pens holding hundreds of slaves in wretched conditions, Robey's Pen and Williams' Pen, operated near the Capitol—"that infernal hell which once existed at the corner of Seventh Street and Maryland Avenue," as Giddings put it. Fleets of slave trading ships plied their commerce from the docks of Georgetown and Alexandria. "The tramp of leaden feet crossing Chain Bridge [spanning the Potomac] on a journey into bondage might be heard any month in the year," wrote Helen Nicolay, the daughter of Lincoln's personal secretary. "Or a slave-driver on horseback, with pistols and whip, might march his captives straight past the Capitol, actually in the shadow of the dome, the men in double files, each fastened by a handcuff and a short chain to a longer chain which passed through the whole group from front to rear. The women walked in the same fashion but unchained, while mothers of infants and the little children brought up the rear, huddled in a cart."

Since the founding of Washington, slavery was a source of profit and outrage. Thomas Moore, the national poet of Ireland, visited the new capital in 1806 and wrote "From the City of Washington": "O Freedom! Freedom! how I hate thy cant! . . . / Who can, with patience, for a moment see/ The medley mass of pride and misery,/ Of whips and charters, manacles and rights,/ Of slaving blacks and democratic whites . . . / where bastard Freedom waves/ Her fustian flag, in mockery over slaves." Moore was as famous as Robert Burns, his Scottish counterpart, and Lincoln had read Moore's life of Byron, Moore's intimate friend, memorizing long passages as well as Moore's poetry, lines of which he once recited during a meeting in 1864 with his secretary of the navy, Gideon Welles.

Until he arrived, of course, Lincoln had not personally witnessed the slave trade in Washington that he had proposed abolishing as a state legislator. Now he observed scenes like those that had appalled him as a young man in New Orleans, but he did not publicly mention them until he emerged as a crusader against slavery extension of the Kansas and Nebraska territories in a speech at Peoria on October 16, 1854, describing the "peculiar species of slave trade in the District of Columbia, in connection with which, in view from the windows of the capitol, a sort of negro-livery stable, where droves of negroes were collected, temporarily kept, and finally taken to Southern markets, precisely like droves of horses, had been openly maintained for fifty years."

Mrs. Sprigg's was more than a boardinghouse. It was a station in the Underground Railroad. Beginning in 1842, a highly organized network in Washington began conducting hundreds of slaves to freedom in the north.

Charles T. Torrey, of Massachusetts Puritan stock, a Yale graduate, clergy-man, and Liberty Party man, and Thomas Smallwood, a freed slave, were the clandestine leaders. Repeatedly arrested, tried, and imprisoned, Torrey died in a Maryland jail in 1846, convicted for aiding fugitives. Giddings and others at "Abolition House" were part of this biracial subversive community, and Mrs. Sprigg was undoubtedly privy to its operations.

Ann G. Thornton, a native Virginian, was married to Benjamin Sprigg, a clerk in the House of Representatives who owned eight slaves, according to the 1820 census. When he died, he left her to care for their four children. She began running her boardinghouse in 1839 and the census the next year showed that she owned no slaves. She had eight servants, most of them slaves hired from their owners, and created a system for them to purchase their own freedom. Many vanished via the Underground Railroad. "You recollect that all the table waiters that were here last year have run away," Theodore Weld wrote his wife in 1842. "Whole families disappear like the baseless fabric of a vision and leave not a wink behind," Giddings wrote his son. Mrs. Sprigg then mostly hired free blacks. "Mrs. Sprigg thinks it quite unsafe to have slaves in such close contact with Abolitionists," wrote Weld, "so she has taken care to get free colored servants in their places! Stick a pin there." But pla-toons of slaves still worked at the boardinghouse as waiters while preparing to escape north, runaways in plain sight. (Discovering that Mrs. Sprigg was living in poverty during the Civil War, Lincoln appointed her a clerk in the Treasury Department.)

At the beginning of the 30th Congress, Giddings was as relentless in his antislavery activism as ever. After staging his conspicuous dissent against electing Winthrop as speaker, he filed a petition in early January from "citi-zens of the District of Columbia" calling for the prohibition of the slave trade there. Worse than obnoxious, he actually succeeded with the new Whig ma-jority to have it referred to committee rather than tabled. (Lincoln voted for accepting it.) Southerners were irate.

Henry and Sylvia Wilson, a married couple, worked as waiter and maid at Mrs. Sprigg's. Henry was a slave, but used his job to accumulate savings to buy his freedom, owing just fifty dollars more. Sylvia was a free black, who had been a servant in the White House of William Henry Harrison. Both were well known to Whigs in town, especially for their warm personal relationship with Giddings. On the night of January 14, three men stormed into Mrs. Sprigg's flourishing pistols, gagged and manacled Henry Wilson in front of his wife, and marched him to the nearby Williams Slave Pen. It is likely that Mary Lincoln was present in the house. When Giddings returned from a walk, Sylvia Wilson frantically told him of the kidnapping. He rushed with Strohm and McIlvaine to Williams Pen, where one of the slave dealers explained that "the nigger" had already been sold. "We took him immediately on board ship at Alexandria, and he has sailed for New Orleans," claimed the trader. Giddings, Strohm, and McIlvaine filed a motion for habeas corpus, but Wilson was a slave and the gesture symbolic. On January 17, Giddings explained the "inhuman" circumstances of Wilson's seizure as the preamble to a resolution to abolish the slave trade in Washington or "remove the seat of government to some free state." The measure narrowly lost, 94 to 88, with Lincoln voting in favor. As a last resort Giddings appealed to Duff Green, who apparently grasped that the incident was providing abolitionists with a sympathetic cause and somehow pulled strings for Wilson's miraculous return. Giddings collected the funds to purchase his freedom from his colleagues. It seems highly likely that Lincoln contributed.

The incident inspired Giddings on January 31 to propose an official inquiry into slavery in the District: "That a select committee of five members be appointed to inquire into and report to this House whether the slave trade is carried on within the District of Columbia; if so, by what legal subject is expedient at the present time." Congressman Howell Cobb of Georgia objected, demanding that Giddings's resolution be ruled out of order, but Winthrop decided it was in fact "in order." But it instantly died, never considered.

The animosity toward Giddings apparent in the Henry Wilson incident was vented four years later in 1852 in a debate with Congressman Edward Stanly of North Carolina, a Southern Whig, who rose to answer Giddings after he had declared about the Fugitive Slave Act: "It is not our duty to play the blood-hound for you. . . . Catch them yourselves," adding that the House that passed that law was "weak and effeminate." "If that man," said Stanly, pointing his finger at Giddings, "were in a Southern country, there is not a decent man amongst my constituents who would own such a fellow for a slave. He would be a 'free nigger,' and in less than three weeks would be tied to the whipping-post for stealing or slandering his neighbor." Stanly also vented the anger of Southerners in Washington with Giddings's notorious association with blacks: "Who ever saw him, except upon this floor, with a decent man in Washington City? He receives visits from free negroes sometimes. . . . He remains with his free negro friends when they call to see him, and that is how he spends his extra hours."

In the House of Representatives, on February 21, 1848, the day before Washington's Birthday, at about 1:30 in the afternoon, the clerk began reading a proposed tribute to Mexican War generals. John Quincy Adams voted "no," considering it an affirmation of the extension of slavery, and rising from his seat to speak was seized by a stroke, "catching hold of his desk to sustain himself, but unable to do so," started to fall, but was caught by a member sitting near him. "There was no mistaking his condition," wrote Nathan Sargent, Lincoln's boardinghouse mate, the House sergeant-at-arms, "and he was immediately laid upon a sofa and first carried into the rotunda, and then into the Speaker's room, where a bed was quickly improvised, on which he was placed, and physicians sent for; but he was already beyond their skill." He regained consciousness twice, once to call for Henry Clay, who wept at his side, and finally calmly to announce, "This is the end of earth, but I am composed." Falling back into a coma, he died on February 23, a living link to the founders' generation lost. When Adams had collapsed, Lincoln was in his seat, number 191, in the back row.

On the day that Adams died, a continent away the citizens of Paris stormed to the streets, erected barricades, and overthrew the regime of King Louis Philippe. They established a provisional republic, triggering revolutions throughout Europe, the Springtime of Nations, heralding a new liberal age, but were quickly and bloodily repressed by the forces of reactionary monarchy. Rallies in support of the revolutions were held across the country, hailing the movements for liberty as proof of American revolutionary inspiration. "Here is their model," declared Senator Douglas. But the support for European revolution initially crossing partisan lines soon turned into a peculiarly American conflict over slavery, exposing the deepening fissures among the Democrats, and became an ironic preface to the greatest slave escape in the history of Washington.

Facing the new revolutionary government in France, the American minister Richard Rush recognized it on his own authority. Unlike the damned Nicholas Trist, who had also felt compelled to act on his own, Polk hailed Rush, the former attorney general under Madison and the son of Dr. Benjamin Rush, signer of the Declaration of Independence. The president sent a special message to the Congress on April 3: "The world has seldom witnessed a more interesting or sublime spectacle than the peaceful rising of the French people, resolved to secure for themselves enlarged liberty, and to assert, in the majesty of their strength, the great truth that in this enlightened age man is capable of governing himself."

Lending support to Polk, Senator William Allen of Ohio, so devoted a Jacksonian he had built his home in Chillicothe as a scaled-down version of Jackson's Hermitage, proposed a resolution congratulating the French for establishing "a republican form of government." In his floor speech, Allen emphasized that the issue would at last lift Polk beyond the contentious Mexico debate, which was "distracted with ideas of conquest and had lost sight of ideas of liberty." By this time, Polk was a lame-duck president; yet in looking to the campaign the Democrats for their own sakes still needed to protect his tarnished reputation and deflect criticism. But even the seemingly noncontroversial issue of praising the French for overthrowing a king turned rancorous. As soon as Allen introduced his resolution, two great dissenters from opposite ends of the spectrum rose to oppose it, John P. Hale and John C. Calhoun.

Hale was new to the exclusive club of the Senate, claimed by neither party, the first man carried there by the antislavery movement. He had been a promising Democratic congressman from New Hampshire, but broke with party discipline against the Gag Rule, and seemed to have gone mad, tossing away his career, when he opposed the annexation of Texas. In February 1845, a kangaroo court was convened, under the authority of the state party chairman, former U.S. senator Franklin Pierce, which censured Hale's "treachery" and expunged his name from the party's slate for reelection. Then, unexpectedly, came

John P. Hale

the "Hale storm." On June 9, at Concord's Old North Church, Hale debated Pierce. They had been close friends as classmates at Bowdoin College, but were now bitter rivals. Pierce accused Hale of entering into an "unholy" alliance with abolitionists to advance his career. "I expected to be called ambitious; to have my name cast out as evil. I have not been disappointed," replied Hale, concluding with a ringing declaration: "I may be permitted to say that the measure of my ambition will be full, if, when my earthly career shall be finished and my bones be laid beneath the soil of New Hampshire, when my wife and children shall repair to my grave to drop the tear of affection to my memory, they may read on my tombstone, 'He who lies beneath surrendered office, place, and power, rather than bow down and worship slavery.'" The next year, a new coalition of Independent Democrats, Whigs, and Liberty men elected Hale to the state legislature, made him speaker of the house, and elected him U.S. senator. He went to Washington in 1847 as the first antislavery senator with a state resolution in hand demanding abolition of slavery in the District of Columbia and against the expansion of slavery. Hale's emergence created a model for those seeking to forge a national coalition of antislavery forces, the coalition that would become the Free Soil Party. Pierce, too, politically profited from his inquisition, becoming a Northern hero to Southern Democrats, the legend on which he would rise to the presidency.

Now Hale proposed an amendment to the resolution on the new Second French Republic, praising the revolutionary government for "the immediate emancipation of the slaves of all the colonies of the republic." Calhoun was on his feet to move that the original resolution be tabled. "It is not yet time for congratulation," he said. "A revolution in itself is not a blessing." In private, he sympathized with the reactionary powers. "They are right," he wrote, "because what are called reform, will lead to anarchy, revolution and finally to a worse state of things than now exists." But his effort to table the measure was defeated, as was Hale's amendment, and the resolution passed.

That night, April 13, the Democratic Party of Washington celebrated the European revolution with a torchlight parade of thousands down Pennsylvania Avenue, led by cabinet secretaries, senators, and representatives, to the illuminated White House, where Polk greeted them from a window. Speakers held forth from a specially constructed rostrum at the nearby offices of the *Washington Union* newspaper, climaxed by Mississippi's Senator Henry S.

Foote's ecstatic and ironically unreflective outburst, "The age of tyrants and slavery is rapidly drawing to a close."

While the revelers hailed foreign revolution, a schooner named the *Pearl* unobtrusively docked at the Seventh Avenue wharf on the Potomac River. Two nights later, seventy-seven slaves that belonged to some of the most prominent Washington households, including Dolley Madison (who sustained her standard of living by selling the occasional slave), clambered into the ship's hold, and it set sail for the open sea and then to tack north. The fugitives were the elite of Washington's black community, almost all educated, light-skinned, and many related to free blacks. Some, in fact, were free blacks that felt their status was in jeopardy, always in danger of being kidnapped and being sold into slavery. By the next morning, word of their disappearance spread consternation throughout the city. One slave privy to the plot but who did not join it turned informer. A posse of thirty armed men commandeered a boat and soon caught up with the *Pearl*, anchored to wait out a storm. The manacled slaves, the *Pearl*'s white captain, and his mate were marched through the city, passing a slave pen, where the slave trader rushed them brandishing a knife, shouting, "Damn the law! I have three negroes, and I will give them all for one thrust at this damned scoundrel!" On Pennsylvania Avenue the captives were dragged through the gauntlet of a shrieking mob to the city jail—"Lynch them!"

The next morning, April 18, Giddings submitted a provocative resolution to the House. The captured fugitives, he stated, were not guilty of "any impropriety other than an attempt to enjoy that liberty for which our fathers encountered toil, suffering and death itself, and for which the people of many European governments are now struggling." He proposed appointment of a committee to investigate the "authority" under which the Washington city jail was used to hold escaped slaves. Isaac E. Holmes of South Carolina, a follower of Calhoun, offered an amendment that the inquiry determine "whether the scoundrels who caused the slaves to be there ought not to be hung," a statement that filled the chamber with derisive laughter and ended the debate.

That evening a mob assembled outside the office of the abolitionist newspaper *The National Era*, and bricks were tossed, but police dispersed the crowd. The newspaper had been established two years earlier as the antislavery beacon in the capital, filled with polemics and graphic reports on the slave trade as well as a literary section edited by the poet John Greenleaf

Whittier. Gamaliel Bailey, its editor and publisher, had originally been recruited into the movement by Theodore Weld, and founded the Cincinnati Anti-Slavery Society, where he befriended Salmon Chase. As assistant editor of the abolitionist newspaper *The Philanthropist*, edited by James Birney, of the Liberty Party, he had plenty of experience with crusading journalism and mob violence.

The next morning, Giddings marched into the jail to see Captain Daniel Drayton and his first mate, Edward Sayres, being held as prisoners. He brought along Edward Hamlin, a former Whig congressman, boarder at Mrs. Sprigg's, and the editor of the antislavery *Cleveland Daily True Democrat*. Giddings was "not easily repulsed," though he was "followed into the jail by a crowd of ruffians," recalled Drayton. He promised the men proper legal counsel and financial support. The mob burst into the jail, menaced Giddings, and when he left threatened to "lay violent hands upon me." He identified Hope H. Slatter, the main slave dealer in Baltimore, as the ringleader of a mob consisting of slave traders from "Baltimore, Richmond, Alexandria, Annapolis, and of this city, collected to purchase the persons who were confined there for having fled from slavery." In a speech in the House, Giddings called them "buzzards" and "a mass of moral putridity," but the *Baltimore Sun* defended them as "respectable, quiet, unoffending injured citizens, who were present, pursuant to a public call, for the purpose of identifying their property."

It is almost certain that Giddings knew that three prominent abolitionists had hired Drayton, though it seems he was not informed beforehand. On the night of the escape, as it was already under way, William L. Chaplin visited Giddings at Mrs. Sprigg's to confide in him. Chaplin, Harvard educated and trained by Weld, had taken Torrey's place as the leading figure in the capital's Underground Railroad and was known as "General" Chaplin. Publicly, he headed a group he called the "Bureau of Humanity" to purchase slaves' freedom in Washington, another method of rescue and publicity. Gerrit Smith, the fabulously wealthy heir to the fortune of his father, John Jacob Astor's partner, probably the largest landowner in New York state, was Chaplin's financial angel, as he was of the Liberty Party and much of the movement, and would later become one of the "Secret Six" supporting John Brown's 1859 attack on Harpers Ferry to provoke a slave insurrection. Dr. Charles Cleveland, president of the Philadelphia Anti-Slavery Society, was the third man, who had used Drayton before to transport a fugitive slave and had initially suggested the *Pearl* scheme.

The mob that threatened Giddings in the morning at the jail reassembled that night for another assault on the *National Era* office. Prominent Washingtonians, including members of the city council, seeking to avert violence, visited Gamaliel Bailey at his home to demand that he remove his press and cease publication. "I am one man against many," Bailey answered. "But I cannot sacrifice any right that I possess." Back at the *Era* office, the rowdy crowd began throwing bricks, but once again was routed by the police. Fearing violence they could not control, that would turn into a national scandal, city officials urgently met with President Polk, who authorized the U.S. marshal to impose order. In his diary, Polk blamed the "excitement" on an "outrage committed by stealing or seducing the slaves from their owners, and the attempt of abolitionists to defend the White men who perpetrated it."

It was now April 20, the third day since the capture of the fleeing slaves, a day of recrimination and threats in the Congress. The tumult began in the House with Palfrey's resolution to investigate the "lawless mob" that had committed "acts of violence over the past two nights, menacing individuals of this body"—namely, Giddings. This prompted Congressman Abraham W. Venable of North Carolina to claim the South was "persecuted, taunted, harassed, held up to odium to the world. . . . Were they to be made odious— were their institutions continually to be dragged before the public by the fanatic and hypocrite, to taunt and sneer at, and were their dearest rights to be abandoned by those who represented them? Was there no man from the South who would stand up and say to them what should be said?" Venable declared that the Union would become intolerable and "hailed dissolution with pleasure and joy, if they were continually to be taunted by fanatics and hypocrites—if their wives and little ones were to be assassinated and destroyed by intermeddling men with hearts black as hell." He "denied that slavery was either a moral, social, or political evil. They had nothing to do with it. It was a matter which belonged to the South." Then, he hurled an accusation that he had heard that a member of the Congress had gone to the jail to offer defense to those "who had plundered the owners in the district of their slaves, and were caught with the Negroes in their possession."

The subject swiftly turned to punishing Giddings, even lynching him. "Men on this floor," declared Congressman William Haskell of Tennessee, "under the garb of philanthropy and love of liberty, had been endeavoring to perpetuate felonies for which they ought to swing as high as Haman." Giddings attempted to defuse the hostile atmosphere, rattling on about the American Revolution and the "rights of humanity," but was continually interrupted with pointed questions from a host of Southern members. "Inasmuch as the gentleman has justified this attempt of these slaves to escape from their rightful owners, I call on him to know whether he justifies the thieves who stole them?" demanded Haskell. Under the assault, Giddings conceded that the men who aided the fugitive slaves were criminal. "Unquestionably, if they aided slaves in escaping," he admitted. To which Venable announced his support for Haskell's resolution to investigate "whether members of this House were instrumental in procuring the slaves who were recently decoyed from their owners in this District" and whether they were "guilty of felony" in the attempt to "kidnap slaves." (Venable would later serve in the Confederate Congress.)

Meanwhile, on the same day in the Senate, Hale proposed a bill that would make the District liable for damage caused by "riotous" mobs. "The notes of congratulations, which this Senate sent across the Atlantic to the people of France, on their deliverance from thralldom, have hardly ceased when the supremacy of mob-law and the destruction of the freedom of the press are threatened in this capital of the Union." This immediately roused Calhoun. "I know to what this leads," he said portentously. "I have known for a dozen years to what this is tending. When this subject was first agitated, I said to my friends, there is but one question that can destroy this Union and our institutions, and that is this very slave question." Now, Hale had "so little regard for the laws and the Constitution" that it was being "trampled on." "We are approaching that crisis," announced Calhoun, through the "masked attack on the great institution of the South, upon which not only its prosperity but its very existence depends."

Senator James Westcott of Florida spoke up next, boldly admitting he was "a spectator" of the mob at *The National Era*, denied it was anything but peaceful, and added "I heard nothing by any means so incendiary as I have heard since the honorable Senator from New Hampshire took his seat upon this floor."

Calhoun's vehemence had left him exhausted. "I now leave this matter in the hands of my younger friends from the South," he said, recalled Senator

Foote. "I have stood here long in the front of battle, almost singlehanded and alone, defending the rights of our slave-holding constituents, and I begin to feel it to be high time that such men as your colleague, Mr. Davis, and yourself, should come forward to my relief." The torch was being passed.

Upon receiving this request from Calhoun, Senator Jefferson Davis of Mississippi sprang to his feet. Born in Kentucky in 1808, a year earlier than Lincoln, his ascent ran as a parallel life that would eventually collide, one the follower of Clay, the other the acolyte of Calhoun. Davis was anything but a self-made man, but a child of privilege. The youngest of ten children of a modestly successful Revolutionary War soldier and farmer, who wound up owning six slaves, Davis was mostly raised by his oldest brother. Joseph Davis, twenty-two years older, had elevated himself to the upper echelon of the Mississippi elite, a Natchez lawyer, owning an entire peninsula on the Mississippi River called Davis Bend, a vast plantation of more than five thousand acres he called Hurricane, where 226 slaves labored by 1840. He thought of himself as his younger brother's guardian. The older Davis was childless with his wife, but had numerous illegitimate children who populated Hurricane as "cousins." Jefferson Davis attended Transylvania University in Kentucky and through his brother's connections gained an appointment to West Point. He served in the Black Hawk War, passing Lincoln's way but likely never encountering the Illinois volunteer. In 1835, he married Sarah Knox Taylor, daughter of General Zachary Taylor, who initially opposed the match. Less than three months after their wedding, she was stricken with malaria and died. Seven years later, he married nineteen-year-old Varina Howell, daughter of a bankrupt Natchez businessman who was a close friend of Joseph Davis. After losing his first race for the state legislature, he was elected to the Congress on the tide that brought Polk into the White House. A favorite of the administration politically and socially, he was a war hawk on Mexico, and when war was declared enlisted as a colonel. "It may be that I will return with a reputation," he wrote. Winning laurels commanding the Mississippi Rifles at the Battles of Buena Vista and Monterrey, the conquering hero was elected to the Senate.

Now, summoned by Calhoun, he rose to rebuke Hale. "Is this chamber to be the hot-bed in which plants of sedition are to be nursed?" He described Hale's resolution as "insulting to the South," the language of the Code Duello—a duel of North and South, an invitation to civil war.

Is this debatable ground? No! It is ground upon which the people of this Union may shed blood; and that is the final result. If it be pressed any further, and if this Senate is to be made the theatre of that contest, let it come— the sooner the better. We who represent the Southern States are not here to be insulted on account of institutions which we inherit. And if civil discord is to be thrown from this chamber upon the land; if the fire is to be kindled herewith which is to burn the temple of our Union; if this is to be made the center from which civil war is to radiate, here let the conflict begin. I am ready, for one, to meet any incendiary who, dead to every feeling of patriotism, attempts to introduce it."

This was Davis's first statement using the words "civil war." Then Foote took the floor. He hated Davis and his brother with a passionate intensity, a rivalry that would metamorphose depending on Foote's endlessly inconsistent positions—running as a moderate Unionist he would defeat Davis for governor in 1851, but as a Confederate senator he would excoriate the Confederate president as a despot. Mercurial, provocative, and imaginatively vicious, Foote fixed his animosity for the moment on Hale. "The senator from New Hampshire is evidently attempting to get up a sort of civil war in the country, and is evidently filled with the spirit of insurrection and incendiarism," he declared. Warming to his subject, he continued with baroque eloquence,

If he really wishes glory, and to be regarded as the great liberator of the blacks—if he wishes to be particularly distinguished in this cause of emancipation, as it is called—let him, instead of remaining hero in the Senate of the United States, or instead of secreting himself in some dark corner of New Hampshire, where he may possibly escape the just indignation of good men throughout this republic, let him visit the good State of Mississippi, in which I have the honor to reside, and no doubt he will be received with such hosannas and shouts of joy as have rarely marked the reception of any individual in this day and generation. I invite him there, and will tell him beforehand, in all honesty, that he could not go ten miles into the interior before he would grace one of the tallest trees of the forest, with a rope around his neck, with the approbation of every virtuous and patriotic citizen; and that, if necessary, I should myself assist in the operation.

Thus the debate in both the House and the Senate devolved into calls for lynching.

At the District jail one of the guards offered Captain Drayton $1,000 if he would disclose the names of his backers. Dr. Cleveland, who had originated the plan, served as the agent for handling money raised by a Boston committee and Gerrit Smith to provide for Drayton's wife and counsel. Salmon Chase and William Seward were contacted and offered legal assistance. (Seward traveled to Washington and quietly offered advice.) But the attorney who was secured was Horace Mann, who had arrived in Washington to assume John Quincy Adams's seat in the Congress on the very day that the *Pearl* had embarked on its ill-fated voyage. In Boston, Mann was considered a suitably prestigious replacement for the irreplaceable Adams. Secretary and creator of the Massachusetts Board of Education, he was the national founder of the movement to establish common, secular, and free public schools. He was a reformer with lofty goals but an experienced politician of practical means, having served as president of the state Senate. Resolutely antislavery, he maintained close ties to both the Cotton Whigs and the Conscience Whigs.

The U.S. Attorney, Philip Barton Key, son of Francis Scott Key, composer of "The Star-Spangled Banner," indicted Drayton and Sayres on 110 charges apiece for larceny and illegal transportation of property. The trial, held in late July through early August, transfixed Washington. Mann argued that the slaves were not stolen because they had acted on their own volition— the property in question not property at all, but people animated by nothing less than American ideals. "But a man might lose a slave without his being stolen," he said. "Though we may call men slaves, yet are they not human beings?" He pointed out, "Many of the col-

Horace Mann

ored people can read. Who knows but some of them have read the Declaration of American Independence; and, in their blindness and simplicity of mind, applied its immortal truths to themselves?" The *Pearl*, he reminded the court, had docked at the moment the capital was filled with stentorian speeches about liberty in Europe. Mann read from one of these orations: "the age of tyrants and slavery is rapidly drawing to a close." The judge, Thomas Crawford, an old Jacksonian congressman appointed to the bench by Polk, hammered his gavel angrily. "Such inflammatory language cannot be allowed in this court!" Prosecutor Key interjected, "I demand to know from what paper the gentleman reads." As if revealing the secret to a magic trick, Mann held up the *Washington Union*, the pro-administration newspaper. "From whose speech does the gentleman read?" Key insisted, playing the straight man to the end. "From the speech of the Hon. Henry S. Foote." To which, Judge Crawford declared, "Mr. Mann knows Mr. Foote did not mean his language for *our* slaves," provoking a round of laughter.

Over the next ten months four trials were staged, convictions in the first two overturned, followed by acquittals. Only then did the tenacious Key drop his prosecution of Drayton for larceny in return for a plea of guilty of transporting slaves. The vindictive Judge Crawford, who had become an object of ridicule, levied exorbitant fines and sentenced the men to prison until it was paid. They remained there until Senator Charles Sumner arranged a pardon from President Millard Fillmore in 1852. Sayres simply disappeared into the ether, while Drayton, after delivering a series of antislavery speeches, unable to find work fell into poverty and three years after his release committed suicide.

The slaves, for their part, were divided up by a host of traders—the Baltimore dealer, Hope H. Slatter, who had menaced Giddings, sold more than fifty. Freedom was purchased for a few, notably the light-skinned, educated, and beautiful Edmonson sisters, Mary and Emily. Henry Ward Beecher, the youthful antislavery pastor of Brooklyn's Plymouth Church, raised the funds to secure them. Once freed, the Edmonsons participated in the antislavery movement and attended Oberlin College. But most of the slaves from the *Pearl* were sold into bondage in the Deep South, never to be heard from again.

While rage over the *Pearl* consumed the capital, Lincoln traveled to Philadelphia to attend the national Whig convention at the Chinese Museum, beginning on June 7. Before the balloting, acting on behalf of the Taylor campaign, he tried and failed to deny the seating of two delegates from Illinois he knew were committed to Clay. In the vast crowd he was just one of what he described to his wife as "a multitude of strange faces," but he made a point of introducing himself to a number of them, including Thaddeus Stevens and Horace Greeley. Taylor led from the start with 111 votes, with Clay within striking distance at 97, and Scott at 43 and Webster at 22, keeping Clay from a majority. Clay's slippage began on the second ballot and he collapsed on the third. Apparently his implosion was well planned by the Taylor forces. Congressman Truman Smith, chief of the Young Indians, controlled the Connecticut delegation, and led it to vote for Clay while he was coming up just short. Then, on the third ballot, Smith ended the charade, suddenly switching, creating a sensation. "Smith's smooth-shaven, pink and white face rises before me as I write, and it seems as though I could hear his voice as I heard it," recalled the journalist Oliver Dyer, ". . . when, in answer to the call of his name, he responded in clear, penetrating tones: 'Zachary Taylor.' That vote sounded the knell of Henry Clay. The Taylor men had all got ready for this signal, and when it was given, they burst out with repeated cheers and nearly stampeded the Convention." Lincoln, the Young Indian, would almost certainly have been doing a war dance. On the fourth ballot, Taylor was nominated by 171 votes to Clay's 32. It was Clay's last hurrah. The division of the delegates revealed an underlying North-South schism—Clay got only six votes from slave states and Taylor only 66 from free states. To balance the ticket, Millard Fillmore, a former Whig congressman from Buffalo, New York, and state comptroller, colorless and universally thought inoffensive, at the behest of the Clay camp, was chosen for vice president.

Taylor had no known positions on the issues, nor did he intend to fill them in. The Whig platform was a document of utter vapidity, bravely in favor of "Peace, Prosperity, and Union." Beyond that, it noted that had Taylor voted in 1844, which he did not, he "gives us the assurance" he would have voted for Clay, a gesture at party unity. The platform concluded with "mourning" over the graves of Whigs who had died in battle in the Mexican War, one of them Clay's son and another John J. Hardin, Lincoln's fallen rival whom he had edged out of his congressional seat. Horace Greeley, editor of the *New York Tribune* and a convention delegate, who harbored grandiose political ambitions of his own, and "loved" Clay as the leader to bring about "Gradual

Emancipation," denounced the platform as "a slaughterhouse of Whig principles." "I fear the Whig party is dissolved," lamented Clay, now at the end of his hopes. It had become "a mere personal party," he said, gathered around a military figure whose qualifications for "civil services" were "sleeping forty years in the woods, and cultivating moss in the calves of his legs."

On his return to Washington, Lincoln stopped in Wilmington, Delaware, to attend a local Whig meeting held to ratify the convention's choice, where he was introduced as the "Lone Star of Illinois," and given three cheers. Undoubtedly, he invented the nickname himself, adapting it from Clay, known as the "Star of the West" early in his career. (In a letter sent in September to an influential lawyer among the Whigs of Pennsylvania running that year for the House, Thaddeus Stevens, later to become the Radical Republican leader, Lincoln wrote, "You probably remember seeing me at the Philadelphia Convention—introduced to you as the lone Whig star of Illinois.") Lincoln's speech, as reported by the Wilmington newspaper, roundly assailed Polk for his "abuse of power," the "high-handed and despotic exercise of the veto power" against internal improvements, and for waging "a war of conquest brought into existence to catch votes."

Lincoln was cheerful about the Whig prospects. "By many, and often, it had been said they would not abide the nomination of Taylor; but since the deed has been done, they are fast falling in, and in my opinion we shall have a most overwhelming, glorious, triumph," he wrote Herndon. But Herndon wrote back an anxious letter describing falling support and listing defectors by name, which Lincoln found "heart-sickening." He replied with detailed directions, drawing on his experience from his earliest campaigns with Clary's Grove Boys through those for Harrison and Clay. "You young men get together and form a Rough & Ready club, and have regular meetings and speeches. Take in every body that you can get . . . gather up all the shrewd wild boys about town, whether just of age, or little under age . . . and hundreds such. Let everyone play the part he can play best—some speak, some sing, and all holler. . . . Don't fail to do this."

Yet Lincoln was peevish, "a little impatient," that Herndon kept asking for copies of speeches to provide talking points. "Can I send speeches that nobody has made?" And he was agitated that Herndon still did not accept his version of the Mexican War that had gotten him branded "Ranchero Spotty." "You ask how Congress came to declare that war existed by the act of Mex-

ico. Is it possible you don't understand that yet?" Lincoln also raised an un-
settling political question, not about the campaign at hand, but about the
long-term influence of Sangamon County, his base, once the concentration
of power in Illinois, but now being diluted. "In 1840, for instance, we had
two senators and five representatives in Sangamon; now we have part of one
senator, and two representatives. With quite one third more people than we
had then, we have only half the sort of offices which are sought by men of the
speaking sort of talent." The rapid growth in population was in the northern part of the state, beginning to balance and then outweigh the southern
part populated by Kentucky migrants. With the city of Chicago about to
boom as its industrial center, northern Illinois was not only prosperous but
also antislavery. Illinois was becoming more Northern—the foundation for
a Republican Party that did not yet exist and an Abraham Lincoln who had
not yet emerged.

On July 4th, 1848, a parade a mile and a half long slowly moved down
Pennsylvania Avenue, led by President Polk and his cabinet, followed by
thousands of soldiers, firemen, Masons, delegations of American Indians, and
the members of the Congress in carriages, including Lincoln, and wended
its way to the Independence Mall, where the cornerstone of the Washington
Monument was laid in the presence of the venerable Dolley Madison and
the widow of Alexander Hamilton. Speaker of the House Winthrop delivered an address extolling the "hero" Washington as no "mere politician," and
fireworks lit up the sky. The Mexican War went unmentioned, but this was
as close to a victory celebration that would be held in the capital, connecting
the expansion of the country and by inference the extension of slavery to the
founding fathers. Manifest Destiny was dawning. A few weeks later the trial
of Drayton and Sayres began.

Back in Springfield, the Whig campaign was filled with friction. Lincoln's instructions to Herndon had only caused him to collide with older
Whigs who did not want him organizing groups that they felt would be out
of their control. Herndon leaked his "dispirited view" of "the death throes
of the Whig party" to the *Journal* and sent the clipping with a letter to Lincoln excoriating "the stubbornness and bad judgment of the old fossils of the
party." Lincoln responded that Herndon's letter was "exceedingly painful to
me; and I cannot but think there is some mistake in your impression of the
motives of the old men." He expressed doubt that Herndon's resentment was

well founded and offered Polonius-like advice. "The way for a young man to rise, is to improve himself every way he can, never suspecting that anybody wishes to hinder him." Whatever the impression the letter made on Herndon, Rough and Ready Clubs soon sprang up throughout the district.

Lincoln spent much of the month composing his standard campaign speech defending Taylor against accusations of lacking principles while assailing Lewis Cass, the Democratic nominee, for hiding a supposedly fraudulent military record, engaging in petty corruption, and lacking principles. On July 27, Lincoln held forth on the House floor, delivering the kind of slashing stump speech he had perfected in Illinois. Of the Democrats, he said, "Most of them cannot find out that General Taylor has any principles at all; some, however, have discovered that he has *one*, but that one is entirely wrong. This one principle is his position on the veto power." With that, Lincoln praised Taylor as a true Whig, who would not veto internal improvement bills like Polk. "They are in utter darkness as to his opinions on any of the questions of policy which occupy the public attention," he continued. "But is there any doubt as to what he will do on the prominent questions, if elected? Not the least. It is not possible to know what he will, or would do, in every imaginable case . . . but on the prominent questions of currency, tariff, internal improvements, and Wilmot Proviso, General Taylor's course is at least as well defined as is General Cass'."

Lincoln was confident about Taylor's unexpressed opinions, except when he wasn't, in which case he deduced them from no actual evidence but the fact of his nomination as a Whig. The most perplexing question whose answer Lincoln divined was the extension of slavery.

> I admit I do not certainly know what he would do on the Wilmot Proviso. I am a Northern man, or rather, a Western free state man, with a constituency I believe to be, and with personal feelings I know to be, against the extension of slavery. As such, and with what information I have, I hope and believe, General Taylor, if elected, would not veto the Proviso. But I do not know it. Yet, if I knew he would, I still would vote for him. I should do so, because, in my judgment, his election alone, can defeat General Cass; and because, should slavery thereby go to the territory we now have, just so much will certainly happen by the election of Cass; and, in addition, a course of policy, leading to new wars, new acquisitions of territory and still further extensions of slavery. One of the two is to be President; which is preferable?

To Lincoln, the Democratic candidate was an irresistible figure for fun, having lumbered across the political stage for forty years, a barn door of a target. Lewis Cass was a remainder man whose time had come at last but only when his party was likely to lose. He had compiled a distinguished résumé of upward political mobility that belied his mediocrity, or perhaps was the result of it: a general in the War of 1812, who saw no combat; a governor of the Michigan Territory; secretary of war under Jackson (chiefly charged with Indian removal); minister to France; and U.S. senator. Politically awkward, intellectually pretentious, and not clever, he never quite grasped the mechanics of the new party politics, yet his career was regularly promoted through his usefulness to the dominant Southern Democrats. For decades he had been a remnant of the past, but remained in the party's front ranks. "General Cass was a dull, phlegmatic, lymphatic, lazy man," wrote the journalist Oliver Dyer. "He had an unusually large brain, but it was so torpid that nothing but a powerful appeal to his selfishness or his vanity could arouse it into action; and when it was aroused its activity was spasmodic and could not be counted upon for sustained energy. There was not a bit of chivalry in Cass's character, nor an atom of magnetism in his nature." "He was ignorant on no subject, and was deeply versed on none," observed the journalist Ben Perley Poore. "The world to him was but a playhouse, and that drama with him was best which was best performed." On the political stage, he was an all-purpose supporting actor. Whenever he gained the spotlight his convoluted platitudes administered euthanasia to his audiences. An ardent flag-waver for Manifest Destiny, he spoke so often about war with Britain over Oregon as "inevitable" that whenever he uttered the word he provoked "a general laugh" from his fellow senators, according to the journalist Nathan Sargent. "As to my political views, my friend, I have none," Cass confided to Duff Green, who was seeking to determine whether Cass intended to run for the presidential nomination in 1844. "It is a subject on which I can give no explanations, because I have none to give." Cass, of course, was transparently misleading about his ambition and bypassed that year as though he did not exist in favor of the dark horse Polk.

Acting as Polk's Senate floor leader, he deviated from the party line only in advocating the annexation of the entirety of Mexico until Calhoun embarrassed him in debate over his absurdity and once mistakenly seeming to support the Wilmot Proviso before he became the leader against it. To counter the Proviso, he proposed the doctrine of "squatter sovereignty" that would allow the residents of a territory to decide whether it would be slave or free. Through his effort to finesse the divisive issue he traduced the Ordinance of 1787 that had made Michigan a free state but seized the center ground among the warring Democrats. "Squatter sovereignty," which Douglas would translate as "popular sovereignty," was presented as the pure definition of democracy itself, a solution that could be all things to all people. The unintended future consequences of his opportunistic notion in "Bleeding Kansas" could hardly be foreseen, and Cass's idea proposed to avoid conflict, would later become the catalyst for it.

In taking down Cass, Lincoln resumed his role as "slasher," deploying the techniques of sarcasm, belittlement, and ridicule he had honed against opponents in Illinois. He began his merriment calling the overweight Cass "the great Michigander." Then he derided Cass for his "double position" and "equivocation" on internal improvements, "claimed by the advocates of both sides of this question." He scored Cass for being "for" the Wilmot Proviso before he was "against it." But the heart of Lincoln's polemic was his evisceration of Cass's military record, a credential from the distant War of 1812, deflating him in comparison to the hero of the hour Taylor, "the noblest Roman of them all." "Yes sir, all his biographers (and they are legion) have him in hand, tying him to a military tail, like so many mischievous boys tying a dog to a bladder of beans." In the War of 1812, according to Lincoln's telling, Cass was little more than a buffoon. "He invaded Canada without resistance, and he outvaded it without pursuit." Lincoln then engaged in a humorous bit of self-deprecation in order to scoff at Cass. "By the way, Mr. Speaker, did you know I am a military hero?" said Lincoln. "Yes sir, in the days of the Black Hawk war, I fought, bled, and came away. Speaking of General Cass' career, reminds me of my own." Lincoln pointed out he had seen no combat, just like Cass. "If he saw any live, fighting Indians, it was more than I did; but I had a good many bloody struggles with the mosquitoes; and, although I never fainted from loss of blood, I can truly say I was often very hungry." He finished by satirizing the Democrats for lionizing Cass. "Mr. Speaker, if I should ever conclude to doff whatever our Democratic friends may suppose there is of black cockade federalism about me"—referring to the most anti-Democratic emblem of the Federalist Party—"and thereupon, they shall take me up as their candidate for the Presidency, I protest they shall not make fun of me, as they have of General Cass, by attempting to write me into a military hero." Once again, Lincoln demeaned Cass by self-deprecation. This bit of foolery was the first time Lincoln ever publicly talked about himself as president.

But Lincoln was not done. He detailed hilariously how Cass had exploited his many government positions to pad his expenses, often double and triple billing—"the art of being paid for what one eats, instead of having to pay for it"—another reference to his weight. "General Cass is a general of splendidly successful charges—charges, to be sure, not upon the public enemy, but upon the public treasury."

While Lincoln was having a wonderful time berating the inert Cass, the Whigs in his home district were busy losing his seat. His attempt in his floor speech to spin his position on the Mexican War revealed his anxiety that his record as "Ranchero Spotty" might be a sore spot. Addressing the Democrats, he explained, "But if, when the war had begun, and had become the cause of the country, the giving of our money and our blood, in common with yours, was support of the war, then it is not true that we have always opposed the war."

The Seventh Congressional District was the one Whig stronghold in the state, never before won by a Democrat except "Big Red" May in 1836, who afterward declared himself a Whig. Lincoln's former law partner Stephen T. Logan was the Whig candidate. Judge Logan was considered one of the ablest lawyers, affluent, inhabiting a large house on Aristocracy Hill, but dressed shabbily, never wore a tie, had fits of ill-temper, spoke poorly, and was widely perceived as "a cold, avaricious, and little mean man," according to Herndon. "He was not enough of a politician, not positive enough, and created no enthusiasm," recalled Gustave Koerner, Shields's law partner, leader of the German community, and a Democrat, who later became an ally of Lincoln and governor. Koerner also described Logan as "the most slovenly man."

Logan's Democratic opponent was the dashing Major Thomas L. Harris, who fought at the Battle of Cerro Gordo. The gunnery of the Democratic press bombarded Logan with editorials equating him with "Spotty" Lincoln. Was he, wrote one, "upon the side of his country in the war with Mexico" or with "A. Lincoln?" Not only was he charged with being unpatriotic, but also guilty of a new offense. Throughout the year, German refugees from the failed revolution of 1848 had come to Illinois, achieving a critical mass as a new constituency, liberal and antislavery. By 1850, more than 38,000

Germans had settled in Illinois, mostly in the northern part, initially voting for the Democrats but almost all later becoming stalwarts of the Republican Party. Within a decade, by 1860, their number would explode to more than 130,804, a major element in the new party, and Lincoln would assiduously court them. To win them in this election, the Democrats published a phony handbill in old-style German script, claiming Logan was for "the extirpation of all foreigners by fire and sword" and calling for Americans to "rise en masse, and kill every foreigner." In the election held on August 7, Logan lost by 106 votes. "The Whig citadel taken! The 'Dead District' Redeemed!" trumpeted the *Register*, Douglas's paper, which crowed that the German handbill had turned the trick.

Whether Lincoln caused Logan's defeat, the Democrats chalked it up to his "Spotty" stand on Mexico. Despite the complexity of factors, Herndon always attributed the loss to Lincoln's position. Meanwhile, Edward D. Baker, Lincoln's close friend, who had previously held the Seventh District seat, was elected to the Congress, running in a new district, carved out in northern Illinois, centered on the river city of Galena. Shielded from criticism as a war hero, his questioning of the war and opposition to the extension of slavery delivered him a victory with a wide margin. His win was an early sign of the shift in political weight in the state to the north.

The first session of the 30th Congress concluded with a series of three votes on the extension of slavery. Senator John M. Clayton of Delaware, a Whig from a border slave state, proposed that the territories of California and New Mexico be prohibited from limiting slavery and transfer authority on the matter to the Southern-dominated Supreme Court. The Clayton "compromise," "so called," as Horace Mann tartly put it, passed the Senate enthusiastically supported by Jefferson Davis and Calhoun, but was defeated in the House—Lincoln voting against. A few days later, the House passed a bill establishing the territorial government of Oregon under the provisions of the antislavery Northwest Ordinance of 1787—Lincoln voting in favor. Then Polk's proposal to extend the line of the Missouri Compromise to the Pacific coast, opening California and New Mexico to slavery, was voted on and defeated—Lincoln against. With these three votes, Lincoln drew his line against the extension of slavery. This was hardly the end of the matter, but only the beginning. The terms of the coming contest were being set: whether the balance of power through the admission of new free states would be tipped decisively against the South, whether a compromise could be struck, or whether the conflict was irreconcilable. Lincoln had no intimation where the current debate would lead. He had no visions of a day of reckoning that had raged through the mind of John Quincy Adams before his death—nor did he have any premonitions he had staked the position that would be the source of his future political rise to the presidency.

Even before the Congress adjourned on August 14, Lincoln was fully enlisted as a soldier in the national Whig cause, assigning himself to the Whig Executive Committee, working out of the "Whig document room," where he helped frank by hand more than twenty thousand campaign documents a day to mail to voters, and to promote the weekly party paper, *The Battery*, whose logo featured a cannon belching fire at Cass's rear end. "Please get as many subscribers as you can and send them on," Lincoln wrote a Whig friend in Illinois. "I have put you down for one copy, the subscription for which I will pay myself, if you are not satisfied with it."

CHAPTER FIFTEEN

THE HAYSEED

O n August 9, 1848, a crowd in the fervent atmosphere of a revival estimated at ten or twenty thousand, no one really counted, clamored
under a literal big tent raised in Buffalo for the founding convention of the

Martin Van Buren   Free Soil Party Campaign Poster

Free Soil Party. "Free Soilers! Radicals! Liberty Men! All whose throats are not tough enough to swallow Taylor or Cass!" wrote one of the enthusiastic self-appointed delegates, a Brooklyn newspaperman, Walt Whitman, who subsequently founded a short-lived paper, *The Freeman*, to advance the cause. In Buffalo gathered true believers and politicos, the guileless and cunning, righteous and cynical, virtuous and vengeful, prophets and hacks. They flowed into the common stream from three main tributaries: the Liberty Party, Conscience Whigs, and antislavery New York Democrats known as Barnburners.

Salmon P. Chase had been maneuvering for four years to supplant the Liberty Party, gingerly handling its most fervent abolitionist supporters, in order to form a grand antislavery party that would become the True Democracy, the real Democratic Party living up to its Jeffersonian legacy as he interpreted it. He was at once perhaps the most practical politician of the antislavery movement not in public office and yet only a little less delusional than those unyielding idealists he considered obstacles to political influence. He had fended off the Eastern abolitionists, such as former Congregationalist minister Joshua Leavitt, descendant of a wealthy Massachusetts family and founder of the New York Anti-Slavery Society, and the trust fund abolitionist Gerrit Smith, who rejected as shameful compromise the opposition to slavery in the new territories, the issue Chase saw as unifying. They clung to the purity of the shell of the Liberty Party and had contempt for Chase's "designs" and his "clique," as Leavitt called it. Chase struck back, pushing aside Leavitt and installing his friend Gamaliel Bailey as founding editor of *The National Era*, establishing the antislavery voice in Washington.

Chase, meanwhile, angled to marginalize Giddings, a Whig who took Whig economic policies seriously and didn't quite grasp that Chase thought of himself as a Democrat beneath sheep's clothing. Giddings had tarnished his credibility in the movement by touting the presidential candidacy of Senator Thomas Corwin of Ohio in 1847 as the man to head off Taylor. While thunderous in a famous oration against the Mexican War, Corwin cowered on the Wilmot Proviso. When the Corwin balloon deflated, Giddings's influence as potential kingmaker waned. Eastern Liberty leaders, for their part, touted the new man John P. Hale as their ideal candidate, but Chase tried to stall his coronation, fearing it would perpetuate the Liberty Party as it was and thwart his plan for its replacement. Hale met with the abolitionist leaders in Boston in July 1847 and accepted an early nomination at a rump Liberty convention in October, though he did not completely share their views, believing that slavery in the Southern states was constitutionally protected and should be left alone. Yet by allowing himself to be embraced as the Liberty standard-bearer he tainted himself as a factional figure in the grips of radicals. Still relatively unknown, Hale's bold entrance onto the national stage never occurred and he remained standing in the wings.

The ultras, Gerrit Smith and his followers, split from the already reduced Liberty Party, rejecting it as not radical enough, and formed the Liberty League, which nominated the utterly unsuitable Smith as its presidential candidate. Its political slogan disdained politics: "Duty is ours, results are God's." Instead of these momentary messiahs, Chase encouraged the unlikely candidacy of his wife's uncle, Supreme Court Justice John McLean, an Old Whig regarded warily by abolitionists, and who in the end was too autonomous to allow Chase to manipulate him, too much a shrewd Whig to trust a crypto-Democrat, and lacked a larger constituency outside the Old Whigs, who were hardly about to abandon their party. Charging down the path for a new party, Chase rode no horse.

Charles Sumner, former Harvard Law professor, well regarded, well read, and well traveled, was the ringleader of the Conscience Whigs. "The impression he made was that of a gentleman of refinement and self-respect, reminding me of some Englishmen of distinction I had seen," Carl Schurz, the German revolutionary exile who would become an important Republican, would observe upon first meeting him a decade later. "He was tall and well-built, his handsome but strong face shadowed by a wealth of dark locks." His elevated mind combined classical learning, an exalted sense of morality, absolute certitude, equally absolute contempt for those who disagreed, and an almost absolute inability to read the motives of others. He gathered Charles Francis Adams and the other young well-born crusaders for regular meetings at his Court Street law office in Boston, the group's unofficial headquarters, where they plotted against the Cotton Whigs, the oligarchy entrenched in the banks and firms of nearby State Street with lucrative links to Southern interests.

Abbott Lawrence, owner of the largest textile mills in Massachusetts, founder of the city of Lawrence, named after him, former congressman and philanthropist, was chief of the Whigs. He had always been a Clay man and now he was for Taylor. As the leading supporter of Clay in Massachusetts,

Lawrence had clashed with Webster, who he concluded from long experience was corrupt, selfish, and the ultimate self-destructive obstacle to his own ambition. Once again, Webster's ambition to become president burned brightly. He began his campaign at the Whig state convention of 1847, to secure its endorsement. Lawrence invisibly ensured that Sumner, Adams, and the Conscience Whigs were well represented. When Webster's men moved that the convention make his endorsement for president unanimous, the Conscience Whigs were permitted by Lawrence's agents to introduce a resolution against the nomination of any candidate "but those who are known by their acts or declared opinions to be opposed to the existence of Slavery." Threatened with embarrassment, Webster declared himself fervently in favor of the Wilmot Proviso. "Have I ever departed from it in the slightest degree? I must be permitted, sir, to say that I do not consent that more recent discoverers shall take out a patent for the discovery. I do not quite consent that they shall undertake to appropriate to themselves all the benefit and honor of it. Allow me to say, sir, it is not their thunder." Lawrence and his men moved quietly to give him his coveted endorsement, having perfectly choreographed the scene by which he threw himself before the Conscience Whigs, making him unacceptable to the South, and thwarting his nomination. Then Lawrence orchestrated rejection of a Conscience Whig resolution in favor of the Wilmot Proviso that would prohibit the expansion of slavery into the territory gained from the Mexican War. Sumner was guileless about how he had been used. Convinced that Webster was the true Conscience Whig standard-bearer, he urged Lawrence, who had made a deal to become Taylor's vice presidential running mate, to oppose Taylor instead. "I am your friend," said Sumner with complete naive sincerity. "I now plead with you to withdraw from this movement in which you are involved." "What can I do about it?" replied the candid Lawrence. "I am in up to the eyes."

At the national convention, the Massachusetts Conscience Whigs, who came as Webster delegates and were disappointed at his poor showing, vengefully opposed Lawrence's nomination as Taylor's vice president. "Their protests had an immediate effect on the vote for Vice President, which resulted in the defeat of Abbott Lawrence," recalled a triumphant Sumner. One of those delegates, Henry Wilson, a state legislator and shoemaker (a working-class background unlike that of the elite Conscience Whigs), loudly staged a walkout, proclaiming he would do all in his power to defeat Taylor. They would not "have King Cotton at both ends of the ticket." "It was generally conceded beforehand that he was to receive the nomination on the same ticket with General Taylor," wrote Lawrence's authorized biographer, "and, but for the defection of some of the Massachusetts delegates,—Henry Wilson and others, who at that time were supporters of Mr. Webster,—he undoubtedly would have had it." (Wilson would become a powerful anti-slavery U.S. senator, chairman of the Committee on Military Affairs during the Civil War, and vice president under Grant.) So the vice presidential nomination instead went to Millard Fillmore, the New York state comptroller, a cipher, pleasant and dull, "bland as ever," as Seward described him. In two years, His Accidency II would be president. If not for the Conscience Whigs, the capable Lawrence would have been in the White House.

Sumner was already corresponding with Liberty leaders, Giddings, and dissident Democrats in New York seeking to form a third party. The battle royal inside the New York Democracy ripped apart the oldest state political party in the country, the pillar of Jefferson's original Democratic Party and foundation of Jackson's. Van Buren had once ruled the party with an iron hand through his Albany Regency, delivering it to Jackson twice, and elevating himself into his vice president and successor. When he was thwarted from gaining the presidential nomination at the 1844 convention by the Southern imposition of the two-thirds rule, Van Buren still played the party loyalist supporting the nominee, who won the presidency on the very narrow margin in New York. But Polk embraced Van Buren's factional enemy, William L. Marcy, appointing him secretary of war, and ran patronage through his wing of the local party while starving the Van Buren wing. Marcy had coined the Jacksonian dictum, "To the victor belong the spoils." Now, in New York, to Marcy belonged the spoils.

These warring factions were dubbed the Barnburners, after the apocryphal farmer who torched his barn to destroy the rats inside, and the Hunkers, who "hunkered" or hungered after office. The Barnburner issues ranged across the lot of old Jacksonian economic nostrums on taxation, hard currency, and internal improvement, but the one that unified and galvanized them was the Wilmot Proviso. The factions fought for control of the party at the state convention in October 1846, where Barnburners prevailed in passing a resolution charging the Hunkers with waging "war for the extension of slavery" and nominated Silas Wright, who was outspoken against the

Mexican War, as their candidate for governor. Polk and his Hunker cabinet member, Secretary of War Marcy, retaliated, throwing their patronage army of workers in the state against Wright, who lost. In the embittered aftermath Barnburners touted Wright as their natural candidate for president to oust the usurpers, but he suddenly died of a heart attack. "It was believed by his friends that he was politically assassinated by the Old Hunkers," wrote the journalist Oliver Dyer. At the September 1847 Democratic state party convention, just weeks after Wright's death, the Hunkers gained complete control over nominations and defeated all antislavery resolutions. "In the convention someone spoke of doing justice to Silas Wright," recalled Henry B. Stanton, who was present. "A Hunker sneeringly responded, 'It is too late; he is dead.' Springing upon a table, Wadsworth"—James Wadsworth, who would become one of Lincoln's political allies and a Civil War general—"made the hall ring as he uttered the defiant reply: 'Though it may be too late to do justice to Silas Wright, it is not too late to do justice to his assassins.'" The Barnburners stormed out and a month later gathered in the town of Herkimer, where they heard Wilmot's oration against the "slave power." "Are we so tame, so servile, so degenerate, that we cannot maintain the rights of a free soil, and a free people? Let us hurl back the defiance of the South, and in a voice of thunder proclaim that the North will not yield." And then the aroused delegates passed a resolution "that free white labor cannot thrive upon the same soil with slave labor."

Van Buren operated behind the scenes, guiding the Barnburners, tamping down its young radicals, while aiming to oust the Hunkers as the New York delegation at the national convention, and regain his influence within the party. (His youthful amanuensis, a lawyer, Samuel Tilden, learning the political ropes, aided him.) At the convention both delegations were recognized, dividing New York's delegates between them, provoking the Barnburners to stalk out again. The nomination of Cass, who had conspired against Van Buren in 1844 by supporting the two-thirds rule, provoked the Barnburners to issue a proclamation that the convention had been "unjust" and "absurd." A month later, in June, they met in Utica, where they nominated Van Buren for president, and heard the oration of Benjamin F. Butler, a former attorney general and secretary of war during the Jackson administration, pronouncing the "breach between the Democracy of New York and the slave power of the South." This set the stage for the Free Soil convention.

Thus the men of New York, Massachusetts, and Ohio—and Owen Lovejoy of Illinois, bringing along three Underground Railroad conductors—assembled in Buffalo to unite into a new party. Hale arrived with the most committed votes, but he was a reluctant candidate and an outsider to any of the organizations. At the convention of the most principled activists in the country, the nomination was decided in a smoke-filled room before the delegates cast a single vote. The Liberty men, represented by Joshua Leavitt and Henry B. Stanton, cut a deal with the Barnburners, whose negotiators were Tilden, Butler, and "Prince" John Van Buren, the former president's son and the New York state attorney general. Chase was in the room as a kind of mediator. Ditching Hale, the Liberty group supported Van Buren for the nomination in exchange for having their platform adopted. The Conscience Whigs, still suspected by the others as Whigs after all, received a symbolic reward: Charles Francis Adams would be permitted to preside as the convention chairman. Chase wrote the platform, including its enduring slogan: "Free Soil, Free Labor and Free Men." Van Buren, "the catchpole of slaveholders," as John Quincy Adams had called him, still appeared as an unlikely antislavery torchbearer. Only after Butler dramatically announced that Van Buren would sign a bill prohibiting slavery in the District of Columbia did the delegates fall into line. Leavitt marched to the platform to declare that the Liberty Party was "not dead, but translated." Then young Adams was selected for vice president, joined on the ticket with his father's ancient enemy. Chase, who had assumed new prominence as a political figure in bargaining away the existence of the Liberty Party, still clung to his vision of the Free Soil Party as the vehicle for taking over the Democratic Party. "I for one," he wrote, "never dreamed of building up at Buffalo a mere free soil party."

While the Free Soil Party was organized Lincoln spoke at several Whig rallies in Maryland towns near Washington, entertaining audiences with versions of his floor speech ridiculing Cass. The Whig Executive Committee, meanwhile, received dire reports from Massachusetts, the historic bedrock of the Whig Party, never wavering for Whig presidential candidates, but now endangered. It was a shell of its former formidable self. Eight of ten Whig congressmen had declined to run for reelection in protest against Cotton Whig control. Winthrop, the speaker of the house, stood virtually isolated in his own bailiwick. Webster, sullen at his final rejection as the Whig nominee for president, belatedly issued a grudging statement of support for Taylor, and sat on his hands.

Lincoln had developed a few contacts in Massachusetts, one of them a Boston attorney and Whig state legislator with whom he had once tried a case in Illinois, Junius Hall, who urged him to come there to speak for the beleaguered party. Lincoln also corresponded with William Schouler, editor of the staunchly Whig newspaper the *Boston Atlas*, who was engaged in a running spat with the Conscience Whigs. Lincoln related to him how his seat came to be lost to the Whigs. "I would rather not be put upon explaining how Logan was defeated in my district," Lincoln wrote on August 28, attributing the loss to Logan's unpopularity and his opponent's war record. "These two facts and their effects, I presume tell the whole story." But there was another factor, one that undoubtedly gave Lincoln a motive for trying to stanch the flow of Whig support to the Free Soilers. Among the reasons Logan lost was that there was a Free Soil candidate in the race, Erastus Wright, the Springfield businessman and Underground Railroad conductor. (In time, he would become a good friend of Lincoln, who would handle his legal work.) Wright had gained one percent of the vote, but almost all of it was drained from the Whigs, enough to throw the election to the Democrat. Lincoln would have keenly remembered that the Liberty Party candidate had taken enough votes in New York in 1844 to deliver that state and the presidency to Polk, defeating Clay. Instead of heading home, he veered to a political tour of Massachusetts.

"I have wondered how Mr. Lincoln happened to come in '48," said Edward L. Pierce, who heard him speak. Winthrop had a slight opinion of Lincoln, if he had one at all. "Mr. Lincoln in Congress did not make much impression on Mr. Winthrop," recalled Pierce, at the time a young man from a prominent Massachusetts political family, who became Chase's confidential secretary, Sumner's authorized biographer, and an influential figure in his own right in the Republican Party. Pierce later asked Winthrop who had invited Lincoln and Winthrop replied that he thought it was Congressman Charles Hudson, the one loyal Whig member of the delegation besides the speaker. There was no formal invitation, or at least evidence of it, for Lincoln to appear in the Bay State. But given his close working relationship with the Whig Executive Committee and his party discipline it is likely he was sent, rather than wandered off on his own.

Lincoln arrived in Worcester on September 12, the day before the regular Whigs, dispirited and disorganized, held their state convention. The local Rough and Ready Club had planned a rally that evening, but it had no speaker. When the head of Worcester Whig Executive Committee learned of Lincoln's presence he hurried him to the platform. Wearing a long linen duster, he began with self-deprecation about being "this side of the mountains" and then attacked the Free Soil Party for laboring to produce the result they were pledged against. In standing against the extension of slavery, "Mr. Lincoln believed that the self-named 'Free Soil' party was far behind the Whigs," the *Boston Advertiser*, a Whig newspaper, reported. "Both parties opposed the extension. As he understood it, the new party had no principle except this opposition. If their platform held any other, it was in such a general way that it was like the pair of pantaloons the Yankee peddler offered for sale, 'large enough for any man, small enough for any boy.' They therefore had taken a position calculated to break down their single important declared object." Van Buren could not be elected by the Free Soil effort, but Cass might well be. "To unite with those who annexed the new territory to prevent the extension of slavery in that territory seemed to him to be in the highest degree absurd and ridiculous." The true Free Soil Party was, declared Lincoln, the Whig Party. "The 'Free Soil' men in claiming that name indirectly attempted a deception, by implying that Whigs were *not* Free Soil men."

Paraphrasing the tiny evangelical breakaway Liberty League's credo, "Duty is ours, results are God's," as "Do their duty and leave the consequences to God," the freethinker Lincoln ridiculed the notion of associating theology with the mundane Van Buren. In his seamless weaving of logic and light humor, while exalting "reasoning," this was the most characteristically Lincolnian part of his Worcester speech: "If there were divine law, or human law for voting for Martin Van Buren, or if a fair examination of the consequences and first reasoning would show that voting for him would bring about the ends they pretended to wish—then he would give up the argument. But since there was no fixed law on the subject, and since the whole possible result of their action would be an assistance in electing Gen. Cass, he must say that they were behind the Whigs in their advocacy of the freedom of the soil."

One eyewitness, Henry J. Gardner, a future governor, recalled Lincoln's appearance. "No one there had ever heard him on the stump, and in fact knew anything about him. When he was announced, his tall, angular, bent form, and his manifest awkwardness and low tone of voice, promised nothing interesting. But he soon warmed to his work. His style and manner of speaking were novelties in the East. . . . His sarcasm of Cass, Van Buren and the Democratic Party was inimitable, and whenever he attempted to stop, the shouts of 'Go on! go on!' were deafening."

The Whig newspaper account described Lincoln as "a very tall and thin figure, with an intellectual face, showing a searching mind, and a cool judgment. He spoke in a clear and cool, and very eloquent manner, for an hour and a half, carrying the audience with him in his able arguments and brilliant illustrations—only interrupted by warm and frequent applause." A local Free Soil publication called *The Spy*, however, identified him wrongly as "the recently defeated Taylor candidate in the 7th Illinois district in Illinois for reelection to Congress," but conceded his remarks were "rather witty, though truth and reason and argument were treated as out of the question, as unnecessary and not to be expected." "His speech," wrote Edward L. Pierce, "was not on a high level, and gave no promise of future leadership in the antislavery conflict."

The next evening, after the opening day of the convention, the former governor, Levi Lincoln, "a fine specimen of a gentleman of the old school," hosted a dinner at his mansion for the notables of Massachusetts Whiggery and the visitor from Illinois. When Gardner encountered Lincoln again in Washington after his election as president, Lincoln instantly recalled the event. "Yes, I had been chosen to Congress then from the wild West, and with hayseed in my hair I went to Massachusetts, the most cultured State in the Union, to take a few lessons in deportment. That was a grand dinner—a superb dinner; by far the finest I ever saw in my life. And the great men who were there, too!" Upon meeting the august Levi Lincoln, a very distant relative, the "hayseed" joked, "I *hope* we both belong, as the Scotch say, to the same clan; but I *know* one thing, and that is, that we are both good Whigs."

Lincoln was promptly recruited to deliver campaign speeches throughout the state. It seems he gave the same one he did in Worcester. (The only detailed account of what he said on his tour appeared in the *Boston Advertiser* report on the Worcester speech.) After ten days in Cambridge and Lowell, Dorchester and Dedham, he mounted the stage at the Tremont Temple in

Boston to speak at the biggest rally of the campaign. The principal speaker was the former governor of New York, William Seward. "The time would come when the free people would free the slaves in this country," he declared. "This is to be accomplished by moral force . . . without injustice . . . by paying a full remuneration for so great a blessing." The difference between the Democratic and Whig parties on the question, he pointed out, was the basis for profound antagonism, one rooted in "its foundations in South Carolina, the other on the Rock of Plymouth." The danger of the Free Soil Party, he warned, was that if it would "draw off all the advocates of liberty . . . we shall have left the two great parties, ready to bow before the aristocracy of the South."

Then Lincoln delivered his by-now stock speech with its entertaining arguments and jokes. And the crowd, according to a report, "gave three hearty cheers for 'Old Zack,' three more for Governor Seward, three more for Mr. Lincoln, and then adjourned." "It is evident from all the contemporaneous reports," wrote Edward L. Pierce, "that Mr. Lincoln made a marked impression on all his audiences. Their attention was drawn at once to his striking figure; they enjoyed his quaintness and humor; and they recognized his logical power and his novel way of putting things. Still, so far as his points are given in the public journals, he did not rise at any time above partisanship, and he gave no sign of the great future which awaited him as a political antagonist, a master of language, and a leader of men."

Years later, Seward recalled that he and Lincoln traveled to Worcester, where they spent the night in the same hotel, and that Lincoln spoke with him about his remarks at the Tremont Temple. "Governor Seward, I have been thinking about what you said in your speech. I reckon you are right. We have got to deal with this slavery question, and got to give much more attention to it hereafter than we have been doing." "This was his first meeting with Abraham Lincoln," wrote Seward's son Frederick in his biography of his father, "one which Mr. Lincoln recalled when they met again in 1860, remarking that it 'had probably made a stronger impression on his memory than it had on Governor Seward's.'" Many Lincoln biographers have taken the anecdote as the basis for locating the time and place that Lincoln "began . . . to realize that something must be done," as Ida Tarbell wrote. Yet Seward and Lincoln did not happen to be together in Worcester that night, according to Seward's biographer Walter Stahr. So the event must have been either misremembered or apocryphal. Yet it is possible that the conversation or a version of it did happen, but not in the hotel. Lincoln's position on the extension of slavery was little different than Seward's, though Seward's was much more thought through and advanced, which he would make clear in a speech after his Boston appearance, in Cleveland, drawing the distinction between "the two antagonistical elements of society in America—freedom and slavery," and arguing for complete abolition, the end of the "aristocratic and odious" Black Codes in the Northern states, and, most radical of all, black voting. There can be no doubt that Lincoln and Seward spoke with each other. And in his first meeting with Seward, Lincoln, the "hayseed," knew he was encountering the most formidable leader of his party who had seriously engaged antislavery politics. Seward, eight years older than Lincoln, urbane and cosmopolitan, already having served as governor of New York, was nearly a fully formed character, while Lincoln was still in a state of becoming. What he could not know of course was that Seward would become one of the central characters in his life and indispensable to his presidency.

CHAPTER SIXTEEN

THE FIRM

———————•◦•◦•———————

T here was to me something mysterious in the slim, wiry figure, the thin, sallow face, the overhanging eyebrows, and the muffled voice of Seward," observed Carl Schurz, who would first encounter him in 1850. The mesmerizing effect that William Henry Seward had was unlike that of Webster, who reigned through his thunderous orations and imperious presence.

Seward's major speeches were brilliantly constructed, following the classical structures of Aristotle's rhetoric in which he had been instructed as a boy, filled with apt literary allusions, pithy metaphors, and memorable lines, but he delivered them dully, almost as asides, in a lowly heard voice. They were almost always better read than heard. "The broad sweep of philosophical reasoning and the boldness of statement and prediction I found in them, as well as the fine flow of their language, had greatly captivated my imagination," recalled Schurz.

William Henry Seward

Before seeing him I had pictured him to myself, as one is apt to picture one's heroes, as an imposing personage of overawing mien and commanding presence. I was much disappointed when I first saw that quiet little man who, as he moved about on the floor of the Senate chamber, seemed to be on hardly less friendly terms with the Southern senators than with the Northern—his speeches were always personally polite to everybody—and whose elocution was of dull sound, scarcely distinct, and never sounding a resonant note of challenge or defiance. But he made upon me, as well as upon many others, the impression of a man who controlled hidden, occult powers which he could bring into play if he would. Indeed, I heard him spoken of as a sort of political wizard who knew all secrets and who commanded political forces unknown to all the world except himself and his bosom friend, Thurlow Weed, the most astute, skillful, and indefatigable political manager ever known. It is quite probable that the flavor of weirdness in his personal appearance and voice and the oracular tone of many of his utterances did much to strengthen that impression.

Seward's public tone was certain, sharp, and omniscient. Part of his influence came from his uncanny ability to frame every important event on the broad canvas of an overarching and compelling scene, like one of Thomas Cole's enormous and encompassing paintings in his series *The Course of Empire*. (Seward not only knew Cole, the foremost artist of the Hudson River School, but also commissioned him to paint a picture of the bucolic landscape where the Genesee Valley Canal would be built, an internal improvement Seward engineered as governor—a huge painting that covered a wall in Seward's home at Auburn.) In his scope, Seward was a comparable political artist. "He would compress into a single sentence, a single word, the whole issue of a controversy; and those words became the inscriptions on our banners, the passwords of our combatants," wrote Schurz. "His comprehensive intellect seemed to possess the peculiar power of penetrating into the interior connection and of grasping the general tendency of events and ideas, things and abstractions; he charmed our minds with panoramic views of our political and social condition and the problems to be solved; his telescopic eye seemed to pierce even the veil which covers future developments; and while all his acts and words were marked by a thorough-going and uncompromising consistency, they were, at the same time, adorned with the peculiar graces of superior mental culture."

Seward's private manner was informal, seductive, and indiscreet. Short in height, he had tousled red hair that turned brown and then gray, clear blue eyes, a beaklike nose, was clean shaven, and in perpetual motion. Only occasionally at home at his expansive estate at Auburn, where he assiduously tended his trees, bushes, and flowers, and catalogued the birds, he was usually found after his election as senator in 1849 in a luxurious home in Washington. Donn Piatt, a youthful Ohio journalist who became part of Chase's inner circle, was invited in the late 1850s to Seward's after expressing admiration for his eloquence, and was "ushered into the library, where we found Mr. Seward in a much-faded silk gown and old slippers, busily at work, assisted by two clerks. He received us cordially, but did not suspend his labor. He talked and wrote at the same time until dinner was announced. Without changing gown or slippers, he led the way, followed by his guests and clerks and proceeded at once to the business of dining." Seward, a "charming conversationalist" and "good-naturedly cynical," freely called his most famous utterance about the coming "irrepressible conflict" between the North and South "an imprudent speech, and I ought to have been more careful." "Not if you believe it," argued the shocked visitor. "My young friend," Seward explained, "we are warned to keep to ourselves what we do not believe. It is as well, frequently, to conceal what we do believe. There is apt to be public damnation in both." He then called the Constitution, which Piatt believed to be "Holy Writ," just "a paper kite" that was "held up by a string" in danger of breaking. "Why, Mr. Senator," Piatt asked incredulously, "you certainly do not believe that of our Constitution?" "I certainly do," Seward replied without hesitation, "but I generally keep it to myself. A written Constitution is a superstition that presupposes certain impossibilities. The first is that it can express all the wisdom of the past, and anticipate all the wants of the future. It supposes that its creators were both saints and sages. We have had those two classes, but never the two qualities united in one class. The saints were not sages, and the sages were not saints."

Seward was a rare case combining radicalism and partisanship, reform and ruthlessness. He achieved his ends, virtuous and otherwise, usually through cunning means. He had the intellectual qualities of a statesman informed by the slyness of a practiced and endlessly charming politician. He was ironic rather than earnest, witty rather than self-righteous, pursuing higher morality without sanctimony, strikingly objective in his assessment of friends and foes, and savored well-wrought political gestures like a theater critic, even when he was their target. During the debate over extending slavery into Kansas, he was lambasted by Senator Judah P. Benjamin of Louisiana, later the Confederate secretary of state. "Benjamin," he replied, "give me a cigar, and when your speech is printed send me a copy." Benjamin, a bon vivant, handed him a fine cigar, Seward carried it to the cloakroom, and he lit it.

His father, Samuel S. Seward, son of a Revolutionary War soldier, was the leading citizen of his town near the Hudson River, the pillar of the community, a doctor, merchant, judge, and state legislator, and stern toward his third son of five children. Seward's mother, Mary, provided the kinder impulse. The family owned three slaves, two women and a boy, "a perplexing enigma," Seward wrote later. Emancipation in New York would not come into effect until 1827. "I knew they were black, though I did not know why. If my parents never uttered before me a word of disapproval of slavery, it is but just to them to say that they never uttered an expression that could tend to make me think that the negro was inferior to the white person." Other families also had slaves, one of whom was his close playmate, a boy named Zeno. "He told me one day that he had been whipped severely, and the next day he ran away. He was pursued and brought back, and wore an iron yoke around his neck, which exposed him to contempt and ridicule. He found means to break the collar, and fled forever." Then the boy in the Seward household ran away. "I early came to the conclusion that something was wrong, and the 'gradual emancipation laws' of the State, soon after coming into debate, enabled me to solve the mystery, and determined me, at that early age, to be an abolitionist."

Seward attended Union College at Schenectady, the first college chartered by New York state, where he distinguished himself as a member of Phi Beta Kappa and was influenced by the college president to whom he remained close over the years, Eliphalet Nott, a Presbyterian minister and social reformer, proponent of universal public education, temperance, and abolitionism. Nott lavishly admired the English abolitionists and invited George Thompson, the English antislavery activist, to the school to lecture. Once, when Dr. Frances Wayland, the president of Brown University, complained to Nott about abolitionists for their "abusive" language that would "inflame the public mind," Nott rebuked him. "This is one of those questions that can never die," he said. "This agitation will spread from city to city, until it involves the whole country, and becomes the leading political question of the day."

Seward became the junior law partner of Judge Elijah Miller, the leading attorney of Cayuga County, and in 1824 married his daughter, Frances, educated at a Quaker school and the Troy Female Seminary, the first college established for women. Inheriting her father's mansion and estate in Auburn, they used it as an Underground Railroad station, funded the purchase of slaves in order to free them, and when the occasion demanded would hire them. "The 'underground railroad' works wonderfully," he wrote Weed on November 18, 1855. "Two passengers came here last night. Watch [Seward's dog] attacked one of them. I am against extending suffrage to dogs. They are just like other classes of *parvenus*." Seward also provided permanent shelter for seven of the descendants of one of his family's female slaves. In 1859, he deeded seven acres and a house to Harriet Tubman, the Underground Railroad conductor, who lived thereafter on his estate. He quietly gave funds to *The North Star*, the newspaper edited by Frederick Douglass, the escaped slave and abolitionist orator. And in Washington, from the beginning of the Civil War, in 1861, a year and a half before Lincoln issued the Emancipation Proclamation, in collaboration with James Wormley, the black Washington hotelier and caterer, he operated a clandestine steamer to ferry fugitive slaves from Virginia to Washington. One evening he introduced Wormley at a dinner, as one of his guests recalled. "Wormley and I went into the emancipation business a year and a half before Mr. Lincoln did, down on the James River," said Seward. "How was it Wormley—how many slaves did we take off on our steamer?" "Eighteen," Wormley replied.

Seward's ascent from aspiring attorney to the commanding political figure of New York was the story of the rise of the Whig Party in the Empire State. In 1828, the twenty-seven-year-old Seward brought a group of John Quincy Adams men from Cayuga County into an alliance with the Anti-Masons, a political movement that suddenly materialized after the drowning of a bricklayer named William Morgan, who, adherents claimed, had been murdered by the Masons when he threatened to expose how their secret society plotted to manipulate the government. The Anti-Masonic paranoia was a genuinely spontaneous and popular movement in upstate New York, breeding ground of evangelicalism, abolitionism, and Mormonism, and provided a broad basis for a new kind of participatory party politics that was unimagined by the patrician Adams, who thought that the best men ought to rule. The Anti-Masonic movement established a democratic-minded foundation that was pro-Adams, who was not a Mason, and anti-Jackson, who was a Mason, that political figures like Seward managed to fuse with the local pro-Adams National Republicans, "combining all branches of opposition in the support of a common ticket for electors, Congressmen, and local officers," he wrote. At their county convention, Seward authored the platform and proclamations, and the grateful Anti-Masons nominated him as their candidate for the Congress, but neglected to first inform him or their National Republican allies, who thought Seward had staged a little coup of his own, which was also a surprise to him. He withdrew, the Anti-Mason candidate lost the race, Adams was swept from the presidency, and the Democrats were in charge. "The National Republican organization had fallen to pieces, and the party virtually ceased to exist," Seward recalled. The fiasco was the beginning of his political education. And the creation of the Whig Party out of the pieces of parties and movement would become preparation a quarter century later after the Whig collapse for the formation of the Republican Party.

While the National Republicans evaporated as an identifiable party, the Anti-Masons thrived, the first third party in American history and the first to hold a national convention. It was infused with Protestant moral intensity that transcended the group's early narrow focus and broadened into a reform movement that eventually influenced the Whigs and Republicans. In 1830, Seward, bridging factions, was nominated as the obvious consensus candidate of the Anti-Mason Party for the state Senate and elected in 1830.

The following year he made a pilgrimage to meet his hero John Quincy Adams at his home in Quincy, Massachusetts. For three hours the former president and his disciple discussed politics and personalities. Then a candidate for the House of Representatives as an Anti-Mason, Adams held forth on Clay—he supported his former secretary of state for president, but wished he had resigned from the Masons—Calhoun ("the sin of unchastened ambition") and Jackson ("ruinous"). Seward found Adams thoroughly admirable and thoroughly dry, "all the time plain, honest, and free, in his discourse; but with hardly a ray of animation or feeling in the whole of it." Seward understood "as I left the house, I thought I could plainly answer how it happened that he, the best President since Washington, entered and left the office with so few devoted personal friends." Seward remained close to Adams, virtually a member of his extended family when Seward was in Washington, until Adams's death. In 1843, Adams even journeyed to visit Seward at Auburn. Over breakfast, Adams ventured his opinion on the fate of slavery: "I am satisfied it will not go down until it goes down in blood!"

Seward upheld Adams as a mentor, his household god, but learned the lesson that cold rectitude was ill suited for the new democratically propelled politics. He could not have been like Adams if he had tried, but instead was naturally his temperamental opposite: warm, loquacious, gossipy, preferring the company of politicians, cigar in one hand, wineglass in the other. Seward rose on the raucous partisanship that repelled the puritan. And he relied for his advancement on a modern political boss who combined money, media, and message: Thurlow Weed.

Thurlow Weed, the son of a small farmer in upstate New York, a printer's apprentice, putting him into proximity of newspapers and therefore politics, steadily rose through the political ranks on the basis of sheer craftiness and astuteness. Attaching himself to the fortunes of Governor DeWitt Clinton, he became the editor of a Rochester newspaper and was elected to the state legislature. Observing the party techniques and spoils system invented by Van Buren, he immediately adopted them for his own uses. Meeting Seward by chance on the road, helping him fix his broken stagecoach in 1824, Weed instantly spotted his talent. He was instrumental in arranging the coalition of the Anti-Masons with the Adams men and then in moving the Anti-Masons into the nascent Whig Party. By 1834, his influence, centered in his newspaper, the *Albany Evening Journal*, artfully promoting his friends and punishing his enemies, was extensive enough to manage Seward's nomination for governor of the new party, though he lost to William Marcy, the Jacksonian spoilsman. Weed

Thurlow Weed

was hardly discouraged. He ran Seward again in 1838, recruiting a young journalist named Horace Greeley, then editing a literary magazine called *The New Yorker*, to start a new Whig paper called *The Jeffersonian* to tout the candidate, Greeley's launch into orbit. Greeley would later refer to their partnership as "the political firm of Seward, Weed & Greeley," calling himself distinctly "the junior partner."

In the aftermath of the Panic of 1837 and the wave of revulsion against the Democrats, Seward's election was foretold. There was not even a glitch when Gerrit Smith posed a series of extreme abolitionist positions as questions that could only have the effect of losing votes. Seward belatedly endorsed only one of them—jury trials for fugitive slaves—and Smith and his tiny group of followers endorsed another candidate, who did not happen to win the Whig nomination. Despite favorable political conditions, Weed left little to chance. He raised a slush fund to pay "floaters," working-class men, mostly from Philadelphia, to vote early and often. As it turned out, Seward didn't need the padded votes, winning in a landslide. "God bless Thurlow Weed!" he exclaimed. "I owe this result to him . . . my first last and best of friends." Weed was the highly visible power behind the governor's chair, widely called "The Dictator." "I had no idea that dictators were such amiable creatures," Seward wrote him a month after his victory. From then on, it was commonly said in New York and then national politics: "Seward is Weed and Weed is Seward."

The division of labor and rewards between Seward and Weed was definable. "Thurlow Weed, with his peculiar shrewdness, turned over to his co-worker all the honors of office, while retaining to himself all the emoluments that came from success," wrote Donn Piatt. Weed was the opposite of an overbearing political boss, barking orders and threats, and crudely imposing his will. He was subtle, sinuous, and often silent. "Thurlow Weed was as strange as Seward was remarkable," Piatt recalled.

Tall, slender, awkward, and solemn, in his ways, he had a stoop in his shoulders that did not come from study of books, but from bending over in a confidential way to hear what others had to say. He was the most confidential man in manner I ever encountered. In my first interview with him, after an hour's talk on my part, I left impressed with his superior sagacity, until, in humility, I came to remember that I had done all the talking. He won men as a heartless belle wins lovers, through the use of his ears, and in this he had not only unwearied patience, but a confidential air that impressed his victim, as the belle does her admirer, with the belief that he was the only one in all the world in whom he thus confided. His manner, in this respect, was simply superb. He never spoke save in a subdued tone, as if he feared others might hear what he was very careful never to utter. The intense expression of his mysterious eyes, as he looked at and listened to his victim, discounted the fascination sung of in the Ancient Mariner. What can you do with a man who leads you to a remote corner of a room and, in the most deferential manner, tells you nothing in a low, confidential tone?

Governor Seward was the most effective elected Whig official in the country, advancing Clay's "American System" of internal improvements in one state. He was also sympathetic to immigrants, speaking strongly against the growing nativist movement that would find expression in the Know Nothing Party. Drawing on the advice of his old Union College president, he stirred an enormous controversy proposing not only that the state provide education for immigrant children but also that state aid be given to Catholic schools. But the greatest storm he created came in 1840, when he refused the governor of Virginia's request to extradite three men who had helped a slave escape to New York. Virginia retaliated by refusing to extradite common criminals to New York. Mississippi and South Carolina joined in solidarity with Virginia against New York. Seward issued a defiant statement that gained him the reputation of a radical and made him notorious in the South: "I cannot believe that a being of human substance, form, and image—endowed with the faculties, propensities, and passions common to our race, and having the same ultimate destiny, can, by the force of any human constitution or laws, be converted into a chattel or a thing, in which another being like himself can have property, depriving him of his free will, and of the power of cultivating his own mind and pursuing his own happiness; a property beginning with his birth, and reaching over and enslaving his posterity. I cannot believe that that can be stolen which is not and cannot be property." And then Seward guided passage of state legislation protecting free blacks from being kidnapped into slavery. All of these elements of his record would combine into a radical image that would haunt him as he sought the presidency.

After leaving the governorship, in 1846, Seward took on the cases of two black murderers, offering an insanity defense for both. Democrats be-smirched him as responsible for inflaming the second one because he had defended the first. That same year, he joined Salmon Chase as co-counsel be-fore the Supreme Court representing John Van Zandt, the Ohio abolitionist who sheltered fugitive slaves, arguing that the Ordinance of 1787 protected his action. Van Zandt lost, but Seward and Chase hoped their argument would alter public opinion.

Seward and Chase were already engaged with each other in a private debate about the direction of the major parties in relation to the slavery issue. In 1845, after Polk's election but before the Mexican War, while Chase was maneuvering the Liberty Party as his stalking horse for capturing the Dem-ocratic Party, which he believed could be made into an antislavery vehicle, he charged the Whigs with being pro-slavery. Seward dismissed the whole scenario as a fantasy, but not, he explained, because he was a partisan Whig. "I love the Whig party, but I love it only as the agency through which to promote the good of the country and of mankind," he wrote Chase. Seward refused even to call the Democratic Party "Democratic." "There can be," he asserted,

> but two permanent parties. The one will be and must be the Locofoco party. And that always was, and is, and must be, *the* slavery party. Its antag-onist of course must be, always, as it always was and is, an antislavery party, more or less. Whether more or less at one time or another, depends of course on the advancement of the public mind and the intentness with which it can be fixed on the question of slavery. Nor will the character of that an-tagonist party be greatly changed by any change of organization or name. Strike down the Whig party and raise the Liberty party in its place—if it be possible—and the Liberty party, composed of the same elements, will be only the Whig party as it would have been if left to maintain its original position. I see nothing but loss of time and strength in the attempt at sub-stitution.

Seward continued: "The Liberty party I do not think will succeed in dis-placing the Whig and giving a new name to the same mass (and I repeat, the mass of the opposition will always be the same under any name). You think otherwise. So let it be. We must differ until time shows which was right."

Seward would turn out to be wrong about the eternal nature of the Whig Party, Chase wrong about the essential character of the Democratic Party, and Seward prophetic about the polarization of politics between a slavery party and an antislavery one.

While General Zachary Taylor was earning his laurels in the Mexican War, winning his early battles in 1846, Weed encountered his brother, Colonel Joseph T. Taylor, onboard a steamboat to New York, and inquired into the mystery of the hero's "political opinions." Colonel Taylor explained that the general admired Clay, disliked Jackson, and favored American manufactures, and asked why Weed was interested. "Because," he replied, "your brother is to be the next President of the United States." Weed offered detailed political advice on how to handle the nomination that would fall into his lap if only he would remain above the fray. Colonel Taylor requested that he put his strategy into a letter he would deliver to his brother. Most Whigs in New York were still committed to a Clay resurrection, but Weed editorialized in the *Evening Journal* that it was on "the minds of many" that the military hero, "Rough and Ready," would be elevated to the presidency; then he quietly arranged for other Whig editors to create a Taylor boom and promoted Taylor committees throughout the state.

Weed was closely tracking the split within the New York Democratic Party between the Barnburners and Hunkers, calculating how it might profit the Whigs in general and the firm of Seward & Weed in particular. After the state Democratic convention at Syracuse, in 1847, where the party fractured, Weed discussed prospects with Seward. "Weed came last evening," Seward wrote his wife, "and gave me a full account of the Convention at Syracuse which seems to have proceeded exactly as he wished, in all material respects. The 'Barn-Burners' are bent on defeating the Democratic ticket." By October, Weed was operating at full throttle. "Weed's star is again in the ascendant, and he is as busy in political affairs now as he was in the days of his 'Dictatorship' "—that is, during Seward's governorship. "The sum of his speculations at the present moment is, that the Whig party are to succeed in the State this fall; that matters shape decidedly toward Mr. Clay's nomination next year, with that of a friend of yours for V. P., but that success would be doubtful." But Weed was already working to inflate the Taylor boom and deflate Clay. On January 21, 1848, after dining with Adams, Seward had a long conversation into the night with Clay. "He thinks that he does not personally desire to be a candidate, and thinks that he is ready and willing to withdraw from the canvass, but he does not fully understand the workings of his own mind," Seward wrote. Greeley, the mercurial "junior member" of "The Firm," now editing the *New York Tribune*, was hostile to Taylor and clung to Clay. "He is, of course, unhappy," Seward wrote Weed.

"Seward and Weed understood each other intimately, and worked together in perfect accord," wrote the journalist Oliver Dyer. "In the political contest of 1848, they knew just exactly what they must accomplish in order to win, and they pursued their course with clear vision, fixed purpose and unfaltering steps. They subtly and successfully drew their lines through and around the disaffected political elements in the State, and especially in the City of New York. They had the hearty co-operation of several of the leading Barnburners, who were so determined to wreak vengeance on General Cass and the Old Hunkers that they gladly availed themselves of any means which promised to gratify their desires."

Weed encouraged his Barnburner friends to stage a rally at City Hall Park the day before the Whig convention at Philadelphia, when he held a reception at Astor House, his headquarters, for Whig delegates he had invited to stop over "to have a friendly interchange of views." He brought them to the demonstration to expose them to the virulent denunciations of the Democratic candidate by the Van Buren supporters. He suggested, according to Dyer, that if the Whigs were to nominate Clay, a candidate "obnoxious to Van Buren and his friends, they would not help elect him by bolting. On the other hand, if the Whigs should nominate a candidate who would not be personally objectionable to Van Buren and his friends, the probability was that the Barnburners would organize an independent movement, with Van Buren for their leader. Should they do this, the Empire State would certainly be carried by the Whigs, and that would doubtless give them a majority of the electoral votes, and ensure the election of the Whig candidate. With such ideas were the minds of the Whig delegates inseminated."

Weed's original strategy was to have Seward named the vice presidential nominee but then he favored Abbott Lawrence, having received an assurance from Colonel Taylor that Seward would be appointed secretary of state. At the convention, however, when the Conscience Whigs undermined Lawrence, losing the nomination by six votes, and Fillmore filled the spot, Weed's deal fell through. It was a revolt of the Clay delegates against Weed's pervasive influence in destroying their perennial hero's last hope and elevating "Rough and Ready," who had not voted in decades, much less for Clay for president in 1844. There simply could not be New Yorkers as vice president and secretary of state.

Seward, for his part, thought the Mexican War was "odious" and was privately unenthusiastic about its victor after his nomination. His view of Taylor was little different from the disillusioned Clay supporters. But, of course, he stayed in constant communication with Weed on the Democratic split and its potential ramifications. "If the 'Barn-Burners' continue their conflict, as I suppose they must, they will be able to save this State for us," Seward wrote on June 14. "But if the temper around us is at all like that of New England, Ohio, and Indiana, what is to save us in those regions?" In his letters to Weed, he revealed his disgust with Taylor's lack of substance that he concealed in public. "I am thankful, as you can be, that I am not involved in the surrender that has been necessarily made for a time, of principles, the value of which are beginning to be so justly appreciated now that they have been so foolishly betrayed," he wrote on June 24. And he expressed some shame that the Whigs had not taken a forthright stand against slavery and left it to the Free Soilers. "It is fortunate for us that the Democratic party is divided," he wrote on July 12. "Anti-slavery is at length a respectable element in politics." Two weeks later, Seward was in Washington consulting on the *Pearl* case with Horace Mann, who offered to step down as lead counsel if Seward would take over, an offer he declined.

Clay's supporters remained embittered and Webster's sullen, and their pro forma endorsements of Taylor helped but did not supply any energy. Greeley offered a backhanded and belated endorsement of the party nominee in the *Tribune*. His personal solution to his disdain for Taylor was to run for the Congress himself, to which

Horace Greeley

he was elected, serving one term, the taste for public office never leaving his mouth, the source of his future friction with Seward and Weed, who refused to support his ambition to be slated for governor or lieutenant governor in 1854, instead backing Greeley's hated rival, Henry J. Raymond, editor of the *New York Times*, for the latter position. They clearly understood Greeley's mercurial, quixotic, and uncontrollable character. His rejection prompted a private letter to Seward, not published until years later, when Seward made it known, announcing "the dissolution of the political firm of Seward, Weed and Greeley, by the withdrawal of the junior partner"—a curious proclamation that would not prevent Greeley from returning to the senior partners time and again for political collaboration until he churlishly decided to subvert Seward's nomination for president at the Republican convention in 1860 as payback.

It was widely felt that the election would turn on New York as it had the last time. In the Empire State, moreover, the fate of the governorship, the legislature, and a U.S. Senate seat that might be held by Seward were at stake. Beginning in September, Seward started his speaking tour for the Whig ticket, arguing that a vote for the Free Soil Party was a "negative protest," a wasted vote. "Real friends of emancipation must not be content with protests," he declared. "They must act wisely and efficiently." He moved through New York until by the month's end he found himself on the stage of the Tremont Temple in Boston with the little known but amusing rustic from Illinois. "The Whigs who manage at Boston wanted my help, because I was less obnoxious than themselves to the people," Seward wrote Weed. Seward's main memory of his Boston speech was the "barren report of it in the newspapers, which spoiled it for future use, and yet stripped it of its logical method, and of nearly all that could commend it to perusal. Such is the fortune of political lecturers." Undiscouraged, he pressed on to Pennsylvania, defending the Whigs as the party of "universal freedom" against the Democrats, whose "cause of slavery has been advanced by war, the acquisition of useless territory by conquest, the extension of slavery"—and on to Ohio defining the contest between the parties as between "freedom and slavery."

Lincoln's trek home took him to Niagara Falls, and through the Great Lakes—where he held a public debate with a Free Soil man on a steamer—to Chicago, where he delivered his well-rehearsed stump speech about how a vote for the Free Soil Party betrayed the antislavery cause. But his first stop after leaving Massachusetts was a pilgrimage to Thurlow Weed at Albany, where the political patroon of the Empire State introduced him to none other than Millard Fillmore. The presence of the obscure Lincoln made so little an impression on Weed, however, that when he ventured to Springfield after Lincoln's nomination in 1860 to confer about the presidential campaign he had "forgotten" about their earlier meeting and Lincoln had to remind him.

CHAPTER SEVENTEEN

THE SPOILS

———◆———

Niagara-Falls! By what mysterious power is it that millions and millions, are drawn from all parts of the world, to gaze upon Niagara Falls?" Awestruck at the "world's wonder," Lincoln's logical and scientifically in-clined mind meditated on the amount of water pouring over it per minute, its geology and origins. "The Mammoth and Mastadon—now so long dead, that fragments of their monstrous bones, alone testify, that they ever lived,

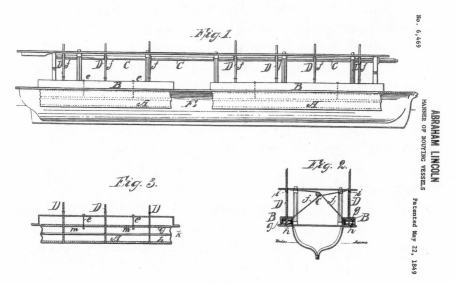

Lincoln Drawings for Patent No. 6,469.

have gazed on Niagara." He later remarked to Herndon, "The thing that struck me most forcibly when I saw the Falls was, where in the world did all that water come from?"

On his way home, steaming through the Great Lakes, his boat became stuck on a sandbar. The captain improvised lashing empty barrels to its sides to buoy it over the barrier. Lincoln may have been reminded of how he had pried Denton Offutt's riverboat from an obstacle on the Sangamon River, his entry into New Salem. His mind remained fixed on the problem and once he returned to Springfield he enlisted a mechanic and Whig activist, Walter Davis, whose shop was near his law office, to help him whittle a wooden model to illustrate his invention for raising ships above sandbars. Carefully carrying the model to Washington, Lincoln presented it at the Patent Office. "Be it known that I, Abraham Lincoln, of Springfield, in the county of Sangamon, in the state of Illinois, have invented a new and improved manner of combining adjustable buoyant air chambers with a steam boat or other vessel for the purpose of enabling their draught of water to be readily lessened to enable them to pass over bars, or through shallow water, without discharging their cargoes." He was granted a patent, the only one ever held by a president, but no steamboat builder ever sought its application. Lincoln's intricate design for clear sailing was stored to gather dust.

The results of the election were a resounding victory for Zachary Taylor. Under the revival tent at the Free Soil convention Giddings had proclaimed to cheers, "I am not waiting for these Taylor men to make war upon me, I will make war upon them, and commence it. I will carry this war into Africa!" While he kept his seat, he could not even help the Free Soilers carry Ohio. "If we have not reached the anticipations of the more sanguine," Sumner nonetheless wrote Giddings optimistically a week after the election, "we have disappointed all the calculations of our enemies. We have . . . taken our place, before the Cass party, as the second party. First we are in principles; I trust we shall soon show ourselves first in numbers." But the Free Soil ticket, in fact, had more than disappointed its fervent adherents, though its tally was five times what the Liberty Party received four years before. It carried only 10 percent of the national vote, 15 percent in the North and not a single electoral vote. Those who voted for it were mostly Democratic supporters of Van Buren, drawn by a combination of nostalgia for Old Hickory's successor, despite his dismal record as president, factional resentment against the two-thirds rule that deprived him of the nomination in 1844 and delivered it to Polk, and, lastly, opposition to the extension of slavery. Nearly half of Van Buren's slender 291,475 votes—120,497—came from his bastion of New York. Van Buren finished second in only three states—New York, Vermont, and Massachusetts—all of which Taylor won. Only if all of Van Buren's votes in New York had gone to Cass would the Democrat have narrowly defeated Taylor there. Even in Massachusetts, where the Conscience Whigs were for all intents and purposes the Free Soil Party, at least 45 percent of their votes came from Democrats. More than 80 percent of its vote in New Jersey and Pennsylvania was also from Democrats. Whigs kept more than 98 percent of its 1844 vote, Democrats only 85 percent. Van Buren split the Democrats more than the Whigs, exposing its internal rift, and showing the limits of his appeal. If the war was carried into "Africa," it was to the Democratic rather than the Whig party. Cass swept all the Northwest states, including Ohio, which had voted Whig four years earlier. His closest margin was in Illinois, capturing it by only two points, but that was due less to the Whig effort than to Democratic defections, especially in northern districts, to Van Buren. Taylor, meanwhile, won most of the South, including the border states of Kentucky and Tennessee, and lost Virginia, Mississippi, and Alabama by only one point. The Free Soil campaign, like the European revolutions of 1848, was a failed revolt, but one that left a lasting legacy.

The unlikely Free Soil standard-bearer, after exacting his revenge in helping to bring about the ignominious defeat of his rivals who had denied him the prize, returned to his party of origin. His fervent pledges to the antislavery cause had been expedients to secure the Free Soil nomination. "Mr. Van Buren's name was in it, but not his head nor his heart," recalled William Allen Butler, the son of Benjamin F. Butler, who was Van Buren's law partner and Jackson's and Van Buren's attorney general. "Great words were inscribed on its banners—'Free Soil, Free Speech, Free Labor, and Free Men.' But they were words of advance and not of strategy, and Mr. Van Buren was too deeply entrenched in his old political notions to utter them in earnest." His private views were unaltered from his long-held previous public ones. "The vagaries and political antics of the Abolitionists and Emancipationists of all descriptions were not at all to his liking." In the next presidential contest, he would abandon the Free Soilers, endorse the pro-Southern Democrat Franklin Pierce, in 1854 endorse the Kansas-Nebraska Act opening the territory to slavery, and then in 1856 endorse the equally pro-Southern James Buchanan for "offering good grounds for hope." With Van Buren's reversion to type antislavery men reverted to their old contempt for him.

The second, brief lame-duck session of the 30th Congress was dominated by a series of antislavery resolutions. In the first session, Lincoln had consistently voted against tabling petitions to abolish slavery in the District of Columbia and to enact the Wilmot Proviso. But when on December 13, Congressman John G. Palfrey of Massachusetts proposed a bill to abolish slavery in the District of Columbia without compensation Lincoln voted with the majority to table it. He never spoke to the question, but the likely reason was in part the bill's failure to provide compensation and in part Palfrey's lack of party loyalty. Palfrey was the pluperfect representative of the high-minded New England moral sensibility in the Congress. Beginning his education as the student of William Ellery Channing, the preeminent Unitarian minister, he graduated from Harvard and its Divinity School, becoming the pastor at the Brattle Street Church, whose parishioners were the cream of the Boston Brahmins—the Adamses, Lowells, and Lodges. An overseer at Harvard, he was appointed dean of the Divinity School, tutoring a whole generation of the most influential Unitarian ministers, among them Theodore Parker. At the same time he was the owner and editor of *The North American Review*, the most important journal in New England, if not the country, a beacon of social reform and literary culture. Palfrey's concern with slavery had a more personal source than revulsion at a distant horror. His father and two brothers owned a large plantation in Louisiana, the family's prosperity resting on a practice he believed "utterly null and void before God." In the event of his father's death, he would inherit one third of the property, a legacy of sin. But even before that, he paid the family's slaves wages. And later he brought sixteen former slaves to Boston, conducted a ceremony at King's Chapel, a Unitarian church in the center of the city, formalizing their emancipation, and arranged for their employment in the households of Boston's leading citizens. Elected to the House of Representatives, Palfrey was a regular participant in Giddings's circle at Mrs. Sprigg's, where Giddings observed the distinguished member's political tin ear. "He is a learned man," Giddings wrote his wife in early 1848. "It is a feast to sit down and chat with him on any moral subject. . . . He knows nothing about politics, but is exceedingly interesting on morals, religion, and science. I am honored to call him my friend." Palfrey's first act as a congressman was to launch a strident campaign against Winthrop's election as speaker, refusing John Quincy Adams's private request after making his initial point that he "forbear further opposition." One of the charter Conscience Whigs, he ran for reelection as a Free Soiler and lost to a Cotton Whig. His symbolic resolution for abolishing slavery in the District was his last act in the Congress, his valedictory gesture. (At Sumner's recommendation in 1861, Lincoln appointed Palfrey postmaster of Boston, where he proved an efficient administrator and which enabled him to complete his voluminous *History of New England*.)

After Palfrey's resolution was tabled, Giddings proposed a bill to hold a referendum on abolition in the District that would include blacks, free and slave, as voters, without any mention of compensation—a measure that received even fewer votes against tabling than Palfrey's motion when it was brought up for a vote on December 18. Lincoln voted with the majority to table. Giddings's proposal was also opposed by his close ally, Gamaliel Bailey, who functioned as the voice of the movement in the press. On the same day that Palfrey and Giddings introduced their bills, Lincoln voted in favor of one that would prohibit "extending slavery" in California and New Mexico. It was crafted by another of Giddings's circle, Joseph M. Root, the former mayor of Sandusky, Ohio, whose home was a station on the Underground Railroad, a Whig who had turned Free Soiler, but unlike Palfrey was reelected. (Root would become an anti-Chase delegate from his home state to the Republican convention in 1860, and a Lincoln presidential elector; Lincoln appointed him the U.S. attorney for northern Ohio, and, as Lincoln wrote upon receiving a patronage request, "I am very partial to Mr. Root.")

Following these bills, on December 21, Daniel Gott, a Whig from New York, who had just defeated a Free Soil challenge to his seat, proposed abolition of the slave trade in the District, but without a referendum of the District's citizens. Greeley, already seated in the House by virtue of winning an early special election, wrote the bill's preamble in the style of a righteous editorial declaring slavery "a reproach to our country throughout Christendom." Lincoln voted for tabling it, though likely not because of Greeley's sanctimony but because it didn't offer a referendum. It passed because Southerners were uniformly absent from the chamber, though when they returned it was defeated.

These resolutions, with the exception of the Root proposal, split the

Whigs. Each of them had a feature that was unacceptable to one group of Whigs or another. For most of the next month, Lincoln crafted a bill that he felt would remedy the defective bills and instead be broadly approved by all factions. He was alone among the Whigs in trying to resolve the dilemma of forging a consensus antislavery position. "Mr. Lincoln called on me this evening and read his bill and asked my opinion which I freely gave," Giddings wrote in his diary on January 8, 1849. A few days later, he recorded that "our whole mess remained in the dining-room after tea, and conversed upon the subject of Mr. Lincoln's bill to abolish slavery. It was approved by all; I believe it as good a bill as we could get at this time, and am willing to pay for slaves in order to save them from the Southern market." Gamaliel Bailey, writing in *The National Era*, obviously informed about Lincoln's coming resolution, predicted in an editorial, "Such a bill, we doubt not, would pass Congress, and we have just as little doubt as to the decision of the citizens of this District under it." Congressman Horace Mann was also likely consulted, at least to receive his benediction. Years later, during the war, Lincoln recalled to Mann's sister-in-law, Elizabeth Peabody, who pioneered the kindergarten system in the United States, that Mann "was very kind to me" and "it was something to me at that time to have him so—for he was a distinguished man in his way—and I was nobody."

Lincoln announced on January 10 he would soon introduce an amendment to the Gott bill to abolish slavery in the District. His inspiration came from several sources—the British Slavery Abolition Act of 1833, which provided £20 million to compensate owners in the West Indies; the emancipation acts of Pennsylvania in 1780 and New York in 1799 that established gradual abolition over a period of years; and his own proposal before the Illinois legislation in 1837 that would require a referendum of District citizens. Lincoln's proposal would, after such a vote, provide federal compensation to owners for "full cash value," children born to slave mothers after 1850 would be free, and to secure Southern support would require city officials "to arrest, and deliver up to their owners, all fugitive slaves escaping into said District." His bill reflected the widely shared feeling of antislavery opinion that slavery would die through strangulation, not by one bold stroke. Nearly all the Free Soil men thought slavery would end in steps, first in the District and then in border states, a strategy that would cause the South finally to recognize that "the peculiar institution" was an anachronism and to abolish it state by state. Those "immediatist" Garrisonians in favor of instant national abolition without compensation remained extraordinarily marginal.

Lincoln felt fairly confident he had wrapped up local support essential to the bill's passage. He had secured the support of Mayor William Seaton of Washington, a conservative Whig and next-door-neighbor of Bailey, and Lincoln announced that "fifteen of the leading citizens of the District of Columbia to whom this proposition had been submitted" were favorable. But learning of Seaton's pledge to Lincoln, a delegation of Southern congressmen visited him, applied pressure, and he reversed himself. With the mayor's withdrawal of support, Lincoln's effort collapsed. Despite his careful preparation, he never introduced the bill. "Finding that I was abandoned by my former backers and having little personal influence," he said in 1861, "I dropped the matter knowing that it was useless to prosecute the business at that time."

During the two-week period in January while Lincoln composed his bill and watched its demise before it was even proposed another slavery issue obsessed the House—the Pacheco case. Antonio Pacheco was a slave owner in the Florida Territory before it became a state. He leased his slave, Louis, who spoke four languages, to the U.S. military as a guide in its war against the Seminole Indians in 1835. The unit to which he was attached was ambushed, Louis was either captured or joined the Seminoles, and was apprehended two years later, only to be sent west with the exiled tribe. Pacheco's heirs sought $1,000 from the federal government for the loss of their property. The case raised the question of whether slavery was recognized legally not simply in the states but also throughout the whole country, "slavery national," as Calhoun had put it. In its discrete form, the Pacheco case encapsulated the extension of slavery. Giddings argued that framers of the Constitution had never intended to enshrine slavery as a national institution and cited the Declaration of Independence. "No man then," he said, "attempted to involve the people of the north in the support of slavery." On one vote, a majority prevailed against compensation to the Pacheco heirs, but on a final reconsideration on January 19 they were awarded the $1,000 they sought. Lincoln voted consistently with the antislavery forces.

Lincoln's stillborn resolution on emancipation in the District left a tincture from which spread over the years enduring but divergent images of him interpreted depending on the vantage point—a political Rorschach test. For some radical abolitionists, he appeared a compromising and unprincipled politician, but for other antislavery crusaders, a trustworthy ally seeking to forge workable solutions, and for Southern ideologues, a wily and ruthless adversary.

"Who is this huckster in politics? Who is this county court advocate?" demanded the abolitionist Wendell Phillips just after Lincoln's nomination for president. He answered his question himself in an article entitled, "Abraham Lincoln, The Slave Hound of Illinois," in *The Liberator* on June 10, 1860. Phillips affixed that label, he explained, because of Lincoln's 1849 bill that included a provision for returning fugitive slaves. This was merely the beginning of a stream of fierce anti-Lincoln polemics from abolitionist critics that did not end until his death.

With Lincoln's vote against the Gott bill, he had "placed himself squarely on the side of the South," wrote George Washington Julian, who was elected as a Free Soiler from Indiana to the next Congress. "He was a moderate Wilmot Proviso man, but his anti-slavery education had scarcely begun." Though Julian wrote those lines in his memoir published in 1884, he suggested the narrative that Lincoln's antislavery sentiments were barely nascent. In his account Julian did not bother to mention Lincoln's resolution, intended to be an amendment to the Gott bill. Raised a Quaker, a Clay Whig turned Free Soiler, running as the Free Soil vice presidential candidate in 1852, Julian married Giddings's daughter, was an early adherent of Salmon Chase's presidential aspirations, then backed Lincoln in 1860, but as a Radical Republican member of the Congress was a harsh critic, despite demanding and receiving patronage favors to help him retain his office, and ultimately held with "the universal feeling among radical men here is that his death is a god-send," as he wrote in his diary the day after the assassination. Julian broke with the Republican Party in 1872, supporting the Liberal Republican–Democratic candidacy of Horace Greeley, who campaigned against Reconstruction, and whose natural death within weeks of his defeat made him, according to Julian, "scarcely less a martyr than Lincoln."

Giddings did not share his son-in-law's estimate of Lincoln then or in the future—or Phillips's.

Answering his "Slave Hound of Illinois" piece, Giddings issued a public statement about Lincoln's 1849 bill. "His conversing with the people of the District, the preparation of the bill, the avowal of his intention to present it, were important" and the measure itself, far from halfhearted or compromised, demonstrated that Lincoln was among "those who were laboring in the cause of humanity. He avowed his intention to strike down slavery and the slave trade in the District; to strike from our statute book the act by which freemen were transformed into slaves; to speak, and act, and vote for the right," and "cast aside the shackles of party, and took his stand upon principle." Giddings then chastised Phillips for his sanctimonious tone: "you speak of that act with great severity of condemnation. I view it as one of high moral excellence, marking the heroism of the man. He was the only member among the Whigs [identifying him apart from the few "antislavery Whigs" in Congress] of that session, who broke the silence on the subject of those crimes."

Giddings's commitment to Lincoln was not confined to words. When Lincoln made his first bid for the U.S. Senate from Illinois, Giddings waded in on his behalf. "I have this moment had a long talk with Giddings and he is your strongest possible friend and say he would walk clear to Illinois to elect you," Congressman Elihu Washburne, one of Lincoln's Illinois friends wrote him on December 26, 1854. "He will do anything in the world to aid you, and he will today write his view fully on the whole subject to Owen Lovejoy, in order that he may present them to all the freesoilers in the Legislature. He will advise them most strongly to go for you en masse." Giddings, in fact, wrote Lovejoy twice, who was avidly trying to recruit Lincoln to the fledgling Republican Party. (In 1861, Lincoln would appoint Giddings the consul general to Canada, where he served until dying during a game of billiards at the St. Lawrence Hall, the leading hotel in Montreal, on May 27, 1864, where five months later John Wilkes Booth would check in, entertain onlookers at the same pool table, and be observed by Union agents conferring with Confederate commissioners.)

By 1849, when Lincoln prepared his District bill, there was no unified group that could be called simply "the abolitionists," though nearly everyone in politics used the sweeping label, usually as a derogatory term. That rubric encompassed congeries of schismatic factions and people offering differing antislavery solutions that changed shape over time, ranging from John P. Hale to Gerrit Smith, engaging or rejecting politics, viewing the Constitution as either a fundamentally antislavery or pro-slavery document, and often at odds with each other. The term "radical" before the war generally meant those opposed to the extension of slavery but who also acknowledged it was protected in the Southern states. Some antislavery and stalwart Old Whigs were called "radical," but separated themselves from those they categorized as "ultras." Those who were contemptuous of politics like Wendell Phillips, or attached to the ambitions of Chase, or would captiously judge every difficulty Lincoln encountered during the war requiring complex strategy as evidence of his moral shortcoming, became so hostile that they sought to overthrow him during the 1864 campaign, which would have inevitably resulted in a Democratic victory and recognition of the Confederacy, a scenario that prompted a more tempered Garrison to break with many of his own disciples. Lincoln would be disdained by a number of prominent Eastern abolitionists, for reasons not always transparent and tenuously related to their high-flown rhetoric, after supporting him for the Republican presidential nomination in 1860 against Seward, the "radical" candidate but their political enemy in New York. To wit, Henry B. Stanton, his wife, Elizabeth Cady Stanton, who was Gerrit Smith's cousin, and her friend Susan B. Anthony (the founders of the feminist movement) were among the chief organizers of the anti-Lincoln third party effort while engaged in a nasty patronage war over the New York Custom House with Thurlow Weed. Yet, in Illinois, nearly all abolitionists embraced Lincoln by 1854 or 1856 at the latest. They came to know him and trust him. None would defend him against other abolitionist critics more unswervingly than Owen Lovejoy. And in the end Lincoln would enlist Seward to wield methods honed in the precincts of New York's sordid politics—lobbyists and slush funds—to secure passage of the Thirteenth Amendment finally abolishing slavery. Even by 1848, at the creation of the Free Soil Party, the movement remained fractionalized, unstable, and its platform essentially one broad plank against the extension of slavery. If the Free Soilers had advocated immediate abolition through an act of the federal government, it would have broken apart. Few of its leaders believed that emancipation in the South should be achieved through federal law. Almost all, like Chase, thought that Southern states would wind up freeing their slaves on their own. That the Free Soil candidate at the peak of its electoral strength was the quintessential opportunist Martin Van Buren revealed the absence of an abolitionist alternative with even his tattered appeal. There was no glass staircase leading to the final stage of emancipation. The movement, of course, would deeply influence public opinion over the next decade both positively and negatively, from Harriet Beecher Stowe's *Uncle Tom's Cabin* to John Brown's raid, and elements of the movement would play an integral part in the organization of the Republican Party as a vanguard. But, as abolitionists like Owen Lovejoy came to understand, the outcome would greatly depend on politics and the attraction of serious political men like Lincoln.

John C. Calhoun glowered at the presidential candidates of 1848, urging at a large public meeting at Charleston on August 19 that South Carolinians "stand aloof from the contest," avoid being drawn to Taylor just because he was a "Southern man" or Cass because he was a Democrat—their campaigns little more than a "distraction." "The time is coming," he warned, "when your united energies will be demanded for the struggle." If California and New Mexico were admitted as free states in the next Congress, "we have nothing to hope or expect from the Federal government." The "Abolition party," as he called it, would become a "mighty party," and "rally on the great question of sectional supremacy." Sifting the leaves of the current campaign, he could discern the dark future. "There are in the body politics, as in the human system, diseases which, if not promptly arrested, become incurable and eventually fatal," and "Abolition," if joined with one or the other major party and the Barnburners, would "in its progress destroy the Union and the institutions of the country." Only through a Southern party pledged to "Southern rights," "above the mere making of Presidents," would the South "command our terms and control the North." If that effort failed, then the choice must be either "resistance or submission"—and "who can doubt the result. Though the Union is dear to us, our honor and our liberty are dearer."

The wild Gold Rush throughout 1849 to California, its population exploding day by day, made its inevitable admittance to the Union as a free state an issue of rising concern for Calhoun, especially when the Congress seemed incapable of settling it in favor of slavery and bills for emancipation in the District were presented. He proposed that all Southerners within the Congress form a united bloc. In response to his call for "firm, prompt, and manly opposition" to the Wilmot Proviso "applied by law to the territory acquired from Mexico," he convened a caucus of eighteen senators and fifty-one congressmen. The first to sign his private resolution was Jefferson Davis, but a number of others went to Calhoun's meetings in order to undermine his influence. Alexander Stephens, a Whig Young Indian, wanted to prevent sabotage of the incoming Whig president, while President Polk counseled Southern Democratic members to attend but not to do anything.

Calhoun composed an "Address of the Southern Delegates in the Congress," a litany of how "aggression has followed aggression, and encroachment," citing Supreme Court rulings justifying the constitutionality of slavery, singling out the statement of Justice Henry Baldwin in a case in 1833: "Thus you see, that the foundations of the Government are laid, and rest on the right of property in slaves. The whole structure must fall by disturbing the cornerstone"—the metaphor that Alexander Stephens would later famously echo in his defense of secession and the Confederacy.

Calhoun recounted the history of the "aggression" of "Abolitionists" since 1835 against "Southern rights," before coming to the latest "series of aggressions," ticking off each depredation until his wrath finally poured out against "the member from Illinois," but not deigning to mention Lincoln's name. If Lincoln's proposal for emancipation in the District were implemented "nothing would be left but to finish the work of abolition at pleasure in the States themselves." And if the North under such men gained control of the federal government, this "fanaticism and the love of power" would produce a constitutional amendment emancipating the slaves, finally giving them "the right of voting and holding public offices." As "political associates of the North, acting and voting with them on all questions," the blacks would push "the white race at the South in complete subjection. . . . We would in a word, change conditions with them—a degradation greater than has ever fallen to the lot of a free and enlightened people."

Calhoun climaxed his nightmarish vision with a scene of whites "abandoning our country to our former slaves, to become the permanent abode of disorder, anarchy, poverty, misery, and wretchedness." And then he struck a defiant yet muffled note. "We hope," he wrote, "if you should unite with anything like unanimity, it may of itself apply a remedy to this deep-seated and dangerous disease; but, if such should not be the case, the time will then have come for you to decide what course to adopt." His muted ending was forced by internal dissension within the ranks of the Southern members, a majority refusing to follow his trumpet call and forcing what Calhoun's ally, Congressman Robert Toombs of Georgia (later the first Confederate secretary of state) called "weak milk and water." Many Southern Democrats were attracted or compelled to Calhoun's movement, but the Southern Whigs went into the caucus "to control and crush it." "We have completely foiled Calhoun in his miserable attempt to form a Southern party," Toombs wrote Governor John J. Crittenden, a Whig of Kentucky.

The debate over the future of California wracked the 30th Congress until its final hour. Time and again, Democrats proposed measures to outflank the Wilmot Proviso. The day after Lincoln proposed emancipation in the District, Senator Stephen A. Douglas introduced a tortuously worded bill employing a double negative construction about applying U.S. law "not inapplicable" that would have had the effect of legalizing slavery in California—"one of the grossest frauds ever perpetrated upon a free people," wrote Giddings. It was referred to the Committee on Territories of which Douglas was chairman.

Then Senator Isaac P. Walker of Wisconsin, a Democrat, tacked on an amendment to an appropriations bill that would have abrogated Mexican law over the newly acquired territories and substituted U.S. law—thereby lifting the Mexican prohibition of slavery and opening all the territories, presumably under the doctrine of popular sovereignty that the Democratic candidate had just run on and been defeated. The Walker amendment passed the Senate. But, on March 2, after tumultuous debate, the House narrowly rejected it, 114 to 100. Lincoln voted against it. The Senate and the House stood at loggerheads over slavery in California.

On the last night of the session, March 3, after Greeley proposed that the name of the United States of America be changed to "Columbia," removing that of "a mere follower" (Amerigo Vespucci) in honor of the "true hero," Christopher Columbus, the tumult resumed over California. Congressman Richard W. Thompson of Indiana, a Whig and friend of Lincoln, proposed an alternative to the Walker amendment that "the existing laws thereof shall be retained" until July 4, 1850—that is, that Mexican law banning slavery would remain in effect. "Great excitement was manifested in all parts of the hall and in the Senate," recalled Giddings. "Members of irregular habits had recourse to artificial stimulants, which rendered the scene more gloomy." "Imagine," one newspaper correspondent reported, "230 tom cats fastened in a room, from which escape is impossible, with tin cans tied to their tails—raging and screaming, and fighting, and flying about from 6 P.M. to 6 A.M., twelve hours—and you will have some idea of the last jubilee in the House. About ten o'clock, [Richard K.] Meade of Virginia, and Giddings of Ohio, had a fight—Meade drunk. About 3 A.M. Sunday morning, [Jacob] Thompson of Mississippi, and [Orlando B.] Ficklin of Illinois, had a knock down—both drunk."

The Thompson amendment passed the House by 111 to 105, Lincoln voting aye. In the wee hours of the morning, the Senate wearily conceded in order to adjourn. That vote, temporarily protecting California from slavery, was Lincoln's last meaningful vote as a congressman. "California and New Mexico had been obtained for the purpose of extending slavery over them," wrote Giddings, "and the establishing of freedom in those territories was a fatal blow to the institution, from which it never recovered. And its downfall may be dated from that eventful night."

The next day was a Sunday and the day after that Zachary Taylor's inauguration. "A small number of mutual friends," recalled Washburne,

including Mr. Lincoln, made up a party to attend the inauguration ball together. It was by far the most brilliant inauguration ball ever given. Of course Mr. Lincoln had never seen anything of the kind before. One of the most modest and unpretending persons present, he could not have dreamed that like honors were to come to him, almost within a little more than a decade. He was greatly interested in all that was to be seen, and we did not take our departure until three or four o'clock in the morning. When we went to the cloak and hat room, Mr. Lincoln had no trouble in finding his short cloak, which little more than covered his shoulders, but after a long search was unable to find his hat. After an hour he gave up all idea of finding it. Taking his cloak on his arm, he walked out into Judiciary square, deliberately adjusting it on his shoulders, and started off bareheaded for his lodgings. It would be hard to forget the sight of that tall and slim man, with his short cloak thrown over his shoulders, starting for his long walk home on Capitol Hill, at four o'clock in the morning, without any hat on.

Only a year earlier Lincoln had been on the floor of the House when John Quincy Adams had fallen and died. His final day concluded amid a drunken melee and standoff proclaimed a triumph by the Proviso men. He had denounced the president for falsely precipitating the Mexican War and in his district gained notoriety as "Ranchero Spotty." He shared a platform in Boston with the prominent Seward and broken bread with the eminent

Brahmins. Calhoun's attack on him as a "member from Illinois," too negligible to dignify by mentioning his proper name, was the greatest public attention he received from a figure of national renown. But just as he found himself thrust into the conflict over the extension of slavery, he was gone.

Lincoln's term in the Congress over, he believed his political service on behalf of his party during the campaign was a credential that should earn him an important federal job. But he no longer held public office. A Democrat had captured his previously safe Whig seat. Illinois had gone for Cass, so Lincoln could not claim to have won it for Taylor. The governor, legislature, and senators of his state were all Democratic. But Lincoln represented himself as the leading Whig in Illinois through which all patronage appointments must flow in tandem with his friend Ned Baker, who had been elected to the Congress from a new district, the only Whig now in the Illinois delegation. Four days after Taylor was sworn in, on March 9, Lincoln sent the new secretary of the treasury, William M. Meredith, a letter announcing the arrangement: "Col. E. D. Baker and myself are the only Whig members of congress from Illinois—I, of the 30th. & he of the 31st. We have reason to think the Whigs of that state hold us responsible, to some extent, for the appointments which may be made of our citizens. We do not know you personally; and our efforts to see you have, so far, been unavailing. I therefore hope I am not obtrusive in saying, in this way, for him and myself, that when a citizen of Illinois is to be appointed in your Department to an office either in or out of the state, we most respectfully ask to be heard."

Lincoln's presumptuous claim to be the patronage boss of Illinois was the beginning of his troubles. He had asserted influence he did not necessarily have, setting himself up for the inevitable blame when disappointed job seekers watched the plums they felt should be theirs fall into the laps of others. And in the end Lincoln turned into one of the disappointed job seekers himself.

Lincoln's first foray was to demand the biggest plum for Baker, who aspired to be appointed secretary of war, though he was just elected to the Congress. The *Illinois Journal* published editorials touting Baker, probably written or edited by Lincoln, and Whigs endorsed him as a cabinet-balancing Western candidate in the state legislatures of Illinois, Iowa, and Wisconsin (states incidentally dominated by Democrats). Lincoln sent the *Journal* article to his friend William Schouler, editor of the *Boston Daily Atlas*, pressing him to republish it. "Desiring to turn public attention, in some measure to this point, I shall be obliged if you will give the article a place in your paper, with or without comments, according to your own sense of propriety."

While championing Baker, however, Lincoln discovered that his friend was not a widely admired man. Another Lincoln friend, Washburne, who had wanted the congressional seat that Baker won, was organizing subterranean opposition. David Davis, one of Lincoln's lawyer friends, who would become one of the most important people in his rise, managing his presidential campaign, had a low opinion of Baker, not an unusual view, saying he did not have "stability of character." A Chicago Whig leader and lawyer, Justin Butterfield, called him "a vain supercilious Englishman." Undeterred, Lincoln wrote Joshua Speed to request that he lobby Kentucky governor John Crittenden, a Taylor intimate, on Baker's behalf, but when approached Crittenden refused to entertain the idea, though he said a kind word about Lincoln. "His career is regarded as erratic," Speed reported about Baker. Learning of the campaign pushing Baker, Senator Jefferson Davis, Taylor's son-in-law, conveyed his disgust to Crittenden: "What would General Taylor say to such impudent dictation and indelicate solicitation?" Unabashed, Lincoln wrote Taylor directly urging that he appoint Baker—a letter that was ignored. Baker, not so much rejected as not even considered for the cabinet, next proposed that the president appoint him as the special representative to organize the new state government of California. Once again, he instigated Lincoln to act as his agent, and Lincoln dutifully wrote Secretary of State John M. Clayton about Baker that he had "a long personal and intimate acquaintance with him, if the plan he proposes is at all practicable, I think, he would be the very man to execute it." But this scheme, too, was dismissed out of hand. Lincoln was not helping himself.

Yet Lincoln managed to secure jobs for a few of his close friends— Dr. Anson Henry was appointed Indian agent for the Oregon Territory and Jesse K. Dubois got receiver of public monies in the town of Palestine, Illinois. In a bit of nepotism, Lincoln gained the directorship of the federal pension agency in Springfield for his brother-in-law, Dr. William Wallace, a post that, according to Wallace's rival for the position, had been sought by Mary Lincoln to resolve "their family difficulties . . . so you see I was offered up as a sacrifice—a sort of burnt offering—to heal family broils." The Todd family felt that Lincoln could miraculously produce loaves and wine and Mary's uncle, David Todd, demanded a position for his son-in-law. Lincoln beseeched the powers-that-be, but was denied, undoubtedly humiliating him before Mary's insistent relatives.

Lincoln was swarmed by job applicants. George W. Rives, a Whig Party stalwart, demanded the position of postmaster of Paris, Illinois, then switched to ask for the more lucrative head of the Land Office in Minnesota, which Lincoln had initially tried in vain to get for Anson Henry before altering his request to Indian agent in Oregon. "You overrate my capacity to serve you," Lincoln wrote Rives. "Not one man recommended by me has yet been appointed to anything, little or big, except a few who had no opposition. Besides this, at the very inauguration I commenced trying to get a Minnesota appointment for Dr. Henry, and have not yet succeeded; and I would not now, lessen his chance, by recommending any living man for anything in that Territory. It is my recollection that you sent me an application to be P.M. at Paris. Am I mistaken?" But then, when Henry took the Oregon job, Rives managed to land the postmaster one after all, and became a lifelong Lincoln supporter.

Walter Davis, the mechanic who helped Lincoln create his ship model, meanwhile, boasted that Lincoln had promised to name him postmaster of Springfield; it was a pledge he had not made, instead promising it to Abner Ellis, Speed's former business partner. An exasperated Lincoln wrote Davis, "When I last saw you I said, that if the distribution of the offices should fall into my hands, you should have something; and I now say as much, but can say no more. I know no more now than I knew when you saw me, as to whether the present officers will be removed, or, if they shall, whether I shall be allowed to name the persons to fill them. It will perhaps be better for both you and me, for you to say nothing about this." He added, "I shall do what I can about the Land claim on your brother Thomas' account."

"There must be some mistake about Walter Davis saying I promised him the Post-Office," Lincoln wrote Herndon. "I did not so promise him." And he noted that Davis had supported Baker over him for the congressional nomination at the Whig convention of 1844. Herndon came up with the clever idea of naming Davis the receiver of the Springfield Land Office and Turner King, the brother of Franklin King, the abolitionist from Tazewell County who had endorsed Lincoln for the Congress, as the register. That plan solved more than Lincoln's problem with the plaintive Davis; it would gratify Billy by ousting the incumbent receiver, Archie Herndon, his father.

Unfortunately, one of Lincoln's oldest friends going back to his New

Salem days and who had cared for him for years, William Butler, also wanted the receivership. So Lincoln sent a letter recommending him to become a local pension agent, an offer Butler refused as an insult, and he generated letters against King. One of Lincoln's former allies, Dr. Richard F. Barrett, who had served on the Whig Central Committee with him during the 1840 campaign, joined the attack on King, calling him "a free drinker, card player, bankrupt, and loafer." Lincoln countered by recruiting another Whig activist, Philo Thompson, to start a letter-writing campaign on King's behalf. "A tirade is still kept up against me here for recommending T. R. King," Lincoln wrote. "This morning it is openly avowed that my supposed influence at Washington, shall be broken down generally, and King's prospects defeated in particular." Lincoln defended himself on the King matter in another letter to Secretary of the Interior Thomas Ewing, in which he acknowledged the "charges" against King but countered that he was "a good man," and pointed out that he himself was the real target: "I am not the less anxious in this matter because of knowing the principal object of the fault-finders, to be to stab me." King finally got the job and performed poorly, but local abolitionists were grateful to Lincoln.

The biggest plum of all was commissioner of the General Land Office, located in Washington, controlling dozens of patronage positions and paying $3,000 a year, three times what the governor of Illinois earned. Lincoln believed the job could be his for the asking. "I believe that, so far as the Whigs in congress, are concerned, I could have the Genl. Land office almost by common consent," he wrote Speed. But he had pledged his support for the post to Cyrus Edwards, his wife's uncle-in-law, a former Whig candidate for governor, considered to have the claim by virtue of his standing within the party hierarchy and the extended Edwards-Todd clan. Baker, however, had his own favorite candidate, a Mexican War chum and Whig state senator, Colonel James L. D. "Don" Morrison, who had a reputation as a corrupt braggart, was an owner of indentured slaves, and the son-in-law of former Democratic governor Thomas Carlin. Edwards lacked a constituency within the party, except for Lincoln, and was considered a cold, imperious figure expecting the job on the basis of deference. Morrison's bid, on the other hand, was widely resented as a Baker power grab and another example of Baker's impulse to be a self-important blowhard. Soon, candidates appeared on the horizon from other states. To fend off competition, Lincoln and Baker decided that Edwards and Morrison should decide between them who should be the candidate and that they would then back that man. "I can do nothing till all negotiation between you and Don is at an end," Lincoln wrote Edwards. But Lincoln's friends, worried that both men were weak and the job would slip to someone from another state, urged him to seize it himself in the cause of true Illinois Whigs. In reply, Lincoln wrote, "In relation to these pledges, I must not only be chaste but above suspicion. If the office shall be tendered to me, I must be permitted to say 'Give it to Mr. Edwards, or, if so agreed by them, to Col. Morrison, and I decline it; if not, I accept.' With this understanding, you are at liberty to procure me the offer of the appointment if you can; and I shall feel complimented by your effort, and still more by its success." Edwards, at this point, graciously decided that it would be best for Lincoln to seek the position in order to thwart Baker's obnoxious friend.

Enter Justin Butterfield. The former U.S. attorney and leading Chicago lawyer, after his hope evaporated to be named general counsel at the Treasury Department, turned his longing gaze to the Land Office. Despite his break with most of his party by supporting the Mexican War, he had a uniquely influential friend in Thomas Ewing, the most powerful Whig from Ohio, the former secretary of the treasury and U.S. senator, and now secretary of the interior, who had authority over the position. (Nobody could have known that Ewing's family arrangements would turn out to have more significance than his control of patronage: when his next door neighbor died, Ewing adopted his boy as his foster son and ensured that he attended West Point—William Tecumseh Sherman, who married Ewing's daughter.)

On June 2, 1849, after months of staunchly standing by Edwards, Lincoln learned he had no chance from a friendly Whig source at the Land Office. Now

Justin Butterfield

suddenly contemplating the job for himself, Lincoln discovered that the contest, according to his source, had been narrowed either to him or Butterfield. Butterfield, having lost no time, had quickly rounded up supportive letters from Clay and Webster. Meanwhile, Butler, Lincoln's old friend, the unhappy job seeker, gathered signatures in Springfield on a petition for Butterfield, which he flourished in Washington to demonstrate that Lincoln would not be a popular choice. "Almost every name obtained by Butler, recommending Butterfield, was obtained through misrepresentation, and I have the first man yet to see, who does not regret having signed it," Anson Henry wrote Lincoln on June 11. Cyrus Edwards, feeling betrayed after encouraging Lincoln, resentfully wrote a letter endorsing Butterfield. Thus Lincoln's good deed was punished.

Lincoln rounded up nineteen letters of support from his former congressional colleagues and urged them to speak with President Taylor on his behalf. He conferred with Duff Green, whose son lobbied Taylor and his chief of staff, reporting back that Butterfield was the frontrunner. Lincoln had already written a letter to Secretary of the Navy William B. Preston, with whom he had served in the Congress, chronicling Butterfield's record of party disloyalty. "In 1840 we fought a fierce and laborious battle in Illinois, many of us spending almost the entire year in the contest. The general victory came, and with it, the appointment of a set of drones, including this same Butterfield, who had never spent a dollar or lifted a finger in the fight." Instead of backing Taylor, moreover, Butterfield was a Clay man to the end. "Again, winter and spring before the last, when you and I were almost sweating blood to have Genl. Taylor nominated, this same man was ridiculing the idea, and going for Mr. Clay; and when Gen: T. was nominated, if he went out of the city of Chicago to aid in his election, it is more than I ever heard, or believe. Yet, when the election is secured, by other men's labor, and even against his effort, why, he is the first man on hand for the best office that our state lays any claim to. Shall this thing be?"

Desperate for a gesture indicating a high level of support, Lincoln wrote Seward, now a U.S. senator, requesting that he write a letter of recommendation. He received no reply.

On June 10, both Lincoln and Butterfield arrived in Washington to press their cases. An Illinois Whig fixer in the capital, who was lobbying for him, Major Nathaniel B. Wilcox, met Lincoln at the train depot. "He had on a thin suit of summer clothes, his coat being a linen duster, much soiled," Wilcox recalled. "His whole appearance was decidedly shabby. He carried in his hand an old fashioned carpet-sack, which added to the oddity of his appearance." Wilcox explained that he had talked with Taylor, who told him "he was favorable to Lincoln, but that Mr. Butterfield was very strongly urged for the place and the chances of appointment were in his favor." Butterfield argued that he should receive the job as the representative of Whigs in northern Illinois. And Taylor told Wilcox that he had already given appointments to people from the southern and center part of the state but not to the north. Lincoln wrote a plea to the President: "I am in the center. Is the center nothing?"

Butterfield's appointment, announced on June 12, disclosed the fait accompli. Lincoln's lobbying had been pointless all along. "I have hardly ever felt so bad at any failure in my life," Lincoln said. The next day he met with Ewing, who told him that he could have had the job in the beginning if he had gone for it himself instead of promoting the hopeless Edwards. In private, Lincoln railed that giving Butterfield the post was "an egregious political blunder." When he learned two months later that Ewing had suppressed his letters of recommendation, he was outraged and contemplated exposing it, but wrote a friend that "my high regard for some of the members of the late cabinet; my great devotion to Gen: Taylor personally; and, above all, my fidelity to the great Whig cause, have induced me to be silent." But, he added, "I would not now accept the Land Office, if it were offered to me." He remained so upset that he wrote Secretary of State John M. Clayton on August 12, "It is fixing for the President the unjust and ruinous character of being a mere man of straw." And he more than suggested that Taylor had been manipulated. "The appointments need be no better than they have been, but the public must be brought to understand, that they are the President's appointments." Usher Linder, serving in the state legislature, undoubtedly voiced Lincoln's sentiments about Ewing, inspired by his treatment, later that year: "He is universally odious, and stinks in the nostrils of the nation. He is as a lump of ice, an unfeeling, unsympathizing aristocrat, a rough, imperious, uncouth, and unamiable man." Lincoln felt compelled to very mildly distance himself from Linder's blast and again pledged his party loyalty, though the former "slasher" must have gained gratification from every harsh word. Lincoln and his allies were not alone among Midwestern Whigs in feeling unfairly treated in the distribution of the spoils. Ewing systematically hoarded the federal jobs for his own state of Ohio and his friends. By the close of 1849 Whig newspaper editors in Chicago, Detroit, Indianapolis, and Des Moines called for his firing.

As a consolation prize, Lincoln was offered the job of secretary of the Oregon Territory. He entertained for a moment making the hazardous journey to the far edge of the continent, but Mary was adamantly opposed. So he declined—and she would later remind him that she had prevented him from "throwing himself away." After he refused, he asked that the position be given to his friend, Simeon Francis, the *Journal*'s editor, who told him he would like to go, but Lincoln's request was dismissed. That final rejection was the precise degree of his influence in Washington. As consolation beyond the consolation prize, he was offered the governorship of Oregon, but he declined that, too. (Francis moved to Oregon in 1859, becoming editor of the *Oregonian* newspaper, and Lincoln, using his powers of patronage, appointed him an army major and paymaster.)

Butler and Edwards would not remain on speaking terms with Lincoln until he ran for president. Butterfield packed his office with his two sons and a dozen relatives, worked closely with Douglas in giving land grants to the Illinois Central Railroad (whose directors in turn helped enrich Douglas through windfall real estate deals), but suffered a debilitating stroke in 1852 and was replaced. Don Morrison, Baker's candidate for the Land Office, campaigned against Lincoln in 1860, calling him "infinitely worse than a Yankee Abolitionist." From the whole squalid affair, Lincoln learned an invaluable lesson. As president he would maintain tight control as the final arbiter of even the slightest federal job. "Old Abe, through his patronage," George W. Julian would complain in 1864 about the appointment of former congressman Richard W. Thompson, a Julian rival in Indiana, to the Court of Claims, "is the virtual dictator of the country."

Years later, on August 13, 1863, John Hay, Lincoln's private secretary, accompanied Lincoln and Seward back and forth to the Capitol from the White House. Seward discussed the foolishness of Democrats like Governor Horatio Seymour of New York who sought short-term political advantage, even encouraging the New York City draft riots, rather than support the administration in prosecuting the war. "A fundamental principle of politics," he said, "is always to be on the side of your country in a war. It kills any party to oppose a war." He brought up the example of President Buchanan's Mormon War from 1857 to 1858, when "our people . . . led off furiously against it. I supported it to the immense disgust of enemies and friends. If you want to sicken your opponents with their own war, go in for it till they give it up." Lincoln, in fact, had clear memories and firm ideas about the Mormons. Seward's recollection of the Mormon War may have reminded him that Joseph Smith's lawyer in Illinois was none other than Justin Butterfield and he reminisced about Butterfield, recounting the story of how he had suffered politically for his opposition as a Federalist to the War of 1812 and leapt to support the Mexican War, recalling Butterfield's explanation: "I opposed one war. That was enough for me. I am now perpetually in favor of war, pestilence and famine."

CHAPTER EIGHTEEN

A HUNDRED KEYS

E dged aside by the more nimble Justin Butterfield, a gloomy Lincoln "escaped one of the greatest dangers of his life," being named commissioner of the Land Office, the well-compensated plum position with enormous patronage at his disposal, "a position so insignificant and incongruous as that which he was more than willing to assume when he left Congress," according to Nicolay and Hay. Then, bowing to his wife, he refused the compensatory appointment as territorial governor of Oregon, which would have removed him to the Pacific coast. Mary Todd Lincoln had no intention of bundling her family into a covered wagon to trek across the plains and the Rocky Mountains into a kind of internal exile. Had Lincoln accepted either position, his faint mark would appear only in the yellowing annals of forgotten minor officials. In-stead, he returned to obscurity in Illinois. He would not appear in Washington again for a dozen years, until he arrived in the dead of night to elude an assassination plot as president-elect.

He moved back to his clap-board frame house with the picket fence on the corner of Eighth and Jackson Streets, a few blocks from

Herman Melville

downtown Springfield. It was not a sprawling brick mansion on Aristocracy Hill, where Mary's sister lived, but a residence of respectability, with two parlors, which Mary decorated in the Victorian style with wallpaper, carpets, and solid mahogany and cherry furniture. It was bright, comfortable, and orderly. While he had risen from shivering as a boy in a lean-to propped in the wintery wilderness and terrified of the cries of animals in the darkness, she had descended from wealth and privilege, and still struggled to instruct him in manners befitting his acquired station in life, which she, above all, thought was not yet the plateau he should achieve. When they first moved into their home, he bought her two books, *Miss Leslie's Cookery* and *Miss Leslie's Housekeeper*, probably at her request. They were partners in propriety, decorum, and upward mobility. They would be partners in tragedy when their son Edward died at the age of five of tuberculosis in 1850. Lincoln, who had suffered from breakdowns and an overbearing dread of mortality, became the compassionate counselor to his wife to console her beyond her desolate mourning. "Eat, Mary, for we must live," he begged her. "Mr. Lincoln showed great consideration for his wife," recalled one of his law clerks, Gibson W. Harris. "She was unusually timid and nervous especially during a storm. If the clouds gathered and the thunder rolled, he knew its effect on his wife and would at once hasten home to remain there with her till the skies cleared and the storm was safely over." She remained the flame for his ambition, even when his flickered, the first and last member of "our Lincoln party." They were always partners in ambition.

The firm of Lincoln & Herndon was located above the post office and a dry-goods store in the Tinsley Building, conveniently across the street from the state capitol, where Lincoln could use its law library. "The furniture, somewhat dilapidated, consisted of one small desk and a table, a sofa or lounge with a raised head at one end, and a half-dozen plain wooden chairs," said Harris. "The floor was never scrubbed. If cleaned at all it was done by the clerk or law student who occasionally ventured to sweep up the accumulated dirt." It was here that Lincoln took on his cases, told stories, read newspapers, journals, histories, and poetry for an hour or two, and often stared into the far distance. "If no important or pressing matters claimed his time," recalled Herndon,

> he would draw his chair up to the table on which rested his elbow, place his chin in the palm of his hand, his gaze fixed on the floor or through the

window into space, and linger thus absorbed for hours or until interrupted by callers or the demands of his profession. On these occasions he was grave, taciturn, unresponsive. But the most significant and noteworthy thing about him was his look of abstraction and melancholy. It was as painful as it was inescapable. I have often watched him in one of these moods. Bent over in his chair, lost to the world in thought, he was the most striking picture of dejection I had ever seen. When in one of these moody spells neither of us spoke. Occasionally it would become necessary to trouble him with a question without eliciting a response. Meanwhile I would forget that I had asked him; but to my surprise a few moments later (once it was over fifteen minutes) he would break the silence and give me an appropriate and satisfactory answer.

Then, he would set out with his horse, Old Bob, and his buggy, to the county courthouses of the Eighth Judicial District of central Illinois, a member of a movable troupe of fellow lawyers and judges, like a traveling frontier theater company, who would become the core of his team of loyalists. As he wandered, taking on clients for ten-dollar fees, he was binding together his future campaign, which he did not anticipate.

By almost every ordinary measure he was a paragon of success. Familiar to everybody in Springfield, he was still a new kind of man. Just as he was of the first generation of men to become part of a class of professional party politicians, he was of the first class of relatively prosperous lawyers in the state capital. He had, one of just a few professional townspeople, reached a high rung of social mobility.

Despite his immersion in his legal work, the former congressman remained an active Whig leader, in constant contact with Whigs around the state. His political activity no longer consumed every waking moment. He was not an elected official and had to make a living, after all. But even in a fallow period he closely observed every gesture, speech, and movement of the politicians on the stage, especially Stephen A. Douglas. He avidly read the comings and goings at Washington, gleaned gossip from whomever he could, and continued to suggest and write editorials for the *Sangamo Journal*. In his practice of law, he honed his forensic skills not only for the juries of the county courthouses but also prospectively for the voters, who were one and the same. Day after day he developed his logic and humor to perfect his persuasion. On the road in crowded boardinghouse rooms, his candlelight study of Euclid's theorems in bed before falling to sleep stretched his intellectual ability to win more than cases; quietly he began drawing the lines of geometric logic through his antislavery thought.

Outwardly, he was living a life of social tranquility, despite the occasional flare-up at home with Mary, and solid middle-class affluence. He had left his grinding poverty and lack of formal education behind him. He was a model of conventional achievement. He had become a man he could not really imagine when he was a barefoot boy in a dirt floor cabin, or even as a young man just arrived in New Salem and taking the first job and then the next offered to him. He had an irresistible momentum that took him twice down the Mississippi River to New Orleans, where he was horrified at the spectacle of brazen open-air auctions of human property, but he had not known where his aspiration to escape his past into an unknown decorous respectability would drive him.

After his stint in the Congress and setup in Springfield, he accepted his purgatory with the disquiet of long staring silences. There was something in this success that was a failure. His private secretary, John G. Nicolay, would later describe his rise as a classic tale of overcoming obstacles and setbacks, and it was not inaccurate. "Almost every success was balanced—sometimes overbalanced by a seeming failure," wrote Nicolay. "Reversing the usual promotion, he went into the Black Hawk War a captain, and, through no fault of his own, came out a private. He rode to the hostile frontier on horseback, and trudged home on foot. His store 'winked out.' His surveyor's compass and chain, with which he was earning a scanty living, were sold for debt. He was defeated in his first campaign for the legislature; defeated in his first attempt to be nominated for Congress; defeated in his application to be appointed commissioner of the General Land Office. . . . He could not become a master workman until he had served a tedious apprenticeship." But there was more to it than a desire for simple success. He was settled but unsettled. His respectability was also the sign of his revolt against his past. Beneath Lincoln's quest for conventionality lay an ambition for an unrealized fate.

During the Civil War, he maintained his relationship with his intimate friend and early Springfield roommate, Joshua Speed, who, as a prudently cautious Kentucky slaveholder, dissented from the Emancipation Proclamation. With Speed, even if they disagreed on the substance, Lincoln could still confide his most personal motives. His friend might disapprove of his actions, but he could understand their inner springs. Speed had known him when he was most broken. "At first I was opposed to the proclamation and so told him," recalled Speed.

> I remember well our conversation on the subject. He seemed to treat it as certain that I would recognize the wisdom of the act when I should see the harvest of good which we would erelong glean from it. In that conversation he alluded to an incident in his life, long passed, when he was so much depressed that he almost contemplated suicide. At the time of his deep depression he said to me that he had done nothing to make any human being remember that he had lived and that to connect his name with the events transpiring in his day and generation and so impress himself upon them as to link his name with something that would redound to the interest of his fellow man was what he desired to live for. He reminded me of the conversation, and said with earnest emphasis I believe that in this measure [meaning his proclamation] my fondest hopes will be realized.

Entering his wilderness in 1849, his own drama of Dante's "dark wood," in the middle of his journey, Lincoln faced the death of his son, the paralysis of his political hopes, and banishment from Washington where Douglas commanded center stage. While his rival forged the Compromise of 1850, Lincoln was learning the compromises required in his marriage. Nobody thought he was entering a crucible from which he would emerge as Lincoln. Nobody imagined him for great things except his wife. Only she thought him extraordinary. He had cut himself off from his dying father and his original family. But he did not seem disenthralled. He offered no vision for a new birth of freedom. He issued no call for a people's contest. He had his tragedies, disappointments, and melancholy, but they were the ordinary passages of a moderately successful lawyer in central Illinois. He was maturing, developing emotional depths, but there was no reason to suppose his personal crisis would lead anyplace in particular. As late as 1852, he delivered one of his silliest and most clownish performances in a lengthy partisan speech on behalf of the Whig presidential candidate, Winfield Scott. Yet two years later, speaking against the Nebraska Act, with Douglas seated directly in front of him in the packed Illinois House of Representatives, observers who knew him felt stunned at the transformation they witnessed before their eyes.

Nor was Lincoln embarked on a foreordained voyage of evolution toward his ultimate port of call as the Great Emancipator. There were no predetermined stages. The freethinking Lincoln was as skeptical of predestination in politics as he was in religion. His politics were hardly on a chartable course under the constant navigational pressure of abolitionists pure of heart. There was no ascending glass staircase to heaven at whose top stood the perfectionist William Lloyd Garrison, his most brilliant protégé, Wendell Phillips, and the freed slave turned orator and editor, Frederick Douglass. The idea that there was at once slights Lincoln's antislavery views and exaggerates the Garrisonians' political importance even among the highly factionalized abolitionists. The most significant abolitionist contributions soon to come would be from those who considered the Garrisonians confounding and counterproductive. Harriett Beecher Stowe, who would write *Uncle Tom's Cabin*, the passion play of the movement, almost in one long semi-hallucinatory trance, and Eli Thayer, the Yankee entrepreneur who would invent the Massachusetts Emigrant Aid Society to claim the territory of Kansas from the clutches of slavery, both disdained the absolutism and sectarianism of Garrison and his circle. Later, during the perilous 1864 campaign, Garrison himself would break with the Garrisonians who founded a third party to topple Lincoln, and make the case for Lincoln to his errant followers who stayed true to his saintly creed.

The world in 1849 had passed Lincoln by, and he would not enter events again until the world fell apart. He could not conceive of the unraveling of American politics as he knew it. He would cling to the banner of the Whig Party longer than most who joined the new Republican camp. His mind slowly wrapped itself around changing circumstances. His thinking was woven through time.

After he finished his one term in the House, Lincoln came face-to-face with slavery as a social and political force in Kentucky, handling his wife's legal case after her father's death to recover the family fortune. He discovered that her cousin, who was at its center, was a slave, and those who had taken the Todd estate were leaders of the pro-slavery party who rewrote the state constitution to end limits there on the slave trade.

His emergence as the recognizable Lincoln with his speech opposing Douglas's Nebraska Act threatening the expansion of slavery was both the synthesis of his life and thought to that moment and yet the beginning of his grappling with the hard questions that would consume him to his last speech as president, delivered three days before his assassination, when he would declare himself in favor of black citizenship.

"I have always hated slavery, I think as much as any Abolitionist," he explained in 1858. "I have been an Old Line Whig. I have always hated it, but I have always been quiet about it until this new era of the introduction of the Nebraska Bill began." Two years earlier, he repeatedly spoke of his "hate" for slavery's extension: "I hate it because it deprives our republican example of its just influence in the world—enables the enemies of free institutions, with plausibility, to taunt us as hypocrites—causes the real friends of freedom to doubt our sincerity, and especially because it forces so many really good men amongst ourselves into an open war with the very fundamental principles of civil liberty—criticizing the Declaration of Independence, and insisting that there is no right principle of action but self-interest."

In that speech, Lincoln did not publicly blame Southerners for slavery, but described them enchained to "the peculiar institution." "Before proceeding, let me say I think I have no prejudice against the Southern people. They are just what we would be in their situation." Yet Lincoln, who came from Kentucky, became a Northerner, one who had fled the South as a child and came as a man to express his hatred for its whole social system. He was a close observer of the South's customs and mores, especially as an adult on his visits to his wife's hometown of Lexington, Kentucky, where in 1849 he saw firsthand the ruthless political triumph of the slaveholders' party over the moderate antislavery forces, led by his father-in-law and Henry Clay, and the rewriting of the state constitution to broaden the commerce and power of slavery. Years before his emergence was marked with his speech against the Nebraska Act in 1854, he was scathing on the subject in private. He not only expressed hatred of slavery but also revulsion toward the class-ridden South and contempt toward slave owners in particular. For him, these were not abstract concepts, but deep feelings rooted in his personal experience. Lincoln related his insights to his friend Joseph Gillespie, a former Illinois state legislator who had served with him, relating how masters had "a darkey trudging at your heels," so "everybody would see him and know that you owned slaves. It is the most glittering, ostentatious and displaying property in the world. . . . The love for slave property was swallowing up every other mercenary passion. Its ownership betokened not only the possession of wealth but indicated the gentleman of leisure who was above and scorned labor. These things Mr. Lincoln regarded as highly seductive to the thoughtless and giddy headed young men who looked upon work as vulgar and ungentlemanly." Gillespie recalled, "Mr. Lincoln was really excited and said with great earnestness that this spirit ought to be met and if possible checked. That slavery was a great and crying injustice, an enormous national crime and that we could not expect to escape punishment for it." But when Gillespie asked Lincoln for the solution, he did not then have the answer. "He confessed that he did not see his way clearly."

For Lincoln, the Kentucky experience of 1849 was a turning point. But it was also the beginning of his hibernation, when his political career went into a deep sleep from which he thought it would not awaken. His few political speeches of this somnambulant interregnum were mostly conventional Whig Party talking points illustrated with ridiculous frontier humor. It was only when he reappeared as a newly energized figure against the extension of slavery that his public and private remarks were aligned, the public and private man made whole.

Over the passage of decades, the pressure of events impressed upon Lincoln's mind the cancerous nature of slavery as a system of power, economic, social, and political. Certain that slavery could not last, he believed, as he declared in his "House Divided" speech of 1858, that it must be set "in the course of ultimate extinction," limiting it to the South and gradually strangling it through restrictive legislation. It was on that basis that he was elected president.

Imagining that slavery might be stopped in its tracks was not wholly fantastic. Were it not for the untimely death of President Zachary Taylor the crisis would likely have come to a head in 1850. The hero of the Mexican War and a Louisiana slave owner generally considered a semiliterate ignoramus swiftly surprised everyone by opposing the extension of slavery and preparing to use armed force to suppress Southern resistance. Southerners who courted secession in response to Taylor's unyielding attitude certainly believed that slavery might be constricted. His death instead opened the door for the inaptly named Compromise of 1850, more an appeasement and capitulation that annulled New Mexico's antislavery constitution and enshrined the Fugitive Slave Act, not the "final settlement" preserving the Union proclaimed by his doughface successor, Millard Fillmore, but the prelude to Civil War.

Lincoln long understood that free labor could remain free only by breaking the bonds of the slave-owning oligarchy. He knew that his father had
been subjugated as a free man within a system of slavery. He knew that slavery not only oppressed the slave, but also through political power dominated
the free man. From the moment he became a Republican, he declared his
aim the breaking of the "slave power"—an old Liberty Party phrase he cited
in his 1858 debates with Stephen A. Douglas—referring to the greatest, most
extensive, and deepest economic power in the country from the plantations
of the Mississippi Valley to the finance houses of Wall Street—and the controlling political power that held the Democratic Party, the Congress, the
Supreme Court, and the presidency in its iron grip. Once he fully entered
into the contest over slavery he understood that he was engaged in a titanic
struggle for ultimate power.

Through Douglas's bill in 1854 to clear the path for a Pacific railroad
by opening the vast Kansas-Nebraska territory to settlement he believed he
would repeat his triumph in orchestrating passage of the Compromise of
1850 that had established him as a national power broker and gave him the
leverage to create the Illinois Central Railroad, the first big railroad of its
kind—a platform fit for a presidential candidate. Douglas was the chairman of the Senate Committee on Territories, but to enact the bill he had to
win the approval of the tight-knit cabal that controlled the Senate, Southern
political heirs to John C. Calhoun, who all roomed together in the F Street
Mess, and whose ex officio member was the secretary of war and the virtual
president of the United States, more influential than any cabinet secretary in
the nation's history, Jefferson Davis. To achieve his end, Douglas cut a deal to
repeal the Missouri Compromise, ending the prohibition on slavery north of
the Mason-Dixon Line. Douglas touted his bill as the triumph of his "great
principle" of "popular sovereignty," his promise of a shining participatory democracy, but which was also an ill-defined demagogic expedient calculated
to appeal to Democrats from different regions who would gratefully give
him the party nomination. "Bleeding Kansas" was the exemplary demonstration of his principle. Rather than fulfilling his dream to become the per-
sonification of the Western "spirit of the age," a catchphrase he freely adapted
from European romanticism to describe Manifest Destiny, the country's and
his own, he opened the floodgates to catastrophe. Pro-slavery and antislavery forces poured into the virgin territory to claim it, the true beginning of

the Civil War. Thus Stephen A. Douglas and Jefferson Davis, each operating from their own motives, joined together to unleash the convulsion that would have the thoroughly unintended consequence of awakening Lincoln's political career. The two men most responsible for triggering the conflict were Lincoln's once and future rivals, drawing him to national prominence, and against whom he would define himself to the end of his life.

Working behind the scenes before the founding Illinois Republican convention in 1856, Lincoln stood as its only unifying figure, welding together a motley collection of abolitionists, Liberty Party men, antislavery Democrats, and Old and Conscience Whigs into the new organization, "without party history, party pride, or party idols," as he described it, but all standing against the extension of slavery into the new territories.

The triumph of the old regime that crushed revolutions in Europe decisively shaped the rise of the Republican Party in Illinois. A mass migration of German liberals cohered into a critical mass of swing voters. At first they were drawn to the Democratic Party as the most open and liberal, but after the Nebraska Act they were repelled. The Germans rallied to the antislavery cause as a New World extension of their battle against tyranny. Their presence aroused the nativist reaction mostly within Whig ranks, accelerating the Whig disintegration and the rise of another political party that was not Republican, but called the American Party, or simply the Know Nothings. Lincoln performed a delicate balancing act. While he was never publicly critical of the Know Nothings, many former Whigs he believed must be won over in a fusion with anti-Nebraska forces, privately scathing of their intolerance. In the making of the new Republican Party, he would make common cause against the Know Nothings with men like George Schneider, a revolutionary who had fled his homeland under a death warrant and was now editor of the influential German language newspaper, the *Illinois Staats-Zeitung*.

Lincoln was not present at the creation by default. His alliance with the political abolitionists of the Liberty and Free Soil parties, which he had campaigned against as a Whig, was not sudden. For two years they had courted him as the indispensable man to make the organization of the new party possible. In early 1856 he had been the only politician at a closed meeting of Republican newspaper editors preparing the groundwork for the new party. For years he had befriended various Illinois abolitionists, one element of the new coalition, though without ever adopting their abolitionism; yet his antislavery sympathy was vouched for by Herndon, his abolitionist law partner, town radical and Whig partisan, temperance crusader and occasional drunk, lately mayor of Springfield and all-around political aide. Lincoln had not anticipated the rise of the Republicans, but he had been carefully playing at these politics, developing relations with the antislavery movement in Illinois, while keeping his distance in public, until veering to assume political command. After the founding convention, he swung around the state giving more than fifty stump speeches, telling a crowd at Bloomington, two years before his "House Divided" speech, "It is my sincere belief that this government cannot last always part slave and part free. Either slavery will be abolished, or it must become equally lawful everywhere, or this Union will be dissolved."

While Lincoln reestablished himself in Springfield after returning from his brief time in Washington, contemplating his political career seemingly at its close, a writer of South Seas tales began his thinking about and writing of an epic work that would encompass an ocean of ideas, passions, and dread. It was also a book written through the debate over the Compromise of 1850 that was thought to define the new American nation for a generation to come. In one of the chapters of *Moby-Dick*, Herman Melville describes the sailor Queequeg weaving onboard the *Pequod* as Ishmael, the narrator, uses his hands as a shuttle—

it seemed as if this were the Loom of Time, and I myself were a shuttle mechanically weaving and weaving away at the Fates. Meantime, Queequeg's impulsive, indifferent sword, sometimes hitting the woof slantingly, or crookedly, or strongly or weakly, as the case might be; and by this difference in the concluding blow producing a corresponding contrast in the final aspect of the completed fabric; this savage's sword, thought I, which thus finally shapes and fashions both warp and woof; this easy indifferent sword must be chance—aye, chance, free-will, and necessity—nowise incompatible—all interweavingly working together. The straight warp of necessity, not to be swerved from its ultimate course—its every alternating vibration, indeed, only tending to that; free-will still free to ply her shuttle between given threads; and chance, though restrained in its play within the right lines of necessity, and sideways in its motions directed by free-will, though thus prescribed to by both, chance by turns rules either, and has the last featuring blow at events.

Melville's tactile description of destiny as practical work on the whaling ship was more closely a portrayal of the political life than Procrustean beds of predetermined scales of ideological evolution or stages of self-actualizing psychology. Lincoln understood himself as living a political life in history as it unfolded.

"Who ain't a slave?" asked Ishmael.

On June 26, 1857, Lincoln spoke in Springfield against the *Dred Scott* decision of the Supreme Court declaring that blacks had "no rights which the white man was bound to respect" and that slavery could not be prohibited in any territory. For Lincoln this ruling traduced the touchstone of his politics, the Declaration of Independence. "In those days, our Declaration of Independence was held sacred by all, and thought to include all; but now, to aid in making the bondage of the negro universal and eternal, it is assailed, and sneered at, and construed, and hawked at, and torn, till, if its framers could rise from their graves, they could not at all recognize it." Then, he conjured terrifying images of a slave with the world conspiring against him, his bondage fastened through a hundred keys by a hundred men.

> All the powers of earth seem rapidly combining against him. Mammon is after him; ambition follows, and philosophy follows, and the Theology of the day is fast joining the cry. They have him in his prison house; they have searched his person, and left no prying instrument with him. One after another they have closed the heavy iron doors upon him, and now they have him, as it were, bolted in with a lock of a hundred keys, which can never be unlocked without the concurrence of every key; the keys in the hands of a hundred different men, and they scattered to a hundred different and distant places; and they stand musing as to what invention, in all the dominions of mind and matter, can be produced to make the impossibility of his escape more complete than it is.

From what source did Lincoln derive his fearful scene of a prisoner held behind bars locked with a hundred keys in the possession of a hundred keepers? Was this inspired by a horror tale of Edgar Allan Poe? Who were these faceless "scattered" oppressors bound to each other as they "stand musing" in "a hundred different and distant" places how to devise the most complex oppression? Were there keys? What was the crime? Who was the criminal?

"Such is the crime which you are to judge," declared Senator Charles Sumner of Massachusetts, rising to deliver his speech arraigning the "slave power" for "The Crime Against Kansas" on May 19, 1856. "But the criminal also must be dragged into day, that you may see and measure the power by which all this wrong is sustained. From no common source could it proceed. In its perpetration was needed a spirit of vaulting ambition which would hesitate at nothing; a hardihood of purpose which was insensible to the judgment of mankind; a madness for slavery which would disregard the Constitution, the laws, and all the great examples of our history; also a consciousness of power such as comes from the habit of power."

Then Sumner described this power with an image—"a combination of energies found only in a hundred arms directed by a hundred eyes." And through these "hundred arms directed by a hundred eyes" the power exercised

a control of public opinion through venal pens and a prostituted Press; an ability to subsidize crowds in every vocation of life—the politician with his local importance, the lawyer with his subtle tongue, and even the authority of the judge on the bench; and a familiar use of men in places high and low, so that none, from the president to the lowest border postmaster, should decline to be its tool; all these things and more were needed, and they were found in the slave power of our Republic. There, sir, stands the criminal, all unmasked before you—heartless, grasping, and tyrannical—with an audacity beyond that of Verres, a subtlety beyond that of Machiavelli, a meanness beyond that of Bacon, and an ability beyond that of Hastings. Justice to Kansas can be secured only by the prostration of this influence; for this the power behind—greater than any president—which succors and sustains the crime. Nay, the proceedings I now arraign derive their fearful consequences only from this connection.

Two days later, as Sumner sat writing in his seat, Congressman Preston Brooks of South Carolina, feeling honor bound to punish Sumner's insulting remarks about his older cousin, Senator Andrew Butler, entered the chamber and beat Sumner over the head relentlessly with his gold-handled cane, the proper whipping for an inferior, even a slave, until he was left lying in a pool of blood running across the Senate floor. Bleeding Kansas had become bleeding Sumner. Brooks was hailed throughout the South as an avenger; Sumner was transfigured into a martyr. Eight days after Sumner was bludgeoned nearly to death, Lincoln stood on the stage at Bloomington to found the Illinois Republican Party.

Lincoln transformed Sumner's metaphor of the slave power from "a hundred arms directed by a hundred eyes" to a hundred keys controlled by a hundred men. He kept the number and its drumbeat repetition, but changed more than the objects, more than arms to keys and eyes to men. He completely shifted the point of view. Instead of the puritan's condemnation of the morally debased slaveholder, the vantage of the pulpit, he assumed the vision of the slave himself.

"Who ain't a slave?"

In Lincoln's description of the cage of hopelessness he identified with the captive who could not find the key to his freedom. But Lincoln had discovered a hundred keys to his own escape. That was why he understood the captivity and why he would become a new political man. Self-educated and self-emancipated, he would, shortly after creating the Illinois Republican Party, stand before a crowd to issue a personal proclamation: "I used to be a slave."

ACKNOWLEDGMENTS

———•◦•———

Anyone approaching the daunting prospect of saying something new about Abraham Lincoln must be endlessly indebted to generations of historians, scholars, and journalists, beginning with his law partner, William Henry Herndon, who created the first oral history of a president. This book inevitably stands on the tower of work that has since accumulated. I am particularly thankful to contemporary historians who have generously shared their knowledge to guide me through the winding pathways of Lincoln's life and thought. Above all, I am indebted to Sean Wilentz, of Princeton University, for his advice, criticism, and erudition, but especially for his warm friendship of many decades. Stephen Holmes, of the New York University Law School, offered his discernment and enthusiasm through evenings of conversation at his home in the Tuscan hills and apartment in New York City. Hillel Schwartz, my college roommate and an historian who can see beyond the noise of isolated events to envision millennia, contributed helpful references, good humor, and the overarching title for this multivolume work. John Ritch, accomplished diplomat and true blue friend for decades, applied his creative mind and eagle eye to the manuscript to offer thoughtful ideas. My friend Ben Gerson provided acutely perceptive observations. Joan Cashin, of Ohio State University, offered crucial insight that informed my understanding of Mary Todd and the society of women of the nineteenth century. Lincoln scholars Harold Holzer, of the Metropolitan Museum, Michael W. Burlingame, of the University of Illinois, Matthew Pinsker, of Dickinson College, and Wayne C. Temple, of the Illinois State Archives, gave me advice on various sources and material. Terry Alford, of the Northern Virginia Community College, provided helpful insights and reassurance.

Two men of letters who lent me support through the years, but died before this book was published, encouraged me in this work. I felt fortunate to have had discussions on Lincoln and political life generally with Michael Janeway, who was the editor of the *Boston Globe*, dean of the Medill School of Journalism at Northwestern, an historian of the age of Franklin D. Roosevelt, and had a rare combination of cogency, wit, and literary grace. I was grateful to have been able to read aloud a chapter of the work-in-progress to Sheldon Hackney, who was president of the University of Pennsylvania, chairman of the National Endowment for the Humanities, and a distinguished historian and civil rights advocate, on the porch of his Vineyard Haven, Massachusetts, home, on a temperate summer day just weeks before his death. I deeply valued Michael's and Sheldon's friendship, confidence, and judgment.

I had written much of the draft of this work before sharing it. Harold Evans, the finest British newspaper editor of his generation and a brilliant book editor, cajoled me with the inimitable twinkle in his eye to show him a piece of the manuscript. Tina Brown, my former editor at *The New Yorker*, persuaded me to write an article on Lincoln as politician for *Newsweek*, which she was then editing. Alice Mayhew, who has edited many of the most important books on Lincoln, wrote me a note expressing interest. Harry suggested I contact Jonathan Karp, the president of Simon & Schuster, who had worked closely with him at Random House and whose professional judgment he trusted. I sent Jonathan and Alice a good part of the entire manuscript, and the short story is that they agreed to publish it in several volumes. I am indebted to Harry and Tina for sending me their way and for their friendship. I feel extraordinarily lucky to be working with Alice, whose editorial wisdom and understanding of Lincoln is matchless.

I am grateful to Robert Barnett for establishing my relationship with Simon & Schuster adroitly. He is more than a superb lawyer, but a man of parts, and who in any earlier era would have played Stephen A. Douglas to prepare Lincoln for debates.

At Simon & Schuster, I appreciated the meticulous editorial help of Stuart Roberts, Alice's assistant editor. I am indebted to Fred Chase for the diligence and care of his copy editing.

Andrew Edwards, an historian working on his doctoral dissertation at Princeton, was a godsend. His organization of my endnotes and bibliography was nothing less than miraculous.

I am grateful to librarians at the Chicago Historical Society, the Moorland-Spingarn Research Center at Howard University, and the Library of Congress for assistance they provided in my research.

While I researched and wrote in between rambling walks in Rock Creek Park in the company of my constant companion, Pepper the dog, who grew a flowing white mane over the years, my patient wife, Jackie, went out and got herself elected to public office—again and again and again—as an Advisory Neighborhood Commissioner in the District of Columbia. She is the one in the family who most effectively practices Lincoln's craft. There are innumerable reasons why I am grateful to and admire her, but her commitment over decades to public service, bettering our community and skill as an urban politician, is inspiring. We both learn from our sons, Max and Paul, who have become remarkable journalists.

Any errors that may appear in this book are entirely my responsibility and cannot be attributed to anyone else. I alone performed the research, which was my pleasure.

This book is dedicated to my mother, Claire Stone Blumenthal Miller. After the death of my beloved father, Hymen, she decided in her eighties to learn Hebrew and have the Bat Mitzvah she never had. Then she married a wonderful, kind, and intelligent man, Bernard Miller. My sister, Marcia, and I are delighted not only to have him as a stepfather but also to have our stepbrother, Anthony Miller, and his family as part of ours. My mother is the most life-affirming person I know.

I would be remiss not to thank here Sam Wiley, first cousin of my grandmother Minnie Stone, who brought me as a boy on a tour of Springfield, beginning my lifelong interest in Abraham Lincoln.

Washington, D.C.
April 15, 2015
The 150th anniversary of the death of Lincoln

NOTES

ABBREVIATIONS

HI—Douglas L. Wilson, Rodney O. Davis, Terry Wilson, William Henry Herndon, and Jesse William Weik, eds., *Herndon's Informants: Letters, Interviews, and Statements About Abraham Lincoln* (Urbana: University of Illinois Press, 1998).

CW—Roy P. Basler, ed., *The Collected Works of Abraham Lincoln* (New Brunswick, N.J.: Rutgers University Press, 1953).

PROLOGUE: THE SLAVE

2 *Emerging from the Whig crack-up:* Emanuel Hertz, *The Hidden Lincoln: From the Letters and Papers of William H. Herndon* (New York: Blue Ribbon Books, 1940), 89–90.

3 *It was at one of those campaign events:* Allen C. Guelzo, *Abraham Lincoln: Redeemer President* (Grand Rapids, Mich.: Wm. B. Eerdmans, 2003), 121.

3 *Lincoln's wry humor drove home his point:* Hertz, *Hidden Lincoln,* 88; CW, 2:268.

4 *Even more startling than Lincoln's self-description:* Guelzo, *Abraham Lincoln,* 121.

5 *Despite his standing for years among the Illinois Whigs:* Samuel Willard, "Personal Reminiscences of Life in Illinois—1830 to 1850," in *Transactions of the Illinois State Historical Society* (Springfield: Illinois State Historical Library, 1906), 11:73–87.

6 *One of Lincoln's fellow boarding house mates:* Nathan Sargent, *Public Men and Events in the United States from the Commencement of Mr. Monroe's Administration in 1817 to the Close of Mr. Fillmore's Administration in 1853* (Philadelphia: J. B. Lippincott, 1875), 2:331.

6 *Lincoln's marriage was indispensable to his rise:* Douglas L. Wilson, "William H. Herndon and Mary Todd Lincoln," *Journal of the Abraham Lincoln Association* 22, no. 2 (Summer 2001).

6 *Lincoln had a deep private life about which he was reserved:* Albert J. Beveridge, *Abraham Lincoln* (New York: Houghton Mifflin, 1928), 1:538; Horace Porter, *Campaigning with Grant* (New York: Century, 1907), 279.

7 *When he stepped onto the national stage in 1860:* Michael Burlingame, *Abraham Lincoln: A Life* (Baltimore: Johns Hopkins University Press, 2008), 1:672; Robert S. Harper, *Lincoln and the Press* (New York: McGraw Hill, 1951), 322; Sarah Forbes Hughes, ed., *Letters and Recollections of John Murray Forbes* (New York:

Houghton Mifflin, 1900), 2:105; Charles A. Dana, *Recollections of the Civil War* (New York: D. Appleton, 1898), 174, 180–1.

7 *Before the eyes of those who dismissed him:* Hertz, *Hidden Lincoln*, 90.

8 *Politics was not for Lincoln a grudging necessity:* J. G. Randall, *Lincoln the President* (New York: Dodd, Mead, 1945), 1:15; Mark E. Neely, Jr., "The Lincoln Theme Since Randall's Call: The Promises and Perils of Professionalism," *Journal of the Abraham Lincoln Association* 1 (1979).

8 *The mythology of Lincoln as too noble for politics:* Hertz, *Hidden Lincoln*, 91.

10 *Lincoln's words were among his greatest weapons:* CW, 2:126.

11 *Lincoln's political mind and sinuous methods:* Richard Hofstadter, *The American Political Tradition* (New York: Knopf, 1948), 169, 171; David Herbert Donald, *Lincoln* (New York: Simon & Schuster, 1995), 14–15.

13 *Lincoln surrounded himself throughout his career with journalists:* Harold Holzer, *Lincoln and the Power of the Press* (New York: Simon & Schuster, 2014), 188–93, 531–7.

15 *Throughout the war, Copperheads:* CW, 7:301–2.

16 *Just as he would use Aesopian stories:* Edward L. Widmer, *Martin Van Buren* (New York: Macmillan, 2005), 146; Wayne Whipple, *The Story-Life of Lincoln* (Philadelphia: John C. Winston, 1908), 482–3.

17 *Lincoln's definition of freedom:* CW, 2:532, 4:438; Eric Foner, *Free Soil, Free Labor, Free Men: The Ideology of the Republican Party Before the Civil War* (New York: Oxford University Press, 1995).

19 *Lincoln would decide finally on a policy:* CW, 8:361.

20 *In 1860, John Locke Scripps:* Burlingame, *Abraham Lincoln*, 1:15–16.

CHAPTER ONE: THE READER

21 *Abraham Lincoln was of the seventh generation:* Ida Minerva Tarbell, *The Early Life of Abraham Lincoln* (New York: S. S. McClure, 1896), 1–2; Caleb Arnold Wall, *The Historic Boston Tea Party of December 16, 1773: Its Men and Objects* (Worcester, Mass.: F. S. Blanchard, 1896), 53; Esther Forbes, *Paul Revere and the World He Lived In* (New York: Houghton Mifflin, 1942); Douglas Harper, "Emancipation in Massachusetts," "Slavery in the North," http://slavenorth.com/massemancip.htm.

22 *John Lincoln, a great-grandson of Samuel:* James Henry Lea and John Robert Hutchinson, *The Ancestry of Abraham Lincoln* (New York: Houghton Mifflin, 1909), 104, 82–4.

22 *Thomas's two older brothers:* Richard Lawrence Miller, *Lincoln and His World: The Early Years, Birth to Illinois Legislature* (Mechanicsburg, Penn.: Stackpole, 2006), 7; Lea and Hutchinson, *Ancestry of Abraham Lincoln,* 124, 126.

22 *Apprenticed at the carpenter's shop:* Louis A. Warren, *Lincoln's Youth: Indiana Years, 1816–1830* (Indianapolis: Indiana Historical Society, 1991), 6–7; Caroline Hanks

Hitchcock, *Nancy Hanks: The Story of Abraham Lincoln's Mother* (New York: Doubleday & McClure, 1899), 24–5.

23 *Stories of Nancy's illegitimacy:* Burlingame, *Abraham Lincoln*, 1:12–3.

23 *"Billy, I'll tell you something":* Douglas L. Wilson, *Honor's Voice: The Transformation of Abraham Lincoln* (New York: Knopf, 1998), 13.

23 *Thomas Lincoln and Nancy Hanks:* Tarbell, *Early Life*, 234.

24 *At the mill he was:* Miller, *Early Years*, 6; Louis A. Warren, *The Slavery Atmosphere of Lincoln's Youth* (Fort Wayne, Ind.: Lincolniana Publishers, 1933).

24 *The year Thomas helped:* John H. Spencer, *A History of Kentucky Baptists: From 1769 to 1885* (Cincinnati: J. R. Baumes, 1885), 162–3.

24 *In 1807, eleven "Emancipationist" ministers:* Tarbell, *Early Life*, 74; William Dudley Nowlin, *Kentucky Baptist History, 1770–1922* (Louisville: Baptist Book Concern, 1922), 71–7.

25 *The Lincolns' first child, Sarah:* Edgar De Witt Jones, *Lincoln and the Preachers* (New York: Harper & Brothers, 1948), 17.

25 *On January 1, 1815, a suit:* William E. Barton, *The Paternity of Abraham Lincoln* (New York: George H. Doran Company, 1920), 263; Warren, *Lincoln's Youth*, 12–13; Miller, *Early Years*, 29.

25 *Thomas Lincoln had to hack:* Warren, *Lincoln's Youth*, 51.

26 *About forty families:* Miller, *Early Years*, 42; Warren, *Lincoln's Youth*, 55–6; Eleanor Atkinson, *The Boyhood of Lincoln* (New York: McClure, 1908), 17.

26 *Eleven-year-old Sarah was now in charge:* Atkinson, *Boyhood,* 19; Burlingame, *Abraham Lincoln*, 1:27–28; HI, 41, 56.

27 *Sarah Bush Lincoln brought civility:* Atkinson, *Boyhood,* 20–3.

27 *The pastor of the church, Thomas Downs:* Warren, *Lincoln's Youth*, 114–5, 119, 121–2; John F. Cady, "The Religious Environment of Lincoln's Youth," *Indiana Magazine of History* 37 (March–December 1941); Jacob Piatt Dunn, *Indiana* (New York: Houghton Mifflin, 1888), 429.

28 *Sarah Bush Lincoln could not help noticing:* Wilson, *Honor's Voice*, 55–7; Ronald White, *A. Lincoln: A Biography* (New York: Random House, 2010), 30; Atkinson, *Boyhood*, 17, 23.

28 *Lincoln read whatever books:* Burlingame, *Abraham Lincoln*, 1:36.

28 *"I induced my husband to":* Tarbell, *Early Life*, 72.

29 *Most people thought of reading as indolence:* HI, 109; Wilson, *Honor's Voice*, 60–1.

29 *Thomas Lincoln was not naturally:* HI, 37, 110, 39; Wilson, *Honor's Voice*, 57; HI, 176.

29 *Life had been starkly unfair to:* HI, 126, 99, 133.

30 *"I never could tell whether":* HI, 176.

31 *In his mid-teens, the hireling Lincoln:* HI, 126–7, 473.

31 *Lincoln borrowed Weems's Washington:* HI, 126; Robert Bray, *Reading with Lincoln* (Carbondale: Southern Illinois University Press, 2010), 14–5.

32 *Lincoln's sister, Sarah, married:* Miller, *Early Years,* 74–5; Burlingame, *Abraham Lincoln*, 1:45; Henry Clay Whitney, *Life of Lincoln* (New York: Baker & Taylor, 1908), 1:56.

32 *"Tom owned Abe's time till":* Atkinson, *Boyhood*, 39.

32 *In 1827, the two teenagers:* Whitney, *Life of Lincoln*, 1:56; Burlingame, *Abraham Lincoln*, 1:44; Jesse W. Weik, *The Real Lincoln* (New York: Houghton Mifflin, 1922), 25–6.

33 *Just over the horizon:* Alice Felt Tyler, *Freedom's Ferment: Phases of American Social History from the Colonial Period to the Outbreak of the Civil War* (New York: Harper Torchbooks, 1962), 196–206; Margaret Bayard Smith, *The First Forty Years of Washington Society* (New York: Scribner, 1906), 196.

33 *New Harmony featured a school:* Frank Podmore, *Robert Owen* (London: Hutchinson, 1906), 1:312; Atkinson, *Boyhood,* 30–1.

34 *Abe was tethered to his father:* Wilson, *Honor's Voice*, 157.

34 *Lincoln had attended:* J. Edward Murr, "Lincoln in Indiana (Concluded)," *Indiana Magazine of History* 14 (1918), 153; Jonathan Todd Hobson, *Footprints of Abraham Lincoln* (Dayton: Otterbein Press, 1909), 30.

34 *After studying the* Revised Statutes*:* HI, 102.

34 *While working as a ferryman:* Reinhold H. Luthin, *The Real Abraham Lincoln* (New York: Prentice Hall, 1960), 12.

35 *Lincoln also wandered to Boonville:* HI, 115.

35 *Lincoln on his own composed articles:* HI, 123–4; William Henry Herndon and Jesse William Weik, *Herndon's Lincoln: The True Story of a Great Life* (New York: Belford, Clarke, 1889), 1:61.

36 *Jones's store became:* Beveridge, *Abraham Lincoln*, 1:86; Whitney, *Life of Lincoln*, 1:48.

36 *"Lincoln would frequently":* HI, 58, 114–5.

36 *The emergence:* Paul Starr, *The Creation of the Media: Political Origins of Modern Communications* (New York: Basic Books, 2004), 86–7.

37 *"Colonel Jones was Lincoln's":* HI, 127, 132.

37 *William Grimshaw's* History*:* Burlingame, *Abraham Lincoln*, 1:45; William Grimshaw, *History of the United States* (Philadelphia: Benjamin Warne, 1821), 270–1; Don C. Seitz, *Lincoln the Politician* (New York: Coward-McCann, 1931), 144; "Grimshaw, Jackson," "The Law Practice of Abraham Lincoln," http://www.law practiceofabrahamlincoln.org/reference/html%20files%20for%20biographies/Bio_1072.html.

38 *Thomas Lincoln, fleeing the slave system:* Jacob Piatt Dunn, *Indiana: A Redemption from Slavery* (New York: Houghton Mifflin, 1888), 322, 348–9; Gordon S. Wood, *Empire of Liberty: A History of the Early Republic, 1789–1815* (New York: Oxford University Press, 2009), 362–3.

38 *Harrison, the son of a wealthy Virginia planter:* Dunn, *Indiana*, 372–3; George R.

Wilson, "General Washington Johnston," *Indiana Magazine of History* 20, no. 2 (June 1924): 123–53.

39 *On the defensive:* Dunn, *Indiana*, 384, 389, 397–8.

39 *Thomas Lincoln undoubtedly voted for Jennings:* Logan Esarey, *A History of Indiana* (Dayton: Dayton Historical Publishing, 1918), 1:1102–3; "Terre Haute Register Mailing List," *Indiana Magazine of History* 22 (1926): 220; Dunn, *Indiana*, 435–6; Sandra Boyd Williams, "The Indiana Supreme Court and the Struggle Against Slavery," *Indiana Law Review* 30, no. 305 (1997): 306.

40 *Even as the slavery issue was closed:* Jacob Piatt Dunn, *Indiana and Indianans* (New York: American Historical Society, 1919), 352.

40 *Edward Coles was the son:* Thomas Ford, *A History of Illinois* (Chicago: S. C. Griggs, 1854), 50–1; Julian P. Boyd, ed., *Papers of Thomas Jefferson* (Princeton: Princeton University Press, 1950), 1:426; Elihu B. Washburne, *Sketch of Edward Coles: Second Governor of Illinois, and of the Slavery Struggle of 1823–4* (Chicago: Jansen, McClurg, 1882), 26.

41 *Coles ran for governor:* Washburne, *Sketch of Edward Coles,* 65, 208–9; John Reynolds, *My Own Times* (Belleville, Ind.: B. H. Perryman & H. L. Davison, 1855), 241; Ford, *History of Illinois*, 51–3.

42 *Coles, however, was not intimidated:* Washburne, *Sketch of Edward Coles,* 233–5; Ford, *History of Illinois*, 54.

42 *Antislavery Baptist preachers were at the heart of the movement:* Reynolds, *My Own Times*, 242–3; Joseph B. Lemen, "The Jefferson-Lemen Antislavery Pact," *Transactions of the Illinois State Historical Society* 13 (1908): 74–84; Willard C. MacNaul, *The Jefferson-Lemen Compact* (Chicago: University of Chicago Press, 1915), 8–9; James A. Edstrom, "'A Mighty Contest,' The Jefferson-Lemen Compact Reevaluated," *Journal of the Illinois State Historical Society* 97, no. 3 (2004): 194.

43 *Almost at the moment:* Auguste Levasseur, *Lafayette in America in 1824 and 1825: or, Journal of a Voyage to the United States* (Philadelphia: Carey & Lea, 1829), 2: 148.

44 *One night, on the Sugar Coast of Louisiana:* HI, 131; Miller, *Early Years*, 82; Warren, *Lincoln's Youth*, 184.

44 *New Orleans was the third largest:* Paul F. Lachance, "The Foreign French," in Arnold Richard Hirsch and Joseph Logsdon, eds., *Creole New Orleans: Race and Americanization* (Baton Rouge: Louisiana State University Press, 1992), 117–9; Solomon Northup, *Twelve Years a Slave* (Buffalo: Derby, Orton & Mulligan, 1853), 82; Burlingame, *Abraham Lincoln*, 1:44; Warren, *Lincoln's Youth*, 185; Warren, *Slavery Atmosphere of Lincoln's Youth*; J. Edward Murr, "Lincoln in Indiana (Continued)," *Indiana Magazine of History* 14, (1918): 20.

45 *Selling their cargo:* HI, 124.

45 *While Lincoln was hammering together:* Warren, *Lincoln's Youth*, 191–2; HI, 103, 105.

46 *"I think when the Lincolns"*: HI, 355, 374, 457.

   Lincoln's mentors: Herndon and Weik, *Herndon's Lincoln*, 1:57; Beveridge, *Abraham Lincoln,* 1:99, 97.

47 *Upon his return to Little Pigeon Creek:* Theodore D. Jervey, *Robert Y. Hayne and His Times* (New York: Macmillan, 1909), 132, 202–3, 251; Merrill D. Peterson, *The Great Triumvirate: Webster, Clay, and Calhoun* (New York: Oxford University Press, 1987), 175; Charles M. Wiltse, *John C. Calhoun: Nullifier, 1829–1839* (Indianapolis: Bobbs Merrill, 1949), 59–60.

47 *Webster's "Second Reply to Hayne"*: Daniel Walker Howe, *What Hath God Wrought: The Transformation of America, 1815–1848* (New York: Oxford University Press, 2007), 368–72; Donald, *Lincoln*, 270.

48 *In the fall of 1829:* Warren, *Lincoln's Youth*, 208; Atkinson, *Boyhood*, 41–2.

48 *The Lincolns settled outside Decatur:* Herndon and Weik, *Herndon's Lincoln*, 1:69, 71; Jones, *Lincoln and the Preachers*, 50; Miller, *Early Years*, 112; Wilson, *Honor's Voice*, 144-5.

49 *At yet another political meeting:* HI, 456; "James Q. Howard, May 1860 (Biographical notes)," Abraham Lincoln Papers, Library of Congress, http://memory.loc.gov /cgi-bin/query/r?ammem/mal:@field%28DOCID+@lit%28d0297401%29%29.

49 *Escaping the milk sickness:* Whitney, *Life of Lincoln*, 1:67.

49 *But John Hanks approached Abe:* HI, 73, 13; "The Horse-Tamers in Court; Mr. Offutt's Suit Against Mr. Rarey," *New York Times,* February 5, 1861; Wilson, *Honor's Voice*, 336.

50 *Offutt had plied the Mississippi:* HI, 373–4, 429.

50 *The boat's voyage almost ended in disaster:* HI, 457; Robert Henry Browne, *Abraham Lincoln and the Men of His Times* (Cincinnati: Jennings & Pye, 1901), 1:139–40.

51 *Herndon later vaguely*: Isaac N. Arnold, *The Life of Abraham Lincoln* (Chicago: Jansen, McClurg, 1885), 31.

51 *When Abe arrived home in June:* Burlingame, *Abraham Lincoln*, 1:50–1, 360; Richard Lawrence Miller, *Lincoln and His World: The Rise of National Prominence, 1843–1853* (Jefferson, N.C.: McFarland, 2011), 3:287–8.

51 *"Lincoln can do anything"*: Burlingame, *Abraham Lincoln*, 1:57; Herndon and Weik, *Herndon's Lincoln*, 1:78–9.

CHAPTER TWO: THE AGE OF REASON

53 *"Can you write?"*: Tarbell, *Early Life,* 118; Miller, *Early Years*, 113; HI, 8, 69.

54 *New Salem was a market town:* Thomas P. Reep, *Abe Lincoln and the Frontier Folk of New Salem* (Middletown, Conn.: Southfarm Press, 2002), 24; "History of the John Miller Camron Family," Ancestry.com, last modified, August 29, 2003, http://www.electricscotland.com/history/world/bios/camron_john.htm; Charles Maltby, *The Life and Services of Abraham Lincoln* (Stockton, Calif.: Daily Independent Steam Power Print, 1884), 27.

54 *"There lived at this time in"*: Benjamin Platt Thomas, *Lincoln's New Salem* (Carbondale: Southern Illinois University Press, 1973), 65; Whitney, *Life of Lincoln*, 5:1, 82; "James Q. Howard, May 1860 (Biographical notes)."

55 *In the winter of 1832:* HI, 384, 365, 539.

55 *One subject of debate*: "James Q. Howard, May 1860 (Biographical notes)"; Maltby, *Life and Services of Abraham Lincoln*, 32–3.

56 *The New Salem club:* "James Q. Howard, May 1860 (Biographical notes)"; Wilson, *Honor's Voice*, 70–1; Reep, *Abe Lincoln and the Frontier Folk of New Salem,* 52; HI, 6, 385; Miller, *Early Years*, 127.

56 *Lincoln launched his political:* Miller, *Early Years*, 143.

57 *Just at that moment a heroic effort:* John Carroll Power and Sarah A. Power, *History of the Early Settlers of Sangamon County* (Springfield, Ill.: Edwin A. Wilson, 1876), 42–3; T. G. Onstot, *Pioneers of Menard and Mason Counties* (Forest City, Ill.: T.G. Onstot, 1902), 48; Beveridge, *Abraham Lincoln*, 1:119; "James Q. Howard, May 1860 (Biographical notes),"1:87; William H. Townsend, *Lincoln the Litigant* (New York: Houghton Mifflin, 1925), 49–51.

57 *About the time of Lincoln's return:* Whitney, *Life of Lincoln,* 1:86.

58 *The first order of business:* "James Q. Howard, May 1860 (Biographical notes)"; Donald, *Lincoln*, 45; Whitney, *Life of Lincoln,* 1:96.

58 *Lincoln saw no combat:* Noah Brooks, "Personal Reminiscences of Lincoln," *Scribner's Monthly* 15 (1878): 563.

58 *Late in the war:* "James Q. Howard, May 1860 (Biographical notes)."

59 *William Cullen Bryant:* Parke Godwin, ed., *Prose Writings of William Cullen Bryant* (New York: D. Appleton, 1884), 20.

59 *John Dixon, the operator:* Isaac N. Arnold, "Isaac N. Arnold's Address," in *Chicago Historical Society, November 19, 1868* (Chicago: Fergus Printing, 1877), 15–6, 19; Beveridge, *Abraham Lincoln,* 1:123; *History of Sangamon County* (Chicago: Inter-State Publishing Company, 1881), 580.

59 *After three months in the militia:* Miller, *Early Years*, 182–3; Herndon and Weik, *Herndon's Lincoln*, 1:103–4.

60 *The* Sangamo Journal *mistakenly:* Miller, *Early Years*, 181–2; "James Q. Howard, May 1860 (Biographical notes)."

60 *Just days earlier:* Rufus Rockwell Wilson, *Lincoln Among His Friends: A Sheaf of Intimate Memories* (Caldwell, Idaho: Caxton Printers, 1942), 63.

61 *Voters could cast their ballots:* Miller, *Early Years*, 188.

61 *In distant Washington:* William W. Freehling, *Prelude to Civil War: The Nullification Crisis in South Carolina, 1816–1836* (New York: Oxford University Press, 1992), 1–3; Reynolds, *My Own Times*, 423.

61 *In New Salem:* Onstot, *Pioneers of Menard and Mason Counties*, 81–3.

62 *Lincoln was much happier:* Beveridge, *Abraham Lincoln,* 1:141; "James Q. Howard, May 1860 (Biographical notes)"; Wilson, *Honor's Voice*, 62; HI, 10.

62 *Lincoln also was appointed:* Miller, *Early Years*, 180, 215.

62 *Mentor Graham, the schoolteacher:* HI, 10.

63 *Lincoln's assistants in surveying:* HI, 528, 374; Wilson, *Honor's Voice*, 73–4.

64 *Milton Hay remembered:* Wilson, *Honor's Voice*, 74; HI, 577.

64 *Burns, the bard of the Scottish Enlightenment:* Alexander Broadie, *The Scottish Enlightenment Reader* (Edinburgh: Canongate Books, 2010), 8.

64 *In the period between the elections:* Herndon and Weik, *Herndon's Lincoln*, 3:439.

64 *Paine, the English radical:* Harvey J. Kaye, *Thomas Paine and the Promise of America* (New York: Hill & Wang, 2006), 36; Thomas Paine, *The Age of Reason* (New York: G. N. Devries, 1827), 6, 179; Charles Francis Adams, ed., *The Works of John Adams* (Boston: Little & Brown, 1841), 3:421.

65 *Volney is a forgotten philosophe:* Jack Fruchtman, Jr., *Thomas Paine: Apostle of Freedom* (New York: Four Walls Eight Windows, 1996), 372; James Grant Wilson and John Fiske, eds., *Appleton's Cyclopaedia of American Biography* (New York: D. Appleton, 1889), 306; Edward Derbyshire Seeber, *Antislavery Opinion in France During the Second Half of the Eighteenth Century* (North Stratford, N.H.: Ayer Publishing, 1937), 159–60; William Spohn Baker, *Washington After the Revolution: 1784–1799* (Philadelphia: J. B. Lippincott, 1897), 325; John P. Foley, ed., *The Jeffersonian Cyclopedia: A Comprehensive Collection of the Views of Thomas Jefferson* (New York: Funk & Wagnalls, 1900), 915; Edwin Scott Gaustad, *Sworn on the Altar of God: A Religious Biography of Thomas Jefferson* (Grand Rapids, Mich.: Wm. B. Eerdmans, 1996), 35; Peter Linebaugh and Marcus Rediker, *The Many-Headed Hydra: Sailors, Slaves, Commoners, and the Hidden History of the Revolutionary Atlantic* (Boston: Beacon, 2001), 342; Richard Buel, *Joel Barlow: American Citizen in a Revolutionary World* (Baltimore: Johns Hopkins University Press, 2011), 259.

66 *Volney had lived for years:* Constantine de Volney, *The Ruins; or, A Survey of the Revolutions of Empires*, ed. Josiah P. Mendum (Boston: The Office of the Boston Investigator, 1869), 170.

66 *In* The Ruins, *Volney mounted an assault:* Ibid., 26–7.

66 *"Volney and Paine":* Ward Hill Lamon, *The Life of Abraham Lincoln* (Boston: James R. Osgood, 1872), 493; John Eleazer Remsburg, *Abraham Lincoln: Was He a Christian?* (New York: Truth Seeker, 1893), 220–1; Herndon and Weik, *Herndon's Lincoln*, 3:439.

67 *Inspired by Paine and Volney:* Lamon, *Life of Abraham Lincoln*, 493–4.

67 *The book burning did not brand him:* Ibid., 489.

67 *Lincoln regarded the primitive evangelical churches:* Burlingame, *Abraham Lincoln*, 1:84.

68 *Jesse Fell, an Illinois friend:* Lamon, *Life of Abraham Lincoln*, 491; Miller, *Early Years*, 259.

68 *There is no record:* Onstot, *Pioneers of Menard and Mason Counties*, 46–8.

68 *Lincoln's study of the law:* HI, 171, 173, 170.

69 *Green recruited Lincoln:* Miller, *Early Years*, 226–41.

69 *Lincoln's duties as surveyor:* HI, 170, 431; Miller, *Early Years*, 303.

69 *By the spring of 1834:* HI, 432, 450.

70 *Lincoln had the approval of the Whigs:* Interview with Stephen T. Logan, July 6, 1875, Abraham Lincoln Papers, Library of Congress.

70 *Before the gambit went into effect:* Miller, *Early Years*, 261.

70 *With his first election:* HI, 8; William Makepeace Thayer, *The Pioneer Boy: And How He Became President, The Story of the Life of Abraham Lincoln* (London: Hodder & Stoughton, 1882), 108; George D. Prentice, *Biography of Henry Clay* (Hartford: S. Hanmer, Jr., and J. J. Phelps, 1831).

71 *I inherited infancy:* Robert V. Remini, *Henry Clay: Statesman for the Union* (New York: Norton, 1991), 1–14, 27, 19–20.

71 *Lincoln's early career closely followed:* Herndon and Weik, *Herndon's Lincoln*, 2:268; Calvin Colton, ed., *The Life, Correspondence, and Speeches of Henry Clay* (New York: A. S. Barnes, 1857), 5:386–7.

72 *In December 1834, Lincoln prepared:* HI, 254; Burlingame, *Abraham Lincoln,* 1:92; Wilson, *Honor's Voice*, 152.

CHAPTER THREE: THE SLASHER

73 *Lincoln, the political apprentice:* Richard Lawrence Miller, *Lincoln and His World: Prairie Politician, 1834–1842* (Mechanicsburg, Penn.: Stackpole, 2008), 5; HI, 481–2; Ford, *History of Illinois*, 89.

73 *Lincoln did not deliver a single speech:* Usher F. Linder, *Reminiscences of the Early Bench and Bar of Illinois* (Chicago: Chicago Legal News, 1879), 37.

74 *Lincoln arrived duded up:* Beveridge, *Abraham Lincoln,* 1:160–1; James Stuart, *Three Years in North America* (Edinburgh: R. Cadell, 1833), 2:408.

74 *Vandalia's nightlife mainly:* Miller, *Lincoln and His World*, 5; Ford, *History of Illinois*, 88.

74 *Illinois was a Northern state:* "Act of Incorporation for the City of Chicago 1837," *Encyclopedia of Chicago,* http://encyclopedia.chicagohistory.org/pages/11480.html.

75 *The first statehouse at Vandalia:* "Vandalia, Illinois History," City of Vandalia, Illinois, http://www.vandaliaillinois.com/history.html.

75 *Vandalia attempted a veneer:* Whitney, *Life of Lincoln*, 1:127.

75 *Political parties were yet:* Ford, *History of Illinois*, 88.

76 *The concept of very limited:* Ibid., 90–1.

76 *Before he departed:* HI, 440.

76 *Lincoln had known Ann:* HI, 409, 403, 608.

77 *After an unusually rainy spring:* HI, 383, 21.

78 *"Lincoln and she was engaged":* HI, 243, 205.

78 *Lincoln's surrogate father:* HI, 236, 11; Wilson, *Honor's Voice*, 116–24.

78 *The death of Ann Rutledge:* Kenneth J. Winkle, *The Young Eagle: The Rise of Abra-*

ham Lincoln (Dallas: Taylor Trade Publishing, 2001), 120; Miller, *Lincoln and His World*, 74.

79 *When the second session:* Miller, *Lincoln and His World*, 72–3; Burlingham, *Abraham Lincoln,* 1:101–2.

79 *Beneath the debate:* Joseph Gillespie, *Recollections of Early Illinois and Her Noted Men* (Chicago: Fergus Printing, 1880), 8.

80 *Among the articles:* Paul Simon, *Lincoln's Preparation for Greatness: The Illinois Legislative Years* (Urbana: University of Illinois Press, 1971), 35; Onstot, *Pioneers of Menard and Mason Counties,* 114; Robert Bray, " 'The Power to Hurt': Lincoln's Early Use of Satire and Invective," *Journal of the Abraham Lincoln Association* 16, no. 1 (Winter 1995).

80 *Hill knew that alongside:* Herndon and Weik, *Herndon's Lincoln,* 1:51–5.

81 *President Jackson was a commanding figure:* Sean Wilentz, *The Rise of American Democracy: Jefferson to Lincoln* (New York: Norton, 2005), 446–52.

82 *One of the most widely circulated:* David Crockett, *The Life of Martin Van Buren* (New York: Nafis & Cornish, 1835), 13, 95.

82 *The Whig strategy lacked:* Nancy N. Scott, *A Memoir of Hugh Lawson White* (Philadelphia: J. B. Lippincott, 1856), 327; Charles Manfred Thompson, *The Illinois Whigs Before 1846* (Urbana: University of Illinois Press, 1915), 54.

83 *Daniel Webster ran:* Thompson, *Illinois Whigs Before 1846,* 52–3.

83 *In Vandalia, the Democrats:* Simon, *Lincoln's Preparation for Greatness,* 34; Miller, *Lincoln and His World,* 50–1.

83 *This set off a rapid-fire game:* Thompson, *Illinois Whigs Before 1846,* 51–2.

83 *Finally, the Whigs:* Miller, *Lincoln and His World,* 53–4.

84 *Lincoln maneuvered on behalf:* Burlingame, *Abraham Lincoln,* 1:109; Miller, *Lincoln and His World,* 55; Thompson, *Illinois Whigs Before 1846,* 51.

84 *Lincoln was likely:* Burlingame, *Abraham Lincoln,* 1:109.

84 *Lincoln was also likely:* Ibid., 1:107, 111.

84 *"Lincoln was by common consent":* Whitney, *Life of Lincoln,* 1:127–8; Herndon and Weik, *Herndon's Lincoln,* 1:167.

85 *Lincoln's sudden surfacing:* Power and Power, *Early Settlers of Sangamon County,* 79; CW, 1:48–9.

85 *The formal campaign was launched:* John Locke Scripps, *The First Published Life of Abraham Lincoln* (Detroit: Cranbrook Press, 1900), 40; HI, 202–3.

86 *The* Sangamo Journal *editorialized:* Simon, *Lincoln's Preparation for Greatness,* 45; Miller, *Lincoln and His World,* 78.

86 *After the Springfield opening debate:* HI, 589; Burlingame, *Abraham Lincoln,* 1:105–6; Thompson, *Illinois Whigs Before 1846,* 92; J. F. Snyder, "Governor Ford and His Family," *Journal of the Illinois State Historical Society* 3, no. 2 (July 1910): 45–51; Miller, *Lincoln and His World,* 82.

87 *Lincoln was the biggest vote getter:* Miller, *Lincoln and His World,* 148–9, 156; HI, 480.

88 *Setting up his new residence:* Linder, *Reminiscences of the Early Bench and Bar of Illinois*, 348; HI, 590; Luthin, *The Real Abraham Lincoln,* 46.

88 *Three quarters of the members:* Linder, *Reminiscences of the Early Bench and Bar of Illinois*, 56; Beveridge, *Abraham Lincoln*, 1:177.

89 *In Stuart's place the second-term:* Whitney, *Life of Lincoln*, 1:140.

89 *The new legislature opened:* John McAuley Palmer, ed., *The Bench and Bar of Illinois: Historical and Reminiscent* (Chicago: Lewis Pub., 1899), 1:24; William Henry Perrin, ed., *History of Effingham county, Illinois* (Chicago: O. L. Baskin, 1883), 133–4; Ford, *History of Illinois*, 220; Linder, *Reminiscences of the Early Bench and Bar of Illinois,* 260.

89 *For his instrument Smith:* Linder, *Reminiscences of the Early Bench and Bar of Illinois*, 260–2.

90 *Lincoln led the debate:* CW, 1:66.

90 *"Mr. Lincoln's remarks":* Miller, *Lincoln and His World*, 130; Simon, *Lincoln's Preparation for Greatness*, 64; Linder, *Reminiscences of the Early Bench and Bar of Illinois*, 262.

90 *Lincoln now took charge:* John Nicolay and John Hay, *Abraham Lincoln: A History* (New York: Century, 1890), 1:131; HI, 203; Beveridge, *Abraham Lincoln,* 1:175.

91 *Many towns scrambled:* Ford, *History of Illinois*, 186–7.

91 *When, at one point:* HI, 204.

91 *But at a low point in the effort:* Burlingame, *Abraham Lincoln*, 1:117, 121; Ford, *History of Illinois*, 186; Miller, *Lincoln and His World*, 131–2.

92 *Lincoln confided to Joshua Speed:* HI, 476.

92 *On February 28:* Luthin, *Real Abraham Lincoln*, 45–6; HI, 206; Whitney, *Life of Lincoln*, 1:138–9.

92 *Twenty-eight years old:* N&H, 1:151; Ford, *History of Illinois*, 34.

CHAPTER FOUR: PARADISE LOST

95 *On his deathbed, Andrew Jackson:* James Parton, *Life of Andrew Jackson* (New York: Mason Brothers, 1861), 3:447

96 *After Calhoun failed to attain:* Ibid., 3:448; Sarah Mytton Maury, *The Statesmen of America in 1846* (Philadelphia: Carey & Hart, 1847), 168–70.

97 *His speeches and writings:* Peterson, *Great Triumvirate*, 412, 408; Edward G. Parker, *Reminiscences of Rufus Choate: The Great American Advocate* (New York: Mason Brothers, 1860), 245; Harriet Martineau, *Retrospect of Western Travel* (London: Saunders and Otley, 1838), 1:243–4; Maury, *Statesmen of America in 1846*, 181.

98 *Calhoun the young champion:* William Edwin Hemphill, ed., *The Papers of John C. Calhoun* (Columbia: University of South Carolina Press, 1999), 25:68.

98 *Henry Clay openly ridiculed:* Robert Seager II, ed., *The Papers of Henry Clay: The Whig Leader, January 1, 1837–December 31, 1843* (Lexington: University Press of Kentucky, 1988), 9:600; William J. Grayson, *The Autobiography of William J. Grayson* (Columbia: University of South Carolina Press, 1990), 129.

99 *"But Mr. Calhoun had no youth":* Peterson, *Great Triumvirate,* 27.

99 *Calhoun's father, Patrick Calhoun:* William M. Meigs, *The Life of John Caldwell Calhoun,* vol. 5 (New York: Neale Publishing, 1917), 1:43–6.

100 *When he returned:* Ibid., 100.

100 *Calhoun arrived in Washington:* Hermann von Holst, *John C. Calhoun* (New York: Houghton Mifflin, 1899), 145; Epes Sargent, *The Life and Public Services of Henry Clay* (Auburn, N.Y.: Derby & Miller, 1852), 39.

101 *Calhoun's maiden speech:* Meigs, *Life of John Caldwell Calhoun,* 124–5, 130–1.

101 *In the aftermath of the War of 1812:* Holst, *John C. Calhoun,* 289, 33–5; Meigs, *Life of John Caldwell Calhoun,* 179–86.

102 *President James Monroe appointed:* John Quincy Adams, *Memoirs of John Quincy Adams* (Philadelphia: J. B. Lippincott, 1875), 5:360–1.

102 *But Calhoun's far-reaching projects:* Ibid., 4:314–5, 2412; Meigs, *Life of John Caldwell Calhoun,* 266–71.

104 *On December 28:* Meigs, *Life of John Caldwell Calhoun,* 290; Adams, *Memoirs of John Quincy Adams,* 5:514–5.

104 *Calhoun launched his own newspaper:* Meigs, *Life of John Caldwell Calhoun,* 295.

104 *Crawford struck back:* David Franklin Houston, *A Critical Study of Nullification in South Carolina* (New York: Longmans, Green, 1908), 60, 59.

105 *While Smith galvanized:* Ibid., 59; Thomas Cooper, *Consolidation: An Account of Parties in the United States from the Convention of 1787 to the Present Period* (Columbia, S.C.: Black & Sweeney, 1824); Peterson, *Great Triumvirate,* 135.

106 *"For the first time":* Henry Adams, *John Randolph* (New York: Houghton Mifflin, 1898), 267–8; Hugh A. Garland, *The Life of John Randolph of Roanoke* (New York: D. Appleton, 1854), 1:306.

107 *"When I speak of my country":* Nicholas Wood, "John Randolph of Roanoke and the Politics of Slavery in the Early Republic," *Virginia Magazine of History and Biography* 120, no. 2 (Summer 2012); Adam L. Tate, *Conservatism and Southern Intellectuals, 1789–1861* (Columbia: University of Missouri Press, 2005), 21, 28–9; Meigs, *Life of John Caldwell Calhoun,* 223; Adams, *John Randolph,* 180–1, 274–5, 270; David Hackett Fischer, *Albion's Seed: Four British Folkways in America* (New York: Oxford University Press, 1989), 412; Peterson, *Great Triumvirate,* 95; Josiah Quincy, *Figures of the Past* (Boston: Roberts Brothers, 1896), 213; James Parton, *Famous Americans of Recent Times* (Boston: Fields, Osgood, 1871), 175–218.

108 *Opposing the War of 1812: Annals of the Congress,* 11th Congress, 2nd Session, 451.

109 *Later, in 1838:* John C. Calhoun, *Works of John C. Calhoun* (New York: D. Appleton and Company, 1883), 3:185.

110 *The presidential contenders:* Parton, *Life of Andrew Jackson,* 60, 66–7, 72, 90.

110 *Calhoun made public statements:* Peterson, *Great Triumvirate,* 152.

110 *Now he hated Clay:* Ibid., 136.

111 *Calhoun began a sub rosa:* Wilentz, *Rise of American Democracy*, 261; William Cabell Bruce, *John Randolph of Roanoke, 1773–1833* (New York: G. P. Putnam's Sons, 1922), 510–12; Adams, *John Randolph*, 287; Peterson, *Great Triumvirate*, 142; John C. Calhoun, *Speeches of John C. Calhoun* (New York: Harper & Brothers, 1843), 16.

111 *Clay struck back at Calhoun:* Peterson, *Great Triumvirate*, 153.

112 *Calhoun thought of himself:* Sargent, *Public Men and Events from the Commencement of Mr. Monroe's Administration*, 108–9, 111.

112 *After the passage of a new tariff:* Houston, *Critical Study of Nullification in South Carolina*, 77–9; Hemphill, ed., *Papers of John C. Calhoun*, 10:506–8.

113 *Calhoun's defenders retrospectively:* Wiltse, *John C. Calhoun: Nullifier*, 17; Parton, *Life of Andrew Jackson*, 321.

113 *During the transition between administrations:* Wiltse, *John C. Calhoun: Nullifier*, 26.

114 *Jackson's beloved wife:* Marquis James, *The Life of Andrew Jackson* (New York: Bobbs Merrill, 1938), 464.

114 *While Jackson was considering:* Margaret Bayard Smith, *The First Forty Years of Washington Society* (New York: Scribner's, 1906), 282.

115 *The campaign against Mrs. Eaton:* Parton, *Life of Andrew Jackson*, 184–205; Wiltse, *John C. Calhoun: Nullifier*, 28–9, 33.

115 *Martin Van Buren, a widower:* Adams, *Memoirs of John Quincy Adams*, 8:185; Wiltse, *John C. Calhoun: Nullifier*, 36.

116 *His feeling toward Calhoun:* Parton, *Life of Andrew Jackson*, 295.

116 *In January 1830 Calhoun:* Peterson, *Great Triumvirate*, 176–7.

116 *By now Jackson firmly believed:* Parton, *Life of Andrew Jackson*, 299.

117 *Jackson was scheduled:* Wiltse, *John C. Calhoun: Nullifier*, 70–1.

117 *Despite everything, Jackson:* Meigs, *Life of John Caldwell Calhoun*, 410.

117 *In November 1829:* Parton, *Life of Andrew Jackson*, 310–24.

118 *After he read it, thoroughly convinced:* Ibid., 325.

118 *Jackson's reply to Calhoun:* Ibid., 332.

118 *Calhoun desperately pled:* Adams, *Memoirs of John Quincy Adams*, 8:306; Wiltse, *John C. Calhoun: Nullifier*, 95.

119 *The feud between the president:* Parton, *Life of Andrew Jackson*, 333–9.

119 *Calhoun refused to make the customary:* Wiltse, *John C. Calhoun: Nullifier*, 94–6; Louis P. Masur, *1831: Year of Eclipse* (New York: Macmillan, 2002), 107.

120 *But Calhoun was persuaded:* Wiltse, *John C. Calhoun: Nullifier*, 100–101; Meigs, *Life of John Caldwell Calhoun*, 425–9.

120 *The next month his allies:* Royce C. McCrary, "'The Long Agony Is Nearly Over': Samuel D. Ingham Reports on the Dissolution of Andrew Jackson's First Cabinet," *Pennsylvania Magazine of History and Biography* 100, no. 2 (April 1976): 231–42.

120 *Days after the cabinet's:* Wiltse, *John C. Calhoun: Nullifier,* 107; John C. Calhoun, *The Works of John C. Calhoun* (New York: D. Appleton, 1855), 6:439.

121 *Calhoun was greeted home: Niles' Register* 40 (1831): 171.

121 *McDuffie was more:* John Niven, *John C. Calhoun and the Price of Union* (Baton Rouge: Louisiana State University Press, 1993), 26–7; Houston, *Critical Study of Nullification in South Carolina,* 36–7; Sam R. Watkins, *"Co. Aytch": A Confederate Memoir of the Civil War* (New York: Simon & Schuster, 2008), 72.

121 *On the wall behind the podium:* Meigs, *Life of John Caldwell Calhoun,* 430–3; James Schouler, *History of the United States of America: Under the Constitution* (New York: Dodd, Mead, 1917), 4:40; Parton, *Life of Andrew Jackson,* 422; Wiltse, *John C. Calhoun: Nullifier,* 111.

122 On July 4th at Charleston: Houston, *Critical Study of Nullification in South Carolina,* 100–3; Meigs, *Life of John Caldwell Calhoun,* 434.

122 *Calhoun finally stepped:* von Holst, *John C. Calhoun,* 96; Wiltse, *John C. Calhoun: Nullifier,* 115, 122.

122 *Duff Green traveled:* Wiltse, *John C. Calhoun: Nullifier,* 121–2.

123 *That summer a house slave:* Ibid., 116–7.

123 *Van Buren's diplomatic nomination:* William M. Meigs, *The Life of Thomas Hart Benton* (Philadelphia: J. B. Lippincott, 1904), 1:449; Parton, *Life of Andrew Jackson,* 196–7.

123 *At the start of the campaign:* Wilentz, *Rise of American Democracy,* 377; Meigs, *Life of John Caldwell Calhoun,* 409.

123 *Events in South Carolina:* Wiltse, *John C. Calhoun: Nullifier,* 141; Thomas Hart Benton, *Thirty Years' View: Or, A History of the Working of the American Government for Thirty Years, from 1820 to 1850* (New York: D. Appleton, 1880), 1:297–8.

124 *The state also authorized:* Parton, *Life of Andrew Jackson,* 459.

124 *Days before this shuffling:* "Proclamation 43—Regarding the Nullifying Laws of South Carolina," American Presidency Project, http://www.presidency.ucsb.edu /ws/?pid=67078.

125 *Jackson dispatched General Winfield Scott:* Wilentz, *Rise of American Democracy,* 383; Parton, *Life of Andrew Jackson,* 474.

125 *South Carolina sought:* Wilentz, *Rise of American Democracy,* 383–4.

126 *In a rage against Jackson:* Parton, *Life of Andrew Jackson,* 470–1; Houston, *Critical Study of Nullification in South Carolina,* 121.

126 *But February 1:* Houston, *Critical Study of Nullification in South Carolina,* 123.

126 *Van Buren had advised:* Parton, *Life of Andrew Jackson,* 476.

126 *Clay killed the Verplanck bill:* Benton, *Thirty Years' View,* 1:316, 321–2; Parton, *Life of Andrew Jackson,* 479–81.

127 *Clay's bill liberated Calhoun:* Benton, *Thirty Years' View,* 1:338, 341; John S. Jenkins, *The Life of John Caldwell Calhoun* (Auburn, N.Y.: J. M. Alden, 1850), 313; Wiltse, *John C. Calhoun,* 190.

127   *Calhoun had already left:* Wiltse, *John C. Calhoun*, 195.

127   *Calhoun hurried to South Carolina: Niles' Register* 45 (1833): 240.

128   *Calhoun had succeeded:* Maury, *Statesmen of America in 1846*, 173; Meigs, *Life of John Caldwell Calhoun*, 419.

128   *Jackson felt all along:* David Maydole Matteson, ed., *Correspondence of Andrew Jackson: 1833–1838* (Washington, D.C.: Carnegie Institution, 1931), vol. 5; Manisha Sinha, *The Counter-Revolution of Slavery: Politics and Ideology in Antebellum South Carolina* (Charlotte: University of North Carolina Press, 2000), 60; Lawrence M. Anderson, *Federalism, Secessionism, and the American State* (New York: Routledge, 2013), 91.

128   *After nullification:* Benjamin Franklin Perry and Hext McCall Perry, *Reminiscences of Public Men* (Philadelphia: J. D. Avil, 1883), 49.

129   *"I cannot describe to you":* Maury, *Statesmen of America in 1846*, 173; Parker, *Reminiscences of Rufus Choate*, 245.

CHAPTER FIVE: OLD MAN ELOQUENT

132   *But Garrison's invocation of the Declaration:* Oliver Johnson, *William Lloyd Garrison and His Times* (Boston: B. B. Russell, 1879), 130, 132, 152; Wendell Phillips Garrison and Francis Jackson Garrison, *William Lloyd Garrison, 1805–1879: The Story of His Life Told by His Children* (New York: Century, 1889), 1:225, 3:331; Frederick J. Blue, *No Taint of Compromise: Crusaders in Antislavery Politics* (Baton Rouge: Louisiana State University Press, 2006), 48–9.

133   *On July 29, a mob:* Peter P. Hinks, John R. McKivigan, and R. Owen Williams, *Encyclopedia of Antislavery and Abolition* (Westport, Conn.: Greenwood, 2007), 540–2; "Postmaster General Amos Kendall's Report on the Delivery of Abolition Materials in the Southern States Report of the Postmaster General," House Documents, 24th Congress, 1st Session, 1835, Appendix, 9.

134   *In Washington, Dr. Reuben Crandall:* Henry Wilson, *History of the Rise and Fall of the Slave Power in America* (Boston: J. R. Osgood, 1875), 1:305–6; Daniel A. Farber, *Security v. Liberty: Conflicts Between Civil Liberty and National Security* (New York: Russell Sage Foundation, 2008), 145; Louis Ruchames, ed., *Letters of William Lloyd Garrison: A House Dividing Against Itself* (Cambridge: Harvard University Press, 1971), 137.

134   *From July to October 1835:* David Grimsted, *American Mobbing, 1828–1861: Toward Civil War* (New York: Oxford University Press, 2003), 3–12.

134   *One after another, Southern state legislatures:* Wilson, *History of the Rise and Fall of the Slave Power in America*, 1:324–5; William Allen Butler, *A Retrospect of Forty Years, 1825–1865* (New York: C. Scribner's Sons, 1911), 79; Drew Gilpin Faust, *James Henry Hammond and the Old South: A Design for Mastery* (Baton Rouge: Louisiana State University Press, 1985), 161.

134   *On August 21, 1835:* Garrison and Garrison, *William Lloyd Garrison*, 2:485–8.

135 *A few weeks later, a gallows:* Ibid., 2:495, 519, 521.

135 *On October 21, 1835:* Wilson, *History of the Rise and Fall of the Slave Power in America* 1:282–4.

135 *The same day as the Boston riot:* Ibid., 1:287–9, 291–2.

136 *In December, stoking the furor:* Ibid., 1:325.

136 *President Jackson, in his annual message:* William Lee Miller, *Arguing About Slavery: The Great Battle in the United States Congress* (New York: Knopf, 1996), 98.

137 *After the Charleston bonfire:* Theodore Dwight Weld, *The Power of the Congress over the District of Columbia* (New York: John F. Trow, 1838), 17; William Slade, *Speech of Mr. Slade, of Vermont, on the Right of Petition* (Washington, D.C.: Gales & Seaton, 1840), 9.

137 *As early as 1834:* J. Franklin Jameson, ed., *Correspondence of John C. Calhoun* (Washington, D.C.: U.S. Government Printing Office, 1900), 327–8.

137 *The idea of submitting petitions:* Miller, *Arguing About Slavery*, 109–12; Wiltse, *John C. Calhoun: Nullifier*, 278–9.

138 *The surfacing of abolitionist petitions:* Wiltse, *John C. Calhoun: Nullifier*, 281.

139 *Suppressing petitions:* James Henry Hammond, *Selections from the Letters and Speeches of the Hon. James H. Hammond* (New York: J. F. Trow & Co., 1866), 15–78.

140 *The slaves were not only naturally inferior:* John C. Calhoun, *The Works of John C. Calhoun* (New York: D. Appleton, 1853), 2: 625–33.

141 *No Carolinian had a more illustrious lineage:* William W. Freehling, *The Road to Disunion: Secessionists at Bay, 1776–1854* (New York: Oxford University Press, 1990), 329–32.

142 *Two future Democratic presidents:* Ibid., 324–8; Wiltse, *John C. Calhoun: Nullifier*, 284–6; Miller, *Arguing About Slavery*, 143.

142 *On the day the Pinckney Report:* Miller, *Arguing About Slavery*, 146–9.

142 *Adams was thwarted from speaking:* John Quincy Adams, *Speech of the Hon. John Quincy Adams in the House of Representatives on the state of the nation: delivered May 25, 1836* (New York: H. R. Piercy, 1836), 15.

143 *The sixth President of the United States:* Wilentz, *Rise of American Democracy*, 258–9; Adams, *Memoirs of John Quincy Adams*, 1:249.

144 *Afflicted with a host of ailments:* Adams, *Memoirs of John Quincy Adams*, 10:79, 9:14.

144 *After his speech:* Ibid., 9:298.

144 *Adams had held private conversations:* Ibid., 4:524, 4:10, 11:284.

145 *Adams was naturally inclined:* Joseph Wheelan, *Mr. Adams's Last Crusade* (New York: PublicAffairs, 2008), 98, 158–9.

145 *Adams deployed every wile:* Ibid., 130–4; Miller, *Arguing About Slavery*, 271.

147 *"He is no literary old gentleman":* Miller, *Arguing About Slavery*, 293, 296; Don Seitz, *Famous American Duels* (New York: Thomas Y. Crowell, 1929), 251–82;

Adams, *Memoirs of John Quincy Adams*, 10: 413, 9:502; Edward Waldo Emerson and Waldo Emerson Forbes, eds., *Journals of Ralph Waldo Emerson* (New York: Houghton Mifflin, 1911), 6:349–50.

147   *By 1838 the abolitionist movement:* Gilbert Hobbs Barnes, *The Antislavery Impulse, 1830–1844* (New York: Harcourt Brace, 1964), 161–7.

147   *A year later, when abolitionists:* Wheelan, *Mr. Adams's Last Crusade*, 176–84; "Argument of John Quincy Adams, Before the Supreme Court of the United States: in the Case of the United States, Appellants, vs. Cinque, and Others, Africans, Captured in the schooner Amistad, by Lieut. Gedney; 1841," Avalon Project, http://avalon.law.yale.edu/19th_century/amistad_002.asp.

148   *By 1840, despite the* Amistad *victory:* Barnes, *The Antislavery Impulse*, 177–9.

149   *Weld was, in effect:* Miller, *Arguing About Slavery*, 404–8; Weld, *Power of Congress over the District of Columbia*, 3.

150   *"I call for the reading":* Miller, *Arguing About Slavery*, 429–39; Seager, ed., *Papers of Henry Clay*, 9:643–4.

150   *Marshall had been standing:* Joshua R. Giddings, *The History of the Rebellion: Its Authors and Causes* (New York: Follet, Foster, 1864), 158–67.

151   *For six years, Adams:* Ibid., 168; Adams, *Memoirs of John Quincy Adams*, 11:80, 84.

151   *"Old Man Eloquent":* Giddings, *History of the Rebellion,* 218.

152   *Adams had started against:* Wheelan, *Mr. Adams's Last Crusade*, 103; William Whiting, *War Powers Under the Constitution* (Boston: Lee & Shepard, 1871), 80; Allen C. Guelzo, *Lincoln's Emancipation Proclamation: The End of Slavery in America* (New York: Simon & Schuster, 2004), 193.

152   *Calhoun would anoint:* Paul Findley, *A. Lincoln: The Crucible of Congress* (New York: Crown, 1979), 139.

CHAPTER SIX: THE SPRINGFIELD LYCEUM

155   *The struggle over the Gag Rule:* Beveridge, *Abraham Lincoln*, 1:189–92.

156   *The Illinois General Assembly:* Ibid., 1:194.

156   *Only one protest was lodged:* Miller, *Lincoln and His World*, 143.

156   *Lincoln and Stone waited:* Herndon and Weik, *Herndon's Lincoln*, 1:179–80.

157   *Five weeks after Van Buren's:* Howe, *What Hath God Wrought*, 502–5; Wilentz, *Rise of American Democracy*, 456–7.

158   *Brilliant financial innovation:* Jessica M. Lepler, "1837: Anatomy of a Panic" (PhD diss., Brandeis University, 2008), 5–13; Peter Temin, *The Jacksonian Economy* (New York: Norton, 1969), 82; Edward E. Baptist, "Toxic Debt, Liar Loans, and Securitized Human Beings: The Panic of 1837 and the Fate of Slavery," *Common-Place* 10, no. 3 (April 2010).

158   *This scheme was pioneered:* Baptist, "Toxic Debt, Liar Loans, and Securitized Human Beings."

159   *Cotton production had almost doubled:* Ibid.

160 *Stephen A. Douglas's rise:* Robert W. Johannsen, *Stephen A. Douglas* (New York: Oxford University Press, 1973), 21; Linder, *Reminiscences of the Early Bench and Bar of Illinois*, 78; William M. Holland, *The Life and Political Opinions of Martin Van Buren* (Hartford: Belknap & Hamersley, 1836), 69.

161 *Douglas was as single-minded:* Allen Johnson, *Stephen A. Douglas: A Study in American Politics* (New York: Macmillan, 1908), 37–8.

161 *In 1836, Douglas replaced:* Ibid., 23, 35.

161 *After Young's election:* Tarbell, *Early Life*, 1:145; H. C. Bradsby, *History of Bureau County, Illinois* (Chicago: World Publishing, 1885), 155–66.

162 *On June 22, Lincoln lifted:* Nicolay and Hay, *Abraham Lincoln*, 1:213–4.

163 *While besmirching Adams:* Miller, *Lincoln and His World*, 160–3; Burlingame, *Abraham Lincoln*, 1:133–6; Howard F. Rissler, "The State Capitol, 1837–1876," *Journal of the Illinois State Historical Society* 61, no. 4 (Winter 1968): 397–430; Joseph Wallace, *Sketch of the Life and Public Services of Edward D. Baker* (Springfield, Ill.: Journal, 1870), 18.

164 *Calhoun lost by a decisive margin:* Miller, *Lincoln and His World*, 164–6; Wallace, *Sketch of the Life and Public Services of Edward D. Baker*, 18.

165 *For the special two-week legislative session:* Linder, *Reminiscences of the Early Bench and Bar of Illinois*, 62–3.

165 *A year earlier, on July 30, 1836:* Beveridge, *Abraham Lincoln*, 1:221; Miller, *Lincoln and His World*, 202.

166 *At once Lovejoy courted trouble:* Joseph C. Lovejoy and Owen Lovejoy, *Memoir of the Rev. Elijah P. Lovejoy: Who Was Murdered in Defence of the Liberty of the Press, at Alton, Illinois, Nov. 7, 1837* (New York: J. S. Taylor, 1838), 126, 140, 154, 157.

166 *In April 1836, a free black worker:* Henry Tanner, *The Martyrdom of Lovejoy: An Account of the Life, Trials, and Perils of Rev. Elijah P. Lovejoy* (Chicago: Fergus Printing, 1881); Lovejoy and Lovejoy, *Memoir of the Rev. Elijah P. Lovejoy*, 172; American Anti-Slavery Society, *The Quarterly Antislavery Magazine* 1, no. 1 (October 1835): 403.

167 *Judge Luke Lawless, appropriately named:* Louis Houck, *A History of Missouri from the Earliest Explorations and Settlements Until the Admission of the State into the Union* (Chicago: R. R. Donnelley & Sons, 1908), 3:19–21; Walter Barlow Stevens, *Centennial History of Missouri* (St. Louis: S. J. Clarke, 1921), 1:223–4.

168 *On July 21, Lovejoy editorialized:* Tanner, *Martyrdom of Lovejoy*, 82; Lovejoy and Lovejoy, *Memoir of the Rev. Elijah P. Lovejoy*, 182.

168 *Lovejoy continued to write occasional antislavery articles:* Tanner, *Martyrdom of Lovejoy*, 105–6.

168 *Within days a committee of town notables:* Ibid., 108–9, 123–4, 131–3: George T. M. Davis, *Autobiography of the Late Col. Geo. T. M. Davis* (New York: Jenkins & McCowan, 1891), 59–63.

169 *Lovejoy traveled to Springfield in October:* Paul M. Angle, *"Here I Have Lived": A*

History of Lincoln's Springfield (New Brunswick, N.J.: Rutgers University Press, 1935), 79–80; H. D. Jenkins, "The History of Presbyterianism in Illinois," *Publications of the Illinois State Historical Library*, no. 19, 65.

169 *Lovejoy had planned strategy over the summer:* Edward Beecher, *Narrative of Riots at Alton: In Connection with the Death of Rev. Elijah P. Lovejoy* (Alton, Ill.: G. Holton, 1838), 24–7.

169 *In order to diffuse the growing hostility:* Tanner, *Martyrdom of Lovejoy*, 134–6; Newton Bateman and Paul Selby, eds., *Historical Encyclopedia of Illinois* (Chicago: Munsell Publishing, 1900), 175; Donald, *Lincoln*, 63; Linder, *Reminiscences of the Early Bench and Bar of Illinois*, 223–4.

170 *Lovejoy answered that he would:* Lovejoy and Lovejoy, *Memoir of the Rev. Elijah P. Lovejoy*, 89–90.

171 *Linder emerged from the meeting:* Ibid., 276; Tanner, *Martyrdom of Lovejoy*, 220.

171 *The new press for the* Observer: Lovejoy and Lovejoy, *Memoir of the Rev. Elijah P. Lovejoy*, 284–92.

171 *The city attorney of Alton indicted:* Theodore Calvin Pease, *The Story of Illinois* (Chicago: University of Chicago Press, 1965), 368; William Sever Lincoln, *Alton Trials* (New York: John F. Trow, 1838), 139, 143.

172 *A distinguished and influential attorney:* J. F. Snyder, "Alfred Cowles," *Transactions of the Illinois State Historical Society* 10 (1910): 167–75; Lincoln, *Alton Trials*, 143–4, 156.

172 *The transfiguration of Lovejoy:* Stephen B. Oates, *To Purge This Land with Blood: A Biography of John Brown* (Amherst: University of Massachusetts Press, 1984), 41–2; Evan Carton, *Patriotic Treason: John Brown and the Soul of America* (Lincoln: University of Nebraska Press, 2009), 82.

173 *In Illinois, the common opinion:* Ford, *History of Illinois*, 238–9.

173 *The trial acquitting the mob leaders:* Thomas F. Schwartz, "The Springfield Lyceums and Lincoln's 1838 Speech," *Illinois Historical Journal* 83 (Spring 1990).

173 *His style at the Lyceum:* Beveridge, *Abraham Lincoln*, 1:210; Coleman McCampbell, "H. L. Kinney and Daniel Webster in Illinois in the 1830's," *Journal of the Illinois State Historical Society* 47, no. 1 (Spring 1954): 35–44; Henry Clay Whitney, *Life on the Circuit with Lincoln* (Boston: Estes & Lauriat, 1892), 574.

174 *Lincoln awkwardly entitled his talk:* Burlingame, *Abraham Lincoln*, 1:141.

178 *Deploring mobs:* Sean Wilentz, *Andrew Jackson* (New York: Macmillan, 2005), 55; Schwartz, "Springfield Lyceums," 49.

181 *Lincoln's forewarning against:* Edmund Wilson, *Patriotic Gore: Studies in the Literature of the American Civil War* (New York: Farrar, Straus & Giroux, 1962), 108; Donald, *Lincoln*, 81.

181 *Once again, Lincoln's description:* Johannsen, *Stephen A. Douglas* 882 Note 4.

182 *The initial article:* Ibid., 63–4.

183 *Then, in the article:* Glenn H. Seymour, " 'Conservative': Another Lincoln Pseud-

onym?," *Journal of the Illinois State Historical Society* 29, no. 2 (July 1936): 135–50; "Lincoln—Author of the Letters by 'A Conservative,' " *Bulletin*, Abraham Lincoln Association, Springfield, Ill., 50, no. 1 (December 1937); Burlingame, *Abraham Lincoln*, 1:139–40.

183 *Lincoln's appeal to reason:* Calhoun, *Speeches of John C. Calhoun*, 626–7.

183 *Lincoln's lament of the passing:* Daniel Webster, *The Bunker Hill Monument Orations* (New York: Maynard, Merrill, 1885), 27.

184 *On December 23, 1837: Niles' Register* 53 (1838): 267; John Quincy Adams, "Introduction," in Lovejoy and Lovejoy, *Memoir of the Rev. Elijah P. Lovejoy*, 12.

CHAPTER SEVEN: THE RIVALS

187 *Stephen A. Douglas's frantic climb:* Johnson, *Stephen A. Douglas*, 39–41.

188 *On March 7, 1838:* Miller, *Lincoln and His World*, 228–31; *History of Sangamon County*, 525.

188 *Stuart's prospects, however:* Wilson, *Honor's Voice*, 302.

188 *Douglas and Stuart traveled*: John M. Palmer, *Personal Recollections* (Cincinnati: R. Clarke Co., 1901), 24; HI, 451.

189 *The Little Giant's fulminating:* CW, 2:283.

189 *John Quincy Adams, in 1844:* Adams, *Memoirs of John Quincy Adams,* 11:510; Roll Ogden, ed., *Life and Letters of Edwin Lawrence Godkin* (New York: Macmillan, 1907), 1:178.

189 *In the climactic Stuart-Douglas clash:* Johannsen, *Stephen A. Douglas*, 44–5, 69; Miller, *Lincoln and His World*, 257–9; C. C. Brown, "Major John T. Stuart," *Transactions of the Illinois State Historical Society for the Year 1902* (Chicago: Illinois State Historical Library, 1902), 110.

190 *Lincoln closely monitored vote:* Nicolay and Hay, *Abraham Lincoln*, 1:179.

190 *One Democrat, however:* Miller, *Lincoln and His World*, 231, 256–7; Linder, *Reminiscences of the Early Bench and Bar of Illinois*, 354–5.

191 *But there was soon another:* "John G. Nicolay, July 6, 1875 (Interview with Stephen T. Logan)," Abraham Lincoln Papers, Library of Congress, http://memory .loc.gov/cgi-bin/query/r?ammem/mal:@field(DOCID+@lit(d4364400)).

191 *When the legislature assembled:* John Moses, *Illinois, Historical and Statistical* (Chicago: Fergus Printing, 1889), 426; Miller, *Lincoln and His World*, 262; Simon, *Lincoln's Preparation for Greatness*, 150–1.

191 *One of the first matters before:* Simon, *Lincoln's Preparation for Greatness*, 134–5; Miller, *Lincoln and His World*, 269–72; Burlingame, *Abraham Lincoln*, 1:146.

192 *The Whigs had great expectations:* Burlingame, *Abraham Lincoln*, 1:148.

192 *On October 7, 1839, delegates:* Thompson, *Illinois Whigs Before 1846*, 63–4.

192 *The political consequences of the Panic:* Wiltse, *John C. Calhoun: Nullifier*, 358, 409; Peterson, *Great Triumvirate*, 273, 270–1, 277; Martin Van Buren, *The Autobiography of Martin Van Buren*, John C. Fitzpatrick, ed. (Washington, D.C.: U.S. Gov-

ernment Printing Office, 1920), 393; Calhoun, *Correspondence of John C. Calhoun*, 2:454.

193 *Clay warned that the:* Calvin Colton, ed., *The Speeches of Henry Clay* (New York: A. S. Barnes, 1857), 2:140–59.

194 *Listening on the floor of the Senate:* Peterson, *Great Triumvirate*, 286–9; Remini, *Henry Clay*, 526–31.

195 *At the first national Whig convention:* Hans L. Trefousse, *Thaddeus Stevens: Nineteenth-Century Egalitarian* (Mechanicsburg, Penn.: Stackpole, 2001), 63–5; Alexander K. McClure, *Our Presidents: And How We Make Them* (New York: Harper & Brothers, 1900), 68.

195 *In the chess game for the nomination:* Henry A. Wise, *Seven Decades of the Union* (Philadelphia: J. B. Lippincott, 1881), 173–4.

195 *For more than a year:* HI, 469; Herndon and Weik, *Herndon's Lincoln*, 1:190.

196 *John C. Calhoun, sensing his opening:* Thompson, *Illinois Whigs Before 1846*, 47; HI, 476; Harry L. Watson, *Liberty and Power: The Politics of Jacksonian America* (New York: Macmillan, 2006), 2089; Wiltse, *John C. Calhoun: Nullifier*, 357–8; Peterson, *Great Triumvirate*, 271; Ford, *History of Illinois*, 186–7.

197 *The first debate, on November 19:* Johannsen, *Stephen A. Douglas*, 76; Wilson, *Honor's Voice*, 198–9.

197 *Round two, on the next night:* Simon, *Lincoln's Preparation for Greatness*, 180; HI, 181.

197 *Round three, the next night:* HI, 388; Herndon and Weik, *Herndon's Lincoln*, 1:196–7.

198 *Lincoln's adversary, Usher Linder:* Linder, *Reminiscences of the Early Bench and Bar of Illinois*, 248–9.

198 *Even while jumping through:* CW, 1:159.

199 *His speech, a brief against:* CW, 159–79.

199 *"He transcended our highest expectations":* HI, 388; CW, 185; Miller, *Lincoln and His World*, 343.

199 *On behalf of the Whig Central Committee:* CW, 1:202–3.

200 *The war between:* Miller, *Lincoln and His World*, 361.

200 *Old Hickory replied:* Angle, *"Here I Have Lived,"* 115; Johannsen, *Stephen A. Douglas*, 80; CW, 1:206; Herndon and Weik, *Herndon's Lincoln*, 1:187.

201 *In early June:* Angle, *"Here I Have Lived,"* 112–4.

202 *And yet Bledsoe still regarded:* Albert Taylor Bledsoe, "Article IV," *Southern Review* 12, no. 25 (Southwestern Book and Publishing, 1873): 328–68; Fred C. Hobson, *Tell About the South: The Southern Rage to Explain* (Baton Rouge: Louisiana State University Press, 1983), 92; Douglas Southall Freeman, *The South to Posterity: An Introduction to the Writing of Confederate History* (Baton Rouge: Louisiana State University Press, 1939), 49.

202 *During that campaign:* Abraham Lincoln Papers, Library of Congress, Nicolay, July 6, 1875, Interview with Logan.

202 *When a Democratic newspaper:* William James Cooper, *The South and the Politics of Slavery, 1828–1856* (Baton Rouge: Louisiana State University Press, 1980), 139–40; *Extra Globe* vols. 6–7 (Washington, D.C.: F. P. Blair, 1840).

203 *In Illinois, the Democrats:* Burlingame, *Abraham Lincoln,* 1:154; Johannsen, *Stephen A. Douglas,* 78.

203 *As a young man in Virginia:* Miller, *Lincoln and His World,* 387–8.

204 *Archie Herndon, the Democratic:* Ibid., 189; Burlingame, *Abraham Lincoln,* 1:160.

204 *Another of the Democratic orators:* Howard's Notes, Abraham Lincoln Papers, Library of Congress; Miller, *Lincoln and His World,* 392; HI, 472, Herndon and Weik, *Herndon's Lincoln,* 1:194–5.

205 *Herndon immortalized Lincoln's: Bulletin of Abraham Lincoln Association of Springfield, Ill.,* 50, no. 1; Bledsoe, "Article IV," 332–3; Herndon and Weik, *Herndon's Lincoln,* 1:197–8.

206 *Though Lincoln won the August contest:* Miller, *Lincoln and His World,* 396.

206 *For months, Lincoln had attempted:* Johannsen, *Stephen A. Douglas,* 78; Holland, *Life and Political Opinions of Martin Van Buren,* 182.

206 *Seeking another element:* Miller, *Lincoln and His World,* 398.

206 *Douglas, who was familiar:* Hertz, *Hidden Lincoln,* 435–6; HI, 471.

207 *To the end of the campaign:* Republican Committee of Seventy-six, *The Northern Man with Southern Principles and the Southern Man with American Principles* (Washington, D.C.: Peter Force, 1840), 7.

207 *Unfortunately, Harrison's calculation:* Wise, *Seven Decades of the Union,* 179–80.

208 *Clay dismissed Tyler:* Freehling, *Road to Disunion,* 363–4; Peterson, *Great Triumvirate,* 317.

208 *In Illinois, after the Harrison victory:* Herndon and Weik, *Herndon's Lincoln,* 161–2; HI, 188.

209 *His rival rose and rose:* Miller, *Lincoln and His World,* 418–24; Johannsen, *Stephen A. Douglas,* 95.

209 *Lincoln signed a statement:* Burlingame, *Abraham Lincoln,* 1:164; Miller, *Lincoln and His World,* 425.

209 *From the opening of the special session:* HI, 133.

CHAPTER EIGHT: THE ROMANCE

211 *"Yes," Frances admitted:* Miller, *Lincoln and His World,* 156; Newspaper Interview with Mrs. Frances Wallace, Springfield, Illinois, September 2, 1895, "Says There Is No Truth in the Statements That Lincoln's Home Life Was Unhappy" (Privately Printed, 1917); Tarbell, *Early Life,* 1:270–1.

213 *Eliza died in childbirth:* Thomas Marshall Green, *Historic Families of Kentucky* (Cincinnati: R. Clarke, 1889), 210, 271–4; Georgie Hortense Edwards, *Historic Sketches of the Edwards and Todd Families and Their Descendants: 1523-1895* (Springfield, Ill.: H. W. Rocker, 1894); Stephen Berry, *House of Abraham: Lincoln*

and the Todds, A Family Divided by War (New York: Houghton Mifflin, 2007), 6–9, 13; W. A. Evans, *Mrs. Abraham Lincoln* (New York: Knopf, 1935), 35.

214 *Lexington in the early:* Marion B. Lucas, *A History of Blacks in Kentucky: From Slavery to Segregation, 1760–1891* (Lexington,: University Press of Kentucky, 2003), 89–90; Frederic Bancroft, *Slave Trading in the Old South* (New York: Ungar, 1959), 1302; Randolph Hollingsworth, *Lexington: Queen of the Bluegrass* (Charleston, S.C.: Arcadia, 2004), 58.

214 *In 1832, a thirteen year-old girl:* Berry, *House of Abraham*, 21–2.

215 *Frances Todd, the second born:* Lincoln's Marriage: Newspaper Interview with Mrs. Francis Wallace, September 2, 1895 (Springfield, Ill.: Privately Printed, 1917).

215 *Mary had visited briefly:* Thomas F. Schwartz, "Mary Todd's 1835 Visit to Springfield, Illinois," *Journal of the Abraham Lincoln Association* 26, no. 1 (Winter 2005); Carl Sandburg, *Mary Lincoln: Wife and Widow* (New York: Harcourt, Brace, 1932), 28–30; Wilson, *Honor's Voice*, 215; Winkle, *Young Eagle*, 162–3; Miller, *Lincoln and His World*, 440.

215 *The romantic history of Lincoln:* HI, 556–7; Walter Barlow Stevens, *A Reporter's Lincoln*, ed. Michael Burlingame (Lincoln: University of Nebraska Press, 1916), 9; HI, 374.

216 *Lincoln's courtship technique:* HI, 262; CW, 1:78, 94.

216 *Later, Owens explained:* HI, 256.

217 *Poor Lincoln lamented:* CW, 1:117–8.

218 *Two years after his breakup:* HI, 443–5.

218 *Mary flourished as a center:* Wilson, *Honor's Voice*, 219–20; Onstot, *Pioneers of Menard and Mason Counties*, 34; Justin G. Turner and Linda Levitt Turner, *Mary Todd Lincoln: Her Life and Letters* (New York: Knopf, 1972), 295; Sandburg, *Mary Lincoln*, 32.

219 *One week before Election Day:* Angle, *"Here I Have Lived,"* 114–5.

219 *Mary's romance with Lincoln:* HI, 443, 474; Onstot, *Pioneers of Menard and Mason Counties*, 34.

220 *Sometime during the special:* HI, 443, 475, 477; Miller, *Lincoln and His World*, 451.

221 *Lincoln's "bad lick":* Ruth Painter Randall, *The Courtship of Mr. Lincoln* (New York: Little, Brown, 1957), 74; Miller, *Lincoln and His World*, 450; CW, 1:282; Joshua Wolf Shenk, *Lincoln's Melancholy* (New York: Houghton Mifflin, 2005), 55.

221 *Unfortunately for the two:* HI, 444.

222 *Ninian W. Edwards later:* HI, 133.

222 *Elizabeth Todd Edwards offered:* HI, 443–4.

222 *But these theories:* Katherine Helm, *Mary, Wife of Lincoln* (New York: Harper Brothers, 1928), 82; Mary Edwards Raymond, "Some Incidents in the Life of Mrs. Benjamin S. Edwards" (Privately published, 1909).

223 *In early January:* HI, 475; Wilson, *Honor's Voice*, 236; Herndon and Weik, *Herndon's Lincoln*, 182–3.

223 *Despite Speed's dramatic talk:* Tarbell, *Early Life*, 180.

223 *Lincoln's isolation may well:* Shenk, *Lincoln's Melancholy*, 59–61.

224 *Lincoln's plight:* Wilson, *Honor's Voice*, 236–8; Randall, *Courtship of Mr. Lincoln*, 112.

224 *On January 20, Lincoln:* CW, 1:228.

224 *Three days later:* CW, 1:229.

225 *Logan was exacting:* Nicolay, "Interview with Logan."

225 *Despite Lincoln's rejection:* Wilson, *Honor's Voice*, 240; Randall, *Courtship of Mr. Lincoln*, 114.

225 *Yet Mary still had thoughts:* Randall, *Courtship of Mr. Lincoln*, 144.

226 *For thirteen years:* Carl Adams, "Lincoln's First Freed Slave: A Review of Bailey v. Cromwell, 1841," *Journal of the Illinois State Historical Society* (Fall–Winter 2008).

226 *Traveling to Texas:* Ibid.

227 *Lincoln and Bailey had known:* Illinois Historical Survey, *Portrait and Biographical Record of Tazewell and Mason Counties, Illinois* (Chicago: Biographical Publishing, 1894), 221–2; Illinois Anti-Slavery Society, *Proceedings of the Illinois Antislavery Convention* (Alton, Ill.: Parks & Breath, 1838), 4.

227 *On July 9, 1841, Lincoln:* Albert A. Woldman, *Lawyer Lincoln* (New York: Carroll & Graf, 1994), 61; Johannsen, *Stephen A. Douglas*, 104.

227 *Lincoln had taken on:* Adams, "Lincoln's First Freed Slave."

227 *"I stick to my promise":* Wilson, *Honor's Voice*, 249.

228 *The longest passage:* CW, 1:259–61.

229 *Nearly fourteen years later:* CW, 2:320, 2:322.

229 *After Speed returned:* CW, 1:265.

230 *One month later:* CW, 1:267–8, 1:270.

230 *On the day of Speed's wedding:* HI, 171.

230 *Unable to compose his emotions:* Miller, *Lincoln and His World*, 486.

231 *One week after Speed's wedding:* Beveridge, *Abraham Lincoln*, 1:325.

231 *Lincoln's freethinking was no secret:* HI, 462.

232 *His peroration, like that:* CW, 1:271–9.

233 *Unsurprisingly, the* Sangamo Journal: Beveridge, *Abraham Lincoln*, 1:330; CW, 1:282–3; Miller, *Lincoln and His World*, 497.

233 *Unfortunately, he was quite wrong:* Herndon and Weik, *Herndon's Lincoln*, 206–7.

233 *Even before Lincoln delivered:* Miller, *Lincoln and His World*, 495–6.

233 *Now known as the:* Holland, *Life and Political Opinions of Martin Van Buren*, 87; Miller, *Lincoln and His World*, 502, 500; CW, 1:285.

234 *For the first time:* HI, 180; Herndon and Weik, *Herndon's Lincoln*, 208; Miller, *Lincoln and His World*, 506.

CHAPTER NINE: THE PROPHET

235 *The founding platform of the Republican Party:* CW, 2:399.

236 *Joe Smith briefly joined:* William Alexander Linn, *The Story of the Mormons: From*

the Date of Their Origin to the Year 1901 (New York: Macmillan, 1902), 13, 18; Pomeroy Tucker, *Origin, Rise, and Progress of Mormonism: Biography of Its Founders and History of Its Church* (New York: D. Appleton, 1867), 16, 18, 21; Fawn N. Brodie, *No Man Knows My History: The Life of Joseph Smith* (New York: Knopf, 1945), 30–1.

237 *While farming on land:* Brodie, *No Man Knows My History*, 77, 205; Paul C. Gutjahr, *The Book of Mormon: A Biography* (Princeton: Princeton University Press, 2012), 50; Linn, *The Story of the Mormons*, 156.

238 *Putting aside the volume's:* For the first analysis of the Book of Mormon, with conjecture about its contemporary sources, see: Eber D. Howe, *Mormonism Unvailed: Or, A Faithful Account of That Singular Imposition and Delusion, from Its Rise to the Present Time* (Painesville, Ohio: Published By the Author, 1834).

238 *The original version of the book:* Tucker, *Origin, Rise, and Progress of Mormonism*, 65; Brodie, *No Man Knows My History*, 84; Linn, *The Story of the Mormons*, 26–7, 38.

239 *At Kirtland:* Linn, *The Story of the Mormons*, 142–53, 157, 195; Tucker, *Origin, Rise, and Progress of Mormonism*, 155.

239 *"God is my right-hand man":* Tyler, *Freedom's Ferment*, 100; Ford, *History of Illinois*, 260; Sally Denton, *American Massacre: The Tragedy at Mountain Meadows, September 1857* (New York: Knopf, 2003), 20; Linn, *The Story of the Mormons*, 196–7, 205.

240 *Lincoln joined in the unanimous:* Ford, *History of Illinois*, 262; CW, 1:206; *The Latter-Day Saints' Millennial Star* 18 (Manchester, England: P. P. Pratt, 1856), 264; Tyler, *Freedom's Ferment*, 103.

241 *Through the Nauvoo Charter:* Ford, *History of Illinois*, 263.

241 *With Joseph Smith's endorsement:* Gary Vitale, "Abraham Lincoln and the Mormons: Another Legacy of Limited Freedom," *Journal of the Illinois State Historical Society* (Fall–Winter 2008).

241 *Douglas, now a judge:* Johnson, *Stephen A. Douglas*, 58.

241 *For more than a year, Governor Thomas:* Miller, *Lincoln and His World*, 477; Johannsen, *Stephen A. Douglas*, 107; John Doyle Lee, *Mormonism Unveiled* (St. Louis: Sun Publishing, 1882), 144.

242 *On December 20, 1841, Smith:* Johnson, *Stephen A. Douglas*, 59; John Francis Snyder, *Adam W. Snyder and His Period in Illinois History, 1817–1842* (Virginia, Ill.: E. Needham, 1906), 387–8; Johannsen, *Stephen A. Douglas*, 108–9.

242 *The Democrats were almost:* Peter Cartwright, *The Backwoods Preacher: An Autobiography* (London: Alexander Heylin, 1858), 198–200.

242 *The Mormon factor grew:* Tyler, *Freedom's Ferment*, 103; W. Wyl, *Mormon Portraits* (Salt Lake City: Tribune Printing and Publishing, 1886), 41; Linn, *The Story of the Mormons*, 257–8, 231.

243 *Smith reigned as an autocrat:* Tyler, *Freedom's Ferment*, 103; Linn, *The Story of the Mormons*, 258–9.

243 *After Smith hailed Douglas:* Miller, *Lincoln and His World*, 508–9.

243 *On May 4, 1842, former governor Boggs:* Brodie, *No Man Knows My History*, 330–1; Charles A. Shook, *The True Origins of Mormon Polygamy* (Cincinnati: Standard Publishing Company, 1914), 127; Charles Kelly and Hoffman Birney, *Holy Murder: The Story of Porter Rockwell* (New York: Minton, Balch, 1934); Wyl, *Mormon Portraits*, 255.

244 *The day after the assassination attempt:* Wyl, *Mormon Portraits*, 28; George Quayle Cannon, *The Life of Joseph Smith, The Prophet* (Salt Lake City: Juvenile Instructor Office, 1888), 380; Johnson, *Stephen A. Douglas*, 61.

245 *Smith collected statements:* Harry M. Beardsley, "The Mormons in Illinois," *Illinois State Historical Society, Transactions for the Year 1933*, 53; Wyl, *Mormon Portraits*, 59–60; Shook, *True Origins of Mormon Polygamy*, 65; Brodie, *No Man Knows My History*, 306, 316, 309–14.

245 *"EXTRA. The Mormon Plot":* Miller, *Lincoln and His World*, 512; John C. Bennett, *The History of the Saints: Or, An Exposé of Joe Smith and Mormonism* (Boston: Leland & Whiting, 1842), 217–67.

245 *The* Register *cast the exposé:* Miller, *Lincoln and His World*, 511–12; Gilbert A. Tracy, ed., *Uncollected Letters of Abraham Lincoln* (New York: Houghton Mifflin, 1917), 8; *Sangamo Journal*, July 15, 1842, http://www.sidneyrigdon.com/dbroadhu /IL/sang1842.htm; Brodie, *No Man Knows My History,* 314.

246 *After Bennett's disclosure:* Kent L. Walgren, "James Adams: Early Springfield Mormon and Freemason," *Journal of the Illinois State Historical Society* (Summer 1982); Brodie, *No Man Knows My History*, 280–2.

247 *There was a further Adams:* Miller, *Lincoln and His World*, 469.

247 *The Bennett scoop seemed:* Sangamo Journal, January 21, 1842, http://www.sidney rigdon.com/dbroadhu/IL/sang1842.htm.

248 *The possible author of that passage:* CW, 4:10–11.

248 *On July 29, the* Journal *assailed:* Sangamo Journal, July 29, 1842, http://www.sidney rigdon.com/dbroadhu/IL/sang1842.htm.

248 *Despite the scandal Duncan:* Earl Schenck Miers and William E. Baringer, eds., *Lincoln Day by Day: A Chronology, 1809–1865* (Washington, D.C.: Lincoln Sesquicentennial Commission, Northern Illinois University, 1960), 1:189; *Sangamo Journal*, August 12, 1842, http://www.sidneyrigdon.com/dbroadhu/IL/sang1842 .htm.

248 *Immediately after the Democrats:* Brodie, *No Man Knows My History*, 327–8; Johannsen, *Stephen A. Douglas*, 114; Vitale, "Lincoln and the Mormons"; Angle, *"Here I Have Lived,"* 99.

249 *Smith hired an accomplished:* Brodie, *No Man Knows My History*, 329; William A. Meese, "Nathaniel Pope," *Journal of the Illinois State Historical Society* 3, no. 4 (January 1911); Josephine E. Burns, "Daniel P. Cook," *Journal of the Illinois State Historical Society* 6, no. 1 (1913); Thomas J. McCormack, ed., *Memoirs of Gustave*

Koerner (Cedar Rapids, Iowa: Torch Press, 1909), 1:478–9, 1: 483–4; Angle, *"Here I Have Lived,"* 126; B. H. Roberts, *History of the Church of Jesus Christ of Latter-Day Saints* (Salt Lake City: Deseret News, 1909), 5:223.

249   *"Smith was too ignorant":* Ford, *History of Illinois*, 316; Brodie, *No Man Knows My History*, 355.

250   *On May 18, Smith hosted Douglas:* Roberts, *History of the Church of Jesus Christ of Latter-Day Saints*, 5:393–5; Ezra Taft Benson, "Joseph Smith: Prophet to Our Generation," November 1981, *Ensign*, http://www.lds.org/ensign/1981/11/joseph -smith-prophet-to-our-generation?lang=eng.

251   *Smith's grand entrance was greeted:* Roberts, *History of the Church of Jesus Christ of Latter-Day Saints,* 5:444, 449, 467; B. H. Roberts, *The Rise and Fall of Nauvoo* (Salt Lake City: Deseret News, 1900), 245; Ford, *History of Illinois*, 316.

251   *Smith's grandiosity led him:* Brodie, *No Man Knows My History*, 340–1; Shook, *True Origins of Mormon Polygamy*, 86–93.

252   *More than any other:* Ford, *History of Illinois*, 327–9.

252   *"I will make war":* Roberts, *History of the Church of Jesus Christ of Latter-Day Saints*, 5:473; Ford, *History of Illinois*, 317; Roberts, *Rise and Fall of Nauvoo*, 244–6.

252   *In a ploy to trump Smith's endorsement:* Calvin N. Smith, " 'Gentile' Champions Church Cause During Tribulations in Nauvoo," *LDS Church News*, Augusts 19, 1989; Roberts, *History of the Church of Jesus Christ of Latter-Day Saints*, 5:326; Ford, *History of Illinois*, 319.

253   *Verily, Hoge received:* Linn, *The Story of the Mormons*, 249; Johannsen, *Stephen A. Douglas,* 122; Ford, *History of Illinois*, 319.

253   *Smith's grandiosity rapidly:* Roberts, *History of the Church of Jesus Christ of Latter-Day Saints*, 6:116; Brodie, *No Man Knows My History*, 356.

253   *Having pitted the Democrats:* Roberts, *History of the Church of Jesus Christ of Latter-Day Saints*, 5:256, 6:322–3, 6:244.

254   *Seized by Texas fever:* Ibid., 6:275–7, 6:373; Brodie, *No Man Knows My History*, 360, 462–4.

254   *Preparing for his presidential:* Roberts, *History of the Church of Jesus Christ of Latter-Day Saints*, 6:152.

254   *William Law, second counselor:* Ibid., 5:285.

255   *Law confronted him:* Brodie, *No Man Knows My History*, 369; Roberts, *History of the Church of Jesus Christ of Latter-Day Saints*, 6:403–5, 6:408–9.

255   *"The Truth, the whole Truth":* Nauvoo Expositor, June 7, 1844, http://www.utlm .org/onlineresources/nauvooexpositor.htm; John Hay, "The Mormon Prophet's Tragedy," *Atlantic Monthly*, December 1869.

256   *As proof, the* Expositor *printed: Nauvoo Expositor*, June 7, 1844, http://www.utlm .org/onlineresources/nauvooexpositor.htm; Linn, *The Story of the Mormons*, 291–2.

256   *Smith summoned an emergency meeting:* Roberts, *History of the Church of Jesus Christ of Latter-Day Saints*, 6:445; Linn, *The Story of the Mormons*, 294–5.

256   *The* Expositor's *editors fled:* Hay, "The Mormon Prophet's Tragedy"; *Warsaw Signal,* June 12, 1844, http://www.sidneyrigdon.com/dbroadhu/IL/sign1844.htm.

257   *Judge Jesse Thomas:* Roberts, *History of the Church of Jesus Christ of Latter-Day Saints,* 6:479; Ford, *History of Illinois,* 328.

257   *Smith's council denounced:* Roberts, *History of the Church of Jesus Christ of Latter-Day Saints,* 6:495–7, 6:499; Brodie, *No Man Knows My History,* 383–5.

257   *In the jail at Carthage:* Roberts, *Rise and Fall of Nauvoo,* 432–8.

258   *In a struggle for power Brigham Young:* Roberts, *History of the Church of Jesus Christ of Latter-Day Saints,* 6:330–2; Ford, *History of Illinois,* 411; Hay, "The Mormon Prophet's Tragedy."

259   *While the new Republican Party:* Vitale, "Lincoln and Mormons"; Johannsen, *Stephen A. Douglas,* 568.

259   *In Springfield, looking forward:* CW, 2:399.

260   *A week after Lincoln's election:* Mary Jane Woodger and Jessica Wainwright Christensen, "Lincoln and the Brethren," *Religious Educator* 11, no. 1 (2010): 109–42; Fred C. Collier, ed., *The Office Journal of President Brigham Young: 1858–1863, Book D* (Hanna, Utah: Collier's Publishing, 2006), 220, 277–8; Scott G. Kenney, ed. *Wilford Woodruff's Journal* (Midvale, Utah: Signature Books, 1984), 5:605–6.

260   *On July 2, 1862:* John Hyde, *Mormonism: Its Leaders and Designs* (New York: W. P. Fetridge, 1857), 65, 69, 307, 310–11.

261   *But Lincoln did not enforce:* Vitale, "Lincoln and Mormons."

CHAPTER TEN: THE DUELIST

263   *Immediately after sweeping:* Miller, *Lincoln and His World,* 515–6.

264   *James Shields was Douglas's indispensable:* Johannsen, *Stephen A. Douglas,* 92; William H. Condon, *Life of Major-General James Shields* (Chicago: Blakely Printing, 1900), 23–6; McCormack, *Memoirs of Gustave Koerner,* 1:414; Nicolay and Hay, *Abraham Lincoln,* 1:214.

264   *"Shields is a fool":* CW, 1:291-6.

265   *If the Democratic plan:* Beveridge, *Abraham Lincoln,* 1:338–40; "Mormon stories," *Sangamo Journal.* http://www.sidneyrigdon.com/dbroadhu/IL/sang1842.htm; Herndon and Weik, *Herndon's Lincoln,* 192; Justin G. Turner and Linda Levitt Turner, *Mary Todd Lincoln: Her Life and Letters* (New York: Knopf, 1972), 293–4.

265   *"I have become the object of slander":* Beveridge, *Abraham Lincoln,* 1:345–9; Louis Vargo, "Abraham Lincoln Prepares to Fight a Saber Duel," *Civil War Magazine* (February 2002); Linder, *Reminiscences of the Early Bench and Bar of Illinois,* 66–7; Angle, *"Here I Have Lived,"* 125; Condon, *Life of Major-General James Shields,* 368.

266   *Escalated into a matter of honor:* "The Age of Political Duels," Missouri Digital Heritage, http://www.sos.mo.gov/archives/education/dueling/political-duels.asp.

266   *On September 22, 1842, a crowd of hundreds:* Miller, *Lincoln and His World,* 525; Onstot, *Pioneers of Menard and Mason Counties,* 18; Randall Parrish, *Historic Illinois: The Romance of the Early Days* (Chicago: A. C. McClurg, 1905), 337–40.

267   *Lincoln, however, returned:* Burlingame, *Abraham Lincoln*, 1:193–4; Parrish, *Historic Illinois*, 340.

267   *The* Alton Telegraph *also disclosed:* Miller, *Lincoln and His World*, 520.

267   *Lincoln, for his part:* Turner and Turner, *Mary Todd Lincoln*, 293–5; Herndon and Weik, *Herndon's Lincoln*, 183; Francis Carpenter, *Six Months at the White House with Abraham Lincoln: The Story of a Picture* (New York: Hurd & Houghton, 1867), 305.

268   *Twenty months before:* CW, 1:282; HI, 623, 444.

268   *Yet according to Sarah Rickard:* Wilson, *Honor's Voice*, 284–5.

268   *According to Mary's account:* Turner and Turner, *Mary Todd Lincoln*, 293–5.

269   *There is one other tantalizing artifact:* Jean H. Baker, *Mary Todd Lincoln* (New York: Norton, 2008), 94; "Elections in Sangamon County, Illinois, for State Representatives," Gilder Lehrman Institute for American History, http://www.gild erlehrman.org/collections/0a3a73b3-ef1e-40a8-aea0-343848508713?back=/mweb /search%3Fneedle%3DLincoln%252C%2520Abraham%2520%281809-1865%29% 2526fields%3D_t301000285; HI, 444.

269   *About two weeks after the duel:* CW, 1:302–3.

269   *Mary had first come:* Eugenia Jones Hunt, "My Personal Recollections of Abraham and Mary Todd Lincoln," *Abraham Lincoln Quarterly* (March 1945); Burlingame, *Abraham Lincoln*, 1:195.

270   *Apparently, Mary made a spirited case:* Stevens, *A Reporter's Lincoln*, 117.

270   *But once Elizabeth Edwards knew:* Newspaper Interview with Mrs. Frances Wallace; Octavia Roberts, "We All Knew Abr'ham," *Abraham Lincoln Quarterly* 4, no. 1 (1946): 27–8; Onstot, *Pioneers of Menard and Mason Counties,* 36.

271   *Lincoln dressed for the wedding:* Hunt, "My Personal Recollections of Abraham and Mary Todd Lincoln"; Herndon and Weik, *Herndon's Lincoln*, 180.

271   *One of the distinguished guests:* HI, 665; Linder, *Reminiscences of the Early Bench and Bar of Illinois*, 73; John Dean Caton, *Early Bench and Bar in Illinois* (Chicago: Chicago Legal News, 1893), 173.

271   *Lincoln had bought the ring:* HI, 251.

272   *I certainly saw him:* Newspaper Interview with Mrs. Frances Wallace; Hunt, "My Personal Recollections of Abraham and Mary Todd Lincoln."

272   *A week after the wedding:* Wilson, *Honor's Voice,* 265–92.

273   *Stories of Mary's uncontrolled temper:* Burlingame, *Abraham Lincoln*, 1:201–6, 197; HI, 453, 577, 713; Wayne C. Temple, *Lincoln: From Skeptic to Prophet* (Mahomet, Ill.: Mayhaven, 1995), 27–8.

273   *There is another more plausible theory:* Ruth Painter Randall, *Mary Lincoln: Biography of a Marriage* (New York: Little, Brown, 1953), 70, 19; Helm, *Mary, Wife of Lincoln*, 76; Berry, *House of Abraham*, x.

274   *Mary constantly sought:* Ruth Painter Randall, *I Mary: A Biography of the Girl Who Married Abraham Lincoln* (New York: Little, Brown, 1959), 122; Winkle, *Young Eagle*, 224; HI, 358.

274 *"That Lincoln did not"*: Helm, *Mary, Wife of Lincoln*, 80.

275 *"In her domestic troubles"*: Douglas L. Wilson, "William H. Herndon and Mary Todd Lincoln," *Journal of the Abraham Lincoln Association* 22, no. 2 (Summer 2001).

275 *For all the difficulties:* Helm, *Mary, Wife of Lincoln*, 110.

275 *"It was always, music in my ears"*: Turner and Turner, *Mary Todd Lincoln*, 293–5.

275 *In 1864, at a party:* Jean Baker, "Mary and Abraham: A Marriage," in *The Lincoln Enigma: The Changing Faces of an American Icon*, Gabor Boritt, ed. (New York: Oxford University Press, 2002), 50.

275 *Despite his "plebian" background:* HI, 445.

276 *Lincoln's own ambition:* Herndon and Weik, *Herndon's Lincoln*, 304.

276 *"Miss Todd's ambition"*: Onstot, *Pioneers of Menard and Mason Counties,* 36–7; HI, 63-4.

276 *Together, Lincoln and Mary:* Baker, "Mary and Abraham," 51.

CHAPTER ELEVEN: COUP D'ÉTAT

277 *Encouraged by his wife:* CW, 1:307.

277 *Illinois' rapid population:* Miller, *Lincoln and His World*, 3:6–7.

277 *Lincoln proposed adoption:* CW, 1:309–18.

278 *Lincoln faced a field:* CW, 1:320.

279 *Lincoln's problem was that:* CW, 1:319; Tarbell, *Early Life*, 1:195.

279 *"Immediately after the nomination"*: Tarbell, *Early Life*, 1:195; Herndon and Weik, *Herndon's Lincoln*, 214.

280 *Lincoln was designated a statewide presidential elector:* Angle, *"Here I Have Lived,"* 130; Miller, *Lincoln and His World*, 3: 41, 46–7; Beveridge, *Abraham Lincoln*, 1:367; Hertz, *Hidden Lincoln*, 79.

281 *They debated almost exclusively:* Burlingame, *Abraham Lincoln*, 1:226.

281 *Lincoln's preparation for his debates:* Francis Wayland, *Elements of Political Economy* (New York: Sheldon, 1879), 103; Donald, *Lincoln*, 110.

281 *Casting aside Wayland:* Hertz, *Hidden Lincoln*, 117; Henry C. Carey, *Essay on the Rate of Wages* (Philadelphia: Carey, Lea & Blanchard, 1835), 18; Gabor S. Boritt, *Lincoln and the Economics of the American Dream* (Chicago: University of Illinois Press, 1994), 122.

282 *Carey had special contempt:* Carey, *Essay on the Rate of Wages*, 247, 244; Henry Charles Carey, *Manual of Social Science* (Philadelphia: H. C. Baird, 1874), 370, 247.

282 *Carey addressed slavery in* The Slave Trade*:* Henry C. Carey, *The Slave Trade* (Philadelphia: H. C. Baird, 1872), 364.

283 *Carey was the first internationally:* Daniel Walker Howe, *The Political Culture of the American Whigs* (Chicago: University of Chicago Press, 1979), 210–16; Michael Lind, *What Lincoln Believed* (New York: Doubleday, 2004), 80.

283 *From 1844 onward, Lincoln:* CW, 1:407–12.

284   *As Lincoln relentlessly hammered:* Miller, *Lincoln and His World*, 3:50–1.

284   *Through most of the Tyler administration:* Peterson, *Great Triumvirate*, 299–301; Charles M. Wiltse, *John C. Calhoun: Sectionalist, 1840–1850* (Indianapolis: Bobbs Merrill, 1951), 38; Seager, ed., *Papers of Henry Clay*, 9:515.

285   *Clay had inserted John Tyler:* Peterson, *Great Triumvirate*, 312–3; Thomas B. Stevenson, ed., *The Works of Henry Clay* (New York: G. P. Putnam's Sons, 1904), 371–2.

286   *On March 31, 1842, Clay retired:* Remini, *Henry Clay*, 599; *Niles' Register* 62 (1842): 88; Remini, *Henry Clay*, 601.

286   *Tyler surrounded himself:* Calhoun, *Correspondence of John C. Calhoun*, 2:478, 495–7.

287   *Calhoun's campaign handlers immediately began:* Wiltse, *John C. Calhoun: Sectionalist*, 89–90, 100, 134–5; Calhoun, *Correspondence of John C. Calhoun*, 2:556, 558.

287   *John Quincy Adams's opposition to Texas: Niles' Register* 64 (May 13, 1843): 175.

288   *Adams's "Address" was a response:* Frederick Merk, *Slavery and the Annexation of Texas* (New York: Knopf, 1972), 8.

288   *The election of 1844 was the turning point:* Sean Wilentz, "The Bombshell of 1844," in *America at the Ballot Box: Elections and American Political History*, Gareth Davies and Julian Zelizer, eds. (Philadelphia: University of Pennsylvania Press, 2016).

288   *In June 1843, Tyler appointed:* Abel P. Upshur, *A Brief Enquiry into the True Nature and Character of Our Federal Government* (Petersburg, Va.: E. and J. C. Ruffin, 1840), 116.

289   *As soon as he was sworn in:* Calhoun, *Correspondence of John C. Calhoun*, 2:376.

289   *Green reported personally to Tyler: Niles' Register* 65–66 (November 4, 1843): 149; Merk, *Slavery and the Annexation of Texas*, 1972, 254–5, 221–3; W. Stephen Belko, *The Invincible Duff Green: Whig of the West* (Columbia: University of Missouri Press, 2006), 24; Miller, *Lincoln and His World*, 3:158.

290   *Calhoun composed for the president:* Merk, *Slavery and the Annexation of Texas*, 20–23.

290   *By the fall of 1843:* Calhoun, *Correspondence of John C. Calhoun*, 908.

290   *By January 20, 1844, Upshur:* Merk, *Slavery and the Annexation of Texas*, 38; Wise, *Seven Decades of the Union*, 221.

291   Carpe diem: Wise, *Seven Decades of the Union*, 221–5.

291   *Now Secretary of State:* Merk, *Slavery and the Annexation of Texas*, 58–9; Richard K. Cralle, ed., *Reports and Public Letters of John C. Calhoun* (New York: D. Appleton, 1867), 337–8.

292   *On the same day as the release:* Robert W. Merry, *A Country of Vast Designs* (New York: Simon & Schuster, 2009), 75, 77; Joel H. Silbey, *Storm over Texas, The Annexation Controversy and the Road to Civil War* (New York: Oxford University Press, 2005), 63–5; De Alva Stanwood Alexander, *A Political History of the State of New York: 1833–1861* (New York: H. Holt, 1906), 67–8; Charles Seller, "Election of

1844," in Arthur M. Schlesinger, Jr., et al., eds., *History of American Presidential Elections, 1789–1968* (New York: Chelsea House, 1971), 1:762; Wayne Cutler, ed., *Correspondence of James K. Polk: September–December 1844* (Knoxville: University of Tennessee Press, 1993), 192.

292 *Just as Van Buren expected:* Peterson, *Great Triumvirate*, 359–60.

293 *"Texas is all now":* Cooper, *South and the Politics of Slavery*, 203.

293 *Senator Robert J. Walker of Mississippi:* Robert V. Remini, *Andrew Jackson and the Course of American Democracy* (New York: Harper & Row, 1984), 3:493–6; Merry, *A Country of Vast Designs*, 79; Edward Morse Shepard, *Martin Van Buren* (New York: Houghton Mifflin, 1896), 345; Freehling, *Road to Disunion*, 417.

294 *Adams always understood Calhoun's game:* Adams, *Memoirs of John Quincy Adams*, 1:29.

294 *On April 22, four days after:* Meigs, *Life of Thomas Hart Benton*, 347.

294 *At the convention at Baltimore opening:* William E. Dodd, *Robert J. Walker, Imperialist* (Chicago: Chicago Literary Club, 1914), 23; Calhoun, *Correspondence of John C. Calhoun*, 959.

296 *Like Benton, Blair clearly recalled:* Jon Meacham, *American Lion: Andrew Jackson in the White House* (New York: Random House, 2008), 167.

296 *Two weeks after:* Benton, *Thirty Years' View*, 2:614, 596, 599; Meigs, *Life of Thomas Hart Benton*, 351, 354, 357.

297 *Tyler still wished to be president:* Merry, *A Country of Vast Designs*, 107; Perry and Perry, *Reminiscences of Public Men*, 167–8.

297 *In July, Clay tried to appeal to the South:* Peterson, *Great Triumvirate,* 364–5; Cooper, *South and the Politics of Slavery*, 217; Melba Porter Hay, ed., *The Papers of Henry Clay* (Lexington: University Press of Kentucky, 1991), 10:91; Merry, *A Country of Vast Designs*, 109; Wilentz, *Rise of American Democracy*, 573.

298 *The Alabama Letters did Clay:* Cooper, *South and the Politics of Slavery*, 214; Robert J. Walker, *The South in Danger* (Washington, D.C.: Democratic Association, 1844).

298 *Clay's running mate was a paragon of virtue:* Richard J. Carwardine, "Lincoln, Evangelical Religion, and American Political Culture in the Era of the Civil War," *Journal of the Abraham Lincoln Association* 18, no. 1 (Winter 1997); Remini, *Henry Clay*, 651–2.

299 *Lashed as an abolitionist:* Wilson, *History of the Rise and Fall of the Slave Power in America*, 1:275–9; Peterson, *Great Triumvirate,* 362; Reinhard O. Johnson, *The Liberty Party, 1840–1848: Antislavery Third-Party Politics in the United States* (Baton Rouge: Louisiana State University Press, 2009), 42.

299 *Clay lost the entire Deep South:* Freehling, *Road to Disunion*, 438; Shepard, *Martin Van Buren*, 356.

300 *In Illinois the election was foretold:* Miller, *Lincoln and His World*, 3:64; Tarbell, *Early Life*, 1:106; CW, 1:378.

300   *The motley array of political forces:* Adams, *Memoirs of John Quincy Adams,* 12:110.

300   *After the election Tyler repackaged:* Merk, *Slavery and the Annexation of Texas,* 110–11, 281–8; Adams, *Memoirs of John Quincy Adams,* 1:25.

301   *Visions of Texas divided:* Freehling, *Road to Disunion,* 440, 446–8; Wise, *Seven Decades of the Union,* 230.

302   *Calhoun had once again failed:* Charles Henry Ambler, *Thomas Ritchie: A Study in Virginia Politics* (Richmond, Va.: Bell Book & Stationery, 1913), 231, 238–43, 252–3; Wiltse, *John C. Calhoun: Sectionalist,* 223–4; Thomas M. Leonard, *James K. Polk: A Clear and Unquestionable Destiny* (Lanham, Md.: Rowman & Littlefield, 2001), 42.

CHAPTER TWELVE: INFIDELS

304   *But Lincoln confessed that he had not:* CW, 1:347–8.

304   *Lincoln's correspondent was Williamson Durley:* CW, 1:347.

304   *The Liberty Party of Illinois won:* Theodore Calvin Pease, *Frontier State: 1818–1848* (Springfield: Illinois Centennial Commission), 371; Richard H. Sewell, *Ballots for Freedom: Antislavery Politics in the United States, 1837–1860* (New York: Oxford University Press, 1976), 31–3.

305   *Only 121 delegates from six Eastern states:* Sewell, *Ballots for Freedom,* 71–3, 77, 79.

306   *When his apprenticeship in Washington:* Frederick J. Blue, *Salmon P. Chase: A Life in Politics* (Kent, Ohio: Kent State University Press, 1987), 2; J. W. Schuckers, *The Life and Public Services of Salmon Portland Chase* (New York: D. Appleton, 1874), 38; Albert Bushnell Hart, *Salmon Portland Chase* (New York: Houghton Mifflin, 1899), 54.

307   *The movement to rescue and guide runaway slaves:* Hart, *Salmon Portland Chase,* 30–44.

307   *Beneath Cincinnati's veneer of propriety:* Ohio Antislavery Society, *Narrative of the Late Riotous Proceedings Against the Liberty of the Press, in Cincinnati* (Cincinnati: NP, 1836), 24, 27, 30.

308   *On that terrifying night:* Hart, *Salmon Portland Chase,* 49–50.

308   *For his defense of free speech:* Schuckers, *Life and Public Services of Salmon Portland Chase,* 41–4, 52.

309   *The Garrisonians had condemned the Constitution:* Wilson, *History of the Rise and Fall of the Slave Power in America,* 1:367.

309   *Adams had never called himself:* Adams, *Memoirs of John Quincy Adams,* 9:365, 10:43–44; Wilson, *History of the Rise and Fall of the Slave Power in America,* 1:435–6.

310   *The words Adams had reclaimed:* Wilson, *History of the Rise and Fall of the Slave Power in America,* 1:433–4.

310   *The break between Garrisonian abolitionism:* James Oakes, *Freedom National: The Destruction of Slavery in the United States, 1861–1865* (New York: Norton, 2013), 15–22.

311   *But it was not until Chase that a compelling:* Hart, *Salmon Portland Chase*, 56.

311   *In 1842, Chase took the case:* Schuckers, *Life and Public Services of Salmon Portland Chase*, 55–62.

312   *After the negligible showing:* Sewell, *Ballots for Freedom*, 123–5.

312   *Tall, erect, with a high forehead:* Donn Piatt, *Memories of the Men Who Saved the Union* (New York: Belford, Clarke, 1887), 96, 100.

313   *Chase was driven by an overriding:* Blue, *Salmon P. Chase,* 26, 28; Hart, *Salmon Portland Chase*, 16; Charles Frederic Goss, *Cincinnati, the Queen City, 1788–1912* (Chicago: S. J. Clarke Publishing, 1912), 1:169.

314   *The plausibility of Chase's constitutional theory:* Reinhard O. Johnson, *The Liberty Party, 1840–1848: Antislavery Third-Party Politics in the United States* (Baton Rouge: Louisiana State University Press, 2009), 252–3.

314   *Chase saw his mission as the vindication:* Sewell, *Ballots for Freedom*, 90–1; Foner, *Free Soil, Free Labor, Free Men*, 80.

314   *Chase clarified his views:* Salmon P. Chase, "The Address of the Southern and Western Liberty Convention," in *Anti-slavery Addresses of 1844 and 1845,* Charles Dexter Cleveland, ed. (London: Sampson Low, Son, & Martson, 1867), 75–125.

316   *The Chicago meeting also approved:* Edward Magdol, *Owen Lovejoy: Abolitionist in Congress* (New Brunswick, N.J.: Rutgers University Press, 1967), 24, 30, 34, 61, 59; Victor B. Howard, "The Illinois Republican Party, Part I, A Party Organizer for the Republicans in 1854," *Journal of the Illinois State Historical Society* 64, no. 2 (Summer 1971): 127; Zebina Eastman, *The Black Code in Illinois* (Chicago: University of Illinois Library, 1883), 1.

316   *Lovejoy was named as one of the five:* Sewell, *Ballots for Freedom*, 63–4.

317   *Shortly after the Liberty convention:* Hannah Maria Preston Codding, "Ichabod Codding," in *Proceedings of the Annual Meeting of the State Historical Society of Wisconsin,* vols. 44–50 (Madison: The Society, 1898), 175; Barnes, *The Antislavery Impulse*, 107, 197; N. Dwight Harris, *The History of Negro Servitude in Illinois, and of the Slavery Agitation in That State, 1719–1864* (Chicago: A. C. McClurg, 1904), 153–4.

317   *The Liberty Party was not only:* A. T. Andreas, *History of Chicago* (New York: Arno Press, 1884), 1:605–6; Wilbur Henry Siebert, *The Underground Railroad from Slavery to Freedom* (New York: Macmillan, 1898), 41–2; Harris, *The History of Negro Servitude in Illinois*, 379; Johannsen, *Stephen A. Douglas*, 102–3.

317   *In Chicago, the chief conductors:* Andreas, *History of Chicago*, 607.

318   *Lovejoy would be elected:* HI, 149–50; *Biographical Sketches of the Leading Men of Chicago* (Chicago: Wilson & St. Clair, 1868), 76.

318   *Lincoln's interlocutor with the Illinois abolitionists:* Herndon and Weik, *Herndon's Lincoln*, xiv.

319   *Stephen T. Logan had decided after the 1844 election:* Ibid., 252.

320   *The partners:* David Herbert Donald, *Lincoln's Herndon* (New York: Knopf, 1948), 25.

320 *Herndon was more than a worker bee:* Ibid., 54, 198; Angle, *"Here I Have Lived,"* 192; David Herbert Donald, *We Are Lincoln Men* (New York: Simon & Schuster, 2003), 80.

321 *Lincoln was always the indisputable:* Donald, *Lincoln's Herndon*, 199; Donald, *We Are Lincoln Men*, 76; Douglas L. Wilson, "William H. Herndon and His Lincoln Informants," *Journal of the Abraham Lincoln Association* 14, no. 1 (Winter 1993); John Y. Simon, "Abraham Lincoln and Ann Rutledge," *Journal of the Abraham Lincoln Association* 11, no. 1 (Winter 1990).

322 *Lincoln recruited Herndon just as he planned:* Frank E. Stevens, "Autobiography of Stephen A. Douglas," *Journal of the Illinois State Historical Society* 5 (1913): 324; CW, 1:351, 353.

323 *Hardin proposed a direct primary of Whig voters:* CW, 1:356, 359, 360–5.

323 *The first caucus to choose delegates:* Beveridge, *Abraham Lincoln*, 1:374; Burlingame, *Abraham Lincoln*, 1:235.

324 *On May 1, the Whig convention:* Beveridge, *Abraham Lincoln*, 1:375.

324 *For weeks, the Democrats were without a candidate:* Herndon and Weik, *Herndon's Lincoln*, 218.

324 *Cartwright, known in his youth:* Onstot, *Pioneers of Menard and Mason Counties*, 106, 109, 111.

325 *Thirteen days after the Whig convention:* Merry, *A Country of Vast Designs*, 240–51.

325 *The Democratic-controlled House permitted:* Adams, *Memoirs of John Quincy Adams*, 1:202.

325 *Hardin immediately enlisted as a colonel:* Miller, *Lincoln and His World*, 3:104; CW, 1:381.

326 *At a State House recruitment rally:* Miller, *Lincoln and His World*, 3:105; Francis Fisher Browne, *The Every-day Life of Abraham Lincoln* (New York: G. P. Putnam, 1915), 131.

326 *Baker's 4th Illinois Regiment:* Angle, *"Here I Have Lived,"* 132; CW, 1:383.

326 *The attack on Lincoln as an infidel:* Remini, *Henry Clay*, 649–50.

326 *Lincoln was swinging through:* Ida Tarbell, *Abraham Lincoln and His Ancestor* (Lincoln: University of Nebraska Press, 1924), 270–1.

327 *But Cartwright's campaign against the unbeliever:* HI, 432; Herndon and Weik, *Herndon's Lincoln*, 218.

328 *Finally, he ended with affirmation:* CW, 1:382; Wilson, *Honor's Voice*, 310–12.

328 *In the future Lincoln would not stray:* Lamon, *Life of Abraham Lincoln*, 520.

328 *While fending off Cartwright's infidelity charge:* Cartwright, *Backwoods Preacher*, 246.

329 *Two abolitionists:* HI, 700.

329 *Lincoln was already known as one:* Noah Brooks, *Abraham Lincoln and the Downfall of Slavery* (New York: G. P. Putnam's Sons, 1894), 126–7.

329 *Brooks's story was not apocryphal:* Samuel Willard, "Personal Reminiscences of Life in Illinois—1830–1850," *Transactions of the Illinois State Historical Society* 11 (1906): 85–7.

330   *In 1845, as he prepared to run:* Richard E. Hart, "Lincoln's Springfield, The Underground Railroad," *Abraham Lincoln Association Newsletter* 8, no. 1–2, 2006; Miller, *Lincoln and His World*, 3:89–90.

330   *The documentation for some of these cases:* Hart, "Lincoln's Springfield, The Underground Railroad"; *History of Sangamon County,* 514.

330   *Among the Underground Railroad conductors:* Hart, "Lincoln's Springfield, The Underground Railroad."

331   *Lincoln won his congressional race:* Hertz, *Hidden Lincoln,* 253.

331   *While Lincoln campaigned:* Johannsen, *Stephen A. Douglas,* 194–6.

331   *In private, Douglas debated the war:* Browne, *Abraham Lincoln and the Men of His Times,* 1:364–6.

332   *Within the Congress, Douglas had befriended his home state:* Johannsen, *Stephen A. Douglas,* 195–6, 187–9.

332   *Shields came back a hero:* Isaac N. Arnold, *Reminiscences of the Illinois Bar Forty Years Ago* (Chicago: Fergus, 1881), 15; Johannsen, *Stephen A. Douglas,* 259–61; James L. Huston, *Stephen A. Douglas and the Dilemmas of Democratic Equality* (Lanham, Md.: Rowman & Littlefield, 2007), 72–3.

333   *When Shields was wounded attacking*: James H. Matheny, "A Modern Knight Errant—Edward Dickinson Baker," *Journal of the Illinois State Historical Society* 9 (1916): 27–8; Miller, *Lincoln and His World*, 3:204.

333   *John J. Hardin came home in a coffin:* John Frost, *Life of Major General Zachary Taylor* (New York: D. Appleton, 1847), 290.

333   *On July 4, 1847, Springfield:* Beveridge, *Abraham Lincoln,* 1:389–90; Miller, *Lincoln and His World*, 3:146.

CHAPTER THIRTEEN: GREAT EXPECTATIONS

335   *The newly elected congressman:* William Mosley Hall, *Chicago River-and-Harbor Convention* (Chicago: Fergus, 1882), 14–16.

336   *More than one thousand delegates:* Miller, *Lincoln and His World*, 3:134.

336   *One notable voice was heard:* Hall, *Chicago River-and-Harbor Convention*, 141; Miller, *Lincoln and His World*, 3:136.

336   *The* Chicago Journal *went out:* Hall, *Chicago River-and-Harbor Convention*, 138.

337   *Only thirty-six years old:* Allen Thorndike Rice, *Reminiscences of Abraham Lincoln by Distinguished Men of His Time* (New York: North American Publishing, 1886), 16.

337   *Lincoln's reply to Field was his first speech:* Robin L. Einhorn, *Property Rules: Political Economy in Chicago, 1833–1872* (Chicago: University of Chicago Press, 2001), 66–75; Joshua A. T. Salzmann, "Safe Harbor: Chicago's Waterfront and the Political Economy of the Built Environment, 1847–1918" (PhD diss., University of Illinois, 2008), 23–65.

337   *While the River and Harbor Convention met:* Harris, *The History of Negro Servitude in Illinois,* 235; Winkle, *Young Eagle,* 260–1.

338 *Before departing for Washington:* Miller, *Lincoln and His World*, 3:151; Charles R. McKirdy, *Lincoln Apostate: The Matson Slave Case* (Jackson: University Press of Mississippi, 2011), 43.

338 *Robert Matson, of Bourbon County, Kentucky:* Duncan T. McIntyre, "Matson Slave Trial," *Tuscola Review* (September 7, 1922); Mark E. Steiner, *An Honest Calling: the Law Practice of Abraham Lincoln* (DeKalb: Northern Illinois University Press, 2006), 106–8; McKirdy, *Lincoln Apostate*, 44.

339 *Matson swore in his affidavit:* Steiner, *An Honest Calling*, 110–13.

339 *On the eve of the trial:* Jesse W. Weik, "Lincoln and the Matson Negroes: A Vista into the Fugitive-Slave Days," *The Arena* 17 (1897): 755.

340 *Linder delivered a stentorian speech:* Ibid., 756; McIntyre, "Matson Slave Trial."

340 *Lincoln completely ignored Linder's pro-slavery:* Weik, "Lincoln and the Matson Negroes," 756; McIntyre, "Matson Slave Trial"; HI, 58; "Stephen T. Logan Talks About Lincoln," *Bulletin of the Abraham Lincoln Association* 12, no. 1 (1928): 5.

341 *Lincoln would have been as aware:* Weik, "Lincoln and the Matson Negroes," 757; Steiner, *An Honest Calling*, 120–1; Beveridge, *Abraham Lincoln*, 1:397.

341 *The American Colonization Society took charge:* Steiner, *An Honest Calling*, 125; Weik, "Lincoln and the Matson Negroes," 757; Delores Archaimbault and Terry A. Barnhart, "Illinois Copperheads and the American Civil War," Illinois Periodicals Online, http://www.lib.niu.edu/1996/iht319615.html.

342 *"It was a cold day in November":* "Abraham Lincoln's Classroom," http://www.abrahamlincolnsclassroom.org/Library/newsletter.asp?ID=55&CRLI=135.

342 *At last, in Lexington, Lincoln:* "Henry Clay and Abraham Lincoln," Ashland— The Henry Clay Estate, http://www.henryclay.org/henry-clay/henry-clay-and-abraham-lincoln/.

342 *Distressed by his son's death:* Remini, *Henry Clay*, 670–1, 684–5, 687–8, 697; George Washington Julian, *The Life of Joshua R. Giddings* (New York: A. C. McClurg, 1892), 209.

343 *And he concluded with an eight-point program:* Remini, *Henry Clay*, 692–4.

344 *After Clay's speech, Lincoln was introduced:* J. G. Holland, *Life of Lincoln* (Springfield, Mass.: G. Bill, 1866), 95–6; HI, 569; Alexander K. McClure, *Abe Lincoln's Yarns and Stories* (Philadelphia: International Publishing, 1901), 200.

344 *But Lincoln was leaning to Taylor:* John Hill, *Opposing Principles of Henry Clay and Abraham Lincoln* (St. Louis: G. Knapp, 1860), 13; Burlingame, *Abraham Lincoln*, 1:274; William C. Harris, *Lincoln's Last Months* (Cambridge: Harvard University Press, 2004), 107–11.

345 *The questions that Clay raised in his speech:* Burlingame, *Abraham Lincoln*, 1:256; Miller, *Lincoln and His World*, 3:156.

346 *At these lines Lincoln:* Elizabeth Todd Grimsley, "Six Months in the White House," *Journal of the Illinois State Historical Society* 19 (October–January 1926–27): 57; Burlingame, *Abraham Lincoln*, 1:255–6.

CHAPTER FOURTEEN: RANCHERO SPOTTY

347 *Lincoln arrived at the city of his dreams:* William Allen, "History of Slave Labor-ers in the Construction of the United States Capitol," History, Art and Archives of the U.S. House of Representatives, http://artandhistory.house.gov/art_artifacts /slave_labor_reportl.pdf; Charles Dickens, *American Notes* (London: Chapman & Hall, 1842), 281–2.

348 *The Capitol's looming grandeur:* Guy Gugliotta, *Freedom's Cap: The United States Capitol and the Coming of the Civil War* (New York: Macmillan, 2012), 9–26.

348 *Yet the shabbiness, noise, and filth:* Ben Perley Poore, *Perley's Reminiscences* (Tecum-seh, Mich.: A. W. Mills, 1886), 1:341.

348 *On December 6, he caucused:* Ibid., 1:42; Robert C. Winthrop, Jr., *A Memoir of Rob-ert C. Winthrop* (Boston: Little, Brown, 1897), 71; *Congressional Globe*, 30th Con-gress, 1st Session, December 6, 1847, 2; David Herbert Donald, *Charles Sumner and the Coming of the Civil War* (Chicago: University of Chicago Press, 1960), 144–8; Luthin, *Real Abraham Lincoln*, 102–3; Julian, *Life of Joshua R. Giddings*, 222, 232, 226–32.

349 *Mary had once confided:* Sarah Meer, *Uncle Tom Mania: Slavery, Minstrelsy, and Transatlantic Culture in the 1850s* (Athens: University of Georgia Press, 2005), 151; Baker, *Mary Todd Lincoln*, 139–41; Rice, *Reminiscences of Abraham Lincoln by Dis-tinguished Men of His Time*, 222.

350 *Almost the instant Lincoln landed:* Michael F. Holt, *The Rise and Fall of the Whig Party: Jacksonian Politics and the Onset of the Civil War* (New York: Oxford Uni-versity Press, 2003), 288–9; Alexander H. Stephens, *Recollections of Alexander H. Stephens* (New York: Doubleday, Page, 1910), 21–2; CW, 1:448; Arnold, *Life of Abraham Lincoln*, 77.

351 *"I have to say I am in favor":* CW, 1:455.

351 *Lincoln envisioned Taylor:* CW, 1:455, 467, 453.

352 *The political unraveling of Polk's presidency:* Wilentz, *Rise of American Democracy*, 577.

353 *Polk's two main generals:* Sargent, *Public Men and Events from the Commencement of Mr. Monroe's Administration*, 2:292–4, 304, 326.

353 *When Scott had protested:* Ibid., 2:320.

353 *The "fire in the rear" also happened:* Winfield Scott, *Memoirs* (New York: Sheldon, 1864), 2:416; Nathaniel Cheairs Hughes and Roy P. Stonesifer, *The Life and Wars of Gideon J. Pillow* (Chapel Hill: University of North Carolina Press, 1993), 325.

354 *In September 1847, after Scott's great victories:* Walter R. Borneman, *Polk: The Man Who Transformed the Presidency and America* (New York: Random House, 2009), 295; Eugene Irving McCormac, *James K. Polk: A Political Biography* (Berkeley: University of California Press, 1922), 532.

355 *On December 7, the next day:* James K. Polk, "Third Annual Message," Ameri-can President Project, http://www.presidency.ucsb.edu/ws/index.php?pid=29488;

Borneman, *Polk,* 298; Merry, *A Country of Vast Designs,* 408; John D. Eisenhower, *Agent of Destiny; The Life and Times of General Winfield Scott* (Norman: University of Oklahoma Press, 1999), 313; Scott, *Memoirs,* 2:415, 417.

355 *Trist's treaty, the Treaty of Guadalupe Hidalgo:* Richard M. Ketchum, "The Thankless Task of Nicholas Trist," *American Heritage* 21, no. 5 (August 1970); McCormac, *James K. Polk,* 527, 532, 526, 529, 530, 534, 541, 544; Merry, *A Country of Vast Designs,* 441–2.

356 *Under the stress of war and strain:* Howe, *What Hath God Wrought,* 798–90; Wilentz, *Rise of American Democracy,* 611; Blue, *No Taint of Compromise,* 191–4; CW, 2:252.

357 *Senator Cass of Michigan:* Howe, *What Hath God Wrought,* 798–90; Wilentz, *Rise of American Democracy,* 611.

357 *Calhoun had become a rancorous enemy:* Wiltse, *John C. Calhoun, Sectionalist,* 220, 227, 297, 301–2; Sargent, *Public Men and Events from the Commencement of Mr. Monroe's Administration,* 2:266–8; McCormac, *James K. Polk,* 468.

357 *Calhoun's stem-winding speech:* Hemphill, ed., *Papers of John C. Calhoun,* 24:169–75.

358 *Calhoun's speech was the most radical:* Wiltse, *John C. Calhoun,* 294–5.

358 *In the midst of the Democrats' disarray:* Howe, *Political Culture of the American Whigs,* 289.

358 *One week after the opening of the first session:* Benjamin Perley Poore, *Veto Messages of the Presidents of the United States* (Washington, D.C.: U.S. Government Printing Office, 1886), 194–211.

359 *Calhoun, constantly probing for Polk's vulnerability: Congressional Globe,* 30th Congress, 1st Session, December 20, 1847, 54–5.

359 *The next day, Joshua Giddings, the abolitionist Quixote: Congressional Globe,* 30th Congress, 1st Session, December 21, 1847, 60.

359 *On December 21, Stephens launched the Young Indian offensive: Congressional Globe,* 30th Congress, 1st Session, December 21, 1847, 61–2.

360 *It was this claim about the war's source:* Congressional Globe, 30th Congress, 1st Session, December 22, 1847, 64.

360 *Lincoln's "Spot Resolution" was undoubtedly coordinated:* Beveridge, *Abraham Lincoln,* 1:423–4.

360 *Lincoln had not yet delivered a proper speech:* CW, 1:430.

360 *On January 12, Lincoln took the floor:* CW, 1:431–42.

361 *Lincoln's maiden speech dripped:* CW, 6, 392.

361 *Reaching his peroration Lincoln:* CW, 1:441–2.

361 *On February 1, the new senator: Congressional Globe,* 30th Congress, 1st Session, February 1, 1848, 221–6; *Congressional Globe,* 30th Congress, 1st Session, February 2, 1848, 159–63.

362 *The Lincoln-Douglas debate over the Mexican War:* Herbert Mitgang, *Abraham Lincoln: A Press Portrait* (New York: Fordham University Press, 2000), 55–8.

362 *From Springfield, Herndon wrote Lincoln:* Hertz, *Hidden Lincoln*, 172.

363 *"I will stake my life":* CW, 1:446–7.

363 *Months after delivering the speech that got him branded:* Elliott Anthony, "The Need of a Constitutional Convention, Historically Considered," *Proceedings of the Illinois State Bar Association* (1891), 115; John Mason Peck, *Forty Years of Pioneer Life* (Philadelphia: American Baptist Publication Society, 1864), 195.

364 *One place Lincoln found reinforcement:* Samuel Clagett Busey, *Personal Reminiscences and Recollections of Forty-Six Years' Membership in the Medical Society of the District of Columbia and Residence in this City, with Biographical Sketches of Many of the Deceased Members* (Washington, D.C.: Dornan, 1895), 25–28.

364 *Since Jefferson's day, legislators:* James Sterling Young, *The Washington Community, 1800–1828* (New York: Columbia University Press, 1966), 98–109.

365 *Giddings was the dominant personality:* Miller, *Arguing About Slavery*, 341; James Brewer Stewart, "Joshua Giddings, Antislavery Violence and Congressional Politics of Honor," in *Antislavery Violence: Sectional, Racial, and Cultural Conflict in Antebellum America,* John R. McKivigan and Stanley Harrold, eds. (Knoxville: University of Tennessee Press, 1999), 155, 184.

366 *The members of the Congress residing:* McClure, *Our Presidents*, 95; Joseph H. Bausman, *History of Beaver County, Pennsylvania* (New York: Knickerbocker Press, 1904), 2:1151; Charles L Blockson, "The Underground Railroad in Pennsylvania," *Milestones* 20, no. 2 (Summer 1995); A. R. McIlvaine, *Speech of Honorable A. R. McIlvaine of Pennsylvania on the Mexican War in the House of Representatives, February 4, 1847* (Washington, D.C.: Blair & Rives, 1847).

366 *Lincoln befriended another messmate:* Holt, *Rise and Fall of the Whig Party*, 441; John J. Hight, *History of the Indiana Fifty-eighth Regiment of Volunteer Infantry* (Princeton: Press of the Clarion, 1895), 572; William Henry Egle, *Life and Times of Andrew Gregg Curtin* (Philadelphia: Thompson Publishing, 1896), 49–51.

366 *James Pollock of Pennsylvania:* Reginald Horsman, *Race and Manifest Destiny: The Origins of American Racial Anglo-Saxonism* (Cambridge: Harvard University Press, 1981), 240; Tyler G. Anbinder, *Nativism and Slavery: The Northern Know Nothings and the Politics of the 1850s* (New York: Oxford University Press, 1994), 58.

367 *Patrick W. Tompkins of Mississippi:* James Daniel Lynch, *The Bench and Bar of Mississippi* (New York: E. J. Hale & Son, 1881), 285.

367 *The other boarders included Nathan Sargent:* "Baseball in Washington During the Civil War," Civil War Washington, D.C., http://civilwarwashingtondc1861-1865 .blogspot.com/2011/08/baseball-in-washington-during-civil-war.html.

367 *"The Wilmot Proviso was the topic of frequent conversation":* Busey, *Personal Reminiscences*, 25–28.

368 *The growing band of antislavery:* Stanley Harrold, *Subversives: Antislavery Community in Washington, DC, 1828–1865* (Baton Rouge: Louisiana State University Press), 203, 109.

368 *Washington was a Southern city:* Bancroft, *Slave Trading in the Old South*, 45–66; Helen Nicolay, *Our Capital on the Potomac* (New York: Century, 1924), 350.

369 *Since the founding of Washington, slavery was a source:* Wilson, *Honor's Voice*, 275; Bray, *Reading with Lincoln*, 102; Marcus Wood, ed., *The Poetry of Slavery: An Anglo-American Anthology, 1764–1865* (New York: Oxford University Press, 2004), 238; Gideon Welles, *Diary of Gideon Welles* (New York: Houghton Mifflin, 1911), 1:26.

369 *Until he arrived, of course:* CW, 2:253.

369 *Mrs. Sprigg's was more than a boardinghouse:* Wilson, *History of the Rise and Fall of the Slave Power in America*, 2:74–9.

370 *Ann G. Thornton, a native Virginian:* Theodore Weld, *Letters of Theodore Dwight Weld, Angelina Grimké Weld and Sarah Grimké, 1822–1844* (New York: D. Appleton-Century, 1934), 2:948; Harrold, *Subversives*, 68–84, 82; Clark Evans, "Cornucopia of Lincolniana," Library of Congress, http://www.loc.gov/loc/lcib/0903/lincolniana.html.

370 *Henry and Sylvia Wilson, a married couple:* Harrold, *Subversives*, 108–11; Giddings, *History of the Rebellion*, 269; *Congressional Globe*, 30th Congress, 1st Session, January 17, 1848, 250.

371 *The incident inspired Giddings:* *Congressional Globe*, 30th Congress, 1st Session, January 31, 1848, 326.

371 *The animosity toward Giddings:* *Congressional Globe*, 32nd Congress, 1st Session, February 11, 1852, 534–5.

372 *In the House of Representatives:* Sargent, *Public Men and Events from the Commencement of Mr. Monroe's Administration*, 2:331–2; Wheelan, *Mr. Adams's Last Crusade*, 246–8.

372 *On the day that Adams died:* Johannsen, *Stephen A. Douglas*, 329.

372 *Facing the new revolutionary government in France:* Wiltse, *John C. Calhoun, Sectionalist*, 2:340; James K. Polk, "Special Message," American Presidency Project, http://www.presidency.ucsb.edu/ws/index.php?pid=67998.

373 *Lending support to Polk:* Jean Baker, *Affairs of Party: The Political Culture of Northern Democrats in the Mid-Nineteenth Century* (New York: Fordham University Press, 1998), 42–5.

373 *Hale was new to the exclusive club of the Senate:* Daniel Hall, *Addresses Commemorative of Abraham Lincoln and John P. Hale* (Concord, N.H.: Republican Press Association, 1892), 54; Jonathan H. Earle, *Jacksonian Antislavery and the Politics of Free Soil, 1824–1854* (Chapel Hill: University of North Carolina Press, 2004), 93; Sewell, *Ballots for Freedom*, 127–9.

374 *Now Hale proposed an amendment:* *Congressional Globe*, 30th Congress, 1st Session, 567–9; Wiltse, *John C. Calhoun, Sectionalist*, 2:339.

374 *That night, April 13, the Democratic Party:* Wiltse, *John C. Calhoun, Sectionalist*, 2:340; Horace Mann, *Slavery: Letters and Speeches* (Boston: B. B. Mussey, 1851), 105–6.

375 *While the revelers hailed foreign revolution:* Harrold, *Subversives*, 116–21; Daniel Drayton, *Personal Memoir of Daniel Drayton* (New York: B. Marsh, 1855), 40.

375 *The next morning, April 18, Giddings: Congressional Globe*, 30th Congress, 1st Session, 41.

375 *That evening a mob assembled outside:* Mary Kay Ricks, *Escape on the Pearl: The Heroic Bid for Freedom on the Underground Railroad* (New York: William Morrow, 2007), 114–17.

376 *The next morning, Giddings marched:* Drayton, *Personal Memoir of Daniel Drayton*, 45; Joshua R. Giddings, *Speeches in Congress* (Boston: John P. Jewett, 1853), 227–8; Ricks, *Escape on the Pearl*, 105.

376 *It is almost certain that Giddings:* Harrold, *Subversives,* 94–115; Ricks, *Escape on the Pearl,* 21–3.

377 *The mob that threatened Giddings in the morning:* Drayton, *Personal Memoir of Daniel Drayton*, 51; Ricks, *Escape on the Pearl*, 123; Milo Milton Quaife, ed., *The Diary of James K. Polk During His Presidency, 1845–1849* (New York: A. C. McClurg, 1910), 428–9.

377 *The subject swiftly turned to punishing Giddings: Congressional Globe*, 30th Congress, 1st Session, 649–55.

378 *Meanwhile, on the same day in the Senate: Congressional Globe*, 30th Congress, 1st Session, 500.

378 *Senator James Westcott of Florida: Congressional Globe*, 30th Congress, 1st Session, 500.

378 *Calhoun's vehemence had left him exhausted:* Henry S. Foote, *Casket of Reminiscences* (Washington, D.C.: Chronicle Publishing, 1874), 75.

379 *Upon receiving this request from Calhoun:* Davis, *Autobiography of the Late Col. Geo. T. M. Davis,* 1:13; Joan E. Cashin, *First Lady of the Confederacy: Varina Davis's Civil War* (Cambridge: Harvard University Press, 2006), 32–53; William J. Cooper, Jr., *Jefferson Davis, American* (New York: Knopf, 2000), 72–7, 128.

379 *Now, summoned by Calhoun: Congressional Globe*, 30th Congress, 1st Session, 501.

380 *Then Foote took the floor: Congressional Globe*, 30th Congress, 1st Session, 502.

381 *At the District jail one of the guards:* Ricks, *Escape on the Pearl*, 162–9; Frederick W. Seward and William H. Seward, *1846–1861* (New York: Derby & Miller, 1891), 73.

381 *The U.S. Attorney, Philip Barton Key:* Mann, *Slavery*, 100–8.

382 *Over the next ten months four trials were staged:* Ricks, *Escape on the Pearl*, 170, 202–3, 288–9; Harrold, *Subversives,* 140–1.

382 *The slaves, for their part:* Harrold, *Subversives,* 137; Harriet Beecher Stowe, *A Key to Uncle Tom's Cabin* (Cleveland: John P. Jewett & Co., 1853), 381–412.

382 *While rage over the* Pearl *consumed the capital:* CW, 1:495; Oliver Dyer, *Great Senators of the United States Forty Years Ago, 1848–1849* (New York: R. Bonner's Sons, 1889), 76; Remini, *Henry Clay*, 706–7.

383 *Taylor had no known positions on the issues:* "Whig Party Platform of 1848," Amer-

ican Presidency Project, http://www.presidency.ucsb.edu/ws/index.php?pid=25855; Don C. Seitz, *Horace Greeley* (Indianapolis: Bobbs-Merrill, 1926), 96; Wilentz, *Rise of American Democracy*, 617; Remini, *Henry Clay*, 710.

384 *On his return to Washington, Lincoln stopped in Wilmington:* Beveridge, *Abraham Lincoln*, 1:462; CW, 1:475–6.

384 *Lincoln was cheerful about the Whig:* CW, 1:476–7, 490–1; Miller, *Lincoln and His World*, 3:195.

384 *"Yet Lincoln was peevish:* CW, 1:491.

385 *On July 4th, 1848, a parade a mile:* Robert C. Winthrop, *Oration* (Washington, D.C.: J. & G. S. Gideon, 1848), 3–8, 27.

385 *Back in Springfield, the Whig campaign:* Herndon and Weik, *Herndon's Lincoln*, 227; CW, 1:447–8; Miller, *Lincoln and His World*, 3:195.

387 *Acting as Polk's Senate floor leader:* Dyer, *Great Senators of the United States Forty Years Ago*, 45; Poore, *Veto Messages of the Presidents of the United States*, 344–5; Willard Carl Klunder, *Lewis Cass and the Politics of Moderation* (Kent, Ohio: Kent State University Press, 1996), 121; Sargent, *Public Men and Events from the Commencement of Mr. Monroe's Administration*, 2:272.

389 *But Lincoln was not done:* CW, 1:501–16.

389 *The Seventh Congressional District:* Hertz, *Hidden Lincoln*, 172; McCormack, *Memoirs of Gustave Koerner*, 1:478–9.

389 *Logan's Democratic opponent was the dashing:* Miller, *Lincoln and His World*, 3:198–200; Pease, *Story of Illinois*, 393–4; Arthur Charles Cole, *Centennial History of Illinois: The Era of the Civil War, 1848–1870* (Springfield, Ill.: A. C. McClurg, 1922), 3:16.

390 *Whether Lincoln caused Logan's defeat:* Miller, *Lincoln and His World*, 3:204–5.

390 *The first session of the 30th Congress:* Mann, *Slavery*, 402; Burlingham, *Abraham Lincoln*, 1:285.

391 *Even before the Congress adjourned:* CW, 1:498.

CHAPTER FIFTEEN: THE HAYSEED

393 *On August 9, 1848, a crowd in the fervent:* David S. Reynolds, *Walt Whitman's America* (New York: Knopf, 1995), 126.

395 *The ultras, Gerrit Smith and his followers:* Niven, *John C. Calhoun*, 88–9, 94, 100, 107–8; Sewell, *Ballots for Freedom*, 135–8, 141; Wilson, *History of the Rise and Fall of the Slave Power in America*, 2:110.

395 *Abbott Lawrence, owner of the largest textile mills:* Carl Schurz, *The Reminiscences of Carl Schurz* (London: J. Murray, 1909), 2:35; Donald, *Charles Sumner and the Coming of the Civil War*, 155–65; Wilentz, *Rise of American Democracy*, 608.

396 *At the national convention, the Massachusetts Conscience Whigs:* Wilson, *History of the Rise and Fall of the Slave Power in America*, 2:124; Edward L. Pierce, *Memoir and Letters of Charles Sumner* (Boston: Roberts Brothers, 1894), 3:162; Harriet A.

Weed, *Autobiography of Thurlow Weed* (New York: Houghton Mifflin, 1884), 1:578; Hamilton Andrews Hill, *Memoir of Abbott Lawrence* (Cambridge, Mass.: Wilson, 1883), 78; Seward and Seward, *1846–1861*, 107.

397 *These warring factions were dubbed the Barnburners:* Ransom Hooker Gillet, *The Life and Times of Silas Wright* (Albany, N.Y.: Argus, 1874), 2:1789–91; Shepard, *Martin Van Buren*, 356; Dyer, *Great Senators of the United States Forty Years Ago*, 48; Henry B. Stanton, *Random Recollections* (New York: Harper & Brothers, 1887), 160; Wilentz, *Rise of American Democracy,* 609; Sewell, *Ballots for Freedom*, 145–8; O. C. Gardiner, *The Great Issue; or Three Presidential Candidates* (New York: W. C. Bryant, 1848), 56.

398 *Van Buren operated behind the scenes:* Sewell, *Ballots for Freedom*, 148–9; Gardiner, *The Great Issue*, 106–36.

399 *Thus the men of New York, Massachusetts, and Ohio:* Magdol, *Owen Lovejoy*, 88; John Niven, *Salmon P. Chase* (New York: Oxford University Press, 1995), 109–11; Sewell, *Ballots for Freedom*, 159.

400 *Lincoln had developed a few contacts:* Findley, *A. Lincoln*, 189–90; CW, 1:518–9; Winkle, *Young Eagle*, 245.

400 *"I have wondered how Mr. Lincoln":* HI, 681; George F. Hoar, "Edward Lillie Pierce," *Proceedings of the American Antiquarian Society* 13 (October 1897): 197–210.

401 *Paraphrasing the tiny evangelical breakaway:* Arthur P. Rugg, "Abraham Lincoln in Worcester," *Proceedings of the Worcester Society of Antiquity* 25 (1912): 226–40.

402 *The Whig newspaper account:* HI, 699; Rugg, "Abraham Lincoln in Worcester"; Pierce, *Memoir and Letters of Charles Sumner*, 3:173.

402 *The next evening, after the opening day:* HI, 698–9.

402 *Lincoln was promptly recruited to deliver campaign:* Beveridge, *Abraham Lincoln*, 1:475–6.

403 *Then Lincoln delivered his by-now stock speech:* Walter Stahr, *Seward: Lincoln's Indispensable Man* (New York: Simon & Schuster, 2012), 110; HI, 691.

403 *Years later, Seward recalled that he:* Frederick Seward, *Seward at Washington: 1846–1860* (New York: D. Appleton, 1891), 79–80; Tarbell, *Early Life*, 220; Stahr, *Seward,* 110–11; Seward, *1846–1861*, 86.

CHAPTER SIXTEEN: THE FIRM

405 *"There was to me something mysterious":* Carl Schurz, *Henry Clay* (New York: Houghton Mifflin, 1899), 2:33–4.

406 *Seward's public tone was certain:* Frederick Seward, *William H. Seward, 1831–1846* (New York: Derby & Miller, 1891), 439–40; Schurz, *Reminiscences of Carl Schurz*, 2:174.

407 *Seward's private manner was informal:* Piatt, *Memories of the Men Who Saved the Union*, 136–7.

407 *Seward was a rare case combining radicalism:* Stanton, *Random Recollections*, 204.

408 *His father, Samuel S. Seward:* William H. Seward and Frederick Seward, *Autobiography of William H. Seward, from 1801 to 1834: With a Memoir of His Life, and Selections from His Letters from 1831 to 1846* (New York: D. Appleton, 1877), 27–8.

408 *Seward attended Union College:* Stahr, *Seward,* 12; Cornelius Van Santvoord and Tayler Lewis, *Memoirs of Eliphalet Nott: For Sixty-two Years President of Union College* (New York: Sheldon, 1876), 212–14.

409 *Seward became the junior law partner:* Seward and Seward, *Autobiography of William H. Seward,* 62; William Henry Seward and Frederick W. Seward, *Seward at Washington as Senator and Secretary of State, 1846–1861* (New York: Derby & Miller, 1891), 258; Peter Wisbey, "In the 'Emancipation Business': William and Frances Seward's Abolition Activism," Ancestry.com, http://www.rootsweb.ancestry.com/~nycayuga/ugrr/seward.html#14.

409 *Seward's ascent from aspiring attorney:* Wilentz, *Rise of American Democracy*, 272–9; Seward and Seward, *Autobiography of William H. Seward*, 1:171–3.

410 *While the National Republicans evaporated:* Howe, *What Hath God Wrought*, 268–70.

410 *The following year he made a pilgrimage:* Frederick Seward, *Reminiscences of a Wartime Statesman and Diplomat: 1830–1915* (New York: G. P. Putnam's Sons, 1916), 57.

411 *Seward upheld Adams as a mentor:* Seward and Seward, *Autobiography of William H. Seward*, 1:205–6.

411 *Thurlow Weed, the son of a small farmer:* "Personal Politics; Horace Greeley's Letter to Wm. H. Seward," *New York Tribune*, June 15, 1860.

412 *In the aftermath of the Panic of 1837:* Stahr, *Seward*, 53–7, 93; Seward and Seward, *Autobiography of William H. Seward*, 1:381.

412 *The division of labor and rewards:* Piatt, *Memories of the Men Who Saved the Union*, 191.

413 *Governor Seward was the most effective:* Frederic Bancroft, *The Life of William H. Seward* (New York: Harper & Brothers, 1900), 1:103–4.

413 *After leaving the governorship:* Stahr, *Seward*, 99–105.

414 *Seward and Chase were already engaged:* Bancroft, *Life of William H. Seward*, 1:162; Schuckers, *Life and Public Services of Salmon Portland Chase*, 72.

415 *While General Zachary Taylor was earning his laurels:* Harriet A. Weed, ed., *The Life of Thurlow Weed* (New York: Houghton Mifflin, 1884), 570–2; Stahr, *Seward*, 106–9; Bancroft, *Life of William H. Seward*, 1:157.

415 *Weed was closely tracking the split:* Seward, *1846–1861*, 55, 61, 67.

416 *"Seward and Weed understood each other intimately":* Dyer, *Great Senators of the United States Forty Years Ago*, 60–2.

416 *Weed encouraged his Barnburner friends:* Ibid., 63.

416 *Weed's original strategy was to have Seward:* Bancroft, *Life of William H. Seward*, 1:157; Seward, *1846–1861*, 69.

417   *Seward, for his part, thought the Mexican War:* Seward, *1846–1861,* 70–1, 73.

417   *Clay's supporters remained embittered:* Seitz, *Horace Greeley,* 158–60.

418   *It was widely felt that the election:* Seward, *1846–1861,* 77, 79–80; Stahr, *Seward,* 110–12.

418   *Lincoln's trek home took him to Niagara Falls:* Miller, *Lincoln and His World,* 3:213–4; Weed, *Life of Thurlow Weed,* 3:602–3.

CHAPTER SEVENTEEN: THE SPOILS

422   *On his way home, steaming:* CW, 2:10–11; Herndon and Weik, *Herndon's Lincoln,* 238–40.

422   *The results of the election were a resounding victory:* Oliver Dyer, *Oliver Dyer's Phonographic Report of the Proceedings of the National Free Soil Convention* (Buffalo, N.Y.: G. H. Derby, 1848), 20; Donald, *Charles Sumner and the Coming of the Civil War,* 178–9; Wilentz, *Rise of American Democracy,* 630, 920; Johannsen, *Stephen A. Douglas,* 233–4.

423   *The unlikely Free Soil standard-bearer:* William Allen Butler, *Martin Van Buren: Lawyer, Statesman and Man* (New York: D. Appleton, 1862), 33–4; William Allen Butler, *A Retrospect of Forty Years, 1825–1865* (New York: C. Scribner's Sons, 1911), 191; Shepard, *Martin Van Buren,* 439, 379.

424   *The second, brief lame-duck session:* John G. Palfrey, *A Letter to a Friend* (Cambridge, Mass.: Metcalf, 1850), 17.

425   *After Palfrey's resolution was tabled: Congressional Globe,* 30th Congress, 2nd Session, 38–9; Thomas G. Mitchell, *Anti-slavery Politics in Antebellum and Civil War America* (Westport, Conn.: Greenwood, 2007), 54–5; *Firelands Pioneer* 1–4 (1882), 65; Stevens, *A Reporter's Lincoln,* 108.

425   *Following these bills:* Mitchell, *Anti-slavery Politics in Antebellum and Civil War America,* 54–5.

425   *These resolutions, with the exception of the Root proposal:* Burlingame, *Abraham Lincoln,* 1:290; Arlin Turner, "Elizabeth Peabody Visits Lincoln, February, 1865," *New England Quarterly* 48, no. 1 (March 1975).

427   *Lincoln felt fairly confident he had wrapped:* CW, 2:20–22; William Dean Howells, *Life and Speeches of Abraham Lincoln and Hannibal Hamlin* (Columbus, Ohio: Follett, Foster, 1860), 64.

427   *During the two-week period in January: Congressional Globe,* 30th Congress, 2nd Session, 172–3, 302–3; Julian, *Life of Joshua R. Giddings,* 262–6; Eric Foner, *The Fiery Trial: Abraham Lincoln and American Slavery* (New York: Norton, 2010), 59–60.

428   *"Who is this huckster in politics?":* Lucia A. Stevens, "Growth of Public Opinion in the East in Regard to Abraham Lincoln Prior to November, 1860," in Illinois State Historical Society, *Papers in Illinois History and Transactions* (1906), 299–300.

428   *With Lincoln's vote against the Gott bill:* Julian, *Life of Joshua R. Giddings,* 261, 351;

"George W. Julian's Journal—The Assassination of Lincoln," *Indiana Magazine of History* 11, no. 4 (December 1915): 324.

428   *Answering his "Slave Hound of Illinois" piece:* Burlingame, *Abraham Lincoln*, 1:292.

429   *Giddings's commitment to Lincoln:* Abraham Lincoln Papers, Library of Congress, Elihu B. Washburne to Abraham Lincoln, December 26, 1854.

429   *By 1849, when Lincoln prepared:* Lawanda Cox and John H. Cox, *Politics, Principle, and Prejudice, 1865–1866* (New York: Free Press, 1963), 274, n. 59; Niven, *Salmon P. Chase*, 117.

431   *John C. Calhoun glowered at the presidential candidates:* Clyde N. Wilson and Shirley B. Cook, eds., *The Papers of John C. Calhoun, 1848–1849* (Columbia: University of South Carolina Press, 2001), 15–18.

432   *Calhoun climaxed his nightmarish vision:* Richard K. Cralle, ed., *The Works of John C. Calhoun* (New York: D. Appleton, 1855), 6:285–312; Freehling, *Road to Disunion*, 480; Holt, *Rise and Fall of the Whig Party*, 387; George Fort Milton, *The Eve of Conflict: Stephen A. Douglas and the Needless War* (New York: Octagon, 1969), 47.

433   *Then Senator Isaac P. Walker of Wisconsin:* Giddings, *History of the Rebellion*, 294; *Congressional Globe*, 30th Congress, 2nd Session, 665.

434   *The Thompson amendment passed: Congressional Globe*, 30th Congress, 2nd Session, 694, 696; Burlingame, *Abraham Lincoln*, 1:293; Giddings, *History of the Rebellion*, 298–9.

434   *The next day was a Sunday:* E. B. Washburne, "Abraham Lincoln in Illinois," *North American Review* 141 (1885), 314–5.

435   *Lincoln's term in the Congress over:* CW, 2:32.

436   *While championing Baker, however:* CW, 2:25, 30, 38; Miller, *Lincoln and His World*, 3:228–9.

436   *Yet Lincoln managed to secure jobs:* Burlingame, *Abraham Lincoln*, 1:294; Miller, *Lincoln and His World*, 3:228.

437   *Lincoln was swarmed with job applicants:* CW, 2:46; Burlingame, *Abraham Lincoln*, 1:294–5.

437   *Walter Davis, the mechanic who helped Lincoln:* CW, 2:18.

437   *Unfortunately, one of Lincoln's oldest friends:* CW, 2:19, 44–5, Miller, *Lincoln and His World*, 3:227–8.

438   *The biggest plum of all:* CW, 2:29, 41; Miller, *Lincoln and His World*, 3:233; Burlingame, *Abraham Lincoln*, 1:296–7.

439   *On June 2, 1849, after months of staunchly standing:* "Anson G. Henry to Abraham Lincoln," Monday, June 11, 1849, Abraham Lincoln in Land Office, Abraham Lincoln Papers, Library of Congress; CW, 2:57; Thomas F. Schwartz, "An Egregious Political Blunder: Justin Butterfield, Lincoln, and Illinois Whiggery," *Journal of the Abraham Lincoln Association* 8, no. 1 (1986).

440   *Lincoln rounded up nineteen letters of support:* Miller, *Lincoln and His World*, 3:237; CW, 2:59, 49.

440 *Desperate for a gesture:* Stahr, *Seward*, 119.

440 *On June 10, both Lincoln and Butterfield:* Browne, *Every-Day Life of Abraham Lincoln*, 106–8; Burlingame, *Abraham Lincoln* 1:301–2; CW, 2:54.

441 *Butterfield's appointment:* Arnold, *Life of Abraham Lincoln*, 81; CW, 2:58; Miller, *Lincoln and His World*, 3, 238; Michael F. Holt, "Politics, Patronage, and Public Policy: The Compromise of 1850," in Paul Finkelman and Donald R. Kennon, eds., *Congress and the Crisis of the 1850s* (Athens: Ohio University Press, 2012), 28.

442 *As a consolation prize, Lincoln was offered:* Burlingame, *Abraham Lincoln*, 1:307; Beveridge, *Abraham Lincoln*, 1:493.

442 *Butler and Edwards would not remain:* Miller, *Lincoln and His World*, 3:238; Burlingame, *Abraham Lincoln*, 1:631; Charles Roll, *Colonel Dick Thompson: The Persistent Whig* (Indianapolis: Indiana Historical Bureau, 1948), 193.

442 *Years later, on August 13, 1863:* John M. Hay and Tyler Dennett, eds., *Lincoln and the Civil War* (New York: Da Capo, 1939), 79–80.

CHAPTER EIGHTEEN: A HUNDRED KEYS

445 *Edged aside by the more nimble:* Nicolay and Hay, *Abraham Lincoln*, 1:294–6.

445 *He moved back to his clapboard frame house:* Winkle, *Young Eagle,* 223, 278–9; Octavia Roberts, *Lincoln in Illinois* (Boston: Houghton Mifflin, 1918), 67; Weik, *Real Lincoln*, 108.

446 *The firm of Lincoln & Herndon:* Weik, *Real Lincoln*, 105.

448 *After his stint in the Congress:* John G. Nicolay, *Abraham Lincoln* (New York: The Century Co., 1902), 552–3.

448 *During the Civil War, he maintained:* HI, 197.

455 *While Lincoln reestablished himself in Springfield:* Herman Melville, *Moby-Dick: Or the Whale* (New York: Scribner, 1902), 186.

456 *On June 26, 1857, Lincoln spoke in Springfield:* CW, 2:404.

457 *Then Sumner described this power:* Charles Sumner, *The Crime Against Kansas* (Boston: John P. Jewett, 1856), 6–7.

BIBLIOGRAPHY

Adams, Henry. *John Randolph.* New York: Houghton Mifflin, 1898.

Adams, John Quincy. *Memoirs of John Quincy Adams.* Philadelphia: J. B. Lippincott, 1875.

Alexander, De Alva Stanwood. *A Political History of the State of New York: 1833–1861.* New York: H. Holt, 1906.

Ambler, Charles Henry. *Thomas Ritchie: A Study in Virginia Politics.* Richmond, Va.: Bell Book & Stationery, 1913.

Anbinder, Tyler G. *Nativism and Slavery: The Northern Know Nothings and the Politics of the 1850s.* New York: Oxford University Press, 1994.

Anderson, Lawrence M. *Federalism, Secessionism, and the American State.* New York: Routledge, 2013.

Andreas, A. T. *History of Chicago.* New York: Arno Press, 1884.

Angle, Paul M. *"Here I Have Lived": A History of Lincoln's Springfield.* New Brunswick, N.J.: Rutgers University Press, 1935.

Arnold, Isaac N. *The Life of Abraham Lincoln.* Chicago: Jansen, McClurg, 1885.

———. *Reminiscences of the Illinois Bar Forty Years Ago.* Chicago: Fergus, 1881.

Atkinson, Eleanor. *The Boyhood of Lincoln.* New York: McClure, 1908.

Baker, Jean. *Affairs of Party: The Political Culture of Northern Democrats in the Mid-Nineteenth Century.* New York: Fordham University Press, 1998.

———. *Mary Todd Lincoln.* New York: Norton, 2008.

Baker, William Spohn. *Washington After the Revolution: 1784–1799.* Philadelphia: J. B. Lippincott, 1897.

Bancroft, Frederic. *The Life of William H. Seward.* New York: Harper & Brothers, 1900.

——— *Slave Trading in the Old South.* New York: Ungar, 1959.

Baptist, Edward E. "Toxic Debt, Liar Loans, and Securitized Human Beings: The Panic of 1837 and the Fate of Slavery." *Common-Place* 10, no. 3 (April 2010).

Barnes, Gilbert Hobbs. *The Antislavery Impulse, 1830–1844.* New York: Harcourt Brace, 1964.

Barton, William E. *The Paternity of Abraham Lincoln.* New York: George H. Doran Company, 1920.

Basler, Roy P., ed., *The Collected Works of Abraham Lincoln.* New Brunswick, N.J.: Rutgers University Press, 1953.

Beecher, Edward. *Narrative of Riots at Alton: In Connection with the Death of Rev. Elijah P. Lovejoy.* Alton, Ill.: G. Holton, 1838.

Belko, W. Stephen. *The Invincible Duff Green: Whig of the West.* Columbia: University of Missouri Press, 2006.

Bennett, John C. *The History of the Saints: Or, An Exposé of Joe Smith and Mormonism.* Boston: Leland & Whiting, 1842.

Benton, Thomas Hart. *Thirty Years' View: Or, A History of the Working of the American Government for Thirty Years, from 1820 to 1850.* New York: D. Appleton, 1880.

Berry, Stephen. *House of Abraham: Lincoln and the Todds, A Family Divided by War.* New York: Houghton Mifflin, 2007.

Beveridge, Albert J. *Abraham Lincoln.* New York: Houghton Mifflin, 1928.

Blockson, Charles L. "The Underground Railroad in Pennsylvania." *Milestones* 20, no. 2 (Summer 1995).

Blue, Frederick J. *No Taint of Compromise: Crusaders in Antislavery Politics.* Baton Rouge: Louisiana State University Press, 2006.

———. *Salmon P. Chase: A Life in Politics.* Kent, Ohio: Kent State University Press, 1987.

Boritt, Gabor S. *Lincoln and the Economics of the American Dream.* Chicago: University of Illinois Press, 1994.

Borneman, Walter R. *Polk: The Man Who Transformed the Presidency and America.* New York: Random House, 2009.

Boyd, Julian P., ed. *Papers of Thomas Jefferson.* Princeton: Princeton University Press, 1950.

Bray, Robert. "'The Power to Hurt': Lincoln's Early Use of Satire and Invective." *Journal of the Abraham Lincoln Association* 16, no. 1 (Winter 1995).

———. *Reading with Lincoln.* Carbondale: Southern Illinois University Press, 2010.

Brodie, Fawn N. *No Man Knows My History: The Life of Joseph Smith.* New York: Knopf, 1945.

Brooks, Noah. *Abraham Lincoln and the Downfall of Slavery.* New York: G. P. Putnam's Sons, 1894.

Browne, Francis Fisher. *The Every-day Life of Abraham Lincoln.* New York: G. P. Putnam, 1915.

Browne, Robert Henry. *Abraham Lincoln and the Men of His Times.* Cincinnati: Jennings & Pye, 1901.

Bruce, William Cabell. *John Randolph of Roanoke, 1773–1833.* New York: G. P. Putnam's Sons, 1922.

Buel, Richard. *Joel Barlow: American Citizen in a Revolutionary World.* Baltimore: Johns Hopkins University Press, 2011.

Burlingame, Michael. *Abraham Lincoln: A Life.* Baltimore: Johns Hopkins University Press, 2008.

Cady, John F. "The Religious Environment of Lincoln's Youth." *Indiana Magazine of History* 37 (March–December 1941).

Cannon, George Quayle. *The Life of Joseph Smith, The Prophet*. Salt Lake City: Juvenile Instructor Office, 1888.

Carey, Henry C. *Essay on the Rate of Wages*. Philadelphia: Carey, Lea & Blanchard, 1835.

———. *Manual of Social Science*. Philadelphia: H. C. Baird, 1874.

———. *The Slave Trade*. Philadelphia: H. C. Baird, 1872.

Carpenter, Francis. *Six Months at the White House with Abraham Lincoln: The Story of a Picture*. New York: Hurd & Houghton, 1867.

Carton, Evan. *Patriotic Treason: John Brown and the Soul of America*. Lincoln: University of Nebraska Press, 2009.

Cartwright, Peter. *The Backwoods Preacher: An Autobiography*. London: Alexander Heylin, 1858.

Carwardine, Richard J. "Lincoln, Evangelical Religion, and American Political Culture in the Era of the Civil War." *Journal of the Abraham Lincoln Association* 18, no. 1 (Winter 1997).

Cashin, Joan E. *First Lady of the Confederacy: Varina Davis's Civil War*. Cambridge: Harvard University Press, 2006.

Cole, Arthur Charles. *Centennial History of Illinois: The Era of the Civil War, 1848–1870*. Springfield, Ill.: A. C. McClurg, 1922.

Condon, William H. *Life of Major-General James Shields*. Chicago: Blakely Printing, 1900.

Cooper, Thomas. *Consolidation: An Account of Parties in the United States from the Convention of 1787 to the Present Period*. Columbia, S.C.: Black & Sweeney, 1824.

Cooper, William J., Jr. *Jefferson Davis, American*. New York: Knopf, 2000.

———. *The South and the Politics of Slavery, 1828–1856*. Baton Rouge: Louisiana State University Press, 1980.

Cralle, Richard K., ed. *Reports and Public Letters of John C. Calhoun*. New York: D. Appleton, 1867.

Crockett, David. *The Life of Martin Van Buren*. New York: Nafis & Cornish, 1835.

Cutler, Wayne, ed. *Correspondence of James K. Polk: September–December 1844*. Knoxville: University of Tennessee Press, 1993.

Dana, Charles A. *Recollections of the Civil War*. New York: D. Appleton, 1898.

Davis, George T. M. *Autobiography of the Late Col. Geo. T. M. Davis*. New York: Jenkins & McCowan, 1891.

Denton, Sally *American Massacre: The Tragedy at Mountain Meadows, September 1857*. New York: Knopf, 2003.

Dickens, Charles. *American Notes*. London: Chapman & Hall, 1842.

Dodd, William E. *Robert J. Walker, Imperialist*. Chicago: Chicago Literary Club, 1914.

Donald, David Herbert. *Charles Sumner and the Coming of the Civil War*. Chicago: University of Chicago Press, 1960.

———. *Lincoln*. New York: Simon & Schuster, 1995.

———. *We Are Lincoln Men*. New York: Simon & Schuster, 2003.

Dunn, Jacob Piatt. *Indiana: A Redemption from Slavery.* New York: Houghton Mifflin, 1888.

———. *Indiana and Indianans.* New York: American Historical Society, 1919.

Dyer, Oliver. *Great Senators of the United States Forty Years Ago, 1848–1849.* New York: R. Bonner's Sons, 1889.

Eastman, Zebina. *The Black Code in Illinois.* Chicago: University of Illinois Library, 1883.

Edstrom, James A. "'A Mighty Contest,' The Jefferson-Lemen Compact Reevaluated." *Journal of the Illinois State Historical Society* 97, no. 3 (2004).

Einhorn, Robin L. *Property Rules: Political Economy in Chicago, 1833–1872.* Chicago: University of Chicago Press, 2001.

Eisenhower, John D. *Agent of Destiny: The Life and Times of General Winfield Scott.* Norman: University of Oklahoma Press, 1999.

Erle, Jonathan H. *Jacksonian Antislavery and the Politics of Free Soil, 1824–1854.* Chapel Hill: University of North Carolina Press, 2004.

Esary, Logan. *A History of Indiana.* Dayton, Ohio: Dayton Historical Publishing, 1918.

Evans, W. A. *Mrs. Abraham Lincoln.* New York: Knopf, 1935.

Farber, Daniel A. *Security v. Liberty: Conflicts Between Civil Liberty and National Security.* New York: Russell Sage Foundation, 2008.

Faust, Drew Gilpin. *James Henry Hammond and the Old South: A Design for Mastery.* Baton Rouge: Louisiana State University Press, 1985.

Findley, Paul. *A. Lincoln: The Crucible of Congress.* New York: Crown, 1979.

Fischer, David Hackett. *Albion's Seed: Four British Folkways in America.* New York: Oxford University Press, 1989.

Foner, Eric. *Free Soil, Free Labor, Free Men: The Ideology of the Republican Party Before the Civil War.* New York: Oxford University Press, 1995.

Foote, Henry S. *Casket of Reminiscences.* Washington, D.C.: Chronicle Publishing, 1874.

Forbes, Esther. *Paul Revere and the World He Lived In.* New York: Houghton Mifflin, 1942.

Ford, Thomas. *A History of Illinois.* Chicago: S. C. Griggs, 1854.

Freehling, William W. *Prelude to Civil War: The Nullification Crisis in South Carolina, 1816–1836.* New York: Oxford University Press, 1992.

———. *The Road to Disunion: Secessionists at Bay, 1776–1854.* New York: Oxford University Press, 1990.

Freeman, Douglas Southall. *The South to Posterity: An Introduction to the Writing of Confederate History.* Baton Rouge: Louisiana State University Press, 1939.

Frost, John. *Life of Major General Zachary Taylor.* New York: D. Appleton, 1847.

Fruchtman, Jack, Jr. *Thomas Paine: Apostle of Freedom.* New York: Four Walls Eight Windows, 1996.

Gardiner, O. C. *The Great Issue; or Three Presidential Candidates.* New York: W. C. Bryant, 1848.

Garland, Hugh A. *The Life of John Randolph of Roanoke*. New York: D. Appleton, 1854.

Garrison, Wendell Phillips, and Francis Jackson Garrison. *William Lloyd Garrison, 1805–1879: The Story of His Life Told by His Children*. New York: Century, 1889.

Gaustad, Edwin Scott. *Sworn on the Altar of God: A Religious Biography of Thomas Jefferson*. Grand Rapids, Mich.: Wm. B. Eerdmans, 1996.

Giddings, Joshua R. *History of the Rebellion: Its Authors and Causes*. New York: Follet, Foster, 1864.

———. *Speeches in Congress*. Boston: John P. Jewett, 1853.

Goss, Charles Frederic. *Cincinnati, the Queen City, 1788–1912*. Chicago: S. J. Clarke Publishing, 1912.

Grayson, William J. *The Autobiography of William J. Grayson*. Columbia: University of South Carolina Press, 1990.

Grimshaw, William. *History of the United States*. Philadelphia: Benjamin Warne, 1821.

Grimsted, David. *American Mobbing, 1828–1861: Toward Civil War*. New York: Oxford University Press, 2003.

Guelzo, Allen C. *Abraham Lincoln: Redeemer President*. Grand Rapids, Mich.: Wm. B. Eerdmans, 2003.

———. *Lincoln's Emancipation Proclamation: The End of Slavery in America*. New York: Simon & Schuster, 2004.

Gugliotta, Guy. *Freedom's Cap: The United States Capitol and the Coming of the Civil War*. New York: Macmillan, 2012.

Gutjahr, Paul C. *The Book of Mormon: A Biography*. Princeton: Princeton University Press, 2012.

Hall, Daniel. *Addresses Commemorative of Abraham Lincoln and John P. Hale*. Concord, N.H.: Republican Press Association, 1892.

Harper, Robert S. *Lincoln and the Press*. New York: McGraw Hill, 1951.

Harris, N. Dwight. *The History of Negro Servitude in Illinois, and of the Slavery Agitation in That State, 1719–1864*. Chicago: A. C. McClurg, 1904.

Harris, William C. *Lincoln's Last Months*. Cambridge: Harvard University Press, 2004.

Harrold, Stanley. *Subversives: Antislavery Community in Washington, D.C., 1828–1865*. Baton Rouge: Louisiana State University Press, 2002.

Hart, Albert Bushnell. *Salmon Portland Chase*. New York: Houghton Mifflin, 1899.

Helm, Katherine. *Mary, Wife of Lincoln*. New York: Harper Brothers, 1928.

Herndon, William Henry, and Jesse William Weik. *Herndon's Lincoln: The True Story of a Great Life*. New York: Belford, Clarke, 1889.

Hertz, Emanuel. *The Hidden Lincoln: From the Letters and Papers of William H. Herndon*. New York: Blue Ribbon Books, 1940.

Hill, John. *Opposing Principles of Henry Clay and Abraham Lincoln*. St. Louis: G. Knapp, 1860.

Hinks, Peter P., John R. McKivigan, and R. Owen Williams. *Encyclopedia of Antislavery and Abolition*. Westport, Conn.: Greenwood, 2007.

Hitchcock, Caroline Hanks. *Nancy Hanks: The Story of Abraham Lincoln's Mother*. New York: Doubleday & McClure, 1899.

Hobson, Fred C. *Tell About the South: The Southern Rage to Explain*. Baton Rouge: Louisiana State University Press, 1983.

Hobson, Jonathan Todd. *Footprints of Abraham Lincoln*. Dayton, Ohio: Otterbein Press, 1909.

Hofstadter, Richard. *The American Political Tradition*. New York: Knopf, 1948.

Holland, J. G. *Life of Lincoln*. Springfield, Mass.: G. Bill, 1866.

Holland, William M. *The Life and Political Opinions of Martin Van Buren*. Hartford, Conn.: Belknap & Hamersley, 1836.

Hollingsworth, Randolph. *Lexington: Queen of the Bluegrass*. Charleston, S.C.: Arcadia Publishing, 2004.

Holt, Michael F. *The Rise and Fall of the Whig Party: Jacksonian Politics and the Onset of the Civil War*. New York: Oxford University Press, 2003.

Holzer, Harold. *Lincoln and the Power of the Press*. New York: Simon & Schuster, 2014.

Horsman, Reginald. *Race and Manifest Destiny: The Origins of American Racial Anglo-Saxonism*. Cambridge: Harvard University Press, 1981.

Houck, Louis Houck. *A History of Missouri from the Earliest Explorations and Settlements Until the Admission of the State into the Union*. Chicago: R. R. Donnelley & Sons, 1908.

Houston, David Franklin. *A Critical Study of Nullification in South Carolina*. New York: Longmans, Green, 1908.

Howe, Daniel Walker. *The Political Culture of the American Whigs*. Chicago: University of Chicago Press, 1979.

———. *What Hath God Wrought: The Transformation of America, 1815–1848*. New York: Oxford University Press, 2007.

Hughes, Nathaniel Cheairs, and Roy P. Stonesifer. *The Life and Wars of Gideon J. Pillow*. Chapel Hill: University of North Carolina Press, 1993.

Hughes, Sarah Forbes, ed. *Letters and Recollections of John Murray Forbes*. New York: Houghton Mifflin, 1900.

Huston, James L. *Stephen A. Douglas and the Dilemmas of Democratic Equality*. Lanham, Md.: Rowman & Littlefield, 2007.

James, Marquis. *The Life of Andrew Jackson*. New York: Bobbs Merrill, 1938.

Jenkins, John S. *The Life of John Caldwell Calhoun*. Auburn, N.Y.: J. M. Alden, 1850.

Johannsen, Robert Walter. *Stephen A. Douglas*. New York: Oxford University Press, 1973.

Johnson, Allen. *Stephen A. Douglas: A Study in American Politics*. New York: Macmillan, 1908.

Johnson, Oliver. *William Lloyd Garrison and His Times*. Boston: B. B. Russell, 1879.

Johnson, Reinhard O. *The Liberty Party, 1840–1848: Antislavery Third-Party Politics in the United States*. Baton Rouge: Louisiana State University Press, 2009.

Jones, Edgar De Witt. *Lincoln and the Preachers.* New York: Harper & Brothers, 1948.

Julian, George Washington. *The Life of Joshua R. Giddings.* New York: A. C. McClurg, 1892.

Kaye, Harvey J. *Thomas Paine and the Promise of America.* New York: Hill & Wang, 2006.

Kelly, Charles, and Hoffman Birney. *Holy Murder: The Story of Porter Rockwell.* New York: Minton, Balch, 1934.

Klunder, Willard Carl. *Lewis Cass and the Politics of Moderation.* Kent, Ohio: Kent State University Press, 1996.

Lamon, Ward Hill. *The Life of Abraham Lincoln.* Boston: James R. Osgood, 1872.

Lea, James Henry, and John Robert Hutchinson. *The Ancestry of Abraham Lincoln.* New York: Houghton Mifflin, 1909.

Lee, John Doyle. *Mormonism Unveiled.* St. Louis: Sun Publishing, 1882.

Leonard, Thomas M. *James K. Polk: A Clear and Unquestionable Destiny.* Lanham, Md.: Rowman & Littlefield, 2001.

Lepler, Jessica M. "1837: Anatomy of a Panic." PhD diss., Brandeis University, 2008.

Levasseur, Auguste. *Lafayette in America in 1824 and 1825: or, Journal of a Voyage to the United States.* Philadelphia: Carey & Lea, 1829.

Lincoln, William Sever. *Alton Trials.* New York: John F. Trow, 1838.

Lind, Michael. *What Lincoln Believed.* New York: Doubleday, 2004.

Linebaugh, Peter, and Marcus Rediker. *The Many-Headed Hydra: Sailors, Slaves, Commoners, and the Hidden History of the Revolutionary Atlantic.* Boston: Beacon, 2001.

Linn, William Alexander. *The Story of the Mormons: From the Date of Their Origin to the Year 1901.* New York: Macmillan, 1902.

Lovejoy, Joseph C., and Owen Lovejoy. *Memoir of the Rev. Elijah P. Lovejoy: Who Was Murdered in Defence of the Liberty of the Press, at Alton, Illinois, Nov. 7, 1837.* New York: J. S. Taylor, 1838.

Lucas, Marion B. *A History of Blacks in Kentucky: From Slavery to Segregation, 1760–1891.* Lexington: University Press of Kentucky, 2003.

Luthin, Reinhold H. *The Real Abraham Lincoln.* New York: Prentice Hall, 1960.

MacNaul, Willard C. *The Jefferson-Lemen Compact.* Chicago: University of Chicago Press, 1915.

Magdol, Edward. *Owen Lovejoy: Abolitionist in Congress.* New Brunswick, N.J.: Rutgers University Press, 1967.

Maltby, Charles. *The Life and Services of Abraham Lincoln.* Stockton, Calif.: Daily Independent Steam Power Print, 1884.

Mann, Horace. *Slavery: Letters and Speeches.* Boston: B. B. Mussey, 1853.

Masur, Louis P. *1831: Year of Eclipse.* New York: Macmillan, 2002.

McCampbell, Coleman. "H. L. Kinney and Daniel Webster in Illinois in the 1830's." *Journal of the Illinois State Historical Society* 47, no. 1 (Spring 1954).

McClure, Alexander K. *Abe Lincoln's Yarns and Stories.* Philadelphia: International Publishing, 1901.

————. *Our Presidents: And How We Make Them.* New York: Harper & Brothers, 1900.

McCormac, Eugene Irving. *James K. Polk: A Political Biography.* Berkeley: University of California Press, 1922.

McCormack, Thomas J., ed. *Memoirs of Gustave Koerner.* Cedar Rapids, Iowa: Torch Press, 1909.

McKirdy, Charles R. *Lincoln Apostate: The Matson Slave Case.* Jackson: University Press of Mississippi, 2011.

Meacham, Jon. *American Lion: Andrew Jackson in the White House.* New York: Random House, 2008.

Meer, Sarah. *Uncle Tom Mania: Slavery, Minstrelsy, and Transatlantic Culture in the 1850s.* Athens: University of Georgia Press, 2005.

Meigs, William M. *The Life of John Caldwell Calhoun.* New York: Neale Publishing, 1917.

————. *The Life of Thomas Hart Benton.* Philadelphia: J. B. Lippincott, 1904.

Merk, Frederick. *Slavery and the Annexation of Texas.* New York: Knopf, 1972.

Merry, Robert W. *A Country of Vast Designs.* New York: Simon & Schuster, 2009.

Miers, Earl Schenck, and William E. Baringer, eds. *Lincoln Day by Day: A Chronology, 1809–1865.* Washington, D.C.: Lincoln Sesquicentennial Commission, Northern Illinois University, 1960.

Miller, Richard Lawrence. *Lincoln and His World: Prairie Politician, 1834–1842.* Mechanicsburg, Penn.: Stackpole, 2008.

————. *Lincoln and His World: The Early Years, Birth to Illinois Legislature.* Mechanicsburg, Penn.: Stackpole, 2006.

————. *Lincoln and His World: The Rise of National Prominence, 1843–1853.* Jefferson, N.C.: McFarland, 2011.

Miller, William Lee. *Arguing About Slavery: The Great Battle in the United States Congress.* New York, Knopf, 1996.

Mitgang, Herbert. *Abraham Lincoln: A Press Portrait.* New York: Fordham University Press, 2000.

Nelly, Mark E., Jr. "The Lincoln Theme Since Randall's Call: The Promises and Perils of Professionalism." *Journal of the Abraham Lincoln Association* 1 (1979).

Nicolay, Helen. *Our Capital on the Potomac.* New York: Century, 1924.

Nicolay, John G. *Abraham Lincoln.* New York: The Century Co., 1902

Nicolay, John G., and John Hay. *Abraham Lincoln, A History.* New York: Century, 1890.

————. *Abraham Lincoln: A History.* New York: Century, 1914.

Niven, John. *John C. Calhoun and the Price of Union.* Baton Rouge: Louisiana State University Press, 1993.

————. *Salmon P. Chase.* New York: Oxford University Press, 1995.

Northrup, Solomon. *Twelve Years a Slave.* Buffalo: Derby, Orton & Mulligan, 1853.

Nowlin, William Dudley. *Kentucky Baptist History, 1770–1922.* Louisville, Ky.: Baptist Book Concern, 1922.

Oakes, James. *Freedom National: The Destruction of Slavery in the United States, 1861–1865*. New York: Norton, 2013.

Oates, Stephen B. *To Purge This Land with Blood: A Biography of John Brown*. Amherst: University of Massachusetts Press, 1984.

Paine, Thomas. *The Age of Reason*. New York: G. N. Devries, 1827.

Parrish, Randall. *Historic Illinois: The Romance of the Early Days*. Chicago: A. C. McClurg, 1905.

Parton, James. *Life of Andrew Jackson*. New York: Mason Brothers, 1861.

Pease, Theodore Calvin. *Frontier State: 1818–1848*. Springfield: Illinois Centennial Commission.

———. *The Story of Illinois*. Chicago: University of Chicago Press, 1965.

Peck, John Mason. *Forty Years of Pioneer Life*. Philadelphia: American Baptist Publication Society, 1864.

Peterson, Merrill D. *The Great Triumvirate: Webster, Clay, and Calhoun*. New York: Oxford University Press, 1987.

Piatt, Donn. *Memories of the Men Who Saved the Union*. New York: Belford, Clarke, 1887.

Pierce, Edward L. *Memoir and Letters of Charles Sumner*. Boston: Roberts Brothers, 1894.

Podmore, Frank. *Robert Owen*. London: Hutchinson & Co., 1906.

Porter, Horace. *Campaigning with Grant*. New York: Century, 1907.

Prentice, George D. *Biography of Henry Clay*. Hartford, Conn.: S. Hanmer, Jr., and J. J. Phelps, 1831.

Quaife, Milo Milton, ed. *The Diary of James K. Polk During His Presidency, 1845–1849*. New York: A. C. McClurg, 1910.

Quincey, Josiah. *Figures of the Past*. Boston: Roberts Brothers, 1896.

Randall, J. G. *Lincoln the President*. New York: Dodd, Mead, 1945.

Randall, Ruth Painter. *The Courtship of Mr. Lincoln*. New York: Little, Brown, 1957.

———. *I Mary: A Biography of the Girl Who Married Abraham Lincoln*. New York: Little, Brown, 1959.

———. *Mary Lincoln: Biography of a Marriage*. New York: Little, Brown, 1953.

Reep, Thomas P. *Abe Lincoln and the Frontier Folk of New Salem*. Middletown, Conn.: Southfarm Press, 2002.

Remini, Robert V. *Andrew Jackson and the Course of American Democracy*. New York: Harper & Row, 1984.

———. *Henry Clay: Statesman for the Union*. New York: Norton, 1991.

Remsburg, John Eleazer. *Abraham Lincoln: Was He a Christian?* New York: Truth Seeker, 1893.

Reynolds, David S. *Walt Whitman's America*. New York: Knopf, 1995.

Rice, Allen Thorndike. *Reminiscences of Abraham Lincoln by Distinguished Men of His Time*. New York: North American Publishing, 1886.

Ricks, Mary Kay. *Escape on the Pearl: The Heroic Bid for Freedom on the Underground Railroad*. New York: William Morrow, 2007.

Roberts, B. H. *History of the Church of Jesus Christ of Latter-Day Saints*. Salt Lake City: Deseret News, 1909.

———. *The Rise and Fall of Nauvoo*. Salt Lake City: Deseret News, 1900.

Salzmann, Joshua A. T. "Safe Harbor: Chicago's Waterfront and the Political Economy of the Built Environment, 1847—1918." PhD diss., University of Illinois, 2008.

Sandburg, Carl. *Mary Lincoln: Wife and Widow*. New York: Harcourt, Brace, 1932.

Sargent, Epes. *The Life and Public Services of Henry Clay*. Auburn, N.Y.: Derby & Miller, 1852.

Sargent, Nathan. *Public Men and Events in the United States from the Commencement of Mr. Monroe's Administration in 1817 to the Close of Mr. Fillmore's Administration in 1853*. Philadelphia: J. B. Lippincott, 1875.

Schouler, James. *History of the United States of America: Under the Constitution*. New York: Dodd, Mead, 1917

Schuckers, J. W. *The Life and Public Services of Salmon Portland Chase*. New York: D. Appleton, 1874.

Schurz, Carl. *Henry Clay*. New York: Houghton Mifflin, 1899.

Scipps, John Locke. *The First Published Life of Abraham Lincoln*. Detroit: Cranbrook Press, 1900.

Seeber, Edward Derbyshire. *Antislavery Opinion in France During the Second Half of the Eighteenth Century*. North Stratford, N.H.: Ayer Publishing, 1937.

Seitz, Don C. *Famous American Duels*. New York: Thomas Y. Crowell, 1929.

———. *Lincoln the Politician*. New York: Coward-McCann, 1931.

Seller, Charles. "Election of 1844." In *History of American Presidential Elections, 1789–1968*, Arthur M. Schlesinger, Jr., et al., eds. New York: Chelsea House, 1971.

Seward, Frederick. *Reminiscences of a Wartime Statesman and Diplomat: 1830–1915*. New York: G. P. Putnam's Sons, 1916.

———. *Seward at Washington: 1846–1860*. New York: D. Appleton, 1891.

———. *William H. Seward, 1831–1846*. New York: Derby & Miller, 1891.

Seward, William Henry, and Frederick W. Seward. *Seward at Washington as Senator and Secretary of State, 1846–1861*. New York: Derby & Miller, 1891.

Sewell, Richard H. *Ballots for Freedom: Antislavery Politics in the United States, 1837–1860*. New York: Oxford University Press, 1976.

Seymour, Glenn H. " 'Conservative': Another Lincoln Pseudonym?" *Journal of the Illinois State Historical Society* 29, no. 2 (July 1936).

Shenk, Joshua Wolf. *Lincoln's Melancholy*. New York: Houghton Mifflin, 2005.

Shepard, Edward Morse. *Martin Van Buren*. New York: Houghton Mifflin, 1896.

Shook, Charles A. *The True Origins of Mormon Polygamy*. Cincinnati: Standard Publishing Company, 1914.

Siebert, Wilbur Henry. *The Underground Railroad from Slavery to Freedom*. New York: Macmillan, 1898.

Silbey, Joel H. *Storm over Texas: The Annexation Controversy and the Road to Civil War.* New York: Oxford University Press, 2005.

Simon, Paul. *Lincoln's Preparation for Greatness: The Illinois Legislative Years.* Urbana: University of Illinois Press, 1971.

Sinha, Manisha. *The Counter-Revolution of Slavery: Political and Ideology in Antebellum South Carolina.* Charlotte: University of North Carolina Press, 2000.

Smith, Margaret Bayard. *The First Forty Years of Washington Society.* New York: Scribner, 1906.

Snyder, John Francis. *Adam W. Snyder and his Period in Illinois History, 1817–1842.* Virginia, Ill.: E. Needham, 1906.

Spencer, John H. *A History of Kentucky Baptists: From 1769 to 1885.* Cincinnati: J. R. Baumes, 1885.

Stahr, Walter. *Seward: Lincoln's Indispensable Man.* New York: Simon & Schuster, 2012.

Starr, Paul. *The Creation of the Media: Political Origins of Modern Communications.* New York: Basic Books, 2004.

Steiner, Mark E. *An Honest Calling: The Law Practice of Abraham Lincoln.* DeKalb: Northern Illinois University Press, 2006.

Stephens, Alexander H. *Recollections of Alexander H. Stephens.* New York: Doubleday, Page, 1910.

Stevens, Walter Barlow. *A Reporter's Lincoln*, ed. Michael Burlingame. Lincoln: University of Nebraska Press, 1916.

Stewart, James Brewer. "Joshua Giddings, Antislavery Violence and Congressional Politics of Honor." In *Antislavery Violence: Sectional, Racial, and Cultural Conflict in Antebellum America,* John R. McKivigan and Stanley Harrold, eds. Knoxville: University of Tennessee Press, 1999.

Stowe, Harriet Beecher. *A Key to Uncle Tom's Cabin.* London: Sampson Low, Son, 1853.

Tanner, Henry. *The Martyrdom of Lovejoy: An Account of the Life, Trials, and Perils of Rev. Elijah P. Lovejoy.* Chicago: Fergus Printing, 1881.

Tarbell, Ida. *Abraham Lincoln and His Ancestor.* Lincoln: University of Nebraska Press, 1924.

———. *The Early Life of Abraham Lincoln.* New York: S. S. McClure, 1896.

Tate, Adam L. *Conservatism and Southern Intellectuals, 1789–1861.* Columbia: University of Missouri Press, 2005.

Temin, Peter. *The Jacksonian Economy.* New York: Norton, 1969.

Temple, Wayne C. *Lincoln: From Skeptic to Prophet.* Mahomet, Ill.: Mayhaven, 1995.

Thayer, William Makepeace. *The Pioneer Boy: And How He Became President, The Story of the Life of Abraham Lincoln.* London: Hodder & Stoughton, 1882.

Thomas, Benjamin Platt. *Lincoln's New Salem.* Carbondale: Southern Illinois University Press, 1973.

Thompson, Charles Manfred. *The Illinois Whigs Before 1846.* Urbana: University of Illinois Press, 1915.

Townsend, William H. *Lincoln the Litigant.* New York: Houghton Mifflin, 1925.

Tracy, Gilbert A., ed. *Uncollected Letters of Abraham Lincoln.* New York: Houghton Mifflin, 1917.

Trefousse, Hans L. *Thaddeus Stevens: Nineteenth-Century Egalitarian.* Mechanicsburg, Penn.: Stackpole, 2001.

Tucker, Pomeroy. *Origin, Rise, and Progress of Mormonism: Biography of Its Founders and History of Its Church.* New York: D. Appleton, 1867.

Turner, Justin, G., and Linda Levitt Turner. *Mary Todd Lincoln: Her Life and Letters.* New York: Knopf, 1972.

Tyler, Alice Felt. *Freedom's Ferment: Phases of American Social History from the Colonial Period to the Outbreak of the Civil War.* New York: Harper Torchbooks, 1962.

Upshur, Abel P. *A Brief Enquiry into the True Nature and Character of Our Federal Government.* Petersburg, Va.: E. and J. C. Ruffin, 1840.

Van Buren, Martin. *The Autobiography of Martin Van Buren*, John C. Fitzpatrick, ed. Washington, D.C.: U.S. Government Printing Office, 1920.

Vargo, Louis. "Abraham Lincoln Prepares to Fight a Saber Duel." *Civil War Magazine* (February 2002).

von Holst, Hermann. *John C. Calhoun.* New York: Houghton Mifflin, 1899.

Walker, Robert J. *The South in Danger.* Washington, D.C.: Democratic Association, 1844.

Wall, Caleb Arnold. *The Historic Boston Tea Party of December 16, 1773: Its Men and Objects.* Worcester, Mass.: F. S. Blanchard, 1896.

Warren. Louis A. *Lincoln's Youth: Indiana Years, 1816–1830.* Indianapolis: Indiana Historical Society, 1991.

———. *The Slavery Atmosphere of Lincoln's Youth.* Fort Wayne, Ind.: Lincolniana Publishers, 1933.

Watkins, Sam R. *"Co. Aytch": A Confederate Memoir of the Civil War.* New York: Simon & Schuster, 2008.

Watson, Harry L. *Liberty and Power: The Politics of Jacksonian America.* New York: Macmillan, 2006.

Weed, Harriet A. *Autobiography of Thurlow Weed.* New York: Houghton Mifflin, 1884.

Weik, Jesse W. *The Real Lincoln.* New York: Houghton Mifflin, 1922.

Weld, Theodore. *Letters of Theodore Dwight Weld, Angelina Grimké Weld and Sarah Grimké, 1822–1844.* New York: D. Appleton-Century, 1934.

———. *The Power of the Congress over the District of Columbia.* New York: John F. Trow, 1838.

Welles, Gideon. *Diary of Gideon Welles.* New York: Houghton Mifflin, 1911.

Wheelan, Joseph. *Mr. Adams's Last Crusade.* New York: PublicAffairs, 2008.

Whipple, Wayne. *The Story-Life of Lincoln.* Philadelphia: John C. Winston, 1908.

White, Ronald. *A. Lincoln: A Biography.* New York: Random House, 2010.

Whiting, William. *War Powers Under the Constitution.* Boston: Lee & Shepard, 1871.

Whitney, Henry Clay. *Life of Lincoln.* New York: Baker & Taylor, 1908.

————. *Life on the Circuit with Lincoln.* Boston: Estes & Lauriat, 1892.

Widmer, Edward L. *Martin Van Buren.* New York: Macmillan, 2005.

Wilentz, Sean. "The Bombshell of 1844." In *America at the Ballot Box: Elections and American Political History,* Gareth Davies and Julian Zelizer, eds. Philadelphia: University of Pennsylvania Press, 2016.

————. *The Rise of American Democracy: Jefferson to Lincoln.* New York: Norton, 2005.

Williams, Sandra Boyd. "The Indiana Supreme Court and the Struggle Against Slavery." *Indiana Law Review* 30, no. 305 (1997).

Wilson, Douglas L. *Honor's Voice: The Transformation of Abraham Lincoln.* New York: Knopf, 1998.

————. "William H. Herndon and Mary Todd Lincoln." *Journal of the Abraham Lincoln Association* 22, no. 2 (Summer 2001).

Wilson, Douglas S., Rodney O. Davis, Terry Wilson, William Henry Herndon, and Jesse William Weik, eds. *Herndon's Informants: Letters, Interviews, and Statements About Abraham Lincoln.* Urbana: University of Illinois Press, 1998.

Wilson, Edmund. *Patriotic Gore: Studies in the Literature of the American Civil War.* New York: Farrar, Straus & Giroux, 1962.

Wilson, George R. "General Washington Johnston." *Indiana Magazine of History* 20, no. 2 (June 1924).

Wilson, Henry. *History of the Rise and Fall of the Slave Power in America.* Boston: J. R. Osgood, 1875.

Wilson, Rufus Rockwell. *Lincoln Among His Friends: A Sheaf of Intimate Memories.* Caldwell, Idaho: Caxton Printers, 1942.

Wiltse, Charles M. *John C. Calhoun: Nullifier, 1829–1839.* Indianapolis: Bobbs Merrill, 1949.

————. *John C. Calhoun: Sectionalist, 1840–1850.* Indianapolis: Bobbs Merrill, 1951.

Winkle, Kenneth J. *The Young Eagle: The Rise of Abraham Lincoln.* Dallas: Taylor Trade Publishing, 2001.

Winthrop, Robert C. *Oration.* Washington, D.C.: J. & G. S. Gideon, 1848.

Wise, Henry A. *Seven Decades of the Union.* Philadelphia: J. B. Lippincott, 1881.

Woldman, Albert A. *Lawyer Lincoln.* New York: Carroll & Graf, 1994.

Wood, Gordon S. *Empire of Liberty: A History of the Early Republic, 1789–1815.* New York: Oxford University Press, 2009.

Wood, Marcus, ed. *The Poetry of Slavery: An Anglo-American Anthology, 1764–1865.* New York: Oxford University Press, 2004.

Wood, Nicholas. "John Randolph of Roanoke and the Politics of Slavery in the Early Republic." *Virginia Magazine of History and Biography* 120, no. 2 (Summer 2012).

Wyl, W. *Mormon Portraits.* Salt Lake City: Tribune Printing and Publishing, 1886.

Young, James Sterling. *The Washington Community, 1800–1828.* New York: Columbia University Press, 1966.

ILLUSTRATION CREDITS

Endpapers: V. O. Hammon Publishing Co., Chicago (*front*), Library of Congress (*back*)
Frontispiece: Library of Congress.

21 Library of Congress
26 Wikimedia Commons
41 Wikimedia Commons
53 National Portrait Gallery
73 Illinois State Historical Library
77 Library of Congress
88 Filson Historical Society
95 Beinecke Rare Book & Manuscript Library
106 National Portrait Gallery
131 The Metropolitan Museum of Art
132 The Metropolitan Museum of Art
138 Library of Congress
155 Wikimedia Commons
164 Library of Congress
187 Library of Congress
195 White House Collection
211 Library of Congress
235 Library of Congress
263 National Archives and Records Administration, College Park
278 Library of Congress
303 National Archives and Records Administration, College Park
319 Library of Congress
324 Wikimedia Commons
335 The Henry Clay Estate
347 Library of Congress
352 Library of Congress
365 Library of Congress
373 Library of Congress
381 Library of Congress
393 The Metropolitan Museum of Art

405 Wikimedia Commons
411 Library of Congress
417 Library of Congress
421 Wikimedia Commons
439 Wikimedia Commons
445 Library of Congress

INDEX

Page numbers in *italics* refer to illustrations.

ABOUT THE AUTHOR

SIDNEY BLUMENTHAL is the former assistant and senior adviser to President Bill Clinton. He was a journalist at *The Washington Post*, *The New Yorker*, *The New Republic*, and a columnist for *The Guardian* of London. He is the author of seven previous books, including *The Permanent Campaign*, *The Rise of the Counter-Establishment*, and *The Clinton Wars*. He was executive producer of the Academy Award– and Emmy Award–winning documentary *Taxi to the Dark Side*. He was born and raised in Chicago, Illinois, and lives in Washington, D.C.